D1260601

STANDARD DICTIONARY OF COMPUTERS AND INFORMATION PROCESSING

martin h. weik

Information Systems Analyst
Defense Communications Agency
Washington, D.C.

Chairman
Subcommittee X3K5 (Terminology
  and Glossary)
American National Standards Committee X3
  (Computers and Information Processing)
American National Standards Institute

Chief USA Delegate
Subcommittee 1, Vocabulary
Technical Committee 97
Computers and Information Processing
International Organization for
  Standardization

Chairman
Subcommittee on Glossary
Federal Telecommunications Standards
  Committee

Co-Chairman
Computer-Communications Glossary
  Subcommittee
Computer Society
Institute of Electrical and Electronics
  Engineers

Formerly, Chief
Data Management Division
U.S. Army Research and Development
  Information Systems Office

Formerly, Chief
Special Systems Section
Computing Laboratory
Ballistic Research Laboratories
U.S. Army

Formerly, Chairman
Information Retrieval Group
Information Systems Subdivision
Manufacturing Systems Division
American Society of Tool and
  Manufacturing Engineers

Formerly, Chairman
Subcommittee 1 (Glossary)
Technical Data and Standardization
  Policy Committee
Department of Defense

Formerly, Chairman,
Task Group on Glossary
Committee on Scientific and Technical
  Information
Office of Science and Technology
Executive Office of the President

Formerly, Secretary
Subcommittee 8.4 (Electronic Computer
  Definitions)
Institute of Electrical and Electronics
  Engineers

Formerly, Member
Task Force on Glossary
Federal Interagency Automatic Data
  Processing Committee

STANDARD DICTIONARY OF COMPUTERS AND INFORMATION PROCESSING

REVISED
SECOND EDITION

MARTIN H. WEIK

HAYDEN BOOK COMPANY, INC.
Rochelle Park, New Jersey

*To my wife and children, whose
patience with me was often tried during
the years of preparation, and to the
many wonderful friends with whom I have
worked in many vocabulary efforts.*

Library of Congress Cataloging in Publication Data

Weik, Martin H.
    Standard dictionary of computers and information
processing.

    Bibliography: p.
    1.   Electronic data processing — Dictionaries.
2.   Electronic digital computers — Dictionaries.
I.   Title.
QA76.15.W4   1977   001.6'4'03   77-22664
ISBN   0-8104-5099-2

Printed in the United States of America

1	2	3	4	5	6	7	8	9	PRINTING
77	78	79	80	81	82	83	84	85	YEAR

Preface to the Second Edition

"When I use a word," Humpty Dumpty said in rather a scornful tone, "it means just what I choose it to mean—neither more nor less."
"The question is," said Alice, "Whether you can make words mean so many different things."
"The question is," said Humpty Dumpty, "which is to be master – that's all."

From *Through the Looking Glass*

For effective communication, perhaps there can be no master. Both sender and receiver must have arrived at a basic agreement on the meaning of the terms and their codes in a given message. If agreement has not been reached, the sender must include definitions of the words and codes that are in the message, in which case there must have been prior agreement on the definition of the terms used in the definitions, ad infinitum. *Standard Dictionary of Computers and Information Processing* is designed to advance the ability of men and machines to communicate with one another.

Vocabulary development in the broad field of information processing, particularly in computers and automatic data processing, passed a major milestone when the first *American Standard Vocabulary for Information Processing* was published by the United States of America Standards Institute (now the American National Standards Institute) in 1966. It required three years of painstaking effort on the part of Technical Committee XK35, a highly skilled group of professional experts in information processing. Each member of the group headed a glossary effort for either a computer manufacturer, a technical society, an educational institution, or the federal government. In addition to this standard, six other major vocabulary efforts were undertaken and completed. They included:

(1) *The First Glossary of Programming Terminology,* published in 1954, and *Glossary of Terms in the Computer and Information Processing Field,* both prepared by the Association for Computing Machinery.

(2) *Computer Programming and Engineering Terminology,* glossaries prepared from 1954 through 1964 by the author of this dictionary as a series of revised vocabularies that were published both separately and as part of the Computer Surveys conducted by the Computing Laboratory of the Ballistic Research Laboratories. These glossaries were reprinted by many trade associations, computer manufacturers, and technical societies.

(3) *Standard Definitions of Terms for Digital Computers,* a series of glossaries prepared and published from 1956 to 1963 by the Institute of Electrical and Electronics Engineers.

(4) *Automatic Data Processing Glossary*, a comprehensive and popular glossary prepared in 1962 by the Washington, D.C., Area Interagency Automatic Data Processing Committee Task Force on Glossary under the direction of the Bureau of the Budget of the Executive Office of the President.

(5) *Glossary of Terms Relating to Automatic Data Processing,* prepared by the British Standards Institution and published in 1962.

(6) *Vocabulary for Information Processing*, prepared jointly by the International Federation for Information Processing and the International Computation Center and published by the North-Holland Publishing Company in 1965.

In 1970, the American Standard Vocabulary for Information Processing was expanded. The American National Dictionary for Information Processing, prepared under the auspices of the American National Standards Institute, is expected to be published in the near future. In addition, during the last several years, the International Organization for Standardization has published several sections of a vocabulary of information processing.

All the major computer manufacturers prepared and published or reprinted various general and specialized data-processing and communications glossaries, as did many technical societies, industrial firms, government agencies, and publishers. Approximately eighty data-processing vocabularies, in addition to the seven major works cited above, have been published during the last decade. These were primarily devoted to computer engineering, computer programming, data transmission, and communications. More than fifty percent of the terms and definitions found in the eighty vocabularies are contained in the seven major vocabularies cited above. The seven major vocabularies have had the greatest normative influence on vocabulary usage in the United States and many other English-speaking countries.

Many of the eighty vocabularies, as well as the seven major vocabularies, were excellent works, prepared mostly by technical committees made up of professional experts, such as computer programmers, logic designers, system analysts, and educators. Each vocabulary, or glossary, was often designed to meet a specific purpose or was restricted to a limited subject area. Some were meant for programmers, some for engineers, and some were for users, operators, or designers of equipment. Many were reprints or extracts of others. Whole definitions were taken verbatim from one another, creating a high redundancy rate among the terms and their definitions appearing in the various vocabularies. Very often, definitions in one vocabulary were only special cases or more general definitions for the same term in another vocabulary.

The task of preparing this dictionary involved the collection, correlation, and analysis of over 50,000 terms and definitions over a period of twenty years. A complete and comprehensive definition was prepared for each term. The definitions reflect the best popular usage consistent with professional practice and compatible with national and international standards. Appropriate additional explanations, illustrations, examples, and cross-references for further clarification of concepts and meanings were added to the basic defining phrases.

Specifically, the primary task became one of recognizing conflict and agreement among the source definitions, removing inconsistencies, reflecting the best standard current usage, and legislating to a minimum. During this task, the author found that in thousands of entries among the many vocabularies examined, definitions were logically inconsistent. Many definitions were absolutely redundant. Terms that were stated to be synonymous were defined differently in different glossaries and even in the same glossary. Many definitions were merely descriptions of examples, illustrations, or special cases of what might be considered the basic definition.

This task would have been nearly impossible were it not for the fact that the author enjoyed the unique experience of playing a direct, personal, and active role in all of the many major vocabulary efforts cited above. This experience permitted a thorough understanding of the strengths and weaknesses of the major vocabulary efforts as well as an understanding of the relationships among the definitions in each of the vocabularies. The author headed or played a leading role in many vocabulary efforts in computer and information processing within the United States Government, the American National Standards Institute, the International Organization for Standardization, and the Institute of Electrical and Electronics Engineers. In addition, the contents of *Standard Dictionary of Computers and Information Processing* is tempered by the expertise and logical consistency developed by the author during twenty-six years of experience in computer research, digital computer logic circuit design, computer systems evaluation, information systems research and engineering, management information systems, and in teaching electronics and electrical engineering in several universities. Of course, the definitions in this dictionary do not necessarily reflect the official position of the Defense Communications Agency, with which the author is currently employed.

In summary, *Standard Dictionary of Computers and Information Processing* is consistent with the latest and best professional usage approved by technical society, government, national, and international standards bodies.

The new Second Edition contains some 2,500 additional entries. About 500 entries were revised to reflect new usage and improve upon the earlier definitions. No material from the First Edition has been deleted.

Martin H. Weik

Arlington, Virginia

Contents

How to Use This Dictionary

Introduction

The best professional general practice developed for the arrangement of technical dictionaries, particularly the arrangement that has been developed by the American National Standards Institute (formerly the American Standards Association) has been used in the preparation and arrangement of this dictionary. The definitions are concise and informative. Each definition is a description of a concept. Some concepts are somewhat separate and independent and some are closely interrelated with others. Nevertheless, each defined term tends to serve as a label for the concept described by the definition.

The terms in this dictionary are arranged in an inverted word order, with regard to the noun-modifier relationship, and the resulting multiword combinations are alphabetized. Of course, modified nouns alphabetically immediately follow the noun itself. For example, definitions of all types of registers would follow the definition of register. Inverted word order means inverted with respect to natural or spoken English word order. Many foreign languages, particularly the Latin-based languages, are already "inverted" with respect to English, in the sense that the modifier follows the noun. Many lists, indices, thesauri, and structured vocabularies are arranged in this manner. The independent and precise definitions in this dictionary are supplemented with further explanations, illustrations, and examples. Cross-references are added where appropriate. The definitions and supplementary information are based on the contents of many authoritative vocabularies. The definitions in some eighty vocabularies were collated to serve as the data base for the preparation of this dictionary.

The concise, independent, and informative defining phrases, alphabetically arranged under the term being defined, provide immediate cross-referenced access to concepts in computer programming, engineering, operation, and maintenance, as well as general data processing and communications. The proper logical format for definitions developed by the American National Standards Institute have been precisely followed. The additional essay-type supplementary information provides additional background information in the subject area of the definition. This permits the reader to arrive at a better understanding of the definition and the concept described by the definition, than the shorter, authoritative, and professionally accurate definition itself will allow. Adding supporting information to the definitions has been the policy of the British Standards Institution, the International Federation for Information Processing, and the International Computation Center. Cross-referencing permits various forms of threading through the dictionary in order to enhance understanding of related aspects. In short, the "best of everything" has been fully exploited in the preparation of this comprehensive dictionary on computers, information processing, communications, and related subjects.

Construction of the Definitions

The material in this dictionary has been organized to meet the needs of every type of user. It is designed to meet the needs of those who are new to information processing and those who have become skilled professionals. All terms that retain their original meanings in the context of ordinary English have not been included. Those terms that have acquired meanings different from the conventional English meanings found in authoritative English-langauge dictionaries have been included. In many instances, it is these very conventional English-language terms that have been assigned new meanings in the field of information and data processing that require definition. Much confusion has been caused by assigning new meanings to these conventional terms. Each definition has been specifically prepared so as to be independent of other definitions. This was done so as to avoid multiple look-up as much as possible. Circularity of definition was avoided. The defining phrase of each definition is concise, direct, and explicit.

Words were used in the defining phrase in their conventional English-language sense as defined in standard English-language dictionaries. Thus the reader need not be well-grounded in the field of information and data processing in order to grasp the meanings that have been given to the terms in this dictionary. The explanatory remarks that have been added to the defining phrases are designed to assist the reader in developing a complete concept of the full meaning of the term. The definitions meet the highest professional standard of precision and accuracy required by the most experienced professional expert. They were particularly written for such purposes as preparing contracts, manuals, logic designs, advertising, tutorial materials, textbooks, and many other documents wherein high accuracy and precision are required. This dictionary will also appeal to the discerning student and teacher.

All entries are in alphabetical order. Multiple-word terms are alphabetically arranged both in spoken, or natural English word order, as well as in inverted word order. This arrangement permits rapid location of all terms and their modifiers. Many specialized areas, such as addressing, storing, coding, programming, and checking utilize terms consisting of a basic term and a modifier. The definitions of these terms were placed at the alphabetical position of the inverted word order. Thus, the reader will find the definition of the unmodified basic term immediately followed by all the definitions of the modified form of the basic term. He may readily review the definitions of all the related modified forms of a given basic term at the same time and place. This simplifies comparisons. It reduces the necessity of multiple searching. It also provides immediate access to the definitions of the terms that are related to the basic term. The following list of terms, which are defined in the dictionary, shows how related concepts are immediately at hand by this alphabetical arrangement:

word	word, instruction	word generator, manual
word, alphabetic	word, long	word indexing
word, call	word, machine	word length
word, computer	word, numeric	word length, fixed
word, control	word, parameter	word length, variable
word, data	word, reserved	word mark
word, double	word, short	word-organized storage
word, fixed-length	word, variable-length	word space
word, index	word capacity	word-time
word, information	word gap	

For the case of synonyms, the definitions are placed at the alphabetical position of the inverted word order form of the term being defined. Thus, deprecation of the use of a term is indicated by simply pointing out that the term is synonymous with another term. A cross-reference to the preferred usage is placed at the alphabetical position of the synonym. For the sake of avoiding ambiguity and to promote precise and effective communication among those in the information processing field, it is recommended that the preferred terms be used rather than their synonyms. At the end of a definition, all synonyms of the defined term are listed. A further discussion on synonyms and their treatment in this dictionary is given below under the use of the cross-referencing phrases. The following example shows how synonyms are handled and preferred usage is indicated:

character, illegal—A character that is not acceptable as a valid representation by a data-processing system or by a specific program; for example, the binary notation 1011 for a binary-coded decimal system of numeral representation, where the binary numerals 0000 through 1001, or 0 through 9, are used to represent the ten digits. (Synonymous with *false code*, with *nonexistent code*, with *unused code*, with *forbidden digit*, with *unallowable instruction digit*, with *forbidden combination*, with *illegal command*, with *improper command*, with *unused command*, with *forbidden character*, and with *improper character*.)

3

false code—Same as *character, illegal.*

---

nonexistent code—Same as *character, illegal.*

---

unused code—Same as *character, illegal.*

It is most important that a reader of a definition be confronted with examples of the term being defined, not examples of a term given in the text of a definition. Confusion can often be caused and the wrong impression can be left in the mind of a reader if the proper distinction is not made between examples of the term being defined and examples of terms in its definition. Stated in another way, the reader must be left with the impression that the examples he read were examples of the term he looked up, not examples of some word that happened to appear in the text of the definition, if such is the case. If this is not the case, proper indication must also be made. As a matter of convention in this matter, "for example" is used to indicate an example of the *term being defined,* not some illustration of an item mentioned in the definitions.

The term "such as" is used to indicate examples or illustrations that occur within the text of the definitions and that are not examples of the term being defined. Naturally, the use of both "for example" and "such as" can occur in the same definition.

The various parts of speech of the term being defined are simply indicated by the first word of the defining phrase. Nouns are indicated by the use of a, an, the, any, or each of.

Verbs are written in their infinitive form. They are indicated by the use of "to" as the first word of the defining phrase.

Adjectives are indicated by the consistent use of "pertaining to" as the initial words of the defining phrase, as in the following examples:

bandpass—Pertaining to the operation of a circuit or device, such as a filter, that permits the passage of a specified frequency range. The range of frequencies is expressed as the difference between the limited frequencies at which the power transferred is one-half, or down 3 decibels, of the power transferred at the midfrequency between the limiting frequencies. The midfrequency is also specified. (Contrast with *lowpass* and *highpass*.)

---

decimal—A characteristic or property involving a selection, choice, or condition in which there are 10 possibilities. Pertaining to ten; for example, pertaining to the numeration system with a radix of ten. Many systems, such as the metric system of weights and measures and the United States currency system are decimal systems. Decimal systems are rapidly becoming standard systems for human use. Machine binary systems are usually converted to and from decimal at input and output points.

---

processing, parallel—Pertaining to the simultaneous execution of two or more sequences of instructions by a device having multiple processing units, such as by a computer having multiple arithmetic or logic units. (Contrast with *multiprogramming.* Synonymous with *simultaneous working.*)

It often becomes necessary to place a usage label before a defining phrase to inform, if not warn, the reader that the particular definition he is about to read is written for a specific area of applicationn, such as computer programming, communications, optical character recognition, or mathematics. Such labels are necessary especially when the same term has different meanings in other areas of interest. Where no usage label is given, it is implied that the term is defined according to general usage in the broad field of data processing. The usage label is illustrated in the following examples:

trunk, final—In telephone communications, the last long-distance trunk that connects switching centers which are adjacent to each other in the line of communication, such as a local center to its secondary center, a secondary center to its primary center, a primary center to its zone center, or one zone center to another.

---

sort—In data processing, to arrange data items in groups according to specific rules, fields, or keys used to identify and group them; for example, the items may be segregated into pigeonholes, pockets, storage locations, or printed lists in order to collect like items in one place. Sorting does not necessarily involve sequencing, but sorting is usually a prerequisite to sequencing and ordering. In actual practice, many sorts are made according to numerical or alphabetic sequences, resulting in a sort by letters or numbers, and so a resultant ordering occurs in accordance with the collating sequence.

Following the usage label is the the defining phrase, which actually is the basic definition itself. The additional remarks that tend to clarify the definition are contained in complete sentences following the defining phrase. The defining phrase is the complete definition. The explanatory remarks serve to illustrate and cite additional examples, cross-references, and related matters. The cross-references are always placed at the end of the definition.

Interrelationships among and between related terms are indicated at the end of the definition by inserting one or more phrases each introduced by one of the following sets of terms as appropriate:

5

Synonymous with ...	Further clarified by ...	Contrast with ...
Closely related to ...	Illustrated by ...	Compared with ...
Related to ...	Illustrative of ...	See ... and Same as ...

In each case of the use of the above terms, the definitions are cross-referenced to and from one another. The following paragraphs discuss the use of each of these cross-referencing phrases.

Synonymous with ...

Placed at the end of appropriate definitions, this indicates the terms that are used synonymously with the term that is being defined. The synonyms are written here in natural English-language word order, since there is no need to look up the definition of a synonym. Synonyms are not and need not be separately defined. At the alphabetical location of the synonym, only a back reference to the preferred term will be found. The reference "Same as..." is placed at the location of the synonym. This means that the definition for this term is the *same as* the definition found under the preferred term. Use of the synonym is deprecated in the interest of promoting unambiguous communication and general improvement of information exchange. In summary, the term that has the definition printed along with it is the preferred term.

Closely related to ...

Often there are terms with just a sufficient shade of difference from another term to justify a separate definition. In such cases, a separate definition is given, but the close proximity to the other term is indicated by this phrase. A reader interested in a particular term may properly distinguish between various shades of meaning by reviewing the definitions of closely related terms. This allows the most accurate and precise usage obtainable for a given situation.

Related to ...

Many terms represent associated and perhaps overlapping concepts. A given concept is more firmly grasped and understood when related concepts are also reviewed. This two-way, cross-referencing scheme permits the reader to develop a full understanding of a given definition by facilitating immediate review of definitions of related concepts. Regardless of the direction from which or to which the reader is referred, he will be led to a completely developed concept. This permits the definition originally sought to be placed in its proper perspective with respect to related definitions.

Further clarified by . . .

Oftentimes a definition, though complete and independent, leaves a great deal more to be desired in terms of the development of a full understanding of the concept being defined. Further understanding of a given definition may be found by reading definitions of other terms, even though the concepts are not specifically related very closely. Other definitions may contain information that expands on the definition that was originally sought. Tracing these cross-references permits the reader to obtain additional knowledge in the subject area of the definition. It is strongly recommended that the reader review these references contained in the definition he is seeking. They will round out his grasp of the meaning of the term whose definition he is seeking. Of course, even further information can be obtained if the reader will review the definition of the terms used in a definition. In the interest of brevity, some definitions were written with terms defined elsewhere in this dictionary. However, special care was taken in the preparation of this dictionary to use ordinary English in the definitions whenever possible to reduce multiple look-up to an absolute minimum.

Illustrated by . . .   and   *Illustrative of* . . .

Very often a given term is an example or illustration of another term. For example, one term might be the name of a set and another term the name of a member of the same set; or, the other term may be the name of a subset. In such instances, a two-way cross-reference has been established in order to show the proper relationship.

In many instances, the above kind of relationship is also clearly indicated when the definitions of modified forms of basic terms are placed alphabetically immediately following the definition of the basic term. In order to place such entries in close proximity, the entries containing a comma, which indicates a modified version of a basic or generic term, precede a space in alphabetical order.

Contrast with . . .

Very often a definition bears a specific and distinct relationship to another concept. One of these relationships is that a concept may be an inverse, reverse, reciprocal, or opposite of another term. A concept may be the "other half" of a simple dichotomy. For example, if a reader is interested in such a term as *shop, open,* then he might also want to review the definition of *shop, closed.* It will soon become obvious to the reader that the truly contrasting terms, that is, the inverse, reverse, reciprocal, or opposite terms, differ in their definitions by just a few words, sometimes by only one or two. Often the words that differ are antonyms that describe the contrast. Such pairs of definitions are very carefully paraphrased with parallel wording for maximum consistency.

7

Compare with . . .

Rather than contrasting the various aspects of two or more concepts, it may be more advantageous to the reader to learn of the similarities of the several concepts. In this case, the wording of the cross-reference suggests that the reader compare this definition with other definitions to develop a full grasp of the original definition being sought. In this case, emphasis is placed on the commonality of two definitions rather than on particular differences.

See . . . and *Same as* . . .

These references will always appear without definition. They are separate entries. "See" is used to refer the reader from the natural or spoken word order to the inverted word order, where the definition is. "Same as" indicates specifically that the definition that should appear there for the term given will be found alphabetically under another term. This reference is used to refer the reader from a synonym to the preferred term, where the definition is. This device is used to indicate preferred usage and is aimed at providing some normative influence. Of course, the definitions themselves also tend to promote proper usage. This arrangement also relieves the reader from having to know all the modified forms of a term in order to locate the term he may be seeking. Normally the reader should seek the definition of multiword terms at the alphabetical position of the inverted word order. Thus, the definition of *index register* will be found under *register, index*. Of course, the basic term and its modifier may also be separately defined, as they are in this case. The natural word order is also indexed. For example, if one is reading a report with a sentence containing *volatile storage,* he may decide to seek the definition of *volatile,* feeling that he knows what storage means. If so, he will find an entry under *volatile storage,* where he will find all other things that are volatile, and he will be directed to *storage, volatile,* where he will find all sorts of other types of storage. This arrangement provides maximum flexibility and universal usage of this dictionary, permitting the reader to cope with every type of situation that may arise.

When it is necessary to have several definitions for the same term, the separate definitions are numbered and are considered as separate concepts. Cross-references to these terms are also appropriately numbered. For example, a given term might be synonymous with only the second definition of another term, and not the first definition.

In summary, this dictionary permits browsing among associated terms and concepts in a chainlike fashion through the use of specific references located at the end of the definitions. This permits the reader to develop a full understanding of meanings and concepts to any desired degree of specificity and generality.

a

A AND NOT B gate—See *gate, A AND NOT B.*
A EXCEPT B gate—Same as *gate, A AND NOT B.*
A ignore B gate—See *gate, A ignore B.*
A ignore B gate, negative—See *gate, negative (A ignore B).*
A implies B gate—Same as *gate, B OR NOT A.*
A implies B gate, negative—Same as *gate, A AND NOT B.*
A OR NOT B gate-See *gate, A OR NOT B.*
A-register —Same as *register, arithmetic.*
abacus—The abacus was introduced to the Orient through early trade with the Romans and has been highly developed by both Chinese and Japanese mathematicians. Today there are three basic types of abacus; the Chinese abacus (illustrated), the Japanese abacus, which has one bead above instead of two, and the relatively new abacus for the blind, with four beads below and one above the wire. Instructions for each type are quite different, and an expert on one cannot necessarily operate any other with efficiency. (Synonymous with *soroban.*)
ABC Coding System—An automatic coding system and programming language developed and used at the Atomic Research Establishment, Berkshire, England.
abnormal termination—See *termination, abnormal.*
absolute accuracy—See *accuracy, absolute.*
absolute address—See *address, absolute.*
absolute addressing—Same as *addressing, absolute.*
absolute code—See *code, absolute.*
absolute coordinate—See *coordinate, absolute.*
absolute data—See *data, absolute.*
absolute error—See *error, absolute.*
absolute instruction—See *instruction, absolute.*
absolute language—Same as *language, machine.*
absolute loader—See *loader, absolute.*
absolute vector—See *vector, absolute.*
abstract—1: A summary or an abridged version of a larger body of information. The abstract is generally used to disseminate information concerning the

contents of a larger body of information, thus permitting the individual to determine whether the information is of further or particular interest to him. An abstract may be descriptive or informative. Generally, abstracts are made from written documents; however, there are also film, tape, card, and other types of abstracts. Many abstracting services and information agencies prepare and distribute abstracts in bound volumes, cards, and microfilm. (Further clarified by *autoabstract;* by *abstract, descriptive;* and by *abstract, informative.*) **2:** To prepare a summary or abridged version or to describe the contents of a larger body of information.

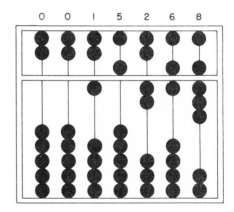

An abacus *representing 15,268.*

abstract, descriptive—An abstract that summarizes the nature or kind of information contained in a larger body of information.
abstract, informative—An abstract that summarizes the important results or significant facts contained in a larger body of information.
abstract, telegraphic—An abbreviated stylized abstract written in short, meaningful phrases, and generally considered suitable for machine input and processing.

9

ac−1: A suffix used to indicate automatic computer; for example, ORDVAC, EDVAC, ENIAC, SEAC, UNIVAC, and ILLIAC. **2:** An abbreviation of alternating current, a sinusoidal variation of voltage, which, when applied to linear passive elements, produces a sinusoidal variation of current. Thus, one does speak of an a-c voltage, although it is not strictly correct usage. The standard power frequency in the United States is 60 Hz. In Europe it is 50 Hz. In many industrial and control applications such as aircraft and missiles, 400-Hz a-c equipment is utilized. **3:** An abbreviation of accumulator.

a-c-coupled flip-flop−See *flip-flop, a-c-coupled.*

a-c coupling−See *coupling, a-c.*

a-c dump−See *dump, a-c.*

a-c flip-flop−Same as *flip-flop, a-c-coupled.*

ACC−1: An abbreviation of accumulator. It is used to signify an accumulating register in many computer instruction codes; for example, in the IBM 709 instruction code, it signifies the accumulator register. **2:** An abbreviation of Air Coordinating Committee, Air Control Center, Allied Control Commission, Astronomical Great Circle Course, and Army Chemical Center.

acceleration time−See *time, acceleration.*

acceptor−An element that is introduced in small quantities as an impurity to semiconductor materials and that has a negative valence less than the valence of the pure semiconductor. For example, if germanium, with a valence of −4, is doped with small amounts of boron, with a valence of −3, the covalent bonds that form in the crystal structure have an electron missing at each boron atom. These boron centers are waiting to accept an electron. If one enters, it necessarily leaves a "hole" in a neighboring germanium atom, thus creating a mobile hole, since another neighbor will supply an electron and so on. Thus, the hole is free to move about. Since each hole can accept an electron, the doping material or impurity is called an acceptor of electrons, or simply, acceptor. The resulting material is called p-type germanium semiconductor. Conduction occurs as a migration of holes, that is, positive charges; thus the semiconductor is called p-type. (Further clarified by *semiconductor, intrinsic;* by *donor;* by *hole;* by *transistor, n-p-n;* by *transistor, p-n-p;* and by *semiconductor, p-type.*)

ACCESS−(Aircraft Communication Electronic Signaling System). Developed by Motorola and General Precision, Inc.

access, direct−1: Same as *access, random.* **2:** A method of accessing data without regard to the sequence in which they are stored.

access, immediate−1: Pertaining to the ability to transfer information into or out of a storage location or register without delay due to other units of data and usually

without delay due to parts of the data itself; that is, the transfer is performed in parallel fashion rather than serial. **2:** Pertaining to a relatively short access time or relatively rapid transfer of information. **3:** Pertaining to a device that is directly connected or available to another device; for example, a register directly connected to an input device or to an arithmetic unit. The arithmetic unit registers themselves can be considered immediate-access registers. Other terms that have been used interchangeably with immediate access are zero access and instantaneous access. Both are deprecated. (Synonymous with *instantaneous access* and with *zero access.* Further clarified by *addition, zero-access.*)

access, indexed−A method of accessing data in which the locations of the data are determined from an index or a table.

access, instantaneous−Same as *access, immediate.*

access, keyed−1: A method of accessing data in which the locations of the data are determined algorithmically from keys, labels, flags, tags, pointers, or indicators. **2:** Pertaining to a method of accessing data by means of hardware recognition of physically recorded keys, labels, tags, flags, pointers, or indicators.

access, multiple−Pertaining to a system in which input and output may be dispatched or received at more than one geographic location or with more than one device at a single location.

access, parallel−The process of transferring information to or from a storage device wherein all the elements of a unit of information are transferred simultaneously; for example, in transferring a 40-binary-digit word from an electrostatic or core storage unit, 40 wires would be used, from 40 cores and, in the case of electrostatic storage, usually from 40 cathode-ray tubes. (Synonymous with *simultaneous access.* Contrast with *access, serial.*)

access, queued−1: Pertaining to the automatic synchronization of the transfer of data among devices under program control so as to eliminate delays in operation. **2:** A method of accessing data in which the data is stored in a queue in main storage to eliminate a wait for transmission from an input device when a record is requested.

access, random−1: Pertaining to a storage device in which access to a particular address is such that the time required to transfer a unit of information to or from the storage is independent of the location or address which is accessed. Thus, the access time for each storage cell is the same for each location. This is in contrast to serial access, in which the access time for a particular unit of information in storage depends on the selected address. In this case, one can speak of an average random access time, which is the average access time to or from storage locations selected at random. **2:** Pertaining to a storage device in which random access, as defined in (1), can be achieved automatically and without a time penalty; for example, by queuing or through the used of a buffer. Access is considered random if the conditions under which the next storage position to be accessed by the program is in no way dependent upon the previously accessed position. **3:** Pertaining to a semirandom or partially random access storage unit, in which a channel or track is a random access type, but in which the individual addresses or locations are serial. Thus, on a magnetic drum, the time required to select a particular track is the same as for any other track. However, it is better to refer to a device as random access only if it is completely so, as defined in (1) and (2). (Contrast with *access, serial*.)

access, sequential–1: A method of accessing data in which physically consecutive records in storage are processed sequentially. **2:** Pertaining to a device that processes data in a sequential manner, such as a card reader or tape unit.

access, serial–1: Pertaining to a storage device in which access to a particular address is such that the time required to transfer a unit of information is dependent on the storage location or address that is accessed. (Contrast with *access, parallel* and with *access, random*.) **2:** Pertaining to a device in which information is stored in such a manner that it is read or obtained in time sequence. Thus, in a serial access storage device, there is a sequential process of retrieving or storing information in the device. This process depends on the sequential relation existing between successive storage locations; for example, an address or location can be arrived at simply by counting previous locations.

access, simultaneous–Same as *access, parallel*.

access, zero–Same as *access, immediate*.

access arm–See *arm, access*.

access coding, minimal–Same as *coding, minimal latency*.

access control, data–See *control, data access*.

access control, file–See *control, file access*.

access line–See *line, access*.

access mode–See *mode, access*.

access storage, serial–See *storage, serial access*.

access time–See *time, access*.

accordion–A type of printed-circuit connector contact in which the spring is given a corrugated or "Z" shape to permit a greater deflection without overstressing the spring.

accounting machine–See *machine, accounting*.

accounting machines, electric–See *EAM*.

accumulator–A device in which representations of numbers are stored, and, upon the receipt of other numbers, certain operations are performed and the results stored. Simply stated, the accumulator is a device that stores the augend and on receipt of the addend adds the two numbers and stores the sum. The actual adding is performed within or by the accumulator itself. In some applications, the accumulator can be cleared, that is, reset to zero, after which time all numbers received are added to what is already stored. In other applications, the accumulator can control or modify another quantity in another register or storage location. It can also serve as the register or the arithmetic and logic unit. Perhaps because of its close association with the arithmetic and logic unit, which uses the accumulator as an integral part, the accumulator has been erroneously called the zero-access register.

accumulator, running–Same as *storage, push-down*.

accuracy–1: A measure of or the quality of freedom from error; the degree of exactness possessed by an approximation or measurement. A high degree of accuracy implies a low degree of error. Accuracy is also a measure of or the degree of conformity to a rule or to truth. Accuracy denotes the absolute quality of computed results. In contrast, precision refers to the degree to which computed results reflect theoretical values. Thus, four-place results are less precise than six-place results; nevertheless, four-place results might be more accurate than six-place results that contain computational errors, human mistakes, print errors, etc. Thus, humans make mistakes, machines malfunction, and programs contain errors. All these contribute to accuracy. (Contrast with *error*, with *precision*, with *malfunction*, and with *mistake*.) **2:** A quantitative measure of the magnitude of error, preferably expressed as a function of the relative error, a high value of the measure corresponding to a small error.

accuracy, absolute–The accuracy that is determined or measured from a specified reference point or origin, rather than from a relative point as a difference value.

AC-DC ringing–See *ringing, AC-DC*.

ACE–An algebraic system utilized by the Canadian Atomic Energy Commission for the Burroughs 205 computer.

ACK–The acknowledge character.

acknowledge character–See *character, acknowledge*.

acknowledge character, negative–See *character, negative acknowledge*.

ACM–(Association for Computing Machinery). A technical society devoted to advancing the art of computer technology, logical design, programs usage, and other computer-related activities.

ACM Committee on Nomenclature–The committee of the Association for

Computing Machinery that, under the chairmanship of Grace Murray Hopper, published in June, 1954, the first glossary of programming terminology. The influence of this glossary is evident in every glossary of computer engineering and programming published since.

ACM-GAMM—(Association for Computing Machinery-German Association for Applied Mathematics and Mechanics). An organization devoted to the development of the computer language ALGOL.

ACOM—An automatic coding system utilized by General Motors Corporation for the IBM 701 and 705 computers.

acorn tube—See *tube, acorn.*

acoustic delay-line—See *delay-line, acoustic.*

acronym—A word formed from the initial letter, letters, or syllables taken from a succession or group of words, and capable of being articulated: for example, *snafu* for *situation normal, all fouled up.* An acronym may also be constructed from the initial letters plus the terminal letters of words: for example, motel for motor hotel. Hundreds of acronyms have been used to label computer programs, compilers, translators, and subroutines; some of them include ENIAC, EDVAC, SAGE, COBOL, ALGOL, and FORTRAN. Note also that letters taken from internal parts of successive words do not form true acronyms nor do simple abbreviations, such as RCA for Radio Corporation of America, since acronyms must be capable of being pronounced.

ACSIMATIC—(Assistant Chief of Staff for Intelligence). An information storage, processing, and retrieval system used for the processing of intelligence information by the Office of the Assistant Chief of Staff for Intelligence. A special computer language called Acsimatic is used. The equipment used is a Sylvania S9400 and a Telex Mass Memory Module disc file.

ACT—1: (Automatic Code Translator). A translator developed by Sperry-Rand Corporation for the Univac systems. **2:** Army Chemical Typewriter.

ACT I—(Algebraic Compiler and Translator). A compiler developed by Royal McBee Corporation for the LGP 30 computer.

ACT III—An extension of ACT I developed by National Carbon Corporation for use on the LGP 30 computer.

action, spring-finger—Pertaining to the operation of an electrical contact that permits a stress-free spring action to provide contact pressure and retention. Contacts of these types are used in the sockets of printed-circuit and other types of electrical connectors.

action, wiping—Pertaining to the sliding of one electrical contact surface against another under some force for the purpose of cleaning or polishing the surfaces and thus improving the contact. Such sliding action will tend to wear away or break through surface films and metallic corrosion such as oxides, sulfides, and chlorides.

action line—See *line, action.*

action period—See *period, action.*

action spot—See *spot, action.*

action time—See *time, action.*

activate button—Same as *button, initiate.*

activate key—Same as *button, initiate.*

active—1: A dynamic or used state. Examples include: a record or file that is being used or referred to or that is pending such usage; an electrical device, such as a tube or transistor, which is capable of amplifying, controlling, modulating, and mixing signals; an element in its excited state in contrast to a ground state. Components of computing systems are active when their operation is directed by the control unit. **2:** Pertaining to the general class of devices that require a power supply separate from the controls; for example, a transistor, since it requires a power supply and a controlling signal, such as an input signal; or a fluidic amplifier, that enables one or more signals to control a source of power and thus is able to deliver at its output an enlarged reproduction of the characteristics of the input signal.

active element—See *element, active.*

active file—See *file, active.*

activity—The use of, alteration of, or referral to a file of information. The level of activity of a record is a measure of the number of referrals or transactions requiring the use or modification of the information in the file or record. For example, the activity of a checking account might be measured by the sum of the number of checks drawn, the number of deposits tallied, and the number of statements prepared during a given period. The activity of an inventory control file might be the number of requisitions, the number of restocking shipments, and the number of inventories made on a given item.

activity ratio—Same as *ratio, file activity.*

activity ratio, file—See *ratio, file activity.*

actual address—Same as *address, absolute.*

actual key—See *key, actual.*

actual time—Same as *time, real.*

ADAPSO—An association of United States and Canadian data-processing service organizations, devoted to operating and maintaining computers and providing computer time to users in government, industry, and education.

ADAPT—A data-processing compiler, somewhat similar to COBOL, developed by Computer Sciences Corporation, for the IBM 1401 computer.

add, Boolean—Same as *OR.*

add, false—To add without carries; that is, to perform a logic add. For example, to create a partial binary sum by adding two binary numerals without considering carries.

add, logic—An operation performed in the Boolean algebra on two binary digits at a time, such that the result is a one if either one or both digits are a one. However, if both digits are a zero, the result is a zero. Logic addition is the operation. The operator is referred to as the OR operator. OR implies the inclusive-OR operation. The word OR comes from the English statement, if either one digit or the other or both, is a one, the result is a one. The operation is only somewhat related to arithmetic addition: $1 + 0 = 1$, $0 + 1 = 1$, $0 + 0 = 0$, but $1 + 1 = 1$. The + sign is often used to indicate the logic add. (Synonymous with *logical add*. Further clarified by *OR*, and by *sum, logic*. Contrast with *AND*, with *multiply, logic*, and with *addition*.)

```
A    0 1 0 0 1 0 1 1

B    0 0 0 1 1 0 1 0

LOGIC SUM   A+B   0 1 0 1 1 0 1 1

ARITHMETIC SUM   A+B   0 1 1 0 0 1 0 1
```

The logic sum that results from a logic add operation, contrasted with the arithmetic sum that results from an arithmetic add operation.

add, logical—Same as *add, logic.*

add, special—An addition operation that permits the addition of numbers having twice as many digits as the computer register is capable of holding; a kind of "double-precision addition." Use of the term is not recommended, as it is misleading.

add operation—See *operation, add.*

add operation, Boolean—Same as *operation, disjunction.*

add time—See *time, add.*

add-without-carry gate—Same as *gate, exclusive-OR.*

addend—A quantity or number that is to be added to another number, called the augend, producing a result called the sum. The addend is an arithmetic operand in the summing operation. The augend is usually on hand or considered first; for example, the augend is the number already in an accumulator and the addend is added to it.. However, when coincident combinational logic is used, as in a binary adder, the distinction between augend and addend is academic. (Further clarified by *adder* and by *augend*.)

adder—A device that is capable of forming the algebraic or arithmetic sum of two or more quantities, i.e., representations of numbers which are presented as inputs. Usually, the adder cannot retain the sum, i.e., the sum is present only as long as the inputs are time coincidentally present. In other cases, the sum is presented to a register or an accumulator, where it may be temporarily stored prior to its transfer to another location. Thus the adder can be considered a logic element with three input channels, to which signals, representing the addend, augend, and carry, may be applied; and two output channels, from which the sum and carry digits emerge. This device is more precisely called a full-adder, which includes a digit delay element for the carry and which therefore has only two external input signal channels for addend and augend, and one output channel, for the sum. Adders may be serial or parallel, digital or analog. An accumulator, a differential gear assembly and some desk calculators are also sometimes called adders. Three-input adder and full-adder are usually implied by the term adder alone. (Synonymous with *three-input adder* and with *full-adder*. Contrast with *half-adder* and with *subtracter*. Further clarified by *addend* and by *augend*.)

adder, analog—Same as *amplifier, summing.*

adder, half—See *half-adder.*

adder, hard—An adder consisting of a digital integrator in which increments of several input variables and of the output integral itself contribute to the total Δy input, without a reversal in sign. If Δy is the total input increment, then in operation, an oscillation develops because of repeated overflow of y between maximum positive and maximum negative values. The integrator output is effectively represented in binary form, irrespective of the normal representation used. The average output represents the average of minus the sum of the inputs. Binary incremental representation is used. Thus, the value of an increment is rounded to one of the values of $+1$ or -1. The extreme values of the rate of change of a variable that can be represented in this system are plus

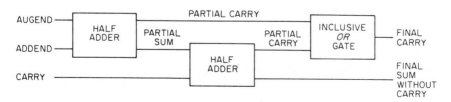

A block diagram of an adder.

and minus one quantum per step. Values between the extremes can be represented as an average of the different rounded values over a sufficiently large number of steps. The hard adder is used in incremental-type computers. (Contrast with *adder, soft.* Further clarified by *computer, incremental.*)

adder, one-digit—Same as *half-adder.*

adder, parallel—A digital adder in which addition is performed concurrently on digits in all of the digit places of the operands. (Contrast with *adder, serial.*)

adder, serial—A digital adder in which addition is performed by adding the corresponding digits of the operands digit place after digit place. (Contrast with *adder, parallel.*)

adder, soft—An adder, used in incremental computers, consisting of a digital integrator in which increments of several input variables and of a sign-reversed version of the output integral itself all contribute to the Δy input. Thus, the output is equal to minus the sum of the inputs. The output is smoothed and delayed. (Contrast with *adder, hard.* Further clarified by *computer, incremental.*)

adder, three-input—Same as *adder.*

adder, two-input—Same as *half-adder.*

adder-subtracter—A device or logic element made to behave as an *adder* or a *substracter* in accordance with the nature of a control signal applied to it. (Further clarified by *adder* and by *subtracter.*)

addition—An arithmetic process or operation that produces the sum of two or more numbers. For example, $6 + 5 = 11$ is an addition operation. The numbers to be added are the addend and augend. The augend is considered as *augmenting,* supplementing, or increasing the addend, that is being added to it. The result of the addition operation is the sum. (Contrast with *add, logic.*)

addition, arithmetic—Same as *addition.*

addition, destructive—Addition performed on a computer wherein the sum appears in the storage location, register, or accumulator, previously occupied by an operand, usually the augend, that becomes lost. (Contrast with *addition, nondestructive.* Further clarified by *operation, arithmetic.*)

addition, nondestructive—Addition performed on a computer in such a manner that the first operand placed in the arithmetic register is the augend. The addend is then added. The sum becomes the new augend. (Contrast with *addition, destructive.* Further clarified by *operation, arithmetic.*)

addition, parallel—Addition in which all the digits of the augend and addend are simultaneously available and are processed concurrently. Thus addition is performed concurrently on digits in all the digit places of the operands, with

appropriate propagation of carries. (Contrast with *addition, serial*).

addition, serial—Addition that is performed by adding the corresponding digits of the operands digit place after digit place. As the digits of each pair of digits in corresponding digit places are added, the generated carry digit is added to the digits at the next more significant digit place. (Contrast with *addition, parallel.*)

addition, zero-access—Addition performed by adding a number to a number already held in an accumulator and forming the sum in the same accumulator. When addition is completed, the sum is available for the next operation and no access time is involved for either the addend or storing the sum. Only the augend had to be fetched. However, this can be accomplished during the addition process. Hence the term *zero-access* has been coined and is often incorrectly applied. (Further clarified by *access, immediate.*)

addition record—See *record, addition.*

addition-without-carry—Same as *operation, non-equivalence.*

addition-without-carry gate—Same as *gate, exclusive-OR.*

additional character—Same as *character, special.*

address—1: An identification, such as a name, label or tag, represented by a number or another set of symbols, that specifies a register, location in storage, or other data source or destination. 2: The part of an instruction that specifies the location of an operand involved in the instruction. Addresses are usually numerical. Thus, an address serves the same purpose as index tabs in a filing system. 3: The representation of the destination of a message. If the address is a person, he is called the addressee. 4: To refer to data, a device, or storage location by its address, or to assign an address to data, a device, or storage location.

address, absolute—1: The specific designation assigned to a storage location, device, or register by the machine designer. The absolute address is inherent in the design of the computer. Usually, the absolute addresses are arrived at by systematically numbering the storage locations in spatial sequence. Thus, adjacent locations are assigned adjacent numbers. The absolute addresses are used to assist in fault diagnosis, so as to permit finding the faulty circuit physically. Thus, the absolute address defines the physical location in the equipment. It might be likened to a bin number in a warehouse. It can be used directly in a program. (Synonymous with *specific address,* with *actual address,* with *machine address,* and with *explicit address.* Clarified by *address, base;* by *address, relative;* and by *address, effective.*) 2: An address, usually written in a computer language, that identifies a storage location, or a device, without the use of an intermediate reference.

address, actual—Same as *address, absolute.*

address, base—An address, usually a number, that is used to modify all the relative addresses of a particular program in order to convert all relative addresses to absolute addresses. Thus, a programmer, when writing a program chooses relative addresses, that is, relative to the particular program. The machine can transfer words to and from storage locations and specific registers only on the basis of absolute addresses. The reference point for each program is the base address. Usually, the relative addresses plus the base address yield the absolute addresses. The base address for each program may be stored in an index register. Each relative address of each instruction is added to the base address in order to obtain each absolute address. (Synonymous with *presumptive address* and with *reference address.* Clarified by *address, relative*; by *address, absolute*; and by *address, effective.*)

RELATIVE ADDRESS	ABSOLUTE ADDRESS
0 0 1	4 0 1
0 0 2	4 0 2
0 0 3	4 0 3
0 0 4	4 0 4
⋮	⋮
1 8 9	5 8 9
1 9 0	5 9 0

BASE ADDRESS = 400

Absolute addresses computed from the program relative addresses and the base address.

address, binary-coded—1: Any address that is written in binary form, that is, using a binary system of number representation. **2:** In certain specific computing systems and programs, the addresses on decks of punched cards containing data and instructions in binary form, but lacking the absolute or machine address, and therefore, in this special instance, considered as a relative address coded in binary form.

address, calculated—Same as *address, synthetic.*

address, direct—An address, usually in a machine instruction, that specifies the location of an operand. The number, given in the address part of the instruction word, is the direct address if it is the number of the storage location in which an operand for the instruction is stored. (Synonymous with *one-level address*, with *first-level address*, and with *single-level address.* Further clarified by *addressing, direct.* Contrast with *address, indirect* and with *addressing, indirect.*)

address, double—Same as *two-address.*

address, effective—The address used in the execution of a particular instruction. Usually it is obtained by modifying the base address of the particular program instruction by the contents of an index register. The address thus obtained is effective for that program and will be treated or used as the valid or effective address as far as that program is concerned. It still may be a relative address and not the absolute address. (Further clarified by *address, absolute*; by *address, relative*; and by *address, base.*)

address, explicit—Same as *address, absolute.*

address, first-level—Same as *address, direct.*

address, floating—An address that is not necessarily related or referenced to a particular base, but is written so that it can be easily converted to an absolute address by any means. A floating address is usually written as a symbolic address and as a relative address, to be automatically converted to an absolute address. (Synonymous with *variable address.*)

address, four—See *four-address.*

address, four-plus-one—A computer instruction that contains four operands, or instruction addresses, and a control address.

address, generated—Same as *address, synthetic.*

address, hash—A pseudorandom address generated by performing operations on a key or identifier. Repeating the operations must yield the same address each time the operations are performed.

address, immediate—An instruction address that is used as an operand by the instruction itself. Thus, the operation part of the instruction word designates an operation, such as compare, that operates upon the address part of the same instruction. (Synonymous with *zero-level address*, with *virtual address*, and with *real-time address.* Further clarified by *addressing, immediate.*)

address, indexed—An address that is to be or has been modified by the contents of an index register or similar device.

address, indirect—An address that indicates the location of a direct address or another indirect address. When executing an instruction containing an indirect address, the machine will interpret the storage contents of the indirect address as the address of the operand that is to be operated upon. It is possible that this second-level storage location does not contain the ultimate operand, but contains the address of the operand, in which case the operand is said to be located at the third-level address. This chaining or multiple-leveling of addresses must be terminated by direct hardware control or a termination symbol in the program, which will cause the machine to halt the interpretation of storage contents as addresses. Thus, one-level addressing, two-level addressing, three-level addressing, etc., are special cases of indirect addressing. Indirect addressing is a powerful replacement for or supplement to the use of index registers in scientific and business data processing, since it allows the program to contain the addresses of the addresses. (Contrast with *address, direct*. Illustrated by *address, second-level* and by *address, two-level*. Further clarified by *addressing, indirect;* by *addressing, two-level;* and by *address, third-level*.)

address, initial—Same as *origin, computer program*.

address, instruction—The address of the location, usually in storage, where the instruction word is stored. The machine control automatically refers to these addresses sequentially unless otherwise directed to skip or branch or, as in the case of four-address and certain other addressing schemes, the control refers to another storage location not necessarily the next or adjacent address in a given sequence of operations. Thus, the next instruction to be executed is determined by programmed control of the instruction addresses.

address, machine—Same as *address, absolute*.

address, multiple—Pertaining to a machine instruction that has or explicitly refers to two or more addresses and usually one operation to be performed on or with the contents of the specified locations; the addresses may specify the location of operands, subsequent instructions, or the destinations of results. Examples of multiple-address instructions are the two-address, three-address, and four-address instructions. There are many modifications and variations of these. (Synonymous with *multiaddress*. Further clarified by *one-address*, by *two-address*, by *three-address*, by *four-address*, by *one-plus-one address*, by *four-plus-one address*, by *modified three-address*, by *variable address*, and by *one-and-one-half address*.)

address, Nth-level—An indirect address written at the Nth addressing level; for example, a second-level address that specifies the address of the desired operand or the third-level address. (Illustrated by *address, second-level*.)

address, one—See *one-address*.

address, one-level—Same as *address, direct*.

address, one-plus-one—A method of addressing in a computer program such that each instruction includes or specifies an operation and two addresses, one address for a register or storage location containing the item to be operated upon and the other address for the register or storage location containing the next instruction to be performed.

address, presumptive—Same as *address, base*.

address, quadruple—Same as *four-address*.

address, real—The address part of a computer instruction word that refers to an actual location in main storage. The real address may be coded, mnemonic, symbolic, relative, direct or possess any other feature, as long as a specific actual location in main storage is referenced. (Further clarified by *translator, address*. Contrast with *address, virtual*.)

address, real-time—Same as *address, immediate*.

address, reference—Same as *address, base*.

address, regional—An address within a series of consecutive addresses; for example, B17, B18, and B19 are three particular regional addresses in the B region of consecutive addresses.

address, relative—An address in a computer instruction that specifies the storage location pertaining to that specific instruction in relation to a particular program. Thus, a complete program may be written completely independently of another set of programs or data addresses, using a set of relative addresses. Base addresses, one for each program or data set, will establish the storage locations for each program and set of data. Then, when executing a particular program, each absolute address will be determined by modifying each relative address by the contents of a register that for each program or set of data is set to the particular base address for that program or set of data. Thus, in most instances, the absolute addresses are obtained by adding the base address to the relative addresses. The base address quite often is the same value as the absolute address assigned to the first instruction word of the routine; that is, if relative address instructions specify addresses by *r*, and the absolute address of the first word in the routine is *a*, then all the absolute addresses of the routine are given by *r* + *a*. (Further clarified by *address, absolute*; by *address, base*; by *address, effective*; and by *coding, relative*.)

address, relocatable—An address that is appropriately amended when the computer program containing the address is relocated.

address, return—Same as *point, entry*.

address, second-level—In an indirect or multilevel addressing scheme, the address cited or stored in the storage location whose address was specified in the instruction. The second-level address specifies the storage location of either the desired operand or the third-level address of the operand. Thus, a special case of an indirect address. (Synonymous with *two level address*.)

address, self-relative—A relative address that uses the address of the computer instruction in which it appears as the base address for calculating the absolute or machine address.

address, single—Same as *one-address*.

address, single-level—Same as *address, direct*.

address, specific—Same as *address, absolute*.

address, symbolic—An instruction or data address that has been or is to be modified; usually an address, or label, chosen for convenience by a programmer to specify a storage location in the context of a particular program. The symbolic addresses must be converted or translated into the absolute address, for use by the machine, by means of a machine program. Thus, programs are first written using symbolic addresses that are converted by the computer itself into absolute addresses for subsequent use. Occasionally, floating addresses, indexed addresses, and variable addresses may be referred to as symbolic addresses when the floating, indexing, and variability conditions are also present in the symbolic addresses.

address, synthetic—An address determined or generated by instructions contained in the program that uses the address; for example, the synthetic address may be calculated or determined as a result of some process or it may be dependent upon some criterion. (Synonymous with *generated address* and with *calculated address*.)

address, third-level—In an indirect or multilevel addressing scheme, the third address encountered in attempting to ultimately arrive at the location of an operand by having the machine interpret the contents of the first two storage locations as addresses rather than operands. Thus, a special case of a multilevel addressing scheme. (Further clarified by *address, indirect*.)

address, three—See *three-address*.

address, triple—Same as *three-address*.

address, two—See *two-address*.

address, two-level—Same as *address, second-level*.

address, variable—Same as *address, floating*.

address, virtual—1: Same as *address, immediate*. 2: A symbol that is used as an address part of a computer instruction word but does not necessarily designate an actual location. 3: The address of a storage location that is notional or conceptual in a virtual storage. (Further clarified by *translator, address*. Contrast with *address, real*.)

address, zero-level—Same as *address, immediate*.

address computation—See *computation, address*.

address constant—Same as *address, base*.

address format—See *format, address*.

address instruction, functional—Same as *instruction, source-destination*.

address instruction, operational—Same as *instruction, source-destination*.

address modification—See *modification, address*.

address part—See *part, address*.

address register—See *register, address*.

address register, instruction—See *register, instruction address*.

address track—See *track, address*.

address translator—See *translator, address*.

addressability—In micrographics, the number of addressable positions on a specified film frame. The addressability is specified as the number of addressable horizontal positions by the number of addressable vertical positions, for example 5,000 by 5,000.

addressable horizontal position—See *position, addressable horizontal*.

addressable point—See *point, addressable*.

addressable vertical position—See *position, addressable vertical*.

addressing, absolute—A method of addressing such that the address part of each instruction contains, or is, an absolute address.

addressing, deferred—A method of addressing in which an indirect address is replaced by another address a specified number of times or until the process is terminated, usually by an indicator character.

addressing, direct—A method of specifying an operand by citing, in an instruction, the storage location of the operand. The number representing or referring to the storage location is the direct address. (Further clarified by *address, direct*. Contrast with *addressing, indirect* and with *address, indirect*.)

addressing, immediate—A mode of specifying the locations of operands and instructions in a computer program by placing the operands and instructions in the same storage location, that is, at the same address. When the program or control unit refers to a storage location, it will find both the instruction and the operands at that location. This is in contrast to the more usual manner of addressing, wherein the instruction word, stored at one address or location, contains the addresses of other storage locations in which the operands are stored. (Synonymous with *zero-level addressing*, with *virtual addressing*, and with *real-time addressing*.)

addressing, implied—A method of addressing in which the operation part of a computer instruction implicitly addresses the operands.

addressing, indirect—A method of addressing used in computer programs wherein each instruction contains the address of a location in which the address of the pertinent operand, operator, or another address may be found. A sequence of addresses of addresses may be terminated by such means as control signals, characters contained in the addresses, or by prior specifications of the length of the sequence. Thus, indirect addressing is somewhat analogous to addressing a letter to someone by placing on the envelope the number of the box where the current address of the recipient is

17

stored. (Synonymous with *multilevel addressing*. Illustrated by *addressing, two-level.*)

addressing, multilevel—Same as *addressing, indirect.*

addressing, one-ahead—A method of addressing in which the operation part of a computer instruction addresses the operands in the location following the location of the operands of the last instruction executed.

addressing, real-time—Same as *addressing, immediate.*

addressing, repetitive—A method of addressing applicable to zero-address or immediate address instructions in which the operation part of the computer instruction word implicitly addresses or contains the addresses of the operands of the last instruction executed.

addressing, second-level—Same as *addressing, two-level.*

addressing, self-relative—Computer program addressing in which the address part of an instruction contains a self-relative address.

addressing, three-level—A method of addressing in which instruction words contain the address specifying the storage location of the address of the storage location containing the address of the operand. Thus, a special case of indirect addressing involving three references to storage locations for obtaining the desired operand. A three-level addressing scheme will use an instruction that cites the indirect address that specifies the storage location where the second-level address is found. Upon referring to the storage location specified by the second-level address, the third-level address is found.the third-level address specifies the storage location of the desired operand, result, or instruction. (Illustrative of *level, addressing.*)

addressing, two-level—A method of addressing in which the instruction words contain addresses specifying the storage locations where the addresses of the operands are to be found. Thus, a special case of indirect addressing involving two references to storage locations for obtaining the desired operand. A two-level addressing scheme will use an indirect address and a second-level address. (Synonymous with *second-level addressing*. Further clarified by *address, indirect* and by *addressing, three-level.* Illustrative of *level, addressing.*)

addressing, virtual—Same as *addressing, immediate.*

addressing, zero-level—Same as *addressing, immediate.*

addressing level—See *level, addressing.*

addressing system—See *system, addressing.*

ADES—(Automatic Digital Encoding System). A programming language used by the United States Naval Ordnance Laboratory

on the IBM 704 automatic data-processing system.

ADES-II—(Automatic Digital Encoding System). A programming language used by the United States Naval Ordnance Laboratory on the IBM 650 automatic data-processing system.

ADI—American Documentation Institute. Now American Society for Information Science (ASIS).

ADIS—(A Data Interchange System). A communication system developed by Teletype Corporation.

adjacency—In character recognition, a printing condition in which the reference lines that designate character spacing between two consecutive characters on the same row are separated by less than a specified distance.

adjacent channel—See *channel, adjacent.*

adjacent channel interference—See *interference, adjacent channel.*

adjacent channel selectivity—See *selectivity, adjacent channel.*

administrative data processing—Same as *data processing, business.*

admissible mark—See *mark, admissible.*

ADP—(Automatic Data Processing). Same as *Processing, Automatic Data.*

ADPE—An abbreviation for automatic data-processing equipment.

ADPS—An abbreviation for automatic data-processing system.

ADSUP—(Automatic Data Systems Uniform Practices). A programming language developed and used by Sandia Corporation, Albuquerque, New Mexico.

advance, item—A technique for permitting successive operations on different records in storage by a method of record grouping and moving from one item to another item in a given record and from record to record.

AFAC—An automatic coding system developed for Allison G.M. for use on the IBM 704 automatic data-processing system.

AFCAL—(Association Française de Calcul). The French computing association.

AFIP—American Federation for Information Processing. (Former designation of AFIPS)

AFIPS—(American Federation of Information Processing Societies). The present designation of AFIP.

AGE—(Aerospace Ground-Support Equipment). Equipment developed by Laboratory for Electronics, Inc., for use with space studies, space vehicles, and communications.

AIA—Aerospace Industries Association.

AIB—American Institute of Banking.

AIChE—American Institute of Chemical Engineers.

AID—A computer algebraic language for conversational mode applications.

AIEE–(American Institute of Electrical Engineers). Now merged with the Institute of Radio Engineers, IRE, to form the Institute of Electrical and Electronics Engineers, IEEE.

AIMACO Compiler–(Air Materiel Command). A program compiling system developed for the Air Materiel Command, USAF, for use on the Univac 1105 automatic data-processing system.

aiming device–See *device, aiming.*

AIP–American Institute of Physics.

air movement data–See *data, air movement.*

AIRS–(Automatic Information Retrieval System). An automatic information storage and retrieval system using an IBM 7090 computer and FAP as a programming language. About 70,000 documents are described in its files. A uniterm or keyword coordination scheme is used to print accession numbers and abstracts. The system has been productive since 1958. Associated with James R. Hubbell, Business Systems Computations, Flight Propulsion Laboratory Department, General Electric Company, Cincinnati, Ohio.

alarm–A visual or audible signal indicating the occurrence of an error or emergency condition that would or did interfere with the proper execution or completion of a program.

alarm, audible–A sound signal or device used to indicate that a certain condition has been met or detected, that a malfunction has occurred in the equipment, or that there is an error or improper condition in the program.

alarm display–See *display, alarm.*

ALCOM –(Algebraic Compiler). A mathematical program compiler developed by Bendix Corporation for use on the Bendix G-20 automatic data-processing system.

ALD–(Analog Line Driver). A power amplifier used on an analog computer to permit a given point to drive several or many loads, which permits an output channel to drive may input channels. No logic function is performed.

ALERT–(Automated Linguistic Extraction and Retrieval Technique). A technique used in indexing and retrieval of textual information and developed by Ramo Wooldridge Corporation, Canoga Park, California, for use on the RW 400 automatic data-processing system. It serves as an aid in indexing, storage, and retrieval of large quantities of data and as a standardized language for development of man-computer cooperative action.

algebra, Boolean–An algebra of classes and propositions, like ordinary algebra, but dealing with truth values as variables and having basic operators such as AND, OR, NOT, EXCEPT, and IF...THEN. It is a branch of symbolic logic, named after George Boole (1815-1864), an English mathematician, and lends itself readily to adaptation and implementation of logic propositions and statements, in the form of on-off circuits and coincidence gates, permitting fabrication of many logic and switching circuits to perform arithmetic and logic operations automatically and giving rise to the modern digital computer. Since it is technologically more practical to build a system out of identical units, the Boolean algebra can be used to determine the combinations of common, or similar, logic elements that will be required to automate a particular logic function. The Boolean algebra permits expression of conditional statements and statements of facts in symbolic form, and by means of prescribed operations allows arrival at valid conclusions. For example, in considering the presence or absence of three things; namely, A, B, and C, the statement, if A is present, then B is not, is written as $A + \overline{B}$, which may be read as NOT A or NOT B; the statement, B is present alone, is written as $\overline{A}B\overline{C}$, read as not A and B and not C. If B cannot be present alone, the entire expression is negated, which yields $\overline{ABC}$, or $A + \overline{B} + C$, which may be read A or not B or C. There is a direct relationship between English language statements and Boolean statements or expressions. (Further clarified by *gate;* by *gate, AND;* by gate, OR; by *gate, NOT;* and by *calculus, Boolean* .)

B	AND	B =	BB	= B
B	OR	B =	B+B	= B
B	AND NOT	B =	B$\overline{B}$	= 0
B	OR NOT	B =	B+$\overline{B}$	= I
B	AND	0 =	B0	= 0
B	OR	0 =	B+0	= B
B	AND	I =	BI	= B
B	OR	I =	B+I	= I
		$\overline{AB}$ =	$\overline{A}+\overline{B}$	
		AB =	$\overline{\overline{A}\overline{B}}$	

Some axioms and propositions of Boolean algebra.

algebraic language–See *language, algebraic.*

algebraic manipulation–See *manipulation, algebraic.*

Algebraic Oriented Language–A misnomer for ALGOL.

ALGO–An algebraic compiler based on the international ALGOL and used on the Bendix G-15 automatic data-processing system.

ALGOL–(Algorithmic Language; Algorithmic Oriented Language). An algebraic and logic language that has been adopted by many computer groups as a common international language used for the precise presentation of numerical procedures in a standard form to a computer. Developed by an ACM-GAMM committee, the language permits the concise, efficient expression of arithmetic and logic processes and allows their control. The language not only serves as a means of directly presenting any numerical procedure to any suitable computer for which a compiler exists, but also serves as a means of communicating numerical procedures among individuals. The language is a result of international cooperation to obtain a standardized algorithmic language.

ALGOL 60–The 1960 version of ALGOL.

ALGOL 68–A standard programming language that is more powerful than, but not an extension of, ALGOL 60. It is intended for several application areas. The term is derived from the expression, *"ALGOrithmic Language 68."*

algorithm–1: A statement of the steps to be followed in the solution of a problem. **2:** A procedure, process, or rule for the solution of a problem in a finite number of steps. The process may be carried out according to a precise prescription or problem description, leading, under fixed or variable conditions, to a definite result. An algorithm may be a set of computational rules for the solution of a mathematically expressed problem or for evaluating a function; for example, a statement of an arithmetic procedure for evaluating sin x to a given precision. Thus, the algorithm is a statement of the step-by-step procedure for solving complex problems by simple steps. (Contrast with *heuristic* and *stochastic.*)

algorithm, scheduling–The rules and criteria according to which a computer operating system schedules system events, such as data entry, program execution, and roll-out-roll in.

algorithm, translation–A set of rules, a defined procedure, or specific method for obtaining a translation from one language to another. Use may be made of automatic data-processing equipment employing computational methods to effect the algorithm. Mechanical translation of languages requires the use of such algorithms.

algorithmic language–See *language, algorithmic.*

Algorithmic Language–Same as ALGOL.

algorithmic routine–See *routine, algorithmic.*

ALGY–An algebraic manipulation program prepared by Philco Corporation for use on the Philco 2000 automatic data-processing system.

alias–An alternate label, or another name for the same thing; for example, a synonym. Usually the primary name is considered the actual name and all secondary or alternative names are the aliases. The question of which name is the alias is a relative one. For example, in a data system, the *performing agency*, the *responsible agency*, or the *cognizant organization* may be aliases for the same data element.

alignment, contact–The amount of movement or side-play that a contact may have within the insert cavity so as to permit self-alignment of mated contacts and easy insertion of the plug or other contact surface. (Synonymous with *contact float.*)

all-magnetic–In electronic computers, pertaining to the construction and nature of electrical and electronic circuitry in which all storage, delay, and decision-making elements make specific use of the magnetic properties of materials.

allocate–1: To assign, allot, commit, or reserve specific parts of a data-processing system for a specified purpose; for example, to assign units of data or instructions to storage locations or registers. Parts of programs, routines, or subroutines, and data may be assigned to specific storage locations or main frames. Thereby symbolic and relative addresses may be converted to absolute addresses. The process of assigning storage locations to these items fixes the absolute values of the addresses. In some situations, allocation may require segmentation. (Synonymous with *reserve.* Further clarified by *segment.*) **2:** In a computer operating system, to grant, assign, or reserve a system resource for a using entity, such as a user, subtask, task, job, program, routine, subroutine, or supervisor. Allocation is usually accomplished in accordance with priorities.

allocate storage–See *storage, allocate.*

allocation, dynamic–1: In a military tactical defense system, the assignment or commitment of weapons by messages composed or routed by a computing system. In one defense system, these messages are initiated by switch action at the various combat control centers. **2:** In a computer operating system, the provision of system resources, such as storage areas, input-output devices, and programs, to a job, task, program, or other using entity, on demand, rather than by prior scheduling.

allocation, dynamic storage–1: Storage allocation in which the location of programs and data is determined by application of specific criteria as needed. **2:** A method of allocating storage such that the storage areas that are assigned to programs and data are assigned at the moment of need in accordance with criteria applied at that moment. **3:** Assignment of storage in real time as a computer program is executed.

allocation, resource–The allocation of the hardware and software items available to a system to the various tasks, jobs, job steps, or runs.

allocation, storage–The assignment of storage locations or regions to specific routines, subroutines, or blocks of data. In many computing systems, this is done automatically. Absolute addresses are assigned as required, and all symbolic and relative addresses are converted accordingly by means of a master control program at the target program running time. One such system that performs this function automatically is the Burroughs B5000. (Further clarified by *storage, allocate.*)

Allocator–A program assembler and compiler developed by Univac for preparing programs and for patching programs by calling subroutines, system interfaces, communication links, and other parts.

alphabet–A set of unique representations, or characters, various combinations and permutations of which are used to denote and distinguish data, in accordance with various rules and conventions. The characters of the alphabet in a given language-forming set are assigned specific functions; for example, in the English language alphabet, a certain subset called vowels; namely, *a, e, i, o,* and *u,* are assigned certain sounds, and so are the consonants and the diphthongs; certain other characters serve as markers, such as periods, commas, semicolons, question marks, exclamation points, hyphens, etc., all of which convey meaning. The characters may be assigned pulse codes, as in the Morse Code, or binary codes for machine processing. Some characters, such as the numerals *0, 1, 2, 3, 4, 5, 6, 7, 8,* and *9* are assigned numerical values to permit the construction of a system of numbers. Usually the set of characters in a given alphabet are finite and are assigned a rank; for example, *a* first, *b* second, *c* third, etc., so that they may be ordered; consequently, the expressed information can be located. The ordering is arbitrary and is usually established by convention historically. A space is usually considered as a character in most alphabets. Sometimes a spacing symbol is used, particularly in some computer applications in order to ensure that an inadvertent omission is not simply interpreted as a space by a machine or an operator. The characters in an alphabet may be represented in any sensible form; for example, dots and dashes, numerals, smoke puffs, light flashes, written letters, semaphore or flag positions, strings of lights, colored lights, sounds, odors, finger orientations, or any other signs, symbols, or conventions, such as squeezes of the hand, movements of the head, or shrugs of the shoulder, even oil lamps in a tower. The most popular alphabet used in computers is the 0 and 1, having the indicated numerical value for representing numbers, and used in combinations and permutations to represent letters, special symbols, and instructions. Sometimes alphabets are considered to include only the letters, exclusive of the numerals and special marks, in which case "alphabet" is considered to mean "letters of the alphabet" and alphanumeric is considered to include the numerals and even other signs and symbols. (Contrast with *set, character.*)

alphabetic character set–See *set, alphabetic character.*

alphabetic character subset–See *subset, alphabetic character.*

alphabetic code–See *code, alphabetic.*

alphabetic coded character set–See *set, alphabetic coded character.*

alphabetical code–Same as *code, alphabetic.*

alphabetic-numeric–Same as *alphanumeric.*

alphabetic word–See *word, alphabetic.*

alphameric–A contraction of *alphanumeric.*

alphameric code–Same as *code, alphanumeric.*

alphanumeric–A contraction of alphabetic-numeric, a set of characters including letters, numerals, and usually a set of additional special symbols used as punctuation marks, special meaning marks, etc. (Synonymous with *alphabetic-numeric,* with *alphameric,* and with *numeric-alphabetic.* Further clarified by *alphabet.*)

alphanumeric character subset–See *subset, alphanumeric character.*

alphanumeric code–See *code, alphanumeric.*

alphanumeric coded character set–See *set, alphanumeric coded character.*

alphanumeric data–See *data, alphanumeric.*

alphanumeric instruction–See *instruction, alphanumeric.*

ALPS–(Advanced Linear Programming System). An operations research technique used to optimize a given set of conditions through the use of a set of linear equations and linear programming; developed by Honeywell Data Processing Division of Minneapolis-Honeywell, Inc.

ALTAC–The Transac Algebraic Translator, a program language translator, developed by Philco Corporation for the Philco 2000 automatic data-processing system.

alteration switch–See *switch, alteration.*

alternate routing–See *routing, alternate.*

alternation–A technique of using two or more input-output units in time sequence so as to speed up input and output operations during a run; for example, three card readers may serve the same input buffer by acceptance of data from each card reader in turn. If there are two devices, they may be used alternately. Sometimes double feed hoppers are used on dual reading stations to speed up card reading. This is a kind of alternation if the purpose is to provide an increased effective reading rather than a collation of information.

alternation gate–Same as *gate, OR.*

alternative denial gate–Same as *gate, NAND.*

ALTRAN–An algebraic translator developed by El-tronics Corporation for use on the ALWAC III E data-processing system.

ALU–An abbreviation for arithmetic and logical unit.

AM–Same as *modulation, amplitude.*

AMA–American Management Association.

ambiguity–Having more than one meaning, interpretation, significance, or representation. In data processing, ambiguity can result during changes of state in a given system. For example, a transient gross error may occur in reading the digital representation of a member when it is changing due to a lack of synchronization of the changes in different digit positions; thus, when passing from 199 to 200, either 299, 209, 109, 100, or 190 may be read momentarily. Such ambiguity can be avoided by using a unit distance, or gray, code or by a guard signal. Other forms of ambiguity include semantic, lexical, and morphological.

Amble's Method–Same as *connection, regenerative.*

AMD–(Air Movement Data). Same as *data, air movement.*

American National Standards Institute–Same as ANSI.

American Standards Association–Same as *ASA.* USASI, and ANSI.

amphiboly–The uncertain meaning of a proposition in logic, such as might result from faulty syntax, ambiguity, or ambiguous language; for example, the statement A OR B AND C, which might mean (A OR B) AND C, or A OR (B AND C), which are different. The question, "Do you A or B?" may have the answers yes, no, A, B, both or neither. Some of the possible answers may be surprising to the interrogator.

amplification, flow–In a fluidic amplifier, the ratio of the change of the flow in a specified load connected to the fluidic amplifier to the change in the flow applied to the input of the amplifier.

amplification, pressure–In a fluidic amplifier, the ratio of the change in pressure drop accross a specified load to the change in the pressure drop applied to the input of the amplifier.

amplifier–A device for increasing the magnitude of an effect, phenomenon, or action, such as electric waves, torques, forces, and light intensity. Usually amplification is achieved by exercising control over a source of energy. Various types of voltage, current, power, torque, and force amplifiers are used in analog and digital computing systems, particularly in order that logic decision-making operations and their results can be propagated through the system and that dynamic storage of information may take place without deterioration or evaporation. Thus amplification is required to compensate for attenuation introduced by unavoidable losses inherent in energy-transfer systems. There are many types of amplifiers that combine the amplification function with an actual operation on the input signal or signals. (Further clarified by *amplifier, buffer.*)

amplifier, buffer–An amplifier used to drive a circuit without drawing much current or power from the circuit that provides the signal. This is the common voltage, current or power amplifier and may be of many forms, using transistors or vacuum tubes. Buffer amplifiers include resistance-coupled, capacitance-coupled, and transformer-coupled vacuum-tube amplifiers, with regenerative or degenerative feedback, including cathode-followers; as well as resistance-coupled, resistance-capacitance coupled, and transformer-coupled transistor amplifiers, including emitter-followers. Signals can pass in one direction only, thus preventing interaction between input and output circuits. (Further clarified by *amplifier.*)

amplifier, capstan–A torque amplifier whose output torque is delivered through a sprocketed shaft or spindle, that is, a capstan. (Further clarified by *amplifier, torque* and by *gear, integrating.*)

amplifier, chopper-stabilized–An amplifier consisting of a signal modulator, an a-c amplifier, that is, a capacitance or resistance-capacitance (RC) amplifier, which is stable and can have appreciable gain at the modulation frequency, and a demodulator to restore the original signal. The net result is drift-free amplification and stable operation, which is difficult to obtain in direct-coupled amplifiers with ordinary circuit elements and d-c or slowly varying input signal levels. The modulator is often a mechanical contact, that is, a vibrator or a transistor or vacuum-tube switch, called a chopper. The chopper simply interrupts the input signal periodically. The chopping permits signal insertion by means of capacitors, which prevent drifting by blocking dc. Drift-free amplifiers are essential to the successful operation of analog computers, since drift of output signals will introduce errors. Note that chopping is in a certain sense, a step toward quantization, or digitalization, although digital techniques are not involved. (Further clarified by *amplifier, drift-corrected* and by *amplifier, direct-coupled.*)

amplifier, closed–In fluidics, an amplifier that has no vent port. (Contrast with *amplifier, open.*)

amplifier, computing–An amplifier that combines the function of amplification with the performance of an operation upon the input signal or signals. Examples of computing amplifiers are summing amplifiers, or analog adders; sign-reversing amplifiers, integrating amplifiers, and differentiation amplifiers. All are used in analog computing systems. (Synonymous with *operational amplifier.*)

amplifier, d-c–Same as *amplifier, direct-coupled.*

amplifier, differential—An amplifier that has two signal-input channels and one signal-output channel and whose behavior is such that the instantaneous output signal is directly proportional to the difference between the instantaneous values of the input signals. Differential amplifiers are primarily used in analog computing systems. Differential amplifiers are often double-ended; that is, they have a set of output terminals, which permits positive and negative output signals with reference to a fixed voltage level, such as ground-level.

amplifier, differentiating—An analog computer amplifier whose output voltage or current is proportional to the derivative, with respect to time, of the input voltage or current. In a type of differentiating amplifier, if the input impedance is a capacitor, then the feedback impedance is a resistor. The use of differentiating amplifiers is avoided in analog computers as much as possible, because they increase the magnitude of the unwanted and spurious signals which in practice accompany analog signals. This and other limitations hinder the attainment of high accuracy as an analog computer element.

amplifier, direct-coupled—An analog computer amplifier that uses resistors for coupling signals in and out of the active element, such as a vacuum tube or transistor, and thus is capable of amplifying input signal currents or voltages no matter how slowly the input signals vary as a function of time. Direct-coupled amplifiers must be stabilized to avoid drifting of the output signal current or voltage level. Stabilization can be accomplished by chopping. (Synonymous with *direct-current amplifier*, with *d-c amplifier*, and with *resistance-coupled amplifier*. Further clarified by *amplifier, drift-corrected* and by *amplifier, chopper-stabilized*.)

amplifier, direct-current—Same as *amplifier, direct-coupled*.

amplifier, drift-corrected—A direct-coupled analog computer amplifier that can prevent or reduce drift; that is, prevent the output voltage or current from changing its value without a corresponding change in the input signal current or voltage. Direct coupling is sometimes called d-c coupling or resistance coupling in contrast to a-c, capacitance, or resistance-capacitance coupling. Direct-coupled amplifiers can follow slow variations of input signal levels no matter how slowly they occur, but they must be drift-stabilized. One method of drift stabilization is accomplished by chopping. (Further clarified by *amplifier, chopper-stabilized* and by *amplifier, direct-coupled*.)

amplifier, feedback—An amplifier that makes use of the principle of feeding some function of the output signal as a part of the input signal to produce desired performance and execute desired operations on the input signal or signals. Stability, gain, and frequency response are influenced by the nature of the feedback signal; however, these are secondary to the primary function of performing operations on the input signal or signals. A particularly common circuit uses a single-ended, direct-coupled amplifier with a negative gain; that is, the output signal decreases when the input signal increases. The input signals are fed through input inpedances to a single input point, called a summing junction. The feedback impedance is connected between the output point and the summing junction. The output point is the actual output channel of the amplifier. Amplifiers using the feedback principle to perform operations on signals are used in analog computers. The feedback principle is used in digital computer amplifiers to achieve desired noncomputational effects, such as fast response, stability of operation, and storage effects.

amplifier, impact modulator—A fluidic amplifier in which the position of the impact plane of two opposed streams is controlled to alter the output.

amplifier, integrating—An analog computer amplifier whose output voltage or current is proportional to the time integral of the input voltage or current. Thus, the output voltage or current is proportional to the area under a time-curve plot of a variable between a given reference time and an arbitrary point in time. In a type of integrating amplifier, if the input impedance is a resistor, then the feedback impedance would be a capacitor. When several inputs are provided through several resistors, the output voltage or current is proportional to the integral of the weighted sum of the input voltages or currents. The device is then called a summing integrator. (Further clarified by *integrator, summing*.)

amplifier, inverting—Same as *amplifier, sign-reversing*.

amplifier, open—In fluidics, an amplifier that has a vent port. (Contrast with *amplifier, closed*.)

amplifier, operational—Same as *amplifier, computing*.

amplifier, resistance-coupled—Same as *amplifier, direct-coupled*.

amplifier, reversing—Same as *amplifier, sign-reversing*.

amplifier, see-saw—Same as *amplifier, sign-reversing*.

amplifier, sign-changing—Same as *amplifier, sign-reversing*.

amplifier, sign-reversing—An analog computer amplifier whose output voltage or current is equal in magnitude to the input voltage or current, but opposite in sign. In one type, there would be but one input inpedance and one feedback impedance, most likely resistors of equal magnitude. (Synonymous with *inverting amplifier,* with *sign-changing amplifier,* with *see-saw amplifier,* with *see-saw circuit,* and with *reversing amplifier.*)

amplifier, stream deflection—A fluidic amplifier that utilizes one or more control streams to deflect a power stream, thus controlling or altering the output.

amplifier, summing—An analog computer amplifier whose output voltage or current is the weighted sum of the input voltages or currents. The weights, corresponding to positional significance in a given number system, would be proportional to the conductances of the circuit elements in the input leads. If there is only one input resistor, the amplifier serves simply to establish proper scaling of numbers. (Synonymous with *analog adder.* Further clarified by *integrator, summing.*)

amplifier, torque—A device that has an input shaft for inserting torques and an output shaft for turning a loading shaft; the output shaft is turned through the same angle as the input shaft, but with a much greater torque supplied at the output shaft than at the input shaft. Thus, the torque amplifier must supply energy to the output shaft. Normally, very little torque should have to be supplied to the input shaft to position it, while the output shaft will provide sufficient torque to position the shaft of the device that it is driving. Such torque amplifiers are required in mechanical analog computers; for instance, to drive wheel and disc integrators. (Further clarified by *amplifier, capstan* and by *gear, integrating.*)

amplifier, turbulence—A fluidic amplifier in which the power jet is at a pressure such that it is in the transition region of laminar stability and can be caused to become turbulent by application of some outside stimuli, such as a secondary jet, sound waves, or vibration, which thus controls or alters the output.

amplifier, vortex—A fluidic amplifier in which the angular rotational rate of a vortex is controlled by some outside stimuli, such as a jet stream, to control or alter the output.

amplifier, wall-attachment—A fluidic amplifier in which the attachment and detachment of a stream to a wall is used to control or alter the output. The attachment of a stream to a wall is known as the Coanda effect.

amplify—To multiply or increase the amplitude of a signal or action; for example, to increase the voltage, current, or power level of a signal. The amount of amplification is usually expressed as gain; that is, the ratio of output signal strength to input signal strength, both expressed in the same units, the gain thus being dimensionless. (Contrast with *attenuate.*)

amplitude, pulse—The maximum instantaneous value, magnitude, size or strength of a signal. Sometimes the amplitude of a pulse is defined as the average value of a signal between the time it has reached 10 percent of the maximum on the rise or ascent and 10 percent of the maximum on the fall or descent. This eliminates the counting of minor spikes or peaks, on a relatively square wave or pulse, as determining the amplitude.

amplitude modulation—See *modulation, amplitude.*

amplitude modulation, pulse—See *modulation, pulse amplitude.*

amplitude vs. frequency distortion—See *distortion, amplitude vs. frequency.*

ANA—An operation called "AND to accumulator" in the IBM 709 automatic data-processing system program instruction code.

analog—1: Pertaining to a device that represents numerical quantities by means of physical variables; for example, by translation, as in a slide-rule; by rotation, as in a mechanical gear system; and by voltage or current as in analog networks that use resistance to represent mechanical losses, capacitors and inductors to store energy and simulate the action of springs, etc. Thus, variables are represented by other variables that have similar properties; for instance, electric current would serve as an analog for water flow, voltage as the analog for pressure, resistors as pipe or channel resistance to flow, etc. In this manner, a mechanical system can be represented or simulated by an electrical network. The equations that express the current, voltage, energy and power relations of the electrical network also apply to the mechanical system. Thus, the compression of a spring or the lifting of a pendulum might be equivalent to the charging of a capacitor. The analog is the one system that is used to study the behavior of the other. Some old mechanical analog computers used integrating balls or spheres in contact with discs to accomplish integration. Modern analog computers use combined electrical-mechanical units, such as potentiometers, whose resistance is proportional to the sine, cosine, or tangent, or is a logarithmic or exponential function of the angular shaft position. Thus, many problems may be solved analytically, by writing the equations that describe the system and solving them mathematically. This might be termed a mathematical analog, or popularly, a mathematical model. In a loose sense, any model is in effect an analog. A model may be a direct analog, such as a network, or a functional analog, in which there is a one-to-one correspondence between the mathematical operations defining the original system and its analog. It is possible to have an analog of an original complex system that will have fewer components than on a one-to-one basis. Such an analog could consist of one operational unit and a storage device. The operational unit performs one operation at a time, stores the result in the memory, resets itself to zero, then proceeds with the next operation, until the complete system is simulated, as in the Turing machine. Thus, simultaneous components in the complex system, or space, is traded for time in the simple system. Such a simple unit is called a serial sequence analog. A digital computer is such a serial analog. An analog computer is a parallel sequence analog. Basically, all data processors, computers, etc., are analog, that is, either parallel sequence or serial sequence machines. In each type, the data may be either continuous, sampled, quantized, or digitized. Analog computers are rightfully called parallel sequence analog processors with continuous data. Digital computers are serial sequence analog processors with digitized information. In popular usage, analog is contrasted with digital. (Further clarified by *device, analog;* by *computer, analog;* by *analog, network;* and by *network, analog.*) 2: Pertaining to representation of information by means of physical quantities that are continuously variable.

analog, network—A model of a network, usually an electrical network, by some system other than a network. Thus, a digital computer and a program can be used to simulate the behavior of a network and so can be called a network analog. The analog is that system that serves as a model for another system. A set of equations can serve as an analog for an electrical network, and thus the equations are a mathematical model of the network and may rightfully be called a network analog. (Further clarified by *analog* and by *network, analog.*)

analog adder—Same as *amplifier, summing.*

analog channel—See *channel, analog.*

analog computer—See *computer, analog.*

analog data—See *data, analog.*

analog device—See *device, analog.*

analog divider—See *divider, analog.*

analog line driver—See *ALD.*

analog multiplier—See *multiplier, analog.*

analog network—See *network, analog.*

analog regenerative connection—Same as *connection, regenerative.*

analog representation—See *representation, analog.*

analysis—1: The resolution or separation of any whole into its component parts to discover or investigate their nature, behavior, proportion, function, relationship, etc. 2: The investigation of a problem, situation, or condition by a consistent and usually systematic method

of separation into related units or phases for detailed study. Analysis usually precedes programming in the sequence of events leading to the solution of problems using electronic computers. Analysis is preceded only by problem statement or problem definition. (Contrast with *synthesis.*)

analysis, fault—The detection, location, and correction of software errors and hardware malfunctions. Fault analysis is often accomplished by the operating system when faults occur for purposes of automatic recovery from error or malfunction conditions, such as by system reconfiguration or by dynamic system maintenance.

analysis, flow—1: An analysis used in compiling a computer program to determine the specific interdependencies of the elements of the computer program. 2: The detection, recording, and review of the sequence of instructions in computer programs. Flow analyses may be used in monitors and debugging routines.

analysis, inferential—In computer simulation, the determination of the consequences of the assertions about a simulation system by direct inference. (Contrast with *analysis, non-inferential.*)

analysis, logic—The study or determination in a process, program, or computer run of the specific steps required to produce the desired output information from the given input data.

analysis, non-inferential—In computer simulation, the determination of the consequences of the assertions about a simulation system through the application of probabilistic and sampling techniques, such as Monte Carlo methods. (Contrast with *analysis, inferential.*)

analysis, numerical—The study and analysis of methods of obtaining useful quantitative solutions to physical problems expressed in mathematical forms or abstractions, whether or not analytic solutions to the mathematical statements exist. Numerical methods are employed. Numerical analysis also includes the study of the errors and their bounds in obtaining such solutions. Sometimes such error analysis is considered as a separate activity, although error analysis may also include a study of errors introduced by equipment; for instance, by measurements, computations, and malfunctions.

analysis, operations—Same as *research, operations.*

analysis, parametric—In computer simulation, an analysis of the performance of a simulation system in which system parameters are varied so as to give an indication of the behavior of the system and other parameters.

analysis, surface—An analysis of the surface conditions of data media, such as

25

magnetic tapes, discs, cards, and drums, by making reliability checks of the surface to detect failing areas, blemishes, inclusions, and other defects that would preclude proper operation. (Further clarified by *replacement, track,* and by *maintenance, volume.*)

analysis, system—The overall and thorough analysis of an activity, procedure, method, technique, or business to arrive at the most appropriate way of accomplishing that which needs to be done. The result of such analysis is a specification of the steps that should be taken, in proper order, so that a specific objective is achieved or a procedure is optimized. For example, a systems analysis is made to arrive at the minimum cost of an operation or to minimize the labor, material, or the computer time required to solve a specific problem. The result is a specification of what is to be accomplished, how it is to be accomplished, what will be utilized to accomplish it, and the relation the accomplishment or activity has to other activities.

analyst—A person specially trained, experienced, and particularly skilled in the definition and solution of a problem; thus, one skilled in analysis. The analyst will usually seek a definition of the problem, develop an algorithm for the solution of the problem, seek its implementation or solution on a computer, and evaluate the results. Usually, he is skilled in specific branches of science, is well-trained in higher mathematics, and possesses a knowledge of digital computer techniques. He is usually assisted by programmers, coders, and problem sponsors, although he has a knowledge of programming. In most cases he is responsible for either formulating the mathematical model for a specific physical phenomenon or he evaluates those proposed. An analyst generally is skilled in such areas as statistical analysis, numerical analysis, error analysis, and applications of digital computers.

analytical engine—See *engine, analytical.*

analytical-function generator—See *generator, analytical-function.*

analyzer—1: A computer program designed to study or perform an analysis of another program that has been written for the same or a different computer. The analysis or study usually consists of tabulating, logging, counting or summarizing certain operations; for instance, summarizing references to storage or tracing sequences of transfer. (Synonymous with *program analyzer*, with *routine analyzer*, and with *subroutine analyzer.*) 2: An abbreviation for differential analyzer or network analyzer. (Further clarified by *analyzer, differential* and by *analyzer, network.*)

analyzer, differential—A mechanical or electrical analog device primarily designed and used to solve differential equations.

For example, a computer, usually analog, using specially designed interconnected mechanisms for solving differential equations. Loosely, any computer designed primarily for automatically solving differential equations. Thus, differential analyzers may be electronic, electromechanical, or mechanical; digital or analog; or any combination of these, as an electronic digital differential analyzer. Some differential analyzers are designed to solve a certain type or class of differential equations; others are general purpose. (Synonymous with *DA.* Further clarified by *analyzer.*)

analyzer, digital differential—A type of incremental computer that combines the properties of a digital computer with the characteristics of a differential analyzer. Thus, for example, instead of performing integration by spheres, discs, and cams, digital values expressing increments of the functions are summed in the integration process in a regular digital or Kirchhoff adder. Greater precision and increased flexibility are achievable in a digital differential analyzer. In essence, such an analyzer uses digital representations for the analog quantities represented in an analog differential analyzer. (Synonymous with *DDA.* Contrast with *computer, analog.*)

analyzer, electronic differential—A computer, usually analog, that uses interconnected electronic integrators to solve differential equations. An electronic digital differential analyzer utilizes digital circuitry and techniques to accomplish integration (summation) and differentiation (differencing) involved in the solution of differential equations. Operation of the electronic differential analyzer may be quite similar to the mechanical differential analyzer, except that electronic analogs of the mechanical parts are used.

analyzer, mechanical differential—An analog computer using interconnected mechanisms, such as gears, cams, and discs, to solve differential equations. An early mechanical differential analyzer, the Vannevar Bush of Massachusetts Institute of Technology, used differential gear boxes to perform addition and a combination of wheel and disc mechanisms to perform integration. Mechanical analyzers were used to perform scientific calculations until the early 1940's, when they were replaced first by digital relay calculators and then by the electronic digital computers, with the famous ENIAC as the forerunner of the modern computer. Torque amplifiers always proved a major source of trouble on the mechanical differential analyzer.

analyzer, network—A network, usually electrical, that is used to simulate a large, complex, usually electrical, network; for example, a large interurban and cross-country network of transmission lines and their loads can be simulated with small lumped electric circuit elements made up of resistors, inductors, and capacitors that behave precisely like the actual network when stimulated with various sources of electrical energy. Behavior of the actual system, responses to transients, peak loads, overloads, various types of fault effects and related phenomena can be studied, analyzed, and checked out to determine methods of minimizing losses, power re-routing, fault elimination, transient analysis and general operational procedures. Other networks may be used to simulate mechanical systems, as an analog, to permit study of the mechanical behavior of the system. Hydraulic systems and networks may also be used to simulate other much larger hydraulic systems. (Further clarified by *analog, network;* by *network, analog;* and by *analyzer.*)

analyzer, program—Same as *analyzer (1).*

analyzer, routine—Same as *analyzer (1).*

analyzer, subroutine—Same as *analyzer (1).*

ancillary equipment—Same as *equipment, peripheral.*

ANCP—An automatic coding system developed by Burroughs Corporation for use on the Burroughs 205 (formerly Electrodata or Datatron 205) automatic data-processing system.

AND—A logic operator having the property that if P is a statement, Q is a statement, R is a statement, . . ., then the AND of P, Q, R, . . ., is true if all statements are true, false if any statement is false. P AND Q AND R is often represented by P · Q · R, PQR, P∩Q∩R, P∧Q∧R. The positive AND is implied. (Synonymous with *AND operator,* with *conjunction,* with *intersection,* with *collation operation,* and with *meet.* Further clarified by *multiply, logic* and by *gate, AND.* Contrast with *NAND* and *OR.*)

AND circuit—Same as *gate, AND.*

AND element—Same as *gate, AND.*

AND gate—See *gate, AND.*

AND gate, negative—same as *gate, NAND.*

AND gate, positive—Same as *gate, AND.*

AND NOT gate—1: Same as *gate, A AND NOT B.* **2:** Same as *gate, B AND NOT A.*

AND operation—Same as *operation, conjunction.*

AND operator—Same as *AND.*

AND unit—Same as *gate, AND.*

angle, elevation—An angular measurement made in a vertical plane from a specific reference, usually the horizontal plane. Thus, elevations are vertical angles. Sometimes vertical angles below the horizontal are called angles of depression.

angle modulation—See *modulation, angle.*

anglicize—To convert from symbolically coded statements to English phrases; for example, to translate from programming language "MPY (A) B" to the anglicized statement of "multiply the contents of storage position A by the contents of storage position B, leaving the product

stored in position A." Usually the translation from code to clear English is called anglicizing. This is required only for the benefit of the human operator and very seldom for use by the computer.

Angstrom—A unit of length equal to 10^{-8} centimeters, used conveniently in expressing the wavelength of visible light, which ranges from 4000 Angstroms for the violet to 7500 Angstroms for the red. Angstrom is abbreviated Å.

annex storage—See *storage, annex.*

annotate—To add explanatory or descriptive notes or remarks to specific portions of information or data. Annotations are usually added to explain relations, avoid ambiguities, lend significance, demonstrate relationships, or otherwise clarify or explain special matters; for instance, an annotated bibliography would cite statements regarding the pertinence, nature, purpose, value, content, or intent of each reference.

annotation—A note that has been added to a document. An annotation usually explains or describes a specific point raised in the main text.

anodize—A process of imparting a corrosion-resistant film of oxidized metal on metal surfaces by connecting the metal as an electrode in an electrolytic bath. When current is passed, the metal oxidizes at the surface. The oxide coating can serve many purposes: for example, as a protective coating to inhibit further oxidation and other forms of corrosion that would occur if the base metal is exposed to corrosive atmospheres . and, most important, as a dielectric storage surface, with a conductive film behind it, since the anodized film is an insulator. The surface can be used as is the surface in a cathode-ray tube, where glass is the dielectric surface and a metal foil or screen is cemented to the outside of the tube to produce the effect of a large number of parallel-plate capacitors. Thus, the anodized surface can be used as a digital data-storage device.

ANSI—American National Standards Institute (Formerly American Standards Association and also formerly United States of America Standards Institute.) ANSI Committee X3 is responsible for developing standards for computers and information processing, with technical Committee X3K5 responsible for vocabulary.

answer, auto—See *auto-answer.*

anticipatory buffering—See *buffering, anticipatory.*

anticoincidence gate—Same as *gate, exclusive-OR.*

anticoincidence unit—Same as *gate, exclusive-OR.*

AP2—A compiler, similar to ALGOL, developed by Rice University for use on the Rice University computer.

27

APAR—(Automatic Programming and Recording). An automatic programming technique developed by Sandia Corporation; thus, a type of compiler.

aperture—1: The part of a mask or filter that permits retention or passage of corresponding portions of data. 2: One or more characters, usually adjacent, in a mask or filter that cause retention of the corresponding characters in the pattern, such as a computer word, that is being masked or filtered.

aperture card—See card, aperture,

aperture core, multiple—See core, multiple aperture.

APL—A programming language with a syntax and character set designed for mathematical applications, especially those involving numeric or literal arrays. The term is derived from the expression, "A Programming Language," and is often used in a conversational, that is, interactive mode.

application, computer—The specific problem or job to be solved or accomplished by automatic data-processing machinery; for instance, payroll, inventory, airline reservations, scientific calculations, file maintenance, and cost accounting. (Further clarified by study, application; and by study, feasibility.)

application, inquiry—A computer application that involves the use of a computer for updating and interrogating stored information, including associated processing when necessary, usually on an intermittent basis. The inquiries can be queued, that is, held up for processing in batches; or they can be processed immediately upon receipt. The inquiry can be effected by card, tape, or direct console input or by remotely located inquiry stations or keysets, such as are used in transportation reservation systems. An inventory control application usually implies a system capability of permitting online inquiries on the status of various stock levels. The inquiry can be handled on an interrupt basis: that is, when an inquiry is inserted, whatever program is being run is temporarily halted until the inquiry is completed, whereupon the machine returns to the program that had been interrupted.

application, slave—A computer application in which one computer is so closely tied to another, the master computer, that the slave computer is at every instant performing the same step in the same program with the same data as the master computer. If any error or malfunction occurs in the master computer, the slave merely continues the execution of the program without perceptible interruption. In some applications, resorting to slave operation as the primary system might result in a deterioration of operation, such as a reduction of precision. The master-slave relationship permits maintenance of the slave, and the roles can

be interchanged without loss of continuity of operations, a significant consideration in some real-time applications, resulting in improved system reliability. (Further clarified by computer, slave.)

application, standby—A computer application involving the use of two or more computers that are tied together in such a manner that in the event of a specific requirement, diversion, or failure of the active system, another system can be fed the program and continue the processing or operation substantially without interruption of the operation. The standby system could be processing another application, standing ready to be interrupted and activated on the application for which it is standing by. A standby application is not the same as a slave application, in which the second system is slaved or tied to the system it is supporting, even to the extent of executing the same programs and receiving the same data at the same time.

application-oriented language—See language, application-oriented.

application software—See software, application.

applications study—See study, applications.

applied epistemology—See epistemology, applied.

approach—Same as method.

APT—(Automatic Programming Tool). A computer program for numerically controlled machine tools, such as flame cutters, drafting machines, and cloth cutters. APT was developed by Univac Division of Sperry-Rand Corporation and Aerospace Industries of America for several machines.

APT III—An extension of APT developed by Sperry-Rand Corporation for use on the Univac 1107.

APX III—An extended automatic programming system, or compiler, developed by Burroughs Corporation for use on the Burroughs 201, 204, and primarily 205 automatic data-processing systems.

aquadag—A graphite coating on the inside of some cathode-ray tubes. The purpose of the coating is to collect secondary electrons emitted by the screen. Cathode-ray tubes are used as electrostatic storage tubes on many computers developed in the early 1950's.

arbitrary-function generator—See generator, arbitrary-function.

architecture, computer—The specification or description of the interrelationships between the parts of a computer, computing system, or data processing system.

area, clear—Same as band, clear.

area, code—In microfilm data systems, the area of a film frame that is used for storing a retrieval code.

area, constant—A section or part of the total storage of a computing system specifically designated for the storage of all the constants required for a particular program, in which case an interlock may be provided so as to preclude the possibility of inadvertently altering the contents of these storage positions. In some special-purpose digital computing systems, these constants are *never* changed, in which case the contents of these storage locations are permanently wired in, such as by removal of cores where a zero is to be permanently stored. These are fixed-storage areas. The FADAC system is one in which the values stored in the constant area are not changed until a new program tape inserts a new program for a different application of the system. Interlocks on the system prevent the alteration of any of the constants. (Synonymous with *constant storage*.)

area, contact—The surface in common between two conductors, between a connector and a conductor, or between two connectors. Electricity flows across the area in common. The contact area must be large enough so as to reduce current density to a value low enough to avoid heating or excessive potential drop across the contact surface. Thus, the contact resistance is inversely proportional to the contact area, and is dependent on other factors, such as the contact material, the cleanliness of the contact surfaces, and the applied pressure.

area, image—On microfilm, that part of the film frame reserved for an image.

area, input—The section or part of a computer's internal storage used for storing data or instructions received directly from an input unit as the immediate result of a program input instruction, such as, "Read the next 100 cards." The input area may be further subdivided into other areas: card input area, tape input area, and drum input area. The input area may be a regular part of the addressable storage or it may be a section or sections addressable only as a single location in an input-output instruction; hence, the contents are transferrable to and from the regular storage by means of input and output instructions. The input area can serve as a kind of buffer unit. (Synonymous with *input storage*. Contrast with *area, output*.)

area, input-output—A section or part of a computer's internal storage allocated specifically for the storage of data or instructions received or to be transferred directly from or to an external input or output device or to another section of the internal storage that is usually used as a working storage. Thus, there are two major input-output areas: one in which the areas are sections of the regular working storage of the system and another in which the areas are separate storage units that are addressable only as a single location in an input-output instruction. In

this second case, the entire contents of the area, or a part of the area, is addressed, and the data is transferred either to a block of the working area or to an output device, or conversely, a block of data is transferred from the working storage or input device to the area. (Synonymous with *input-output storage*.)

area, instruction—A section or part of a computer storage in which program instructions are stored. This area, used for instruction storage, may be simply the regular addressable working storage of a computing system or it may have special features, such as possessing a shorter access time, since the instructions may have to be transferred repeatedly, or it may be provided with interlocks so as to prevent its being inadvertently addressed during a computer run, which might cause an undesirable change in the program. In some special-purpose systems, the programs can never be changed because they are permanently wired in. In others, the fixed instructions are altered by changing permanently wired, pluggable storage units as a field modification. (Synonymous with *routine storage* and *subroutine storage*. Closely related to *storage, program*.)

area, output—The section or part of a computer's internal storage used for storing data or instructions that are to be transferred directly to an output unit such as a tape perforator, card punch, or printer. The output area may be further subdivided into other areas; for instance, card output area, tape output area, and drum output area. The output area may be a regular part of the addressable storage or it may be a section or sections addressable only as entire areas or subareas; that is, as a single location in an input-output instruction, and hence the contents are transferrable to and from the regular, main, or working storage by input and output instructions. In some instances, all the data stored in the output area will be discharged to an external output medium; therefore, it is a kind of release area or buffer. (Synonymous with *output storage*. Contrast with *area, input*.)

area, recording—Same as *frame, film*.

area, save—A part of computer main storage in which the contents of registers may be stored.

area, storage—A specified location or locations in a storage unit; for example, the locations 000 through 099 in a magnetic core storage unit. Usually, specified storage areas are used for specific purposes, such as program storage, constants storage, scratch-pad storage, and input-output buffer storage. (Synonymous with *zone*.)

area, transient—In a computer system, a main storage area, usually within the supervisor area, used temporarily by subroutines, routines and programs while they are being executed or are suspended.

area, working—Same as *storage, temporary.*

area discriminator, initiation—See *IAD.*

area search—See *search, area.*

area service, extended—See *service, extended area.*

argument—An independent variable upon whose value the value of a function or an operation depends; for example, in the function $y = a$ sin bx, the x would normally be considered the argument, just as it would in the function $y = ax^2 + bx + c$ and in the function $y = ae^x$. Thus, the argument is an operand in any indicated operation to be performed on any number of arguments. Normally one argument at a time is considered; however, when several are considered simultaneously, we are talking of multidimensional space. Arguments held constant during a variation of another argument are considered parameters. However, arguments and parameters are members of a given set of variables. The parameters usually provide a family of functions; that is, one function, curve, surface, or volume is defined for each given value of each parameter. For example, in $y = ae^x$, a different exponential curve is obtainable for each value of the parameter a as the argument x ranges through all its values from plus to minus infinity. Since the value of an argument determines the value of a function or an operation, then a determinant, a matrix, or a vector may also serve as an argument. The key used in a search is an argument. The numbers or codes used in a tabular look-up to specify the location of a desired value or to permit the identification of a desired result are arguments. Thus, in general, any representation of a value on which the result of an operation is dependent, is considered an argument.

ARGUS—(Automatic Routine Generating and Updating System). An automatic program compiler system developed for the Honeywell 800 computer and including a symbolic assembly language, an assembly program, automatic selection of routines, and checking and operating systems.

Arith-matic—An automatic coding system and compiler developed by Univac Division of Sperry-Rand Corporation for use on the Univac II automatic data-processing system.

arithmetic, external—Arithmetic operations performed by buffering, peripheral, or satellite equipment, or equipment outside the central processing unit or main arithmetic unit of a computing system. (Contrast with *arithmetic, internal.*)

arithmetic, internal—Arithmetic operations performed by the arithmetic unit of a computer, within the main frame, central processing unit, or main arithmetic unit, rather than arithmetic operations performed by buffering, peripheral, or

satellite equipment. (Contrast with *arithmetic, external.*)

arithmetic, multiple—A system or method of performing ordinary arithmetic with a digital computer, where several parts of one or more numbers are utilized in an arithmetic operation yielding several results. (Further clarified by *arithmetic, partial.*)

arithmetic, parallel—Arithmetic operations performed in such a manner that all of the digits of a numeral are processed or operated upon simultaneously, usually on as many lines as there are binary digits in the numerals of the operands. Partial sums are formed, carries are formed or propagated, and numerals or partial sums are shifted. (Contrast with *arithmetic, serial.*)

TIME	A	0 1 1 0 1 1	AUGEND
INTERVAL	B	1 0 1 1 0 1	ADDEND
t_1		1 1 0 1 1 0	PARTIAL SUM
	0	0 1 0 0 1	PARTIAL CARRY
t_2		1 0 0 1 0 0	PARTIAL SUM
	0	1 0 0 1 0	PARTIAL CARRY
t_3		0 0 0 0 0 0	PARTIAL SUM
	1	0 0 1 0 0	PARTIAL CARRY
t_4		1 0 0 1 0 0	FINAL SUM
	0	0 0 0 0 0	FINAL CARRY

Parallel arithmetic (addition) performed in four time intervals with minimal parallel logic.

arithmetic, partial—A system or method of performing ordinary arithmetic with a digital computer so that portions or parts of computer words or numbers may be utilized in a particular operation, usually yielding a single result. (Further clarified by *arithmetic, multiple.*)

0	1	1	1	0	0		CARRY
	0	1	0	1	1	0	AUGEND
	0	0	1	1	0	1	ADDEND
	1	0	0	0	1	1	SUM
	6	5	4	3	2	1 ← TIME	

Column time 1 added to yield sum digit 1 and carry digit 0 to column time 2, column time 2 added to yield sum digit 1 and carry digit 0 to column 3, and column time 3 added to yield sum digit 0 and carry digit 1 to column time 4, in the serial arithmetic illustrated above.

arithmetic, serial—Arithmetic operations performed so that each digit of a numeral is processed or operated upon one at a time, usually the digits of like significance being processed together in an adder-subtracter or comparator. Thus, to perform addition, all that is required is a full serial adder, which adds two binary digits and a carry at a time and which is used repeatedly until all the bits of the operands have been added. As many addition operations are required as there are binary digits in the operands. Considerably less hardware is required for a serial adder than for a parallel adder. However, the parallel adder is faster. (Contrast with *arithmetic, parallel.*)

arithmetic, significant-digit—A method of performing calculations using a modified floating-point numeration system such that the number of significant digits in the result is determined with reference to the number of significant digits in the operands, the operation performed, and the degree of precision available.

arithmetic check—Same as *check, mathematical.*

arithmetic instruction—See *instruction, arithmetic.*

arithmetic-logic unit—Same as *unit, arithmetic.*

arithmetic operation—See *operation, arithmetic.*

arithmetic operation, binary—See *operation, binary arithmetic.*

arithmetic point—See *point, arithmetic.*

arithmetic product—See *product, arithmetic.*

arithmetic register—See *register, arithmetic.*

arithmetic section—Same as *unit, arithmetic.*

arithmetic shift—See *shift, arithmetic.*

arithmetic sum—See *sum, arithmetic.*

arithmetic unit—See *unit, arithmetic.*

ARM—(Automated Route Management). A program developed by International Business Machines Corporation, which permits control of such items as sales and production reports for businesses with route distribution operations, such as dairies and bakeries.

arm—To allow an interrupt on a system to take place in accordance with specified plans and priorities. (Contrast with disarm.)

arm, access—A mechanical device that positions another device or subunit of itself in proper geometrical position relative to another unit or device, so as to perform a specific function; for example, a mechanical linkage system that mobilizes a reading head to position it properly to read the information recorded at a specific location on a magnetic recording disk; or the arm that positions the needle on an ordinary automatic home record player. Some disc storage units have one access arm and some have many. The quantity of such arms has a direct bearing on the degree of random access possessed by the unit. The access arm positions the head for both reading and writing. (Further clarified by *disk, magnetic.*)

Army Fieldata code—Same as *code, Fieldata.*

Army Fieldata system—See *system, Army Fieldata.*

Armydata—Same as *system, Army Fieldata.*

array—An orderly arrangement of things or of representations of things; for example, data in the form of signs, symbols, alphanumeric characters, etc., such that the arrangement or relative position of an element of an array has some bearing on the operation that will be performed on the element. Each array usually has a rule or set of rules that, when executed, will yield a value; for instance, when two arrays are used as operands, a new array is generated when the specified operation is executed. A magnetic-core storage plane, with rows and columns of magnetic cores, is a matrix, the position of each core being significant in the sense that the core's position corresponds to a specific digit position in the word or number it represents. An ordinary display of items with no significance attached to the relative position of each item is considered an array, only in a very loose sense.

$$a_1 \quad b_1 \quad c_1 \quad d_1$$

$$a_2 \quad b_2 \quad c_2 \quad d_2$$

$$a_3 \quad b_3 \quad c_3 \quad d_3$$

$$a_4 \quad b_4 \quad c_4 \quad d_4$$

An array.

array, closed—An array that cannot be extended inasmuch as the addition of more elements changes the value of the entire array. Certain tabular arrays can be extended simply by increasing the number of elements. The newly added elements should not alter the value of the old elements, for such an array would not be a closed array.

array, data—An array of data or information in the form of representations of data, such as signs, symbols, and characters, recorded on a medium such as tapes, cards, printed sheets, or working storage.

array pitch—Same as *pitch, row.*

ART—An assembly system that accepts English language statements and produces target (object) working routines, makes equipment assignments, provides for error and input-output control, library maintenance, and retrieval. ART was developed by Univac Division of Sperry-Rand Corporation.

artificial cognition—Same as *perception, artificial.*

artificial intelligence—See *intelligence, artificial.*

artificial language—See *language, artificial.*

artificial perception—See *perception, artificial.*

ARTOC—(Army Tactical Operations Center). A unit of Aeronutronics Division of Ford Motor Company devoted to the study and analysis of tactical operations such as weapon requirements, personnel distributions, logistical requirements, battlefield conditions and environments, terrain analysis, and data systems requirements.

ASA–(American Standards Association). Now American National Standards Institute (ANSI). An institute responsible for the establishment of American standards; for example, ANSI Sectional Committee X3 is responsible for the establishment of standards in the field of computers and information processing. Various X3 subcommittees propose standards in subareas such as optical character recognition, coded character sets, data transmission, programming languages, definitions of computer and information processing terms, problem definition and magnetic ink character recognition.

ASCII–(American Standard Code for Information Interchange). A standard code that assigns specific bit patterns to each sign, symbol, numeral, letter, and operation in a specific set.

ASIS–American Society for Information Science. Formerly American Documentation Institute (ADI).

ASIST–(Advanced Scientific Instruments Symbolic Translator). An assembly program developed by Advanced Scientific Instruments, Inc.

ASLIB–Association of Special Libraries and Information Bureaus.

aspect–In an information retrieval system, a feature of information contained in a unit of information, such as a block, a record, a document, an article, or a paragraph. Aspects are usually represented by keywords or descriptors that are somewhat descriptive of the content of the information unit.

aspect card–See *card, aspect.*

aspect indexing, multiple–Same as *indexing, coordinate.*

ASPER–(Assembly System for Peripheral Processors). An assembly program stored on control cards that hold information for the loader to use at execute time, causing the system to assign a peripheral processor from the pool; developed by Control Data Corporation.

assemble–To prepare a machine language program from a symbolic language program by substituting absolute operation codes and addresses for symbolic operation codes and addresses. The assembly process may involve the translation of symbolic codes into machine codes, the allocation of storage at least to the extent of assigning storage locations to successive instructions, the computation of absolute addresses from symbolic addresses, the insertion of routines or subroutines, and the generation of sequences of symbolic instructions by the insertion of specific parameters into macroinstructions. Thus, to assemble is to put subprograms together into a complete program. The subprograms may be adapted for the specific purpose of the particular assembled program or problem. The net result of the assembly process is a complete, new program.

assemble-and-go–A technique of operating a computer in such a manner that there are no stops or halts between the assembling, loading and execution of a computer program.

assembled origin–See *origin, assembled.*

assembler–A computer program that directs a computer to operate upon a symbolic language program and produce a machine language program which then may be directly executed by the machine. The assembler differs from a compiler in the sense that the assembler does not make use of the overall logical structure of the program, while the compiler does. The assembler evaluates each symbolic instruction independently, as if it stood alone, or at most, in the immediate context of a few preceding instructions. There is a one-to-one correspondence between the symbolic instructions written by the programmer and the machine instructions produced by the assembler. The symbolic instructions will have the same format as the machine instructions. In general, the assembler puts two or more routines or subroutines together to form a single program. The assembler thus serves as a translating routine, which accepts or selects required subroutines, assembles parts of a routine, and usually makes the necessary adjustments required for cross-referencing. (Synonymous with *assembly program* and *assembly routine.* Further clarified by *coding, automatic,* by *assemble,* by *generator,* by *interpreter,* by *translator,* and by *compiler.*)

assembling time–Same as *time, assembling.*

assembly, connector–The combination of a plug inserted into a mated receptacle, not necessarily in use. When in use, electrical separation is accomplished by removing the plug from the receptacle.

assembly, print-wheel–A group of print wheels keyed and fastened to a shaft and rotated at high speed. There is a print wheel at each print position. A hammer forces the ribbon against the paper at the instant the desired character to be printed at a position is aligned with the line of print. (Further explained by *wheel, print* and by *printer, wheel.*)

assembly language–See *language, assembly.*

assembly phase–See *phase, assembly.*

assembly program–Same as *assembler.*

assembly routine–Same as *assembler.*

assignment statement–See *statement, assignment.*

assisted management compter–See *management, computer-assisted.*

Association for Computing Machinery–Same as *ACM.*

associative storage–See *storage, associative.*

astable multivibrator–Same as *multivibrator, free-running.*

asynchronous—A mode of operation such that the execution of the next instruction or the next event is initiated by a signal that is generated upon completion of the previous command or event. Thus, the system operates at the speed determined by the time constants of the circuitry rather than at a speed determined by a clock pulse or timing signal. Most digital computing systems use a timing signal, thus operate synchronously rather than asynchronously. (Contrast with *synchronous.*)

asynchronous computer—See *computer, asynchronous.*

asynchronous data transmission—See *transmission, asynchronous data.*

asynchronous machine—See *machine, asynchronous.*

asynchronous operations—See *operations, asynchronous.*

asynchronous working—Same as *operation, asynchronous.*

asyndetic—The omission of conjunctions or connectives, such as in catalogs, programs, or dictionaries without cross-references.

ATS—(Administrative Terminal System). A system developed by International Business Machines Corporation for permitting a typist to communicate with a computer for handling large volumes of texts, such as legal briefs, so as to avoid repetitive copying of large volumes that have been edited.

attach—1: In an operating system, to present a task or subtask to a supervisor. 2: To reserve or designate a system resource for the exclusive use of a specific program; for example, to associate a storage unit or a file description with a process or routine, or to reserve a system resource, such as a tape station, disc pack, storage area, or output channel for the exclusive use of a specific program.

attention device—See *device, attention.*

attention key—Same as *key, attention.*

attenuate—To obtain a fractional part or to reduce the amplitude of a signal or an action; for example, to reduce a voltage level by means of a voltage divider, to reduce a signal strength by means of absorption or line losses, or to muffle a sound signal. The amount of attenuation may be expressed as a percentage of the magnitude of the original signal strength; the attenuated signal may be expressed as a percentage of the original signal strength. The percentages may be expressed in per unit measure rather than percent, or the attenuation may be expressed in decibels. (Contrast with *amplify.* Further clarified by *attenuation.*)

attenuation—The reduction in the strength or magnitude of a signal or action. (Further clarified by *attenuate.*)

attenuation, echo—The ratio of the transmitted power at an output terminal to the echo power received at or reflected back to the same output terminal (output of the transmitter, input to the transmission line). Echoes usually occur in two- or four-wire signal transmission circuits equipped with repeaters or multiplexing equipment, particularly in those lines in which the two directions of transmission can be separated from each other. The echo attenuation is usually expressed in decibels. In general, the echo attenuation is the ratio of the transmitted power to the power reflected back to the point of transmission.

attribute—In computer simulation, a distinguishing feature or characteristic of an entity.

attribute, data—A characteristic of data, such as length, value, method of representation, form, format, or shape.

attribute list—Same as *list, description.*

audible alarm—See *alarm, audible.*

audio—The range of frequencies that can be heard by the human ear, which responds from about 15 to about 15,000 hertz, although some cases of audio perception exist to 20,000 hertz. Many electronic computers use an audio method of determining continued operation. Signals in a particular circuit, for instance, the control unit, are detected and the resultant envelope of high-frequency signals is fed into an audio amplifier to a loudspeaker. Since random numbers and instructions are detected during normal operation, a rather erratic kind of static is heard. If the system halts, a continuous signal is produced notifying an attendant technician that a malfunction has occurred or that a program is completed. By judicious programming, the same speaker can be made to play music.

audit—An operation or check designed to ascertain the validity of data. In data processing, the audit may be performed at any point. The validity of data is verified through the use of check sums, hash totals, maximas, minimas, redundancies, inversions, cross-totaling, and various other methods.

augend—A quantity or number to which another number, the addend, is to be added, producing a result called the sum. The augend is an arithmetic operand in the summing operation. The augend is usually on hand or considered first; for example, the augend is the number already in an accumulator. Then, the addend is added to it and the sum is formed. When coincident combinational logic is used, as in a binary adder, the distinction between augend and addend is academic. (Further clarified by *adder* and by *addend.*)

augmented operation code—See *code, augmented operation.*

autoabstract—1: The information abstracted from a larger body of information through the use of machine methods. The machines used to prepare autoabstracts are usually stored-program, electronic, digital computing systems or automatic data-processing systems. (Further clarified by *abstract*.) **2**: To prepare an abstract of a larger body of information by machine methods. The process usually is accomplished by programming the selection of key words, which are then printed out, along with the titles of each document, article, or report being abstracted.

auto-answer—To respond automatically by means of a transmission control unit or remote terminal to a call that is received over a switched line.

autobalance—A mechanism made of shafts, wheels, discs an integrating gear, and a differential gear connected in such a way as to perform approximate differentiation of one input variable with respect to another input variable. If a variable u is to be differentiated with respect to a variable x, the two inputs to the differential gear are u and the output z of the integrating gear. The integrating gear output, z, is given by $z = \int y \, dx$. The differential gear output, y, and the input variable, x, are the inputs to the integrating gear. The differential gear output, y, is given by $y = u - z$. The y signal is then the output of the unit and is then given by $y = du/dx - dy/dx$. If $y = k \, du/dx$, then $dy/dx = kd^2u/dx^2$. If, further, kd^2u/dx^2 is small, then $y = du/dx$ (approximately). The diagram helps to clarify the relationships involved. The autobalance device is used extensively in mechanical analog computers. (Further clarified by *gear, integrating* and by *gear, differential*.)

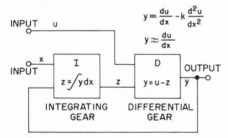

Relationships in an autobalance *expressed mathematically.*

auto-call—To initiate a call automatically by means of a transmission control unit or remote terminal over a switched line.

autocode—A scheme for automatically converting, by means of a computer, a symbolic code for operations and addresses into a machine code for operations and addresses. Thus, an autocode simplifies programming, often through the use of a mnemonic code, which more probably uses macro-instructions. (Synonymous with *automatic code*.)

Autocoder—A specific autocode developed by International Business Machines

Corporation for use on IBM automatic data-processing systems.

Autocoder, Basic—An autocode developed by International Business Machines Corporation specifically for the IBM 7070 automatic data-processing system. This autocode is fundamental to other IBM systems.

AUTOCOMM—A procedure developed by Control Data Corporation for preparing computer programs for the solution of commercial data-processing problems. Originally developed for the Control Data 160A computer, the procedure minimizes programming for computing systems. It is decimally oriented and an abbreviated form of COBOL.

autoindex—**1**: An index prepared automatically through the use of a machine. Thus, a computer may be programmed so that certain data will be selected automatically from the storage unit and used at a later time as the index for scanning and searching the contents of the storage unit. **2**: To prepare an index automatically.

automata theory—See *theory, automata*.

automated data medium—Same as *medium, machine-readable*.

Automath—A compiler used on the Honeywell automatic data-processing systems.

Automath 1800—A compiler and an advanced version of Automath, designed for the Honeywell 1800 computer and compatible with FORTRAN IV. Automath 1800 compiles over 1000 statements per minute.

automatic—Pertaining to a process or device that, under specified conditions, functions without intervention by a human operator.

automatic branch exchange, private—See *exchange, private automatic branch*.

automatic carriage—See *carriage, automatic*.

automatic check—See *check, automatic*.

automatic code—Same as *autocode*.

automatic coding—See *coding, automatic*.

automatic computer—See *computer, automatic*.

automatic control—See *control, automatic*.

automatic control engineering—See *engineering, automatic control*.

automatic controller—Same as *control, automatic*.

automatic crosstell—See *crosstell, automatic*.

automatic data processing—See *processing, automatic data*.

automatic data-switching center—See *center, automatic data-switching*.

automatic dictionary—See *dictionary, automatic*.

automatic error correction—See *correction, automatic error*.

automatic exchange—See *exchange, automatic*.

automatic exchange, private—See *exchange, private automatic*.

automatic feed punch—See *punch, automatic feed*.

automatic grouping—See *grouping, automatic*.

automatic message switching—See *switching, automatic message.*

automatic programming—See *programming, automatic.*

automatic restart—See *restart, automatic.*

automatic routine—See *routine, automatic.*

automatic tape punch—See *punch, automatic tape.*

automatic tape transmitter—Same as *reader, tape.*

automation—1: The entire field of investigation devoted to the design, development, and application of methods and techniques for rendering a process or group of machines self-actuating, self-moving, or self-controlling. Automation pertains to the theory, art, or technique of making a machine, a process, or a device more fully automatic. Simply, the implementation of a process by automatic means. Computers and information-processing equipment play a large role in the automation of a process because of the inherent ability of a computer to develop decisions that will, in effect, control or govern the process from the information received by the computer concerning the status of the process. Thus, automation pertains to both the theory, art, and techniques of using automatic systems in industrial or commercial applications and the processes of investigation, design, and conversion to automatic methods. Automatic control, automatic materials handling, automatic testing, automatic packaging, for continuous as well as batch processing, are all considered parts of the overall or completely automatic process. A fully automatic automobile assembly line, automatic oil refinery, automatic bakery, or automatic blast-furnace are examples of the application of the principles and practices of automation. The use of tape-controlled machine tools is an example of automation in the control aspect as well as in the materials handling and processing aspect. Automatic testing, packaging, and shipping are also a part of the process included in the concept of automation. Thus, the concept of automation includes the concept of labor-saving, since automation embraces the element of decision-making. 2: The implementation of processes and procedures by automatic means, such as the conversion of a procedure or equipment to automatic means or operation.

automation, source data—The creation of data in machine readable media at the place of origin of the data; for example, using a cash register to record the identification of the article sold in order to establish stock levels for reordering; or to prepare a perforated tape or punched card reflecting charges to a project at the point where the charges are incurred.

automaton—A machine or control device that responds automatically to predetermined operations or instructions. Thus, a self-acting system capable of forming logical decisions on the basis of information and rules that have been made available to it. Generally, an automaton exhibits living properties and is responsive to its environment or to stimuli.

automonitor—1: To instruct an automatic computing system to make a record of its own operations; thus, to supervise itself, and verify the correctness of its own program and its operations during the execution of the program. 2: The program or the routine that accomplishes the self-supervision and self-recording.

autonomous working—See *working, autonomous.*

AUTOPIC—(Automatic Personal Identification Code). A computer program code developed by International Business Machines Corporation.

AUTOPROMT—(Automatic Programming of Machine Tools). A technique of directing the operations of machine tools by computer-prepared or computer-executed programs; developed by International Business Machines Corporation.

AUTOPSY—(Automatic Operating System). A program compiler and assembly system developed by Westinghouse Electric Company and International Business Machines Corporation for use on the IBM 704 automatic data-processing system.

auxiliary data—See *data, auxiliary.*

auxiliary equipment—Same as *equipment, peripheral.*

auxiliary operation—See *operation, auxiliary.*

auxiliary storage—See *storage, auxiliary.*

availability, system—The length of time that a manufacturer requires to insure satisfactory operation of his system at the customer's site assuming that the customer does not present obstacles or introduce delays in the installation. Availability can sometimes be measured in terms of the number of machines already in operation at customer sites. Availability is indicated by the anticipated date of the first installation, which in some instances can be months, even years, away. (Further clarified by *time, available* and by *ratio, operating.*)

available time—See *time, available.*

average calculating operation—See *operation, average calculating.*

average data-transfer rate—Same as *rate, effective data-transfer.*

average effectiveness level—See *level, average effectiveness.*

average information rate—See *rate, average information.*

average operation time—See *time, average operation.*

average transinformation content—Same as *content, mean transinformation.*

average transinformation rate—See *rate, average transinformation.*

average transmission rate—Same as *rate, effective data-transfer.*

awaiting-repair time—See *time, awaiting-repair.*

axis, reference—A fixed horizontal or vertical line used as a guide for the specification of character designs such that the location of the character as well as the shape of the character can be specified. This consideration is significant in the specification of the character fonts for optical character recognition purposes.

azimuth—The angular measurement in a horizontal plane in a clockwise direction. The measurement is made from a specific reference direction; for example, a true azimuth is the angle measured from true north to the direction to be specified, magnetic azimuth from magnetic north, or

grid azimuth from grid north. Any base line or thrust line in a horizontal plane may be used as a reference. Azimuth angles may be measured in degrees (360 per full circle); in artillery mils (6400 per full circle); in engineers' mils (an angle whose tangent is $1/1000$); or in radians (2π radians form a full circle).

azimuth, head—In magnetic tape recording devices, the angle between a line determined by the gap centers of the two extreme heads of a group and the reference edge of the magnetic tape.

A0 A1 A2—Automatic coding systems developed by Univac Division of Sperry-Rand Corporation to compile and assemble programs for use on the Univac automatic data-processing systems.

b

B AND NOT A gate—See *gate, B AND NOT A.*

B-box—Same as *register, index.*

B EXCEPT A gate—Same as *gate, B AND NOT A.*

B ignore A gate—See *gate, B ignore A.*

B ignore A gate, negative—See *gate, negative (B ignore A).*

B implies A gate—Same as *gate, A OR NOT B.*

B implies A gate, negative—Same as *gate, B AND NOT A.*

B-line—Same as *register, index.*

B OR NOT A gate—See *gate, B OR NOT A.*

B-register—Same as *register, index.*

B-store—Same as *register, index.*

babble—In teleprocessing systems, the aggregate crosstalk from a number of interfering data communications channels.

BACAIC—(Boeing Airplane Company Algebraic Interpretive Computing System). An interpretive routine developed by Boeing Airplane Company for use on the IBM 701 and IBM 650 automatic data-processing systems.

back-mounted—A connector mounted from the inside of a panel or box. The mounting flanges are on the inside of the equipment.

back-wall photovoltaic cell—See *cell, back-wall photovoltaic.*

background—1: Lower priority tasks, jobs, programs, routines, or subroutines that are executed when higher priority programs are not using the system's

resources. 2: Pertaining to the execution of lower priority computer programs when higher priority programs are not using the system's resources. (Contrast with *foreground.*)

background, display—In computer graphics, those portions of a display image that cannot be altered by the user of the display system. (Contrast with *foreground, display.*)

background reflectance—See *reflectance, backgound.*

backing storage—Same as *storage, auxiliary.*

backspace—To move a recording medium, such as roll paper, paper tape, or magnetic tape, in a backward direction for a unit distance, such as one character, one row, one line, one record, one file, one word, or one space. As an extension of this concept, one could successively backspace, thus causing continual motion of the medium in the reverse direction. For the case of certain accounting machines and typewriters, the entire carriage or paper holder must be moved backward, usually for corrections or deletions.

backspace character—See *character, backspace.*

Backus-Naur form—Same as *form, Backus normal.*

Backus normal form—See *form, Backus normal.*

backward channel—See *channel, backward.*

backward-linked list—See *list, backward-linked.*

backward supervisor—See *supervisor, backward.*

bail—A loop of wire used to prevent separation of two or more parts assembled together. The wire is usually wrapped or snap-fitted around the two parts.

balanced—Electrical symmetry with respect to ground, a particular characteristic, or some other reference; for example, a Wheatstone bridge is balanced when the ratio of the impedances on each of two pairs of legs are equal; two tubes connected in parallel or tandem are said to be balanced when their characteristics are identical and their load current or voltages are equally shared; two transmission lines or the three legs of a wye-connected three-phase load are balanced when the impedances or the currents are the same; a three-wire single-phase circuit is said to be balanced when the neutral wire current is zero; the loads on two parallel-operating generators are balanced when each generator is loaded equally, if they are identical, or proportionate according to maximal efficiency or some other criterion.

balanced circuit—See *circuit, balanced.*

balanced error—See *error, balanced.*

balanced line—See *line, balanced.*

balanced merge—See *merge, balanced.*

balanced merge sort—See *sort, balanced merge.*

BALITAC—An automatic coding system developed by Massachusetts Institute of Technology for use on the IBM 650 automatic data-processing system.

ball resolver—See *resolver, ball.*

band—1: A group of circular recording tracks on storage devices, such as drums and disks. The group of tracks are treated as a logical unit; for example, a single word may be expressed as a set of parallel bits, one from each track in the band; or one particular drum may contain 25 main storage bands, two buffer bands, and one timing band; or four parallel tracks forming a band may be used to record, in binary-coded-decimal form, decimal digits serially. (Further clarified by *track.*) 2: A range of frequencies in the frequency spectrum between two defined frequency limits. 3: A group of radio channels assigned to a particular type of radio service; for example, amateur band, police band, aircraft band, etc. Article 2 of the 1959 Geneva Radio Regulations has divided the radio spectrum into nine frequency bands, each of which shall be designated by the whole numbers 4 through 12. Band number N extends from 0.3×10^N to 3.0×10^N hertz. Frequencies are expressed in kilohertz up to and including 3000 kHz; in megahertz thereafter up to and including 3000 MHz; and in gigahertz up to and including 3000 GHz. Reasonable departures from these rules may be made if necessary. Abbreviations used are Hz (hertz); k (kilo, 10^3); M

(mega, 10^6); G (giga, 10^9); and T (tera, 10^{12}). Abbreviations for adjectival bands are very low frequency for Band 4 (VLF, 3 kHz to 30 kHz); low frequency for Band 5 (LF, 30 kHz to 300 kHz); medium frequency for Band 6 (MF, 300 kHz to 3000 kHz); high frequency for Band 7 (HF, 3 MHz to 30 MHz); very high frequency for Band 8 (VHF, 30 MHz to 300 MHz); ultrahigh frequency for Band 9 (UHF, 300 MHz to 3000 MHz); superhigh frequency for Band 10 (SHF, 3000 MHz to 30,000 MHz); and extremely high frequency (EHF, above 30,000 MHz).

band, clear—In optical character recognition, a specified area on a document that is to be kept free of unrelated printing or any other markings unrelated to machine reading. The clear band is used by optical character recognition equipment, and therefore must be kept free of extraneous ink. (Further clarified by *ink, extraneous.*)

band, dead—A specific range of values of the parameters defining an incoming signal, over which the signal parameter values can be altered without changing or altering the outgoing signal. Thus, the output is "dead," that is, independent of the input, for the period of time involved. (Synonymous with *dead zone.*)

band, frequency—Same as *band (3).*

BAND NO.	FREQUENCY RANGE	METRIC SUBDIVISION (WAVES)
4	3 TO 30 KHz	MYRIAMETRIC
5	30 TO 300 KHz	KILOMETRIC
6	300 TO 3000 KHz	HECTOMETRIC
7	3 TO 30 MHz	DECAMETRIC
8	30 TO 300 MHz	METRIC
9	300 TO 3000 MHz	DECIMETRIC
10	3 TO 30 GHz	CENTIMETRIC
11	30 TO 300 GHz	MILLIMETRIC
12	300 TO 3000 GHz 3 THz	DECIMILLIMETRIC

Frequency bands.

band, guard—An unused frequency band between two assigned frequency channels to provide a margin of safety against mutual interference and the reception of two or more channels through a single discriminator.

band, pass—The range of frequencies that are attenuated less than one-half the midfrequency power value. The power level at the limits of the range is one-half, or down 3 decibels, of the midfrequency level.

band, proportional—Same as *range, proportional.*

banding, rubber—See *rubber-banding.*

bandpass—Pertaining to the operation of a circuit or device, such as a filter, that permits the passage of a specified frequency range. The range of frequencies is expressed as the difference between the limiting frequencies at which the power transferred is one-half, or down 3 decibels, of the power transferred at the midfrequency between the limiting frequencies. The midfrequency is also specified. (Contrast with *lowpass* and *highpass*.)

bandwidth–The difference in frequency between the highest and lowest frequency in a band. (Further clarified by *bandwidth, R-F emission*.)

bandwidth, nominal–The maximum band of frequencies, including guard bands, that are assigned to a given channel.

bandwidth, R-F emission–The frequency difference between the highest and the lowest emission frequencies of a radio-frequency signal in the region of the carrier or principal carrier frequency, beyond which the amplitude of any frequency resulting from modulation by signal or subcarrier frequencies and their distortion products is less than 5 percent, or −26 dB, of the rated peak output amplitude of the carrier or a single-tone sideband, whichever is greater, for a single-channel emission; or any subcarrier or single-tone sideband thereof, whichever is greater, for multiplex emission. (Synonymous with *R-F bandwidth*.)

bank, data–1: A comprehensive collection of data; for example, several automated files, a library, or a set of loaded discs. 2: A collection of data, or part of a collection of data, usually consisting of at least one file and usually sufficient for a given purpose or for a given data processing system.

BANKPAC–A computer software package developed by General Electric Company for the banking industry.

bar, cross–See *cross-bar*.

bar, fixed type–A bar of type that cannot be removed by the operator, thus somewhat permanently fixing the alphabet available to a printer. (Further clarified by *type, bar*. Contrast with *bar, interchangeable type*.)

bar, interchangeable type–A bar of type that can be removed from a printer by the operator to change the alphabet available to a print position. (Further clarified by *type, bar*. Contrast with *bar, fixed type*.)

bar, type–A long, narrow box or magazine that holds type and from which the type projects. A particular character is selected for printing by moving the box, usually vertically, until the desired character is opposite the printing position. Each bar contains an entire font; that is, the entire alphabet available to the particular print position. The type bar in a given printer may be interchangeable, permitting the available alphabet to be changed by the operator, or it may be fixed and not subject to being changed by the operator. The bar printer obtains its name from the type bar. (Further clarified by *bar, fixed type* and by *bar, interchangeable type*.)

bar printer–See *printer, bar*.

Barker code–See *code, Barker*.

barrel–The cylindrical portion or part of a terminal post, contact, or connector, that accepts or accommodates a conductor or conductors; the barrel usually forms the central or main part of a binding post, plug, jack, or cylindrical receptacle.

barrier layer–See *layer, barrier*.

base–1: The electrode in a point contact or the region in a junction transistor that is considered to lie between the two oppositely doped semiconducting media, that is, the collector and the emitter. Thus, in an n-p-n transistor, the base is positively doped with a trivalent element, while the collector and emitter are negatively doped with pentavalent atoms. Transistor action takes place at the surface region of transition between base and collector and between base and emitter. Commonly, collector current is controlled by the emitter current or bias with respect to the base, which can be considered common to both emitter and collector circuits. Operation can also take place with the emitter or collector common. The base can be considered to correspond somewhat to the grid of a vacuum tube, inasmuch as base potential or base current can control the emitter-to-collector current. (Further clarified by *transistor*.) 2: Same as *radix*.

base, data–A collection of data that is fundamental to an enterprise.

base, tape–A non-magnetic material used as a support of a magnetic coating for recording.

base address–See *address, base*.

base complement–A specified numeral that contains the digits from which the corresponding digits of a given numeral are subtracted to obtain the complement of the given numeral.

base metal–See *metal, base*.

base notation–Same as *notation, radix*.

base notation, mixed–See *notation, mixed-base*.

base numeration system, mixed–See *system, mixed-base numeration system*.

base point–Same as *point, arithmetic*.

base register–Same as *register, index*.

base-address register–See *register, base-address*.

Baseball–An automatic question-answerer using an information-processing language, developed by Lincoln Laboratories of Massachusetts Institute of Technology for the IBM 7090 automatic data-processing system. The technique draws its name from baseball as it is similar to that which would be required to answer questions concerning baseball, a game subject to precise rules. The technique is universally applicable to any similar question-answer situations on any subject.

baseball computer program–See *program, baseball computer*.

basic–Pertaining to the concept of a structure that is the innermost part of a nested structure. For example, a statement is basic to a procedure, whereas the procedure can be nested, or reduced to a set of statements, and so cannot be considered basic.

BASIC–1: (Battle Area Surveillance and Integrated Communications). The technique, including the programming language, used for the detection, transmission, reception, transformation, processing, and dissemination of information in a tactical situation on a specific set of equipment. 2: A computer programming language developed at Dartmouth College. It is a standard programming language with a small repertory of commands and a simple syntax. The word BASIC is derived from the expression "Beginner's All-purpose Symbolic Instruction Code."

Basic Autocoder–See *Autocoder, Basic.*

basic code–Same as *code, absolute.*

basic linkage–See *linkage, basic.*

batch data processing–See *data processing, batch.*

batch processing–See *processing, batch.*

batch processing, concurrent–See *processing, concurrent batch.*

batch processing, remote–See *processing, remote batch.*

batch processing, sequential–See *processing, sequential batch.*

batch query–See *query, batch.*

batch total–See *total, batch.*

Batten–Same as *peek-a-boo.*

Batten check–Same as *check, sight.*

baud–A unit of modulation rate; a unit of signaling speed. One baud corresponds to a rate of one unit-time interval per second. The speed in bauds is equal to the number of times the line condition changes per second. Thus, the signalling speed in bauds is the number of discrete conditions or signalling events per second. Usually, a code element or character occurs in the given unit time interval. If the duration of the unit interval for the signaling device is 20 milliseconds, then the modulation rate is 50 bauds. If the code elements of a printing telegram system, such as mark-and-space or on-and-off code elements, occur at the rate of 100 code elements per second, the unit is said to be operating at the rate of 100 bauds. If a teleprinter runs at such a speed that the maximum line frequency is 22.5 hertz, then the system is operating at 45 bauds, since an off condition occurs for each on condition, and each is considered as a code element. Thus, the duration of the shortest code element must be taken into account in determining the number of bauds.

Baudot code–See *code, Baudot.*

BC–The block cancel character.

BCD–(Binary Coded Decimal). See *decimal, binary-coded.*

BCO–(Binary Coded Octal). See *octal, binary-coded.*

BCS–British Computer Society.

beam, holding–A diffuse beam of electrons in a cathode-ray tube. The beam is used for restoring the negative charges on the inside dielectric storage surface of the cathode-ray tube and serves as a source of charges for the replenishment of those that leak off between storage references. Regeneration is continual and is interrupted only for the interrogation of a specific location. (Further clarified by *gun, holding.*)

beam recording, electron–See *recording, electron beam.*

beam-switching tube–See *tube, beam-switching.*

beat–Same as *word-time.*

begin–A procedure delimiter in ALGOL. (Further clarified by *delimiter.*)

beginning-of-tape marker–See *marker, beginning-of-tape.*

BEL–The bell character.

Bell–A complete floating-point interpretive programming system developed by Bell Telephone Laboratories, Inc., for use on the IBM 650 computer. A similar system was used by Shell Oil Company on the Datatron 205 (Burroughs 205 computer), by the Burroughs Corporation on the Datatron 220 (Burroughs 220 computer), and by the IBM Corporation on the IBM 704 computer.

bell character–See *character, bell.*

belled mouth–See *mouth, belled.*

BEMA–(Business Equipment Manufacturers Association). A trade association of computing and data-processing equipment manufacturers. BEMA is the industrial sponsor of the American National Standards Institute's Sectional Committee X3, which is devoted to the development of USA standards on computers and information processing. (Synonymous with *CBEMA.*)

benchmark–A fixed point of reference from which measurements to other fixed or moving points can be made.

benchmark problem–See *problem, benchmark.*

benchmark program–See *program, benchmark.*

BEST–(Business EDP Systems Technique). A concept developed by National Cash Register Company for programming business problem solutions on NCR computers. Logic flow charts are readily converted to computer programs to reduce programming time.

bias–1: The departure from a reference value of the average of a set of values; thus, a measure of the amount of unbalance of a set of measurements or conditions; that is, an unbalanced error or error having an average value that is not zero. Some examples include: the results produced by using a shrunken measuring tape; the results of computations involving certain truncation errors; the nonrandomness of a distribution or sequence; or leaning toward one side of an issue or a situation.

39

(Contrast with *error, balanced.*) 2: The average d-c voltage maintained between the cathode and the control grid of a vacuum tube or the average d-c voltage or current maintained between a control electrode and the common electrode in a transistor. The bias is measured with respect to the cathode for the tube and with respect to the common electrode for the transistor.

bias, internal—A bias in marking or spacing that may occur within a printing receiving mechanism, such as a teletypewriter. The bias will have the same effect on the limits of operation as bias external to the receiver.

bias, ordering—1: The degree to which items of data, such as collections of numerals or alphabetic words, are already in a desired order, such as alphabetical or numerical order. 2: The amount, manner, or degree by which the order of a set of items is different from a random distribution. The ordering bias possessed by a set of items will make the effort necessary to place the set of items in a specific desired order more or less than the effort required to order the same set from a random distribution, depending on whether the ordering bias favors the specific desired order.

bias check—Same as *check, marginal.*

bias distortion—See *distortion, bias.*

bias error—See *error, bias.*

bias port—See *port, bias.*

bias test—Same as *test, marginal.*

bibliography—A list of documents or an annotated catalog of documents pertaining to a given subject or author and generally listed by author, title, publisher, date, and other annotation at the end of a given document. (Further clarified by *index, citation* and by *reference.*)

biconditional gate—Same as *gate, exclusive-NOR.*

bidirectional flow—See *flow, bidirectional.*

bidirectional list—See *list, bidirectional.*

bifurcated contact—See *contact, bifurcated.*

bigit—Same as *bit.*

billibit—Same as *kilomegabit.*

billisecond—Same as *nanosecond.*

bin, tape—A magnetic-tape storage device containing many closed loops of magnetic tape and having either one or more movable read/record heads or a fixed head for each loop. The principle of operation permits semirandom access, as the heads and loops can move to specified locations on tape; the access time is therefore more rapid than on serial reels of magnetic tape, which must be wound. The tape bin resembles a deep-freeze chest, with the head mechanism in the lid and the loops of tape hanging down in the "freezer locker." The Datafile is an example of a tape bin.

binary—A characteristic or property involving a selection, choice or condition in which there are two possibilities; pertaining to two. Pertaining to the numeration system

with a radix of two. A binary choice is a choice between two alternatives; a binary operation involves or combines two quantities; a binary search makes a determination as to whether a number or quantity is greater or less than a reference number, and so, with repeated trials, locates or determines the number. Use of a binary system is predicated on the supposition that a duality exists: that is, a thing, state, or condition is or is not.

binary, Chinese—Same as *binary, column.*

binary, column—The representation of binary data on punch cards in which adjacent positions in a column, as in Chinese writing, correspond to adjacent bits of data; for example, each column in a 12-row card can represent 12 consecutive bits of a 36-bit word. The presence of a zero or a one is determined by the absence or presence of a hole. Thus the binary numbers are read vertically and the card can be sensed vertically, or row-by-row. (Synonymous with *Chinese binary.* Contrast with *binary, row.* Further clarified by *column, card* and by *deck, binary.*)

A card punched in column binary *with the binary numeral 11010111110 in the first* column.

binary, normal—Same as *binary, straight.*

binary, ordinary—Same as *binary, straight.*

binary, pure—Same as *binary, straight.*

binary, regular—Same as *binary, straight.*

binary, row—The representation of binary data on punch cards in which adjacent positions in a row correspond to adjacent bits of data. For example, each row of an 80-column card can represent 80 consecutive bits or two 40-bit words. The presence of a zero or a one is determined by the absence or presence of a hole. Thus, the binary numbers are read by eye horizontally, while the card can be sensed vertically, or row by row, obtaining two words at a time, all bits in parallel on 80 lines, or horizontally, column by column, obtaining say 12 (rows) words at a time, serially by bit, on 12 lines. (Contrast with *binary, column.* Further clarified by *card, row-binary* and by *deck, binary.*)

binary, straight—A binary numeration system in which the binary numerals are expressed in a positional notation system, such that each successive digit position is weighted by a factor of two times the weight of the prior position. For example, a numeral is written as $a_1 2^n + a_2 2^{n-1} + a_3 2^{n-2} + \ldots + a_n 2^1 + a_0 2^0 + a_{-1} 2^{-1} + a_{-2} 2^{-2} + \ldots$, where the binary point occurs to the right of the a_0 term. Thus, the straight binary numeral 101101.1 represents $1 \times 2^5 + 0 \times 2^4 + 1 \times 2^3 + 1 \times 2^2 + 0 \times 2^1 + 1 \times 2^0 + 1 \times 2^{-1}$, or $32 + 0 + 8 + 4 + 0 + 1 + 0.5 = 45.5$ decimal. (Synonymous with *normal binary*, with *ordinary binary*, with *pure binary*, and with *regular binary*.)

DECIMAL		STRAIGHT BINARY		
I	I 0	I	I 0 I 0	
2	I I	I 0	I 0 I I	
3	I 2	I I	I I 0 0	
4	I 3	I 0 0	I I 0 I	
5	I 4	I 0 I	I I I 0	
6	I 5	I I 0	I I I I	
7	I 6	I I I	I 0 0 0 0	
8	I 7	I 0 0 0	I 0 0 0 I	
9	I 8	I 0 0 I	I 0 0 I 0	

Counting sequence of straight binary numerals and their decimal equivalents.

binary arithmetic operation—See *operation, binary arithmetic.*
binary card—See *card, binary.*
binary cell—See *cell, binary.*
binary chain—See *chain, binary.*
binary code—See *code, binary.*
binary code, dense—See *code, dense binary.*
binary-coded address—See *address, binary-coded.*
binary-coded character—See *character, binary-coded.*
binary-coded decimal—See *decimal, binary-coded.*
binary-coded decimal interchange code, extended—See *code, extended binary-coded decimal interchange.*
binary-coded decimal notation—See *notation, binary-coded decimal.*
binary-coded digit—See *digit, binary-coded.*
binary-coded notation—See *notation, binary-coded.*
binary-coded octal—See *octal, binary-coded.*
binary counter—See *counter, binary.*
binary deck—See *deck, binary.*
binary digit—See *digit, binary.*
binary digits, equivalent—See *digits, equivalent binary.*
binary element—See *element, binary.*
binary element string—See *string, binary element.*
binary equivalent—Same as *digits, equivalent binary.*
binary half-adder—Same as *half-adder (1).*
binary incremental representation—See *representation, binary incremental.*
binary notation—See *notation, binary.*
binary number—Same as *numeral, binary.*
binary number system—Same as *notation, binary.*

binary numeral—See *numeral, binary.*
binary numeration system, pure—See *system, pure binary numeration.*
binary one—See *one, binary.*
binary operation—Same as *operation, dyadic.*
binary operator—Same as *operator, dyadic.*
binary pair—Same as *flip-flop.*
binary point—See *point, binary.*
binary scale—Same as *notation, binary.*
binary search—See *search, binary.*
binary-state variable—Same as *variable, two-valued.*
binary symmetric channel—See *channel, binary symmetric.*
binary-to-decimal conversion—See *conversion, binary-to-decimal.*
binary variable—Same as *variable, two-valued.*
binary zero—See *zero, binary.*
bind—1: To assign a value to a variable or to a parameter; for example, to set a variable at a specified constant value. 2: In an operating system, the action of relating absolute or machine addresses with the symbolic addresses of a computer program. (Synonymous with *set.*)
binder-hole card—See *card, binder-hole.*
binding—Transforming one or more object program modules into a program that is a composite of the modules and is suitable for execution. (Synonymous with *collecting* and with *editing, linkage.*)
bionics—The study of functions, characteristics, behavior, and phenomena of living organisms and systems of all species and the application of the knowledge gained in this study to develop operating hardware, techniques, methods, and procedures useful to mankind. Since the studies involve biology and the application involves electronics, the word bionics was coined from these two words. However, bionics is not limited only to these two fields. Neurology, psychology, mechanics, physics, and other fields and subfields are also involved; thus, bionics involves man's attempt to imitate, improve on, and benefit from living systems. Hardware can thus be created that will perform functions in a manner analogous to the more sophisticated functions of the living system. For example, the ultrasonic sensing system of a bat has a figure of merit several thousand times greater than our finest radar, in terms of size, weight, power, and range.
BIOR—(Business Input Output Rerun.) A compiling system developed by Univac Division of Sperry-Rand Corporation for use on the Univac I and Univac II computers.
BIPCO—(Built-In-Place Components). A development of the Burroughs Corporation for construction of equipment.
bipolar—A signal system wherein a logic true input is represented by an electrical voltage or current of a given polarity and a

logic false input is represented by an electrical voltage or current of opposite polarity. (Contrast with *unipolar*.)

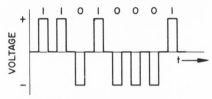

A binary numeral represented by a time sequence of bipolar *signals.*

biquinary—A number representation system in which each decimal digit is represented by a pair of digits, AB, where the biquinary number N equals 5A plus B, and where A equals 0 or 1, and B equals 0, 1, 2, 3, or 4; for example, 7 would be represented in biquinary by 12. This system is an example for a mixed radix system; that is, the radices are 2 and 5. The digits for a biquinary numeral are set off in pairs. Thus decimal 486 would be biquinary 04 13 11. (Further clarified by *quinary*.)

BIQUINARY		DECIMAL	
0 1	0 1 0 0	1	1 0
0 2	0 1 0 1	2	1 1
0 3	0 1 0 2	3	1 2
0 4	0 1 0 3	4	1 3
1 0	0 1 0 4	5	1 4
1 1	0 1 1 0	6	1 5
1 2	0 1 1 1	7	1 6
1 3	0 1 1 2	8	1 7
1 4	0 1 1 3	9	1 8

Counting in biquinary *and decimal.*

biquinary code—See *code, biquinary*.
biquinary notation—See *notation, biquinary*.
bistable—Pertaining to the capability of a device or object to assume either one of two stable or given states at a particular instant of time. The transition period from one state to the other must be relatively short. With this inherent or intrinsic characteristic, the device will have the ability to store a bit of information while in the stable state, since a zero or a one or truth or falsity can be assigned to either state. Thus, bistable, binary pair, trigger pair, Eccles-Jordan circuit, bistable circuit, and bistable trigger circuit are all British terms for *flip-flop*. (Contrast with *monostable*.)
bistable circuit—Same as *flip-flop*.
bistable multivibrator—Same as *flip-flop*.
bistable trigger circuit—Same as *flip-flop*.
bit—1: A contraction or abbreviation of binary digit. One of the characters of a two-valued or binary number system; is thus a single character of a language or alphabet that employs only two distinct kinds of characters. Various permutations

of members of strings or groups of these two characters, such as 0 and 1, may be used to designate characters in other alphabets employing a larger number of character designs; for example, 101010 may represent U. A bit has come to signify the smallest piece or smallest unit of information, which is an added meaning derived from the early usage of bit to mean a small piece of something: a bit-part, a bit of string, a bit of time and a little bit of energy. However, a bit of information in a technical sense no longer means a small amount, but actually the smallest amount. The information must be expressed in a form such as on-off, yes-no, stop-go, truth-falsity, zero-one, or dot-dash. Thus, when the information capacity of a storage device is expressed in bits, the capacity is the logarithm to the base two of the number of stable states that the device is capable of assuming. The unit of information is selective; that is, the amount of information expressed by the bits is derived from the knowledge of the occurrence of one of two equiprobable, mutually exclusive and exhaustive events. The use of *bigit* in place of *bit* is deprecated. (Synonymous with *bigit*. Further clarified by *digit, binary*.) 2: Same as *shannon*.
bit, check—A binary digit used for checking purposes; for example, a redundant bit placed within a group of bits comprising a larger unit of information, such as an alphanumeric character or a word, so as to make the count of all the ones always odd or always even, or all the zeros always odd or always even. Thus, the inaccurate retrieval, transfer, or expression of the character or word is detectable. (Further clarified by *check, parity* and by *digit, check*.)
bit, detail—One of a group of four bits within the Army Fieldata code, which represents the specific symbol, character, or number within a given class. The class is specified by the indicator bit.
bit, indicator—One of a group of two bits used in the Army Fieldata code to indicate to which class (character or keyboard-format-control) a character belongs.

BINARY NUMERAL	BIT TO MAINTAIN EVEN PARITY
1 0 1 1 1	0
1 1 0 1 0	1
1 1 1 1 0	0
1 0 0 1 0	0
0 1 0 1 0	0
0 1 1 1 0	1

Parity bit to maintain even parity for a set of binary numerals.

bit, parity—A bit assigned to a group of bits, such as the group used to specify a character or word, so as to place a constraint on the number of ones or zeros in the group of binary digits. For example, a bit is set when the word is first formulated, so that the number of ones in the word is always even. Whenever the word is stored, transferred, or used by the computer in any way, a count is made to ensure that the number of ones is always even. If it is not this is an indication that at least one bit has been changed and that a single, or at least an odd-bit error has occurred. Of course, if two bits are changed, the change (error) would not be detected; however, it is not likely that the kind of machine malfunction that caused the change of two digits would continue to do so for an extended period, in which case, the malfunction will be detected almost immediately. Thus, there are odd-parity and even-parity checking systems, usually determined by whether the number of ones or zeros to be counted will be odd or even. Usually, by even parity we mean that the number of ones will be maintained even.

bit, presence—A single sentinel bit appearing in a descriptor to indicate whether or not the information to which reference is made is in the high-speed storage at this time. The term is used particularly in connection with equipment manufactured by Burroughs Corporation.

bit, redundancy check—A check bit derived from a record in accordance with some algorithm and appended to the record so that when the transmitted record is received or read the same algorithm can be applied to the read message and the same bit can thus be derived and compared with the original bit.

bit, sign—1: A bit used to designate the algebraic sign of a quantity as plus or minus. The convention is quite arbitrary; that is, it does not matter which digit is used to designate either sign. In most systems, the state used to represent a one is used to represent a plus sign, which makes the positive numbers numerically larger than the negative numbers. In this case, if the presence of a pulse is used to signify a one and the absence of a pulse represents a zero, then the presence of a pulse in the sign position of the number signifies a positive number and the absence of a pulse in the sign position signifies a negative number. This must not be confused with the assignment of a permutation of binary digits to the minus sign, or hyphen, as a symbol within a set of alphanumeric characters and used to display the negative quality of a number when printed for human reading or optical machine sensing. 2: A bit that occupies a sign position and that indicates the arithmetic sign of the number represented by the numeral with which it is associated.

bit, start—In a start-stop communication system, a binary character that precedes each n-bit character and that permits machine recognition of the character; for example, a signal sent to or reviewed by a mechanism designed to receive data alerting the mechanism to assume a state of readiness to perform a function, such as receive data. (Synonymous with *start element* and with *start signal*. Contrast with *bit, stop*.)

bit, stencil—A bit in a set of binary digits in the operation part of an instruction word, used for designating a particular type of operation. For example, in the Litton Data Assessor computer, stencil bits allow full-word, half-word, or shifted half-word transfer. In this computer, it also is possible to transfer a word logically multiplied by a stencil word.

bit, stop—In a start-stop communication system, a binary character that terminates each n-bit character for control purposes; for example a signal sent to, or received by, a mechanism designed to receive data, indicating that it should remain in a state of readiness to receive the next signal. (Synonymous with *stop element* and with *stop signal*. Contrast with *bit, start*.)

bit, zone—One of the bits in a set of bits used to designate some specific grouping of characters, instructions, and delimiters in a binary representation system. For example, in a digital computer in which six bits are used for alphanumeric characters and the four rightmost are used for decimal digits, the two leftmost are the zone bits. Thus, in this case, all the decimal digits will have two zeros as zone bits. If either or both of the zone bits is a one, then the character being represented is not a decimal digit, but is perhaps an alphabetic character. (Further clarified by *zone, minus* and *zone, plus*.)

bit density—See *density, bit*.

bit interleave—See *interleave, bit*.

bit pattern—See *pattern, bit*.

bit position—See *position, bit*.

bit rate—See *rate, bit*.

bits, information—In data transmission, bits generated by the data source that are not used for error control or checking purposes.

Bizmac—(Business Machine Computer). A computer name coined to designate computing and data-processing machines manufactured by Radio Corporation of America. The term is falling into disuse in favor of RCA as a designator for machines manufactured by that corporation.

BKS—An automatic control system developed by Philco Corporation for use on the Philco 2000 computer.

black box—See *box, black*.

black out—A vacuum-tube phenomenon in which a dielectric film is formed on the control grid of the tube, causing objectional effects at high frequencies and thus reducing the frequency at which the tube may operate. The dielectric film increases the time constant of the grid-voltage decay. Thus, a negative bias voltage, with respect to cathode, is built up on the grid. As the dielectric film builds up, the electrons remain permanently during a signal cycle, causing the tube to tend toward cutoff, that is, to black out or fail.

BLADES—(Bell Laboratories Automatic Design System). A program developed by Bell Telephone Laboratories for automating the design process.

blank —A part, area, or section of a data medium in which data is not entered or recorded.

blank character—See character, blank.

blank instruction—Same as instruction, dummy.

blank paper tape coil—See coil, blank paper tape.

bleed, ink—The flow of ink beyond the original or intended edges of a printed character. Ink bleed is due primarily to the capillary action of the fibers of the paper and the spaces between them. (Contrast with smudge, ink.)

BLESSED—(Bell Little Electrodata Symbolic System for the Electrodata.) A symbolic assembly program developed by Michigan Bell Telephone Company and Arthur D. Little, Inc., for use on the Burroughs 220 computer.

blind—To render a device nonreceptive to unwanted data.

blip—A document mark in micrographics; for example, a mark that may be made on a cathode ray tube.

BLIS—(Bell Laboratories Interpretive System). An interpretive routine, or program, developed by Bell Telephone Laboratories.

block—In information processing, a group of information units handled as a single unit; for example, a string of words transferred as a single group; a group of words or messages stored on a single track or channel of a magnetic drum; or a series of 120 characters on a length of magnetic tape, separated by block markers. In many bulk storage units, such as magnetic drums, discs and tapes, only entire blocks of words can be addressed and so transferred to and from the unit. The block length may be fixed or variable, depending upon the particular equipment. Usually the words in the block are handled serially; hence, they are transferred, extracted, operated upon, or stored consecutively. The section of storage that stores a block also may be called a block. The blocks are marked or addressed for convenient access. Thus, there may be blocks of information, blocks of storage, even blocks of logic and blocks of equipment, shown in a logic block diagram or an electrical equipment block diagram. Each block of a logic or equipment block diagram indicates equipment grouped together to perform a specific function; for example, a block each for input,

output, storage units, control units, and arithmetic and logic units. A programming flow chart is, in a sense, a block diagram showing an assembly of blocks or boxes with each block showing a logical unit of computer programming.

block, control—An area of computer storage used to store data required for controlling the operating system of a computer.

block, input—1: A section of the internal storage of a computer reserved for receiving and storing the input information and instructions read in by the input device. 2: The block of data being read-in or transferred into a computer. (Further clarified by buffer (1). Illustrated by buffer, input.)

block, message—A group of characters transmitted as a unit to or from a terminal in a communications environment. The block may vary in length.

block, output—1: A section of the internal storage of a computer, reserved for storing the output information that is to be transferred out through the output devices. 2: The block of information being transferred out of a computer. (Further clarified by buffer (1). Illustrated by buffer, output.)

block, program—In problem-oriented languages, a subdivision of a computer program that contains a set of instructions for performing or accomplishing a specific purpose, such as group related statements, delimit routings, specify storage allocation, delineate the applicability of labels, or segment parts of the program for other specific purposes.

block, standby—A block of data stored in internal storage of a computer so as to be ready and waiting for processing by the central processing unit or for transfer to an output device. The storage of these extra, reserve, or spare blocks avoids waiting by the central computer and makes more efficient use of buffers so as to reduce the queuing problem on data flow into and out of the processing unit. (Further clarified by buffer.)

block, storage—A part or section of computer storage, usually smaller than a storage area. A storage block may hold one block of data; for example, a fixed number of words in a given computer system.

block, table—A specific part or subdivision of a table of data. Table blocks are usually labeled for identity and access.

block cancel character—See character, block cancel.

block character, end-of-transmission—See character, end-of-transmission-block.

block diagram—See diagram, block.

block gap—Same as gap, interblock.

block length—See length, block.

block sort—See sort, block.

block structure—See structure, block.

block transfer—See *transfer, block.*

blockette—A relatively small block of information or a part or subdivision of a block. Usually the blockette is in the form of a subgroup or subdivision of a group of consecutive machine words and is transferred or stored as a unit, particularly with reference to input and output. For example, in a Univac system, the blockette is a fixed unit of data, with 120 characters of information stored on metallic or Mylar magnetic tape, six of which are equivalent to one Univac block.

blocking—Assigning or combining two or more data units, such as words, records, or messages, into a single block.

blowback—In micrographics and in display systems, an image enlargement, ususally on a screen or a CRT.

blue-ribbon program—Same as *program, star.*

blunder—Same as *mistake.*

BMEWS—Ballistic Missile Early Warning System.

BNF—Backus normal form.

board, bread—See *breadboard.*

board, key—See *keyboard.*

board, pin—See *pinboard.*

board, plotting—The surface portion of a plotter; that is, a device, considered as an output unit with reference to computing machines, which plots curves or displays symbols presenting a graphical representation of analog or digital data, usually for human use. (Synonymous with *plotting table* and with *output table.* Further clarified by *plotter.*)

board, plug—See *plugboard.*

board, problem—Same as *plugboard.*

board, wiring—Same as *plugboard.*

bobbin core—See *core, bobbin.*

body—The largest or main portion of a connector to which other parts are attached.

body, loop—1: The main part of a loop, usually that part that accomplishes the primary purpose of the loop. 2: In a counter, a part of the program loop control.

Boeing compiler—See *compiler, Boeing.*

boldface—A form of lettering in which thicker lines are used so as to produce more black area relative to white area than when printing letters in standard type. Boldface lettering permits the letters to stand out for stress, emphasis, or easy lookup; for instance the entry words in a dictionary.

booboo—Same as *mistake.*

book, run—Same as *file, problem.*

bookkeeping operation—Same as *operation, red-tape.*

Boolean—Pertaining to logic or algebraic operations on two-valued variables and the functions constructed from two-valued variables. The two-valued variables represent dual systems: truth and falsity, coexistence and noncoexistence, go and no-go, zero and one, and yes and no. Boolean algebra, propositional calculus, and set algebra or algebra of classes are all essentially equivalent mathematical systems that find application in switching theory and computer design. The simple Boolean functions are implemented by means of gates, of which the simplest are AND, OR, NAND, NOR, and negation. (Further clarified by *gate, AND* and by *gate, OR.*)

Boolean add—Same as *OR.*

Boolean add operation—Same as *operation disjunction.*

Boolean algebra—See *algebra, Boolean.*

Boolean calculus—See *calculus, Boolean.*

Boolean complementation—Same as *NOT.*

Boolean function—See *function, Boolean*

Boolean operation—See *operation, Boolean.*

Boolean operation, dyadic—See *operation, dyadic Boolean.*

Boolean operation, monadic—See *operation, monadic Boolean.*

Boolean operation, n-adic—See *operation, n-adic Boolean.*

Boolean operation table—See *table, Boolean operation.*

Boolean operator—See *operator, Boolean.*

Boolean variable—See *variable, Boolean.*

boot—A form placed around the wire termination of a multiple-contact connector to contain the liquid-soft potting compound before it hardens. Sometimes, a protective housing, usually made from a resilient material, to prevent the entry of moisture into a connector.

bootstrap—1: A procedure for initiating the reading of a program by a computer, consisting of a technique or device that is designed to produce a desired state by means of its own action. For example, a machine routine whose first few instructions are sufficient to bring the rest of itself into the machine, the use of a special key or set of keys, or the execution of the first few instructions manually from the console. Usually the first few instructions cause the next few to be read in, which cause the next few to be read in, until the entire program is read, assembled in storage, or executed. The bootstrap may be on the first few cards or at the beginning of a tape, and the only bootstrap instruction may be to read the first card or to start reading tape, after which the programmed instructions are used to call in the rest. Thus, the bootstrap is usually in the form of a loading routine. When pertaining to circuits, a positive feedback or regenerative circuit is a bootstrap whose output is fed back in phase to the input terminal, which tends to raise itself up to higher-gain levels of output. Care must be taken to avoid instability of such circuits. 2: An existing or primitive version of a computer program that is used to establish another version of the program.

bootstrap loader—See *loader, bootstrap.*

border-punched card—Same as *card, edge-punched.*

bore–The diameter of a hole; for example, the internal or inside diameter of the hole in a magnetic core, the diameter of the hole or hub on a magnetic tape reel, or the diameter of the holes in a drilled-hole, optically sensed card, punched cards, or paper tape.

borrow–A signal, expression, or number that arises in direct subtraction when the difference between two digits is negative. Thus, it is a negative form of carry. The borrowing takes place when it becomes necessary to raise a lower order digit, and thereby compensating by lowering a higher order digit. For example, in subtracting 67 from 92, a tens digit is borrowed from the nine. Thus, the seven of 67 is subtracted from 12, yielding five as the units digit of the difference. Then six is subtracted from eight, since one was borrowed, yielding two as the tens digit. (Compare with *borrow, end-around* and with *carry*.)

borrow, end-around–The action of transferring a borrow digit from the most significant digit position to the least significant digit position. (Compare with *borrow* and with *carry*. Contrast with *carry, end-around*.)

borrow digit–See *digit, borrow*.

BOSS –(Boeing Operational Supervisory System). A supervisory program developed by Boeing Aircraft Company for use on the IBM 704 computer.

both-way list–Same as *list, bi-directional*.

both-way operation–Same as *operation, full-duplex*.

bound, tape–Same as *limited, tape*.

boundary, character–In character recognition, the largest rectangle with a side parallel to the reference edge of the document and each of whose sides is tangential to the printed outline of a given character.

boustrophedon–In the layout of microforms, the placing of successive frames in rows alternately from left to right and from right to left. This reduces the amount of backtracking to locate successive frames at the end of a row. This requires a knowledge of which direction the next frame is in.

box–A logical unit of computer programming, treated as a unit, shown surrounded by a rectangle on a flow chart, and often identified by requiring transfer of the instructions referred there into and out of the program storage, usually high-speed storage.

box, B–Same as *register, index*.

box, black–A device, processor, or operator that performs a specific function, process, or action or that produces a special effect or output from known inputs, but whose detailed operation or internal behavior is not specified; that is, the internal behavior is not pertinent to the discussion at hand.

box, connection–An electrical distribution panel, which permits the altering of the destination of signals, usually used with punch-card machines with mechanical sensing, by changing wires to different terminals. The connection box has a purpose similar to that of a plugboard.

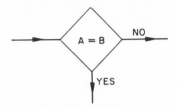

A flowchart symbol for a decision box.

box, decision–**1:** A flowchart symbol used to indicate a choice, a branching, or a decision in the information processing path or sequence of programming. Usually, the box is diamond-shaped and one connector or flowline enters the box and two connectors leave the box. The selection or decision criterion is written inside the box. **2:** In computer simulation flowcharts, a symbol indicating an event, the event being that a decision must be made according to the network logic, applicable rules, and computational results available at the place and time of decision.

box, loop–A register specifically used, as an index register, only to modify instructions just prior to their being executed. A number stored in the loop box is added to an instruction just before the instruction is executed, thus modifying it without changing the instruction as contained in storage.

box, stunt–A terminal device used to determine and control the nonprinting functions, such as carriage return, skip line, space, and stop, of a teletype machine.

branch–**1:** A set of instructions in a routine that lie between two successive decision instructions. **2:** To select such a set of instructions. **3:** Same as *jump*. **4:** To select one of a number of sets of instructions in the execution of a computer program.

branch, conditional–Same as *jump, conditional*.

branch, unconditional–Same as *jump, unconditional*.

branch exchange, automatic private–See *exchange, automatic private branch*.

branch exchange, private–See *exchange, private branch*.

branch instruction–See *instruction, branch*.

branchpoint–A point in a program where one of two or more choices is selected under the control of the program; a decision must be made at the branchpoint in accordance with the stated criterion and the information at hand. Examples include decisions such as whether to execute subroutine A or subroutine B; whether to read in another card or to perform a calculation; or whether to stop or do another iteration, according to a count in a control counter.

breadboard–A roughly constructed experimental circuit used to test the design parameters, make specific alterations in circuit design, and test for operational behavior prior to the construction of an engineering model, which is used for making final changes based on an exact model of the final circuit to be manufactured in quantity or for operational use.

break–In communication circuits, to interrupt a communication channel for the purpose of taking control of the channel. Usually the receiving user does the breaking on the sending user for some specific purpose. Primary usage occurs in connection with half-duplex telegraph circuits and two-way wire and radiotelephone circuits equipped with voice-operated interrupt devices. The break may be scheduled, as in radio broadcast station breaks.

breakage resistance–See resistance, breakage.

breakpoint–A place in a computer program specified by an instruction, an instruction digit, or other condition, where the program or routine may be interrupted by external intervention or by a monitor routine. The breakpoint may be used to permit a visual check, printout, or analysis by stopping or jumping, or performing an event other than continuing the main program. A special instruction inserted at the breakpoint causes the computer to interrupt its main program. The place in a computer program at which the breakpoint occurs can be a complete halt in the execution of instructions for accomplishing some specific action such as hardware or software debugging, jump, or transfer operation. Usually, a breakpoint is placed in a routine, program, or subroutine in order to permit some kind of human intervention. The breakpoint is useful in debugging. (Further clarified by interrupt.)

breakpoint halt–Same as instruction, breakpoint.

breakpoint instruction–See instruction, breakpoint.

breakpoint instruction, conditional–See instruction, conditional breakpoint.

breakpoint switch–See switch, breakpoint.

breakpoint symbol–See symbol, breakpoint.

bridge duplex system–See system, bridge duplex.

brush-compare check–See check, brush-compare.

brush station–See station, brush.

Brussels classification system–Same as classification, universal decimal.

BS–The backspace character.

BSI–(British Standards Institution). A British organization similar in purpose to the USA Standards Institute and pub-

lishers of the British Standard 3527 : 1962, UDC 001.4 : 681.3 : 621.37/.39, a glossary of terms used in automatic data processing.

BSR–An abbreviation for blip-scan ratio, pertinent in radar display systems.

bubble sort–See sort, bubble.

bucket–A place or unit of storage; for example, a section of storage or storage area, the storage location of a word, a storage cell, a part of a word, or a part of a cell. Thus, any place where a piece of data or item may be put. (Illustrated by double-bucket.)

bucket, double–See double-bucket.

buffer–1: A storage device used to compensate for the difference between the rate of data flow from a transmitting device and the rate of data flow that a receiving device can receive; or a device used to store data for the purpose of improving the efficiency of transfer of information between two devices. Thus, the buffer serves the same purpose in a data flowline as an air bell or storage tank in a hydraulic or gas flowline; namely, it smooths out the flow and satifies peak or sudden demands as they occur without requiring excessive channel capacity. The buffer may also receive information in the format of the transmitting medium and transmit the information in the format of the receiving medium. Through the use of buffers, the high-speed storage never needs to become involved with the slow and cumbersome external devices, but needs only to communicate with the buffers associated with each piece of external equipment; thus the high-speed storage is free to operate at electronic speeds and can devote itself to calculations and data processing. (Synonymous with synchronizer (1). Further clarified by block, standby.) 2: An isolating circuit used to avoid any action of a driving circuit from affecting another driving circuit whenever two or more driving circuits are driving a common load; or a circuit used to avoid any reaction of a driven circuit upon a corresponding driving circuit. The first instance is the same situation as occurs in an OR gate; the second instance is the same situation as occurs in the use of a single diode, which permits current to flow in only one direction, thus allowing the desired isolation. A buffer amplifier also may be used to prevent one or more circuits from loading the driving circuit. 3: To allocate and schedule the use of buffers. 4: To perform the function or operate the devices described in (1) and (2), e.g. to store data temporarily so as to smooth the flow of data in a channel or store data temporarily from a slow input channel for rapid input to a computer.

buffer, chained-segment–A buffer composed of a chain of fragmented areas of main storage with each area containing a pointer to the next area in the chain. The chained-segment buffer is normally used to process records of varying lengths, such as personnel files and teleprocessing messages.

buffer, data—Same as *buffer (1)*.

buffer, input—A buffer used to receive and store data being transmitted into a computer. Data includes instructions. (Illustrated by *block, input.*)

buffer, output—A buffer used to receive and store data being transmitted out of a computer. Data includes instructions. (Illustrated by *block, output.*)

buffer, storage—A section of the internal storage of a computer reserved for receiving or storing either input or output data or instructions, or both. (Illustrated by *block, input* and by *block, output.* Further clarified by *storage, buffer.*)

buffer amplifier—See *amplifier, buffer.*

buffer drum—See *drum, buffer.*

buffer gate—Same as *gate, OR.*

buffer pool—See *pool, buffer.*

buffer storage—See *storage, buffer.*

buffered computer—See *computer, buffered.*

buffering—In a computer operating system, the managing of buffers, particularly input-output buffers. Buffering techniques include simple buffering, exchange buffering, locate-mode buffering, and move-mode buffering.

buffering, anticipatory—A method of buffering in which the next set of data is buffered before it is needed.

buffering, dynamic — A method of operating a buffer in such a manner that the buffer is provided to a program in response to a demand by the program when the program is in need of buffering. The buffer is released to other use when no longer needed by that program.

buffering, exchange—A method of buffering that eliminates the need to move data in main storage by exchanging a system buffer area for a user buffer area. (Contrast with *buffering, simple.*)

buffering, locate-mode—A method of buffering in which data is pointed to, relabelled, or a new virtual location indicated, rather than moved. (Contrast with *buffering, move-mode.*)

buffering, move-mode—A method of buffering in which data is actually moved between the buffer and a computer user's work area in storage. (Contrast with *buffering, locate-mode.*)

buffering, simple—A method of buffering in which buffers are permanently assigned to a program until execution of the program is completed. (Contrast with *buffering, exchange.*)

bug—A mechanical, electrical, electronic, or logical defect in a piece of equipment or in its operation, or a defect or error in a coded program; thus, a malfunction or a mistake. Diagnostic programs and test routines are used to locate bugs, and programmed and built-in checks are used to locate programming and coding mistakes. Checking devices, such as dual units, parity checkers, transfer checkers, and forbidden or illegal combination detectors, are used to reveal equipment bugs.

BUIC—(Back-Up Interceptor Control). A modular computing system developed by Burroughs Corporation for the D825 military systems and used as surveillance and warning systems for continental air defense.

built-in check—Same as *check, automatic.*

bulk storage—Same as *storage, mass.*

burn-in—Pertaining to the operation of a device for the purpose of stabilizing failure rates of components, since many circuit elements, particularly vacuum tubes, have a higher failure rate during the first few hours of operation than later on. For example, before being inserted into operational circuits, vacuum tubes are heated and nominal plate and grid voltages are applied so as to induce early failures. After the preburning period, they are tested against specifications and inserted in active circuits, which results in an improvement in the mean time between failures (MTBF). (Synonymous with *preburning.*)

burst—**1:** To separate the sheets of a continuous form along its perforations; thus, also to detail or spread the summarized data; for example, to explode an assembly drawing by showing the individual parts in the order in which they are disassembled or assembled. **2:** In data transmission, a set of characters grouped in accordance with specified and specific criteria.

burst, error—In data transmission, the group of bits in which two successive erroneous bits are always separated by less than a specified number of correct bits. The last erroneous bit in a burst and the first erroneous bit in the successive burst are separated by the specified number of correct bits. The number must be specified in order to permit a counting of the error bursts.

bus—One or more conductors used for transmitting signals or power from one or more sources to one or more destinations. Usually a multiplicity of connections are made to the common bus for the mutual use of many circuits. Thus a bus may run between registers, between computers, from power sources to power sinks, serve as common ground, distribute clock pulses, a-c filament voltages, or synchronizing signals. A single wire or lead serving one source and one load is not usually considered a bus, whereas several generators operating in parallel are all joined to and by the same bus. (Synonymous with *trunk (2)*, with *common lead*, and with *highway.*)

bus, check—A group of parallel lines used for transmitting data to a checking device, such as a check register, a dual unit, a comparator, or a parity checker. (Synonymous with *check trunk*.)

bus, digit transfer—A set of wires used to transfer numbers, in the form of electrical pulses, that represent data and instructions, among the various registers and counters of a computing system. On-off and similar control-signal, transfer lines are not considered as digit transfer buses. (Synonymous with *digit transfer trunk*.)

bus, high-speed—Same as *register, storage*.

bus driver—See *driver, bus*.

bushing, floating—A design feature that aids in the alignment of plug and receptacle shells during insertion of the plug into the receptacle. The floating bushing usually is an eyelet-type bushing, which is fitted into the plug mounting holes so that there is freedom of motion in all directions between the plug and the receptacle.

business data processing—See *data processing, business*.

butt—Pertaining to the joining of two conductors end-to-end, without overlapping, and with their axes in line. Such a joint requires special welding or some method of forming a strong mechanical bond, otherwise the joint is mechanically weak. Most joints are not butted but are lapped or twisted.

button, activate—Same as *button, initiate*.

button, initiate—A switch, usually on the control panel, used to cause the first step of a sequence of programmed steps to be executed or to start the cycling or movement of actions. (Synonymous with *start button*, with *start key*, with *initiate key*, with *activate button*, and with *activate key*.)

button, intervention—Same as *button, panic*.

button, panic—A button designed to prevent destruction or further destruction of a device in the event of a sudden emergency, usually of an unknown kind and for which the operator is not fully aware of the proper corrective action. (Synonymous with *emergency switch*, with *intervention switch*, and with *intervention button*.)

button, start—Same as *button, initiate*.

byte—1: A small group of adjacent binary digits, such as 4, 6, or 8 bits, that form a sub-unit of information and that are usually operated upon as a unit; for example, a six-bit byte may be used to specify a letter of the alphabet; a four-bit byte, or tetrad, may be used to specify a decimal digit and is usually handled as a unit in the arithmetic unit during arithmetic operations; an eight-bit byte may be used to specify an instruction or indicate an address; or an arithmetic unit may handle carry propagation in four-bit bytes at a time. 2: A binary element string usually operated upon as a unit. The byte is normally shorter than a computer word and is often used to represent a character, such as a letter, a digit, or a special sign or symbol.

byte, eight-bit—Same as *octet*.

byte, five-bit—Same as *quintet*.

byte, four-bit—Same as *quartet*.

byte, n-bit—A byte that has exactly n bits, that is, binary digits or elements; for example 1101 would be a four-bit byte.

byte, seven-bit—Same as *septet*.

byte, six-bit—Same as *sextet*.

byte, three-bit—Same as *triplet*.

byte, two-bit—Same as *doublet*.

B15—An automatic coding system developed by Texas Instruments, Inc., for use on the IBM 650 computer.

C

cable—One or more electrical conductors usually within a sheath for electrical isolation and mechanical and chemical protection and constructed so as to permit use of the conductors separately or in groups. The conductors may be solid, hollow, segmented, twisted, or a combination of these.

cable, coaxial—A cable used as an unbalanced transmission line and consisting of one conductor placed concentrically within and insulated from an outer conductor of larger diameter. The inner conductor is usually a small copper tube or wire. The outer conductor is usually copper tubing or braiding and may or may not be grounded. Radiation from this type of line is nearly zero at high frequencies. Several coaxial cables may be combined into a single bundle and installed as a unit.

cable, combination—A cable having conductors placed or bundled in groups of twos or fours, called pairs or quads. Thus, in cables having hundreds of conductors, the pairs or quads are more easily identifiable from one end or terminal to another.

cable, composite—A cable consisting of two or more conductors of two or more different gauges and types, all combined under one sheath.

cable, flat—Same as *cable, tape.*

cable, paired—A cable in which the individually insulated conductors are twisted together two at a time for easy selection, identification, and use.

cable, quaded—A cable in which some or all of the conductors are arranged in groups of four.

cable, tape—A cable consisting of flat conductors, that is, metallic ribbons, all lying in the same plane, side by side, and imbedded in insulating material, which insulates as well as binds. (Synonymous with *flat cable.*)

CAGE—(Compiler and Assembler by General Electric). A compiler developed by General Electric Company for use on the IBM 704 computer.

calculated address—Same as *address, synthetic.*

calculating operation, average—See *operation, average calculating.*

calculating operation, representative—Same as *operation, average calculating.*

calculating punch—See *punch, calculating.*

calculation—The determination of a result by addition, subtraction, multiplication, and division. These arithmetic operations may be considered fundamental to all other calculations, such as evaluating logarithms and extracting square roots. However, even multiplication is but shifting and adding and division is but shifting and subtracting, which is performed by complementing and adding. Thus addition is perhaps the only basic arithmetic operation, and so calculation is simply the manipulation of numerals along with addition. A high-speed adder is the primary and basic unit in all digital computer arithmetic and logic units.

calculation, fixed-point—A calculation involving numbers in which the arithmetic point, such as the binary point or the decimal point, is always assumed to be or is held in a specific relative position in each number, such as at the left end, in which case all numbers have an absolute value of less than unity. All values or numbers must be scaled in a given system so as to maintain proper significance of all digits in all calculations, maintaining a record of all scaling. (Contrast with *calculation, floating-point.*)

calculation, floating-point—A calculation involving numbers whose arithmetic point, such as decimal point or binary point, is movable; that is, in different locations in each number. The location is specified by citing a power of the base. The base, raised to this power serves as a multiplier, or a coefficient, of a fixed-point number, the product serving to represent the floating-point number. Thus, an operand in a floating-point calculation may be written as 49.6×10^{-3}, which locates the decimal point as in 0.0496. Floating-point calculations involve less of a scaling problem, since the possible number ranges are larger; however, the scaling problem is not entirely eliminated, as operand values must still be scaled between the largest negative value and the largest positive value that can be expressed by the floating-point number. (Contrast with *calculation, fixed-point.*)

	NORMAL NOTATION	MACHINE REPRESENTATION
MULTIPLICAND	423×10^6	$423 + 06$
MULTIPLIER	211×10^3	$211 + 03$
PRODUCT	892×10^{11}	$892 + 11$

Floating-point calculation *using machine notation. (The exponent signs can be eliminated with appropriate biasing of the exponent.)*

calculator—A device that performs arithmetic and some limited logic operations and displays the results, but that usually cannot itself alter its own program; thus, a calculator is a computer capable of interpreting and executing a small number of different instructions. Usually, a calculator operates with data and instructions that are entered manually, as opposed to a stored-program computer, although data may be entered by cards as in a card-programmed calculator or by other means. Many calculators are controlled by a plugboard.

calculator, network—Same as *analyzer, network.*

calculus, Boolean—An extension of Boolean algebra that includes other variables, such as time, changes of state, delay, step functions, additional operations of before, during, and after, and combinations of these. Therefore, where the Boolean algebra is implemented in hardware by combinational logic elements, the Boolean calculus is implemented with sequential logic elements also, and circuit elements are considered or used whose type and nature change with time. (Further clarified by *algebra, Boolean.*)

calculus of variations—See *variations, calculus of.*

calendar—In computer simulation, a timing base created by an algorithm. The calendar is used to schedule events during a simulation, is usually in the form of a civil calendar; and permits the timing of events precisely. The creating algorithm is usually a computer program.

CALINT—An interpretive programming system developed by Control Data

Corporation for the Control Data 160 computer.

call—1: In data processing, to transfer control of a computer to a specified closed subroutine from some point in a program. Usually the purpose of calling is to insert a sequence of operations to fulfill a subsidiary purpose. The routine that is called in may be a member of a set of specific subroutines available for special purposes. Sometimes the calling action is represented by a set of characters that spell out the action that is to take place with regard to the data involved, such as to call a subroutine, an operand, or a descriptor. (Synonymous with *call-in*. Further clarified by *word, call* and by *number, call*.) 2: In communications, the action performed by the person who places a call, the operations necessary in making a call, or the effective use made of a connection between two stations, such as a telephone call, an overseas call, a long-distance call, or a conference call.

call, subroutine—A set or list of characters that initiates a subroutine and contains the parameters or serves to identify and locate the parameters that are required for the execution of the subroutine.

call, supervisor—In a computer operating system, a request for a service to be performed by the supervisor or executive. The request may be initiated by a job, task, subtask, job step, program, routine, or subroutine.

call-in—Same as *call (1)*.

call number—See *number, call*.

call word—See *word, call*.

called station—See *station, called*.

calling, selective—Pertaining to the ability of a transmitting station to specify which of several stations are to receive a message.

calling sequence—See *sequence, calling*.

calling station—See *station, calling*.

CAM—(Content Addressed Memory). Same as *storage, associative*.

camfer—The angle on the inside edge of the barrel entrance of an electrical connector to permit easier insertion of the cable into the barrel.

CAMP—(Computer Applications of Military Problems). A computer user group with a common interest in military problems.

CAN—The cancel character.

cancel character—See *character, cancel*.

cancel character, block—See *character, block cancel*.

CAOS—(Completely Automatic Operational System). A computer programming system developed by Lockheed Aircraft Corporation for use on the Univac 1103A computer.

capacitance—The property of two or more bodies to store energy in an electrostatic field between the bodies; a measure of the ability to store electric charge. The basic unit of capacitance of an electric capacitor is the farad. The property to store charge is useful and deliberate in some applications, as in the tank or oscillating circuit of an oscillator, and detrimental and undesirable in other situations, such as inducing undesirable cross-talk among circuits or preventing operation at high frequencies. Capacitance is often used to couple one circuit to another, in order to transfer data from one circuit to another.

capacitance-coupled flip-flop—Same as *flip-flop, a-c coupled*.

capacitive coupling—See *coupling, capacitive*.

capacitor storage—See *storage, capacitor*.

capacity—In electric circuits, the same as capacitance; that is, the ability of a device to hold an electric charge with a given voltage or potential difference across its terminals. Thus, capacity, whose basic unit is the farad, is the charge to voltage ratio: $c = q/v$, where q is measured in coulombs and v in volts.

capacity, channel—1: The limiting rate at which data can be communicated over a single channel. The frequency of errors must tend toward zero. Channel capacity is usually expressed as data units per unit of time, such as bits per second, characters per second, or words per minute. The channel capacity depends upon its physical and electrical properties, such as noise level, bandwidths, signal power, and physical configuration. 2: A measure of the ability of a channel to transmit data from a data source to a data sink. The channel capacity may be expressed as either the maximum possible mean transinformation content per character or as the maximum average transinformation rate.

capacity, computer—Same as *range, number*.

capacity, exceed—To generate a word or number whose length or magnitude is too great or too small to be represented by the computer, such as might be obtained by dividing by zero. If the computer exceeds capacity, operation is usually interrupted, since erroneous results may be obtained.

capacity, memory—Same as *capacity, storage*.

capacity, register—Same as *length, register*.

capacity, storage—The quantity of data a device can hold; for example, the number of digits, words, or bits a storage unit or a register can hold, and so, the number of binary cells or their equivalent. Accumulators, certain buffers, and special registers are not normally included as part of storage and therefore not counted as part of storage capacity. The storage capacity may be expressed in any of several data units, such as bits, decimal digits, alphanumeric characters, 40-decimal-digit words, or 120-word blocks. The storage capacity in bits is the number obtained by taking the logarithm to the base two of the number of distinguishable states in which the storage can exist. (Synonymous with *memory capacity*.)

capacity, word—Same as *length, word*.

capstan amplifier—See *amplifier, capstan*.

carbon, spot—Carbon paper that has been carbonized only in selected areas so that certain entries made on the original will not be reproduced on the copy.

carbon cleanliness—See *cleanliness, carbon.*

carbon stability—See *stability, carbon.*

card—A piece of relatively thin material of specific geometrical dimensions designed to meet a specific purpose, such as store data in the form of a pattern of holes, serve as a base or substrate for holding a magnetizable material for the storage of binary data, or provide a base for mounting electrical components; for example, punched cards, magnetic ledger cards, or printed-circuit cards.

card, aperture—A card, usually of the size and shape of a normal 80-column punch card, with a rectangular opening or hole large enough to permit a microfilm frame, or frames, to be mounted.

card, aspect—A card on which is entered the identity or accession numbers of documents that have a relationship to the concept or data element for which the card was established. Each aspect is an item in a coordinate indexing system. The accession number may be written on the card, drilled as a hole at a coordinate location, punched as holes on standard 80-column cards, or edge-punched on an edge-punched card. The aspect in such a data-retrieval system might be a uniterm, descriptor, data element, docuterm, or any data code. Thus, assuming a peek-a-boo system is used for the aspect cards, if the aspect is captain for one card and German language ability for another card, then by superimposing the two cards all German-speaking captains will be identified.

card, binary—A card containing data in binary form, such as column binary or row binary.

card, binder-hole—A card that has one or more holes intended or used for binding.

card, border-punched—Same as *card, edge-punched.*

card, check—A punched card that is used for a bank check, containing such data as the names of the maker, the payee, and the bank on which it is drawn; the dollar amount, the number of the check, and the data.

card, column-binary—A punched card that contains data in a column-binary format; that is, binary numbers have their digits represented as punched holes, serially, in each column, usually expressed as vertical or transverse to the direction of the long axis of a standard 80-column card. Thus, one 12-bit word would fit in each column. If the card is read end-wise, each bit in a given word is read simultaneously in parallel fashion. (Contrast with *card, row binary.* Further clarified by *binary, column.*)

card, control—A card that contains input data, parameters, or special instructions for a specific application of a general routine. The data on the control card usually represents information for executing a computer program other than the actual input data or the actual program to be run.

card, double—A card that is about twice the length of a general purpose paper card, usually consisting of two separable general purpose paper cards.

card, ducol-punched—A punched card that has 12 rows of punching positions in each column; namely, zero through nine, and X and Y, in which one of the numerals zero to 99 may be represented by multiple punching in each column. The digit order or digit duplication is indicated by punching or not punching the X or Y position. For example, if there are two numeric punchings in a column, the lower-value digit position is treated as the tens digit and the higher value digit position as the units digit. If the Y position is also punched, the significance of the two numeric punchings is reversed. If the digits are the same, as in 33 or 11, the X position is punched in addition to the numeric punch.

card, edge-coated—A card that has been strengthened along one or more edges by application of a coating, an impregnation, or stronger material.

card, edge-notched—A card in which notches, generally V-shaped, are cut or punched around the edges to represent binary data. A blank card usually has a single row of holes near all four edges; data is enterered by notching the card at the holes. Edge-notched cards are commonly associated with manual data-retrieval or processing systems. The cards are selected and sorted by passing long needles through the holes of the stacked cards; the stack is vibrated, and those cards having holes through which the needles pass are retained, while those having notches will drop down.

card, edge-perforated—Same as *card, edge-punched.*

card, edge-punched—A card in which one or more rows of holes are punched along the edges to represent binary data. A blank card is perforated around all its edges; data is inserted by punching or by not punching away the hole. The cards are selected and sorted by passing long needles through the holes of the stacked cards; the stack is vibrated, and those cards having holes through which the needles pass are retained, while those having punches or notches will drop down. Another type of edge-punched card has several rows of holes along one or more edges; the card is read by machine in much the same way a paper tape is read. The center of the card is often used for written or printed information. (Synonymous with *margin-punched card*, with *verge-perforated card,* with *verge-punched card,* with *margin-perforated card,* and with *edge-perforated card.*)

card, 80-column–A card, punched or to be punched, that has 80 vertical columns with 12 punch positions in each column. The card is divided into two sections: the top, labeled with zone punch positions 11 and 12, also called X and Y; and the bottom, labeled with punch positions zero through nine. Since each column can be used to represent a character, 80 characters can be represented on each card. If column binary is used, each column can represent a binary number ranging from zero to decimal 4095. In many cases, the 11 and 12 punch positions, or the X and Y zones, are not so printed on the card.

card, flash–A target, in micrographics, printed with certain distinctive markings such that when it is photographed the indexing of microfilm is facilitated when the distinctive markings on the card are transferred, or photographed, onto the frames of the microfilm.

card, general-purpose paper–A paper card that meets the specifications contained in applicable standards, usually national or international standards. Printed card forms are not considered as general-purpose cards. (Contrast with *card, special-purpose paper.*)

card, header–A card that contains information concerning data in cards that follow.

card, Hollerith–A punch card that has 80 columns and 12 rows of punch positions. A card with these features has been adopted as a standard by the American National Standards Institute.

card, laced–A card in which holes are punched that are in excess of the hole patterns of the character set used. The card may be laced accidentally or intentionally. Often, a card that is punched so as to materially weaken the card may also be said to be laced.

card, magnetic–A card, usually a rectangular flat surface of any material, such as plastic, fiber, laminate, aluminum, cardboard, or paper, coated with a magnetic substance, such as iron oxide or ferrite, on which data is recorded that can be read by automatic devices. The cards are usually stacked in racks, selected by a mechanical device, read or recorded on, and returned to their appropriate location. A card is selected in accordance with its address, which identifies its physical location. (Further clarified by *storage, magnetic card.*)

card, margin-perforated–Same as *card, edge-punched.*

card, margin-punched–Same as *card, edge-punched.*

card, moisture-proof paper–A card made of specially-treated paper, such as plasticized paper.

card, 90-column–A card, punched or designed to be punched, that is divided in half horizontally, the upper half containing columns one through 45 and the lower half containing columns 46 through 90. Each column contains six punch positions, and as each of the six-position columns can be punched to represent one of 64 different characters or meanings, 90 characters can be represented on the card.

card, port-a-punch–A card that has prescored punch positions and that can be perforated with a hand-held stylus and manually removed from a portable punch. The card can then be read as any other punched card. The card is handy for placing data in machine-readable form at the source where sophisticated card punches may not be available or easily accessible.

card, printed-circuit–A card, usually of laminate or resinous material of an insulating type, on which an electrical circuit is mounted. The blank card is usually clad with copper; portions of the copper are etched away, leaving conducting links to electrical components. Such cards are used in digital computers to perform various functions. They are inserted into frame-mounted plugs that are wired together in the back of panels. Thus, by mounting a standard set of gates on a printed-circuit card, an entire computer's logic, set of registers, and control equipment may be constructed. (Further clarified by *circuit, printed.*)

card, processable scored–A card that contains one or more scored lines to facilitate precise manual folding or separation of parts of the card and that has at least one separable part that can be processed or read after it is separated.

card, program–A card that contains the instructions that a machine is to execute; for example, a punched card whose pattern of holes expresses the routine of operations a computer is to perform in contrast to a card that contains the data the machine is to process in accordance with the instructions.

card, punched–A card that is or is to be punched with a pattern of holes to represent information. The punched card is commonly used as an input-output medium for digital computers. The cards are made of stiff paper of uniform size and shape. The punched holes are sensed electrically by wire brushes, mechanically by metal feelers, or photoelectrically. One standard card is $7\frac{3}{8}$ in. long and $3\frac{1}{4}$ in. wide. Eighty columns and 12 rows of holes may be punched in each card, representing 960 binary digits or bits of data. Cards are handled by such devices as

53

readers, punches, sorters, collators, and converters, like card to tape, tape to card, and card to printer.

card, row-binary—A punched card containing data in binary numbers whose digits are represented as punched holes, serially, in each row, usually expressed as horizontally, that is, in the direction of the long axis of a standard 80-column card. Thus, two 40-bit words would fit in each row. (Contrast with *card, column-binary*. Further clarified by *binary, row*.)

A row-binary card *punched with two 16-bit numerals. The upper numeral is 1100111001101110 and the lower numeral is 1111001100010000.*

card, scored—A card that has one or more lines impressed, or scored, on it to facilitate precise folding or separating of parts of the card. The card will fold or tear readily along the scored lines.

card, short—A card that is shorter in length than a standard or a general-purpose paper card; for example a 51-column card.

card, source date—A card that is used for manually or mechanically recording data that is subsequently punched into the same card somewhat automatically by a card punch or a key punch.

card, special-purpose paper—A card that does not meet one or more specifications in applicable standards. The special-purpose nature of the card is usually relative to a given system, use, or application. (Contrast with *card, general-purpose paper*.)

card, stub—A special-purpose paper card consisting of a separable stub attached to a general-purpose paper card. The stub card may be scored or perforated to assist in separating the special card, or stub, from the general-purpose card, or main card, thus a stub card may be a scored card.

card, trailer—A card containing information related to the data on preceding cards.

card, transfer—Same as *card, transition*.

card, transition—In reading a deck of punched program cards by a computing machine, a card that causes a termination of the reading, or loading, and a commencement of the execution of the program. In modern computers, the

reading of new data can continue while data that has been read is processed in accordance with the program. The transition card might be used to signal to the computer that the cards that follow it contain data that are to be interpreted as ordinary data, such as numbers or names, rather than as coded instructions as has been the ·case thus far, and that since the program has been loaded, its execution may now begin. (Synonymous with *transfer card*.)

card, verge-perforated—Same as *card, edge-punched*.

card, verge-punched—Same as *card, edge-punched*.

card code—See *code, card*.

card column—See *column, card*.

card deck—See *deck, card*.

card editor—See *editor, card*.

card face—See *face, card*.

card feed—See *feed, card*.

card field—See *field, card*.

card form, printed—See *form, printed card*.

card hopper—See *hopper, card*.

card image—See *image, card*.

card input—See *input, card*.

card input magazine—Same as *hopper, card*.

card jam—See *jam, card*.

card leading edge—See *edge, card leading*.

card machine, punched—See *machine, punched-card*.

card mode—See *mode, card*.

card-programmed—The capability of being directed by instructions contained on punched cards.

card punch—See *punch, card*.

card punching—See *punching, card*.

card reader—See *reader, card*.

card reader-punch—See *reader-punch, card*.

card receiver—Same as *stacker, card*.

card row—See *row, card*.

card set—See *set, card*.

card stacker—See *stacker, card*.

card storage, magnetic—See *storage magnetic card*.

card-to-magnetic-tape converter—See *converter, card-to-magnetic-tape*.

card track—See *track, card*.

card trailing edge—See *edge, card trailing*.

card transceiver—See *transceiver, card*.

cards, continuous form—Cards that are attached together in continuous strips, usually to facilitate printing or other operations upon them. The cards can be separated into individual cards, for punching, mailing, or other purposes.

caret—A symbol in the shape of an inverted v (∧), used to indicate the exact location of an insertion, usually the insertion of characters in a line of text, but sometimes an arithmetic point in a number. The item to be inserted must be identified or associated with each caret.

carousel—A rotary device that handles film clips, film frames, small fiche, or other similar data media, making the data media available at a reading or recording station in accordance with positioning data that identifies specific locations.

carriage, automatic—The part of a typewriter or of some printers that holds and guides the paper and is automatically controlled by information stored on paper or magnetic tape. Thus, the carriage movements, such as line spacing, moving right or left, ejecting or tabulating, may be programmed with carriage or format-control symbols and placed on a loop of tape on the device. The paper that is moved about, in space, by the carriage may be separate forms or continuous sheets of one or more parts. The paper is moved by the carriage with reference to a set of print members. The carriage may be under control of a computer program so that the dispersion of data on paper is subject to computer program control. The automatic carriage controls the feeding, spacing, skipping, and ejecting of paper or preprinted forms.

carriage, tape-controlled—An automatic carriage whose movement, except for character spacing, is controlled by data recorded on paper or magnetic tape.

carriage control tape—See *tape, carriage control.*

carriage return—See *return carriage.*

carriage return character—See *character, carriage return.*

carrier—1: A periodic or steady-state signal suitable for modulation by the intelligence-bearing signal that is to be transmitted over a communication system; for example, a continuous, radio-frequency sinusoidal wave; a direct current; a continuous constant-pitch sound wave; or a continuous column of smoke generated by wet leaves. The continuous radio-frequency sinusoidal wave may be modulated by an audio-frequency wave for voice transmission; the direct-current signal may be modulated by a telegraph key; the continuous-pitch sound wave may be modulated by turning the generator on and off, such as in an alert alarm; and the smoke column may be modulated by a blanket, which produces puffs of smoke with controlled spacing and controlled size. (Further clarified by *modulation, frequency,* by *modulation, phase,* and by *modulation, amplitude.*) 2: The mode of conduction of charge in a semiconducting material. The carrier may be a mobile electron or a less mobile hole. The net current is the sum of the electron flow and the hole flow. (Further clarified by *hole* and by *semiconductor, intrinsic.*)

carrier, common—A company, usually a public utility, that is recognized by an appropriate regulatory agency as having a vested interest and responsibility in furnishing communication or transport services to the general public; for example, Western Union, American Telephone and Telegraph, the Penn-Central Railroad, the Greyhound Lines, or American Airlines. A company that leases or utilizes such facilities may also be considered a common carrier if it serves as an intermediary to the ultimate user. Usually, the operating firm is considered the common carrier. Computers may be tied together or fed over common carrier lines.

carrier, data—A medium, such as cards, tapes, paper, and discs, for recording or entering data, usually easily transportable independently of the mechanism used to sense or record the data. Thus, data carriers are used as input-output media for computers. The characters on the carriers are considered as characters themselves, rather than representations of characters. Thus, an array of holes in a card column is as much an A as the printed symbol. (Further clarified by *medium* and by *medium, input-output.*)

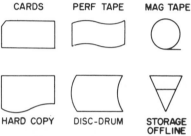

Some typical data carriers.

carrier, majority—The predominant charge carrier in a semiconductor. If the predominant method of conduction in a semiconductor is by means of holes, as in the case of p-type material, then holes are the majority carrier. If the major portion of the conduction takes place by means of electrons, then electrons are the majority carrier, as in n-type material. (Contrast with *carrier, minority.* Further clarified by *semiconductor, n-type* and by *semiconductor, p-type.*)

carrier, minority—The minor or nondominant charge carrier in a semiconductor. If the predominant method of conduction in a semiconductor is by means of holes, as in p-type material, then electrons are the minority, carrier, and holes are the majority carrier. In n-type material, holes are the minority carrier, while electrons, are the majority carrier. (Contrast with *carrier, majority.*)

carrier frequency—See *frequency, carrier.*

carrier noise level—See *level, carrier noise.*

carrier power-output rating—See *rating, carrier power-output.*

carrier reception, exalted—See *reception, exalted carrier.*

carrier shift—See *shift, carrier.*

carrier system—See *system, carrier.*

carrier transmission, suppressed—See *transmission, suppressed-carrier.*

carrier wave—See *wave, carrier.*

carry—A character or characters, such as numerals, signals, or expressions, produced in connection with an arithmetic operation, usually addition, at one digit place of two or more numerals written in positional notation and forwarded to another column for processing there. Thus, an overflow in a single digit column, following an addition operation. Usually, in regular manual arithmetic, the carry from a given column is forwarded to the next left, or more significant, column. The carry arises when the sum of two or more digits equals or exceeds the base of the number system. A carry may also be considered as borrow, the act of forwarding a carry, or the command directing that a carry be forwarded. When the carry is a signal, it is called a carry signal; when the carry is a digit, it is called a carry digit. Thus, carry might be the digit, to forward a carry digit, or to direct that the carry digit be forwarded (Compare with *borrow,* and with *borrow, end-around.*)

AUGEND	1	0	0	1	1	0	1	1
ADDEND	0	1	0	0	1	1	1	0
PARTIAL SUM	1	1	0	1	0	1	0	1
PARTIAL CARRY	0	0	0	0	1	0	1	0
PARTIAL SUM	1	1	0	0	0	0	0	1
CASCADED CARRY	0	0	0	1	0	1	0	0
FINAL SUM	1	1	1	0	1	0	0	1
	0	0	0	0	0	0	0	0

A cascaded carry.

carry, cascaded—A carry digit that results in a digit position only from the carry digit introduced by a previous digit position, when adding two numbers expressed in a positional notation system. For example, when 47 is added to 856, the addition of 4 and 5 in the second column, whose sum is 9, does not give rise to a carry, but the sum of 6 and 7 in the first column, whose sum is 13, gives rise to a carry of 1, which, when added to the 9 in the second column, makes 10, and this does give rise to a cascaded carry into the third column. Thus, the cascaded carry was due only to a carry-in from the previous position, and not from the digits in that column. The cascading can occur several times. Also, the cascaded carry is the carry signal that emerges from a circuit due only to a carry-in. Usually, the cascaded carry is considered as such only when the normal adding circuits are used to handle it, rather than special circuits set up specifically to handle this carry. When two numerals are added and a partial sum and a carry numeral are obtained, if the partial sum and the carry numeral are added and a second carry numeral is obtained along with a second partial sum, then the carries are said to be cascading. The process has to be repeated until no more carries are obtained. In serial addition, carries are propagated, since a carry generated at one digit position is added when the next two succeeding digits are added in a full-adder. In parallel addition, the carries are cascaded, causing a sequence of parallel additions of partial sums and carry numerals until the cascading ceases, that is, the carry numeral becomes zero.

carry, complete—The process of allowing the carries that result from the addition of the carry digits to propagate from place to place; for example, when the partial product is formed in one step of a multiplication process, the carry digits can be propagated or not. If they are allowed to propagate, the process is a complete-carry process; if they are not allowed to propagate, the process is called a partial-carry process. The partial-carry process involves temporarily holding the carry digits and simultaneously adding them later, rather than allowing the single carry digit to propagate from place to place. Thus, in the complete-carry process each carry is introduced into the next stage as part of the same cycle in which it is developed. (Further clarified by *carry, partial.*)

carry, end-around—A carry that is generated at the most significant digit position of a positional notation number system and is sent to the least significant digit position, in order to implement arithmetic operations (addition and subtraction) in a radix-minus-one complement arithmetic system. Many arithmetic units in digital computers accomplish subtraction by adding the nines complement (or the ones complement, in binary) of the minuend to the subtrahend and then "correcting" the sum by adding one to get the proper answer (difference); for example, 562 less 173 equals 389 by ordinary subtraction. In a six-place arithmetic register, the nines complement of 173 is 999,826. The sum of 999,826 and 562 is 1,000,388, which must be corrected by dropping the 1,000,000 and by adding one to 388 in order to produce the correct answer (difference), namely 389. We can think of "carrying" the one from the most significant digit position to the least significant position, and adding it to the least significant digit. Hence, it is called an end-around carry. The end-around carry is required when performing diminished-radix complement arithmetic. (Contrast with *borrow, end-around.*)

carry, high-speed—1: A carry digit generated in one digit position from the carry digit introduced from another digit position and not from the addition of the digits themselves, when adding two numbers expressed in a positional notation system and when the normal adding circuit is bypassed to generate the new carry. For example, when 47 is added to 856, the addition of 4 and 5 in the second column does not give rise to a carry, but the addition of 6 and 7 in the first column gives rise to a carry of one, which, when added to the sum of 9 in the second column, makes 10, and this does give rise to a cascaded carry into the third column. If the normal adding circuit is bypassed, the carry is called a high-speed carry rather than an ordinary cascaded carry. A special circuit brings the carry to the column where it is actually added. The cascaded carry can occur several times. For the decimal system, an example is the standing-on-nines carry. (Synonymous with *ripple-through carry.* Further clarified by *carry, cascaded.*) **2:** Any carry technique in parallel addition for speeding up carry propagation.

carry, partial—The process of temporarily holding the set of carries formed at all the digit positions that result from the addition of all previous carries; for example, when forming the partial product in one step of a multiplication process, the carry digits are temporarily stored, then added to previous carries, and a new set of carry digits is obtained. This is done in lieu of allowing all carries in each addition step to propagate through all stages or places. The set of carry digits temporarily stored may be called the partial carry. Thus, the partial carry is not introduced into the arithmetic process in the cycle during which it is developed. (Further clarified by *carry, complete.*)

carry, ripple-through—Same as *carry, high-speed.*

carry, standing-on-nines—In parallel addition of decimal numbers, a high-speed carry in which carry input to a given digit place is bypassed to the next digit place if the current sum digit in the given place is nine.

carry-complete signal—See *signal, carry-complete.*

carry time—See *time, carry.*

CART—(Computerized Automatic Rating Technique). A freight rate, route selector, and shipment monitor program developed by Honeywell Electronic Data Processing Division for use by common carriers.

cartridge—A small unit of a storage medium capable of being easily removed and inserted; for example, a magazine containing a wound bobbin of magnetic wire and a take-up spool or a magazine with a small reel of magnetic tape and a take-up reel. In computer usage, the entire cartridge is removed from or inserted into the drive-control unit. New data or programs may be inserted into the computer by changing the cartridge.

cartridge, tape—A device that accomodates one or more spools and hubs for handling a magnetic tape while reading, writing, or for static storage of the tape when not in use. The cartridge is made so that it can be inserted into a magnetic tape device that can drive and record or read the tape.

cascade control—See *control, cascade.*

cascaded carry—See *carry, cascaded.*

case, test—A set of sample input data and conditions used to verify the correctness of a proposed program for a computer.

Case SOAP III—Same as *SOAP III.*

casting-out-nines check—See *check, casting-out-nines.*

catalanguage—In computer programming, the object or target language of a translator, compiler, or assembler. (Contrast with *metalanguage.*)

catalog—A list of item labels and descriptive data arranged in accordance with a rule of order to permit location; for example, a list of the labels of a set of documents that best describe the contents of each document.

catalog, dictionary—A catalog in which all the entry classifications are maintained in the same file; for example, a library card catalog in which the author, title, subject, and series entry cards are arranged together in one general alphabetical sequence. (Contrast with *catalog, split.*)

catalog, split—A catalog in which different entry classifications are maintained in separate files; for example, a library card file arranged alphabetically under subject fields such as chemistry, embryology, and entomology; another file alphabetically arranged by author, and still another file arranged alphabetically by title. (Contrast with *catalog, dictionary.*)

catastrophic failure—See *failure, catastrophic.*

category, display—A type or class of data presented for visual display; for example, the target present position presentation on a radar oscilloscope.

catena—**1:** A series of things linked or connected together; for example, a series of records in which each record is a member of a chain and has a linking field for tracing the chain; a routine consisting of segments that are run through the computer in tandem, only one being within the computer at any one time and each using the output from the previous segment as its input; a set of connected terms of a geometric series; or a power series derived from the binomial expansion theorem. (Further clarified by *chain (1)* and *concatenate.*) **2:** A string of characters and therefore part of a computer word.

catenate—Same as *concatenate.*

cathode-follower—An electronic circuit, employing a vacuum tube, in which the input signal is applied to the grid, the load is in the cathode circuit, and the output signal is taken off of the cathode. The circuit possesses a high input impedance and a low output impedance. The name is derived from the fact that the voltage follows that of the grid, with little or no phase shift. Although there is current and power gain, the voltage gain is always less than unity. The circuit is ideal for driving a low-impedance load, such as many gates, solenoids, or small motors used in analog or digital computers. (Further clarified by *emitter-follower.*)

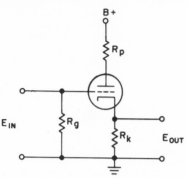

A vacuum triode, cathode-follower electrical schematic diagram.

cathode—ray tube—See *tube, cathode-ray.*

cathode-ray tube storage—Same as *storage, electrostatic.*

CBEMA—1: Computers and Business Equipment Manufacturers Association. Formerly BEMA. **2:** Same as *BEMA.*

CCITT—Comite Consultatif Iternationale Telegraphie et Telephonie.

CDS—1: An abbreviation for Compatible Duplex System, **2:** An abbreviation for Comprehensive Display System.

cell, back-wall photovoltaic—A photovoltaic cell in which light must pass through the front electrode and a semiconductor layer before reaching the barrier layer. (Further clarified by *cell, photovoltaic.*)

cell, binary—A storage cell capable of storing one binary digit; that is, a zero or a one. Thus, the binary cell is capable of remaining in one or the other of two stable states.

cell, data—A storage device that makes use of strips of magnetic tape.

cell, disturbed—A binary storage cell, usually a magnetic or ferroelectric type, polarized, and containing a one or a zero, which has received a drive pulse tending to partially switch the state of the cell to the opposite state, but that does not switch to the opposite storage state. (Further clarified by *signal, disturbed-zero output* and by *signal, disturbed-one output.*)

cell, magnetic—A binary storage cell in which the two values of a binary digit are represented by different magnetic polarization configurations, such as a dipole on magnetic tape faced in one direction to store a one and in the opposite direction to store a zero. The magnetic cell usually includes the necessary storing and sensing wires. The basic requirement for a cell is that electric conductors be associated with magnetic material capable of remaining magnetized after the current is removed.

cell, photovoltaic—A cell that produces an electric potential when exposed to electromagnetic radiation, usually visible light. (Further clarified by *cell, back-wall photovoltaic.*)

cell, storage—An elementary unit of a multiunit storage device, usually a unit of storage capable of holding an elementary unit of data, such as a bit, a character, or a word. The size or capacity of the cell is usually standardized for a given system, and in a computer its location is specified by an address. Specific terms such as block, channel, field, location, or file are preferable when appropriate. In most instances, the cell is the smallest unit of storage, and is capable of storing one binary digit.

cellar—Same as *storage, push-down.*

CELLSCAN—A blood-cell scanning system; specifically, a leucocyte pattern analyzer, developed by Perkin-Elmer Corporation.

CEMON—(Customer Engineering Monitor). A monitor of customer engineering developed by IBM Corporation.

center, automatic data-switching—A data-switching center that senses the contents of a message and relays it without intervention by a human operator. (Synonymous with *electronic data-switching center.* Further clarified by *center, data-switching* and by *switching, automatic message.*)

center, data-processing—A general-purpose computer installation that provides a data-processing service on a customerlike basis. The center may be part of a larger organization with expenses charged to overhead; it may or may not charge for machine and personnel time, or it may be a separate organization in business for a profit.

center, data-switching—A center in which data in the form of messages is relayed or routed in accordance with information contained in the message or in accordance with specific operating instructions or programs. Usually, the installation is in a communication system in which switching equipment is used to interconnect communication circuits. Thus, data coming in on one circuit is transferred to the proper outgoing circuit. (Synonymous with *message-switching center,* with *relay center,* and with *switching center.* Further clarified by *center, automatic data-switching* and by *center, semiautomatic data-switching.*)

center, display—An arbitrarily selected position on a display screen for displaying information to an advantage; for example, the area of a radar scope used to display course or track information.

center, electronic data-switching—Same as *center, automatic data-switching.*

center, local—Same as *center, local switching.*

center, local exchange—Same as *center, local exchange switching.*

center, local exchange switching—A telephone switching center that is not included in the family of switching centers designated in the switching plan to handle traffic in the long distance (LD) trunk network. (Synonymous with *local exchange center* and with *telephone local exchange center.*)

center, local switching—A telephone switching center, usually an automatic switching center, of the family of switching centers designated in the switching plan to handle traffic in the long distance (LD) trunk network. All trunks used for interconnecting any one with any other in this family of switching centers are of such grade as to permit the necessary tandem linkages required by the long distance traffic. (Synonymous with *center, local* and *center, telephone local.*)

center, message-switching—Same as *center, data-switching.*

center, primary—Same as *center, primary switching.*

center, primary switching—A telephone switching center, usually automatic, that is both a selected secondary switching center and a local switching center and to which all secondary centers of the group of secondary centers to which it belongs are connected by trunk circuits. (Synonymous with *primary center,* and with *telephone primary center.*)

center, relay—Same as *center, data-switching.*

center, secondary—Same as *center, secondary switching.*

center, secondary switching—Selected local switching telephone center of a group of local switching centers to which all local centers of the group are connected by trunk circuits. (Synonymous with *telephone secondary center.*)

center, semiautomatic message-switching—A data-switching center at which a human operator routes the messages in accordance with data contained in them. (Further clarified by *center, data-switching.*)

center, switching—Same as *center, data-switching.*

center, technical information—An organization for acquiring, processing, and disseminating technical information. A technical information center may include a library, a staff of scientists and engineers for extracting, indexing, and evaluating technical literature, a roster of consultants on call, or a document center. Capabilities for writing handbooks, reviews, and reports may also be included.

center, telephone local—Same as *center, local switching.*

center, telephone local exchange—Same as *center, local exchange switching.*

center, telephone primary—Same as *center, primary switching.*

center, telephone secondary—Same as *center, secondary switching.*

center, telephone zone—Same as *center, zone-switching.*

center, torn-tape switching—A data-switching center at which messages are produced in a physical form and then forwarded or retransmitted to the proper destination.

center, zone—Same as *center, zone-switching.*

center, zone-switching—A telephone trunk switching center that serves as a switching center for a group of primary centers and that is directly connected to every other zone center by trunk circuits. A zone center does not have loop circuits or trunk circuits from local exchanges terminating on the switchboard. (Synonymous with *telephone zone center* and with *zone center.*)

centerline, stroke—A line used on a printed character specification drawing to designate the position and shape of the locus of character stroke midpoints.

central processing unit—See *unit, central processing.*

central office exchange—See *exchange, central office.*

centralized data processing—See *data processing, centralized.*

CFM—1: An abbreviation for cathode-follower mixer, 2: An abbreviation for cubic feet per minute, 3: An abbreviation for Combat File Maintenance.

chad—A piece of material removed from a paper tape, card, or other medium, when forming a hole or notch in the medium for the purpose of storing or recording data. (Synonymous with *chip (2).*)

chadded tape—See *tape, chadded.*

chadless—Pertaining to cards or tape in which each chad is left fastened by about a quarter of the circumference of the hole, ususally at the leading edge. Chadless punching is useful where it is undesirable to destroy information written or printed on the cards or tape or undesirable to produce chad. Only mechanical-feeler type reading mechanisms can be used to sense or read chadless tape or cards, since the presence of a chad in the tape would seriously hamper the reliable electrical or photoelectric reading of the paper tape or punched cards. (Further clarified by *chad.*)

chadless tape—See *tape, chadless.*

chain—1: A series of parts, events, data, or other items linked together by some means; examples include a series of steel rings linked together, a series of mountains, a column of ships roped together, or a series of data items joined by a reference to each other, such as by means of an address of the adjacent data item. (Further clarified by *catena.*) 2: A sequence of binary digits used to construct a binary code. The chain must not permit a recurrence of the same sequence of bits that may represent digits. The chain is used by selecting n-bit sequences, starting at one end, each successive n-bit word is generated by moving one digit position to the right or left, to the other end of the chain, completing a cycle by carrying around the end as though the bits of the chain were in a circle. It is possible to start anywhere; for example, the chain 00010111 might yield a three-bit code as 000 from the first three bits starting at the left end, 001 moving one position right, 010 moving two right, and so on, to obtain 101, 011, 111, 110, 100 and back to 000. Note that there are no ambiguities, and these might be used to encode the octal digits 0 through 7. (Further clarified by *code, chain.*)

chain, binary—A series of binary circuits, such as flip-flops or one-shot multivibrators, existing in either one of two states, such that each circuit can affect or modify the next circuit.

chain, data element—Same as *macroelement, data.*

chain, Markov—A model for a sequence of events in which the probability of a given event is dependent only on the preceding event.

chain code—See *code, chain.*

chain printer—See *printer, chain.*

chain search—See *search, chain.*

chained file—See *file, chained.*

chained list—See *list, chained.*

chained-segment buffer— See *buffer, chained-segment.*

chance parameter—See *parameter, chance.*

change, control—The change of function that occurs when successive punched cards being read differ in the data punched in a specified field called the control field; for example, change from addition to printing when the last of the items to be added has been added. Usually, a control change stops the card feed for a time long enough to allow the new operation to be performed. Cards are always sorted according to the contents of their control fields before being processed; for example, in calculating a payroll, cards might be sorted on a control field of employee numbers; every time the employee number changed, a control change would occur to cause a pay slip to be printed. (Further clarified by *change, intermediate control;* by *change, major control;* and by *change, minor control.*)

change, intermediate control—A control change of average or relatively moderate magnitude. (Further clarified by *change, control.*)

change, major control—A control change of greater importance or a control change of relatively larger magnitude. (Further clarified by *change, control.*)

change, minor control—A relatively less important control change or a control change of relatively smaller magnitude; for example, in a sales analysis of a large shop, totals might be required for each sales assistant, a minor control change; for each sales point, an intermediate control change; and for each department, a major control change. (Further clarified by *change, control.*)

change, step—To go from one value to another value in a single increment. Usually, the absolute value of the difference of the two values is the smallest value the system is capable of handling.

change character, face—Same as *character, font change.*

change character, font— See *character, font change.*

change dump—See *dump, change.*

change tape—See *tape, change.*

change-on-ones recording, non-return-to-zero—See *recording, non-return-to-zero change-on-ones.*

changeable storage—See *storage, changeable.*

channel—1: A physical path along which data may be transferred or transmitted; or a physical path along which data may be stored serially for subsequent recovery. (Synonymous with *data channel.*) 2: In communication, a means of one-way transmission. (Contrast with *circuit (2).*) 3: The part of a communication system that connects the message source with the message sink.

channel, adjacent—A channel whose frequency band is immediately above or below the referenced channel or whose time slot on a serial communications link is just before or after the referenced channel.

channel, analog—A channel used to transmit data in analog form. This implies that the data can assume any value between the defined limits of the channel; for example, a channel, with a frequency range of 220 to 230 kilohertz that is used to represent or transmit temperature in the range −150°F. to +400°F. and where the 550°F. temperature range is proportionately scaled over the 10-kilohertz range.

channel, backward—A data channel in which the direction of transmission is the opposite of that in which information is being transferred and which is used for transmission of supervisory or error-control signals. (Contrast with *channel, forward.*)

channel, binary symmetric—A channel that conveys messages consisting of binary characters and that has the property that the probabilities of changing any one character to the other character are equal.

channel, data—Same as *channel.*

channel, dedicated—A communication channel that has been committed, obligated, allocated, or otherwise set aside or earmarked for a specified use or user; for example, a channel used only for emergency calls or for use by the president of a corporation. (Synonymous with *dedicated circuit.*)

channel, duplex—A channel that provides simultaneous transmission paths in both directions.

channel, forward—A data channel in which the direction of transmission is the same as that in which information is being transferred. (Contrast with *channel, backward.*)

channel, four-wire—A channel that provides separate and distinct transmission paths simultaneously in both directions.

channel, half-duplex—A channel that transmits and receives signals, but in only one direction at a time.

channel, input—A channel for introducing or impressing a signal or state on a device, such as a logic element or gate. (Contrast with *channel, output*.)

channel, input-output—A channel that allows independent simultaneous communication between any storage unit, certain internal registers, buffers, or other specified units of a computing system, and any of the several input or output units such as card readers, card punches, printers, magnetic or paper tape stations, or display devices. Usually the channel controls certain peripheral devices and sometimes performs validity checks on all data transfers.

channel, output—A channel for removing, obtaining, or conveying data from a device, such as a logic element. (Contrast with *channel, input*.)

channel, simplex—A channel that transmits in one direction only.

channel, two-wire—A channel that transmits in both directions, but in only one direction at a time.

channel, voice-grade—A channel that transmits speech, that is, a channel that permits transmission of frequencies within the voice band, about 200 to 3500 hertz.

channel capacity—See *capacity, channel*.

channel queue—See *queue, channel*.

channel scheduler—See *scheduler, channel*.

character—1: An elementary mark or event used in combination with others to represent data. A character often occurs in the form of a graphic or spatial arrangement of connected or adjacent strokes; for example, A, 1, 5, or —. A character is usually a member of a set of characters, such as the English alphabet. Characters are usually arranged in linear strings or rows and columns, and are combinable in groups to form words, phrases, sentences, paragraphs, chapters, and books for the representation of data in accordance with natural, machine, or artificial languages. The characters are classified into subgroups, such as alphabetic characters, or letters; numeric characters, or numerals; special characters, such as punctuation marks, and other special signs and symbols; and instructional characters that direct machine operations, such as start, stop, shift, back-space and move paper. Characters may be represented in many forms, such as print (A); as a written set of binary digits (100001); as the set of binary digits in the form of electrical pulses; as a specific sound wave of certain frequency component structure; as the word Able in phonetic spelling for voice transmission of letters; or as · — in International Morse Code. The word MISSISSIPPI contains eleven characters, but only four are distinctly different. In most computers, up to 64 distinctly different characters are represented by a six-bit code. Many computer systems use a seventh bit as a parity check on all characters. The primary purpose of characters is to convey information; hence, they are ideograms; however, no significance is attached to minor discrepancies between nominally identical representations, such as flaws in printing or variations in pulse amplitudes. The concept common to different specimens of the same graphic, such as two specimens of an italic A, is called a grapheme. Usually a character does not refer to one bit where the bit is processed as a unit. Many pieces of computing equipment store characters in quantity, expressing storage capacity as total number of characters, or handle characters at certain rates, as in printing or reading, expressing handling rates as so many characters per second or characters per minute. In most alphabets, an arbitrary sequence is fixed for storage and retrieval of data. called alphabetical order. (Further clarified by *code, character*.) 2: A member of a set of elements used for the organization, control, or representation of information. Normally, agreement must be reached as to their usage. Characters may be letters, digits, punctuation marks or other symbols, often represented graphically in the form of a spatial arrangement of adjacent or connected strokes or in the form of other physical conditions in data media.

character, acknowledge—A transmission control character transmitted by a station as an affirmative response to a station with which a connection has been established. Abbreviated as ACK. (Contrast with *character, negative acknowledge*.)

character, additional—Same as *character, special*.

character, backspace—A format effector that causes a print or display position to move one position backward along a line without producing the printing or display of a graphic character. Abbreviated as BS.

character, bell—A control character that is used to call or signal for human attention or intervention by activating an alarm or other attention device.

character, binary-coded—A character represented in the form of a set or sequence of binary digits; for example, 1000001 to represent A. Usually, six binary places are required, allowing a representation of 64 different characters, such as the letters A through Z, numerals 0 through 9, and certain special marks such as . , — and /. Thus, the set of 64 would comprise a single alphabet. The number of binary places used in a given binary code for the alphabet is usually fixed. Some codes utilize an additional bit for error detection, such as an odd or even parity bit. Additional bits may be used for error correction. An example of binary coding for the English alphabet is given in the USA Standard Code for Information Interchange. (Illustrative of *character, coded.*)

character, blank–1: A character used to separate groups of characters, usually when recorded in printed form. In most instances, the space between the groups is left blank and a printed character is not used. However, in some systems a specific symbol, such as a plus sign (+) is used to designate a blank, in order to ensure that the blank space did not result from a machine malfunction. The blank space can mean the absence of information; however, in some information systems, the presence of a blank space at a print position can, and usually does, convey information, even if the information is redundant. A blank must be assigned a code within the system if the position of the blank is to be subject to the operator's discretion. Thus, in one sense, the blank is an instruction for a machine motion, such as a "move carriage," while in another sense, the blank is a character in a given character set, such as on a print wheel, and is selectable as is any other character on the wheel. 2: A graphic representation of the space character.

character, block cancel–A cancel character that is used to indicate that the preceding portion of the block is to be disregarded. The preceding portion of the block is that portion of the block between the block cancel character and the most recently, or last, occurring block mark. Abbreviated as BC.

character, cancel–A control character used to indicate that the data with which it is associated are in error or are to be disregarded. In a certain sense, the cancel character is an operator, and the data it is to operate upon must be identified. Abbreviated as CAN. (Synonymous with *ignore character.*)

character, carriage return–A format effector that causes the print or display position to move to the first position on the same line; for example, a character that would cause the next alphabetic character on a teleprinter to be printed at the first print position; conventionally at the left margin of the paper. A feed character would move the paper to a particular line or row. Abbreviated as CR.

character, check–A character used to perform a check. The character is usually associated with a word or a part of a word, such as an address, a command, or even a character. Frequently, the check character is a check digit, such as a check bit used as the parity bit for an alphanumeric character recorded on magnetic tape.

character, code extension–1: A character used to indicate that succeeding characters or code values are to be interpreted according to a different code. 2: A control character used to indicate that succeeding coded representations are to be interpreted or are written according

to a different code or according to a different coded character set. (Closely related to *character, escape.*)

character, coded–A character represented by a code; for example, · — is the International Morse coded character for the letter A, and 1000001 is the USA Standard Code for Information Interchange binary code for the letter A. (Illustrated by *character, binary-coded.*)

character, command–Same as *character, control.*

character, communication control–Same as *character, transmission control.*

character, control–1: A character that specifies an operation to be performed by a device, particularly a peripheral device, and usually represented as a pattern of binary digits or holes in tapes or cards. When its occurrence is detected, operations such as back space, new line, paper throw, skip line, and rewind are executed by the applicable devices. Thus, the occurrence in a particular context initiates, modifies, or stops a control operation, such as to control or initiate carriage return. 2: A character that is used to initiate, modify, or stop a control function. A control character may be recorded or stored for use at any time, and though it is not a graphic character, it may have a graphic representation, in some circumstances, for human or machine identification. When actually used, the control character is usually in electrical form so as to be interpretable by circuitry. (Synonymous with *command character,* with *functional character,* with *operational character,* and with *instruction character.*)

character, data link escape–A transmission control character used to effect a change in meaning of a limited number of immediately following characters or coded representations and used exclusively to provide supplementary transmission control characters. Abbreviated as DLE.

character, delete–A control character used primarily to obliterate or erase an unwanted character. On perforated tape, the delete character is a code hole in each punch position, thus any character on the tape can be easily deleted simply by punching a hole at each of the unpunched positions. From then on, the appearance of all holes at a character position is ignored. Abbreviated as DEL. (Synonymous with *rub-out character* and with *erase character.* Compare with *character, ignore.*)

character, device control–A control character used for controlling devices associated with a data processing or data communication system. The device control character may be used, for example, to switch devices on or off.

character, end-of-medium–A control character used to identify or indicate the physical limits of a data medium, the limits of the used portion of a data medium, or the limits of the wanted portion of data on a data medium. Abbreviated as EM.

character, end-of-message—The specific character, or group of characters, that indicates the termination of a message; for instance EOM, OUT, ROGER, or WILCO.

character, end-of-text—A transmission control character that signals or marks the end of transmitted text in a message. Abbreviated as ETX.

character, end-of-transmission—A transmission control character that indicates the conclusion of a transmission, the transmission usually consisting of a number of texts, messages, and any associated message headings. Abbreviated as EOT.

character, end-of-transmission-block—A transmission control character used to indicate the conclusion or end of a transmitted block of data. The block may include one or more texts and associated message headings and endings. Abbreviated as ETB.

character, enquiry—A transmission control character used to request a response from a station with which a connection has been made. The response may include station identification, type of equipment in service, the status of the remote station, and other data according to established conventions. Abbreviated as ENQ.

character, erase—Same as *character, delete.*

character, escape—A character used to indicate that the succeeding one or more sequenced characters are expressed in a code different from the code currently in use. Thus, new graphic representation and new meanings are assigned to the coded representations; for example, 1000001, which heretofore meant the decimal numeral 1, now means the English letter A. The use of the escape character allows a limited code to represent a wider range of characters by assigning more than one meaning to each character code representation. For certain programming and engineering purposes, it is usually convenient in the second and third cases for the escape character code representation to be identical in all alphabets. Abbreviated as ESC. (Further clarified by *escape, locking; escape, non-locking;* and by *escape, general.* Closely related to *character, code extension.*)

character, face change—Same as *character, font change.*

character, floating—A character placed in the position that is one place more significant than the otherwise most significant position.

character, font change—A control character that selects and effects a change in the shape, size, or style of the graphics for a set of graphemes, that is, for a set of printed characters. Abbreviated as FC.

(Synonymous with *face change character.*)

character, forbidden—Same as *character, illegal.*

character, form feed—A character, i.e. a format effector, that causes the print or display position to move to the next prescribed first line on the next form or next page or card. Abbreviated as FF.

character, format effector—A control character used to control the positioning or arrangement of data in or on a data medium; for example, a character used to control the location of data when printed, displayed, or recorded. Abbreviated as FE.

character, functional—Same as *character, control.*

character, gap—A character included in a group or string of characters, such as a computer word, for a specific purpose other than to represent data or instructions.

character, graphic—A character that is normally represented by a graphic, that is, a character made visible on a medium by a process such as handwriting, drawing or printing.

character, heading—Same as *character start-of-heading.*

character, horizontal tabulation—A character that causes the print or display position to move forward to the next of a series of positions along a line of characters. The horizontal tabulation character is a format effector, since it is used, along with other format effectors, to control the position of data on or in a medium. Abbreviated as HT.

character, ignore—1: A character that represents, in a particular context, that the character itself is to be ignored; that a preceding or following item is to be ignored, in accordance with some fixed convention; or that some previously specified action is not to be taken; for example, seven holes in a single row of a seven-level tape used to erase a character by punching all holes in a given row. (Compare with *character, delete.*) 2: Same as *character, cancel.*

character, illegal—A character that is not acceptable as a valid representation by a data-processing system or by a specific program; for example, the binary notation 1011 for a binary coded decimal system of numeral representation, where the binary numerals 0000 through 1001, or 0 through 9, are used to represent the ten digits. (Synonymous with *false code,* with *nonexistent code,* with *unused code,* with *forbidden digit,* with *unallowable instruction digit,* with *forbidden combination,* with *illegal command,* with *improper command,* with *unused command,* with *forbidden character,* and with *improper character.*)

character, improper—Same as *character, illegal.*

63

character, instruction—Same as *character, control.*

character, line feed—A character, such as a format effector, that causes the print or display position to move to a corresponding position on the next line of a printed page, of a page to be printed, or of any other medium. Abbreviated as LF.

character, negative acknowledge—A transmission control character transmitted by a station as a negative response to a station with which the connection has been established. Abbreviated as NAK. (Contrast with *character, acknowledge.*)

character, new-line—A character that is a format effector and that represents the signal or that causes a print or display position of a printing or display device to move to the first position on the next line so that the next character can be printed or displayed on the next line. Abbreviated as NL.

character, null—A control character used to fill space on a data medium or occupy the time of data handling equipment, that is, accomplish media-fill or time-fill. Null characters may be inserted into or removed from a series of characters without affecting their meaning, however control equipment may be affected. Abbreviated as NUL.

character, numeric—Same as *digit.*

character, operational—Same as *character, control.*

character, print control—A control character for controlling printing operations, such as line spacing, paper ejection or feeding, carriage return, and type-font selection.

character, protection—Any character used to replace a zero that has been suppressed to avoid error, ambiguity, or false statements; for example, an asterisk used for such a purpose.

character, rub-out—Same as *character, delete.*

character, separating—Same as *separator, information.*

character, shift-in—A code extension character used to terminate a series of characters that has been introduced by the shift-out character, making effective the standard set of graphic characters rather than the alternate set. Abbreviated as SI. (Contrast with *character, shift-out.*)

character, shift-out—A code extension character that causes the substitution of an alternate set of graphic characters for the graphic characters of the standard set. Certain agreement has to be reached concerning the manner of substitution and the use of the code extension characters. Abbreviated as SO. (Contrast with *character, shift-in.*)

character, sign—A character that occupies a sign position and indicates the algebraic sign of the number represented by the numeral with which it is associated.

character, space—A graphic character that is usually represented by a blank location or site in a sequence of graphic characters. The space character could be a graphic character for explicit representation, to distinguish the space character from inadvertent omission of a graphic character. The space character, though not a control character, has a function equivalent to that of a format effector in that it can cause the print or display position to move one position forward, with or without producing the printing or display of any graphic. Also, the space character may have a function equivalent to that of an information separator, in that words are separated, thus the space character bears information; for example, *a synchronous* is different in meaning than *asynchronous.* Abbreviated as SP.

character, special—1: A character, such as a punctuation mark, ignore character, and instructional or operational character, that is a member of a specified alphabet, but is neither a letter nor a numeral. Specific meanings must be assigned to the character in order to use it for conveying information. A space is usually not considered a special character. (Synonymous with *special sign,* with *special symbol,* and with *additional character.*) 2: A member of a graphic character set that is neither a letter, a digit, nor a space character.

character, start-of-heading—A transmission control character used as the first character in the heading of a message to indicate the beginning of the heading of the message. Abbreviated as SOH. (Synonymous with heading character.)

character, start-of-text—A transmission control character that preceded the text of a message and that may be used to terminate the message heading. Abbreviated as STX.

character, substitute—A control character used in lieu of a character that is considered to be invalid or in error, or that cannot be represented on a given device. Abbreviated as SUB.

character, synchronous idle—A transmission control character used by synchronous data transmission systems to provide or cause synchronism to be maintained or to bring about synchronism when it is lost between data terminal equipment. The character is used particularly when no other character is being transmitted. Abbreviated as SYN.

character, transmission control—A control character used to control the transmission of data between data terminal equipment. (Synonymous with *communication control character.*)

character, vertical tabulation—A format effector that is a format control character and that causes a print or display position to move to the corresponding position on the next of a series of predetermined lines. Abbreviated as VT.

character, who-are-you—A transmission control character used to switch on an answer-back unit in the station with which the connection has been set up, or to initiate a response including station identification, and in some applications, the type of equipment in service, and the status of the station. Abbreviated as WRU.

character boundary—See boundary, character.

character check—See check, character.

character code—See code, character.

character-controlled generator—See generator, character-controlled.

character crowding—See crowding, character.

character density—See density, character.

character design—See design, character.

character display device—See device, character display.

character edge—See edge, character.

character emitter—See emitter, character.

character fill—See fill, character.

character generator, display—See generator, display character.

character mean entropy—See entropy, character mean.

character outline—See outline, character.

character pitch—See pitch, character.

character printer—See printer, character.

character reader—See reader, character.

character recognition—See recognition, character.

character set—See set, character.

character set, alphabetic—See set, alphabetic character.

character set, alphabetic coded—See set, alphabetic coded character.

character set, alphanumeric—See set, alphanumeric character.

character set, alphanumeric coded—See set, alphanumeric coded character.

character set, coded—See set, coded character.

character set, numeric—See set, numeric character.

character set, numeric coded—See set, numeric coded character.

character-spacing reference-line—See reference-line, character-spacing.

character style—See style, character.

character subset—See subset, character.

character subset, alphabetic—See subset, alphabetic character.

character subset, alphanumeric—See subset, alphanumeric character.

character subset, numeric—See subset, numeric character.

character string—See string, character.

characteristic—The part of the logarithm of a number that specifies the integral part of the logarithm; that is, the largest power of the base that is contained within the number. For example, for the number 300, the characteristic is 2, since 10^2 is 100, which is smaller than the 300, but 10^3 is

1000 which is larger than the number. Thus, the $\log_{10}$ of 300 is 2.478, where the 2 is the characteristic and the 0.478 is the mantissa. Thus for floating-point numbers, the characteristic is the portion that indicates the exponent.

characteristic impedance—See impedance, characteristic.

chart, flow—See flowchart.

chart, process—Same as flowchart.

chart, plugboard—A chart that shows, for a given job, where plugs or wires must be inserted into a plugboard. Usually the chart also shows the required settings of switches and selective digit emitters and other related information concerning the use of the board. (Synonymous with plugging chart.)

chart, plugging—Same as chart, plugboard.

chart, Veitch—Same as diagram, Veitch.

check—A process for determining accuracy; for example, a test for the absence of error or improper performance, such as to test for errors in a set of data or to determine the correctness of performance of a machine process. The check may be used to determine whether certain prescribed conditions within a computer have been met, whether the results produced by a program are correct, or whether the computer program itself is correct. A check may be made on the program before it is run, during the run, and after the run. Checks may be made to determine the accuracy, precision, or relevancy of the data to be used by a program. (Synonymous with verify (3).)

check, arithmetic—Same as check, mathematical.

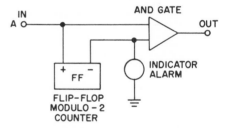

An automatic checking device. Flip-flop inhibits AND gate and sets off alarm if odd (or even) number of bits is present in any character on Line A.

check, automatic—A check performed by circuits or components built into a system specifically for checking purposes and automatically accomplished each time the pertinent operation is performed; for example, a check performed by the parity detection circuit to assure that digits were not deleted or added during storage or a check performed by using twin arithmetic units and continually comparing the

65

results. The programmer need not program the automatic check; however, in some systems, he may exercise an option as to whether or not the automatic check is to be performed. The "extent of automatic checking" may imply either the proportion of machine processes checked in relation to the machine processes performed, or it may imply the proportion of hardware devoted to checking in relation to the total hardware. (Synonymous with *built-in check*. Contrast with *check, programmed*.)

check, Batten—Same as *check, sight*.

check, bias—Same as *check, marginal*.

check, brush-compare—A check performed by using a set of electrical brushes to sense what has just been punched in cards or tape, comparing what has been punched with what is desired, and then signaling any disagreement between the two.

check, built-in—Same as *check, automatic*.

by the remainder of the quotient, to which is added the sum of the digits of the true arithmetic remainder of the division operation, to obtain the remainder of the dividend. The check by this method will fail under certain circumstances, such as when the digits of a sum, quotient, difference, or product are recorded or mistakenly developed in reverse order. Thus, the verification of accuracy is partial. (Synonymous with *nines check*.)

check, character—A check that assures that the rules for the formation of characters have been observed; for example, a check to verify that a particular character has been properly coded by the addition of an appropriate check digit to the basic character code.

check, code—To isolate and remove mistakes from a routine; thus, to debug a routine or program that has been coded.

check, Cordonnier—Same as *check, sight*.

	ADDITION	MODULO-9 SIDEWAYS SUM	
	4583	2	
	456	6	
	644	5	
	723	3	
	637	7	
	764	8	
SUM	7807	31	SUM
SIDEWAYS SUM	22	4	SIDEWAYS SUM
MODULO-9 SUM	4 =	4	CHECK

Casting-out-nines check *for addition. This is a modulo-n check in which n equals nine.*

check, casting-out-nines—A check on an arithmetic operation through the use of a remainder obtained from the operand by dividing by nine and performing the same operations on the remainders as are performed on the operands. The remainder can be obtained by dividing by nine or by adding the digits of the operand. Thus, the casting-out-nines remainder for 923 is 5. The sum of the digits of 923 is 14, adding the digits again, for 14, is again 5. The 5 is also obtained simply by striking out all combinations of digits that sum to 9. Thus the remainder for 6,397,243 is simply 7, since the 6 and 3, the 9, and the 7 and 2 each sum to 9; all that remains is 4 and 3, or 7. To use the casting-out-nines check, perform all indicated operations on the remainders; for example 4327 × 728 is 3,150,056. To check this, multiply the remainder of the multiplier, 7, by the remainder of the multiplicand, 8, to obtain 56. The remainder of 56 is 2, obtained from 6 + 5 = 11 and 1 + 1 = 2. The remainder of the product digits is also 2; thus the multiplication is checked. To check addition, simply add the remainders of all the operands. The remainder of the sum should be the same as the sum of the remainders. Substraction is checked as in addition, and division is checked by multiplying the remainder of the divisor

check, diagnostic—A specific routine designed to assist in locating a malfunction in a computer or a mistake in a program; for example, a diagnostic routine that tests the ability of every storage location to function properly by storing a given number in the first location, transferring it successively to all locations, always testing to ensure it has not changed, and recording the address of the storage location, which causes the number to change.

check, dump—A check performed during a dumping operation; for example, adding all the digits when the contents of the high-speed storage are dumped into the auxiliary storage, and verifying the sum when the data is retransferred.

MULTIPLICATION	SIDEWAYS SUMS MODULO-9		
7348	4		
293	5		
2152964	20	2	CHECK
SIDEWAYS SUM OF PRODUCT DIGITS = 2			

Casting-out-nines check *for multiplication. Note: The digits 5, 4, and 9; or the digits 5, 2, 2, and 9; or the digits 6, 2, 1, 5, 4, and 9 may be cast out when determining the modulo-9 sideways sum of the product digits.*

check, duplication—A check based on a comparison for the consistency of two or more independent performances or measurements, either concurrently on duplicate equipment or at different times on the same equipment; for example, a comparison of the results of the same program run twice on the same machine. The duplication check may be programmed, performed automatically, or performed manually. Sometimes, a test or search made to determine the existence of duplicate items, such as words, records, cards or numbers, in a given collection is considered a duplication check. (Contrast with *check, twin*.)

check, echo—A check on the accuracy of transmission of data in which the received data is returned to the sender for comparison with the data orginally sent. The data is stored at the sending end in order to perform the comparison with the data that are "echoed" back; for example, the check in many output devices, such as printers, whereby the hardware that is about to accomplish an action, such as printing or punching, sends a signal back to the computer in order that the computer may verify that the called-for action and the action about to be accomplished are the same. Thus, a *print A* command is interpreted and a *ready to print A* statement is returned for verification of the command to print an A. (Synonymous with *read-back check*.)

check, even-odd—Same as *check, parity*.

check, false code—Same as *check, forbidden-combination*.

check, forbidden-combination—A check, usually an automatic check, that tests for the occurrence of codes for which no valid or real meaning has been assigned, such as illegal characters. One method of implementing such a check would be to add additional logic elements on the instruction decoding matrix, so that if one of the forbidden instructions or illegal characters were to occur, a flip-flop would be set to indicate and record the event. This can easily be accomplished provided that all of the pulse code combinations are not used up for legal codes. If four bits are used to express the command, about four of the sixteen possible codes should be made illegal. An equipment malfunction or a programming error, such as requiring that an address or a piece of data be interpreted as an instruction, will cause detection of a wrong combination within a few program steps, or within microseconds on modern high-speed electronic computers. A parity check failure represents the occurrence of a forbidden pulse combination. Redundancy checks are also forbidden-combination checks, since if the redundancy check shows an error, then a forbidden combination of digits must also be present. (Synonymous

with *false-code check*, with *nonexistent code check*, with *forbidden-digit check*, with *unallowable-instruction check*, with *illegal-command check*, with *improper-command check*, and with *unused-command check*.)

check, forbidden-digit—Same as *check, forbidden-combination*.

check, hardware—Same as *check, machine*.

check, high-low bias—Same as *check, marginal*.

check, illegal-command—Same as *check, forbidden-combination*.

check, improper-command—Same as *check, forbidden-combination*.

check, machine—A check that tests the proper functioning of the parts of equipment; for example, a programmed check that ensures that all instructions are properly decoded by the decoder, or an automatic check that tests the proper functioning of the arithmetic unit by the use of a dual arithmetic unit, or that checks proper storage functioning through the use of a parity bit. (Synonymous with *hardware check*.)

check, marginal—A check based on a procedure in which certain equipment operating conditions, such as supply voltage, signal amplitudes, or frequency are varied about their nominal values to detect and locate incipient defectiveness of parts; for example, a preventive computer maintenance procedure in which the negative bias voltage on tubes is made slightly less negative to allow the detection of those tubes that show excessive leakage and are not sufficiently cut off or are showing signs of being gassy. Marginal checks are helpful to assure extended running periods, that is, an increased mean time between failures. (Synonymous with *bias check* and with *high-low bias check*. Further clarified by *test, marginal*.)

check, mathematical—A programmed check that makes use of mathematical identities or other inherent properties of arithmetic operations; for example, a check of multiplication by multiplying with A as the multiplier and B as the multiplicand, then multiplying with B as the multiplier and A as the multiplicand, and comparing the two products; the operation $10(A + B)$ may be verified by also performing the operation $10A + 10B$ and then comparing both results, or a tabulated function may be verified by certain differencing operations. The nature of the mathematical check is usually based on the structure of the computation task that is to be accomplished by the computer program. Frequently, some degree of discrepancy between the results obtained by each of the mathematical methods must be made acceptable as a tolerance. The mathematical check verifies the results of the operation as well as the behavior of the various circuits of the

check, modulo-n — check, redundancy

arithmetic unit, since the operation of the unit will be entirely different for each of the cases involved in the checking procedure. (Synonymous with *arithmetic check*.)

check, modulo-n—A check based on the formation of a remainder, modulo-n; for example, a check on numbers in which each number, A, is accompanied by the remainder obtained by dividing the number A by n, the remainder then being used as the check digit. The remainder is written as *A mod n*. The check may be used to establish, with some degree of certainty, the correctness of the performance of arithmetic operations. This is due to the relation that $(A \text{ op } B)$ mod n equals $[(A \text{ mod } n) \text{ op } (B \text{ mod } n)]$. In this equation, op is the arithmetic operation. As an example, $14 \times 15 = 210$. Now 14 has a remainder of 2 mod 4, and 15 has a remainder of 3 mod 4. The product of the remainders is 2×3 or 6, which has a remainder of 2 mod 4. But 210 also has a remainder of 2 mod 4, and therefore the multiplication operation is checked. The method is also called verification by congruences, of which casting-out-nines is another illustration. Casting-out-nines is a modulo-nine check. In this case, as in other $n = b^n - 1$, where b is the base of the number system, such as ten, and n is a positive integer, such as one, the remainder modulo-n = $b^n - 1$ is obtained simply by adding the digits of the numeral. Thus, the remainder mod 9 for 67313 is 2, also called a sideways sum. (Synonymous with *residue check*. Illustrated by *check, casting-out-nines*. Further clarified by *residue, modulo-n* and by *check, summation*.)

check, nines—Same as *check, casting-out-nines*.

check, nonexistent code—Same as *check, forbidden-combination*.

check, odd-even—Same as *check, parity*.

check, parity—A check that tests whether the number of ones or zeros in an array of binary digits is odd or even. Usually, the check is performed by summing the number of ones, affixing a parity bit so as to make the count even, or odd; and then at other times and places, such as after transfer out of storage, counting the digits again including the parity bit to see if the total number of bits is still even, or odd; if not, an error has occurred, because of a machine malfunction in storage. If the number of ones or zeros in a character, number, or other data unit, is required to be odd, the check is called an odd parity check; when even, an even parity check. Thus, the parity check is a type of summation check, using modulus 2. Any array of digits required to form a computer character, word, or other data unit may be parity checked. (Synonymous with *odd-even check* and with *even-odd*

check. Further clarified by *parity, even* and by *parity, odd*.)

check, programmed—A check specified by a program or part of a program and implemented specifically as part of the program. The check is carried out by the computer as a set of programmed operations; for example, a mathematical or logic check, such as comparing the product of A and B with the product of B and A. The programmed check is designed by the programmer and made a part of his regular problem-solving program. The reliability of the check is based on the high probability of correctness, rather than on the duplication of equipment or in built-in error-detecting circuitry. Thus, the computer's own ability to execute instructions is used to have the computer check itself. (Synonymous with *routine check*. Contrast with *check, automatic*.)

check, programmed marginal—A marginal check accomplished by a computer under the supervision of a program; for example, a computer program that initiates and controls the variation of voltage on a tube or other component, controls its performance by requiring certain operations to be performed by the tube, diagnoses the results, and prints out its findings concerning the component. This type of check might be performed as part of a preventive maintenance check.

check, read-back—Same as *check, echo*.

check, read-write—A check on the accuracy of reading, writing, recording, sensing, punching, and similar operations by sensing what has been written and comparing it with that that was to be written or by writing what has been sensed and comparing it with that that was to be read; for example, reading punched cards, punching what has been read, and running the original cards that were read and the new cards that were punched through a comparator to determine if any errors were made.

check, redundancy—A check based on the use of more data symbols than are required to represent the information being expressed. The additional characters, such as binary digits attached to a binary-coded character, do not in themselves carry any information. They reduce the probability of an undetected alteration of the data, such as a change in the bit pattern of a binary-coded character. The redundancy may be incorporated in the code or may be provided by extra characters. The redundancy check is usually arranged so that it is short of complete duplication. A redundancy check is usually automatic, though it may be programmed, such as a summation check. The redundancy checks; for example, modulo-n checks, parity checks, and summation checks, usually make use of check characters, such as check bits, parity bits, hash totals, and zone bits. Some redundancy checking schemes permit error correction as well as error detection.

check, residue—Same as *check, modulo-n.*

check, routine—Same as *check, programmed.*

check, selection—A check, usually automatic, made to verify that the correct register or other device has been selected for the execution of an instruction.

check, sequence—A check designed to check the order of items in a file assumed to be already in sequence.

check, sight—A check performed by sighting through the holes of an aligned deck of punched cards toward a source of light to verify the punching; for example, to determine if a specific hole has been punched in all cards, to verify sorting, or to determine the column wherein commonality of punching occurs or does not occur. (Synonymous with *peek-a-boo check*, with *Batten check*, and with *Cordonnier check*.)

check, sum—Same as *check, summation.*

check, summation—A check performed by addition, usually based on the formation of the sum of the digits of a number. A summation check may verify the validity of a number or the validity of an operation. Each of these involves the use of a check sum which is previously computed, and a check sum digit or numeral, which is carried along with the number or the operation being checked. If the check sum is obtained by summing individual digits in the representation of a number without regard to position or significance of the digits, the sum is called a sideways sum. (Synonymous with *sum check*. Further clarified by *sum, check* and by *check, modulo-n.*)

check, system—A check made on the overall performance of a system, component, or program, usually not made by built-in circuitry or other hardware, but more often by controls imposed on the flow of data at various checkpoints by programming means, such as summation checks, hash totals, duplications, redundancy, and the use of special control data.

check, transfer—A check on the accuracy of the transmission and reception of data, usually performed automatically by built-in circuitry; some examples include an echo check, the use of redundancy, or the inclusion of a fixed set of characters in each message to test the transmitting and receiving equipment.

check, twin—A check performed by continuously comparing the results from duplicate equipment; for example, by using two arithmetic units, two reading or punching stations, or two complete computing systems. Thus, the check is accomplished by performing the same operations simultaneously on different pieces of equipment, whereas in a duplication check the same set of operations is repeated on the same equipment at different times. (Contrast with *check, duplication.*)

check, unallowable-instruction—Same as *check, forbidden-combination.*

check, unused-command—Same as *check, forbidden-combination.*

check, validity—A check based on known conditions or on reasonable limits relative to given information or computer results; for example, a check based on the fact that a calendar month will not be numbered higher than 12, that a week will not have more than 168 hours, that an absolute temperature scale will never show all zeros, or that a coded character shall always have three binary ones.

check bit—See *bit, check.*

check bit, redundancy—See *bit, redundancy check.*

check bus—See *bus, check.*

check card—See *card, check.*

check character—See *character, check.*

check digit—See *digit, check.*

check digit, sum—See *digit, sum check.*

check indicator—See *indicator, check.*

check indicator, overflow—See *indicator, overflow.*

check indicator, read-write—See *indicator, read-write check.*

check indicator, sign—See *indicator, sign-check.*

checking program—See *program, checking.*

checkout—The application of diagnostic or test procedures to a program or to equipment; to make a determination as to the existence of mistakes in a program or malfunctions in a piece of hardware.

checkout, program—A checkout of a program by running it on the computer to determine whether it runs as it is designed.

check problem—See *problem, check.*

check program—See *program, check.*

check register—See *register, check.*

check routine—Same as *routine, test.*

check sum—See *sum, check.*

check trunk—Same as *bus, check.*

checking code, error—See *code, error-checking.*

checking feature—See *feature, checking.*

checking routine, sequence—See *routine, sequence-checking.*

checking time, code—See *time, code checking.*

checkpoint—A point in a program at which a computation could be restarted, because sufficient data or results have been stored from previous computations, or a point in a program where the results of a number of checking operations may be examined. The checkpoints may be periodic points in time of a computer run at which processing is halted to make a record of the status of all variables, working storage, input-output tapes, and other conditions. One primary purpose of checkpoints, used in conjunction with restart routines, is to minimize reprocessing time occasioned by computer malfunction. The use of nonvolatile storage, such as tapes and cores, rather than volatile storage, such as electrostatic and delay-line storage, has reduced the requirement for such checkpoints in more modern computers. A rerun may begin from each checkpoint.

Chinese binary—Same as *binary, column.*

chip—1: A logic element, containing electronic circuit components, both active and passive, embedded in a cohesive material of any shape. The electric circuit, such as a logic element consisting of several AND and OR gates, is embedded in a material that results in a package resembling a small coin, a triangular cookie, or a wafer of plastic. Connections may be made by wires, tape conductors, or pins and holes that permit stacking. **2:** Same as *chad.* **3:** An interpretive subroutine for packed floating-point operands, developed by Wright Air Development Center for use on the Univac 1103 computer. **4:** A small piece of microfilm that can be handled as a unit. The chip can contain data, such as a drawing, be coded, indexed, sorted, stacked, and stored by a mechanical storage and retrieval system.

chop—Same as *multiplex, time-division.*

chopper-stabilized amplifier—See *amplifier, chopper-stabilized.*

cine-oriented image—See *image, cine-oriented.*

circuit—1: A complete closed-loop path for current to flow, usually including the source of electromotive force. For the sake of clarity, the circuit that is broken so that current cannot flow, is called an open circuit, and when the opening is closed, the circuit is called a closed circuit, thus describing the state of closure of the loop. Thus, a circuit becomes a communication link between two or more points, since a controlled variation in current at one point in a circuit can be sensed at another point in the same circuit. **2:** In communication, a means of two-way communication between two points, consisting of *go and return* channels (Contrast with *channel (2)*.)

circuit, AND—Same as *gate, AND.*

circuit, balanced—A circuit consisting of two signal branches in the presence of ground or a neutral branch capable of being operated in such a way that the voltages of the two branches at all corresponding points on both branches are equal in magnitude and opposite in polarity with respect to ground or the neutral branch.

circuit, bistable—1: Same as *flip-flop.* 2: A trigger circuit that has two stable states (Synonymous with *bistable trigger circuit.*)

circuit, bistable trigger—1: Same as *flip-flop.* 2: Same as *circuit, bistable.*

circuit, clamping—A circuit that prevents the electrical potential of one point from exceeding a certain value with reference to another point, usually a stabilized reference, like a low-impedance source or infinite bus; for example, a tube, transistor, or diode, properly connected to a d-c supply level of potential that prevents the voltage of a point from exceeding the voltage level of the power supply, or a voltage regulator gas tube (argon, neon, xenon, or krypton) that breaks down and conducts at 80 volts and extinguishes at 60 volts will hold a voltage level so that it does not exceed 80 volts. Clamping circuits are commonly used in computer logic circuits. The clamp is designed to hold a particular part of a waveform at a predetermined voltage level, sometimes at a particular instant of time. (Synonymous with *clamp.*)

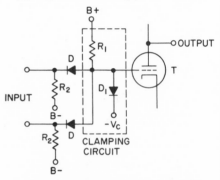

A typical clamping circuit. Diode D_1 prevents grid of tube T from going more positive than $-V_c$ volts when diodes D of AND gate are cut off by positive voltages appearing simultaneously at both inputs.

circuit, clear-to-send—A teletype communication circuit that transmits signals originating in the signal converter and that is not required for receive-only service. For send-only and for full-duplex service, the signal converter will hold the clear-to-send circuit in the on condition at all times. For half-duplex service, when the send-request signal is switched to the on condition, the clear-to-send circuit will be switched to the on condition after a time delay sufficient to effect the reversal of direction of transmission of data on the communication channel and all associated equipment. When the send-request circuit is switched back to the off condition, the clear-to-send circuit will be switched back to the off condition.

circuit, clipping—A circuit that removes the portion of a voltage or current waveform that would otherwise extend above or below a specified level. Clipping may be accomplished by tubes, transistors, diodes, or any other type of clamp; for example, if a clipping circuit is energized with a triangular wave, a trapezoidal wave is obtained; if energized with a sine wave, a nearly rectangular wave is obtained; or if sharp spikes are riding on a square wave, the clipping circuit will clip them off. For certain low-energy transients, an ordinary capacitor can be made to do a certain amount of clipping. (Synonymous with *clipper*.)

circuit, coincidence—Same as *gate, AND*.

circuit, combinational—A logic device whose output values at any given instant depend only upon the input values at that instant. The combinational circuit does not have a storage capability and is thus a special case of a sequential circuit.

circuit, control—A circuit used to maintain control of situations or events; for example, a circuit that effects the execution of instructions in a computer in proper sequence.

circuit, data telephone—A telephone circuit that permits the transmission of digital data, such as the digital data transmitted by the Data-phone, developed by American Telephone and Telegraph Company and used by Bell Telephone System or the Autodin circuits of the Department of Defense. (Further clarified by *Data-phone*.)

circuit, dedicated—Same as *channel, dedicated*.

circuit, deflection—The circuit used in a cathode-ray tube to direct the electron beam so as to strike the desired spot on the screen, thus establishing the storage location of the data bit to be stored. Usually, the deflection is accomplished by applying a voltage to a set of deflecting plates, between which the beam must pass. The resulting electric field magnitude and polarity, in two planes, horizontal and vertical, determines the location of the strike on the surface of the tube. Thus, the addressing determines the deflection of the beam, and the beam on or off determines whether the zero or the one is to be stored in a digital computer electrostatic storage tube. The same technique is used in other cathode-ray tube applications, such as in radar displays, digital data displays, print-out devices, and oscilloscopes. The deflection may also be accomplished magnetically by means of a magnetic yoke around the neck of the tube. The electron beam is deflected by the resultant magnetic field.

circuit, differentiating—Same as *differentiator*.

circuit, Eccles-Jordan—Same as *trigger, Eccles-Jordan*.

circuit, etched—An integrated electronic circuit constructed on a single piece of semiconducting material by controlling the geometry of various paths and forming active elements by an etching process.

circuit, four-wire—A two-way communication circuit using two paths, so arranged that signals are transmitted in one direction only on one path and in the other direction on the other path. The transmission cable may or may not employ four wires, for the same ground or ground wire may serve both ways.

circuit, frame grounding—A conductor that is electrically bonded to the machine frame and to any conducting parts that are normally exposed to operating personnel. This circuit may be further connected to external grounds as may be required by applicable Fire Underwriters codes.

circuit, gigahertz—Same as *circuit, nanosecond*.

circuit, integrated—An electronic circuit in which passive and active elements are all made of a single piece of semiconducting material by controlling the geometry and purity of conducting and semiconducting paths. The integrated circuit is usually a complete circuit containing active and passive elements fabricated and assembled as a single unit, which results in an assembly that cannot be disassembled without destroying it. For example, an AND gate etched on a single germanium crystal by control of geometry to provide active junctions for diode and transistor action; a thin ceramic wafer with inserted transistors and diodes, deposited or applied geometrically controlled resistive inks as resistors, deposited capacitors, and conductive inks, forming a complete integrated flip-flop; or a logic element potted in a thin chip. Abbreviated IC.

circuit, integrating—Same as *integrator*.

circuit, interlock—A teletype signal transmission circuit that transmits a signal originating in the signal converter and that is in the on condition only when both the internal switching circuits are arranged for signaling on a communication facility and there is not any abnormal or test condition that disables or impairs any normal function associated with the class of service being used.

circuit, large-scale integrated—An integrated circuit of densely packed digital storage and logic elements (10,000 per sq. in.) on a single chip of semiconducting material. Abbreviated LSI.

circuit, monolithic integrated—Several electronic active circuits, logic circuits, such as gates and flip-flops for computer applications, etched on a single semiconductor crystal or material, fabricated by controlling geometry through etching and deposition techniques; for example, 15 silicon transistors and 13 resistors, with interconnections on a 0.05 in. by 0.05 in. hermetically sealed chip.

circuit, monostable—A circuit, usually a trigger circuit, that has one stable state and one unstable state.

circuit, multipoint—A circuit that interconnects several locations such that data transmitted over the circuit are available at all the locations simultaneously. Provision must be made to ensure that a receiving station does not interrupt the data signals to other stations.

circuit, nanosecond—An electronic circuit, such as a computer logic circuit, that has a

71

pulse rise time or a pulse fall time of the order of several nanoseconds or less; that is, billionths (U.S.) of a second or less.

circuit, OR—Same as *gate, OR.*

circuit, printed—A circuit whose circuit elements, such as resistors, capacitors, diodes, and transistors, are mounted on a card on which the interconnecting conductors are deposited. The card is prepared in the same way printing plates are prepared: it is clad with copper, then covered with a light-sensitive emulsion, and exposed to light. The light fixes the areas that are to be retained; when the card is emersed in an acid bath, those portions that have not been fixed are eaten away. (Further clarified by *card, printed-circuit.*)

circuit, received data—A teletype circuit that carries signals originated by the receiving signal converter in response to signals received over the communication media. The circuit is not required for send-only service. In half-duplex service, the receiving signal converter holds the marking condition on the received data circuit when the remote data terminal equipment has its send-request circuit in the off conditon. Optionally, in half-duplex service, the received data circuit may be used to monitor transmitted signals, such as for producing local copy of transmissions. (Contrast with *circuit, transmitted data.*)

circuit, request-send—Same as *circuit, send-request.*

circuit, see-saw—Same as *amplifier, sign-reversing.*

circuit, send-request—A teletype circuit that carries signals originating in the data terminal equipment and that selects whether the signal converter is to be conditioned to transmit or to receive. For half-duplex service, when the signal on the send-request circuit is switched to the transmit condition, the signal converter will switch to the receive condition, without regard to any signals that may be received from the communication facility. When this signal is switched to the off condition, the signal converter will switch to the receive condition without regard to any signals on the transmitted data circuit. Data terminal equipment intended for use with send-only service will hold the send-request circuit in the on condition at all times. Data terminal equipment intended for use with receive-only service will hold the send-request circuit in the off condition at all times. This circuit is not required for full-duplex service.

circuit, sequential—A logic device that has output values, at a given instant, that depend upon its input values and internal state at that instant, and wherein the internal state depends upon the immediately preceding input values and internal state. A sequential circuit can

assume a finite number of internal states and may thus be regarded as a finite automation.

circuit, tank—An electric circuit consisting of inductance and capacitance connected together at both ends and used to sustain electrical oscillations, such as are used in tuned amplifiers. (Synonymous with *tank.*)

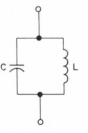

A tank circuit.

circuit, transmitted data—A teletype circuit on which signals are orginated by the data terminal equipment for transmission on the data communication channel. This circuit is not required for receive-only service. (Contrast with *circuit, received data.*)

circuit, trigger—A circuit that has two or more stable states or unstable states at least one of which is stable, and is designed so that transition to another state can be initiated by the application of a suitable pulse.

circuit, two-wire—A communication circuit limited to communication in one direction at a time. One of the wires is usually grounded, or if one conductor is used, the return path is by ground. If one conductor is used, along with ground, the system is still called a two-wire circuit. (Further clarified by *circuit, four-wire.*)

circuit, video—A circuit capable of handling nonsinusoidal waveforms involving frequencies of the order of megahertz.

circuit card, printed—See *card, printed-circuit.*

circuit switching—See *switching, circuit.*

circular list—See *list, circular.*

circular shift—Same as *shift, cyclic.*

circulating register—See *register, circulating.*

circulating storage—See *storage, circulating.*

CISCO—Compass Integrated System Compiler.

citation—A statement of reference to another source of data.

citation index—See *index, citation.*

CL-1—A programming system developed by Technical Operations, Inc., for use on the IBM 704 and IBM 709 computers.

clamp—Same as *circuit, clamping.*

clamping circuit—See *circuit, clamping.*

clamp-on—A method of holding a telephone call for a line that is in use and of signaling when it becomes free.

class—A set of items, such as persons, documents, data, or articles, that have some characteristic or set of characteristics in common; for example, a subdivision of a category, such as trucks as a class of motor vehicles or synchronous computers as a class of digital computers.

CLASS–(Computer-based Laboratory for Automated School Systems). A project of System Development Corporation.

classification, colon–A faceted classification scheme developed by S. R. Ranganathan.

classification, concept–A classification scheme for arranging information in storage for subsequent retrieval on a conceptual or image basis. Each information unit is identified or labeled by a word or group of words that is used to search for and retrieve the desired information; for example, concepts are assigned to documents that are then identified during searching. Usually a multidimensional analysis is required; or an English dictionary is concept classified in that each word represents the concept or image defined by the definition of the word; thus one retrieves the definition. (Synonymous with *concept coordination.*)

classification, Dewey decimal–A classification system, utilizing specific ranges of decimal numbers, to classify and order books, usually in a library, so as to permit location of a specific text. The Dewey decimal number on the text is obtained by the searcher from a card catalog, which may be alphabetically arranged by author, title, or subject. The librarian assigns a number to a given book from a list of specific numbers assigned to specific subject headings, such as biology, zoology, mathematics, history, and chemistry. Further breakdowns of these major fields are identified by the addition of digits to the right of the decimal point. The system was devised and developed by Melvil Dewey. (Synonymous with *Dewey decimal system.*)

classification, universal decimal–An expansion and extension of the Dewey decimal classification system, initiated by P. Otlet in Brussels. (Synonymous with *Brussels classification system.*)

classification system, Brussels–Same as *classification, universal decimal.*

classify–To assign, group, or arrange items, such as machines, data, or persons, into segregrated classes in accordance with a specific criterion or characteristic, such as level of secrecy of information, type of computing machine, genus of plant, or blood type.

cleanliness, carbon–The freedom of a sheet of carbon paper or a carbon ribbon from the tendency to transfer to hands and paper while in use and in storage.

clear–1: To put every cell in a storage device in the same prescribed state, usually that denoting zero or blank. Clear usually returns all storage contents to zero, while erase removes all data, leaving no form of data representation whatever, not even symbols for blank or zero, and delete removes all data, but may leave a trace of the event, such as a complete row of holes across a paper tape, the only manner in which nonerasable storage contents may be erased. Thus, data in a bank of flip-flops is usually not *erased* or *deleted,* but is *cleared.* (Further clarified by *erase* and *delete.* Synonymous with *erase.*) **2:** Same as *reset.*

clear area–Same as *band, clear.*

clear band–See *band, clear.*

clear-to-send circuit–See *circuit, clear-to-send.*

CLIP–(Compiler Language for Information Processing). A programming language developed by System Development Corporation.

clipper–Same as *circuit, clipping.*

clipping circuit–See *circuit, clipping.*

clock–1: A device that generates periodic signals used for synchronization or that measures and indicates time. In a digital synchronous computer, clocks control the generation of pulses that occur at specified fixed time intervals, which govern the timing of events, such as the enabling or inhibiting of gates. The clock may record real time or any referenced time, such as machine time, in a register that is available to the computer program in order that certain events may be scheduled, certain delays measured, or events synchronized. Any elapsed time, such as real time, may be recorded for logging purposes. (Synonymous with *timer* and *synchronizer (2).*) **2:** A device that measures or indicates time; for example, a register whose contents change at regular intervals in such a way as to measure or indicate time. For a given system, such a register might control the rate or instant at which events can occur. In this instance, the clock might be said to control time for the system.

clock, master–The clock that generates the basic timing pulses used in a system; for example, a one-megahertz, crystal-controlled oscillator that generates a clock pulse at microsecond intervals. The output of a master clock in a digital computer may be utilized to generate clock pulses, such as a pulse that occurs once every word time. The master clock may develop multiple phases, so that a five-phase clock will have a pulse at one-microsecond intervals on each of five lines, staggered 0.2 microseconds apart. (Synonymous with *master synchronizer* and *master timer.*)

clock frequency–See *frequency, clock.*

clock pulse–Same as *pulse, timing.*

clock-pulse generator–See *generator, clock-pulse.*

clock rate–See *rate, clock.*

clock signal–Same as *pulse, timing.*

clock track–Same as *track, timing.*

clock unit—See *unit, clock.*

closed amplifier—See *amplifier, closed.*

closed array—See *array, closed.*

closed, contact, normally—See *contact, normally-closed.*

closed entry—See *entry, closed.*

closed loop—See *loop, closed.*

closed routine—See *routine, closed.*

closed shop—See *shop, closed.*

closed subroutine—See *subroutine, closed.*

cluster—In a document retrieval system, a group of related documents.

clutch cycle—See *cycle, clutch.*

coalesce—1: In filing, to combine two or more files into one file. 2: To combine two or more sets into one set.

coated card, edge—See *card, edge-coated.*

coaxial cable—See *cable, coaxial.*

COBOL—(Common Business Oriented Language). A business data-processing language developed by CODAYSL, a U.S. Department of Defense sponsored committee. COBOL was designed to express data manipulation and processing problems in English narrative form, in a precise and standard manner. The language is intended as a means for directly presenting any business program to any suitable computer for which a compiler exists, and it is a means for communicating such procedures among individuals.

COBOL, Compact—A subset of USASI COBOL.

CODAP—(Control Data Assembly Program). An assembly program designed and developed by Control Data Corporation. Also, the symbolic assembler of programs for use on the Control Data 1604A computer.

CODASYL—(Conference on Data System Languages). A committee organized and sponsored by the United States Department of Defense and responsible for COBOL, the business data-processing language.

code—The set of rules used to convert data from one form of representation to another; for example, the set of correspondences in the USA Standard Code for Information Interchange. Thus, the set of representations defined by the rules may also be considered as the code, as in the USA Standard Codes. For computers, the repertoire of instructions also constitute a computer code. Most codes, then, are merely a system of symbols, usually with a one-to-one relationship between the symbols of the two languages, such as 1000001 for A. To code a computer program implies the preparation of a description of the steps involved in the program in the language of the computer, or simply the translation and writing of information in a computer language, usually in a symbolic notation. Labeling or identifying objects, routines, locations, operators, operands, names, or similar things is a form of coding. Thus, English language statements are a form of coding for the thoughts and ideas that are expressed. Coding may also be considered the transformation of a computer program into the instruction code appropriate for the preparation of the input media. It is essential that the agreed transformation, whereby any given data in one alphabet may be represented in another alphabet, be unambiguous. (Further clarified by *coding, relative.*)

code, absolute—A code in which computer instructions are written using machine addresses, locations, and registers, machine operation codes, and actual operands; for example, an absolute code for the EDVAC System would appear as follows: 1100110011/1100110100/1100110101/1100110110/0100, which defines where the augend and addend are stored, where to put the results, where the next instruction is stored, and the operation to be performed, namely addition, all in machine language, or binary notation. Even if octal or sexadecimal notation were to be used, the code would still be absolute. An absolute code uses the names, numbers and symbols for storage locations, channels, registers, indexes, and the like, that have been assigned by the machine designer. (Synonymous with *specific code* and *basic code.* Contrast with *coding, relative* and *code, symbolic.*)

code, alphabetic—1: A code that uses an alphabet, usually the 26 letters of the English alphabet, to represent information; for example, 26 of the International Morse Code characters and their English letter equivalents; sets of English letters used to represent information or instructions, such as BN for Boston, NY for New York, AD for addition, and CN for carriage return; a binary code used to represent letters of the alphabet, such as parts of the USA Standard Code for Information Interchange; or a computer instruction repertoire in which the instructions are defined in terms of letters or groups of letters, such as MPY for multiply and ADD for addition. (Further clarified by *code, numeric.*) 2: A code in which data is represented using an alphabetical character set. 3: A code whose code set contains letters; may contain control characters, space characters, and other special characters such as punctuation marks; but does not contain digits. (Synonymous with *alphabetical code.*)

code, alphabetical—Same as *code, alphabetic.*

code, alphameric—Same as *code, alphanumeric.*

code, alphanumeric—A combined alphabetic and numeric code; a code that makes use of letters and digits for the representations involved in the code; for example, a code that uses letters of the English alphabet, decimal digits, and certain other signs and symbols, such as the American Standard Code for

Information Interchange. (Synonymous with *alphameric code*. Further clarified by *code, numeric*.)

code, augmented operation—An operation code that is further defined, modified, or limited by information found in another portion of the instruction. Sometimes all the distributed parts of an operation code are considered as constituting the operation code, in which case the concept of augmentation is not necessary; for example, the entire instruction word except the addresses may be considered as the operation code.

code, automatic—Same as *autocode*.

code, Barker—A binary code suitable for pulse code modulation from synchronization having optimal correlation properties and having relative immunity to phase displacement by random pulses immediately adjacent to the pattern, and relative immunity to phase displacement by error in the transmitter code. The Barker codes are, for 3 bits: 110; for 7 bits: 1110010; and for 11 bits: 11100010010.

code, basic—Same as *code, absolute*.

code, Baudot—A binary code that uses five binary digits to represent a character; for example, five rows of holes on punched paper tape, each row capable of representing a single character. The code is also designated as the Standard Teletypewriter code. An upper- and lowercase signal must also be associated with the character to distinguish between letters (specified by lowercase), numbers (uppercase), special signs and symbols (uppercase), and operations (both upper and lowercase). The code is used in standard commercial teletype transmissions involving the use of punched paper tape and Teletypewriters. The standard five-channel Teletypwriter code consists of a start impulse and five character impulses, all of equal length, and a stop impulse whose length is 1.42 times the start or character impulses. The code is also known as the 1.42 unit code. (Synonymous with *Teletype code*.)

code, binary—A code that uses two distinct characters; for example, a code in which the characters in at least one of two transliterated alphabets are in the form of binary digits or their equivalents, such as yes-no, on-off, true-false, hole-no-hole, polarized clockwise or counterclockwise, or zero-one. Usually, binary coding implies the use of bits to represent characters; for example, 1000001 for A, binary 1101 for decimal 13, or a code for the ten decimal digits 0 through 9, where each is represented by its radix 2 binary equivalent number. It is entirely possible that any arbitrarily assigned combination of binary digits may be used to represent decimal digits; however, if arithmetic is to be performed, there must be a definite relationship between the binary-coded numbers, such as exists in the straight binary or excess-three binary codes.

code, biquinary—A code in which a decimal digit n is represented by the pair of numbers a and b, where $n = 5a + b$, in which a may be 0 or 1, and b may be 0, 1, 2, 3, or 4. Examples of biquinary codes using a binary form of representation and a decimal form of representation are as follows:

Decimal Digit	Biquinary	
	A Binary Form	A Decimal Form
0	01 00001	00
1	01 00010	01
2	01 00100	02
3	01 01000	03
4	01 10000	04
5	10 00001	10
6	10 00010	11
7	10 00100	12
8	10 01000	13
9	10 10000	14

code, CP—Same as *code, gray*.

code, card—A code in which one set of the coded characters is in the form of patterns of holes punched in a card, the other set of correspondences of the code being the characters of some alphabet, such as letters of the English alphabet, decimal digits, and punctuation marks; for example, the Hollerith code. (Illustrated by *code, Hollerith*. Further clarified by *Hollerith*.)

DECIMAL	0 0 0 I 0 I I I CHAIN CODE
0	0 0 0
I	0 0 I
2	0 I 0
3	I 0 I
4	0 I I
5	I I I
6	I I 0
7	I 0 0

A three-bit chain code *derived from the chain-numeral 00010111, with decimal equivalents.*

code, chain—A code derived from a chain; that is, a binary code derived by arranging in a cyclic sequence some or all of the different M-bit words that are linked by the relationship that each binary word is derived from its neighbor by displacing the binary digits one digit position to the left (or right), dropping the leading bit and inserting the next bit at the end. The value of the inserted bit needs only to satisfy the requirement that a word must not recur before the cycle is complete. Thus, if the chain is 011010, then a three-bit derived code would be 011, the first three digits; 110, the next three digits; followed by 101, and 010. (Further clarified by *chain*.)

code, character—A code used to represent a character in a computer or its peripheral equipment; for example, a set of electrical pulses whose polarity is used to represent a pattern that represents the character, or a set of pulses of two different time lengths, such as dots and dashes, used to represent characters. Prevalent usage indicates that the electrical, magnetic, mechanical, or any other physical profile of a character is also a character in its own right. Thus, a set of large and small smoke signals is as much a representation of the first letter of the English alphabet as a set of penciled lines on a piece of paper. (Further clarified by *character*.)

code, command—Same as *code, operation*.

code, computer—A code that is written in machine language or that can be translated into machine language, enabling a person to inform and instruct a computer. The code usually defines the built-in hardware features and characteristics of a computer, such as the storage addressing scheme, indexing scheme, arithmetic and logical operations, and other programming options; for example, the repertoire of instructions that a computer is capable of executing or the code used to identify addresses, registers, storage devices, data links, and input-output devices. (Further clarified by *code, instruction* and by *code, operation*.)

code, continuous-progression—Same as *code, unit-distance*.

code, continuous progressive—Same as *code, unit-distance*.

code, correcting—Same as *code, error-correcting*.

code, cyclic—A code formed from a positional notation system for numbers, in which any two numbers whose arithmetic difference is one are represented by characters, such as decimal digits, that are the same except in one place or column and in that place or column differ by only one unit as defined by the specified sequence of characters. Cyclic codes, such as the cyclic binary code, or Gray code, are used to advantage in certain mechanical and electrical devices because of the reduced ambiguity possible at change points, since there is only one change at a time, which reduces demands on the system. An example of a cyclic code, corresponding to a decimal count from 0, is 0, 1, 2, ..., 9, 19, 18, 17, ..., 11, 10, 20, 21, ..., 29, 39, 38, ... The change from code 10, which is decimal 19, to code 20, which is decimal 20, requires only a change in the second place, whereas in ordinary notation, the change from decimal 19 to decimal 20 requires changes in both places, usually at once, which can be a burden in some systems. The Gray code is an example of a binary cyclic code.

code, cyclic binary unit-distance—Same as *code, Gray*.

code, cyclic permuted—Same as *code, unit-distance*.

code, data—1: Sets of symbols used to represent the data items for a data element on a one-for-one basis; for example, 01, 02, 03, ...12 used to represent the names of the months of the year of the Gregorian calendar. 2: A set of rules and conventions according to which signals representing the data should be formed, transmitted, received, or otherwise processed. 3: In information retrieval, a set of characters used to represent data items, for example, the codes, 01, 02, ..., 12 may be used to represent January, February ..., December, for the data element called months of the year. (Contrast with *set, code*.)

code, dense binary—A binary code in which all possible binary patterns are used; for example, straight binary representation for sexadecimal or octal digits, or a cyclic binary using all possible patterns, in contrast to a binary-coded decimal system of representing decimal digits that does not use six out of the 16 possible patterns.

DATA NUMERAL	CHECK CODE MODULO-9	TRANSMITTED NUMERAL
4 3 2	0	4 3 2 0
1 2 8	2	1 2 8 2
5 6 8	1	5 6 8 1
1 9 6	7	1 9 6 7
4 9 8	3	4 9 8 3
8 1 4	4	8 1 4 4
3 4 8	6	3 4 8 6

Examples of modulo-9 error-checking codes.

code, error-checking—A code designed either to detect or to detect and correct errors in the representation of information,

MNEMONIC CODE	NUMERIC CODE	EXPLANATION
ADD	1	ADDITION
DPA	2	DOUBLE PRECISION ADD
SQA	3	SQUARE ROOT
VLS	5	VARIABLE LENGTH SQUARE ROOT
CAN	12	COMPARE A AND N
TBP	18	TRANSFER IF B IS POSITIVE
STB	24	STORE B
RSI	72	RIGHT SHIFT AND INCREMENT
RTK	84	READ TYPEWRITER KEYBOARD

A computer code showing part of the instruction repertory of a computer.

particulary in the storage and transmission of data handled by computers and data processors; for example, a parity bit used only to check, with some uncertainty, the occurrence of an error, such as a changed digit.

code, error-correcting–A code, usually an error-detecting code, that use redundant characters to assist in the restoration of a word that has been multilated. Only certain kinds of errors may be corrected if the redundancy is less than 100 percent. The redundancy is usually so arranged that the multilated word still resembles the orginal word more closely than any other valid representation of another possible word in the vocabulary. When a partial loss or an error has occurred that the code has not been designed to correct, the adjustment that is made may be erroneous. In most applications, the code is in the form of additional digits in a computer word; the digits are moved or transmitted with the word from one part of a computer to another and used to reconstruct the moved number in case of a partial loss. Each acceptable expression in an error-correcting code conforms to specific rules of construction that also define one or more equivalent nonacceptable expressions, so that if certain errors occur in an acceptable expression, the result will be one of its equivalents and the error can be corrected. (Synonymous with *correcting code.* Further clarified by *correction, automatic error.*)

$$\begin{vmatrix} 1 & 1 & 0 & 0 \\ 0 & 1 & 1 & 0 \\ 0 & 0 & 1 & 1 \\ 1 & 0 & 0 & 1 \end{vmatrix} = 6 \qquad \begin{vmatrix} 1 & 1 & 0 & 0 \\ 0 & 1 & 1 & 0 \\ 0 & \boxed{1} & 1 & 1 \\ 1 & 0 & 0 & 1 \end{vmatrix}$$

EVEN PARITY   ERROR

In the error-correcting code above, even parity is not satisfied in the third row and second column. Hence, the digit at the intersection is wrong and must be corrected to a zero.

code, error-detecting–A code in which each representation conforms to specific rules of construction so that for certain errors the mutilated representation is not valid and hence is detectable as unallowable in the alphabet or language being used, unless the mutilation is of a special kind, which the code may be unable to detect. The presence of errors is detectable without reference to the original message. Such codes require more than the minimum number of code elements that could represent the message; for example, an odd parity code. The code requires redundant data that detects the presence of certain unintentional alterations of the data. The biquinary code and a modulo-n check code make use of redundancy to assist in error detection. (Synonymous with *self-checking code.*)

code, excess-fifty–Same as *representation, excess-fifty.*

code, excess-three–A code for representing binary-coded decimal digits in which the decimal digit n is represented by the straight binary equivalent of $n + 3$. In this code, the nines complement of a decimal digit is formed simply by changing all ones to zeros and all zeros to ones. This is convenient in hardware, since any register consisting of a bank of flip-flops always has stored in it the complement of numbers in the form of the condition of the side of the flip-flop other than that being used to represent the number. The excess-three code also simplifies the generation of carries.

DECIMAL	STRAIGHT BINARY	EXCESS-THREE
0	0 0 0 0	0 0 1 1
1	0 0 0 1	0 1 0 0
2	0 0 1 0	0 1 0 1
3	0 0 1 1	0 1 1 0
4	0 1 0 0	0 1 1 1
5	0 1 0 1	1 0 0 0
6	0 1 1 0	1 0 0 1
7	0 1 1 1	1 0 1 0
8	1 0 0 0	1 0 1 1
9	1 0 0 1	1 1 0 0

An excess-three code with decimal and straight-binary equivalents.

code, extended binary-coded decimal interchange–A coded character set that consists of eight-bit coded characters. Thus, each character comprises an eight-bit byte. Abbreviated as EBCDIC.

code, false–Same as *character, illegal.*

code, Fieldata–A code constructed from a specially chosen assignment of alphabetic and numeric characters and other special signs and symbols to each of the 64 possible patterns of 6 binary digits, each for use in expressing data in devices such as computers and data transmission and input-output devices. The Fieldata code was developed and adopted as a United States Army standard, particularly for data communications. (Synonymous with *United States Army Fieldata code.*)

code, forbidden–Same as *code, illegal.*

code, four-address–Same as *instruction, four-address.*

code, Gray–A cyclic binary unit-distance code; a positional binary code system for consecutive numbers, whose digits are the same in every place except one, and in that place the digits differ by one unit. Thus, it is a cyclic unit-distance binary code, the distance being the Hamming distance. The code proves valuable for encoding devices, since only one digit changes at a time, which provides for smoother operation and reduced

DECIMAL	STRAIGHT BINARY	GRAY CODE
0	0 0 0 0	0
1	0 0 0 1	1
2	0 0 1 0	1 1
3	0 0 1 1	1 0
4	0 1 0 0	1 1 0
5	0 1 0 1	1 1 1
6	0 1 1 0	1 0 1
7	0 1 1 1	1 0 0
8	1 0 0 0	1 1 0 0
9	1 0 0 1	1 1 0 1

A Gray code *table with decimal and straight binary equivalents.*

ambiguities at change points; that is, where many digits might change at the same time, such as 1111 to 10000 in binary. To convert from straight binary to a Gray code proceed as follows: Starting from the left end of the straight binary number, copy any initial zeros and the first occurrence of a one. If the next binary digit is different from one; that is, zero, write a one, if the same, write a zero. If the next digit is different from the previous digit, write a one, if the same, write a zero. Each time the next digit in the straight binary changes, write a one for the Gray code; when there is no change, write a zero, until the end of the number. For example, binary 1011011 is equivalent to 1110110 in a Gray code. Note that except for the first digit, each occurrence of a one in the Gray code represents a change of digits in straight binary. In order to convert the Gray code back to binary, start counting the Gray code ones from the left. If the count is odd, write a one, and as long as the count remains odd as position by position is passed, continue writing ones. Whenever the count is even, write zeros, and continue writing zeros as long as the count is even. For example, given the Gray code number 1110110, the straight binary equivalent will be one, for the first one in the Gray code number, zero for the second one because the count of ones from the left is two, or even; one for the third one because the count of ones is now odd, one again because the count is still odd; zero because the count of ones is again even, and so on, to yield 1011011 in straight binary. The code may be constructed, in a cyclic fashion, by writing reflections of sequence. Thus, it is a type of cyclic binary and is also called a reflected binary code. Begin with 0,1 written in a column, as

0
1

then reflect the 0,1 by writing its mirror image under it; that is; in reverse sequence, to obtain:

0
1
1
0

Now prefix the forward sequence with 0 and the reverse sequence with 1, to obtain:

00
01
11
10

Now, with this as the forward sequence, reflect it by writing its reverse sequence under it, to obtain:

00
01
11
10
10
11
01
00

Now prefix the forward sequence with 0 and the backward with 1, to obtain:

000
001
011
010
110
111
101
100

This process may be continued indefinitely. Therefore, to construct an $(n+1)$-bit Gray code from an n-bit Gray code, write the n-bit twice in sequence, first in forward and then in reverse sequence of code words. Then prefix an extra bit to each word, the prefix taking the value zero for the forward sequence of the n-bit code and the value one for the reverse sequence. (Synonymous with *cyclic binary unit-distance code,* with *reflected binary unit-distance code,* and with *CP code.*)

code, Hamming—An error-correction code named after the inventor.

code, Hollerith—The set of hole patterns that may be punched in a card and that corresponds with a set of alphanumeric characters, usually consisting of the subset of 26 letters of the English alphabet, the subset of ten digits of the decimal number system, and a subset of certain punctuation marks and other special signs and symbols used in commerical and literary English composition, such as the dollar sign, hyphen, comma, period, and question mark. Each specific pattern of holes of the Hollerith code is placed in a column on a card and corresponds to a specific character. The Hollerith code-hole pattern was originally designed for the widely used 80-column, 12-row punched card. The columns on the card are numbered consecutively one through 80. The rows are labeled Y, X, and zero through nine consecutively from top to bottom. For example, letters are represented on the card by a hole in the Y, X, or zero row and also in one of the numbered rows, both holes in the same column. The decimal digits are represented by a single hole in the row corresponding to the digit being represented. Other special combinations of three holes in the same column are used to represent other special signs and symbols. (Illustrative of *code, card*. Further clarified by *Hollerith*.)

code, illegal—A code element, character, or symbol that appears or purports to be a proper element, but is, in fact, not a member of the defined alphabet or language; for example, four-binary-digit patterns, that is, tetrads, are used to represent the ten decimal digits, six need not be used, and so may be declared illegal, in which case their use is forbidden. Should a forbidden pattern present itself, it may be assumed that a mistake or a malfunction of equipment has occurred. (Synonymous with *forbidden code* and *improper code*.)

code, improper—*Same as* code, illegal.

code, input instruction—An instruction code that is more convenient to the programmer, since it is usually more mnemonic; that is, the operations are coded so as to have some of the appearances of the actual operations, such as MPY for multiply, SHR for shift right, and CPR for compare. The computer interprets these and translates these into the machine instruction codes for execution. Thus, the input instruction code is a kind of pseudocode that the computer can interpret and the programmer understands more readily.

INSTRUCTION	CODE
ADD	0 0 0 1
MULTIPLY	0 0 1 0
SUBTRACT	0 0 1 1
DIVIDE	0 1 0 0
SQUARE ROOT	0 1 0 1
SHIFT RIGHT	0 1 1 0
SHIFT LEFT	0 1 1 1
COMPARE	1 0 0 0
READ	1 0 0 1
WRITE	1 0 1 0

A computer *instruction code in machine language with explanations.*

code, instruction—1: A code used to represent the instructions that a computer is capable of executing. The code is used by a coder or programmer to prepare a program for computer execution. Thus, a stored-program, electronic digital computer accepts the sequence of coded instructions that represent the program, stores, and then proceeds to execute them. The code itself can be a list of symbols that defines a code of operations that a computer can recognize, along with the English equivalents that define the codes; for example, MPY when sensed by the computer means to multiply. The instruction codes are usually written in programming languages, such as COBOL, FORTRAN, and ALGOL, which a machine can sense, and a translator is used to translate them into machine language instructions. Thus, the code represents the basic instructions that a computer has been built to execute. (Synonymous with *machine instruction code*, with *code repertoire*, and with *code repertory*. Further clarified by *instruction, multiple-address*.) 2: Same as *code, operation*.

code, lock—A code used in a computer operating system to provide protection against or prevent improper use of main storage areas, input-output files, or input-output devices.

code, m-out-of-n—A binary code, of fixed weight in each digit position, in which m of the n digits that comprise a word, character, or digit, are the same for every word, character, or digit. For example, a two-out-of-five code in which every five-bit character has exactly two binary ones and three binary zeros. (Further clarified by *code, two-out-of-five*.)

code, machine—An operation code that a machine can sense, read, interpret, or recognize.

code, machine instruction—Same as *code, instruction*.

code, macro—See *macrocode*.

code, MICR—A magnetic ink character recognition code, consisting of a set of 10 numeric symbols and four special symbols, standardized as Font E-13B of the American Bankers Association. The characters of the code are imprinted by standard printing techniques and are readable visually and by magnetic sensing heads in magnetic ink character recognition equipment. The special symbols are amount, on us, transit number, and dash. The code is published in ABA Publication 147 and 149. The USA Standards Institute Subcommittee X3.7 is engaged in continuing the standardization efforts of MICR.

code, micro—See *microcode*.

code, minimum distance—A code for representing the characters of an alphabet and developed so that the signal distance between any two words consisting of the coded characters is not less than a specified minimum value. If the minimum distance is specified as $2n + 1$, then errors in up to $2n$ digit places in a word can be detected or errors in up to n digit places can be corrected. (Further clarified by *distance, signal*.)

code, mnemonic—A code that can be comparatively easily remembered by a

GERMAN	MNEMONIC	SCHLÜSSEL CODE	MNEMONIC	ENGLISH
WAGENRÜCKLAUF	WRL	0 0 1	CR	CARRIAGE RETURN
RECHTSVERSCHIEBUNG	RVS	0 1 0	RS	RIGHT SHIFT
LINKSVERSHIEBUNG	LVS	0 1 1	LS	LEFT SHIFT
DRUCKBEFEHL	DBF	1 0 0	PR	PRINT INSTRUCTION
LOCHKARTENLESEN	LKL	1 0 1	RC	READ CARDS
SPRUNGBEFEHL	SBF	1 1 0	JP	JUMP INSTRUCTION
WEITERSCHALTEN	WSN	1 1 1	CF	COUNT FORWARD

A mnemonic code depends on the language familiar to the user.

human being. Thus, some aspect of the code must be familiar to the user, although a code that may be mnemonic to one person may not be mnemonic to another; for example, to an English-speaking person, ACC for accumulator, AC for alternating current, SHR for shift right, and SUB for subtract might be a good mnemonic code; however, for a German-speaking person, the respective codes might be AKK for Akkumulator, WS for Wechselstrom, VSR for Verschieben Recht and ABZ for Abziehen. The code INT for integrate might be entirely mnemonic to a mathematician but not to a biologist, even if both are familiar with the machine process defined by the code.

code, mnemonic instruction—An instruction code for a computer written in such a manner that it is easier for the computer programmer to remember; for example, MPY for multiply, DIV for divide, and ACC for accumulator. The mnemonic code programs must be converted to machine language codes by the computer or by a human coder prior to being executed by the computer. The benefit of mnemonic code is that the human programmer, who should be occupied with mathematical analysis and methods of solution, does not have to be preoccupied with unwieldy codes and laborious and tedious coding of his sequence of operations. Thus, many mnemonic codes are pseudocodes. Many of the programming languages, such as ALGOL, FORTRAN, and COBOL are mnemonic instruction codes; in fact, they closely resemble English statements. (Synonymous with *code, mnemonic operation.*)

code, mnemonic operation—Same as *code, mnemonic instruction.*

code, multiple-address—A computer instruction code in which more than one storage location is referenced and utilized. Thus, the data and the instructions are stored in various storage positions, registers, accumulators, and other storage media available to the computer. If each instruction refers to two or more locations, the instruction code is a multiple-address code; for example, each instruction might contain the addresses of two operands, or it might contain the addresses of two operands and the address of the location for storing the results of the operation, such as the sum or product. (Contrast with *code, single-address.* Further clarified by *instruction, multiple-address.*)

code, nonexistent—Same as *character, illegal.*

code, numeric—A code that permits the use of numerals, such as integers, decimal digits, and binary numbers; for example, 01 for Washington, 23 for Boston, or 46 for addition, rather than WA for Washington, BN for Boston, and ADD for addition, which allows letters. Thus, a numeric code may be used to prepare data for computer acceptance by reducing all information to numerical quantities whose meaning can be interpreted by the built-in circuitry of the computer. (Further clarified by *code, alphabetic* and by *code, alphanumeric.*)

code, numeric data—A digital code used to represent numerals and some special characters such as 1110 to represent +6 and 0110 to represent −6.

code, object—The code produced by a compiler or an assembler which can be executed.

code, one-address—Same as *instruction, one-address.*

code, operation—A code used to represent the specific operations to be performed or that may be performed by a computer; for example, AD for addition, SU for subtraction, SH for shift, and EX for extract. Usually the operation code is a portion of the instruction code which specifies all the elements of a computer instruction, such as the addresses, sentinels, tags, and the operation itself. Often the operation code is written in absolute machine language as a combination of bits, but it may also be written in a pseudocode, such as a mnemonic code, or in a common language, such as COBOL, ALGOL, or FORTRAN. (Synonymous with *order code* and with *command code.* Further clarified by *address* and by *code, instruction.*)

code, order—Same as *code, operation*.

code, own—A code incorporated into a standard routine to modify or extend the routine to accomplish particular tasks that otherwise would not be accomplished by the standard routine.

code, paper-tape—Same as *code, punched-tape*.

code, perforated-tape—Same as *code, punched-tape*.

code, pseudo—See pseudocode.

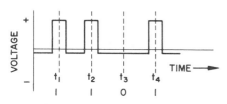

A pulse code *representing the binary number 1011, showing the least-significant digit first in time.*

code, pulse—A code in which data is represented in groups or patterns of pulses, usually electrical, occurring as a function of time or space. Pulse codes are usually binary representations of characters; for example, zero represents the absence of a pulse, and one the presence of a pulse; then in a serial computer, a time sequence of pulses representing binary 1011 would mean a positive voltage at time t_1, corresponding to the least significant digit, a positive voltage at t_2, corresponding to the next significant one digit, zero voltage at time t_3, and a positive voltage at t_4, where the time intervals are equal. Particular meanings are assigned to the various pulse patterns.

code, punched-tape—A code consisting of patterns of holes punched in a tape. Most codes are arranged so that each character occupies one row of holes, although some codes use several rows to represent a character. The holes correspond to binary digits. Numerous kinds of punched tape codes are in use; for example, Standard Teletype, Flexowriter, Fieldata, and the USA Standard. The number of channels, or columns, of holes varies from five to eight for most of the one-row-a-character, or one-level, tapes. (Synonymous with *perforated tape code* and with *paper-tape code*.)

code, quibinary—A code for representing decimal digits in which each decimal digit is represented by seven binary digits, a group of five, and a group of two digits, which are coefficients of 8, 6, 4, 2, 0, 1, and 0, respectively; for example, quibinary 00100 01 is equivalent to decimal 5.

code, reentrant—Same as *program, reentrant*.

code, reflected binary unit-distance—Same as *code, Gray*.

code, retrieval—A code used to retrieve data from a file or bank; for example, a code used in micrographics for manual or automatic retrieval of microimages.

code, return—A code, usually established by a computer program, routine, or subroutine, that is used to notify the system of the status or availability of all peripheral equipment, such as input-output devices, remote terminals, and consoles.

code, self-checking—Same as *code, error-detecting*.

code, self-demarcating—A code in which the symbols are so arranged and selected that the generation of false combinations by interaction of segments from two successive codes is prevented.

code, single-address—Same as *instruction, one-address*.

code, skeletal—A code, such as a set of computer instructions, in which some parts, such as addresses, must be completed or specified in some detail each time the code is used.

code, specific—Same as *code, absolute*.

code, symbolic—Any code that uses signs and symbols. Usually a computer instruction code that uses symbols rather than machine language statements to represent machine operations and addresses. Often the symbols are mnemonic, particularly for operations, as an aid to programming. When symbolic codes are used, symbolic notations may also be used for operators and operands. When the symbolic language is not the machine language, a translation to machine language becomes necessary, for either machine or human interpretation. There is hardly a distinction between a symbolic code and a pseudocode, except that pseudocodes tend to direct attention to meaning while symbolic codes tend to direct attention to representation. (Closely related to *pseudocode*. Contrast with *code, absolute*.)

code, Teletype—Same as *code, Baudot*.

code, thirty-nine feature—A code that represents, on punched cards, all numerals from 0 to 39 by not more than two punchings in any column.

code, three-address—Same as *instruction, three-address*.

DECIMAL	QUIBINARY	
0	0 0 0 0 1	0 1
1	0 0 0 0 1	1 0
2	0 0 0 1 0	0 1
3	0 0 0 1 0	1 0
4	0 0 1 0 0	0 1
5	0 0 1 0 0	1 0
6	0 1 0 0 0	0 1
7	0 1 0 0 0	1 0
8	1 0 0 0 0	0 1
9	1 0 0 0 0	1 0

A quibinary code *with* decimal equivalents.

code, twenty-nine feature—A code that represents, on punched cards, all numerals from 0 to 29 by not more than two punchings in any column.

code, two-address—Same as *instruction, two-address*.

DECIMAL	TWO-OUT-OF-FIVE CODE
0	0 0 0 1 1
1	0 0 1 0 1
2	0 0 1 1 0
3	0 1 0 0 1
4	0 1 0 1 0
5	0 1 1 0 0
6	1 0 0 0 1
7	1 0 0 1 0
8	1 0 1 0 0
9	1 1 0 0 0

A two-out-of-five code *with decimal equivalents.*

code, two-out-of-five—A binary code for representing decimal digits in which each decimal digit is represented by five binary digits, of which, in every numeral, three are ones and two are zeros; or, in every numeral, two are ones and three are zeros. This code is an error-detecting code. Some errors can be corrected. (Further clarified by *code, m-out-of-n*.)

code, unit-distance—A positional code for numbers having the property that when some or all of them of a given length, are arranged in sequence, the signal distance between consecutive numbers is one. It is essential that no two numbers representing two different quantities are the same. This type of code reduces the possibility of ambiguity at the transition point from cycle to cycle, as at 0999 to 1000, where all four positions must change at once. In a unit-distance code, not more than one digit position may undergo a digit change at a time. The Gray code is a cyclic binary unit-distance code. (Synonymous with *continuous-progression code*, with *continuous progressive code*, and *with cyclic permuted code*.)

code, unused—Same as *character, illegal*.

code area—See *area, code*.

code check—See *check, code*.

code check, false—Same as *check, forbidden-combination*.

code check, nonexistent—Same as *check, forbidden-combination*.

code-checking time—See *time, code-checking*.

code distance—Same as *distance, signal*.

code element—See *element, code*.

code extension character—See *character, code extension*.

code frame—See *frame, code*.

code holes—See *holes, code*.

code-line index—See *index, code-line*.

code modulation, pulse—See *modulation, pulse-code*.

code position—See *position, code*.

code repertoire—Same as *code, instruction*.

code repertory—Same as *code, instruction*.

code set—See *set, code*.

code transparent—See *transparent, code*.

code value—Same as *representation, coded*.

coded character—See *character, coded*.

coded character set—See *set, coded character*.

coded character set, alphabetic—See *set, alphabetic coded character*.

coded character set, alphanumeric—See *set, alphanumeric coded character*.

coded character set, numeric—See *set, numeric coded character*.

coded decimal—Same as *decimal, binary-coded*.

coded-decimal digit—See *digit, coded-decimal*.

coded-decimal notation—See *notation, coded-decimal*.

coded notation, binary—See *notation, binary coded*.

coded program—See *program, coded*.

coded representation—See *representation, coded*.

coded stop—Same as *halt, programmed*.

CODEL—An automatic coding system developed by Computer Developments, Ltd., and International Computers and Tabulators, Ltd.

coder—A person who writes but does not necessarily design computer programs; for example, a person who writes specific machine language instructions from a symbolic language program.

coding, automatic—Preparing a code with the use of a digital computer in such a manner that the machine translates a routine written in a nonmachine language into coded machine instructions; for example, assembling, compiling, and interpreting. Thus, automatic coding involves techniques in which a computer is used to help bridge the gap between some

DECIMAL	UNIT DISTANCE	DECIMAL	UNIT DISTANCE	DECIMAL	UNIT DISTANCE
0	0 0 0	1 0	1 2 1	2 0	2 1 2
1	0 0 1	1 1	1 2 2	2 1	2 2 2
2	0 0 2	1 2	1 0 2	2 2	2 2 0
3	0 1 2	1 3	1 0 0	2 3	2 2 1
4	0 1 0	1 4	1 0 1	2 4	2 0 1
5	0 1 1	1 5	1 1 1	2 5	2 0 2
6	0 2 1	1 6	1 1 2	2 6	2 0 0
7	0 2 2	1 7	1 1 0		
8	0 2 0	1 8	2 1 0		
9	1 2 0	1 9	2 1 1		

A unit-distance code (radix 3, ternary) with decimal equivalents.

intellectually and manually easier way of describing the steps to be followed in solving a given problem and a time-and-space-wise more efficient final coding of the same problem for a given computer. The computer is usually used to perform a significant part of the coding. The automatic code conversion may occur prior to the execution of the program, as a compiler; during the execution, as an interpreter; or at both times. Usually the computer is used to aid in the preparation of computer programs by converting a higher level language, such as English language or other mnemonic language, one relatively easy for a human being to use, into a lower level, usually tedious machine language. All computers can be directly instructed in their own built-in machine language, such as in strings of binary digits. This type of early programming is generally awkward, inconvenient and error-prone. To aid the human in communicating with the computer, various other higher languages have been devised, such as FORTRAN, COBOL, and ALGOL. These languages have been arranged in a hierarchy, consisting of assemblers, compilers, and generators. Thus, automatic coding involves the preparation of machine language routines with the assistance of a computer.

coding, forced—Same as *programming, minimum-access.*

coding, minimal-latency—Coding in such a manner as to minimize the computer time devoted to transferring words to and from storage, for those computers in which the waiting time for transfers to and from storage depends on the location in storage. Thus, locations for data are so chosen that access time is reduced; for example, coding in a manner such that the next word called for in the program is the next word that would be read from a revolving drum; inserting a word in an acoustic delay line at the moment the address involved is at hand; or having the data arranged in a delay line so that the next instruction is the one just emerging from the end of the line. (Synonymous with *minimum-access coding* and with *minimum-delay coding.* Closely related to *programming, minimum-access.* Illustrative of *coding, optimum.*)

coding, minimum-access—Same as *coding, minimal-latency.*

coding, minimum-delay—Same as *coding, minimal-latency.*

coding, optimum—Preparing a routine for a computer with a view toward optimizing or idealizing a specific situation; for example, minimizing storage access time to speed up operations; minimizing the use of storage to handle larger quantities of data; minimizing the use of magnetic tape stations or punched cards to reduce wear on mechanical equipment, or making maximum use of the low capacity but ultra high-speed thin-film storage unit. (Illustrated by *coding, minimal-latency.*)

coding, pence—Same as *coding, single-column pence.*

coding, relative—Coding for a computer, using relative addresses in the program instructions. (Further clarified by *address, relative* and by *code.* Contrast with *code, absolute.*)

coding, single-column pence—Punched card coding in which a single digit from 0 to 11, inclusive, is represented in a column by a single punch. (Synonymous with *pence coding.*)

coding, skeletal—Coding that consists only of the framework of a routine and that is to be completed by a generator; that is, a generalized routine, using input parameters. Thus, the skeletal code is only an outline of a routine. (Further clarified by *generator.*)

coding, straight-line—Computer coding in which repetition of sequences of instructions, with or without address modification, is achieved, by explicitly writing the instructions for each repetition. Generally, straight-line coding will require less execution time than equivalent loops. If the number of repetitions is large, the coding becomes tedious unless a generator is used. The feasibility of straight-line coding is limited by the space required and the difficulty of coding a variable number of repetitions.

coding, symbolic—1: Coding that uses machine instructions with addresses expressed in symbols convenient to the programmer. The use of arbitrary characters to represent addresses facilitates programming. particularly if the programming or coding is in machine language. The use of common languages such as FORTRAN, ALGOL, and COBOL involves symbolic coding. Machine addresses may be assigned automatically. (Synonymous with *symbolic programming.*) **2:** The preparing of computer software, such as programs, routines, compilers, and assemblers using a symbolic language.

coding line—Same as *word, instruction.*

Coding System, ABC—See *ABC Coding System.*

coefficient, floating-point—The part of a floating-point numeral (representation) that expresses the number of times that the number base with exponent is to be multiplied; for example, 6.07, in the numeral 6.07×10^{19}, is the floating-point coefficient. (Synonymous with *fixed-point part.*)

coefficient, phase-distortion—In a transmission system, the difference between the maximum transit time and the minimum transit time for frequencies within a specified band.

coefficient, reflection—The ratio of incident to reflected light intensity at a point on a surface. (Further clarified by *ratio, print contrast* and by *contrast.*)

coefficient, scale—Same as *factor, scale.*

coefficient, switching—The derivative of the applied magnetizing force; that is, the magnetic field intensity, with respect to the reciprocal of the resultant switching time. Expressed mathematically as $S_w = dH/d(1/T_s)$. Thus, if a magnetic field intensity H_1 (oersteds) is applied to a volume of magnetic material, and it takes T_s time (seconds) for the material to orient its molecular structure in the direction of the applied field, and if H is plotted as the ordinate with $1/T_s$ plotted as the abscissa, then the slope of the resultant curve is the switching coefficient. This value is significant when designing logic and storage circuits that require the reversal or change in direction of polarization of magnetic materials. The coefficient is fairly constant over not too great a range of values. If the coefficients for different materials are plotted on the same set of axes, a family of nearly straight lines is obtained.

coefficient unit—Same as *scalar.*

coefficient unit, multiplier—Same as *scalar.*

cognition, artificial—Same as *perception, artificial.*

cognition, machine—Same as *perception, artificial.*

COGO—A coordinate geometry computer program developed by Massachusetts Institute of Technology.

COGO-10—A civil engineering problem-oriented language.

Coherent Light Detection and Ranging—Same as *COLIDAR.*

coil, blank paper-tape—A coil of paper tape that can be punched with a pattern of holes to represent data, but that has been punched with feed holes only. (Contrast with *coil, virgin paper-tape.*)

coil, paper-tape—A roll of paper tape, which may be a virgin, blank, or punched coil, used to record data.

coil, virgin paper-tape—A coil of paper tape that can be punched with a pattern of holes to represent data, but that is completely devoid of all holes, such as feed or code holes, and therefore has not been perforated at all. (Contrast with *coil, blank paper-tape.*)

coincidence circuit—Same as *gate, AND.*

coincidence gate—Same as *gate, AND.*

coincidence unit—Same as *gate, AND.*

coincident-current selection—See *selection, coincident-current.*

COL—(Computer Oriented Language). Any programming language having terms, such as address and instruction codes, that are applicable to a particular computer or a particular set of similar computers. Machine language programs are written in a computer oriented language.

COLASL—(Compiler Los Alamos Scientific Laboratories). A computer program compiler developed by Los Alamos Scientific Laboratories of the University of California for the IBM STRETCH computer.

COLIDAR—(Coherent Light Detection and Ranging). A sensing system developed by Hughes Aircraft Company.

collate—1: To compare and merge two or more similarly ordered, or sequenced, sets into one ordered set; for example, to arrange the set 1, 4, 9, 12, 18 and the set 2, 5, 10, 19 as the single set 1, 2, 4, 5, 9, 10, 12, 18, 19; or to merge sequences of punched cards, each ordered on some key into a single sequence ordered on the same key. (Related to *merge.*) 2: To change the arrangement of items, from two or more ordered sets each containing a number of items, into one ordered set such that the resulting ordered set is composed of items not necessarily in the same order in which they were in the original sets.

collating sequence—See *sequence, collating.*

collation operation—Same as *AND.*

collator—A computer program or device that collates sets of sequenced cards or stored data into a single sequence of cards or data. A typical card collator has two input feeds for entering two ordered sets, four output stackers for stacking four ordered sets generated by the process, and three comparison stations for routing the cards to one or the other stacker on the basis of comparison criteria that has been specified by a plugboard. The machine is capable of matching detail cards with master cards and merging them in proper sequence. The machine thus feeds and compares two decks of punched cards in order to match or merge them or to check their sequence. The cards that match can be separated from those that do not match, thereby making it possible to select and file cards automatically. Basically, the collator compares selected fields, in cards contained in its input magazines, for equality and relative magnitudes, and then stores the cards in selected stackers on the basis of the outcome of these comparisons. A collating program arranges sequenced sets of data into a single sequence. (Synonymous with interpolator.)

collecting—Same as *binding.*

collection, garbage—The reclamation of space in storage, usually by rearranging its contents and by eliminating unneeded data.

collection station, data—Same as *station, data input.*

collector—The electrode in a point-contact transistor or the region in a junction transistor that serves as an area to which electrons or holes, that is, ions, may migrate under the influence of applied electric fields. The collector in a transistor corresponds to the plate in a tube, in so far as the function is concerned. Usually, the load to be driven by the transistor is placed in series with or just external to the collector lead for many amplifier applications. If the collector is made of p-type material, it is biased negative and vice versa. (Further clarified by *transistor.*)

collision—The generation of the same address when an address computation technique is applied to the keys of two different records.

colon classification—See *classification, colon.*

color—In optical character recognition, the characteristic of an image that causes its appearance to be dependent upon the spectral reflectance of the image itself, the spectral response of the observer or observing instrument, and the spectral composition of the incident light; for example, a characteristically green-reflecting image will appear black when illuminated with red light. The property of color itself is determined by the frequency of the electromagnetic radiation that is incident upon the retina of the eye, coupled with the response of the eye to the particular frequency. Color problems are inherent in optical character sensing devices, since the spectral characteristics of the image, the incident light, and the response of the photosensitive surface of the optical sensing device affect the operation of the system. Thus, the color actually is the spectral composition; that is, the combination of wavelengths and intensities of measured light from an image.

color-bleeding resistance—See *resistance, color-bleeding.*

COLT—(Communication Line Terminator). Developed by International Business Machines Corporation.

column—A line of vertical elements in a rectangular matrix of elements; for example, one of the 80 vertical sets of 12 punch positions of an 80-column card or 6 positions in a 90-column card; a vertical line of numerals in a table of values, or one of the places in a numeral or a register. Columns are usually numbered from left to right. Thus, the physical device corresponding to a position in a number, a table, or other vertical arrangement of characters or expressions. (Contrast with *row.*)

column, card—A column of punch positions on a card; that is, a vertical line of places where holes may be punched so as to represent data. Typical cards have 45, 80, or 90 vertical columns, each column capable of representing or holding a character. (Further clarified by *binary, column.* Contrast with *row, card.*)

column, digit—A place or position of a digit in a numeral; for example, the position held by the 8 in 4786, or the vertical group of computer elements used to handle the particular position of a number in a computer.

column, mark-sense—A line or column of mark-sense positions. The column is usually considered to be parallel to the Y-datum line of a data medium, such as a card or sheet of paper. The Y-datum line is at right angles to the X-datum line, usually passing through the midpoint of the right edge of the medium when held in its normal viewing position. (Contrast with *row, mark-sense.*)

column, punch—A line of punch positions that is parallel to the Y-datum line of a punch card, the Y-datum line being parallel to a card column, which is parallel to the shorter edge of a card or is vertical when the card is held for normal human reading of any data printed on the card. (Contrast with *row, punch.*)

column binary—See *binary, column.*

column-binary card—See *card, column-binary.*

column split—See *split, column.*

COM—1: Computer Output Microfilm. 2: Computer Output Microfilmer. 3: Computer Output Microfilming. 4: Computer Output Microform.

COMAC—Continuous Multiple-Access Collator

combination—A specific association or grouping of one or more selected members of a set; for example, ab and bc are two possible combinations that can be made from the letters abc. When dealing with combinations, the arrangements ab and ba are the same combination, but different permutations. Thus, the number of combinations that can be made of n things taken r at a time is always equal to or less than the number of permutations of the same n things also taken r at a time; or $nCr \leqslant nPr$. (Contrast with *permutation.*)

combination forbidden—Same as *character illegal.*

combination cable—See *cable, combination.*

combination check, forbidden—See *check, forbidden-combination.*

combinational circuit—See *circuit, combinational.*

combinational logic element—See *element, combinational logic.*

combined head—Same as *head, read-write.*

comic-strip-oriented image—See *image, comic-strip-oriented.*

COMIT—A programming language developed and used by Massachusetts Institute of Technology for information storage and retrieval with the IBM 704, IBM 709, and IBM 7090 computers. It is a machine-oriented language.

COMLOGNET—(Combat Logistics Network). A communications network set up by the United States Department of Defense for logistics data.

command—Loosely, a control signal, an instruction for a computer in machine language, an operation to be performed by a computer, or an operator itself. Thus, the command portion of the instruction word for a digital computer specifies the operation to be performed by the computer; the command may be a set of signals that occurs as a result of decoding an instruction, the command initiating the individual steps that form the process of executing the instruction. Instruction operation, operator, or other more specific terms should be used in preference to command.

command, illegal—Same as *character, illegal.*

command, improper—Same as *character, illegal.*

command, operator—A statement or instruction issued to the control program, executive, or operating system of a computer via a console or other input device, in order to achieve a specified result, such as to cause the control program to provide certain information, initiate a new operation, alter operations, or terminate a run or job.

command, unused—Same as *character, illegal.*

command character—Same as *character, control.*

command check, illegal—Same as *check, forbidden-combination.*

command check, improper—Same as *check, forbidden-combination.*

command check, unused—Same as *check, forbidden-combination.*

command code—Same as *code, operation.*

command language—See *language, command.*

comment—In computer programming, a description, reference, explanation, note, annotation, or remark added to or interspersed among the statements of a source language that have no effect on the target language.

Commercial Translator—An automatic coding system developed by International Business Machines Corporation for use on IBM 705III, IBM 709, IBM 7070, IBM 7080, and IBM 7090 computers.

Committee on Nomenclature—Same as *ACM Committee on Nomenclature.*

common-battery signaling—See *signaling, common-battery.*

common carrier—See *carrier, common.*

common field—See *field, common.*

common hardware—See *hardware, common.*

common software—See *software, common.*

common language—See *language, common.*

common language, OCR—See *language, OCR-common.*

common page—See *page, common.*

common program—See *program, common.*

communication—The process of transferring information or the information so transferred.

communication, data—1: The transferring of the representation of information from one point, person, or equipment to another. 2: The transmission and reception of data. 3: The transmission, reception, and validation of data. Validation may include interpretation, checking, verifying, translating, screening and other operations to insure that the received data and the transmitted data have the same meaning.

communication control character—Same as *character, transmission control.*

communication link—See *link, communication.*

communication region—See *region, communication.*

communication theory—See *theory, communication.*

commutator—Same as *distributor.*

commutator pulse—See *pulse, commutator.*

COMPACT—A computer program compiler similar to the FORTRAN II, developed by Royal McBee, Inc., for the RPC 4000 computer.

Compact COBOL—See *COBOL, Compact.*

compaction, curve-fitting—A method of data compaction accomplished by substituting an analytical expression for the data to be stored or transmitted; for example, if the curve can be broken into a series of straight line segments, it may only be necessary to specify the slope, intercept, and applicable range for each segment; or a method of successive differences can be used to reduce the volume of data; or a polynomial can be used to express the data as a curve rather than as a large set of data. This method is slightly more sophisticated and more general than the slope-keypoint compaction method.

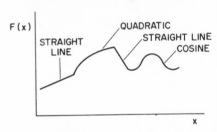

Data compaction by means of curve-fitting.

compaction, curve-pattern—A method of data compaction accomplished by specifying the code name or title given to a single or a set of prearranged curves or functions; for example, if the data is a set of exponential functions; it merely becomes necessary to store or transmit the parameter that specifies which member of the family the particular set of data best matches. The same is applicable to any set of straight lines, sine waves, etc. Thus, it may only become necessary to compare the data with a given family of curves and transmit the identity of the curve that most nearly matches the phenomena. This method is more sophisticated, but is generally more prone to the introduction of errors than the slope-keypoint method of data compaction.

compaction, data—Pertaining to the reduction of space, bandwidth, cost, and time for the generation, transmission, and storage of data by employing techniques designed to eliminate repetition, remove irrelevancy, and employ special coding techniques. Simply squeezing regular, or noncompacted, data into a smaller space, say by transferring data on punched cards to the same data on magnetic tape is not considered as data compaction. Some data compaction methods employ fixed tolerance bands, variable tolerance bands, slope-keypoints, sample changes, curve patterns, curve fitting, floating-point coding, variable precision coding, frequency analysis, and probability analysis.

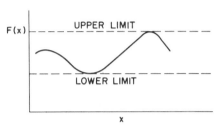

Data compaction *through the use of* fixed tolerance bands.

compaction, fixed-tolerance-band—A method of data compaction in which storage or transmission of data only becomes significant when the data deviates beyond preordained limits; for example, transmission will not take place unless the temperature is above or below a pair of values. The recipient of this information will assume that the value is in range unless a signal to the contrary is received. Since, in the usual case, the value is within range most of the time, transmission requirements are reduced. Procedures to make the system fail-safe must be implemented. This technique will reduce transmission space and time requirements.

compaction, floating-point coding—A method of numerical data compaction that employes the use of exponents to specify the scale or range, that is, set the decimal point, of a number. Each number is expressed as a number, called a coefficient, that is to be multiplied by a power of ten to express the actual magnitude. If the number is to be precise to four significant digits, then the coefficient of the power of 10 will have four digits; for example, the number 42,860,000 is expressed as 4286×10^4 or 4286(4) or 42864, where the last digit is always the exponent. The same number, rounded to two significant digits, might be sent or stored as 436, where again, the last digit is the exponent. Note that the original number occupied 8 positions, the last one only 3, only 38 percent of the original space.

compaction, frequency-analysis—A method of data compaction that uses an expression composed of a number of different frequencies of different magnitudes to express a curve; for example, a frequency or Fourier analysis of a periodic or nonperiodic function yields a set of fixed frequencies, usually harmonics of a fundamental variation, so that only the fundamental frequency of the sine wave and the coefficients of the harmonics are all that need be expressed to express the curve. The sum of these harmonics will reconstitute the curve at every point.

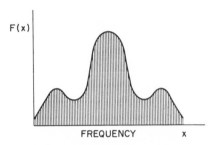

Data compaction *by means of* frequency analysis.

compaction, incremental—A method of data compaction in which only the initial value and all subsequent changes are stored or transmitted; for example, if a line voltage or a speed measurement is to be recorded or measured at each time interval or independent variable interval, only the change or deviation over the interval is stored, transmitted, or processed. Thus, instead of transmitting the numbers 102, 104, 105, 103, 100, 104, and 106, only the values 102, +2, +1, −2, −3, +4 and +2 are transmitted, which requires much less time and space.

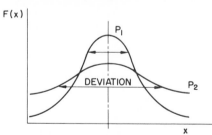

Data compaction *through the use of* probability analysis.

compaction, probability-analysis—A method of data compaction employing an analytical formulation characterized by expressing a distribution of a set of measurements or data by certain numbers; for example, the median and the deviation. Thus, one could transmit only the median value, and only those values that exceed one, two, or three standard deviations. This method is based on the assumption that only these large deviations are surely significant and require attention, action, or interpretation. All other data values need not be stored, transmitted, recorded, or considered.

compaction, sample-change—A method of data compaction accomplished by specifying a constant level or easily definable varying level of a value, parameter, or variable, and also specifying the deviations in discrete or continuous values; for example, the same degree of precision can be expressed with smaller numbers as can be expressed if the absolute values are stored, transmitted, or processed. Thus, by storing the average or median value, or if the average or median is transmitted, the entire curve can easily be reconstructed.

compaction, slope-keypoint—A data compaction method that employs the statement of a specific point of departure and a direction or slope of departure, until the deviation from a prescribed condition exceeds a specified value, whereupon a new keypoint and a new slope are specified. The storage requirement and the transmission time and space, therefore, are reduced from the uncompacted method of sending or storing absolute values.

compaction, storage—Increasing the efficiency of utilization of storage area, that is increasing the ratio of data stored to storage capacity, by relocating data in the storage unit; for example maximizing available main storage area in a computer by relocating active programs from fragmented to contiguous areas.

compaction, variable-precision coding—A method of data compaction that utilizes the concept that the precision required of a set of data can vary with the magnitude of the function, with time, or with the independent variable or other parameter; for example, in the countdown of a rocket launch, timing signals every 15 minutes are sufficient several days or hours before the launch. As time proceeds, time gets critical, intervals get shorter until at launch, fractions of a second become very significant.

compaction, variable-tolerance-band—A method of data compaction that uses several discrete bands to specify the operational limits of a quantity or parameter. Thus, several fixed-tolerance bands are specified; for example, a transmission will be made only if the variable, parameter, or quantity lies outside of the cited tolerance limits during specific time intervals. (Further clarified by *compaction, fixed-tolerance band.*)

comparative linguistics—See *linguistics, comparative.*

comparator—A device used to determine whether or not there is any difference

between two statements and if there is a difference, to determine a relationship between the two statements; for example, a device used to determine relationships between A and B, such as whether A is equal to, larger than, or smaller than B, and the difference between them. The device usually consists of a subtractor. Then, if A and B are equal, the output is zero. If A is larger, the output may be positive; if A is smaller, the output may be negative. Electrical signals usually represent the data. Sometimes the comparator is used to determine only agreement or disagreement, and so functions as a verifier or a checking device for various checks such as echo, duplicate equipment, duplicate recording, or read and compare what was written. Thus, the comparator may only be used to verify the accuracy of transmission. (Synonymous with *comparing unit*. Further clarified by *comparison, logic.*)

comparator, tape—A machine that automatically compares two supposedly identical tapes row by row and stops when there is a discrepancy. (Compare with *verifier, tape.*)

compare—To examine the representation of two quantities to determine their relative magnitudes or whether they are equal, for such purposes as checking, sorting, collating, placing them in a prescribed sequence, or discovering their relationship to zero. The comparison is often accomplished in a comparator. If only a determination as to whether or not two representations of quantities are identical is to be made, the operation is called a logic comparison. (Further clarified by *comparison, logic.*)

compare check, brush—See *check, brush-compare.*

comparing unit—Same as *comparator.*

comparison—The process of examining the representations of two quantities to determine their similarity or dissimilarity; thus, their identity, relative magnitude, or polarity. Usually the process terminates with a decision that initiates an action.

comparison, logic—A determination as to whether or not the representations of two quantities are identical. The comparison may be accomplished by an exclusive-OR gate. (Further clarified by *comparator,* by *compare,* and by *gate, exclusive-OR.*)

COMPASS—A computer program compiler and assembler developed by the United States Air Force for specific computers of the SAGE system.

compatibility, equipment—The ability of one device to accept and handle data that have been prepared, processed, or handled by another device without data conversion or code modification.

compatibility test—See *test, compatibility.*

compatible—Pertaining to a feature of a device, such as the width of tape acceptable to a computer, that permits it to perform operations or functions intended for execution by another device.

compile—In computer programming, to prepare a machine language program from a computer program written in another programming language by performing the usual functions of an assembler, or by making use of the characteristics of the overall logical structure, generating more than one machine instruction for each symbolic instruction, or both. Thus, one sequentially ordered machine language routine is the result.

compile-and-go—A computer operating technique or program execution technique in which there are no stops between the compiling, loading, and execution of a computer program.

compile phase—See *phase, compile.*

compiler—A computer program that prepares a machine language program from subroutines written in other programming languages by performing the usual functions of an assembler, or, by making use of the overall logical structure of the program, generating more than one machine instruction for each symbolic instruction, or both. A compiler is more complex than an assembler because a symbolic language instruction is not directly translatable by the compiler into a single machine instruction on a one-for-one basis. Also, extensive syntactic analysis of the symbolic language instructions is frequently required to arrive at the correct translation into machine code. The compiler may be required to direct operations, such as conversion selection, generation, allocation, interpretation, assembly, and recording; for example, a compiler may determine the intended meaning of a program element in the symbolic code, select or generate the required subroutine, transform the subroutine into machine language code, allocate specific storage locations or registers, enter it as an element in the machine language program, make a record of progress, and continue to the next element of the symbolic code. Sometimes a compiler contains its own library of closed subroutines. A compiler may convert a problem-oriented program into a machine-oriented program; hence, it is a useful automatic programming tool. (Synonymous with *compiling routine* and with *compiling program.* Further clarified

by *assembler,* by *interpreter,* by *translator,* and by *generator.*)

compiler, Boeing—A compiler developed by Boeing Airplane Company for use on the Univac 1103A computer.

compiler, Dow—An automatic coding system developed by Dow Chemical Company for use on the Burroughs 205 computer.

compiler generator—See *generator, compiler.*

compiler interface—See *interface, compiler.*

compiler library support—See *support, compiler library.*

compiling program—Same as *compiler.*

compiling routine—Same as *compiler.*

compiling time—See *time, compiling.*

COMPLEAT—A programmer developed by Burroughs Corporation for the Burroughs 205, 220, and E101 computers.

complement—A numeral derived from another numeral in accordance with one or more specified rules and bearing a specified relation to the other numeral. A complement does not come into being until the defining rule is stated and applied. The type of complement is determined by the rule that defines or generates it. The rule also defines the method of obtaining the particular complement. Complements have many useful purposes in digital computer computations. In many computers, a negative number is represented as the complement of the corresponding positive number. Thus, binary -101, which is octal -5, has as its complement binary $+010$, which is octal $+2$. However, 2 is the radix-minus-one complement of 5. Thus, in many digital computer registers, a negative number is represented by the complement of the absolute value of the number. When the excess-three binary-coded decimal system is used, a number and its negative are usually readily available in flip-flop registers. Thus, 1 0110 is equivalent to $+3$ and 0 1001 is equivalent to -6 in the excess-three binary-coded decimal system. In Boolean algebra, the complement of an element is the entire specified universe except the element; that is, the result of the NOT, negation, or all except operation. Thus, the complement of a Boolean element A is NOT A, symbolized as $\bar{A}$, A', or $\sim A$.

complement, diminished-radix—Same as *complement, radix-minus-one.*

complement, nines—The decimal numeral obtained by taking each digit of the

NUMERATION SYSTEM						
		BINARY		OCTAL		DECIMAL
NUMERAL		1 011000		6 30600		498900
COMPLEMENT	ONES	0 100111	SEVENS	1 47177	NINES	501099
	TWOS	0 101000	EIGHTS	1 47200	TENS	501100

Complements *for several numeration systems.*

decimal numeral whose nines complement is desired, subtracting it from nine, and writing the digits down, place by place. No carries are involved. For example, the nines complement of 5783 is 4216. Note that the sum of the numeral and its nines complement is a numeral consisting of all nines. Also, there are usually as many digits in the complement as in the original numeral. Either numeral is the complement of the other. A practical application of the nines complement is the excess-three binary-coded-decimal system of notation. Decimal three is represented as 0110. If the three is stored in a flip-flop register the opposite sides of the four flip-flops storing the three indicate 1001, which represents six. Thus, each decimal digit and its nines complement are immediately available. This situation has many practical advantages for performing calculations. In general, a nines complement is a radix-minus-one complement whose radix equals 10.

complement, noughts—Same as *complement, radix.*

complement, ones—The binary numeral obtained by taking each digit of the binary numeral whose ones complement is desired, subtracting it from one, and writing the digits down, place by place. No carries are involved. For example, the ones complement of 101101 is 010010. Note that the sum of the numeral and its ones complement is a numeral consisting of all ones. Also, there are usually as many digits in the complement as in the original numeral. Either numeral is the complement of the other. For a practical application, note that a ones complement of a binary numeral, and it can only be a binary numeral, is obtained simply by changing all its zeros to ones and its ones to zeros. A binary ones complement is always available at the other side of every flip-flop in a register storing a numeral. This proves to be very valuable in arithmetic computations, such as subtraction. In general, a ones complement is a radix-minus-one complement whose radix equals two.

complement, radix—In a given radix notation, the numeral obtained by taking each digit of a numeral whose radix complement is desired, subtracting it from the radix minus one, writing down each difference digit, place by place, and then adding a one to the least significant digit, executing all carries as required; for example, the tens complement in radix ten (decimal) notation and the twos complement in radix two (binary) notation; thus, the tens complement of 4830 is 5170 and the twos complement of 100100 is 011100. Radix complements prove valuable in calculations using digital computers. (Synonymous with *true complement*, with *noughts complement*, and with *zero complement*.)

complement, radix-minus-one—In a given radix notation, the numeral obtained by taking each digit of a numeral whose radix-minus-one complement is desired, subtracting it from the radix minus one, and writing down each difference digit, place by place. No carries are involved. For example, the nines complement in radix ten (decimal) notation and the ones complement in radix two (binary) notation, with the nines complement of 4830 equal to 5169 and the ones complement of 100100 equal to 011011. The radix complements prove valuable in calculations using digital computers. The radix-minus-one complements are readily available in many types of computer registers. (Synonymous with *diminished-radix complement*.)

complement, tens—A radix complement whose radix equals 10; for example, 5220 is the tens complement of 4780, in the decimal system. Note that the nines complement of 4780 is 5219, to which one must be added to the least significant digit and all carries propagated to obtain the tens complement, namely 5220.

complement, true—Same as *complement, radix.*

complement, twos—A radix complement whose radix equals two; for example, in the binary system, 011000 is the twos complement of 101000. Note that the ones complement of 101000 is 010111, to which one must be added to the least significant digit and all carries propagated to obtain the twos complement.

complement, zero—Same as *complement, radix.*

complement base—See *base, complement.*

complement on n—To determine the radix complement.

complement on n−1—To determine the radix-minus-one complement.

complementary operation—See *operation, complementary.*

complementary operator—See *operator, complementary.*

complementation, Boolean—Same as *NOT.*

complementer—1: Same as *element, negation.* 2: A device whose output is a representation of the complement of the number represented by its input; for example, a device whose output is 468 when its input is 531, that is, a nines complementer.

complete carry—See *carry, complete.*

complete operation—See *operation, complete.*

complex, equipment—A large interconnected group of equipment intended for a specific purpose; for example, several connected, large-scale, high-speed, electronic digital computing machines.

complex number—See *number, complex.*

component, quadrature—The reactive component of a current or a voltage caused by the inductive or capacitive reactance in a circuit. Thus, if a reference sinusoidally varying voltage is applied to a

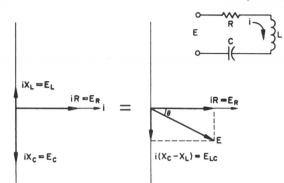

For the RLC series circuit, note how the voltage across capacitor C, inductor L, the combination of LC, and resistor R are quadrature components *of applied voltage E. Since capacitive reactance X_C is larger than inductive reactance X_L, the net reactance is capacitive, causing the current to lead the applied voltage by angle θ. Hence, E_R leads E_{LC} by the quadrature angle of 90°.*

pure inductance, the current that would flow would be lagging behind the voltage by 90 electrical degrees, and is said to be in quadrature. If a sinusoidally varying voltage is applied to a circuit made up of an inductance and a resistance in series, the voltage drops across the resistor and inductor are quadrature components of the applied voltage.

component, solid-state—An electrical or electronic component whose operation depends on the control of electric or magnetic phenomena in solids; for example, a transistor, crystal diode, resistor, or ferrite. The term is used to distinguish these components from those that depend on phenomena that occur in a vacuum or rarefied gas, such as vacuum tubes or gas tubes. Solid-state components are proving to be of greater reliability, increased life, decreased size, and greater efficiency.

COMPOOL—A communications pool developed by System Development Corporation; for example, a collection of information relating all item tags, table tags, constants, parameters, and programs to absolute storage locations. A COMPOOL may be on magnetic tape, on cards, or in print.

composite cable—See *cable, composite.*

compound statement—See *statement, compound.*

COMPREHENSIVE—A system of automatic coding developed by Massachusetts Institute of Technology for use on the Whirlwind I computer.

compression, data—A method of increasing the amount of data that can be stored in a given space or reducing the amount of storage space required to store a given amount of data.

compression, digit—Any technique used to increase the number of digits that may be stored in a given space; for example, storing three binary-coded decimal digits in the same space as two six-bit characters.

computation, address—A computation that produces or modifies the address part of an instruction word.

computational stability—See *stability, computational.*

computer—1: A device capable of solving problems by accepting data, performing prescribed operations on the data, and supplying the results of these operations. In information processing, usually an automatic, stored-program computer is implied. Types of computers are so varied and abundant that it is usually necessary to specify the type of system, such as analog, digital, internally stored program, and electronic. The typical computer, or automatic data processor, is capable of performing sequences of arithmetic and logic operations, not only on data, but also on its own program, which is usually stored internally, although some computers store programs externally, in such media as cards, paper tapes, and plugboards. If the program is inserted manually, the term calculator is used, rather than computer. If the program is held on tape or cards during execution, the machine is also usually called a calculator. A computer should be able to accept, store, execute, and modify its own program; otherwise it is a trivial processor. In a very narrow sense, a computer can only perform arithmetic operations, make logic decisions or manipulate data. However, these functions are usually relegated to the arithmetic and logic unit, and we speak of the computer as having (1) an input; (2) a storage, or memory; (3) an arithmetic and logical unit; (4) a control unit; and (5) an output. Without any one of these five main units, the system is not a computer in the full sense. Of course it may have a multiplicity of any of these units. A computer is a piece of machinery. A person is no longer implied by the term. **2:** A data processor that can perform computation, such as arithmetic or logic operations, usually without intervention by a human operator during a run.

computer, analog—A computer that solves problems by operating on continuous variables that represent continuous data, rather than by operating in discrete form as in digital computers. Thus, the physical variables are represented by means of an analog. Various types of amplifiers, properly connected, perform various kinds of arithmetic operations, such as summation, multiplication, integration, and differentiation. Accuracy is limited by the precision with which parts can be made, and the extent to which electrical circuit elements change with environmental variations, such as changes in temperature, whereas the precision of a digital computer is dependent upon the number of digit positions or places handled by the computer's components, taking both time and space into consideration. Both input and output data are in analog form. Analog systems are usually faster than digital systems, since only electrical propagation time through the system limits the speed. Briefly, an analog computer measures values, like an ordinary voltmeter, whereas a digital computer counts, as a counter counting weighted pulses. The analog computer solves problems by translating physical conditions, such as numbers, flow, temperature, pressure, angular position, or speed into related mechanical or electrical quantities and uses mechanical or electrical circuits as an analog for the physical phenomenon being represented. Usually a one-to-one correspondence exists between (1) each numerical variable occurring in the problem, with its solution; and (2) a varying physical measurement, such as voltage or rotation, in the analog computer; that is, an analog computer is a physical system in which the analysis or solution of the problem is mirrored by the varying behavior of the physical system. A Honeywell Electrik Tel-O-Set process temperature controller is an example of an analog computer. The measured temperature is converted into an electrical quantity (milliamperes) that varies in magnitude as the temperature varies. This electrical quantity is the input to the computer. The electrical circuitry of the controller is analogous to the problem to be solved; that is, maintenance of the measured temperature at some preset value. This circuitry weighs the measured value of the temperature, calculates the amount of resetting of the final control element, such as a valve or damper, needed to return the temperature to the desired value, and sends the resulting corrective signal to the final control element. Most analog computers work in real time: they continuously offer the solution of the problem they are solving. (Contrast with *computer, digital* and with *analyzer, digital differential.* Further clarified by *analog* and by *device, analog.*)

computer, arbitrary sequence—A computer in which each program instruction explicitly specifies the location of the next instruction to be executed.

computer, asynchronous—A computer in which each event or the performance of

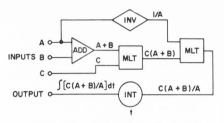

A connection of the parts of an analog computer *for a specific set of operations on a set of input variables A, B, and C.*

each operation is initiated by a signal generated by the completion of a previous event or operation or by the availability of the parts of the computer required for the next event or operation. Thus, an asynchronous computer will run slightly faster if it is cooled down, because circuit response time, or the time constant, is decreased as resistances are lowered at reduced temperatures. A clocking pulse is not required for an asynchronous computer. (Contrast with *computer, synchronous.*)

computer, automatic—A computer that can execute groups or sequences of arithmetic and logic operations without continuous human intervention.

computer, buffered—A computer that has a special storage device used to hold input data, output data, or both and that arrives or is to depart at irregular intervals and not at the time it is needed or at the time an output device is ready to accept it. This permits a computer to read, write, and compute simultaneously and obviates the need for frequently testing for the availability of a data channel for the transfer of data between the input-output units and the main processing unit. Buffering also permits matching an asynchronous source of data with a synchronous computer. Thus, while a buffer is being filled or emptied, the computer can work away at earlier data.

computer, concurrent—A computer that executes two or more instructions simultaneously, such as read, print, and compute. The concurrent actions occur under the control of the program or can be accomplished automatically by the computer as they are detected. (Contrast with *computer, sequential;* with *computer, program-controlled sequential;* and with *computer, logic-controlled sequential.*)

computer, consecutive—Same as *computer, sequential.*

computer, consecutive sequence—A computer that executes instructions in an implicitly defined sequence, unless a jump instruction specifies the location of the next instruction to be executed.

computer, digital—A computer that solves problems by operating on variables expressed as data in discrete form and by performing arithmetic and logic operations on these data. Numbers in a digital computer are represented as space-time distributions in media such as punched-holes, magnetic-core arrays, strings of electrical pulses on a line in time sequence or in space sequence, magnetized spots in a surface of tapes, drums, and discs, charged spots on a cathode-ray tube screen, or characters printed on a page. Digital data is discontinuous in form, represented by such models as combinations of binary digit patterns. In an analog computer, data is represented in a continuous form. The typical digital computer is the internally stored program, electronic type that can store instructions calling for the execution of sequences of operations, execute these instructions, and modify them according to the results obtained, as well as store and utilize the data to be operated upon. (Contrast with *computer, analog.*)

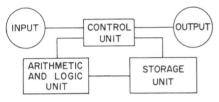

Basic parts of a digital computer.

computer, duplex—A pair of identical computers operated so that when one is shut down for maintenance, checkout, or improvements, the other can operate without a reduction in capability of the total system. One computer might be slaved to the other for continuity of operations in the event of a malfunction, to avoid the slightest interruption. One of the computers might continuously check the results of the other, or it might be only running test problems. Use of each computer might alternate, providing time for preventive maintenance on both. One might run relatively low priority problems.

computer, electronic—A computer composed of electrical and electronic circuits that perform all control, arithmetic, and decision-making operations through the use of elements such as tubes, transistors, diodes, capacitors, magnetic cores, and magnetic thin-films. An electronic computer is usually an automatic computer.

computer, fixed-point—A computer that requires that the arithmetic point, such as the decimal or binary point, remain in a fixed location in all registers, storage locations, and number expressions, with the result that all numbers lie between −1 and +1. This requires that all numbers and results be scaled between these values. In most general-purpose, fixed-point digital computers, floating-point operations can

only be accomplished by programming. (Contrast with *computer, floating-point.*)

computer, floating-point—A computer that has the built-in circuitry for automatically controlling the location of the arithmetic point, such as the decimal or binary point, without the use of programming steps specifically for that purpose. In many automatic, electronic, digital, general-purpose computers, floating-point operations may only be programmed. These are not floating-point computers. A floating-point computer accepts data in floating-point notation; usually, a single bit in the instruction word specifies whether a fixed-point or a floating-point operation is intended. The automatic floating-point feature facilitates scaling of numbers to ensure that they remain within the range of numbers the machine is capable of handling and expressing. (Contrast with *computer, fixed-point.*)

computer, general-purpose—A computer designed to solve a broad class of problems; typically, a stored-program, digital computer used in applications where the exact nature of many problems may not be known before the machine is designed. The program can be changed rapidly to permit many different sequences of computations to be performed. (Contrast with *computer, special-purpose.*)

computer, hybrid—1: A mixed analog and digital computing system. 2: A computer that makes use of both analog and discrete representation of data.

computer, incremental—A computer in which changes in the variables rather than the variables themselves are represented in absolute value. The changes that occur correspond to a change in some common independent variable. Usually the correspondence is that which is defined by the equations being solved. This method of representing variables is called incremental representation. The principal type of computing unit in many incremental computers is a digital integrator. The operation of a digital integrator is similar to that of an integrating mechanism, and such computers are often referred to as digital differential analyzers (DDA). These incremental computers do not make use of adders, but they use the digital integrator, connected in a manner so as to perform approximate addition. (Further clarified by *adder, soft* and *adder, hard.*)

computer, logic-controlled sequential—A sequential computer that executes instructions in a sequence determined by the built-in logic of the computer; thus, a fixed sequence, unless overridden by an instruction; for example, a computer that contains a storage unit and a number of different units used to perform different portions of the computation in turn, the intermediate results being stored for subsequent reuse. Since practical storage units are usually digital, sequential computers are usually digital computers. The control unit has built-in logic that controls the sequence of operations, one at a time, with little or no concurrent action. (Contrast with *computer, program-controlled sequential* and with *computer, concurrent.*)

computer, parallel—A digital computer that handles all digits of the same word simultaneously. Thus, if 40 binary digits comprise a single word and the 40 bits are transferred to storage, each bit is transferred over one of 40 separate wires and all 40 bits at the same time. For a computer to qualify as parallel, the main arithmetic and logic unit must process all digits at the same time, except in carry propagation or some similar action. Thus a computer using a serial adder is not a parallel computer. It is usually implied that a parallel computer has a parallel access storage unit, such as a random-access, coincident-current, magnetic-core storage unit rather than a serial-access storage unit, such as a magnetostrictive delay-line storage unit. (Contrast with *computer, serial.*)

computer, program-controlled sequential—A sequential computer that executes instructions in a sequence determined by the program. Thus, each instruction determines the location of the next instruction to be executed, such as the usual four-address digital computer. (Contrast with *computer, logic-controlled sequential* and with *computer, concurrent.*)

computer, self-adapting—1: A computer that can change its performance characteristics in response to changes in its environment; for example, a computer that can change its configuration so as to more effectively handle changes in the nature of problems it is required to resolve. 2: A computer that can perform its designed function without interruption in spite of changes in its environment.

computer, self-organizing—A computer that can automatically rearrange its internal structure; for example, a digital computer that automatically rearranges its internal logic connections in order to minimize the running time for the execution of a program.

computer, sequential—A computer that executes instructions in a prescribed sequence, one instruction at a time, without any concurrent action, such as reading while computing or reading while writing while computing. The sequence may be determined *a priori* by the built-in logic or by the program, or it might be controlled by computer-made decisions based on results of operations. (Further clarified by *computer, program-controlled sequential* and by *computer, logic-controlled sequential.* Contrast with *computer, concurrent.*)

computer, serial—A digital computer that handles the digits of the same word in time sequence, one at a time. Thus, if 40 binary digits comprise a single word, and two words are added, a serial adder adds corresponding bits by corresponding bits starting with the least significant digit pair; the resultant carry is added in with the next digit pair, using a full serial adder. Usually, in a serial machine, numbers are transferred over one wire, and a serial storage device is used, such as an acoustic delay line. A computer is considered serial if it handles characters serially, even if the bits of a character are handled in parallel fashion. This method is often called the serio-parallel fachion of handling characters. (Contrast with *computer, parallel.*)

computer, simultaneous—A computer organized in such a manner that a separate unit is available to perform each portion of the entire computation, usually a new portion being initiated before a previous portion is completed, and therefore executing operations somewhat concurrently. The units may be interconnected in a way determined by the computation; for example, a differential analyzer. (Synonymous with *simultaneous-operation computer.*)

computer, simultaneous-operation—Same as *computer, simultaneous.*

computer, slave—A computer used in a slave application. (Further clarified by *application, slave.*)

computer, solid-state—An electronic computer whose active circuit elements are magnetic elements, semiconductors, or other solid-state devices that do not involve the use of electrons or ions in free space or gases. Thus, a solid-state computer does not make use of vacuum tubes or gas tubes, except, perhaps, for a cathode-ray tube for display purposes or sets of neon bulbs for indicator lights. Until 1955, none of the dozens of types of electronic computers were solid-state computers; now nearly all systems being manufactured are of the solid-state type.

computer, special-purpose—A computer designed to solve a restricted class of problems more efficiently than a general-purpose computer; for example, a computer designed to receive target information and compute and dispatch projectile trajectory instructions or a computer designed specifically to control a particular industrial process, such as a steel-rolling mill operation. Most special-purpose computers operate from a fixed, internally stored program or from built-in, fixed-logic networks, although some operate from a program stored on an external storage medium, such as a punched card or a punched tape. (Contrast with *computer, general-purpose.*)

computer, stored-program—A digital computer that, under the control of an initial set of instructions, can synthesize, interpret, alter, and store instructions as though they were data and can execute these new instructions as though they were the initial instructions. In the simplest situation, the program that is stored is executed without modification. In most electronic computers, the program is stored internally, usually in high-speed storage, so that instructions are rapidly accessible. The program can be stored externally, such as on a wired plugboard, a punched card that is read as needed, or a strip of punched paper tape, also read as needed.

computer, synchronous—A computer in which each event or the performance of each operation is started or controlled by a signal generated by a clock. Clock signals are usually equally spaced pulses that are distributed throughout the computer. These pulses assist in the timing and shaping of all pulses in the computer, usually a digital computer. (Contrast with *computer, asynchronous.*)

computer, target—The particular computer configuration on which a specific program is to be run.

computer, wired-program—A computer whose program of operations to be executed are specified by the spatial distribution of electrical circuit elements, such as wires, plugs, magnetic slugs, magnetic rope, and diodes. In a wired plugboard computer, the wires are held in a removable plugboard, allowing the plugboard to be removed and saved for later reuse. If the program is wired in permanently, the computer is called a wired-in program computer or a fixed-program computer. A computer with a plugboard memory, or a fixed-core pluggable memory plane, is called a semifixed program computer.

computer application—See *application, computer.*

computer architecture—See *architecture, computer.*

computer-assisted management—See *management, computer-assisted.*

computer capacity—Same as *range, number.*

computer code—See *code, computer.*

computer configuration—See *configuration, computer.*

computer-dependent language—Same as *language, machine-oriented.*

computer graphics—See *graphics, computer.*

computer installation—See *installation, computer.*

computer instruction—See *instruction, computer.*

computer instruction set—Same as *set, machine instruction.*

computer language—Same as *language, machine.*

computer-limited—A condition of computer operation wherein the time required for computation exceeds the time required for some other type of operation, such as card reading, tape reading, card punching, or printing. Such a situation often occurs in computers performing scientific types of calculations. The condition may occur only at certain times during the execution of a routine. The condition is particularly applicable to those computers that allow concurrent reading, computing, writing, and transferring operations. If the computing time is less than that required for other operations, then the system is otherwise limited, such as input-output limited, reader limited, or storage limited.

computer network—See *network, computer.*

computer operation—See *operation, computer.*

computer-oriented language—**1:** Same as *language, machine-oriented.* **2:** Same as *COL.*

computer output microfilm—See *microfilm, computer output.*

computer program—See *program, computer.*

computer program, baseball—See *program, baseball computer.*

computer program origin—See *origin, computer program.*

computer run—Same as *run.*

computer-sensitive language—See *language, computer-sensitive.*

computer service organization—See *organization, computer service.*

computer simulation—See *simulation, computer.*

computer simulator—See *simulator, computer.*

computer store—Same as *storage.*

computer word—See *word, computer.*

computing—The interpretation and execution of operations involving arithmetic and logic calculations in accordance with precisely defined rules and procedures.

computing amplifier—See *amplifier, computing.*

computing machinery—See *machinery, computing.*

concatenate—To unite in a series or to link together or to chain; for example, to form a series of mathematical terms or to form larger mathematical series from several smaller series. (Synonymous with *catenate.* Further clarified by *catena.*)

concentrator—In telecommunications, a multiplexor that is limited in capability in that it cannot handle all the communications channels to which it is connected at once. Thus, a concentrator cannot handle contention if it occurs. For example, if a concentrator is designed to handle up to six lines at once, but twelve are connected, when the seventh subscriber tries to obtain a channel, it will receive a busy signal until one of the busy lines is released. An example of a concentrator is a switched telephone network. All subscribers can access each other theoretically, but the system is configured to expect this situation to never happen. Lines are used on a first-come-first-served basis. If these devices operate under computer control, they should be called front-end processors, not concentrators.

concept classification—See *classification, concept.*

concept coordination—Same as *classification, concept.*

concurrent—Pertaining to the occurrence of two or more events within the same specified time period. (Contrast with *consecutive,* with *sequential,* and with *simultaneous.*)

concurrent batch processing—See *processing, concurrent batch.*

concurrent computer—See *computer, concurrent.*

concurrent operation—See *operation, concurrent.*

condensed deck—See *deck, condensed.*

condenser storage—Same as *storage, capacitor.*

condition, entry—In computer programming, a specified and necessary requirement that must be met before a routine may be entered; for example, that a counter reach a certain number or that the addresses of those locations from which the routine will take its operands and links be specified.

condition, restart—A condition of a system that can be reestablished and that permits restarting a sequence of events or conditions; for example, in the execution of a computer program, a condition that permits the restart of the whole or part of the program.

conditional branch—Same as *jump, conditional.*

conditional breakpoint instruction—See *instruction, conditional breakpoint.*

conditional control transfer instruction—Same as *instruction, conditional jump.*

conditional entropy—See *entropy, conditional.*

conditional implication gate—1: Same as *gate, A OR NOT B.* 2: Same as *gate, B OR NOT A.*

conditional information content—See *content, conditional information.*

conditional jump—See *jump, conditional.*

conditional jump instruction—See *instruction, conditional jump.*

conditional statement—See *statement, conditional.*

conditional transfer—Same as *jump, conditional.*

conditional transfer instruction—Same as *instruction, conditional jump.*

conditioning, signal—Processing the form of a signal so as to make it more easily intelligible to or compatible with a given device or a human; for example, pulse shaping, filtering, clipping, digitizing, and linearizing, analog to digital conversion, differentiating, and amplifying.

configuration, computer—The specific set of equipment connected together to form a single computing system for a given computer run; for example, a main-frame control unit, a high-speed storage unit of $16,384$ words, a $65,000$-word magnetic-disc storage unit, six magnetic tape stations, a card reader, a card punch, and a high-speed online printer.

configuration, contact—The general arrangement of contacts in a multiple-contact connector. The configuration specification includes the number, spacing, location, orientation, and other factors relating to the contacts in the connector.

conjunction—Same as *AND.*

conjunction gate—Same as *gate, AND.*

conjunction operation—See *operation, conjunction.*

conjunctive paths—See *paths, conjunctive.*

conjunctive search—See *search, conjunctive.*

connection—In data networks, a data path between two or more stations.

connection, analog regenerative—Same as *connection, regenerative.*

connection, make—In switching networks, to set up a temporary connection; that is, using switching equipment.

connection, permanent—In switching networks, a connection made without switching equipment.

connection, point-to-point—A data network configuration in which a connection is made between two terminal installations and that usually includes switching facilities.

connection, regenerative—An analog computer connection devised by O. Amble, in which the output of an integrator contributes through an adder to its own input, x, to solve the differential equations of the form: $dx = -(y - 1)dx + u_1du_2 + u_3du_4 + \ldots$, where $y, u_1, u_2, \ldots$ are input variables and x is the output variable. For example, if $u_1 = -x$ and $u_2 = y$, then $x = 1/y$ and u_1du_2, which is also available, allows log y to be obtained. (Synonymous with *Amble's method* and with *analog regenerative connection.*)

connection, release—In switching networks, to break a connection between called and calling station.

connection, temporary—In switching networks, a connection made with switching equipment.

connection box—See *box, connection.*

connective—In Boolean algebra, the symbol that specifies the operation to be performed. The connective is usually written between the operands.

connective, logical—Specific words that make new statements from given, usually conditional statements. The truth or falsity of the new statements can be calculated from the truth or falsity of the given statements and the logical meaning of the connective; for example, AND, OR, NEITHER . . . NOR, IF . . . THEN, EXCEPT, and DON'T CARE. Thus, the statement, "IF it is red, THEN stop," is the same as "EITHER it is not red OR stop." The statement may be written symbolically $\bar{R} + S$, where $\bar{R}$ is not red, S is stop, and + is the OR logical connective or operator. Most logical connectives are operators; however, sometimes a connective pair, such as EITHER . . . OR, may be represented as + and be simply called OR. Thus, A + B may read EITHER A OR B, or simply A OR B. For a method of converting an IF . . . THEN statement to an EITHER . . . OR statement, refer to the illustration. (Synonymous with *logical connector*. Further clarified by *statement, conditional.*)

1.	R	0	0	1	1
2.	S	0	1	0	1
3.	T	1	1	0	1
4.	R̄	1	1	0	0
5.	R̄+S	1	1	0	1

A truth table of designation numbers for various Boolean functions and variables showing the equivalence of the logical connectives IF R THEN S and EITHER NOT R OR S.

connector, electrical—Any device used to terminate or connect electrical conductors; for example, a multicontact device used to join many conductors of one cable to many conductors of another cable. (Synonymous with *plug*.)

connector, feed-through—An electrical connector or terminal block, usually with double-ended terminals that permit simple distribution and busing of electrical circuits; or a bushing in a wall or a bulkhead separating compartments at different pressure levels with terminations or caps on both sides.

connector, flowchart—A symbol used to represent the junction of two consecutive lines of flow on a flowchart, a block diagram, or a logic diagram; the divergence of one flowline into more than one; or a break in a single flowline for continuation in another area.

connector, front-mounted—A connector attached to the outside of a panel. A front-mounted connector can be installed and its mating half inserted and removed only from the outside of the equipment.

connector, hermaphroditic—A connector whose mating parts are exactly alike at their mating face and have no male or female members, but have provisions for maintaining correct polarity, hot-lead protection, sealing, and mechanical and electrical coupling.

connector, interchangeable—A connector of one manufacturer that can mate with another made by a different manufacturer, or a connector that has inserts for various contact configurations that can be interchanged in the standard shell or holder.

connector, logical—Same as *connective, logical*.

connector, modular—An electrical connector that has similar or identical attachable sections that can be assembled to provide an ideal connector type or size for a given application.

connector, multiple—A flowchart connector used to indicate the convergence of several flowlines into one line, or the divergence of one flowline into several lines.

connector, right-angle edge—A connector whose plug is mounted on a chassis or back panel and whose receptacle is mounted along an edge of a printed-circuit board. The receptacle is soldered to the circuits. Its pins usually are of simple rod stock bent at right angles and molded into the receptacle insert. The board and receptacle assembly is inserted into the plug to complete the circuit wiring.

connector, socket—A connector that has socket contacts into which a plug connector having male contacts is inserted.

connector, umbilical—A connector used to connect electrical cables and materiel hoses, such as fuel, oxidizer, and water, to a vehicle, such as a rocket, missile, aircraft, or railroad car, and that is removed at time of launch or departure.

connector, variable—In flowcharting, a flowchart connector that represents a connection that is not fixed but that can be varied by the flowcharted procedure itself; or an instruction in a computer program that corresponds to a variable connector appearing in a flowchart. Thus, the variable connector indicates the joining of one flowline to one of two or more related lines of flow. It is the option of connecting a given point to more than one other point in a flowchart that brings about the variation. (Synonymous with *N-way switch* and with *programmed switch*.

connector assembly—See *assembly, connector*.

connector flange—See *flange, connector*.

connector frame—See *frame, connector*.

consecutive—Pertaining to the occurrence of two events in time or space sequence without the occurrence of any other such event between them. (Contrast with *concurrent*, with *sequential*, and with *simultaneous*.)

consecutive computer—Same as *computer, sequential*.

consecutive sequence computer—See *computer, consecutive sequence*.

consistent network—See *network, consistent*.

consistent unit—See *unit, consistent*.

console—The part of a system, such as a computer, process controller, or operations controller, that is used for communication between the operators or service personnel and the system. The console usually contains a panel for lights, keys, switches, and related circuits for man-machine communication. It may be a desklike unit, permitting the seating of personnel, and may be used for manual control; error and malfunction detection, location, and correction; mounting display registers and counters; revising storage contents; entering data; checking data flow; mounting a typewriter, and assisting in various forms of monitoring and supervising. (Further clarified by *desk, control*.)

console, operator—A device or equipment that is used for communication between a human operator and a system.

console, utility control—A computer console used primarily to control utility and maintenance programs.

constant—A quantity or data or data representation that does not vary in value; for example, a fixed computer word used as a constant, that is, a coefficient, in a differential equation being solved by the computer. (Related to *parameter* and *variable*.)

constant, figurative—A name given to or an identifier for a specified constant in a particular programming language.

constant, instruction—A constant written in the same form as a computer instruction, but not to be executed as an instruction, and so usable as a dummy instruction.

constant, time—The ratio of the inductance to the resistance in an electric circuit consisting of inductance and resistance, or the product of the capacitance and the resistance in an electric circuit consisting of capacitance and resistance. The time constant is measured in seconds. After three time constants have expired a particular transient will have a remaining trace of about 5 percent of the original voltage, current, or charge. Thus, if a resistor, R, is connected across a charged capacitor, C, after 3RC seconds have passed from the instant of connection, only 5 percent of the initial charge, current, and voltage will remain in the circuit.

constant area—See *area, constant*.

constant-multiplier coefficient unit—Same as *scalar*.

constant storage—Same as *area, constant*.

constraint—An imposed or natural limit, bound, or condition within which the solution of a problem must be obtained; for example, management policy, economic condition, geographical limit, word length, or room size.

Constructs—A computer-directed system developed by Control Data Corporation for production of construction drawings.

contact, bifurcated—A flat spring contact that has been slotted lengthwise to increase the flexibility of the spring and provide additional points of contact. Bifurcated contacts are used in printed-circuit connectors.

contact, electrical—1: The element in a connector that makes the electrical joint, path, or touch between the two halves of

the connector. **2:** The point of joining in the electrical connection.

contact, normally closed—A pair of contacts on a relay that is open only when the relay coil is energized.

contact, normally open—A pair of contacts on a relay that is closed only when the relay coil is energized.

contact, pin—A male-type contact designed to mate with a socket, or female contact. The pin contact is usually connected to the "dead" side of a circuit, which is the connector half that is not energized when the connector is disconnected.

contact, smooth—A pin or socket contact that has a relatively smooth profile or flush surface. The smooth contact does not have a locking spring projecting from its side, as does the standard contact, but is locked to the connector body by other methods.

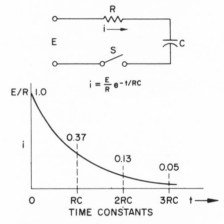

$$i = \frac{E}{R} e^{-t/RC}$$

If current i equals zero when switch S is closed, the initial current is E/R, which decays to E/Re at t equal RC, to E/Re² at t equals 2RC, and to E/Re³ at t equal 3RC. Thus, at t equal 3 times the time constant, i.e., 3RC, the current is 1/e³, or 0.05E/R. Note: e equals the base of the natural log ≈2.718.

contact, socket—A female-type contact designed to mate with a pin, or male socket. The socket contact is usually connected to the "live" side of a circuit, since the contact is usually recessed below the outer surface of the connector. The "live" side is the connector half that is energized when the connector is disconnected.

contact alignment—See *alignment, contact*.

contact area—See *area, contact*.

contact configuration—See *configuration, contact*.

contact engaging force—See *force, contact engaging*.

contact float—Same as *alignment, contact*.

contact separating force—See *force, contact separating*.

contacts, grid-spaced—Electrical contacts, such as pins, surfaces, or spring-type, arranged in parallel, equally spaced rows and columns on any connector, such as a multiple contact connector or on the edge of a printed-circuit board.

content—The data held in a storage device or at a particular storage location, such as the location in storage specified by an address or a particular register. Often the symbol ( ) is used to indicate "the contents of." Thus, in computer programming, (M) means the contents of the storage location whose address is M; (A) indicates the contents of register A; and (T$_2$) indicates the contents of the reel of magnetic tape on unit 2.

content, average transinformation—Same as *content, mean transinformation*.

content, conditional information—The measure of information contained in the occurrence of an event of a specified conditional probability given the occurrence of another event.

content, decision—A measure of the number of decisions needed to select an event from among a number of mutually exclusive events. The decision content is given as the logarithm of the number of events. An event might be the occurrence of a specified character or word in a given position in a message.

content, information—A measure of the information conveyed by the occurrence of an event of definite probability.

content, mean transinformation—The mean or average of the transinformation content that is conveyed by the occurrence of any one of a finite number of mutually exclusive and jointly exhaustive events. Thus, the mean transinformation content is equal to the difference between the entropy of one of two sets of events and the conditional entropy of this set relative to the other set. (Synonymous with *average transinformation content*.)

content, transinformation—The difference between the information content of a set of data conveyed by an event and the conditional information content conveyed by the same event given the occurrence of another event. (Synonymous with *mutual information* and with *transferred information*.)

content-addressed storage—Same as *storage, associative*.

contention—1: In communications, a condition on a communication channel when two or more transmitting locations try to transmit at the same time. 2: In an operating system, a data processing system, or a communication system, a rivalry for the use of a system resource.

context—The text immediately surrounding a given word or group of words. Thus, the context consists of words that occur both before and after a particular group of words. The context tends to have an influence on the intended or implied meaning of a given word. A word might lose its meaning or become ambiguous when it is taken out of context. For instance, in the statement, "The hood was casing the joint," hood is not a head covering, to case is not to enclose, and a joint is not a joining of materials. These words take on new meanings in view of the context.

continuous form cards—See *cards, continuous form*.

continuous progression code—Same as *code, unit-distance*.

continuous progressive code—Same as *code, unit-distance*.

contract, job—An obligation on the part of an operating system to perform a job.

CONTRAN—(Control Translator). A compiler language, developed by Honeywell Data Processing Division, that uses the best features of FORTRAN IV and ALGOL 60 programming languages.

contrast—In optical character recognition (OCR), the difference between the color, reflectance, or shading of one area of a surface and the same characteristic of another area. (Further clarified by *ratio, print contrast;* by *ratio, reflectance;* by *reflectance, ink;* by *reflectance, background;* by *reflectance, spectral;* and by *coefficient, reflection*.)

control—In a digital computer, the section that selects the next instruction, interprets the address and operation parts, and executes the instruction by applying the proper signals to the arithmetic and logic unit and other parts of the computing system in accordance with the interpretation. Thus, the control is one of the five basic parts of any computer: namely, input, storage, arithmetic unit, output, and control. In general, the control may be one or more components, in any machine, that are responsible for interpreting and executing directions. The control might be manual or automatic. Sometimes, a mathematical check or a checking procedure is called a control. Thus, to regulate actions or details, such as details for equipment, data, procedures, or concepts, all within specified control limits. Some of the parts of the control unit are the instruction control, the operation control, the program control, and the selection control. Also, to control a computer is to direct the sequence of execution of the instructions in the program. (Further clarified by *control, program*.)

control, automatic—Control accomplished without human intervention, such as by a device that automatically receives measurements of one or more physical variables involved in a process, automatically performs calculations with these variables, and automatically directs suitable actions so that the process is properly regulated or controlled.

Sometimes the device is called an automatic controller.

control, cascade–An automatic control system in which two or more control units are linked in series, each control unit regulating the operation of the next control unit in line. Thus, the output signals of one are the input to the next.

control, data access–In a data processing system, any of the techniques available to the user for moving data between main storage and an input-output device or channel. The techniques are usually part of the operating system. Examples of data access control techniques include direct, indexed, keyed, queued, and sequential access.

control, dynamic–A method of operating a digital computer in which the computer can alter the instructions as the computation proceeds, the sequence in which the instructions are executed, or both.

control, feedback–Control of a machine, system, or process by allowing the output to affect the input. (Further clarified by *feedback*.)

control, file access–To control access to a file, usually to prevent unauthorized access to a file, including read access, write access, or both. (Related to *password*.)

control, fire–Control over the aiming, timing, and firing of weapons. Many automatic fire-control systems use computers to compute the aiming, timing, and firing of guns and the flight control of missiles.

control, format–Control of the arrangement of data in a given medium; for example, the use of a computer to determine the layout of data through programming instructions, such as spacing instructions and zero suppression.

control, forms–The management function that assures that unneeded forms are not prepared and that needed forms are designed, produced, and distributed economically and efficiently.

control, instruction–In a computing system, the control device that interprets instructions received from storage and sends these instructions to the other units of the computer for execution. The instruction control unit is part of the computer control unit and one of the five basic parts of all computers, the others being input, output, storage, and the arithmetic and logic unit. (Further clarified by *control, selection*.)

control, job–Functions performed by a control program, executive program, or supervisor that regulate the use of system resources for each job; for example, the use of the central processing unit, storage areas, and some peripheral online equipment, though usually not input-output devices. (Closely related to *management, job*.)

control, loop–The parts of a loop that operate upon the loop control variables so as to determine whether to execute the instructions in the main part of the loop, that is, execute the loop, or exit from the loop. (Further clarified by *variable, loop control*)

control, manual–The direction of a machine by manual methods, such as the direction of a computer by means of the console operator rather than by a stored program or the control of an aircraft directly by the pilot rather than by the autopilot.

control, master–Same as *program, master-control*.

control, numerical–1: The general field of design, development, manufacture, and application of digital-control equipment for regulating, controlling, or directing industrial processes or operations. Numerical control began by using digital media, such as punched cards, punched tape, and digital computers to program and control machine tools, such as automatic screw machines. The lathe operations, such as drilling, turning, and knurling, are controlled in accordance with a pattern of holes. Thus, a binary number would specify the depth of drill or cut. Numerical control includes the use of digital computers to program and control industrial processes. 2: The automatic control of a process, or device that performs a process, that uses numerical data usually introduced while the process or device is in operation.

control, operation–In a computing system, the control device that directs the arithmetic operation involved in the execution of an instruction. The operation control may assist the instruction control unit; it may be part of the computer control unit, one of the five basic parts of all computers, the others being input, output, storage, and the arithmetic and logic unit.

control, process–1: The control of industrial processes, usually continuous processes, for the manufacture of material, such as refining oil or making paper; or for the transformation of energy, such as generating electricity or producing illuminating gas from coal; or for providing a service, such as processing airlines trip reservations. Usually automatic process control is inferred, as well as continuous process control, while numerical control implies control of discrete processes, such as the control of sets or sequences of automatic machine tool operations. 2: The control of a process by automatic means, such as one in which a computer is used for the regulation of continuous or sequential operations.

control, program–In a computing system, the control device that controls each step in the program; for example, it sets up each arithmetic operation prior to execution by making arrangements within certain circuits. The program control unit is usually a part of the computer control unit, one of the five basic parts of all computers, the others being input, output, storage, and the arithmetic and logic unit. (Further clarified by *control*.)

control, program structure—To control or manage the structuring of computer programs during the program loading and execution process; for example, to control the structures of programs in a simple, overlay, or dynamic manner.

control, proportional—Control of an action, event, or condition in such a manner that the severity or intensity of the restoration signal is linearly and directly proportional to the amount that the action, event, or condition deviates from the desired value selected as a norm.

control, queue—Control of the functions that are performed to add elements to, remove elements from, and update elements that are in, the various queues of a computer, data processing, or communications system.

control, real-time—The control of a process, usually an industrial process, such as the manufacturing of a commodity, like paper pulp, tooth paste, power generation, or auto assembly, by real-time processing.

control, selection—In a computing system, the control device that assists the instruction control unit in performing the selection of instructions, such as input-output, logic instructions, and other nonarithmetic instructions, to be executed. The selection control unit is part of the computer control unit, one of the five basic parts of all computers, the others being input, output, storage, and the arithmetic and logic unit. (Further clarified by *control*, *instruction*.)

control, sequential—1: A method of controlling the execution of a computer program, whereby the instructions are stored in consecutive storage locations and the control unit obtains from storage one instruction after the other, in the order in which they are stored, unless otherwise specified, such as by a jump instruction. A program counter might be used to develop the addresses of the consecutive instructions. A computer controlled in this manner is usually called a sequential computer. 2: A method of computer operation in which program instructions are executed in an implicitly defined sequence, at least until another sequence is explicitly defined and initiated, such as by a jump instruction that directs the computer to another sequence of instructions stored elsewhere in the computer.

control, supervisory—A control system that furnishes data to a centralized location so that an operator may supervise or monitor the controlling of a process, operation, or calculation. Sometimes a display tube, some display registers, or a typewriter may be used to assist in the supervisory function.

control block—See *block, control.*

control card—See *card, control.*

control change—See *change, control.*

control change, intermediate—See *change, intermediate control.*

control change, major—See *change, major control.*

control change, minor—See *change, minor control.*

control character—See *character, control.*

control character, communication—Same as *character, transmission control.*

control character, device—See *character, device control.*

control character, print—See *character, print control.*

control character, transmission—See *character, transmission control.*

control circuit—See *circuit, control.*

control counter—See *counter, control.*

control data—See *data, control.*

control desk—See *desk, control.*

control engineering, automatic—See *engineering, automatic control.*

control equipment, remote—See *equipment, remote control.*

control field—See *field, control.*

control flow—See *flow, control.*

control function—Same as *operation, control.*

control grid—See *grid, control.*

control hole—Same as *punch, designation.*

control instruction—Same as *instruction, jump.*

control language, job—See *language, job control.*

control line—See *line, control.*

control panel—See *panel, control.*

control panel, operator—See *panel, operator control.*

control port—See *port, control.*

control program—See *program, control.*

control punch—Same as *punch, designation.*

control register—See *register, control.*

control register, sequence—Same as *counter, instruction.*

control routine—Same as *routine, executive.*

control schedule, record—See *schedule, record control.*

control specification—See *specification, control.*

control statement—See *statement, control.*

control statement, switch—See *statement, switch control.*

control station—See *station, control.*

control switch, operation—See *switch, operation control.*

control tape, sequence—Same as *tape, program.*

control-transfer instruction—Same as *instruction, jump.*

control transfer instruction, conditional—Same as *instruction, conditional jump.*

control unit—See *unit, control.*

control unit, main—See *unit, main control.*

control variable, loop—See *variable, loop control.*

control word—See *word, control.*

controlled variable—See *variable, controlled.*

controller, automatic—Same as *control, automatic.*

controller, input-output—A unit in an automatic data processing system that controls peripheral equipment. (Abbreviated IOC.)

conversational mode—See *mode, conversational.*

conversion, binary-to-decimal—The mathematical process of converting a binary numeral to an equivalent decimal numeral. A transformation of notation and representation is involved and/or perhaps a change in the physical recording medium; for example, the binary numeral may be stored in core storage; the decimal numeral may appear on a printed page.

conversion, data—The changing of data from one form of representation to another, or from one physical recording medium to another. (Further clarified by *convert.*)

conversion, decimal-to-binary—The mathematical process of converting a decimal numeral to an equivalent binary numeral. A transformation of notation and representation is involved and/or perhaps a change in the physical recording medium; for example, the decimal numeral may be punched in the form of a pattern of holes on a card and the binary numeral may be stored in a group of polarized magnetic cores.

conversion device—See *device, conversion.*

conversion equipment—See *equipment, conversion.*

conversion equipment, pence—See *equipment, pence conversion.*

convert—To change data from one form of representation to another; for example, to change numerical data from binary to decimal, shaft angular position to binary numerals, punched-hole patterns to electrical signals, fixed-point to floating-point notation, or one code to another code. Conversion also implies changing the physical medium on which data is recorded, such as from punched cards to printed page or from magnetic tape to punched cards. Conversion might also mean changing from one computing system to another; for example, physically removing a set of punched-card machines and installing an automatic data-processing system in its place. (Further clarified by *conversion, data.*)

converter—A device that changes data from one form of representation to another; for example, a device that changes decimal numerals to binary numerals, a device that changes decimal numerals represented as a pattern of holes on a paper tape to decimal numerals graphically printed on a page; or a device that takes data in analog form and converts it to digital form, such as a digital recording voltmeter. A converter may do some editing during the conversion process, such as suppressing zeros where desirable. A converter changes the form of the recorded media or the mode of data representation, usually as peripheral or satellite equipment. When data is moved from without to within the computer, or vice versa, or when data is moved about inside the computing system, it is usually spoken of as being transferred; for example, if it is brought from magnetic core storage to an arithmetic register. (Synonymous with data converter.)

converter, card-to-magnetic-tape—A converter that accepts data punched as a pattern of holes on cards and records the same data as magnetized spots on magnetic tape.

converter, data—See *converter.*

converter, ticket—A converter that reads the data on prepunched tickets, such as is used in merchandising or retail sales, and punches the same data on punched cards for computer processing. The ticket has a basic section and one or more detachable stubs that are prepunched and printed with the same data. When a transaction occurs, a stub is detached from the ticket and placed in the ticket-converter receiver. Cards are punched with the corresponding data and then used as computer input for further processing of the data.

COOP—An automatic coding system developed for Control Data Corporation 1604 computer.

cooperation index—See *index, cooperation.*

coordinate, absolute—A coordinate measured from the origin of a coordinate system. (Contrast with *coordinate, incremental.*)

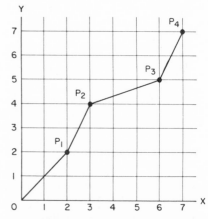

The absolute coordinates *of the points* P_1, P_2, P_3, *and* P_4 *are (2,2), (3,4), (6,5), and (7,7), respectively. The* incremental coordinates *of these same points are (2,2), (1,2), (3,1), and (1,2), respectively.*

coordinate, incremental–A coordinate measured from the preceding, previous, or adjacent coordinate. (Contrast with *coordinate, absolute*.)

coordinate indexing–See *indexing, coordinate*.

coordination, concept–Same as *classification, concept*.

COP–(Computer Optimization Package). A group of routines developed by General Electric Company for automating program testing, operating, and maintenance. Monitoring and scheduling routines to facilitate parallel processing, the use of library and scientific routines, sort, tape handling, simulator, and miscellaneous routines are included.

COPE–(Console Operator Proficiency Examination). An examination for computer operators developed by Computer Usage Company, Inc., for the IBM 705 II computer.

copy–1: To reproduce data in a new location or media, leaving the original data unchanged. Thus, to duplicate; for example, to transfer data stored in one storage location to another storage location, leaving the data stored at the original location unchanged and replacing whatever was previously stored in the second location; to duplicate a printed page by a photographic process; or to make an exact replica of anything. Usually, if data is involved, the form of representation remains the same. Thus, if punched cards contained the same data as is on a printed page, the cards would not usually be considered a copy of the page. (Synonymous with *duplicate*.) 2: To read data from a source, leaving the source data unchanged and to write the same data elsewhere in a physical form or on a data medium that may differ from that of the source; for example, to copy a deck of punched cards (the data on them) onto magnetic tape. Many terms are used as a substitute for copy, though the terms are not exactly synonymous. Among these are read, transmit, write, load, move, and store. Each one of these operations involves the act of copying.

copy, hard–1: Data in printed or written form, usually on paper and usually sensible to a human being, but not readily sensible to a computer. Magnetic tapes and transient displays are not hard copies, whereas printed reports and tabulations are. Recently developed optical character recognition equipment is designed to read hard copy. 2: In graphic systems, a copy, on paper or film, of data that was stored in a computer. Many display systems have a facility for producing a hard copy of data that is displayed so that the user can make a more permanent record. (Contrast with *copy, soft*.)

copy, soft–Data on or in a data medium not as permanent as hard copy, for example, data on volatile media such as cathode ray tubes and delay lines. (Contrast with *copy, hard*.)

CORBIE–A programming system for the IBM 704 computer developed for the National Bureau of Standards.

cord, patch–See *patchcord*.

Cordonnier–Same as *peek-a-boo*.

Cordonnier check–Same as *check, sight*.

core, bobbin–A tape-wound core consisting of a tape of magnetic material wrapped on a spool or bobbin, which provides mechanical support to the tape.

core, magnetic–A configuration of magnetic material that is or is intended to be placed in a certain relationship to electric currents and whose magnetic properties are essential to its use. Thus, the core may be used to concentrate or increase magnetic flux density, as in a transformer, induction coil, or armature; to retain a magnetic polarization for the purpose of storing data; or for its nonlinear properties as in a logic element. A magnetic core may be made of many materials, such as iron, iron oxide, or ferrite, and in many shapes, such as wire, tape, toroid, thin-film, or beads. (Further clarified by *core, storage*.)

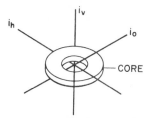

Only the simultaneously combined currents in the vertical and horizontal wires can reverse the polarization of the magnetic core and obtain an output current.

core, multiple aperture–A magnetic core with more than one hole through each of which wires may pass in order to create more than one magnetic closed path. Multiple aperture cores may be used for nondestructive reading of stored data.

core, storage–A configuration of magnetic material that is or is intended to be placed in a certain relationship to electric currents and whose magnetic properties are used to retain data, usually in binary form, such that the direction of polarization determines the storage of a zero or a one. The core material, often in the form of an annulus or toroid, has a high ratio of residual-to-saturated flux density and a threshold value of magnetizing force below which switching to the opposite state of polarization does not occur. The material is called square hysteresis-loop material and is quite often a ferrite. In thin-film magnetic-storage units for digital computers, the storage cores may be small spots deposited on a substrate or base material by evaporative techniques. The cores are arranged in arrays or planes that are stacked to secure a high storage density in binary digits per unit volume. Some cores consist of a tape of magnetic material wrapped on a bobbin. (Further clarified by *core, magnetic.*)

core storage, magnetic—See *storage, magnetic core.*

core, switch—A magnetic core used in a switching device for routing signals to a selected destination. Thus, to send signals to a particular destination, it is necessary only to partially magnetize the switch core linked to that destination. When the signal is sent to all cores, only the core that is partially magnetized will have sufficient magnetizing force to reverse its polarity, generating a signal that proceeds on the selected channel to the destination. The device behaves much like a relay or manual switch, except that the open and closed conditions do not correspond to infinite versus zero impedance but rather to a high versus low impedance or loose versus tight inductive coupling. A proper threshold effect may be obtained by using a biasing magnetizing force, in addition to the biasing force used for switching. Many switching cores are tape-wound cores.

core, tape—Same as *core, tape-wound.*

core, tape-wound—A magnetic core consisting of a piece of ferromagnetic tape wrapped or coiled in spiral form, usually on a spool, spindle, former, or bobbin. Most tape-wound cores are used as switching cores and the tape is usually a metallic foil or ribbon. (Synonymous with *tape core.*)

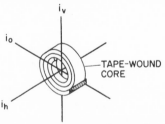

Only the simultaneously combined currents in the vertical and horizontal wires can reverse the polarization of the tape-wound core and obtain an output current.

core image—See *image, core.*

core pool, free—Same as *pool, free-storage.*

core-rope memory—Same as *storage, core-rope.*

core storage—See *storage, core.*

core tape—See *tape, core.*

corner cut—See *cut, corner.*

coronet coupling—See *coupling, coronet.*

correcting code, error—See *code, error-correcting.*

correcting routine, error—See *routine, error-correcting.*

correction, automatic error—A method of automatically detecting and correcting errors that occur in data being stored or transferred; for example, the use of special codes, redundancy of data, or automatic retransmission. (Further clarified by *code, error-correcting.*)

corrective maintenance—See *maintenance, corrective.*

correlation, fact—The automatic recognition, selection, interpretation, and manipulation of words, phrases, whole sentences, or data in any form, particularly in a textual structure, and the relating of these data in order to arrive at useful results and conclusions. The objective may be, for example, to summarize the information content of the data into meaningful statements that convey the explicit as well as the implicit relationships expressed in the original text. Fact correlation forms an integral part of linguistic analysis and adaptive learning. Usually, methods of recognizing and manipulating data elements, data items, or codes are used to respond to requests for information by examining the implicit and explicit relationships of data in a file. Fact retrieval is involved in contrast to document retrieval. Techniques of fact correlation may make use of advanced programming of digital computers.

correlative indexing—Same as *indexing, coordinate.*

count, raster—In data display systems, the product of the number of coordinate positions addressable horizontally and the number of coordinate positions addressable vertically on the display surface of a display device.

countdown—A decreasing tally or integer stored in a counter and representing the remaining number of operations yet to be accomplished in a series of operations. The number is examined to determine whether it has reached zero or minus one. The integer is usually diminished by one each time an operation is performed.

counter—A logic element that stores a number, permits the number to be increased by unity or an arbitrary constant, and is often capable of being set to an arbitrary initial value, such as zero; for example, a register that will advance the number stored by one each time a one is received at the input, a register and an adder in combination, or a bank of flip-flops. Thus, the counter is capable of changing from one to the next of a sequence of distinguishable states upon each receipt of an input signal. The operation of a counter is similar to that of an accumulator. It is used to represent the number of occurrences of an event.

counter, binary—A counter that stores and represents the number of occurrences of an event in binary form; for example, a row of flip-flops connected so that every two pulses into one flip-flop causes one pulse to be fed to the next flip-flop. Each flip-flop counts modulo two; each return to zero causes a one-count pulse to move to the next flip-flop, as an input to it. The first flip-flop of the row, the one receiving the pulses to be counted, represents the least significant digit. The last flip-flop represents the most significant digit.

counter, control—A counter that provides data used to control the occurrence of events in a digital computer; for example, a device that indicates the location of the next computer instruction to be interpreted, by being automatically advanced one count each time an instruction is executed, thus obtaining a sequence of instructions, until a transfer or other special instruction is encountered; a counter that counts words on magnetic tape to determine the end of a block; a counter used to count the number of cycles that have occurred to determine when the sequence is to begin again; or in a Burroughs computer, a 17-bit register that indicates the location of the next syllable to be executed by the processor. (Illustrative of *control register*.)

counter, cycle—A counter that counts, records, and sometimes displays the number of times a specified event or group of repeating events occur. The cycle counter contents could be used, for example, to change the contents of an index register or other control register.

counter, decade—A counter that counts to 10 in one column, position, or place of a decimal number. The old ENIAC computer had 10 decade ring-counters in each accumulator. Each Nixie tube that displays the decimal digits, by being advanced one digit upon the receipt of each count pulse, is a form of decade counter. Any counter that counts to nine and resets to zero at the next count is a decade counter.

counter, delay—A counter used to insert a time delay in a sequence of events; for example, a counter in a computer control unit that can temporarily hold up a program to provide enough time for an operation to be completed or a counter in a computer control unit used to stop the operation of the arithmetic unit long enough to allow the storage unit to complete a cycle.

counter, instruction—A counter that indicates the location of the next instruction to be executed by a computer. The counter, at any given moment, may be indicating the current instruction or the next instruction. In a sequential computer, the instruction counter is advanced by one count at the completion of each instruction, unless a transfer or jump instruction is encountered. Thus, the instruction

counter keeps track of the position in the program that the machine is working on. The number held in the counter is not necessarily the number of operations executed by the computer, due to jump or transfer instructions or to the resetting of the counter to zero after the completion of a cycle of events. (Synonymous with *sequence control register*, with *location counter*, with *program counter*, and with *sequence counter*. Further clarified by *counter, control*.)

counter, location—Same as *counter, instruction*.

counter, modulo-n—A counter in which the number stored reverts to zero in the sequence of counting after it reaches a value of $n - 1$; for example, a modulo-4 counter that stores 0, 1, 2, 3, 0, 1, 2, 3, 0, 1, ... in sequence, as it counts.

counter, program—Same as *counter, instruction*.

counter, reversible—A counter that stores a number that may be increased or decreased in accordance with a control signal.

counter, ring—A closed loop of interconnected bistable elements, such as flip-flops, arranged so that one and only one is in a specified state, such as the one state, the on state, or the set state, at any one time. As counts are made, the element next in sequence assumes the specified state. Thus, if four counts are received, the fourth element from a specified reference point is in the specified state. All other elements are in the opposite state. It might be said that the position of the element in the specified state moves around the loop. Most ring counters in computers are electronic and the counts received are in the form of electrical pulses.

counter, sequence—Same as *counter, instruction*.

counter, step—In a digital computer arithmetic and logic unit, a counter used to count the steps in operations, such as multiplication, division, and shift. Usually, when the count reaches a certain value, the specified operation is completed.

counter, subsequence—An instruction counter used to step through or count microoperations that are parts of larger operations. Thus, it is subordinate to an instruction counter.

counting number—Same as *number, natural*.

coupling—1: The means by which energy is transferred from one medium to another; for example, an electrical network used to transfer an electrical signal from one circuit to another. 2: The common impedance necessary to link two electrical circuits.

coupling, a-c—The coupling of the alternating component of an electrical signal from one circuit to another; for example, the coupling of the plate circuit signal to the load of a vacuum-tube amplifier. The alternating-current mode of coupling is used to prevent the coupling of direct currents; therefore, a capacitor is used to block d-c or very low frequency, while an inductor is used to block very-high-frequency signals. Usually a-c coupling is used to couple high frequencies. (Contrast with *coupling, d-c.*)

coupling, capacitive—A-c coupling accomplished by a capacitor rather than by a transformer, which also may be used to accomplish a-c coupling.

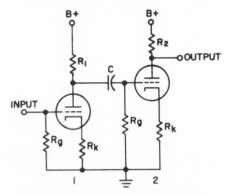

Coupling *of a signal from amplifier stage 1 to stage 2 by means of* capacitor C, *a type of a-c coupling.*

coupling, coronet —A quick-coupling device for plug and receptacle connectors, usually accomplished by rotating the two parts under pressure. Some electric incandescent bulb sockets, particularly auto taillight bulbs, are of this type. Small lugs on the plug (lamp base) engage in cuts in the wall of the receptacle.

coupling, crosstalk—The ratio of the power in a circuit that disturbs another circuit to the induced power in the disturbed circuit observed at definite points in the circuits under specified conditions of termination of the circuits involved. The crosstalk coupling is expressed in decibels; that is, $10 \log (P_1/P_2)$ or $20 \log (V_1/V_2)$.

coupling, d-c—The coupling of the low-frequency or direct-current signals from one circuit to another, usually by resistors. Thus, the slowly varying absolute potential is transferred from circuit to circuit. No series capacitors or transformers may be used. D-c may imply either direct current or direct coupled; however, the latter is ambiguous. (Contrast with *coupling, a-c.*)

C P code—Same as *code, Gray.*

CPC – 1: An abbreviation for card-programmed calculator. **2:** An abbreviation for clock-pulsed control. **3:** An abbreviation for cycle program counter. **4:** An abbreviation for cycle program control. **5:** An abbreviation for computer process control.

CPM—An abbreviation for cards per minute.

CPP–(Card-punching printer). A device capable of punching a card and then printing on both sides of it. It is used as an output device for digital computers.

CPU–Same as *unit, central processing.*

CR–The carriage return character.

CRAM–(Card random access memory). A storage unit that utilizes a card that may be selected at random and on which characters are recorded and read magnetically. The system was developed by National Cash Register Company for use on the NCR 315 computer.

crimp–To deform metal so as to bind or attach, such as compressing a connector barrel around a cable to make an electrical connection.

crimp depth–See *depth, crimp.*

crippled-leapfrog test–See *test, crippled-leapfrog.*

CRIS–A command retrieval system developed by Litton Industries, Inc., for use on the Litton digital computers as a programming system.

criterion, cycle–The criterion that determines when a cycle, such as a group of events, is to be repeated or the total number of times that it is to be repeated. The criterion might be a magnitude, a sign, a fixed number, or the occurrence of any other event. Sometimes the register that stores the criterion is called the criterion register.

criterion, sequencing–Same as *key, sort.*

CRO–An abbreviation for cathode-ray oscilloscope.

cross-bar–An automatic telephone-switching system using cross-bar switches to route calls by selecting specified contacts mounted alongside a straight bar or guide on which a movable contact rides. The dialed number is received and stored by common circuits that select and test the switching paths and control the operation of the switching mechanism.

crosscheck–To verify an operation by performing the operation by two different

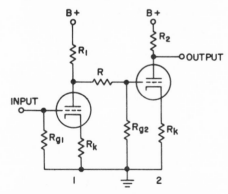

D-c coupling *of a signal from stage 1 to stage 2 of an amplifier by means of resistors* R_1, R, *and* R_{g2}.

methods and comparing the results; for example, to check addition by reversing the addend and augend or the multiplier and multiplicand, or to sum the subtotals and compare with the grand total obtained without the subtotals.

crossed-fields multiplier—See *multiplier, crossed-fields.*

crossfoot—To perform arithmetic operations on numbers in different fields of a punched card and punch the result in another field of the same card.

crosstalk— 1: The unwanted energy transferred from one circuit, the disturbing circuit, to another circuit, the disturbed circuit; for example, a signal detected in one circuit or channel of a communication or transmission system caused by a signal transmitted in another circuit or channel, usually of the same transmission system. If the unwanted signal is caused by a transmission in another system or induced inadvertently, it may be called interference or noise. 2: In information storage and retrieval, the obtaining of undesirable information from a file caused by interrelating elements of the keys or descriptors used in the search; for example, in seeking information from a general file, the obtaining of information concerning bath towels when information only on *bath tubs* and *towel racks,* as fixtures, is being sought. This form of crosstalk is one form of noise in an information storage and retrieval system.

crosstalk coupling—See *coupling, crosstalk.*

crosstell, automatic—The automatic transmission of air surveillance data from one air defense sector to another, usually using a computer to determine the new sets of target coordinates relative to the receiving station.

crowding, character—The reduction of the time or space interval between characters on magnetic tape, usually due to a combination of causes, such as mechanical skew, gap scatter, jitter, and amplitude variation. These phenomena may be additive between the drive that writes the tape and the drive that reads the tape. Thus, tolerances must be maintained on any one drive that does not exceed half of the total tolerance allowed when the tape is read.

CRT—An abbreviation for cathode-ray tube.

CRT storage—Same as *storage, electrostatic.*

cryogenic element—See *element, cryogenic.*

cryogenic storage—See *storage, cryogenic.*

cryogenics—The study and application of the effects of extremely low temperatures on the characteristics and behavior of materials. The temperatures involved are near absolute zero ($-273°$C or $-459.6°$F). Examples of cryogenic studies are superconductivity and uses for the cryostat and cryotron. (Further clarified by *superconductivity.*)

cryostat—A device used to achieve extremely low temperatures, usually by means of

evaporative and condensing cycles, and often used to liquefy gases or for conducting other cryogenic studies. (Further explained by *superconductivity.*)

cryotron—An electric circuit, such as a logic gate or flip-flop, that utilizes the principle that superconductivity is destroyed by applying a magnetic field. The threshold is distinct; that is, when the magnetic field reaches a critical value the superconductive material suddenly becomes resistive; thus, the basic requirement of a switch is met. These phenomena are exhibited at or below $2°$ to $4°$K; or, near absolute zero. The cryotron elements, usually consisting of bits of superconductive wire wrapped in small coils for applying the magnetic field that will control the resistance, and so the current, in the bit of wire, are extremely small, measuring only hundredths of an inch and are packed by the thousands in containers for insertion into the Dewar flasks of the cryostat, in which temperatures are held near absolute zero. By proper interconnection of the logic circuits, computer operation is obtainable, with very small power requirements, except those required to operate the cryostat. For short periods of operation, the entire computer could operate for as long as a supply of liquefied gas will last, and by using a thermocouple as a power source, no external power would be required by the computer. (Further explained by *superconductivity.*)

crystal diode—See *diode, crystal.*

crystal rectifier—Same as *diode, crystal.*

CSL—An abbreviation for Computer Sensitive Language.

cube, N—See *N-cube.*

cue—An instruction, address, or other statement that contains a key used to initiate entry into a closed subroutine at a specified entry point.

CUE—(Cooperating Users Exchange). A users sharing plan, for programs, systems, problem analysis, and similar experience for the Burroughs 220 computer.

cue-response quety—See *query, cue-response.*

cumulative indexing—See *indexing, cumulative.*

cupping—In magnetic tape systems, a cross-curvature of the tape.

curl—1: A measure of the tendency of a sheet of carbon paper to lie flat when exposed to various conditions of temperature and humidity. 2: In mathematics, an operator in the vector analysis, involving the cross-product; that is, the vector product of the del operator and a vector, as contrasted to the dot or scalar product of the del operator and a vector.

cursor—1: A movable device used to indicate a position on the display surface of a device; for example a device used to make a visible mark for position indication of the next unit of input data to a display. 2: A movable visible mark on a display surface; for example, a joy stick or ball cursor. (Further clarified by *stick, joy*.)

curtate–1: A certain horizontal division of the rows of holes on a punched card. Assuming there are 24 rows of holes, designated from bottom to top as 1 through 24, the rows 1 through 18 constitute the lower curtate and rows 19 through 24 constitute the upper curtate division. The even-numbered rows from 2 to 18 are designated as positions 9 to 1, respectively. The even-numbered rows 20, 22, and 24 are designated as positions 0, X, and Y, or positions 0, 11, and 12, respectively. **2:** A group of adjacent rows on a punch card.

curtate, lower–On a punched card, the lower or bottom area of the card. A standard punched card is considered to have 24 rows, of which only 12, the even rows, may have holes punched in them. The odd rows are the spaces between the holes. The bottom 18 rows, containing nine rows of holes, comprise the lower curtate, and are used for the 1 through 9 punches. Use of these rows, along with a punch in the upper curtate, permits the punching of an alphanumeric character in each column. (Contrast with *curtate, upper*.)

curtate, upper–On a punched card, the upper or top area of the card. A standard punched card is considered to have 24 rows, of which only 12, the even rows, may have holes punched in them. The odd rows are the spaces between the holes. The top six rows, containing three rows of holes, comprise the upper curtate, and are used for the 0, X, and Y punches. Use of these rows, along with a numeric 1 through 9 punch in the lower curtate, permits the punching of an alphanumeric character in each column. (Contrast with *curtate, lower*.)

curve-fitting compaction–See *compaction, curve-fitting*.

curve follower–See *follower, curve*.

curve-pattern compaction–See *compaction, curve-pattern*.

cut, corner–A corner cut from a card or film so as to serve as an aid to orientation.

cutoff–1: A facility used in input-output operations to limit the volume of data transferred should it otherwise exceed a preset limit; for example, a facility to prevent an overflow of data into a limited input area or the loss of any characters after the first 80 when punching an 80-column card. **2:** Pertaining to the stopping of the flow of current in a vacuum tube, usually by a highly negative grid bias.

cybernetics–The theory and comparative study of control and communication in organic and machine processes; for example, the study of control and intracommunication of data-handling machines and the nervous system of animals in order to understand and improve communication; the comparative study of complex electronic calculating machines and the human nervous system in order to explain the nature of the brain; or the study of the art of the pilot or steersman as a part of a man-machine, dynamic, closed-loop system.

cycle–1: Same as *loop*. **2:** A set of operations, events, or phenomena repeated as a unit, usually a specified number of times, subject only to a minor variation, such as an address change. **3:** The interval of time or space in which one round of events or phenomenon is completed. The round of events or phenomenon must recur regularly and in the same sequence. **4:** To repeat a set of operations or sequence of events a specified number of times, supplying necessary minor changes with each sequence, such as a new address or a new cycle count number, each time coming back to the first event and repeating the sequence. The cycling of events occurs often in electronic digital computers.

cycle, clutch–The time interval between basic operations on a clutch-driven device; for example, the time interval on input-output operations on fixed-size sections when running at maximum speed.

cycle, grandfather–The period during which records are retained and not used except for the sole purpose of serving as a backup so that records may be reconstructed in the event that they are lost, such as by an erroneous program, a machine malfunction, or a fire. The use of grandfather records is quite prevalent among users of magnetic tape. (Further clarified by *tape, grandfather*.)

cycle, instruction–The series of steps involved in the processing of an instruction word of a digital computer, such as transfer from storage, interpretation or decoding, and checking for validity.

cycle, machine–In the operation of a computer, the shortest period of time at the end of which a sequence of events repeats itself or the sequence of events itself. In many computers, a cycle counter is used to count the steps in the cycle. The counter resets itself to zero when the cycle is complete. Each step or state of the counter determines the events that will take place at that moment in the machine cycle. In some computers, minor cycles and major cycles are distinguished, wherein a major cycle is composed of several minor cycles. (Further clarified by *cycle, major* and *cycle, minor*.)

cycle, major–A fixed number of sequences of events or the time interval required for a fixed number of sequences of events to occur in a machine; for example, in a storage device that provides serial access to storage positions, the time interval between successive appearances of a given storage position; the time required for one rotation of a disc or drum; the time length of a delay line that stores several words; a fixed number of minor cycles; or a fixed number of word times. (Further clarified by *cycle, minor* and by *cycle, machine.*)

cycle, memory—Same as *cycle, storage.*

cycle, minor—A single sequence of events or the time interval required for a single sequence of events to occur in a machine; for example, the time interval between the appearance of corresponding parts of successive words in a storage device that provides serial access, thus, the word time, including spaces between words; the standard least operation time that equipment is capable, usually in parallel operation; or one of the group of cycles that comprise a major cycle. In synchronous computers, pulse lines are used to distribute minor cycle pulses that mark the commencement of each minor cycle as well as signify the completion of the prior minor cycle. After a given number of minor cycles are counted, a major cycle pulse is generated. (Further clarified by *cycle, major* and by *cycle, machine.*)

cycle, search—The sequence of events or the time interval required for a fixed number of events to occur that are required to complete a single search operation, such as decode the key, locate an item, and carry out a comparison.

cycle, storage—A repeated periodic sequence of specific events that take place each time data is transferred into or out of a storage device, such as the decoding, storing, interrogating, and regenerating steps in the storage and retrieval sequence. Usually a pulse-timing chart showing pulses at all times on all leads to a storage cell or location is used to describe the entire cycle of events. (Synonymous with *memory cycle.* Further clarified by *time, cycle.*)

cycle, work—The sequence of events, steps, or operations, or the time interval necessary for a sequence of events, steps, or operations that are required to perform a task or yield a unit of production and that recur in like order for each task or unit of production. For each task or unit of production, the first event, step, or operation is started after the last element of the preceding task or unit of production is completed.

cycle index—See *index, cycle.*

cycle counter—See *counter, cycle.*

cycle criterion—See *criterion, cycle.*

cycle reset—See *reset, cycle.*

cycle time—See *time, cycle.*

cycle time, read—See *time, read cycle.*

cycle time, write—See *time, write cycle.*

cyclic binary unit-distance code—Same as *code, Gray.*

cyclic code—See *code, cyclic.*

cyclic permuted code—Same as *code, unit-distance.*

cyclic shift—See *shift, cyclic.*

cyclic storage—Same as *storage, circulating.*

cylinder—In disc storage units, a set of corresponding tracks on a stack of discs.

d

DA—An abbreviation for differential analyzer.

DAB—1: An abbreviation for display assignment bits; 2: An abbreviation for display attention bits.

DACOM—(Datascope Computer Output Microfilmer). A device developed by Eastman Kodak Company for microfilming computer output data.

DAFT—(Digital-Analog Function Table). A function table developed by Packard-Bell Computer Corporation. (Further clarified by *table, function.*)

DAISY 201—(Double-precision Automatic Interpretive System 201). An interpretive program developed by Bendix Aviation Corporation for use on the Bendix G15 computer.

DAM—1: An abbreviation for Data Association Message. 2: An abbreviation for Descriptor Attribute Matrix.

DAMIT—(Data Analysis Massachusetts Institute of Technology). A computer program for data analysis developed by Massachusetts Institute of Technology and used by Kansas City Air Defense Sector (KCADS) and Experimental SAGE Sector (ESS) to recreate original test runs that made use of live environment and switch-action inputs. This program provides the possibility of repeated tests with a controlled environment and regulated input data.

damping—The characteristic action which is built into electrical circuits and mechanical systems by design or as an intrinsic property and which reduces the amplitude and frequency or rapidity of oscillations which may lead to instability or continued oscillation due to rapid or excessive corrections on the part of a regulatory device; for example, connecting a resistor to the terminals of a pulse transtormer to remove natural oscillations, or placing a moving element in oil or sluggish grease to prevent overshoot of a mechanical system. A regulated power supply will have a tendency to oscillate whenever a load is removed or added. If the supply is critically damped, there will be a gradual recovery to the new load condition without any overshoot.

DAP—A symbolic assembly program that translates programs to a language more closely oriented to the machine language of Computer Control Company DDP-224 computer. FORTRAN compatibility is provided.

DAPAL—Daystrom Powerplant Automation Language.

DARA—(Deutsche Arbeitgemeinshaft für Rechen-anlagen. German Working Committee for Computing Machines).

DAS—(Datatron Assembly System). An automatic program assembly system developed by Westinghouse Corporation for use on the Burroughs 205 computer.

DATA	INFORMATION
40	A MAN'S AGE IN YEARS
COL	A MAN'S RANK IN THE ARMY
7OFEBO8	A MAN'S DATE OF BIRTH
40	A U.S. HIGHWAY ROUTE NUMBER
180	A BOILER WATER TEMPERATURE, °F
180	A MERIDIAN OF EARTH'S LONGITUDE
SOS	A SIGNAL FOR HELP

Data *represents information and information is the assigned meaning. Computers process and handle only data.*

data—1: A representation, such as characters, to which meaning might be assigned; for example, a representation of information expressed in the form of conventional signs and symbols. The signs and symbols are characterized as signals, impressions, imprints, and shapes in such forms as numbers, letters, words, and messages. The data may be suitable for machine consumption, such as distributions of polarized spots on magnetic tape, or it may be suitable for human consumption, such as printed letters on a sheet of paper in the form of ordinary text, as is this writing. Although data and instructions have the same form or expression, a distinction is made between them because of their different nature. In most instances, the instructions convey to the computer the operations which the computer is to perform on the data. Thus, the instructions specify the operators while the data specifies the operands. Data is used as a plural term and may be considered as the commodity handled by computers and data-processing equipment, and thus is material which serves as a basis for discussion or inference, material transmitted or processed to provide information or to control or influence a process. Data is not synonymous with information, although it is used interchangeably in many instances. Information is that which the data conveys or tells a person. Data may be called selective information, while in the ordinary sense of information we mean semantic information; that is, information is the meaning derived from data. 2: A representation of facts, concepts, or instructions in a manner suitable for communication, interpretation, or processing by human or automatic means.

data, absolute—Data expressed in actual or total values from a fixed reference or origin rather than from a relative reference or from a previous or adjacent value; for example the actual coordinates of a point relative to the origin. (Contrast with *data, incremental.*)

data, air movement—Flight-plan data used in reckoning aircraft movement; for example, determining present position, future position, or estimated time of arrival. These data may be presented as situation or digital displays. Abbreviated AMD.

data, alphanumeric—Data that is represented with letters and digits, and that may include control characters, space characters, and other special characters such as punctuation marks.

data, analog—1: Data represented in an analog form by physical variables such as voltage, current, resistance, rotation, reactance, and distance or length as in an ordinary slide rule. (Contrast with *data, digital.* Further clarified by *data* and by *analog.*) 2: Data that is represented by a continuously variable physical quantity and whose magnitude is usually made to be proportional to the data or to a suitable function of the data.

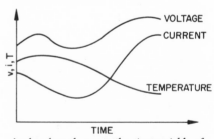

Analog data *shown as the time variable of several quantities.*

data, auxiliary—Any data associated with a set of data, but not forming a part of the main data itself; for example, data associated with a set of position and time coordinates, such as calendar day, location of observation station, name of operator, or wind velocity, which are not actually used in calculations, such as velocity and acceleration information for which the measurements were made.

data, control—Data used to identify, select, execute, modify, or exercise any influence on another set of data, routine, record, file, program, or operation. Thus, the control data is the data required to process the data or information subject to control or processing or the data used to ensure or verify that a process or operation is proceeding properly and correctly; for example, the data used to perform a validity check.

TIME	VOLTAGE	TEMPERATURE
001	78	180
002	76	181
003	74	183
004	70	185
005	64	188
006	59	192
007	48	198

Digital data *in contrast to analog data.*

data, digital—1: Data represented in a discontinuous or discrete form; digital data is usually represented by coded characters; for example, numbers, signs, and symbols. Thus, 101101 might represent a letter or a punctuation mark. Digital data is handled and processed automatically in electronic digital computing and data-processing machines at extremely high speeds. (Contrast with *data, analog.* Further clarified by *data* and by *digital.*) 2: Data that is represented by digits. If special characters, such as decimal points, arithmetic signs, and space symbols are used along with the digits, the data is still considered to be digital.

data, discrete—Data that is represented by characters, such as graphic numerals, holes in cards or tape, magnetized areas on discs, tapes, and cards, magnetized magnetic cores, or patterns of pulses on wires or in delay lines.

data, incremental—Data expressed in values that are relative to previous or adjacent values rather than values from other previous or adjacent coordinates. (Contrast with *data, absolute.*)

data, input—Data intended for processing and impressed on the input channel of a device, such as an optical reader, card reader, logic element or gate. (Contrast with *data, output.*)

data, machine-readable—Data in a form that may be directly sensed or directly acceptable to a machine, such as data in the form of holes in punched cards or tape. Data that is machine-readable to one machine may not be machine-readable to another, because of code, format, medium, or other incongruency; therefore, the term is a relative one, and must be qualified. (Synonymous with *mechanized data* and *machine script.* Further clarified by *readable, machine.*)

data, management—Data that is used to control, direct, organize, plan, supervise, or coordinate the activities of an organization, an enterprise, or a specific endeavor, such as the production of paper; for example financial data, personnel data, inventory data, sales data, or material data. (Contrast with *management, data.*)

data, mass—A relatively larger amount of data than can be stored in the cental processing unit of a computer at any one time.

data, master—A specific set or type of data in a particular data-processing area of application, the data being either infrequently altered or, if it is changed, the change is in a known and invariable way; for example, in the payroll area, names, addresses, badge numbers, pay rates, dates of birth, and deductions are examples of master data. One operational method for a particular application might be to keep all the master data on a single reel of tape, to be read when required. The master data tape is kept up to date independent of the process in which it is used, say to compute the payroll.

data, mechanized—Same as *data, machine-readable.*

data, numeric—Data that is represented by numerals.

data, output—Data that is obtained or to be obtained from a device, such as a logic element, or its output channel. (Contrast with *data, input.*)

data, raw—Data which has not been machine processed or which has not been reduced. The data need not be in machine-readable form.

data, source—Data created by a generator or originator of data, usually an individual, an organization, or data transmission equipment that supplies data.

data, test—Data specifically developed to establish the adequacy of a computer run or a computer system. The data may be artificial or actual data that has been taken from previous operations and perhaps edited to make it more useful for purposes of the test. The data is so organized, constructed, and presented that each subroutine in the program will be tested for performance. The data will usually create conditions which will require entry to basic subroutines to determine whether the program under test can handle the given conditions and produce the desired results.

data, transaction—Data that describes a specific event in a data-processing application area; for example, hours worked, quantities shipped, and amounts invoiced in the application areas of payroll, inventory control, and accounts payable, respectively.

data access control—See *control, data access.*

data array—See *array, data.*

data attribute—See *attribute, data.*

data automation, source—See *automation, source data.*

data base—See *base, data.*

data buffer—Same as *buffer (1).*

data card, source—See *card, source data.*

data carrier—See *carrier, data.*

data cell—See *cell, data.*

data channel—Same as *channel.*

data circuit, received—See *circuit, received data.*

data circuit, transmitted—See *circuit, transmitted data.*

data collection station—Same as *station, data input.*

data communication—See *communication, data.*

data compaction—See *compaction, data.*

data compression—See *compression, data.*

data conversion—See *conversion, data.*

data converter—See *converter.*

data declaration—See *declaration, data.*

data definition—See *definition, data.*

data delay—See *delay, data.*

data delimiter—See *delimiter, data.*

data description statement—Same as *declaration, data.*

data design—See *design, data.*

data element—See *element, data.*

data element chain—Same as *macroelement, data.*

data element use identifier—Same as *identifier, data use.*

data error—See *error, data.*

data evaluation—See *evaluation, data.*

data handling—See *handling, data.*

data input station—See *station, data input.*

data layout—Same as *format.*

data library—See *library, data.*

data link—Same as *link, communication.*

data link escape character—See *character, data link escape.*

data macroelement—See *macroelement, data.*

data management—See *management, data.*

data management system—See *system, data management.*

data medium—See *medium, data.*

data network—See *network, data.*

data origination—See *origination, data.*

Data-phone—One or more of a family of devices used to permit other-than-voice data communication over telephone channels. The term refers to equipment of American Telephone and Telegraph Company. (Further clarified by *circuit, data telephone.*)

data processing—Any operation or combination of operations on data, usually in accordance with a specified or implied set of rules, as a series of discrete steps. including operations such as compute, assemble, compile, interpret, generate, translate, store, retrieve, transfer, select, extract, shift, search, sort, merge, transliterate, read, write, print, erase, and punch. The processing usually results in a solution to a problem. The operations are performed systematically in automatic data processing. Computing leans toward computations involving numerical values, equations, and numerical results as a consequence of arithmetic operations. whereas data processing involves more

data handling in the sense of sorting, merging, account updating, and storage and retrieval. However, a clear-cut distinction between computing and data processing can hardly be drawn. Automatic data processing is accomplished primarily on internally stored program, digital computers. Data may be processed without regard for the meaning assigned to the data. (Synonymous with *information processing.*)

data processing, batch—Data processing in which a number of similar input data items are grouped together and processed during a single machine run with the same program, for operating convenience and efficiency. (Contrast with *data processing, in-line.*)

data processing, business—Data processing involving the handling of data usually encountered in the operation of a commercial enterprise and of an administrative, executive, or management kind, such as payroll computation, inventory control, and cost accounting. These applications are distinguished from scientific data processing, such as computing orbital trajectories from a set of applicable differential equations or predicting a rendezvous in space between maneuverable satellites; it is also to be distinguished from industrial process control, such as controlling the manufacture of sheet steel; or from numerical control, such as using a card or tape to control fabric pattern in a knitting machine or directing an acetylene cutter for cutting ship hull plates and bulkhead plates. Statistical studies, numerical analysis, probability theory, and linear and nonlinear programming has resulted in removing much of the distinction between scientific and business data processing, and single machines are applied to both classes of problems. Scientific problems involve more computation and less mass data handling, although the distinction on this basis is lessening. (Contrast with *data processing, scientific.*)

data processing, centralized—The processing of all data pertaining to a given activity at a single location, usually with a given configuration of equipment in one building. Data to be processed is transmitted to the centralized facility from all parts of the organization for processing and return, or for use there, or elsewhere. No other data-processing capability should exist elsewhere in the organization in a fully centralized activity, except for input preparation prior to transmission, or other minor processing. The term centralized data processing is particularly applicable to an organization that is managerially subdivided or one that is distributed over several geographical locations. All parts of the organization receive their support from or at one location. (Contrast with *data processing, decentralized.*)

data processing, decentralized—The processing of data within each subdivision of an organization or at each geographical location of the parts of an organization. Each subdivision has its own data-processing capability required in the furtherance of its own individual mission. (Contrast with *data processing, centralized*.)

data processing, electronic—Data processing through the use of electronic equipment, such as an internally stored program, electronic, digital computer or an automatic data-processing machine, such as the IBM 360 or RCA Spectra 70 computers.

data processing, in-line—Data processing in which all changes in appropriate records and accounts are made as each transaction or event occurs; for example, if an order is filled, the inventory is adjusted, accounts receivable are augmented, shipping documents are prepared, transportation is requested, and all other ledgers, records, and files are posted. Random access storage is usually required in this type of processing. (Contrast with *data processing, batch*.)

data processing, industrial—See *processing, industrial data*.

data processing, integrated—The processing of data, usually by automatic or electronic means, on an organized, systematic, and correlated basis throughout a given area of interest rather than as a series of disjointed operations. In integrated data processing, the need for massive interface arrangements between successive operations is minimized by eliminating the need for interfaces wherever possible; for example, if a need for a special analog recorder to digital converter is needed, examine the possibility of acquiring a digital recorder in the first place.

data processing, scientific—Data processing involving the solution of mathematical functions or equations. The use of game theory, computing trajectories and orbits, and the application of the laws of aerodynamics, thermodynamics, and magnetohydrodynamics are areas of scientific computation. (Contrast with *data processing, business*.)

data-processing center—See *center, data-processing*.

data-processing machine—Same as *machine*.

data-processing machine, electronic—See *machine, electronic data-processing*.

data-processing system—See *system, data processing*.

data processor—See *processor, data*.

data reduction—See *reduction, data*.

data reduction, online—See *reduction, online data*.

data reduction, real-time—See *reduction, real-time data*.

data reliability—See *reliability, data*.

data retrieval—See *retrieval, data*.

data-signalling rate—See *rate, data-signalling*.

data sink—See *sink, data*.

data source—See *source, data*.

data speed—Same as *rate, telegraph*.

data structure—See *structure, data*.

data structure, graphic—See *structure, graphic data*.

data-switching center—See *center, data-switching*.

data-switching center, automatic—See *center, automatic data-switching*.

data-switching center, electronic—See *center, automatic data-switching*.

data telephone circuit—See *circuit, data telephone*.

data terminal—See *terminal, data*.

data terminal, multiplex—See *terminal, multiplex data*.

data terminal equipment—See *unit, terminal*.

data-transfer rate, average—Same as *rate, effective data-transfer*.

data-transfer rate, effective—See *rate, effective data-transfer*.

data transmission, asynchronous—See *transmission, asynchronous data*.

data transmission, synchronous—See *transmission, synchronous data*.

data-transmission trap—See *trap, data-transmission*.

data-transmission utilization ratio—See *ratio, data-transmission utilization*.

data type—see *type, data*.

data validation—See *validation, data*.

data validity—See *validity, data*.

data word—Same as *word, information*.

DATACODE I—An automatic coding system developed for the Burroughs 205 computer.

datamation—Data and automation, thus implying the combined fields of data processing and industrial automation.

Dataphone—See *Data-phone*.

date, delivery—The date of physical delivery, on-site, of a computer or its components without regard to whether or not they have been unpacked, interconnected, placed in final position, or energized. Delivery of equipment carries no connotation of operational status.

date, installation—The date equipment is ready for on-site use. For example, the date by which a contractor, seller, or lessor must have the contracted equipment ready for use by the buyer or lessee and usually the date on which the contractor, seller, or lessor certifies in writing that the equipment is ready for use. The rental payment is normally accruable from the day following the installation date, subject to the acceptance and standards of performance provisions of the applicable contract; as an example, rental may start on the day following the successful completion of a set of test runs specified in the contract.

dating subroutine—See *subroutine, dating*.

DATOR—Digital data, Auxiliary storage, Track display, Outputs, and Radar display.

datum line, X—See *line, X-datum*.

datum line, Y—See *line, Y-datum*.

DA ZOO2—A supervisory programming system developed by Douglas Aircraft

Company at El Segundo, California, for the IBM 704 automatic data-processing system.

dB−A unit of power ratio, such that $dB = 10 \log_{10}(P_1/P_2)$, where P_1 and P_2 are the two power levels whose ratio is being considered. Thus, if P_1 is 1 watt and P_2 is 1 milliwatt (1×10^{-3} watt), then $dB = 10 \log_{10}(1/10^{-3}) = 30$ dB; or, P_2 is 30 dB below P_1, assuming that P_1 is 0 on the dB scale. (Synonymous with *decibel*. Further clarified by *dBm* and *dBRN*.)

dBm−A unit of absolute power measurement used in electrical communications. The dBm is scaled such that zero dBm equals 1 milliwatt. (A dB is $10 \log_{10}$ of the power ratio.) Thus, 1 watt is $10 \log_{10}(1/10^{-3}) = 30$ dBm above the 1 milliwatt level, which is set at zero. One micromicrowatt is $10 \log_{10}(10^{-12}/10^{-3}) = -90$ dBm; 90 dBm below 1 milliwatt. Also, 1 microwatt is 30 dBm below 1 milliwatt. (Further clarified by *dB* and *dBRN*.)

dBRN−A unit of measurement of the absolute power of electrical circuit noise. The dBRN is scaled such that zero dBRN is equal to a reference power of one micromicrowatt at 1000 hertz as measured by Transmission Measuring Set *TS-569( )/FT*. The zero dBRN; that is, one micromicrowatt of absolute noise level is 90 dB below one milliwatt, the zero of the dBm scale. One watt is 120 dBRN; that is, 120 dB above one micromicrowatt. A −30 dBRN level would represent a power level of one millimicromicrowatt, or 1×10^{-15} watt. (Further clarified by *dB* and *dBm*.)

dc−An abbreviation for direct current, direct coupled, digital computer, direct cycle, direction center, display console, decimal classification, data conversion, design change, or detail condition, depending on the context in which it is used.

d-c amplifier−Same as *amplifier, direct-coupled*.

d-c coupling−See *coupling, d-c*.

d-c dump−See *dump, d-c*.

d-c flip-flop−Same as *flip-flop, d-c-coupled*.

DCA−An abbreviation for Digital Computers Association, Direction Center Active, or Defense Communications Agency, depending on the context in which it is used.

DCR−An abbreviation for data conversion receiver, digital conversion receiver, design change recommendation, or detail condition register, depending on the context in which it is used.

DCTL−An abbreviation for Direct Coupled Transistor Logic.

DD−An abbreviation for delay driver, digital data, digital display, decimal display, or data demand, depending on the context in which it is used.

DDA−1: An abbreviation for Digital Differential Analyzer. See *Analyzer, Digital Differential*. 2: An abbreviation for digital display alarm.

DDCE−An abbreviation for digital data conversion equipment.

DDD−An abbreviation for direct distance dialing, a system developed by American Telephone and Telegraph Company.

DDG−An abbreviation for digital display generator.

DDGE−An abbreviation for digital display generator element.

DDM−An abbreviation for digital display makeup, a specific computer program developed for the United States Air Force.

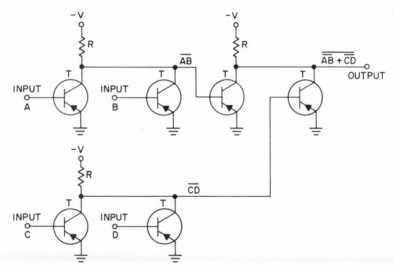

Two two-input positive AND gates driving one two-input negative OR gate using DCTL.

DDOCE—An abbreviation for digital data output conversion equipment.

DDP—An abbreviation for digital data processor.

DDS—An abbreviation of digital display scope.

DDT—1: An abbreviation of digital data transmitter. 2: A symbolic debugging aid that provides dynamic interaction with running programs.

DE—An abbreviation of display element, display equipment, digital element, decision element, or division entry, depending on the context in which it is used.

dead band—See *band, dead*.

dead file—See *file, dead*.

dead-front—The mating or joining surface of a connector designed so that the contacts are recessed below the surface of the connector's insulated body so as to prevent accidental short-circuiting of contacts or to prevent the contacts from coming in contact with any object.

deadlock—In an operating system, a condition that exists when two programs or processes are concurrently executed and each has allocated for its sole use a non-sharable resource that is required by the other before that program or process can continue. When this contention occurs, processing ceases. Deadlocks are broken or prevented by assignment of priorities.

dead reckoning—See *reckoning, dead*.

dead time—See *time, dead*.

dead zone—Same as *band, dead*.

deallocate—To restore the availability of a system resource.

deallocation, resource—The removal of an item of hardware or software from assignment to, or use by, a specific partition, job, job step, or task.

debatable time—See *time, debatable*.

deblock—To separate the parts of a block or blocks; for example to select and remove records or words from a block.

debug—To remove a mistake, malfunction, or a fault; for example, to remove a mistake in a program, to remove a malfunction in a computer, or to remove a fault in a power line. Usually, the debugging process involves the detection, location, isolation, and elimination of the mistake, malfunction, or fault. The process may be assisted by the use of a trace program, that is, a post mortem routine, or a diagnostic or test routine. Nearly every handwritten program must be debugged. Handwritten programs in which no mistakes are found are collequailly called star or blue ribbon programs. (Synonymous with *troubleshoot*.)

decade—1: A group or assembly of 10 items or units; for example, a counter which counts to 10 in one position or column, or a resistor box which inserts resistance quantities in multiples of powers of 10. 2: Pertaining to 10.

decade counter—See *counter, decade*.

decay time—See *time, decay*.

deceleration time—See *time, deceleration*.

decentralized data processing—See *data processing, decentralized*.

decibel—See *dB*.

decimal—A characteristic or property involving a selection, choice, or condition in which there are 10 possibilities. Pertaining to ten; for example, pertaining to the numeration system with a radix of ten. Many systems, such as the metric system of weights and measures and the United States currency system are decimal systems. Decimal systems are rapidly becoming standard systems for human use. Machine binary systems are usually converted to and from decimal at input and output points.

DECIMAL	BINARY CODED DECIMAL	EXCESS THREE BINARY-CODED DECIMAL
0 0	0000 0000	0011 0011
0 4	0000 0100	0011 0111
1 6	0001 0110	0100 1001
2 8	0010 1000	0101 1011
3 3	0011 0011	0110 0110

Two types of binary-coded decimal numerals.

decimal, binary-coded—A form of numeral representation in which binary numerals are used to represent the decimal digits of a decimal numeral. The binary numeral may be in any code, such as the common 8-4-2-1 code, the 5-4-2-1, the excess-three, or the 2-4-2-1 binary code for representing decimal digits. Thus, using the first example; that is, in the binary-coded-decimal notation, the decimal 12 would be represented by 0001 0010, whereas in straight binary decimal 12 would be represented by 1100. There are six-bit codes for decimal digits for such advantages as parity checking and using the decimal digits as members of a larger alphabet such as the alphanumeric alphabet. It is emphasized that each decimal digit is separately and individually coded. The USA Standard Code for Information Interchange assigns specific bit patterns to each decimal digit, as well as to letters and other special signs and symbols. Abbreviated as BCD. (Synonymous with *coded decimal*. Further clarified by *notation, binary-coded-decimal*.)

decimal, coded—Same as *decimal, binary-coded*.

decimal classification, Dewey—See *classification, Dewey decimal*.

decimal classification, universal—See *classification, universal decimal*.

decimal digit—See *digit, decimal.*

decimal digit, coded—See *digit, coded-decimal.*

decimal interchange code, extended binary-coded—See *code, extended binary-coded decimal interchange.*

decimal notation—See *notation, decimal.*

decimal notation, binary-coded—See *notation, binary-coded decimal.*

decimal number—Same as *numeral, decimal.*

decimal number system—Same as *notation, decimal.*

decimal numeral—See *numeral, decimal.*

decimal numeration system—See *system, decimal numeration.*

decimal point—See *point, decimal.*

decimal system, Dewey—Same as *classification, Dewey decimal.*

decimal-to-binary conversion—See *conversion, decimal-to-binary.*

decimal unit, information-content—Same as *Hartley.*

decipher—Same as *decode.*

decipherer—Same as *decoder.*

decision—A choice from among two or more possible courses of action. Thus, decision-making is the process of determining further action based on the relationship among the available choices, their characteristics, or in accordance with given criteria, such as character shape, used to decide which member of a known set a particular character is identified as. Decision-making within a computer is the operation of determining whether or not a certain relationship exists regarding words in storage or in registers, taking alternative courses of action in accordance with the specified conditions. The decision is effected by conditional jumps or equivalent techniques. A decision is usually preceded by, or involves, a comparison.

decision, leading—A decision that is made or executed before a specified sequence of instructions is executed; for example, a loop control decision that is executed before the loop body. (Contrast with *decision, trailing.*)

decision, logic—A decision made in a computing or data-processing system as a direct result of the internal organization of the system, and usually confined to a yes or a no kind of decision. The primary logical decision that can be made pertains to questions regarding equality or relative magnitude; that is, questions may be in the form: Are the contents of A_1 equal to the contents of A_2? If the answer is yes, then execute the instruction stored in B; if the answer is no, then answer the question: Are the contents of A_1 larger than the contents A_2? If the answer is yes, then execute the instruction stored in B_2. If the answer is no, then execute the instruction in B_3. It is pointed out that these same decisions can be accomplished in other ways. (Synonymous with *logical decision.*)

decision, logical—Same as *decision, logic.*

decision, trailing—A decision that is made or executed after a specified sequence of instructions is executed; for example, a loop control decision that is executed after the loop body. (Contrast with *decision, leading.*)

decision box—See *box, decision.*

decision content—See *content, decision.*

decision element—Same as *element, logic.*

decision instruction—See *instruction, decision.*

decision, integrator—Same as *servointegrator.*

decision table—See *table, decision.*

deck—A set, pack, or collection of punched cards used for a definite purpose; for example, a group of cards bearing data for a particular computer run or containing a specific program of instructions. (Synonymous with *pack.*)

deck, binary—A deck of punched cards containing data or instructions punched in binary form. (Further clarified by *binary, column* and by *binary, row.*)

deck, card—A group of punched cards that are related with regard to one or more aspects; for example, a group of cards that contain payroll data for a number of employees in a given department.

deck, condensed—A deck on which the amount of punched data has been increased; for example, if an input deck contains an assembly program with one instruction card, and an output deck is produced containing the equivalent machine-language program, with several instructions per card, then the output deck is considered to be a condensed deck. (Synonymous with *squoze deck.*)

deck, executive—A deck of punched cards on which executive programs, routines, and subroutines have been punched. (Further clarified by *routine, executive.*)

deck, instruction—A deck on which is punched the data that defines the operations to be performed by a data-processing system. The set of instructions comprising the program may be coded in machine language or it may be in the form of a compiler, which will direct the machine to compile the machine-language program, which the machine will then automatically execute.

deck, squoze—Same as *deck, condensed.*

deck, symbolic—A deck on which programs written in symbolic language are punch-coded, as opposed to programs written in binary language.

deck, tape—Same as *drive, tape.*

declaration—In computer programming, a statement that affects or concerns the interpretation of other statements in the source language or generates other declarations in the target language. (Synonymous with *directive.*)

declaration, data—A statement that is not executable by a computer program but describes the characteristics of the data that is to be operated on during the execution of the program. (Synonymous with *data description statement*.)

declaration statement, function—See *statement, function declaration*.

declaration, macro—Same as *definition, macro*.

decode—To utilize a code so as to reverse some previous coding; for example, to ascertain the meaning, expressed in a familiar language or in any other language, of individual characters or groups of characters. Thus, if the letter A was encoded by using the symbol 101101, then to establish that 101101 represented A would constitute decoding. (Synonymous with *decipher*. Contrast with *encode* and *encipher*.)

decoded operation—See *operation, decoded*.

decoder—A device capable of decoding a group of signals, thereby ascertaining the meaning or significance of the group of signals, and capable of initiating an operation within a computer. The device is usually a network in which a specified combination of input lines is excited at one time to produce an output signal on one or more of many output lines. This type of decoder is often called a matrix of switching elements; or briefly, a switch; or simply, a matrix. In reduced form, with only one output line, except for the inverse of the output signal, the decoder or matrix may be a gate. (Synonymous with *decipherer*. Contrast with *encoder* and with *encipherer*.)

decoder, operation—A decoder that examines and interprets the portion of the instruction word that specifies the operation to be performed and sends signals to other circuitry for executing the specified operation. For example, if a specific set of input lines is energized by a positive signal and an addition operation is thus specified, a signal on one of the output lines will cause the immediate addition of whatever two numbers are already stored in two specific arithmetic registers, simply by opening a set of enabling gates in succession and by making proper allowances for carry propagation. Thus, the operation decoder selects control channels in accordance with the statements contained in the operation part of an instruction.

decollate—1: To reverse the collation operation by the separation of members of a collated sequence and thereby obtain a dispersal; for example, to separate the parts of a multipart form and discard the carbons. 2: To separate the plies of a multipart form. (Synonymous with *deleave*.)

decrement—1: The amount by which a specific quantity is reduced. 2: To reduce, or the act of performing the reduction. 3: Rarely, a specific part of the instruction word of some computing systems. (Contrast with *increment*.)

decrement field—See *field, decrement*.

decryption—The interpretation or decoding of coded data.

dedicated channel—See *channel, dedicated*.

dedicated circuit—Same as *channel, dedicated*.

dedicated storage—See *storage, dedicated*.

default—In computer programming, pertaining to an option or value that is to be assumed when none has been explicitly specified.

default option—See *option, default*.

deferred addressing—See *addressing, deferred*.

deferred maintenance time—See *time, deferred maintenance*.

deferred restart—See *restart, deferred*.

define—To establish a value for a variable or a symbol or to indicate that which the variable represents; for example, x is defined by $a^2 + b^2$, or $x = a^2 + b^2$; c is the circumference of the circle, in feet; or $r = \log y$.

defined sequence, recursively—See *sequence, recursively defined*.

definition—The degree to which detail is shown in an image. Thus, if a character is focused on a screen or printed on a page and if the square corners are sharp and clear, the definition is better than if the corners are irregular and fuzzy; again, if the image of a tree is projected on a surface or seen through a lens and if each individual leaf can be seen, the definition is better than if only the general outline of the tree can be distinguished. The definition found in images is significant in visual display devices, such as plotters, cathode-ray tubes, and optical character readers.

definition, data—1: A program statement that describes the features, specifies the relationships, or establishes the context of data. 2: A description of the features, characteristics, or nature of data, such as its forms, formats, shapes, codes, media or other aspects

definition, macro—A statement or declaration that has the skeletal code that a macrogenerator uses in replacing a macroinstruction. (Synonymous with *macro declaration*.)

definition, problem—Same as *description, problem*.

deflection amplifier, stream—See *amplifier, stream deflection*.

deflection circuit—See *circuit, deflection*.

deflection plates—See *plates, deflection*.

DEFT—(Dynamic Error-Free Transmission). A technique developed by Radio Corporation of America and General Dynamics.

degenerative feedback—Same as *feedback, negative*.

degradation, system—A reduction of system capability, without necessarily reducing the quality or quantity of system performance of any specific capability or without resulting in any deterioration of a specified characteristic. System degradation must be measured in terms of specific application. An application requiring six tape stations will not suffer from system degradation if eight out of ten tape stations are available for use. System degradation normally results from a malfunctioning unit, however, degradation can be deliberately planned and caused.

DEL—The delete character.

delay—1: The amount of time that an event or a thing, such as a signal or report, is retarded; for example, the length of time required for information to become available after the close of the reporting period, or the length of time introduced into a circuit by a delay-line. 2: In computer simulation, a network element that is deliberately used to consume time without performing any other function in the simulation system.

delay, data—A delay due to the properties of the data, such as errors in the data, improper data reduction, errors in measurement, wrong data, or incorrectly punched data.

delay, external—Computer time lost due to circumstances beyond the reasonable control of the operator or maintenance engineer, such as failure of the public power supply, ambient conditions outside the prescribed range, tampering, fires not due to a computing equipment fault, delays in the arrival of essential personnel or data, faults in external data-transmission equipment, robbery, or destruction of equipment due to acts of war or violence.

delay, operating—Computer time lost due to the mistakes of operating personnel or users of the system. Mistakes may not halt a run but may hamper it, causing the run to last longer. Time lost due to incorrect data, incorrectly or poorly written programs are not considered operating delays. Thus, failure to mount the correct tape in the correct tape handler or insertion of the wrong deck of cards in the input hopper, would be considered operating delays. (Contrast with *time, down.*)

delay coding, minimum—Same as *coding, minimal-latency.*

delay counter—See *counter, delay.*

delay distortion—See *distortion, delay.*

delay element—See *element, delay.*

delay element, digit—See *element, digit delay.*

delay-line—A device in the nature of a sequential logic element, with one input channel and any number of output channels, in which an output channel state at any given instant t is the same as the input channel state at the instant $t - n$, where n is a constant interval of time for a given output channel; that is, a logic element in which the input sequence undergoes a delay of n time units. The delay line is a device for introducing time lag into the transmission of data, usually for such purposes as bringing data,

available at several points at different distances at different times, to the same place at the same time, for coincidence gating; creating stability in feedback circuits; or storing data by recirculating the same data through the same line by connecting the end of the line to the beginning. For storage of a pattern of pulses representing binary numbers, it is necessary to amplify, reshape, time, and control entry and exit of data before reinsertion at the beginning. Various types and media are used. Types include acoustic, electromagnetic, and magnetic. Acoustic media include mercury, quartz, and nickel. Magnetostrictive effects and piezoelectric effects are used to launch and sense sonic pulses in acoustic lines. Many conductors and cables, acting as a distributed-element, electromagnetic, delay-line, introduce undesirable delay, causing computer operations to be out of synchronism or slowed down. Recirculating loops on discs, drums, and tapes can be made to function like a delay-line by reading from one head and re-recording the read data on another head.

delay-line, acoustic—A delay-line whose operation is based on the time of propagation of sound waves. A pattern of sound pulses, usually consisting of short bursts of higher frequency, ultrasonic sound waves, such as 10 megahertz, spaced one microsecond apart, with a duration of 0.5 microseconds, are launched at one end of the acoustic medium, such as mercury or quartz, and are picked up at the other end. Thus, each binary digit, 1 or 0, is represented by the presence or absence of a short high-frequency packet. If the propagation time is 384 microseconds, and the modulation rate for launching digits is one per microsecond, 384 digits may be stored in the line. Some time external to the line must be allowed for amplification, pulse shaping, gating, and for compensation for variations in geometric tolerances in construction of the the line that would effect its physical length; and so, its time length. The medium must be elastic and have a low change in propagation velocity for changes in temperature. Mercury must be maintained within one-half a degree Centigrade for successful operation. Many early computers used mercury sonic delay lines. A 384-microsecond, one-megahertz sonic line is about one meter long. Some mercury storage lines were glass tubes, one for each line, others were tubs or pots of mercury, cross-talk being prevented because the launched waves are highly directionalized, or beamed. (Synonymous with *sonic delay-line.* Further clarified by *storage, mercury* and by *tank, mercury.*)

delay-line, electric—A transmission line of lumped or distributed capacitive and inductive electric circuit elements in which the velocity of propagation of electric

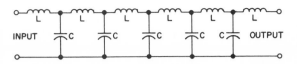

An electric delay-line of lumped inductive and capacitive elements.

pulses is controlled and much smaller than the velocity of light and in which the length, and therefore the delay time, is controlled. Data is stored by recirculating electric pulse patterns representing binary digits. Electric delay-lines are short-time delay-lines compared to sonic delay-lines. A typical electric delay-line might be one foot long and introduce a delay of one microsecond, with for instance, 20 taps 0.05 microseconds apart. In contrast, light would travel a foot in about one millimicrosecond.

delay-line, electromagnetic–A delay-line whose operation is based on the time of propagation of electromagnetic waves through distributed or lumped electrical capacitance, inductance, and resistance.

delay-line, Hg–Same as *delay-line, mercury.*

delay-line, magnetic–A delay-line consisting of a magnetic medium whose operation is based on the time of propagation of magnetic waves. Data is stored in the form of magnetic waves, or data transmission is retarded, since the velocity of propagation of magnetic waves is much smaller than the speed of light. Magnetic lines have a shape approximately like that of an ordinary wooden pencil, circular in cross-section. They are used primarily for short lines.

delay-line, magnetostrictive–A delay-line that utilizes the magnetostrictive property of materials. Magnetostriction is the property of materials that causes them to change in length when magnetized. Thus, pulsing a small coil on the material can launch a shock or sound wave down the length of material. Since magnetostriction effects also include a change in magnetic reluctance, another small coil at the receiving end, carrying a d-c current, can detect the arrival of the pulse. Thus digital data may be stored or simply delayed. The magnetostrictive material need only be at both ends, for launching and detecting pulses. The material in between need only be an acoustic, elastic material to which the magnetostrictive material may be bonded.

delay-line, mercury–A sonic delay-line in which a tube or a tank of mercury is used as an acoustic medium in which sound waves, representing digital data, are propagated over a fixed distance between two transducers. Usually a piezoelectric quartz crystal is used to transmit and pick up the modulated, high-frequency, sonic pulse packets, the presence or absence of which represent the 0 or 1 of binary data. Most early computers used sonic mercury delay-lines. (Synonymous with *Hg delay-line.*)

delay-line, nickel–A delay-line that utilizes the magnetic and/or magnetostrictive properties of nickel to impart delay in a pulse, either for retardation itself or for data storage by circulation.

delay-line, quartz–A sonic delay-line in which a length of quartz crystal is used as an acoustic medium and in which sound waves representing digital data are propagated over a fixed distance. Quartz has an advantage over mercury in that the velocity of sound, and so the time length of the line, does not vary with temperature as sharply as does mercury. Otherwise operation and application is similar to other sonic lines, such as mercury.

delay-line, sonic–Same as *delay-line, acoustic.*

delay-line register–See *register, delay-line.*

delay-line storage–See *storage, delay-line.*

delay unit–See *unit, delay.*

delayed-output equipment–See *equipment, delayed-output.*

deleave–Same as *decollate (2).*

delete–To remove or eliminate; for example, to erase a record in a master file or to change a character from a known, but perhaps wrong character, to no character at all. Sometimes deletion still occupies the space in storage previously occupied by the original data prior to the deletion; for example, to delete a character punched in paper tape, it is usually necessary to punch the entire line across the tape with holes, since this is the only pattern that can be superimposed on every other pattern. Erase removes all data, leaving no form of data representation whatever, not even symbols for blank or zero. Delete removes all data, but may leave a trace of the event, such as a complete row of holes across a paper tape. Thus, data in a bank of flip-flops cannot be erased, but the flip-flops can be cleared. (Further clarified by *clear* and *erase.*)

delete character–See *character, delete.*

deletion record–See *record, deletion.*

delimit–To fix or establish the limits or bounds of anything.

delimiter–A flag, such as a character, which marks the bounds of a series or string of characters and therefore cannot be a member of the string unless it is the first or last member. In most alphanumeric data-transmission codes, certain binary patterns are set aside as data delimiters to be used for markers, such as end of word, end of sentence, end of paragraph, end of record, or end of transmission markers. Thus, the delimiter separates and organizes items of data. (Synonymous with *separator* and with *punctuation symbol.*)

delimiter, data–A delimiter that can also serve to represent information, thus performing functions in addition to marking the bounds of a specific item. Thus, data delimiters come in sets, serving dual functions of placing limits on strings of data as well as expressing other information.

delimiter, location–A delimiter that is used within a storage area or that is part of a storage area, usually to subdivide the area for efficient utilization.

delivery date–See *date, delivery*.

delta signal–See *signal, delta*.

DEM–Same as *demodulator*.

demand processing–See *processing, demand*.

DEMOD–Same as *demodulator*.

demodulation–The process of retrieving an original signal from a modulated signal; for example, if an R-F carrier wave is modulated by an audio wave; that is, if the amplitude of the R-F wave is made to vary in accordance with the amplitude-time variation of an intelligence-bearing signal (AM signal), then the recovery of the intelligence-bearing signal, through the use of a detector, would be called demodulation.

demodulator–A device capable of separating the modulating signal from the carrier and making the modulating signal available for its intended use, such as to be amplified to drive a loudspeaker. Thus, the demodulator performs the demodulation function; for example, it receives audio tones from a telephone or other transmission circuit and converts them to electrical pulses. Demodulation is the reverse of the modulation process. (Synonymous with *DEM* and *DEMOD*.)

denial gate, alternative–Same as *gate, NAND*.

denial gate, joint–Same as *gate, NOR*.

dense binary code–See *code, dense binary*.

density, bit–The number of binary digits stored in a given length, area or volume. On a magnetic tape or drum, the number of bits per linear inch specifies the linear packing density; on drum and disc surfaces, one may speak of the bits per square inch. The volumetric bit packing is also an interesting figure when space is a significant factor, such as in airborne computer systems. (Further clarified by *density, packing* and by *density, character*.)

density, character–The number of characters or symbols recorded or stored in a unit of length, area, or volume; for example, 880 alphanumeric characters per linear inch of tape, or 8,800 alphanumeric characters per square inch of magnetic drum. (Further clarified by *density, packing* and *density, bit*.)

density, packing–The number of units of data stored per unit of length, area, or volume of a storage medium and most usually expressed in bits per inch; for example, 800 bits per inch of magnetic tape or drum track; 12,000 bits per cubic inch of lami-

nated thin-film; 1,200,000 bits per cubic foot of magnetic core storage, and 1200 bits per square inch of magnetic card. Thus, the data-packing density is the number of data units per dimensional unit, as the number of storage cells along a linear inch on a single track, recorded by a single head. (Further clarified by *density, bit*, and by *density, character*.)

density, recording–The number of bits per unit length of a linear track of a recording medium; for example, 1800 bits per inch recorded in a single track on magnetic tape might be the recording density.

density, track–The number of adjacent tracks per unit distance measured in a direction perpendicular to the direction of the individual tracks. The track density is the inverse of the track pitch. Thus, if the track pitch is 0.1 inches, then the track density is 10 tracks per inch. (Contrast with *pitch, track*.)

dependent program–See *program, dependent*.

dependent variable–See *variable, dependent*.

depth, crimp–The thickness of the crimped portion of a connector measured between two opposite points on the crimped surface. (Further clarified by *T-dimension*.)

description, job–A listing of background, education, training, personal characteristics, and skills that must be possessed by a person in order to handle a specific job successfully, along with a list of the duties that are to be performed, sometimes including the percentage of the time spent on each duty.

description, problem–A statement that cites a problem. The statement may also include a description of a method of solving the problem, an explicit or implicit solution, the transformations of data involved, and the relationship of procedures, data, constraints, and environments. Very often results or solutions to problems are useless or invalid because of poorly prepared, improper descriptions of the problem. Often, the true problem is not described, but only some related or quasi-problem. Such aids as flowcharts, computer programs, mathematical formulas, and narrative text may be used in the problem statements. (Further clarified by *language, problem-oriented*.)

description list–See *list, description*.

description statement, data–Same as *declaration, data*.

descriptive abstract–See *abstract, descriptive*.

descriptive linguistics–See *linguistics, descriptive*.

descriptor–A significant word used in and descriptive of the contents of a document and used to classify, store, and retrieve the document from a collection of documents. A list of descriptors chosen from a document is perhaps the shortest descriptive abstract which defines the contents of the document. A set of descriptors for a given document might be *toxic, emulsion, therapeutic, stimulant, dosage,* and *arterial* or *continuous, thin-film, laminar, magnetic, nondestructive,* and *storage.* (Closely related to *entry, index;* to *uniterm;* to *keyword;* and to *docuterm.*)

design, character—The geometric shape or appearance of a character, which permits it to be distinguished from another character; for example, a given letter may have several designs, such as A and a; also A and B are different designs. The word Mississippi has eleven characters, but only four character designs.

design, data—The layout of computer storage, machine storage allocation, and input and output formats that are to be used in the solution of a problem or machine run. The design should be prepared in close coordination with the preparation of flow-charts, programs, or other means of defining the procedure for solving the problem.

design, functional—The specification of the working relationships between all parts of a particular system, taking into account the equipment used and the logic design. The logic design is the application of logic to a given problem, whereas functional design may be considered as the equipment specification; that is, hardware description, that will allow a practical realization of the logic design. (Further clarified by *design, logic.*)

design, item—The specification of the composition or make-up of an item; for example, the description and identification of the fields that make up an item, such as a record, a message, or a block; the order in which the fields are to be recorded; the number of characters to be allocated to each field; and similar data concerning an item.

design, logic—The specification, usually in symbolic form, of the working relations between the various parts of a system. The design is made prior to the detailed engineering design; that is, the preparation of electrical schematic drawings. The logic design may show the synthesis of a network of decision-making logic elements used to perform a specified function. The flow of data and instructions in the form of digital or analog data can be traced through the system on the logic design drawings, showing perhaps networks of gates. The logic design need not have or show regard for the various forms or electrical design of circuits, such as gates, flip-flops, and amplifiers, that may be used to implement the logic design. The logic design will also show the mathematical interrelationships that must be implemented by the hardware. (Synonymous with *logical design.* Further clarified by *half-adder* and by *design, functional.*)

design, logical—Same as *design, logic.*

design objective—See *objective, design.*

designation punch—See *punch, designation.*

designation number—Same as *numeral, designation.*

designation numeral—See *numeral, designation.*

designator—A property or a part of an entity which serves to classify the entity; for example, the left-most bit of a binary number serves to classify a number as a positive number or a negative number; the right-most bit of a binary number serves to classify it as an odd number or an even number, or the speed of a computer serves to determine the classification of high-, medium-, or low-speed systems.

desk, control—A part, in the shape of a desk, in a system, such as a computing system or process controller, that is used for communication between operators or service personnel and the system. It may have all the panels normally found on a console. A person may be seated before it while exercising control over the system. (Further clarified by *console.*)

destination instruction, source—See *instruction, source-destination.*

destructive addition—See *addition, destructive.*

destructive read—See *read, destructive.*

destructive storage—See *storage, destructive.*

destructive test—See *test, destructive.*

detachable plugboard—See *plugboard, detachable.*

detail bit—See *bit, detail.*

detail file—See *file, detail.*

detecting code, error—See *code, error-detecting.*

detection, split—A manual or automatic investigation of the possibility of separating a radar target track into two tracks that are too close together to show separately, that is, to be detected or to be displayed separately on a radar screen.

detent—A bump; a raised or depressed portion projecting from the surface of an object, such as a spring or clamp.

deterministic model—See *model, deterministic.*

device—An appliance, apparatus, mechanism, or contrivance that is created, formed, invented, devised, or constructed by design, such as a mechanical steering device or an input-output device.

device, aiming—In display systems, a part or an attachment to a device, such as a light pen, that emits a pattern of light, such as a circle or dot, on the display surface to permit proper positioning of the pen and describe the field of view of the pen, that usually operates by capacitive coupling.

device, analog—An instrument, mechanism, or machine that depends on or uses an analog for the representation of physical quantities; for example, a slide rule, an analog differential analyzer, a positioning potentiometer, or a watthour meter. (Further clarified by *analog* and by *computer, analog.*)

device, attention—A device used to indicate a new display on a screen that displays many lasting events. Attention is drawn to the new display for possible immediate action by system operators. The device usually is programmed so that new displays may be of higher intensity of illumination or may be enlarged or of different shape; older displays are made smaller, dimmer, or another shape, while still older displays are faded or removed altogether from the display screen.

device, character display—A display device that represents data only in the form of characters. (Synonymous with *readout device*.)

device, conversion—A device which converts data in one form or medium to data in another form or medium, without changing the information content of the data.

device, display—A device that gives a visual representation of data. If the data is displayed temporarily, or if a copy of the displayed data is desired, usually arrangements can be made for making a permanent record or for removing a copy.

device, input—A device capable of accepting data and conveying it to another device. (Contrast with *device, output*.)

device, logic—A device that executes logic operations.

device, mapping—A device that establishes a correspondence or relationship between the members of one set and the members of another set and that performs a transformation from one set to another; that is, a device that performs the function of mapping. An example of a mapping device is a hardware address translator.

device, operating system residence—The external, peripheral, auxiliary, main, or internal storage device used for storing the basic computer operating system before, during or after its utilization by the computer system.

device, output—A device capable of accepting data from another device and usually displaying or recording the data on a data carrier. (Contrast with *device, input*.)

device, read-out—Same as *device, character display*.

device, solid-state—Active or passive circuit elements, or assemblies made from them, which utilize the electric, magnetic, or optical properties of solid materials.

device, storage—A device into which data may be inserted, in which it may be retained, and from which it may be retrieved. (Synonymous with *storage unit*.)

device, terminal—Same as *unit, terminal*.

device control character—See *character, device control*.

device queue—See *queue, device*.

Dewey decimal classification—See *classification, Dewey decimal*.

Dewey decimal system—Same as *classification, Dewey decimal*.

DF—An abbreviation for decimal fraction, direction finder, direction finding, or dual facility.

DFG—An abbreviation for diode function generator.

diad—A group of two items used to express a quaternary digit in binary form. (Contrast with *tetrad* and with *triad*.) (Closely related to *doublet*.)

diagnosis—The process of locating, identifying, and explaining the nature of errors in a computer program, or of malfunctions or faults in equipment.

diagnostic—Pertaining to the detection and isolation of a malfunction or mistake.

diagnostic check—See *check, diagnostic*.

diagnostic logout—See *logout, diagnostic*.

diagnostic routine—See *routine, diagnostic*.

diagnostic test—See *test, diagnostic*.

diagnostics, online—All activities devoted to the detection, location, and correction of program errors and machine malfunctions performed while the system is in operation, including messages resulting from such activities that are output to an operator, usually via a console or output device such as a printer or cathode ray tube.

diagnotor—A computer program that performs a combination diagnostic and edit routine that questions unusual situations in a computer, records the answers, examines the results for possible implications, and draws certain conclusions concerning the sources of error in a program or the faults in a computer.

diagram—A graphic or symbolic representation of the behavioral relationships, in time and space, between the parts of a program or equipment, usually including a portrayal of specific events or causes and their results or effects.

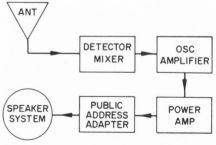

Block diagram *of a receiving public address system*.

diagram, block—1: A diagram of a system, such as an instrument, computer, or program, in which certain portions are represented by annotated boxes and interconnecting lines; thus, the block diagram is a functional drawing which is concerned more with the functioning of component parts than with their physical details. The block diagram usually shows the paths of data or control in a system and is coarser and less symbolic than a flowchart, frequently including descriptions in natural language; for instance, English, written in the boxes. A block diagram of the hardware of a system usually shows the main components; however, any level of detail may be shown. The block diagram of a weapons system may show radar, launcher, computer, data converter, power unit, etc. The block diagram of the computer may show input, output, arithmetic unit, storage, and control unit. Before a computer program or detailed flowchart is written, a rough block diagram may be prepared, which is a graphic representation of the logical sequence of procedural steps for processing the data involved in the program to be written. (Further clarified by *diagram, functional* and by *diagram, logic.*) 2: In computer simulation, a graphic representation of the operations that may occur within a formal system.

diagram, data flow—Same as *flowchart, data.*

diagram, dynamic flow—A diagram showing the operational aspects of a computer program as a function of time and including all references to pertinent items, such as tables, index registers, subroutines, temporary storage, and special tables.

diagram, electrical schematic—A graphic representation of an electrical circuit. A symbol is used for each circuit element, such as resistors, capacitors, inductors, transformers, tubes, transistors, diodes, and switches, and drawn lines are used to represent wires. From the electrical schematic, one can trace the current and voltage paths for both power and signals. Usually the diagram does not show the full manufacturing and other engineering details, such as the dimensions of pluggable units, the chassis, the mechanical details or the materials of construction other than the electrical elements. Electrical schematic diagrams

are usually furnished with all equipment, and may be used to assist in troubleshooting and repair.

diagram, engineering logic—A logic diagram that has been annotated with detailed technical information concerning circuitry, wiring, chassis layout, identification of terminals, and related matters; for example, one showing the electrical structure of the AND, OR, and negation gates used in the logic diagram, including the types and ratings of the circuit elements. (Further clarified by *diagram, logic.*)

diagram, flow—Same as *flowchart.*

diagram, functional—A diagram that shows the operational aspects of a system. Thus, it is a graphic representation of the functional design of a device or program. The functional diagram is more descriptive of the operational behavior, while a block diagram shows the component hardware as well. (Further clarified by *diagram, block* and by *diagram, logic.*)

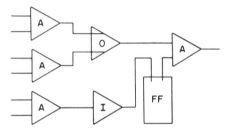

A logic diagram showing a combination of AND and OR gates, with an inverter and a flip-flop.

diagram, logic—A graphic representation of the interconnected logic, or decision-making, elements of a system, such as a computer, control device, or data processor; for example, an interconnected network of AND, OR, and negation gates, in symbolic form, showing related elements, such as flip-flops, counters, registers, delay elements, input-output units, decoders, encoders, storage, and

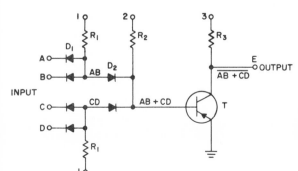

Electrical schematic diagram *of two two-input diode AND gates, left; one two-input diode OR gate, center; and a transistor amplifier inverter, right. Appropriate symbols for resistors, supply voltages, input-output leads, and ground are shown as well as Boolean logic symbols.*

control-signal lines. Usually, only the functioning of the component parts are shown; that is, the role that each part plays in the overall system. Manufacturing and other engineering details, such as the power distribution within a system, the grounding network, framing, air conditioning, and electrical circuit elements, such as tubes, transistors, diodes, resistors, capacitors, and even the clock pulse network, are not shown. Sets of special symbols are used to express the logic events and the flow-path of data through the system. (Synonymous with *logic diagram*. Further clarified by *diagram, block*; by *diagram, engineering logic*; by *diagram, functional*; and by *flowchart*.)

diagram, logical—Same as *diagram, logic*.

diagram, programming flow—Same as *flowchart, programming*.

diagram, set-up—1: A diagram showing how a computing system has been prepared, and what arrangements have been made for operation. 2: A diagram that depicts the specification for the set-up of a computer.

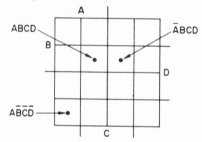

A Veitch diagram *in four variables.*

diagram, Veitch—A table which shows in a compact form all the information contained in a truth table. It is a variation of the Karnaugh map. The Karnaugh map has its columns and rows headed with combinations of the variables in a Gray code sequence, so as to permit elimination of literals by pairing, but the Veitch chart heads the rows and columns in a straight binary number sequence. The Karnaugh map is more convenient to use. (Further clarified by *map, Karnaugh*.)

diagram, Venn—A graphical representation in which sets are represented by closed areas. The closed regions may bear all kinds of relations to one another, such as partially overlap, be completely separate of one another, or be contained totally one within another. All members of a set are considered to lie within or be contained within the closed region representing the set. The diagram is used to facilitate the determination of whether several sets include or exclude the same members.

dial exchange—See *exchange, dial*.

dial-up—A telephone service whereby a dial telephone can be used to initiate and effect a station-to-station telephone call.

DIALGOL—A variation or a dialect of ALGOL written for the IBM 7090 computer at the University of California in Berkeley.

dialing, direct distance—A type of telephone service which enables the individual subscriber to dial a distant exchange and number by dialing the distant or area code number, followed by the area exchange number, followed by the local number in the distant area, all without the intervention of any human operator, except perhaps for billing purposes. The first commercial DDD unit was installed in Englewood, N.J., in 1949. An Englewood subscriber could then dial a California number, if the proper sets of digits were dialed in proper sequence with short pauses between sets for appropriate switching tones. (Synonymous with *DDD*.)

Diamond switch—Same as *storage, core-rope*.

dicap storage—Same as *storage, capacitor*.

dichotomizing search—See *search, dichotomizing*.

dichotomy—A division into two classes which are mutually exclusive and dual in nature; for example, all zero and all nonzero; all solid or all nonsolid; all true or all false; or all identical or all nonidentical. Care must be exercised to ensure that the dichotomy is commensurate with reality.

dictionary—A vocabulary that is alphabetically arranged; each entry term is defined, the part of speech of the term is indicated, and usually hyphenation, pronunciation, origination, and usage are indicated. Often, dictionaries are for words in common usage in a given language, such as a college dictionary, or for language translation, such as an English-French and French-English dictionary. For computer programs, a dictionary might be an alphabetically arranged list of the words of the programming language, along with their accepted or assigned meanings in that language. The list of words can be extended to include the key words or code names in a routine along with their

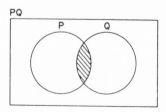

A Venn diagram *showing the AND logic function.*

meaning in that routine. The use of dictionaries tends to stabilize a language and promote acceptance of meanings of words, resulting in more effective and efficient communication among men and between men and machines.

dictionary, automatic—A dictionary whose contents are in machinable form and which forms the fundamental component of a language translating machine which translates on a routine-selected word-for-word basis by straight substitution from one language to another. In automatic searching or coding systems, the automatic dictionary is the component which substitutes codes for words or phrases during an encoding or decoding operation. Any mechanical translation scheme usually requires the use of an automatic dictionary. (Synonymous with *electronic dictionary* and *mechanical dictionary*.)

dictionary, electronic—Same as *dictionary, automatic*.

dictionary, mechanical—Same as *dictionary, automatic*.

dictionary, relocation—The part of a target (object) program, such as an object module or load module, that identifies all the addresses that must be changed when a relocation of the program occurs.

dictionary catalog—See *catalog, dictionary*.

DID–1: (Digital Information Display). A presentation of digital data; for example, in the SAGE computer system, a display of information in tabular form on a 5-inch Typotron tube. **2:** Digital Information Detection.

difference—The result obtained by subtracting one number from another. The value of the subtrahend is subtracted from the value of the minuend to yield the difference. If the difference is added to the subtrahend, the result is the minuend. (Contrast with *sum, product,* and with *quotient*.)

difference, logic—All members of a set, A, which are not also members of a set, B, given two sets of objects A and B; for example, given the set a, b, c, d, e, f, l, m, n and set c, e, f, g, h,; then the logic difference is a, b, d, l, m, and n. (Synonymous with *logical difference*.)

difference, logical—Same as *difference, logic*.

difference gate—Same as *gate, exclusive-OR*.

differential amplifier—See *amplifier, differential*.

differential analyzer—See *analyzer, differential*.

differential analyzer, electronic—See *analyzer, electronic differential*.

differential analyzer, mechanical—See *analyzer, mechanical differential*.

differential gear—See *gear, differential*.

differential state vector—See *vector, differential state*.

differentiating amplifier—See *amplifier, differentiating*.

differentiating circuit—Same as *differentiator*.

differentiator–1: A device whose output is proportional to the derivative of the input with respect to one or more variables; for example, an appropriate resistance-capacitance network. Thus, if the input signal is a square wave, the output is a series of spikelike pulses of alternate polarity; if the input is a triangular wave, the output may be a rectangular or square wave; or if the input is a series of binary numbers of constantly increasing magnitude, the output may be a binary number of constant value or a constant voltage. An example of a differentiating analog circuit would be a resistance-capacitance series network of appropriately sized elements, with the output signal voltage taken from across the resistor. The speedometer in an automobile is an example of a distance differentiator, whereas the odometer (cumulative miles) is an example of a distance integrator. (Synonymous with *differentiating circuit*. Contrast with *integrator*.) **2:** Same as *amplifier, differentiation*.

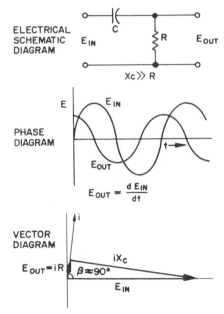

ELECTRICAL SCHEMATIC DIAGRAM

E_{IN} C R E_{OUT}

$X_C \gg R$

PHASE DIAGRAM

E E_{IN} t E_{OUT}

$$E_{OUT} = \frac{d\,E_{IN}}{dt}$$

VECTOR DIAGRAM

$E_{OUT} = iR$ $\beta \approx 90°$ iX_c E_{IN}

For the differentiator shown, if capacitive reactance X_C of capacitor C is very much greater than resistance R, the current, and therefore also output voltage E_{OUT} across R, will lead input voltage E_{IN} by nearly 90°; see the phase and vector diagrams. Hence, E_{OUT} is the time derivative of E_{IN}.

Digiplot—A plotting routine developed by Shell Oil Company for the IBM 650 computer.

Digiralt–A digital radar altimeter developed by Computer Equipment Corporation.

digit–A character used to represent one of the integers smaller than the radix of the number system involved; for example, in decimal notation, one of the characters 0 through 9. The number of different symbols required for a number system is the same as the radix. Thus, the binary numeration system requires two symbols, usually represented as zero and one. One of these symbols is called a digit, which, when unqualified, is assumed to be a decimal digit. Naturally, if the base exceeds 10, additional ideographic characters must be invented. Also, *seven* and VIII are morphemes, as are digits, but they are not digits. Sometimes digits are called numeric characters in contrast to alphabetic characters, punctuation marks, or other special signs and symbols. There is a distinction between digit, integer, number, and numeral. In a computing system, such as a digital computer, a digit is one of the characters of the allowable set of characters that the system is capable of representing. For example, in the ORDVAC computer, a digit might be 0, 1, 2, 3, 4, 5, 6, 7, 8, 9, K, S, N, J, F, and L. (Synonymous with *numeric character.*)

digit, binary–A character used to represent one of the integers smaller than radix two, for example, a zero or a one. In a computer, the binary digits may be represented as states or conditions of circuits, such as on or off, closed or open, conducting or not conducting, resistive or not resistive, lit or extinguished, or magnetized in one direction or the opposite. Numbers in the binary system of notation require about three and one-third times as many digit places as decimal numbers expressing the same magnitude, quantity, or value. Thus, the binary number 1011101110 is equivalent to decimal 750. The binary digit, or bit, is the smallest meaningful unit of information that may be carried in a message. All data may be expressed in symbols which, if the set is finite, can be coded with strings of binary digits using positional notation. Binary digit is often abbreviated as bit.

digit, binary-coded–A digit of any number system represented as a binary number; for example, 1001 is a binary number used to represent the decimal digit nine. Thus, we may speak of the decimal digit as being coded in binary notation; hence, the nine is considered a binary-coded digit, and the group 1001 may also be considered as a binary-coded digit, in particular, a binary-coded-decimal digit.

digit, borrow–A digit that is generated in an arithmetic operation when a difference between the digits in a digit place is negative and that is transferred for processing elsewhere. In a positional representation or numeration system, a borrow digit is transferred to the digit place with the next higher weight for processing there.

digit, check–A digit used to perform a check; for example, a redundant digit carried with a group of digits in such a way that an inaccurate retrieval, storage, transfer, or receipt of that group of digits is detected. The check digit usually represents redundant data. If the check fails, such as a constant sum, the malfunction causing the failure, such as an inappropriate change of a digit of a number, can be detected, unless, of course, two errors occur which are exactly compensating; however, this is not likely to continue to occur for an extended period. A parity bit is a kind of check digit. It is possible to choose binary check digits for rows and columns of digits in such a manner that if a single error of a zero for a one or a one for a zero is made, it can be located immediately by row and column and automatically eliminated by a computer. (Illustrated by *bit, check.*)

digit, coded decimal–A decimal digit that has been coded in a system of notation other than the decimal system; for example, a straight binary-coded-decimal digit, a biquinary-coded-decimal digit, or an excess-three binary-coded-decimal digit. Decimal digits are usually represented by binary codes in most digital computers.

digit, decimal–A digit that is a member of the set of 10 digits; for example, 0, 1, 2, 3, 4, 5, 6, 7, 8, or 9, used in a numerical notation system that has a radix of 10. These digits are also used in other number representation systems. However, *seven* and VII are not decimal digits, but morphemes.

digit, forbidden–Same as *character, illegal.*

digit, gap–Digits included in a computer word for engineering purposes, such as spaces or switching blanks between words in a serial digital computer and which are not used to represent data.

digit, high-order–In a positional notation system, a digit that occupies a more significant or highly weighted position in a numeral; for example, in the numeral 268, the 2 is the high-order digit in conventional notation. (Contrast with *digit, low-order.*)

digit, least significant–The significant digit that contributes the smallest quantity to the value of a numeral; for example, in the numeral 74.382, the 2 is the least significant digit. (Further clarified by *digit, significant.* Contrast with *digit, most significant.*)

digit, low-order–In a positional notation system, a digit that occupies a less significant or lowly weighted position in a numeral; for example, in the numeral 268, the 8 is the low-order digit in conventional notation. (Contrast with *digit, high-order.*)

digit, most significant–The significant digit that contributes the largest quantity to the value of a numeral; for example, in the numeral 74.382, the 7 is the most significant digit. Abbreviated as MSD. (Further clarified by *digit, significant*. Contrast with *digit, least significant*.)

digit, octal—A digit that is a member of the set of eight digits: 0, 1, 2, 3, 4, 5, 6, or 7, used in a numerical notation system that has a radix of eight.

digit, sexadecimal—A digit that is a member of the set of sixteen digits: 0, 1, 2, 3, 4, 5, 6, 7, 8, 9, K, S, N, J, F, or L, used in a numerical notation system that has a radix of 16.

digit, sign—1: A digit in the sign position. In a digital computer, the sign digit is usually represented as a 0 or a 1, and it is used to direct the operation of the arithmetic unit in the handling of negative numbers so as to properly perform addition and subtraction and properly sign the quotients and products. (Further clarified by *position, sign*.) 2: A digit that occupies a sign position and that indicates the algebraic sign of the number represented by the numeral with which it is associated.

digit, significant—1: A digit that contributes to the precision of an accurate number; that is, numeral. The number of significant digits is counted beginning with the digit contributing the most value, called the most significant digit, and ending with the one contributing the least value, called the least significant digit. In positional notation, the significant digits are the digits that are to be multiplied by a power of the radix and are not the digits that are merely used to locate the radix point. In numerals that contain no significant digits on one side of the radix point, any zeros between the radix point and the first nonzero may or may not be significant digits. Significant digits would include all digits including zero in places higher than the highest order nonzero digit. Numerals that are digits by a method of truncation or round-off are not considered significant. If the last two digits are considered irrelevant or inaccurate, then the representation 73524 may be replaced with 73500 to three significant digits. In a system where all numbers are carried to two significant digits, the product of 1200 and 0.0012 is 1.4. In the numeral 80900, the significant digits are most likely 809; since we cannot be certain. However, in the numeral 80901, all the digits are significant unless they are inaccurate. The number 0.00234 most likely has three significant digits, the 2 being the most significant and the 4 being the least significant; 12 million, or 1.2×10^7, has two significant digits, and 300600 probably has four significant digits. If a six-position odometer displays 450,000 miles, there are six significant digits, assuming the digits are all accurate. The numeral 2300.0 has five significant digits. 2: A digit, of a numeral, that is needed for a specified purpose; for example, a digit that must be kept in order to preserve a given accuracy or a given precision. (Synonymous with *significant figure*.)

digit, sum check—A check digit produced by a sum check.

digit, unallowable instruction—Same as *character, illegal*.

digit arithmetic, significant—See *arithmetic, significant digit*.

digit check, forbidden—Same as *check, forbidden-combination*.

digit column—See *column, digit*.

digit compression—See *compression, digit*.

digit delay element—See *element, digit delay*.

digit emitter—See *emitter, digit*.

digit emitter, selective—See *emitter, selective digit*.

digit period—See *period, digit*.

digit place—See *place, digit*.

digit plane—See *plane, digit*.

digit plane driver—See *DPD*.

digit position—Same as *place, digit*.

digit posting, terminal—See *posting, terminal-digit*.

digit punch—Same as *punch, numeric*.

digit selector—See *selector, digit*.

digit time—Same as *period, digit*.

digit transfer bus—See *bus, digit transfer*.

digit transfer trunk—Same as *bus, digit transfer*.

digital—Pertaining to data in the form of digits. Thus, digital data is represented in discrete form, utilizing the quality of numerical notation, namely that of assuming integral values, carried out to any desired degree of precision, whereas analog data is continuous, but is accurate only to the degree of precision of the elements or devices used to express the data. In a digital system, a scale of notation is chosen so that all quantities that occur in a problem may be represented. (Contrast with *analog*.)

digital computer—See *computer, digital*.

digital data—See *data, digital*.

digital differential analyzer—See *analyzer, digital differential*.

digital display—See *display, digital*.

digital multiplier—See *multiplier, digital*.

digital representation—See *representation, digital*.

digital resolution—See *resolution, digital*.

digital sort—See *sort, digital*.

digitize—To express data in a digital form; for example, to change an analog representation of a physical quantity into a digital representation of the same quantity. The digital representation is usually in the form of a number expressed as discrete electrical pulses, such as the binary representation used in a digital computer. It is also possible, for example, to digitize an alphabetical word by assigning digital numbers to the letters according to fixed rules of ordering. This permits sorting, sequencing, or collating by automatic means, as though the letters were numerals.

digits, equivalent binary—The number of binary digit places required to express a given number written in another radix, with the same degree of precision; for example, approximately three and one-third times the number of straight binary places are required to express a decimal number. A sexadecimal number represented in binary requires four times the number of places, as does also a binary-coded-decimal number. Thus the straight binary number 1011101110, requiring 10 binary places, is represented as decimal 750, which requires only three decimal places. The binary-coded-decimal number 1001 0110, requiring eight places (and a space) is represented as decimal 96, which requires two decimal places. For representing a letter of the English alphabet (up to 32 characters), the number of equivalent binary digits is five. If four decimal digits are used to specify a day and a month in a given year, the number of equivalent binary digits is 9, five for the days, to count up to 31, and four for the months, to count up to 12. When one, out of a number of alternatives, is specified by a number of characters, usually a set of digits, the equivalent binary is the number of binary digit places needed to express the same information. The equivalent binary digits are a measure of the amount of selective information only if the alternatives are equiprobable. (Synonymous with *binary equivalent*.)

digits, function—Same as *part, operation*.
dimension, G—Same as *T-dimension*.
dimension, T—See *T-dimension*.
diminished- radix complement—Same as *complement, radix-minus-one*.
diode—An electronic device that has two terminals, allowing electric current to flow through it in one and only one direction. Thus, the forward resistance is several orders of magnitude (orders of 10) lower than the backward resistance; that is, $R_b \approx 10^5 R_f$. The diode, particularly the crystal diode, is used in digital computers for effecting various forms of logic elements. Thus, the diode is a type of rectifier or detector, for either converting ac to dc or detecting radio signals and rectifying them. These characteristics are based on the ability of the diode to permit current flow in one direction and inhibit current flow in the other direction, even at high frequencies.
diode, crystal—A diode formed by a junction of a base metal and some types of crystalline elements, such as silicon and germanium. Crystal diodes are used in modern digital computers for performing logic, buffering, or for converting alternating to direct current for such functions as switching, storage, and control. The crystal diode contrasts with the vacuum diode used in many early computer (ENIAC) and radio circuits for logic, detection, and rectification. The diode is formed from a small piece of the semiconducting crystalline material in

contact with a piece of metal, such as a thin wire. The junction thus formed has a unidirectional flow characteristic to electric current; that is, a high resistance to current flow in one direction and a low resistance to current flow in the opposite direction, as well as a low shunt capacity. (Synonymous with *crystal rectifier*. Further clarified by *diode, germanium* and by *diode, silicon*.)

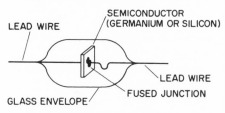

A typical crystal diode.

diode, Esaki—Same as *diode, tunnel*.
diode, germanium—A crystal diode formed with crystalline germanium. (Further clarified by *diode, crystal*.)
diode, light-emitting—A diode that emits light when appropriately excited by electric currents. A matrix of such diodes can be used to display numerals by exciting appropriate combinations of elements of the matrix. The appropriate combinations are selected by combinational logic elements, that is, logic gates. (Further clarified by *display, light emitting diode*.)
diode, silicon—A crystal diode formed with crystalline silicon. (Further clarified by *diode, crystal*.)

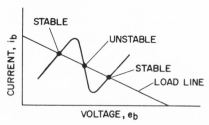

Current-voltage characteristic curve of a tunnel diode.

diode, tunnel—A diode, which, when placed in series with a resistor and a voltage source, has two stable conducting states or regions. As the voltage is increased or decreased, the diode slips from one stable state to another, at very fast speeds, about one nanosecond (10^{-9} seconds), thus making the tunnel diode an attractive computer logic and storage element. The name stems from the fact that the charge carriers seem to tunnel, burrow, or barrel their way through the potential barriers and maintain their new conducting state.

The volt-ampere characteristic of the tunnel diode has a maximum, a minimum, and an inflection. The resistive load line intersects the v-a characteristics in three places, giving rise to two stable states, wherein the diode exhibits positive resistance, and an unstable state of negative resistance. (Synonymous with *Esaki diode.*)

diode display, light-emitting–See *display, light-emitting diode.*

diode function generator–See *generator, diode function.*

dipole modulation–See *modulation, dipole.*

dipole modulation recording, polarized–Same as *recording, polarized return-to-zero.*

direct access–Same as *access, random.*

direct-access storage–Same as *storage, random access.*

direct address–See *address, direct.*

direct addressing–See *addressing, direct.*

direct-coupled amplifier–See *amplifier, direct-coupled.*

direct-coupled flip-flop–See *flip-flop, d-c.*

direct-current amplifier–Same as *amplifier, direct-coupled.*

direct distance dialing–See *dialing, direct distance.*

direct-insert routine–Same as *subroutine, open.*

direct-insert subroutine–Same as *subroutine, open.*

direct instruction–See *instruction, direct.*

direct output–See *output, direct.*

direction, flow–In flowcharting, the antecedent-to-successor relationship between operations, indicated by conventional symbols, such as lines and arrows, on a flowchart.

direction, normal flow–See *flow, normal direction.*

directive–Same as *declaration.*

directory–A list of items or entries with a corresponding related item for each entry in the list; for example, in a computer program, a list of addresses and the symbolic labels of the contents of their respective storage locations; in relative coding, the list of absolute addresses to be taken as reference points for the relative addresses used, such as in various subroutines, the absolute addresses being called address reference numbers; a description of the layout, item by item, of a record within a file; or an ordinary telephone book or office building tenant-room number list. (Illustrated by *symbol, table.*)

disable–To remove or inhibit a normal capability; some examples are to put a unit into a condition in which it is unable to respond to signals from its control unit, to suppress an interrupt feature, or to prevent an AND logic element from functioning as such. (Contrast with *enable.*)

disarm–To disallow the occurrence of an interrupt on a system. (Contrast with *arm.*)

disc, magnetic–A flat circular plate with a magnetic surface on which data can be stored by selective magnetization of portions of the flat surface. The disc rotates, permitting data to be stored in binary form as magnetically polarized spots in concentric circles called recording tracks. The recording heads are usually movable radially and positionable with great precision. Some disc storage devices have many reading and recording heads for permitting some degree of random access. By spacing recording and reading heads in the same set of tracks, relatively faster access recirculating loops of data are formed, which behave very much like delay-lines. A collection of magnetic discs, incorporated into a single unit, is called a magnetic disc storage unit. The disc storage unit permits an overall increased volumetric storage packing density over the magnetic drum storage unit. (Further clarified by *arm, access.*)

disc pack–See *pack, disc.*

disc storage–Same as *disc, magnetic.*

discrete–Pertaining to data consisting of separate and distinct parts, such as holes in a card, electrical pulses, or graphic characters.

discrete data–See *data, discrete.*

discrete programming–Same as *programming, integer.*

discrimination instruction–Same as *instruction, decision.*

discriminator, FM–A device that converts variations in frequency to proportional variations in voltage or current.

discriminator, initiation area–See *IAD.*

disjunction–Same as *OR.*

disjunction gate–Same as *gate, OR.*

disjunction operation–Same as *operation, disjunction.*

disjunctive paths–See *paths, disjunctive.*

disjunctive search–See *search, disjunctive.*

dispatcher–The part of a digital computer that performs the switching to determine the sources and destinations of the computer words being transferred.

dispatcher queue–See *queue, dispatcher.*

dispatching–The allocation of the time of a central processing unit by an operating system supervisor to a specific job or task. Usually tasks or jobs that are eligible for dispatching have already been placed in an execution state by the dispatcher or scheduler and are not waiting for input-output activity, operator responses, or other action that might introduce delay of the central processing unit.

disperse–A data-processing operation in which input items, fields, seconds, or other data units are distributed among more sets than in which they were originally arranged; for example, when an input item, field, record, or other data unit appears in more than one of the output sets.

dispersion gate–Same as *gate, NAND.*

display — display image

display–A visual record; for example, a form of computer output in which the data is intended to be read or visually scanned, and usually acted upon before some subsequent action is to take place, such as the display of the contents of a register for checking purposes; or a reply to a query made by the operator of an inquiry station. A display is usually of a transient nature, such as the presentation of targets on the screen of a radar system or the display of various meter readings on a system or network control board.

display, alarm–A visual alarm; for example,

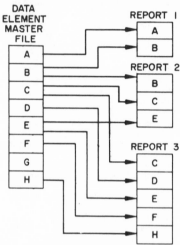

One method of dispersing data items from a master file, generating several reports.

the computer generated display appearing on a radar scope to alert the operator of the control console as to conditions or events requiring his attention.

display, digital–A display of numerals; for example, a table of numerals appearing on the screen of a cathode-ray tube of a radar system or the azimuth and elevation angles digitally displayed on a tracking telescope film. (Synonymous with *DD.*)

display, forced–A display made regardless of whether the operator of the system has asked for it or not.

display, light-emitting diode–A display unit constructed in such a manner that when appropriate leads are energized light-emitting diodes are activated so as to cause the display of specific numerals or other characters. In a typical light-emitting diode (LED) display, such as those made by RCA, Monsanto, or GE, each digit is formed of seven separately wired segments on a single base plate. The segments are so arranged that they can form any digit from 0 to 9. An electric current is sent into the proper combination of segments to form the required digit. (Further clarified by *diode, light-emitting.*)

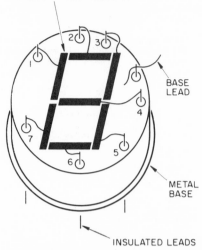

GALLIUM PHOSPHIDE BAR

BASE LEAD

METAL BASE

INSULATED LEADS

A light-emitting diode display element. When terminals 2, 3, 4, 5, and 6 are energized by appropriate logic, the numeral 3 is displayed in an LED display.

display, situation–A maplike display of the past, current, or anticipated situation of a time sequence of events occurring in space; for example, a presentation of air-defense information on a cathode-ray tube mounted in a console; the tactical situation regarding the deployment of enemy and friendly troop units, equipment, materiel, fortifications, terrain features, and related combat data; or the vehicular or railroad traffic pattern or distribution displayed on a screen by projection or other form of representation.

display, status–In the operation of a computer, data processing, or communication system, a visible presentation of the current state of the system or of a component of the system. Display items might include readiness, availability, assignment, degradation, or limitations. Displays may be made on output devices, such as cathode ray tube terminals, printers, typewriters, or console indicators.

display background–See *background, display.*

display category–See *category, display.*

display center–See *center, display.*

display character generator–See *generator, display character.*

display device–See *device, display.*

display device, character–See *device, character display.*

display drum–See *drum, display.*

display element–See *element, display.*

display foreground–See *foreground, display.*

display group–See *group, display.*

display image–See *image, display.*

130

display menu–See *menu, display.*
display terminal–See *terminal, display.*
display tube–See *tube, display.*
display unit–See *unit, display.*
dissector, image–In optical character recognition, a mechanical or electronic transducer that sequentially detects the level of light in different areas of an illuminated sample space or area.
dissemination of information, selective–See *SDI.*
distance, code–Same as *distance, signal.*
distance, Hamming–Same as *distance, signal.*
distance, signal–The number of digit positions in which the corresponding digits of two binary numbers or words of the same length are different. The concept can be extended to numbers of radix other than two; for example, the signal distance between 1011101 and 1001001 is two; between 2143896 and 2233796 is four; between *towed* and *boned* it is two. If two n-digit binary numbers are taken as the coordinates of two points of an N-dimensional hypercube of unit side, that is, in signal space, then the signal distance is the geometrical distance between points, measured along the edges of the cube. This is brought about by the fact that adjacent corners are one unit signal distance apart, or one unit coordinate change apart. (Synonymous with *code distance* and with *Hamming distance.* Further clarified by *code, minimum distance.*)

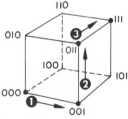

Three-bit numerals showing a signal distance *of three.*

distance code, minimum–See *code, minimum distance.*
distance code, unit–See *code, unit-distance.*
distance dialing, direct–See *dialing, direct distance.*
distance gate–Same as *gate, exclusive-OR.*
distortion, amplitude vs. frequency–Distortion, of a transmission system signal, caused by the nonuniform attenuation, or gain, at different frequencies. Thus, attempts are made to obtain a flat frequency response (gain vs. frequency) over the entire operating range of frequencies of the system. However, impedance conditions throughout the system must be specified, inasmuch as impedance is a function of frequency and gain or attenuation is a function of impedance. Much of the distortion occurs at amplifier stages and transmission lines.

distortion, bias–Distortion caused by the uniform shifting of the beginning or leading edge of all marking pulses from their proper positions in relation to the beginning of the start pulse. Bias distortion pertains to the bias of start-stop teletypewriter signals.
distortion, delay–Distortion resulting from nonuniform speed of transmission of the various frequency components of a signal through a transmission medium or line. (Synonymous with *phase distortion.*)
distortion, end–Distortion caused by the shifting of the end or trailing edge of all marking pulses from their proper positions in relation to the beginning of the start pulse, particularly of start-stop teletypewriter signals.
distortion, fortuitous–Distortion caused by the random displacement of the mark/space and space/mark transitions, or the random distortion of telegraph signals such as the distortion commonly caused by interference as opposed to distortion which is peculiar to the equipment. This pertains to teletypewriter and telegraph transmission systems.
distortion, phase–Same as *distortion, delay.*
distortion, single-harmonic–The ratio of the power of any single harmonic, measured at the output of the transmission system considered, to the power of the fundamental frequency observed at the output of the system because of its nonlinearity, when a single-frequency signal of specified power is applied to the input of the system. The distortion is expressed in decibels.
distortion, teletypewriter signal–Distortion caused by the shifting of the transition points of the signal pulses from their proper positions relative to the beginning of the start pulse of start-stop teletypewriter signals. The magnitude of the distortion is expressed in per cent of a perfect unit pulse length.
distortion, total harmonic–The ratio of the power of all harmonics (summed) measured at the output of the transmission system to the power of the fundamental frequency observed at the output of the system because of its nonlinearity, when a single-frequency signal of specified power is applied to the input of the system. The distortion is expressed in decibels.
distortion coefficient, phase–See *coefficient, phase-distortion.*
distributed infix notation–See *notation, distributed infix.*
distributor–1: A device which distributes signals from a common or one line to several other lines at appropriate time intervals; for example, the electronic circuitry which acts as an intermediate link between an accumulator and a drum storage unit or a circuit for allocating timing or clock pulses to one or more conducting paths, such as control lines, in

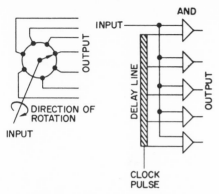

Mechanical and electronic distributors.

a specified sequence. (Synonymous with *commutator.*) **2**: Same as *register, storage.*

distributor, tape transmitter—Same as *reader, tape.*

distributor, time-pulse—A distributor that allocates timing pulses to one or more conductors.

disturb pulse, post-write—See *pulse, post-write disturb.*

disturb pulse, preread—See *pulse, preread disturb.*

disturbed cell—See *cell, disturbed.*

disturbed-one output signal—See *signal, disturbed-one output.*

disturbed-zero output signal—See *signal, disturbed-zero output.*

diversity—Pertaining to a method of radio transmission and/or reception, where, to reduce the effects of fading, a single received signal is derived from a combination or selection of a plurality of signals. The improvement gained is expressed in decibels.

diversity, frequency—Any method of signal transmission or reception wherein the same information signal is transmitted simultaneously in two or more distinct frequency bands in order to minimize the effects of frequency selective fading.

diversity, polarization—Pertaining to a transmission or reception method used to minimize the effects of selective fading of the horizontal and vertical components of a radio signal and generally accomplished by the use of separate vertically and horizontally polarized receiving antennas.

diversity, space—Pertaining to a transmission or reception method which employs antennas having common polarization and spatial separations to minimize the effects of flat or selective fading.

diversity gate—Same as *gate, exclusive-OR.*

dividend—The quantity or number which is or which is to be divided by another number; for example, the numerator of a fraction, the number inside of the dividing bracket ($\overline{)468}$), or the number preceding the division sign, as in 468 ÷ 48. The number that is divided into the dividend is the divisor, as the numeral 48 in the preceding example, and the result of the division operation is the quotient.

divider—A unit that obtains, as an output, the quotient of two input variables, the dividend and the divisor.

divider, analog—A unit with two analog or incremental input variables and one output variable which is proportional to the quotient of the input variables for a limited range of the divisor input. A multiplier with negative feedback can be used as a divider. The input resistor of a scalar amplifier can be made proportional to the divisor input variable.

division—An arithmetic process or operation that produces the quotient of two numbers. The quotient is made up of a whole number and a remainder and tells how many times a divisor goes into a dividend. Division is accomplished on a binary computer by using trial digits for the quotient, successively subtracting the divisor from the dividend, until the difference goes negative, in which case the trial quotient digit was too large.

divisor—The quantity or numeral used or to be used to divide another quantity or number; for example, the denominator of a fraction, the numeral outside of the division bracket (48 $\overline{)}$), or the numeral following the division sign, 468 ÷ 48. Thus, the quotient tells how many times the divisor goes into the dividend.

DLE—The data link escape character.

do-nothing instruction—Same as *instruction, dummy.*

document—A medium in which data has been stored, such as a printed form with data elements printed on it for machine or human reading or use. Examples of documents are magnetic tapes, films, punched cards, a magnetically imprinted card, or a microfilmed copy of a technical report. The most common form of document is the ordinary sheet of paper, such as technical report pages, bills of lading, invoices, marriage and birth certificates, test records, and books. A document must have some degree of permanency. To document a statement is to substantiate it, as by citation of authorities or references to authoritative documents.

document, source—A document that is originally entered into a data-processing system and from which basic data is extracted for use in the data-processing system. Thus, errors in the results can sometimes be attributed to errors in the source document.

document mark—See *mark, document.*

document reference edge—See *edge, document reference.*

document retrieval—See *retrieval, document.*

documentation—The process of collecting, organizing, storing, citing, indexing, retrieving, and disseminating documents or their contents. Documentation involves a group of techniques necessary for orderly presentation, organization, and communication of recorded specialized information in order to give maximum accessibility and utility to the information contained in documents.

docuterm—A word, phrase, or a combination of words or phrases that are descriptive of the contents of a document and which may be used for the later retrieval of the document or its contents. (Closely related to *uniterm*, to *descriptor*, to *keyword*, and to *entry, index.*)

DOD—Department of Defense.

donor—An element which is introduced in small quantities as an impurity to semiconducting materials and which has a negative valence greater than the valence of the pure semiconductor; for example, if germanium, which has a negative valence of four, is doped with small amounts of arsenic or antimony, which have a negative valence of five, in liquid form, the mixture upon cooling is found to consist of a lattice of germanium atoms interspersed with arsenic atoms. However, when all the covalent bonds are complete, there is an extra electron, donated by the arsenic atom, which is fairly free to wander about, thus increasing the ability to conduct. Since the arsenic atoms are not free to move, the donor impurity produces mobile electrons and not holes; therefore, it is called a donor of electrons, or just plain donor; the result is an n-type semiconductor. (Further clarified by *semiconductor, intrinsic;* by *acceptor;* by *hole;* by *transistor, p-n-p;* by *transistor, n-p-n;* and by *semiconductor, n-type.)*

don't-care gate—See *gate, don't-care.*

DOPS—(Digital Optical Projection System). A radar data-plotting system technique wherein targets are projected on a plotting board as a point of light and a plotter in the rear marks the target with a grease pencil. Similar to POPS and TOPS except as to input devices.

DORIS—(Direct Order Recording and Invoicing System). An automatic programming system developed by Shell Oil Company of England and other British petroleum companies.

dot matrix—See *matrix, dot.*

double-address—Same as *two-address.*

double-bucket—A storage device, usually a magnetic core storage unit, that provides complete buffering overlap; that is, while processing data from one section of storage, the other section can be loaded. The two storage sections can be fabricated by using two cores for each bit stored. A double-bucket core storage is used in the Addressograph-Multigraph 943 computer. (Illustrative of *bucket.)*

double card—See *card, double.*

double-ended queue—See *queue, double-ended.*

double-length number—Same as *numeral, double-length.*

double-length numeral—See *numeral, double-length.*

double precision—See *precision, double.*

double-precision number—Same as *numeral, double-length.*

double-precision numeral—Same as *numeral, double-length.*

double-precision quantity—See *quantity, double-precision.*

double-pulse recording—See *recording, double-pulse.*

double punch—See *punch, double.*

double-sideband transmission—See *transmission, double-sideband.*

double word—See *word, double.*

doublet—A byte composed of two binary elements; for example, a group of two binary electrical pulses that might be used to represent a quaternary digit. (Synonymous with *two-bit byte.* Closely related to *diad.)*

doubly-linked list—Same as *list, bi-directional.*

Dow compiler—See *compiler, Dow.*

down time—See *time, down.*

DPD—(Digit Plane Driver). An amplifier that drives a digit plane for a magnetic core storage unit.

DPM—1: An abbreviation for documents per minute. 2: An abbreviation for data-processing machine.

DPMA—Data Processing Management Association.

Dracula—A symbolic assembly program developed by Computer Control Company for use on the CCC DDP 19 computer. The program is part of a complete programming package for the DDP 19.

drift—A slow change in the output of a directly coupled amplifier due to changes in the power supply voltages, in the physical parts of the amplifier, or in ambient conditions. The component of the output voltage that represents the input variable may change indefinitely slowly; thus, it may not be possible to distinguish between it and the component of the output signal due to drift. A-c amplifiers do not suffer this problem because a frequency spectrum is involved and resistance-capacitance coupling is used, which prevents drift. Drift gives rise to an error when the amplifier is used in an analog computer.

drift-corrected amplifier—See *amplifier, drift-corrected.*

drive, tape—The mechanism which moves tape, usually including the capstans, drive motors, reel hubs, and read-record heads. The drive is under the control of a larger system so as to read and record data on command. The tape drive is part of the tape unit or tape station. The tape is moved past a head for reading or writing or for rewinding in accordance with signals to a drive motor sent by a tape drive control unit. (Synonymous with *tape transport* and with *tape deck.)*

drive pulse—See *pulse, drive.*

drive pulse, partial—Same as *pulse, partial write.*

driver, analog line—See *ALD.*

driver, bus—A power amplifier used to drive many points; that is, inputs or devices, such as logic elements, by means of a conductor, usually a low-impedance bus, such as a transfer bus, a checking bus, or a clock-pulse bus, in a digital computer. (Synonymous with *line driver.*)

driver, digit plane—See *DPD.*

driver, line—Same as *driver, bus.*

driver program—See *program, driver.*

DRO—(Destructive Read-Out). Pertaining to the interrogation of the destructive type of storage systems. (Further clarified by *storage, destructive* and by *read, destructive.*)

drop, false—Same as *retrieval, false.*

drop-dead halt—See *halt, drop-dead.*

drop-in—The accidental appearance of an unwanted character, digit, or bit on magnetic recording surfaces, such as tapes, drums, discs, and cards. (Further clarified by *drop-out.*)

drop-out—The accidental failure to read or write a character, digit, or bit on magnetic recording surfaces, such as tapes, drums, discs, and cards. Drop-outs are usually caused by flaws, such as dirt, inclusions, blemishes in the magnetic surface, scratches, and nonmagnetic areas. A drop-in is sometimes used to refer to the accidental appearance of unwanted signals, which cause unwanted characters, digits, or bits to appear. A drop-out may cause a binary one to appear where a binary zero should be, causing a different character to be read from that which was recorded. Much of these failures are detected by parity checking.

DRUCO I—An interpretive floating-decimal programming system developed by International Business Machines Corporation for use on the IBM 650 computer and for the Atomic Energy Commission's IBM 701 computer at Los Alamos, N. M.

drum, buffer—A magnetic drum designed to accept data from input circuits or from an output channel and to retain the data for future use; for example, a drum used to store radar data coming in at a rate greater than the arithmetic unit has the ability to handle, or a drum used to store missile launching orders at a rate greater than the launch site can handle.

drum, display—A magnetic, digital, data buffer, storage drum used to store data that is subsequently to be displayed on visual devices.

drum, log—A magnetic drum used for storing data coming in at random intervals, such as from long range and gap-filler radar inputs, and acting as an output buffer for messages transmitted from the computer by data links; for example, the drum used in the AN/FSQ-7 computer system used for buffering messages transmitted from the computer by ground-to-ground and ground-to-air data-link and automatic teletype.

drum, magnetic—A storage device that makes use of a rotating cylinder coated with a magnetic material for storing data in the form of magnetized spots arranged in circular adjacent rings by a set of heads positioned near the surface. Locations on the cylindrical surface are addressable by the position of the heads, which determine the track, and the angular position of the drum. Data may be read or written only when the drum rotates and the heads are positioned properly. Stored data is nonvolatile, is erasable if desired, and is stored in binary form. (Synonymous with *drum storage.*)

drum, program—A magnetic storage drum on which a computer program is stored.

drum parity—See *parity, drum.*

drum plotter—See *plotter, drum.*

drum printer—See *printer, drum.*

drum storage—Same as *drum, magnetic.*

drum storage, magnetic—See *storage, magnetic drum.*

dual operation—See *operation, dual.*

dual storage—See *storage, dual.*

ducol-punched card—See *card, ducol-punched.*

dummy—1: Pertaining to the characteristic of having the appearance of a specified thing but not having the capacity to function as such, such as a dummy instruction, a dummy address, dummy data, or a dummy name. Thus, a dummy might fulfill prescribed conditions, such as satisfying space requirements in filling in words or blocks, without specifically affecting operations. 2: Pertaining to the characteristic of having the appearance of a specified thing and some capacity to function as such, for example when a dummy instruction is called upon to be executed, the instruction counter may be advanced one count by the dummy instruction.

dummy instruction—See *instruction, dummy.*

dump—1: To copy the contents of all or part of a storage, usually from an internal storage into an external storage; for example, to preserve the contents of a set of locations which are temporarily required for another purpose by storing the data elsewhere, to transmit the contents of an input buffer into internal storage, or to transmit the contents of the high-speed storage to the magnetic disc storage. (Synonymous with *unload.*) 2: The process of copying the contents of all or part of a storage, usually from internal to external storage. 3: The data resulting from copying the contents of all or part of a storage.

dump, a-c—The removal of all alternating-current power supplied to a system or component. Usually an a-c power dump results in the removal of all power. If an a-c power dump occurs and the system being supplied with power, such as a computer is shifted to emergency or auxiliary power, then a dump has not occurred with reference to the computer, but a dump has occurred with reference to the overall system.

dump, change–A selective dump of those storage locations whose contents have changed. Often, during the execution of a computer routine, the change dump is used repeatedly to indicate those locations or their contents that are different from the last execution of a dump.

dump, d-c–The removal of direct-current power supplied to a system or component. Since most dc results from rectified ac, a d-c dump usually occurs if an a-c dump occurs. However, if only the d-c power rectifiers or supplies no longer supply power to the system or component, then only a d-c dump has occurred.

dump, dynamic–A dump performed during the execution of a routine. (Contrast with *dump, static.*)

dump, memory–Same as *dump.*

dump, partial–To transfer a part of the contents of main storage or internal storage to a peripheral device, an output device, external storage, or auxiliary storage.

dump, postmortem–A static dump used for debugging and performed at the end of a computer run, such as at the completion of a routine. (Further clarified by *routine, postmortem.*)

dump, power–The removal of all power to a system or component. In some systems, such as those using volatile storage, a power dump can result in loss of computer time and loss of computed results. The power dump can be accidental, or, for certain special purposes, such as clearing a storage device of its contents, it can be intentional.

dump, selective–A dump of one or more particular or specified storage locations.

dump, snapshot–A selective dynamic dump, usually performed at various points in a computer program or routine. Such dumps are usually in the form of print-outs of selected storage locations at breakpoints, checkpoints, rerun points, branchpoints, or other specific points in a routine. Snapshot dumps might be made at specified times so as to provide a history of a given section of storage for various purposes, such as debugging or tracing. The snapshot dump is a small, partial, fast dump, which is distinguished from one huge static storage dump of the entire contents of storage. (Synonymous with *snapshot.*)

dump, static–A dump performed at a particular time with respect to a machine run, usually at the end of a run. (Contrast with *dump, dynamic.*)

dump, storage–Same as *dump.*

dump check–See *check, dump.*

duodecimal–A characteristic or property involving a selection, choice, or condition

in which there are 12 possibilities; pertaining to twelve. There is some interest in a numeration system with a radix of twelve, since twelve is divisible by more factors than ten, giving the duodecimal system advantages over the decimal system. If men had six fingers on each hand, the duodecimal system most likely would have become standard.

duodecimal number–Same as *numeral, duodecimal.*

duodecimal numeral–See *numeral, duodecimal.*

duplex–The characteristic of being able to serve two purposes, such as the ability of a communication channel to transmit messages in both directions, the ability of a single channel to carry two messages simultaneously, or the ability of a system characteristic to use a second set of equipment in the event of the failure of the primary device.

duplex channel–See *channel, duplex.*

duplex computer–See *computer, duplex.*

duplex operation, full–See *operation, full-duplex.*

duplex operation, half–See *operation, half-duplex.*

duplex service, full–See *service, full-duplex.*

duplex service, half–See *service, half-duplex.*

duplex system, bridge–See *system, bridge duplex.*

duplicate–Same as *copy.*

duplication check–See *check, duplication.*

duration, pulse–Same as *width, pulse.*

duration, run–Same as *time, running.*

duration modulation, pulse–Same as *modulation, pulse-length.*

dyadic Boolean operation–See *operation, dyadic Boolean.*

dyadic operation–See *operation, dyadic.*

dyadic operator–See *operator, dyadic.*

DYANA–(Dynamics Analyzer-Programmer). A computer program developed by General Motors Corporation for use on the IBM 704 computer.

dynamic–Pertaining to a quantity which is changing, usually by the application of power over time; that is, energy. Characteristics of such a quantity are transient or unstable. (Contrast with *static (1).*)

dynamic allocation–See *allocation, dynamic.*

dynamic buffering–See *buffering, dynamic.*

dynamic control–See *control, dynamic.*

dynamic dump–See *dump, dynamic.*

dynamic flow diagram–See *diagram, dynamic flow.*

dynamic model–See *model, dynamic.*

dynamic parameter–Same as *parameter, program-generated.*

dynamic print-out–See *print-out, dynamic.*

dynamic program–See *program, dynamic.*

dynamic program loading–See *loading, dynamic program.*

dynamic program relocation–See *relocation, dynamic program.*

dynamic relocation–See *relocation, dynamic.*

dynamic routine–Same as *subroutine, dynamic*.

dynamic storage–Same as *storage, circulating*.

dynamic storage allocation–Same as *allocation, dynamic storage*.

dynamic subroutine–See *subroutine, dynamic*.

dynamic system maintenance–See *maintenance, dynamic system*.

dynamicizer–A device that converts a space distribution of simultaneously existing states into a time distribution of sequential states; for example, a logic element that converts a binary numeral in the form of the contents of a flip-flop register into a word circulating in a closed-loop delay-line and viewed or sensed as a time sequence of binary states of a single flip-flop. (Contrast with *staticizer*. Synonymous with *serializer*.)

e

EAI–Electronics Associates, Inc.

EAM–(Electric Accounting Machines). Pertaining to the set of punched-card, paper-tape, and similar machines used for data processing, either independently or in connection with automatic data-processing equipment. EAM equipment is predominantly electromechanical in contrast to electronic. Frequently, EAM is used as a euphemism for punched-card machines (PCM).

EASE II–(Engineering Automatic System for Solving Equations). An automatic program compiler developed by General Motors Corporation for use on the IBM 650 computer.

EASI–(Electrical Accounting for the Security Industry). A program developed by International Business Machines Corporation for handling stock broker accounts.

EASIAC–A simulated computer developed by the University of Michigan for use on the now-retired MIDAC computer.

EASY–(Efficient Assembly System). An assembler developed for the Honeywell 400 computer.

EASY FOX–A program assembly system developed by Rand Corporation for use on the Johnniac computer.

EBCDIC–Extended Binary-Coded Decimal Interchange Code.

EBR–Electron Beam Recording.

EC–An abbreviation for error correcting.

ECAP–An electric circuit analysis program.

ECARS–(Electronic Coordinatograph and Readout System). A program developed by Burroughs Corporation to yield information for land use control.

Eccles-Jordan circuit–Same as *trigger, Eccles-Jordan*.

Eccles-Jordan trigger–See *trigger, Eccles-Jordan*.

echo–1: The effect of a wave that has been derived from a primary wave and that arrives at either end of the same circuit or a multiended system with sufficient magnitude and delay to be readily recognizable. **2:** A reflection back to the source of an electromagnetic wave incident on an open-ended transmission line. **3:** The sound wave bounced off the ocean floor for depth determination.

echo attenuation–See *attenuation, echo*.

echo check–See *check, echo*.

ECMA–European Computer Manufacturers Association.

ED–An abbreviation for error detecting or expanded display.

EDGE–(Electronic Data Gathering Equipment). A modular communications system developed by Radio Corporation of America for gathering data from scattered remote locations for computer processing.

edge, card leading–The edge of a card that is forward or leading relative to the direction of motion of the card as it passes along the card track preceding, during, or after reading or punching. Any one of the four edges of a card may be used as the leading edge, depending upon the particular system. Thus, the leading edge of the card is the one which enters the machine first. (Contrast with *edge, card trailing*.)

edge, card trailing–The edge of a card that is opposite the leading edge relative to the direction of motion of the card as it passes along the card track preceding, during, or after reading or punching. The trailing edge of the card is the one that enters the machine last. (Contrast with *edge, card leading*.)

edge, character–An imaginary line running along the optical discontinuity between the printed area and the unprinted area of a printed symbol or character. The optical discontinuity is manifested by a change in the reflectivity along a line transverse to the character edge. The character edge is significant during optical recognition of printed characters.

edge, document reference—The edge of a document from which the location of printed data is specified. The reference edge is significant during the optical recognition of printed characters. The alignment and location of characters are specified with respect to the document reference edge.

edge, guide—1: The edge of a paper tape, magnetic tape, card, printed sheet, or other such media used to determine its transverse position during its movement. 2: Same as *edge, reference.*

edge, reference—The edge of a data medium used to establish specifications or measurements on the medium; for example, the top edge of a punch card or the right edge of a magnetic card. (Synonymous with *guide edge.*)

edge, stroke—In optical character recognition, an imaginary smooth line that is equidistant at all points from the stroke centerline and that divides the edge irregularities of the printed stroke in such a way that the summation of the unprinted areas on the inside or centerline side of the line is approximately equal to the summation of the printed areas on the outside of the line. The stroke edge irregularity is significant during the optical recognition of printed characters. Thus, when the irregularities resulting from the printing and detecting processes are averaged over the length of a stroke, the stroke edge is the line of discontinuity between the side of the stroke and the background.

edge-coated card—See *card, edge-coated.*

edge connector, right angle—See *connector, right-angle edge.*

edge irregularity, stroke—See *irregularity, stroke edge.*

edge-notched card—See *card, edge-notched.*

edge-perforated card—Same as *card, edge-punched.*

edge-punched card—See *card, edge-punched.*

edit—1: To modify the form or format of data. Editing usually involves the arrangement, deletion, selection, or addition to a record in order to conform to the style and conventions of later processes, such as input and output operations. Often editing involves the selection of pertinent data, insertion of special symbols and check characters, and the performance of standard processes, such as zero suppression, code conversion, and general rearrangement for a particular purpose, like publication. Sometimes certain scaling operations on the data are considered as editing. 2: To prepare data for a later operation.

edit routine—Same as *editor.*

editing, linkage—Same as *binding.*

editing subroutine—See *subroutine, editing.*

editing symbol—See *symbol, editing.*

editor—A computer routine that performs certain editing operations on input data and programs prior to or during a computer run or on the output data after the computer run. (Synonymous with *routine, edit.*)

editor, card—A computer subroutine that controls the reading by the computer of information contained on punched cards.

editor, linkage—A utility routine or program that creates another computer program by combining independently translated program modules. The linkage editor may also resolve cross references among the modules to avoid any conflict and remove ambiguities. (Contrast with *program, editor.*)

editor, print-punch—A subroutine that controls the printing and punching of cards and editing operations, such as translating straight binary codes to binary-coded-decimal or Hollerith codes. (Synonymous with *punch-print editor.*)

editor, punch-print—Same as *editor. print-punch.*

editor-loader, linkage—A computer program that produces load modules from object modules by transforming them into a form suitable for execution. In order to execute, all intermodule linkages must be established. The resulting load modules may be located in main storage and immediately executed; or the load modules may be subsequently loaded for execution.

editor program—See *program, editor.*

EDP—(Electronic Data Processing). See *processing, electronic data.*

EDPE—Electronic Data Processing Equipment.

EDPM—Electronic Data Processing Machine.

EDPS—Electronic Data Processing System.

effective address—See *address, effective.*

effective data-transfer rate—See *rate, effective data-transfer.*

effective instruction—See *instruction, effective.*

effective time—See *time, effective.*

effective transmission rate—Same as *rate, effective data-transfer.*

effector character, format—See *character, format effector.*

efficiency ratio, retrieval—See *ratio, retrieval efficiency.*

EHF—(Extremely High Frequency). Frequencies between 30,000 and 300,000 megahertz. (Further clarified by *spectrum, frequency.*)

EIA—Electronic Industries Association.

eight-bit byte—Same as *octet.*

eighty-column card—See *card, eighty-column.*

either-way operation—Same as *operation, half-duplex.*

EJCC—(Eastern Joint Computer Conference). A series of conferences, which, along with the Western Joint Computer Conferences, have been replaced by the spring and fall Joint Computer Conferences.

elapsed time—See *time, elapsed.*
electric accounting machine—See *EAM.*
electric delay-line—See *delay-line, electric.*
electric typewriter—See *typewriter, electric.*
electrical connector—See *connector, electrical.*
electrical contact—See *contact, electrical.*
electrical schematic diagram—See *diagram, electrical schematic.*
Electrical Tough Pitch—See *ETP.*
electrically powered telephone—See *telephone, electrically powered.*
electromagnetic delay line—See *delay line, electromagnetic.*
electron beam recording—See *recording, electron beam.*
electron gun—See *gun, electron.*
electronic computer—See *computer, electronic.*
electronic data processing—See *data processing, electronic.*
electronic data-processing machine—See *machine, electronic data-processing.*
electronic data-switching center—Same as *center, automatic data-switching.*
electronic dictionary—Same as *dictionary, automatic.*
electronic differential analyzer—See *analyzer, electronic differential.*
electronic switch—See *switch, electronic.*
electronics—That branch of science which deals with the motion, emission, and behavior of currents of free electrons and certain ions, especially in vacuum tubes, gas tubes, semiconductors, and superconductors. The difference between electrical and electronic is simply a matter of usage. Thus, whether the study of natural lightning, high-voltage arcing, and magnetic blow-out is an electronic or electrical study is purely academic. No hard-and-fast rule can be drawn. Traditionally, currents in passive elements, such as wires, resistors, and inductors, are considered electric rather than electronic currents. Any distinction that is made between electronic and electrical is usually made on the basis of the nature of the current-carrying medium or device.
electronics, molecular—Electronic circuits in which the components are so small that single or small quantities of molecules are used, such as spin-echo storage that utilizes electron spin direction to effect storage, or monatomic layers of fused or film materials to impart characteristics into sublayers, and single molecular domains to effect magnetic storage. These devices are smaller than miniature, subminiature, microminiature, or microelectronic circuits.
electrostatic storage—See *storage, electrostatic.*
electrostatic storage tube—Same as *tube, Williams.*
electrostrictive—The physical phenomenon involving the change in dimensions which occurs when a dielectric or any other material is polarized. The strain produced in most materials when placed in an electric field is approximately proportional to the square of the field strength. The strain is small, except in certain ferroelectric materials such as barium titanate. These materials may be used as transducers of electrical energy to mechanical energy. (Compare with *magnetostrictive* and with *piezoelectric.* Further clarified by *magnetostriction.*)
element, active—An element, component, or device, usually electronic or chemical, which receives energy from two or more sources and in which one source of energy controls the energy flow or action of the other source.
element, AND—Same as *gate, AND.*
element, binary—An element of data that may assume either of two values or states; for example, a binary digit or a plus-or-minus sign.
element, code—One of the discrete conditions or events in a code; for example, the presence or absence of a pulse in a binary code, a dot or a dash in the International Morse Code, or a stroke in a printed character.
element, combinational logic—A device having at least one output channel and two or more input channels, all characterized by discrete states, such that the state of each output channel is completely determined by the contemporaneous states of the input channels; for example, an AND gate or an OR gate.
element, cryogenic—An electric circuit, usually a circuit capable of high-speed switching, that makes use of the phenomena of superconductivity and low thermal noise at or near absolute zero temperatures and usually the destruction of that superconductivity by magnetic fields.
element, data—The name of a set of data items; for example, the quantity of a supply item issued, a wage rate of an employee or a job, a balance on hand of an item, an employee's middle initial, or the instantaneous speed of a missile. The data element *months of the year* is the name of the set of data items *January, February,. . .December.* (Contrast with *item, data* and with *macroelement, data.*)

DATA ELEMENT	DATA ITEM	DATA CODE
RANK	COL	06
STATUS	CIVILIAN	C
MONTH	FEBRUARY	02
SEX	MALE	M
DAY	TUESDAY	TU
DAY	FRIDAY	FR
SEASON	AUTUMN	AU
STATE	OHIO	OH

Typical data elements, with a sample data item and a possible code for each data item.

element, decision—Same as *element, logic.*

element, delay—An element that introduces a time delay of a signal.

element, digit delay—A delay element that introduces in a line of signals or pulses a delay of one digit period duration. Thus, if digits occur on a line at the rate of 400,000 digits a second, a digit delay element for this system would introduce a delay of 2.5 microseconds.

element, display—In display systems, a basic symbol used in conjunction with others to construct display images; for example, points, line segments of various orientation, and characters.

element, fluidic—In fluidics, the basic structural devices, components, and subassemblies that are used to construct fluidic circuits and assemblies, such as nozzles, volumes, passages and restrictors.

element, function—Same as *element, logic.*

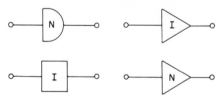

A *larger* logic element *made up of smaller logic elements (AND and OR gates and an inverter).*

element, logic—A device that performs a logic function, in a given computing or data-processing system, usually one, or several gates in association with one another, mounted on a pluggable unit. The element can usually be represented by logic operators in a symbolic logic representation scheme; for example, several AND gates, whose outputs serve as inputs to an OR gate, on a printed-circuit board; a set of four OR gates, with two inputs each, all potted in a one-inch cube of epoxy resin; a pulse transformer, performing the negation function; a half-adder; an AND gate; or a delay element. Logic elements implement the logic operators, permitting logic operations to be performed upon data expressed in electrical codes, usually binary pulse codes. A group of logic elements form the logic design of a system, such as a digital computer. The logic design may be shown graphically on a logic diagram, showing the logic symbols which, when interconnected, describe the system without the use of electrical schematic drawings, which show the detailed circuit elements, such as diodes, capacitors, resistors, and transistors. (Synonymous with *decision element,* with *function element,* and with *functor.*)

element, majority decision—Same as *gate, majority decision.*

element, NAND—Same as *gate, NAND.*

element, negation—A device which is capable of reversing a signal, a condition, a state, or an event into its opposite or alternate. The device is usually an electronic circuit, which more likely consists primarily of an active circuit element, such as a tube or a transistor, but which, though less likely, may be a passive device, such as a transformer. The negation element is applicable in an environment of duality and may be considered as a logical device which changes a given binary input to its opposite value; for example, a positive signal to a negative, a no to a yes, a backward signal to a forward one, a representation of truth to one of falsity, on to off, and a zero to a one. The negation element produces a Boolean complement of the input function, and so may be called an inverter, a complementer, a NOT circuit, or a NOT gate. For example, if the output of a circuit C can be either a high-voltage H or a low-voltage L, and a device attached to C will produce H when C gives L and L when C gives H, then the device attached to C is a negation element. (Synonymous with *inverter,* with *complementer,* with *negation gate,* with *negator,* with *NOT gate,* and with *NOT circuit.* Further clarified by *NOT* and by *negate.*)

Logic symbols used to represent a negation element *or inverter.*

element, NOR—Same as *gate, NOR.*

element, OR—Same as *gate, OR.*

element, passive—An element, component, or device, usually electrical or electronic, which receives energy from one source and performs some operation on that energy; for example, stores the energy in an electric or magnetic field, as a capacitor or inductor, respectively; allows energy to pass, as a wire conductor; attenuates, absorbs, or dissipates energy, as a resistor; restricts the flow of energy to flow in one direction, as in a diode. Hydraulic analogies exist for each of these, such as storage dams (capacitors and inductors), large pipes (conductors), traps (resistors), and gate valves (diodes); as well as mechanical analogies, such as springs (capacitors and inductors), slides (conductors), brakes (resistors), and ratchets (diodes).

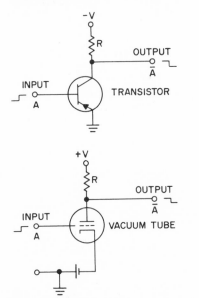

Electrical schematic diagrams for a negation element *with positive input and* negative output.

element, sensing—The part of a transducer that responds directly to the physical or electrical property or condition that is being measured.

element, sequential logic—A device having at least one output channel and one or more input channels such that the state of each output channel is determined by the previous states of the input channels or by the previous states and the contemporaneous states of the input channels.

element, start—Same as *bit, start.*

element, stop—Same as *bit, stop.*

element, threshold—A device that performs the threshold logic operation, the threshold being a general case of the special majority decision. Usually, the truth of each input statement contributes to the output determination a weight associated with that statement. When enough weighted, true input-statement values sum to equal or be greater than the threshold value, the element yields an output signal or statement corresponding to true. (Further clarified by *gate, majority decision.*)

element chain, data—Same as *macroelement, data.*

element string, binary—See *string, binary element.*

element use identifier, data—Same as *identifier, data use.*

eleven-punch—Same as *X-punch.*

ELI—(Equitable Life Interpreter). An interpretive routine developed by Equitable Life Assurance Society for use on the IBM 650 and the IBM 705 computers.

elimination, zero—Same as *suppression, zero.*

elimination ratio—See *ratio, elimination.*

else, or—Same as *OR.*

EM—The end-of-medium character.

emergency maintenance—Same as *maintenance, corrective.*

emergency switch—Same as *button, panic.*

emitter—The electrode in a point contact transistor or the region in a junction transistor which serves as a source of holes or electrons which, under the influence of applied fields and internal barriers, will migrate to the collector and base. The emitter corresponds to the cathode in a vacuum tube. A p-type emitter is a source of holes; an n-type emitter is a source of electrons. The emitter and base form the junction for transistor action, and control the current flow. (Further clarified by *transistor.*)

emitter, character—An electromechanical device that generates and emits in some code pulse groups that correspond to characters. These are used to energize specified lines. Usually the holes in cards or tapes permit these groups to be gated into a common bus for further processing. The characters are usually emitted at fixed intervals.

emitter, digit—A character emitter that is limited to digits to the exclusion of alphabetic characters and other signs and symbols; for example, limited to the twelve row pulses in a punched card column.

IN A	OUT Q
O	I
I	O

A truth table showing the behavior of a negation element *or inverter.*

emitter, half-time—A device that emits synchronous pulses midway in time between the individual row pulses of a punched card.

emitter, selective digit—A part of the control mechanism of a punched card reader by means of which the operator can select which rows of a punched card are to be read.

emitter-follower—An electronic circuit analogous to a cathode-follower, employing a transistor instead of a vacuum tube, the emitter instead of the cathode, and the base instead of the grid. The emitter-follower behaves and performs very much the same functions as the cathode-follower. (Further clarified by *cathode-follower*.)

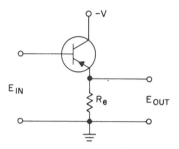

A transistor emitter-follower.

emitter pulse—See *pulse, emitter*.
emitting diode, light—See *diode, light-emitting*.
empiric-function generator—See *generator, empiric-function*.
empirical—A statement or conclusion based on experimental evidence or experience rather than on purely theoretical or purely mathematical reasoning.
empty medium—See *medium, empty*.
empty set—See *set, empty*.
emulate—1: To imitate one system with another such that the imitating system accepts the same data and programs and achieves the same results as the imitated system. There may be a difference in time of performance to achieve the same results. 2: To imitate one system with another using software and additional hardware on the system doing the emulation. (Compared with *simulate*.)
emulator—Hardware built into a computing system, which makes the system appear and behave to certain software, such as programs and routines, as if it were another system. For example, an IBM 7094 emulator for the IBM 360 would permit all programs written for the 7094 to run directly on the 360, without translation or any other intermediate operation.
emulsion-laser storage—See *storage, laser-emulsion*.
enable—To restore to normal operating conditions; for example, to restore a suppressed interrupt feature so that it operates in regular fashion or to remove an inhibiting signal from an AND gate so that it operates as an AND gate again. (Contrast with *disable*.)
enabling signal—See *signal, enabling*.
encipher—Same as *encode*.
encipherer—Same as *encoder*.
encode—To apply the rules of a code, often by representing individual characters or groups of characters in a message with

other individual characters or groups of characters. The substitution of characters, such as letters or numbers for other letters or numbers, is made in order to accomplish a specific purpose, such as make storage or transmission practical or to hide the information in the message from certain persons or groups of persons. Encoding schemes are many and varied and many devices exist for automatic encoding of clear text. (Synonymous with *encipher*. Contrast with *decode* and *decipher*.)
encoded recording, phase—Same as *recording, phase modulation*.
encoder—A device capable of translating from one method of representing data to another method of representing data, such as changing the expression ADDAB, which signifies "add the contents of register A to the contents of register B," to a set of binary digits represented by a set of electrical pulses on a set of wires. Usually the encoder has several inputs, with only one input excited or energized at a time, and each input produces a specified output. Thus, the encoder may have the appearance of a matrix. (Synonymous with *encipherer*. Contrast with *decoder* and with *decipherer*.)
Encore—A utility program for parameter and assembly testing that avoids overlapping of two adjoining operating programs run on the SAGE computer system.
end—The completion of a process; for example, procedure delimiter in ALGOL.
end, leading—1: The end of a wire, tape, ribbon, or similar item that is processed first. (Further clarified by *record, header*. Contrast with *end, trailing*.) 2: The end of a tape or card that first enters a reader, punch, or other device.
end, trailing—1: The end of a wire, tape, ribbon, or similar item that is processed last. (Further clarified by *record, trailer*. Contrast with *end, leading*.) 2: The end of a tape or card that last enters a reader, punch, or other device.
end-around borrow—See *borrow, end-around*.
end-around carry—See *carry, end-around*.
end-around-carry shift—Same as *shift, cyclic*.
end-around shift—Same as *shift, cyclic*.
end distortion—See *distortion, end*.
end instrument—See *instrument, end*.
end mark—See *mark, end*.
end-of-file indicator—See *indicator, end-of-file*.
end-of-medium character—See *character, end-of-medium*.
end-of-message character—See *character, end-of-message*.
end-of-text character—See *character, end-of-text*.
end-of-transmission-block character—See *character, end-of-transmission-block*.
end-of-transmission character—See *character, end-of-transmission*.
end value—See *value, end*.

endogenous event–See event, endogenous.

engaging force, contact–See *force, contact engaging.*

engine, analytical–An early form of general-purpose mechanical digital computer.

engineering, automatic control–The branch of science and technology that deals with the design and use of automatic control devices and systems.

engineering, systems–The implementation of the procedures and plans adopted in an analysis of all the elements in an industrial process, business problem, or control situation. It serves as a systematic method of applying engineering knowledge to all the elements of a system down to the smallest unit.

engineering improvement time–See *time, engineering improvement.*

engineering logic diagram–See *diagram, engineering logic.*

English, ruly–An English in which every word has one and only one meaning and each conceptual meaning has only one word to represent it. The language complies uniformly to a definite set of rules and is devoid of ambiguities. It lends itself to accurate interpretation, machine sensing and interpretation, information retrieval and indexing. It is used by the United States Patent Office for development of index codes.

ENQ–The enquiry character.

enquiry character–See *character, enquiry.*

entity–1: Any item or thing that has individual existence in the mind or in reality; usually, an entity must have some kind of representation or realization that can affect the senses of a human or the sensors of a machine. 2: In computer simulation, an item that is independently identifiable, and usually identified in a simulation by enumerating its particular attributes. The simulated system, the model, and the simulation may also be considered an entity.

entity, permanent–In computer simulation, an entity that exists during the entire period of simulation. (Contrast with *entity, temporary.*)

entity, temporary–In computer simulation, an entity that exists for a part of the period during which the simulation takes place. (Contrast with *entity, permanent.*)

entropy–1: The mean value of the measure of information conveyed by the occurrence of one of a number of mutually exclusive and jointly exhaustive events. Mathematically, the entropy of information is given as:

$$H = \sum_{i=1}^{n} p(x_i) \log (1/ p(x_i))$$

2: The unavailable information in a file, such as a group of documents. 3: The degree of disorganization in a collection of information.

entropy, character mean–The mean entropy per character for all possible messages from a data source.

entropy, conditional–The average of the measure of information contained in the occurrence of any one of a set of mutually exclusive and jointly exhaustive events of specific conditional probabilities, given the occurrence of events of another set of mutually exclusive events.

entry–A way or method of entrance into an item, a collection of items, or one of the items of the collection itself; for example, each word in a list of words that is part of a dictionary, a punched card containing data intended for computer storage, each statement in a program, or each member of a table of values.

entry, closed–An entry in a design that specifically limits a mating part to a certain dimension; for example, the dimension of a lamp socket before the screw base of the bulb is designed.

entry, index–One line or item of data in an index, such as a line-item in a catalog, a line in a table of contents, an entry in a dictionary, or an item in a structured thesaurus. (Closely related to *uniterm,* to *descriptor,* to *keyword,* and to *docuterm.*)

entry, keyboard–An entry to a computing system effected by means of a set of keys, such as a typewriter. Usually, the entry is made to internal storage or to a special register. Thus, the keyboard is a method or channel of access for making entries.

entry, page–In flowchart symbols, the point where a flowline continues from a previous page due to space limitations on the previous page. At that point, a page reference is given in order to locate the point of exit from the previous page. (Further clarified by *page, exit.*)

entry, remote job–The entry of jobs into a computer from a remote station, rather than at the main frame or central processing unit site. A station is considered remote when it is electrically connected but electrically distant from the CPU. If a job is on magnetic tape, and the tape unit is directly connected to the CPU via an input channel for high-speed transfer, then the job entry is not considered to be remote. If a job is entered via a teletype unit and telephone lines, even though the teletype unit is geographically adjacent to the CPU, the job entry is still considered remote.

entry condition–See *condition, entry.*

entry point–See *point, entry.*

environment–The elements or factors that influence or affect the design and operation of a device or system, such as a computer, and to which it must adapt, adjust, readjust, and continue to exist and thrive; for example, the sum of all constraints and limits, ambient conditions, logical considerations, or the totality of equipment available to a program, including data sensors.

EOF—An abbreviation for end-of-file.

EOM—An abbreviation for end of message.

EOT-1: The end-of-transmission character. 2: The end-of-transmission-block character.

EPAM—(Elementary Perceiver and Memorizer). A reading and storing device developed by the University of California.

epistemology, applied—The use of machines, computer programs, or models to simulate the process that handle data, such as perception, recognition, learning, selective recall, indexing, categorization, scanning, storage, search, and retrieval; including the application of principles that apply to the design of machines that perform these functions.

epitaxy—The oriented intergrowth that occurs between two solid crystal phases, the surface of one crystal providing by means of its lattice structure preferred positions for the depositions of the second crystal.

equality gate—Same as gate, exclusive-NOR.

equation solver—See solver, equation.

equalization—The process of reducing frequency or phase distortion or both by introducing networks to compensate for the difference in attenuation and time delay at the various frequencies in the transmission band. For example, a circuit that would favor a frequency that had been attenuated can be introduced to the exclusion of all frequencies.

equipment—1: The hardware, such as electronic computer systems, punched-card machines, devices, and components, that is used to provide a service. 2: In computer simulation, components of a simulation system; for example, storage, logic, and input channels. The equipment usually remains constant during a simulation run and reacts in varying ways with transactions and events.

equipment, ancillary—Same as equipment, peripheral.

equipment, auxiliary—Same as equipment, peripheral.

equipment, conversion—Equipment that transcribes data from one recording medium to another; for example, tape-to-card converters, card-to-printed-page converters, card-to-tape converters, paper-tape-to-magnetic-tape converters, and analog-to-digital converters. Conversion equipment may also change the format of the data in the same medium; for example, magnetic tape to magnetic tape of two different manufacturers. If the data language is changed, the equipment is considered translation equipment. However, in the gray area of overlap between data conversion and data translation lies code conversion, which is a one-to-one conversion of one expression or representation for another. Translation involves some interpretation and contextual analysis of the data involved.

equipment, data terminal—Same as unit, terminal.

equipment, delayed-output—Equipment used to remove data from a computing or data-processing system after processing is completed or in progress; for example, an extra set of tape stations, which accepts data from the main set being used by the computer, and a printer used in conjunction with the extra set of tape stations, thus avoiding the necessity of tying up the computer tape stations during printing.

equipment, high-performance—Equipment whose quality, serviceability, characteristics, and reliability are as good as the best technology permits. (Contrast with equipment, low-performance.)

equipment, input—Equipment used by a computer for accepting data from its outside environment; for example, card readers, paper-tape readers, magnetic-ink character-recognition equipment, optical character-recognition equipment, magnetic tape recorders, and magnetic disc packs. (Contrast with equipment, output.)

equipment, low-performance—Equipment whose performance characteristics are so low that its use is not permitted in trunk or link telephone circuits. However, such equipment may be employed in loop circuits whenever it meets the lower requirements of the loop circuit. (Contrast with equipment, high-performance.)

equipment, output—Equipment used by a computer for transferring data to its outside environment; e.g., printers, punched cards, magnetic tape recorders, paper tape perforators, magnetic disc packs, and cathode-ray display tubes. (Contrast with equipment, input.)

equipment, pence conversion—Card equipment that codes the digits 0 through 11 by a single hole punched in a card column, thus duodecimal coding by means of one hole in a twelve-position column.

equipment, peripheral—Specific devices associated with a data-processing system; for example, magnetic tape units, printers, sorters, plotters, card readers and punches, analog-digital converters, and typewriters. The console and control unit, main internal storage, arithmetic and logic unit, and associated power supplies are not considered peripheral equipment. All else that handles the same data before or after processing is considered peripheral, whether it is or is not under the direct control of the central processing or control unit. Usually peripheral equipment provides a means of communication between a computer and its environment. (Synonymous with ancillary equipment and auxiliary equipment.)

equipment, printing—Equipment that impresses characters on paper with inking techniques for visual sensing.

equipment, remote control—Equipment used for performing a prescribed function or set of functions at a distance. Usually some degree of discretion or decision-making may be exercised upon or by the remote station as to what operations or functions are to be performed, when, and by what means; for example, a console down in a valley used to control a radome up on a mountain peak.

equipment, tabulating—The entire set of equipment that handles or uses punched cards, such as tabulators, sorters, collators, key punches, reproducers, readers, punches, and verifiers. The name tabulating equipment, or simply tab equipment, came into being because the main function of punched cards for many years prior to the advent of automatic digital computers (1944) was to produce tabulations of information resulting from sorting, listing, selecting, and totaling data from punched cards. Many of these functions have been assumed by automatic data processors that manipulate data in internal storage under the control of an internally stored program. Other names that are and have been attributed to tab equipment are punched-card machines (PCM), electrical (or electronic) accounting machines (EAM), and punched-card equipment.

equipment, terminal—The data source equipment, the data sink equipment, or both.

equipment compatibility—See *compatibility, equipment.*

equipment complex—See *complex, equipment.*

equipment failure—See *failure, equipment.*

equivalence—A logic operator having the property that if P is a statement, Q is a statement, R is a statement . . . , then the equivalence of P, Q, R . . . , is true only if all statements are true or all statements are false.

equivalence gate—Same as *gate, exclusive-NOR.*

equivalence operation—See *operation, equivalence.*

equivalent, binary—Same as *digits, equivalent binary.*

equivalent binary digits—See *digits, equivalent binary.*

ERA—(Engineering Research Associates). A manufacturer of electronic equipment, including the 1100 series of computers, which subsequently became the ERA Division of Sperry-Rand Corporation and then part of Remington-Rand Univac.

erasability—In optical character recognition, the ease with which a printed image may be removed without impairing the surface of the medium, such as paper.

erasable storage—See *storage, erasable.*

erase—1: To remove data from storage, leaving the remaining space in a blank condition, or containing no data at all. In a straight binary computer, all storage cells are reduced to the zero condition, in which case the state of storage is the same as if it had been cleared to zero in every storage location. However, in a system in which nonzero pulse codes are used to represent zero, as in the excess-three binary-coded-decimal system, erasing reduces all storage locations to the zero pulse code, such as using a d-c signal to erase a magnetic tape, drum, or disc, or by putting all magnetic cores in the zero state of polarization, in contrast to the one state. Thus, if a one is represented by a positive pulse on the output line, every core shall be in such a state as to produce no pulse or a negative pulse on the output line when the cores are sensed. Then the storage is considered erased. In summary, clearing to zero may leave some binary ones pulse codes, namely those used to represent zero, whereas erasing leaves no binary ones pulse codes anywhere. Most storage devices do not require erasing. Data is simply changed by storing new data in place of the old. Thus each core is polarized in accordance with new data. *Erase* removes all data, leaving no form of data representation whatever, not even symbols for blank or zero. *Delete* removes all data, but may leave a trace of the event, such as a complete row of holes across a paper tape, the only manner in which nonerasable storage contents may be erased; i.e., deleted. Thus, data in a bank of flip-flops cannot be *erased,* but the flip-flops can be *cleared.* (Further clarified by *delete* and by *clear.*) 2: Same as *clear.*

erase character—Same as *character, delete.*

erase head—See *head, erase.*

ERFPI—(Extended Range Floating Point Interpretive System). A system developed by Royal McBee Corporation for the LGP 30 computer.

ergodic—Pertaining to a stochastic process in which every member of a family of processes is statistically representative of the other; for example, in a family of wires carrying telephone voice conversations, since each wire should have the same statistical value of voltage, the process is ergodic, but if a digital tone signal is placed on one or more wires, but not all, then the collection of wires, that is, the process, is no longer ergodic.

error—The deviation of a computed, observed, or measured quantity from the true, specified, or theoretically correct value of the quantity; for example, the difference between a mutilated message and the original message. The error is called positive if the result is greater than the true value, and negative if it is less. Errors are usually due to particular identifiable causes or faults, such as truncation, rounding, cumulation, and measurements. To make a fine distinction, an error is a loss of precision in a quantity, being the difference between an accurate quantity and its calculated approximation. Errors occur in numerical methods, while mistakes are made by humans in such things as programs, codes, and data transcriptions, and malfunctions occur in equipment due to physical limitations in the properties of materials. In automatic control, an error is the difference or variation of a controlled unit compared with the position, setting, or value that it should have. In a restricted sense, the error may be the deviation due to unavoidable random disturbances, or to the use of finite approximations. (Contrast with *accuracy*, with *precision*, with *malfunction*, and with *mistake*.)

error, absolute—1: The error without regard to its algebraic sign or without regard to its direction if it is a vector; thus, the absolute value of an error is only its magnitude. 2: The algebraic result obtained when subtracting a true, specified, or theoretically correct value from the value computed, observed, measured, or achieved.

error, balanced—A set of error values in which the maximum and minimum are opposite in sign and equal in magnitude or a range of error values such that the average of all the values is zero. (Contrast with *error, unbalanced* and with *bias*.)

error, bias—An error that has been introduced or caused by a systematic deviation of a value from a reference value.

error, data—An error introduced by the source data rather than by a mistake in the program or a malfunction of the computer.

error, generated—The total error represented by the combined effect of using inexact or imprecise arguments in an inexact formula; for example, using a rounded number in a truncated series. Thus, if f_a is the value produced by a correct argument in an approximation function, such as a Taylor series, and f* is the value of the actual result because the argument is inexact, then $f_a - f*$ is the generated error. This error is one that builds up as a result of rounding.

error, gross—1: An error of considerable magnitude usually caused by human bungling, such as a major blunder in programming, mounting the wrong reel of tape, or throwing the wrong switch. 2: Same as *mistake*.

error, inherent—Same as *error, inherited*.

error, inherited—The error in quantities that serve as the initial conditions at the beginning of a step in a step-by-step set of operations. Thus, the error carried over from the previous operation from whatever source or cause. The current operation may cause additional error. (Synonymous with *inherent error*.)

error, initial—The error represented by the difference between the true or actual value of an argument and the value used in a computation. Thus, if x is the true value but x* is used in the computation, the x − x* is the initial error.

error, machine—A deviation from correctness of output data caused by a fault or failure in the hardware of a system. Even if the error is made intermittently or only occasionally, the fault must be located and removed for continued successful error-free operation.

error, potentiometer loading—The error in output voltage due to the connection of a load to the slider of a potentiometer as a voltage divider, a potentiometer-multiplier, or a potentiometer scalar. The error is a nonlinear function of the angular setting of the shaft or the position of the slider. It is sometimes avoided by replacing the potentiometer by two or more mechanically linked variable resistors, at least one of which has a nonlinear variation of resistance with angular setting or linear position. Such devices are used in electromechanical analog computers.

error, program—A mistake in a program. Such a mistake can be introduced by a programmer, coder, key puncher, or a machine-language compiler or assembler, due to either a machine malfunction or a mistake in the compiler or assembler. Thus, the error in the program must be corrected before successful operation and error-free results can be obtained.

error, program-sensitive—A malfunctioning of a programmed computer occurring only when a certain program, routine, or combination of operations occurs that is not otherwise logically improper.

error, propagated—An error that occurs in one operation and spreads through later operations. In the later operations it would be called an inherited error.

error, relative—The ratio of the absolute error, which is the algebraic difference obtained by subtracting the true, specified, or theoretically correct value of a parameter from the computed, observed, measured or achieved value of parameter, to the true, specified or theoretically correct value of the parameter that is in error.

error, residual—The error that represents the difference between the optimum result derived from experience or experiment and a supposedly exact result derived from theory.

error, rounding—The error in a numeral caused by deleting the less significant digits of the numeral, and applying some rule of correction to the part retained; for example, +3 and −2 if 2737 is rounded to 2740 and 2682 is rounded to 2680, respectively, according to the rule that if the last digit is 4 or less, drop it and use 0, if it is 5 through 9, add one to the next more significant digit and use 0 for the least significant digit. As computations proceed, rounding errors can build up to the extent of producing completely erroneous and entirely misleading results. (Synonymous with *round-off error*.)

error, round-off—Same as *error, rounding*.

error, truncation—An error introduced by truncating an expression at some point, such as truncating, that is, cutting off or removing the last several letters of a word or digits of a numeral. Truncating the last three digits of the numeral 43.4921 produces 43.4, whereas rounding might produce 43.5.

error, unbalanced—A set of error values in which the maximum and minimum are not necessarily opposite in sign and equal in magnitude; or a range of error values such that the average of all the values is not zero. (Contrast with *error, balanced*)

error burst—See *burst, error*.

error-checking code—See *code, error-checking*.

error-correcting code—See *code, error-correcting*.

error-correcting routine—See *routine, error-correcting*.

error correction, automatic—See *correction, automatic error*.

error-detecting code—See *code, error-detecting*.

error-detecting routine—Same as *routine, diagnostic*.

error range—See *range, error*.

error span—Same as *span, error*.

Esaki diode—Same as *diode, tunnel*.

ESC—The escape character.

escape—To depart from one code or language to another code or language. (Further clarified by *character, escape*.)

ESCAPE—(Expansion Symbolic Compiling Assembly Program for Engineering). A program compiler and assembler developed by Curtiss-Wright Corporation for the IBM 650 computer.

escape, general—An escape to one of two or more possible alphabets, the character immediately following the escape character serving to identify which one of the alphabets are in force until the next escape character is encountered. (Further clarified by *character, escape*.)

escape, locking—An escape in which all characters immediately following the escape character are to be from the alternative alphabet. The action of the locking escape is similar to that of pressing the shift key on a typewriter and also pressing the shift lock. Thus, all succeeding characters are of the new alphabet until the escape character is again encountered; that is, until, in the typewriter, the shift key is unlocked. (Further clarified by *character, escape*.)

escape, nonlocking—An escape in which a specified number of characters, usually only one, immediately following the escape character are to be from the alternative alphabet. The action of the nonlocking escape is similar to that of pressing the shift key on a typewriter without pressing the shift key lock. (Further clarified by *character, escape*.)

escape character—See *character, escape*.

escape character, data link—See *character, data link escape*.

ESD—An abbreviation for electrostatic storage deflection.

ETB—The end-of-transmission-block character.

etched circuit—See *circuit, etched*.

ETP—(Electrical Tough Pitch). A grade of copper that has been refined electrolytically and is used in electrical conductors.

ETX—The end-of-text character.

evaluation, data—The examination and weighing of data in order to obtain an assessment of its inherent meaning, probable accuracy, relevancy, and relationship to a given situation or context. (Further clarified by *center, evaluation*.)

evaluation, performance—In data processing, an on-site analysis of accomplishments with a computer or automatic data-processing system in terms of initial objectives and estimates, to provide a base of experience, to identify corrective actions, and to recommend procedures for performance improvement.

even-odd check—Same as *check, parity*.

even parity—See *parity, even*.

event—1: In a computer operating system, a significant occurrence; for example, the completion of an asynchronous operation such as input-output. 2: In computer simulation, a discrete point in a formal system that is accomplished by an entity and is one of the succession of states in a simulation. Operations that occur at, or as, an event are considered instantaneous since the variable that represents time is kept constant during the occurrence of an event.

event, endogenous—In computer simulation, an event in a simulation system that is internal to the system being simulated and that is initiated or caused by circumstances within the simulation system. (Contrast with *event, exogenous*.)

event, exogenous—In computer simulation, an event in a simulation system that is external to the system being simulated, and that is initiated or caused by circumstances outside the simulation system. (Contrast with *event, endogenous*.)

event monitoring—See *monitoring, event*.

event notice—See *notice, event*.

event posting—See *posting, event*.

exalted carrier reception—See *reception, exalted carrier*.

exceed capacity—See *capacity, exceed*.

except gate—See *gate, except*.

excess-fifty code—Same as *representation, excess-fifty*.

excess-fifty representation—See *representation, excess-fifty*.

excess-three code—See *code, excess-three*.

exchange—An intertransfer or an interchange of devices, a commodity, or information. Examples include the interchange of the contents of two storage devices or locations; a Bendix G-15 computer users' organization, called EXCHANGE, that exchanges programs, system concepts, and operational procedures; or a complex telephone switchgear installation that exchanges, or interchanges or interconnects, telephone circuits in order to route telephone calls.

exchange, automatic—A telephone exchange in which communication between subscribers is effected by devices set in operation by the originating subscriber's instrument, and without the intervention of an operator.

exchange, central office—The place or the equipment that a communication common carrier, such as a telegraph or telephone company, uses to locate the equipment that interconnects subscribers and circuits.

exchange, dial—A telephone exchange, either the place or the equipment, where all the subscribers can originate their calls by dialing. Nearly all exchanges are dial exchanges.

exchange, input-output—An electronic switch used to route input-output messages; that is, messages from various sources intended for various destinations after processing.

exchange, manual—1: A telephone exchange where calls are completed by a human operator. 2: The equipment used to complete telephone calls manually. (Synonymous with *manual telephone switchboard*.)

exchange, memory—Same as *exchange, storage*.

exchange, message—A device that serves as a buffer between a communication line and a computer and that performs communication functions, thus freeing the computer to perform computations while messages are being processed for other operations that do not involve computations.

exchange, private automatic—A dial exchange that provides private telephone service within an organization, but does not allow calls to be transmitted to or from the public telephone network. Abbreviated PAX.

exchange, private automatic branch—A dial exchange that provides private telephone service within an organization and the transmission of calls to and from the public telephone network. Such an exchange is located on a subscriber's site and operated by his employees. Abbreviated PABX.

exchange, private branch—A manual or dial exchange that provides private telephone service within an organization and the transmission of calls to and from the public telephone network. Such an exchange is located on a subscriber's site and operated by his employees. Abbreviated PBX.

exchange, storage—1: The interchange of the contents of two storage locations or two storage devices, such as registers. (Synonymous with *memory exchange*.) 2: A switching device that controls and handles the flow or exchange of data among storage units or other elements of a system. (Synonymous with *memory exchange*.)

exchange buffering—See *buffering, exchange*.

exchange center, local—Same as, *center, local exchange switching*.

exchange center, telephone local—Same as *center, local exchange switching*.

exchange register—Same as *register, storage*.

exchange service—See *service, exchange*.

exchange service, foreign—See *service, foreign exchange*.

Exchange Service, Teletypewriter—See *Service, Teletypewriter Exchange*.

exchange sort—See *sort, exchange*.

exchange switching center, local—See *center, local exchange switching*.

exclusion—Same as *NOT-if-then*.

exclusion gate—1: Same as *gate, A AND NOT B*. 2: Same as *gate, B AND NOT A*.

exclusive-NOR gate—See *gate, exclusive-NOR*.

exclusive-OR—A logic operator having the property that if P is a statement and Q is a statement, then P exclusive-OR Q is true if either but not both statements are true, false if both are true or both are false. The statement P exclusive-OR Q is often represented by $P \oplus Q$, $P \forall Q$. (Contrast with *OR*. Synonymous with *exclusive-OR operator* and with *inequivalence*.)

exclusive-OR gate—See *gate, exclusive-OR*.

exclusive-OR operation—Same as *operation, non-equivalence*.

exclusive-OR operator—Same as *exclusive-OR*.

execute—In computer programming, to interpret a computer instruction and carry out the operations specified by the instruction.

execute phase—See *phase, execute*.

execution time—See *time, execution*.

execution time, program—See *time, program execution*.

executive—Same as *routine, executive*.

executive deck—See *deck, executive*.

executive instruction—See *instruction, executive*.

executive program—Same as *routine, executive*.

executive routine—See *routine, executive*.

executive routine support—See *support, executive routine*.

executive system—Same as *system, operating*.

exhaustivity—In an information retrieval system, the number of keywords or descriptors assigned to a document or record in a file.

exit—1: In computer programming, a way of stopping a repeated cycle of operations or a point at which a repeated cycle of operations may be stopped. Testing the size of a remainder is one way of providing for an exit. If a departure from a routine is involved, the last obeyed instruction of the routine is the exit. A routine may have more than one exit. 2: An instruction in a computer program after the execution of which control is no longer exercised by that computer program. 3: In computer programming, to stop a repeated cycle of operation in a program.

exit, page—In flowchart symbols, the point where a break on the flowline is necessitated by space limitations on the page or paper on which the flowchart is drawn. At that point, a page reference is given in order to locate the point of entry where the flow is continued on another page. (Further clarified by *entry, page*.)

exjunction gate—Same as *gate, exclusive-OR*.

exogenous event—See *event, exogenous*.

exp—The base of natural logarithms, namely 2.718 . . ., or e. Thus, exp bt = ebt = (2.718 . . .)bt.

expanded order—Same as *pseudo-instruction*.

expected-value model—See *model, expected-value*.

explicit address—Same as *address, absolute*.

exponent—A numeral that indicates the number of times a given numeral is to be a factor to produce a product. Thus, when a numeral is raised to a power, the exponent is the numeral indicating the power; for example, in the expression 2^8, the 8 is the exponent. The exponent can be used to indicate the number of zeros that follow a one (1) when a base is raised to the given power; for example, in decimal, 10^4 equals decimal 10,000; in binary, 2^8 equals binary 100000000, or decimal 256. A floating-point numeral uses an exponent to indicate the location of the point; for example, 2.17×10^4, where 4 is an exponent, is equal to 21,700. If the number base is known or implied, only a fractional part and the exponent need be given. The exponent is usually written at the upper right of a numeral or symbol; for example, b^2 or u^v, where 2 and v are exponents.

expression—One or more symbols to which meaning is assigned. Sets of expressions form statements. (Further clarified by *statement*.)

extended area service—See *service, extended area*.

extended binary-coded decimal interchange code—See *code, extended binary-coded decimal interchange*.

extended time scale—See *scale, extended time*.

extensible langauge—See *language, extensible*.

extension character, code—See *character, code extension*.

external arithmetic—See *arithmetic, external*.

external delay—See *delay, external*.

external program parameter—See *parameter, external program*.

external sort—See *sort, external*.

external storage—See *storage, external*.

externally stored program—See *program, externally stored*.

extract—**1:** To remove, from a set of items, a subset whose members meet a specified criterion; for example, to obtain from a computer word digits that are specified by an instruction or a filter, to derive a new computer word from another computer word by filtering, or to remove specific parts of a file, such as a specific passage of text. When dealing with a computer word, the filter is the computer word or part of a word that specifies the digits that are to be removed or retained. **2:** The part of a set that is removed.

extract instruction—See *instruction, extract*.

extractor—Same as *mask*.

extraneous ink—See *ink, extraneous*.

extrapolate—To extend a curve beyond the limits of known points by continuing the trend established over known points.

E 364—A program for the translation of mathematical equations for the Whirlwind I computer.

f

fabricated language—Same as *language, artificial*.

face, bold—See *boldface*.

face, card—The side of a punched card that is printed if one and only one side is printed. Many punched cards have numerals to identify the columns and rows, or punch positions. Some cards are ruled to demarcate zones, fields, or special areas. The side opposite the face is usually blank.

face, inner—The face of a magnetic or punched paper tape that is in contact with the reading, writing, punching, or sensing head, and so the side facing the head. (Contrast with *face, outer*.)

face, outer—The face of a magnetic or punched paper tape that is not in contact with the reading, writing, punching, or sensing head, and so the side facing away from the head. (Contrast with *face, inner*.)

face change character—Same as *character, font change*.

face-down feed—See *feed, face-down*.

face-up feed—See *feed, face-up*.

facility–In computer simulation, a specific piece of equipment that is used by one transaction at a time.

facility, hold–The ability of a computer to keep all variables at the value they had when the computations were interrupted. In such computers, time is usually used to represent the independent variable. Means are included for interrupting the computing action and for allowing the computations to proceed after initiation without repetition or without the insertion of new data or instructions.

FACS–(Floating-decimal Abstract Coding System). A compiler developed by Lockheed Aircraft Corporation for the IBM 650 computer.

facsimile–An exact copy, usually of a document, such as a letter, picture, map, or diagram.

Facsimile–A commercial method developed by American Telephone and Telegraph Company for transmitting images, such as letters, pictures, maps, and diagrams, by electrical means, usually wire.

facsimile posting–See *posting, facsimile.*

FACT–1: (Factual Compiler). A program compiler developed by Ramo-Wooldridge Corporation. 2: (Fully Automatic Compiling Technique). A program compiler developed by Minneapolis-Honeywell Regulator Company for the Honeywell 800 computer for handling the full range of business applications, such as editing, sorting, processing, and report writing. It uses English language statements.

fact correlation–See *correlation, fact.*

factor–1: Any of the numbers or quantities that are the operands in a multiplication operation. 2: Either one of the two numbers that are multiplied.

factor, relocation–The algebraic difference between the assembled origin, i.e. the initial address in main storage assigned by the assembly program, and the initial address in main storage assigned by the loading program, i.e., the initial address of the program when it is loaded into main storage.

factor, scale–1: A number used as a multiplier or divisor and so chosen that it will cause a set of quantities occurring in a problem to fall within a given range of values; for example, if the quantities 856, 432, -95, and -182 were all to be divided by 1000, then the resultant quantities would all lie between $+1$ and -1, and the scale factor would be $1/1000$ or 10^{-3}. In most instances, the scale factor has the effect of moving the arithmetic point, such as decimal or binary, so that all numbers may be held in the computer registers properly and with proper relative significance. The scale factor assures that the significant digits of a number occupy a specified portion or digit position of a computer word. Scaling is particularly required in fixed-point computers. The

scaling problem is somewhat alleviated in floating-point computers, since permissible number ranges are broader. Scale factors must be processed along with the data, in order to interpret the results. Therefore, to multiply 512 by 32, with a scale factor of 1000 for both, the numbers must be converted: 512 is converted to 0.512 and 32 to 0.032, and the product, 0.016384, must be multiplied by 1000×1000, or 10^6, to yield 16,384, the correct product of the two original numbers. Further, the scale factor is a constant for each set of conversions and usually is dimensionless. (Synonymous with *scale coefficient.*) 2: In instrumentation, the coefficient required to convert a scale or instrument reading to the value of a quantity being measured; for example, if 2 in. of deflection of a spot of light is equivalent to 5 coulombs of electrical charge passing through a ballistic galvanometer, then the scale factor is 2.5 coulombs per inch. The scale factor in instrument conversions is usually a dimensional quantity. (Further clarified by *scale* and by *scalar.*)

factor, time scale–The ratio of computer time to the corresponding time of a problem being solved by the computer; for example, if a computer is calculating the trajectory of a missile faster than the trajectory is traversed by the missile, then computer time is shorter than problem time and the time scale factor is less than one, that is, a fast time scale factor is being used.

factorial–The product of the positive integers 1, 2, 3, up to and including a given integer; for example, factorial 5 is $1 \times 2 \times 3 \times 4 \times 5$ or 120.

fading–The fluctuation or temporary loss of strength of any or all components of a signal due to changes in the characteristics of the propagation path; for example, the rising and falling of the intensity of a radio signal.

fading, flat–Fading in which all components of a signal fluctuate in the same proportion simultaneously; for example, the amplitude of all frequency components of a radio signal rising and falling in proportion to their respective amplitudes in the original signal as broadcast.

fading, selective–Fading in which the components of a signal fluctuate independently or disproportionately; for example, the rising and falling of only the high-frequency components of a radio signal.

failure, catastrophic–A failure resulting in the complete lack of useful performance of an item, such as a sudden change in the operating characteristics of a computer power supply rendering all circuits inoperative.

failure, equipment–A fault in equipment that causes improper behavior of the equipment or that prevents a scheduled job from being accomplished, such as the interruption of the execution of a computer program. All external factors must be excluded, such as program errors and human mistakes. (Further clarified by *malfunction.*)

failure, incipient—An equipment failure that is just about to exist. Noticeable or detectable degradation of operation has not occurred. Most incipient failures can be detected by conducting marginal tests. Incipient failures are not considered equipment failures, since an operational interruption has not occurred nor has an error in results been introduced.

failure, induced—An equipment failure that is caused by the environment of the failed item. Thus, a physical condition or phenomenon external to the component caused it to fail; for example, the failure of a tube caused by the positive voltage swing of the control grid, which was caused by the failure of the clamping diode, or the destruction of transistors caused by a rise in the ambient temperature because of the failure of the air conditioner.

failure, mean-time-to- —See *mean-time-to-failure.*

failures, mean-time-between- —See *mean-time-between-failures.*

FAIR—An automatic coding system developed by Eastman-Kodak Company for the IBM 705 computer.

false add—See *add, false.*

false code—Same as *character, illegal.*

false code check—Same as *check, forbidden-combination.*

false drop—Same as *retrieval, false.*

false retrieval—See *retrieval, false.*

fan-in—In fluidics, the number of operating or input controls that individually and in combination produce the same output. (Contrast with *fan-out.*)

fan-out—In fluidics, the number of like devices whose inputs can be connected to the output of a given fluidic device; for example, the number of amplifier control inputs that can be driven by a given amplifier output. (Contrast with *fan-in.*)

FAP—**1:** (Floating-point Arithmetic Package). An automatic coding system developed by Lockheed Missile Systems Division for the Univac 1103A computer for coding floating-point arithmetic. **2:** (FORTRAN Assembly Program, or Procedure). A FORTRAN assembler developed by International Business Machines Corporation for the IBM 704 and IBM 709 computers. AIRS, an automatic information retrieval system, is written in this language.

farad (F)—A measure of the ability of two insulated bodies to hold a static electric charge equal to one coulomb at a potential difference of one volt between the two bodies, or one coulomb per volt. A coulomb of charge passing a point in one second is an ampere of current. Since a coulomb is a large charge, one coulomb

per volt is a large capacity to hold charge. Hence, most capacitors (condensors) are measured in *micro*farads (μF); *millimicro*farads (mμF); and *micromicro*farads ($\mu\mu$F), also called *pico*farads (pF).

FARET—(Fast Reactor Test Facility). An atomic energy reactor test facility at Argonne National Laboratory.

FARGO—(Fourteen-oh-one Automatic Report Generator Operation). A report generator prepared for the IBM 1401 computer.

FAST—1: (Fieldata Applications, Systems and Techniques). A Fieldata computer users group, including Mobidic, Basicpac, Compac and other computers. **2:** (Four Address to SOAP Translator). A program translator developed at Texas A and M College for the IBM 650 computer. **3:** (Flexible Algebraic Scientific Translator). An algebraic translator for scientific problems run by National Cash Register 315 computer users.

fast-access storage—Same as *storage, high-speed.*

fast storage—Same as *storage, high-speed.*

fast time scale—See *scale, fast time.*

fault—The improper behavior of a device, program, component, or element that causes it to fail to perform in a required manner during a specified time period under a given set of environmental conditions. Some examples are a short circuit, an emission-limited cathode, an oscillating power supply, a broken wire, or a wrong logic connection. The fault may be sporadic or permanent. Many computers have automatic circuits for fault detection, location, and even correction. Faults in equipment are usually called *equipment failures* or *malfunctions*, while faults in programs are called program *errors.* Humans make *mistakes.*

fault, pattern-sensitive—A fault that causes a data-handling component to fail only when some particular set of data is used. For other data or for other patterns, the failure does not occur.

fault, program-sensitive—A fault that causes a computer component to fail only when a particular program is executed, such as a particular timing sequence or a set of program steps. The failure does not occur when any other program is run.

fault analysis—See *analysis, fault.*

fault-location problem—See *problem, fault-location.*

fault time—Same as *time, down.*

Fax—A facsimile system developed by American Telephone and Telegraph Company.

FC—The font change character.

FE—The format effector character.

feasibility study—See *study, feasibility.*

FEAT—(Frequency of Every Allowable Term). An inventory computer program used for information storage and retrieval and for linguistic analysis. An IBM 709 computer is used for implementation, applying SCAT symbolic, SOS, and SMASHT programming languages. System Development Corporation is associated with and developed the program.

feature, checking—A built-in capability of a machine that automatically performs a check on its own operations.

feed, card—A mechanism that moves cards one by one into a machine, such as a punched-card reader. The feeder transfers the cards from a hopper to a card track that has one or more reading or sensing stations. The cards usually trail one after the other along the track. In some machines, the cards are read "on-the-fly," appearing as a blur as they move through free space in a fanlike fashion. These are high-speed card readers.

feed, face-down—A card feed that accepts cards in the face-down position.

feed, face-up—A card feed that accepts cards in the card face-up position.

feed, horizontal—To enter a rectangular punch card into a card feed mechanism with a long edge first. Thus, the card travels with the long edge leading and the card rows are read row by row. (Contrast with *feed, vertical*.)

feed, tape—A mechanism that moves tape so that it passes sensing and recording stations. The tape may be paper, metal, plastic, or other material. The most common materials are paper in which holes are punched to record data, and Mylar, coated with an iron oxide, on which data is recorded magnetically.

feed, vertical—To enter a rectangular punch card into a card feed mechanism with a short edge first. Thus, the card travels with the short edge leading and the card columns are read column by column. (Contrast with *feed, horizontal*.)

feed character, form—See *character, form feed*.

feed character, line—See *character, line feed*.

feed holes—Same as *holes, sprocket*.

feed pitch—See *pitch, feed*.

feed punch, automatic—See *punch, automatic-feed*.

feed reel—See *reel, feed*.

feed-through connector See *connector, feed-through*.

feed track—See *track, feed*.

feedback—To return a part of the output of a machine, system, or process to the input; thus, permitting the output to affect the input as well as the input to affect the output. In simple cases, if an increase in output tends to decrease the input, the feedback is negative, or degenerative, whereas if the increase in output tends to increase the input, the feedback is positive, or regenerative. Feedback may be used to stabilize or increase the gain of an amplifier, to self-correct for control purposes in a computer, or to modify or moderate input to a system in accordance with a critique of the output, such as is used in management reporting techniques.

Feedback principles are used in closed-loop systems to bring back information about a condition under control for comparison with a target value. The use of feedback can produce many desired results, in areas ranging from computer operation to pest control. (Further clarified by *control, feedback*; by *feedback, negative*; and by *feedback, positive*.)

feedback, degenerative—Same as *feedback, negative*.

feedback, negative—The technique of returning a part of the output of a machine, system, or process to the input in such a manner that an increase of output results in a larger quantity to be deducted from the input. (Synonymous with *degenerative feedback*. Contrast with *feedback, positive*.)

feedback, positive—The technique of returning a part of the output of a machine, system, or process to the input in such a manner that an increase of output results in a larger quantity to be added to the input. (Synonymous with *regenerative feedback*. Further clarified by *feedback*. Contrast with *feedback, negative*.)

feedback, regenerative—Same as *feedback, positive*.

feedback amplifier—See *amplifier, feedback*.

feedback control—See *control, feedback*.

feeding, form—The positioning of various forms or other documents, usually by mechanisms designed to move the forms singly or in continuous rolls, past printing or sensing devices. The feeding is often controlled by a punched paper or fabric tape that directs a carriage to move the single or multipart forms. Some form feeders handle two or more forms simultaneously, for recording the same data with the same type bars, wheels, or chains, but perhaps with different spacing. The form feed controls both the movement of the form during printing as well as ejection, and the feeding of the next form.

feeding, multicycle—Same as *feeding, multiread*.

feeding, multiread—Feeding punched cards in such a manner that several fields of a single card are sensed sequentially at successive revolutions of the card reader main shaft. Multiread feeding may be used as a card-saving technique, such as when printing names and addresses, because card machines usually require one revolution for each line of print. (Synonymous with *multicycle feeding*.)

feeding, single-sheet—The feeding of separate sheets of paper rather than feeding in roll or fan-folded form. The feeding may be manual or automatic, and the printing is accomplished on each sheet separately and sequentially.

FEP—(Financial Evaluation Program). A program for managing investment, business operations, taxes, costs, manpower, and related items, developed for the IBM 1620 computer.

fermi level—Same as *level, fermi.*

ferrite—A compound of iron oxide and other metallic oxides in a ceramic matrix that has been properly sintered. The material displays a rectangular magnetic hysteresis loop; thus, in an annulus of ferrite, the residual flux remaining after the magnetizing force is removed is nearly equal to the saturation flux. In addition, ferrites display high electrical resistance; low magnetizing force, which is required to switch the material to polarization in the opposite direction; and high switching speed. Most storage cores for digital computers are made of ferrite.

ferroelectric—Pertaining to the property of materials that renders them capable of being electrically polarized in a manner similar to that in which ferrous and some other metals may be magnetized. Certain materials exhibit a characteristic that is explained by the existence of permanent electric dipoles. Thus, if E is the applied electric field strength, measured or expressed as potential difference per unit length, such as electrostatic units of potential difference per centimeter, or volts per centimeter; force per unit charge; or lines of force per unit area; and if P is the amount of polarization that has taken place in the material, measured or expressed as oriented dipoles per unit volume or the amount of charge that moves across a unit area upon the application of the electric field to a virgin or unpolarized piece of material (in ferroelectric materials there will be a residual polarization that remains after the electric field is removed); then the electric displacement vector D, much like the magnetic flux density B, is defined as $D = E + 4\pi P$; or $D = \mu_e E$; and $P = \psi_e E$, where μ_e and ψ_e are the electric permeability and susceptibility respectively, similar to $B = H + 4\pi M$; where $B = \mu_m H$ and $M = \psi_m H$, where μ_m and ψ_m are the magnetic permeability and susceptibility, respectively. Note that the μ_e and ψ_e are also called dielectric constants. Note also the similarity of relationships between the ferroelectric and ferromagnetic cases. Since ferromagnetic behavior is attributed to the ferrous metals, the similarity of expression prompted the use of the word ferroelectric, though perhaps this is somewhat unfortunate and a misnomer, since the materials that demonstrate ferroelectric effects are not at all ferrous metals or materials, such as barium titanate or Rochelle salt. Since ferroelectric materials may be electrically polarized permanently, a rectangular hysteresis loop is obtainable in the *D-E* plane, with a squareness ratio approaching unity, just as ferromagnetic materials do in the *B-H* plane, that is, flux density versus magnetic field intensity. Serious attempts have been made to utilize ferroelectric

effects as a means of storing or switching data in computers. Certain electric insulators display the ferroelectric phenomenon and can be polarized. The polarization can be reversed or reduced by application of an electric field of opposing polarity. (Compare with *ferromagnetic.*)

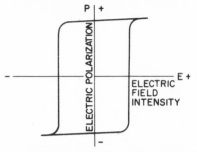

Ferroelectric *polarization of a material through the application of an electric field. (Note the similarity to a ferromagnetic hystersis loop; hence, the term* ferroelectric.*)*

ferromagnetic—Pertaining to the property of materials that renders them capable of being magnetically polarized. Since the polarization has residual effects, the property can be used to store or switch data, by allowing polarization in one direction to represent a numeral one and polarization in the opposite direction to represent a numeral zero. With this binary arrangement, all data can be expressed. A one can easily be changed to a zero by passing a pulse of electric current through an appropriate conductive winding in the opposite direction, which creates a field of opposite polarity. The ferromagnetic effect is prevalently used in digital computer storage units. If the magnetic flux density B is plotted versus the magnetic field intensity H, and H is varied in a positive and then a negative direction, a nearly rectangular hysteresis loop can be obtained. The applicable relationships are $B = H + 4\pi M$; $B = \mu H$ and $M = \psi H$, where B is the magnetic flux density, H is the magnetic field intensity, M is the magnetic polarization, μ is the magnetic permeability, and ψ is the magnetic susceptibility to polarization, (Further clarified by *square-loop* and by *hysteresis.* Compare with *ferroelectric.*)

ferromagnetics—The science devoted to the magnetic polarization properties of materials. It is a subdivision of magnetics and somewhat related to electromagnetics, which is primarily devoted to radiation. The ferromagnetic properties of materials have found wide application in computers for data storage and switching.

ferrule—A short tube used to make solderless connections to a shielded or coaxial cable and sometimes molded into the plastic inserts of multiple-contact connectors to provide strong, wear-resistant shoulders on which contact retaining-springs can bear.

fetch–1: Same as *retrieve.* 2: In computer programming, the portion of a computer operation execution in which the address of the next instruction is located and the next storage location is determined. The instruction in that location is then placed in a register for execution. Thus, the next instruction is fetched from storage.

FF–1: An abbreviation for *flip-flop.* 2: The form feed character.

Fibonacci number–See *number, Fibonacci.*

Fibonacci search–See *search, Fibonacci.*

Fibonacci series–See *series, Fibonacci.*

fiche–A term meaning card and used primarily in Europe. (Further clarified by *microfiche.*)

field–In a record, a specified part of the record. Some examples include a group of card columns used to represent a particular item of data, such as an employee's wage rate; a set of bits in a computer word used to express the address of the operand; the set of bits in a computer word used to indicate the operation to be performed; or the fourth, fifth, and sixth word in every block on a magnetic tape. The particular field is always used to record the same type of information, such as the distance to the target at every given interval of real time. Thus, the contents of a field are usually treated or handled as a whole or as a unit. One may consider a field to contain several, but usually, related units of information.

field, card–A field on a punched card; for example, columns 84 through 90, inclusive, used to record an employee's date of birth. The card columns or rows assigned to a field are usually consecutive. The card field for a particular unit of data may be fixed, or its location may be made relative to another reference field. Thus, corresponding fields on successive cards normally contain similar information.

field, common–A field accessible to two or more routines.

field, control–A particular location used for control in each of all of a set of items, records, or files of data. The location is usually the same for each unit of data; for example, in a deck of punched cards, the 47th to 49th column, used to control or determine whether or not certain operations will be performed.

field, decrement–The part of a computer instruction word used specifically for modifying the contents of a register or storage location. The register or storage location is specified by the tag digits of the same instruction word that the decrement field is a part of. In most digital computers, the decrement is a set of binary digits, and the field is the location of the digits; for example, the 17th through 19th bits of every instruction word.

field, fixed–Pertaining to a method of storing information in a storage medium wherein the same kind of data is placed in the same relative position; for example, using the 15th to 20th digit position, only for an employee's payroll number. Thus, a given part of each computer word, a given area on each frame of film, a specific set of columns of a punched card, or a given set of holes along the margin of a set of edge-punched cards are used for recording a specific characteristic or given item of data. (Contrast with *field, free.*)

field, free–Pertaining to a method of storing data in a storage medium that permits recording the data without regard to preassigned or fixed fields; for example, punching English text, such as titles of books, across the eighty columns of a punched card without restriction as to where particular parts, or the title itself, may lie. (Contrast with *field, fixed.*)

field, signed–A location in a storage medium that can be assigned a plus or minus algebraic sign that applies to the entire number stored at that position.

field length–See *length, field.*

Fieldata–Pertaining to an interim family of automatic data-processing equipment designed and built to be employed in the field by the United States Army. The equipment is completely rugged, militarized, mobile, and makes maximum use of existing state-of-the-art computer components to ensure a high degree of reliability, ease of maintenance, and simplified logistical support. Members of the Fieldata family include DYSEAC, Basicpac, Compac, the Mobidic series of systems, and FADAC. Applications include command, control, logistics, intelligence, and fire direction.

Fieldata code–See *code, Fieldata.*

Fieldata Family–Same as *System, Army Fieldata.*

Fieldata System–Same as *System, Army Fieldata.*

FIFO–First-in-first-out.

figurative–An item of data that is descriptive of its magnitude or value; for example, sin 60°, five, zero, or four hundred three. The data need not be descriptive of the format or code used to represent the figurative.

figurative constant–See *constant, figurative.*

figure–Same as *numeral.*

figure, significant–Same as *digit, significant.*

file–A collection of related records; e.g., a sequence of records on magnetic tape, terminated by an end-of-file mark or a file gap; or in a stock control situation, one line of an invoice might be an item, the entire invoice would be a record, and all the invoices would form the file. The file is usually organized to meet a specific purpose. The records in a file are usually sequenced in accordance with some key contained in each record. Although each record in a file is usually kept together, such as sequentially, it is possible to scatter the records of a file to meet a specific purpose; e.g., an employee's file may be scattered if it is desired to pull all wage-data into one file, all experience information into another file and all personal statistics into another file. Files are not necessarily all the same size, nor need all items or records of a file be in the same class; e.g., in a set of employee files, an experience record may only appear in the professional employee's file. A file might be made up of records, fields, words, characters, bytes, or bits.

file, active—A file currently in use. Thus it is anticipated with a reasonable degree of certainty that an entry or a reference will be made in the immediate future. (Contrast with *file, inactive*. Further clarified by *file, dead*.)

file, chained—A file of data arranged so that each data element, item, or key in a record has an address of another record with the same data element, item, or key. Thus, to retrieve all records that contain a given key, it is necessary to find only the first one; for adjacent to this will be the address of another record containing the same key, which will have the address of another, and so on, until the chain is ended and all the records containing the given key have been retrieved. Computer organized files are thus easily searched. If the chain is broken, data can be lost in the file. Much space can be consumed storing the addresses. Less searching is required, since only the linked records need be accessed and retrieved. (Synonymous with *threaded file*.)

file, dead—A file that is retained but not in current use. Thus, it is anticipated with a reasonable degree of certainty that an entry or reference will not be made in the immediate future. Most likely the file will never be referenced and it is retained only for meeting a legal or other specific requirement. (Further clarified by *file, active* and by *file, inactive*.)

file, detail—A file of data, of a variant or transient nature, containing current data that is processed against a master file at a later time or at periodic intervals, either to update the master file or to compute or determine a specific result. An example would be a file containing all the daily transactions in an inventory control application, such as the quantity of items received, shipped, due in, due out, and spoiled in storage; periodically, the file containing the inventory would be adjusted in view of daily transactions. (Synonymous with *transaction file*. Further clarified by *file, master*.)

file, fixed-length record—A file containing a set of records, each of which contains the same number of characters or a few predetermined specified record lengths. In such a system, the field, word, blocks, or records may be fixed in length. (Contrast with *file, variable-length record*.)

file, flat—A file in which documents, usually papers, are filed unfolded in a vertical, horizontal, or slanted position. Flat filing is usually loose filing, and is distinguished from fastening sheets in a folder.

file, follow-up—A file in which certain matters are automatically brought to one's attention at the appropriate time; for example, a deck of cards containing data about insurance policies, filed in order of expiration date so that at some fixed time prior to expiration, a renewal notice can be sent. (Synonymous with *suspense file*.)

file, forms—A file of all the forms used by an activity, usually filed according to function, such as supply forms (requisition, hand-receipt, and turn-in slip) or personnel forms (Form 57, Personal History, and Withholding Statement).

file, inactive—A once active file that, although not in current use, is expected with a reasonable amount of certainty to be restored to an active status. For example, the medical record of a patient who has been released from the hospital with the expectation that he may return at some future date would be placed in an inactive file. (Contrast with *file, active*. Further clarified by *file, dead*.)

file, inverted—A file, or a method of file organization, in which all item labels are placed in a single record that is identified by some label that describes the contents of the documents; e.g., if *infrared* is descriptive of the contents of documents numbered 47, 52, 58, and 60, then these numbers could be placed on a card, say by punching a hole at a coordinate location that represents each number, and if *detection devices* describe the contents of documents numbered 47, 51, 58, and 59, then these numbers could be placed on a card, again say by punching a hole at a coordinate location that represents each number. The file can be used to identify all documents that treat of infrared detection devices, say by holding the record cards labeled *infrared* and *detection devices* up to the light in peek-a-boo style and noticing that light comes through at holes 47 and 58.

file, master—1: A main reference file containing data that is relatively permanent but that is usually updated periodically by a detail file, which contains relatively less permanent data. (Further clarified by *file, detail*.) 2: A file used as an authority during or with a given job or run and that is relatively permanent, even though its content may be changed.

file, problem—All the material needed or used to document a program run on a computer. It contains such things as a statement of the problem, flowcharts, coding sheets, operating instructions, and notes. (Synonymous with *run book* and *problem folder*.)

file, spike — firmware

file, spike–A vertical, or horizontal for wall mount, spike or pointed rod mounted on a firm base used to hold papers by forcing the spike through the papers. A hole results in the papers that are spiked.

file, string–A piece of tape, wire, or string used to arrange documents for convenient reference. (Synonymous with *tape file* and with *wire file*.)

file, suspense–Same as *file, follow-up.*

file, tape–1: A file consisting of a magnetic or punched-paper tape used to hold records. 2: A set of tapes; for example, a number of reels of magnetic tape placed in an orderly, indexed array, as in a tape library. 3: Same as *file, string.*

file, threaded–Same as *file, chained.*

file, tickler–A file maintained so that its contents can be followed up at definite future dates; for example a suspense file with items filled in the chronological order in which specific actions are due to be completed; or an appointed calendar.

file, transaction–Same as *file, detail.*

file, variable-length record–A file containing a set of records in which the number of characters or the field, word, block, or records may vary in length. (Contrast with *file, fixed-length record.*)

file, visible–A file in which recording media, such as cards, sheets of paper, and films, are so arranged that data placed in the margin can serve as an index that the user can see without thumbing through the file; for example, a deck of cards with visible tabs projecting from the side.

file, wire–Same as *file, string.*

file access control–See *control, file access.*

file activity ratio–See *ratio, file activity.*

file gap–See *gap, file.*

file identification–See *identification, file.*

file maintenance–See *maintenance, file.*

file maintenance, interactive–See *maintenance, interactive file.*

file maintenance, logical–See *maintenance, logical file.*

file management routine–See *routine, file management.*

file owner–See *owner, file.*

file purging–See *purging, file.*

file reorganization–See *reorganization, file.*

file structure, keyed–See *structure, keyed file.*

fill–Same as *pad.*

fill, character–1: To store the repeated representations of the same character in a storage location, in a group of storage locations, or in a complete storage unit of a computer. 2: To insert, as often as appropriate into a storage medium, the representation of a specified character that does not itself convey data but may delete unwanted data.

fill, storage–The storing of a pattern of characters in storage areas that are not used for program or data storage for a particular machine run. Thus, if an error should cause the machine to refer to one of these areas not intended for data or

coding, the machine will stop. This technique serves as an aid to program and machine debugging. This is better than having the machine attempt to execute instructions that are taken from storage locations that were not intended to contain coding. The entire set of instructions and data are loaded into storage, along with the fill, as a logical unit.

filler–One or more characters adjacent to an item of data to bring the representation of the data up to a given size.

film, negative–Film on which the light portions of the image or subject appear dark and the dark portions appear light, which is opposite to the appearance of an image or scene to a human eye. (Contrast with *film, positive.*)

film, positive–Film on which the light portions of the image or subject appear light and the dark portions appear dark, much as an image or scene appears to the human eye. (Contrast with *film, negative.*)

film, thin–Same as *thin-film, magnetic.*

film frame–See *frame, film.*

film reader–See *reader, film.*

film recorder–See *recorder, film.*

Filmorex system–See *system, Filmorex.*

filter–A device or a program that separates data, signals, or materials in accordance with specified criteria; for example, a set of instructions that permits the setting of certain bit positions in a computer word to zero, through the use of a mask. Masking is usually accomplished through the use of a logic AND operation, to eliminate the undesired bits from another word. Thus, the mask is an artificially constructed word which contains zeros in the bit positions that are to be disregarded or thrown away and ones in the bit positions that are to be isolated. By using the logic multiply, AND, or extract instruction with this word and the word to be masked, a masking out of the selected bits will occur, leaving the word that is desired, that is, a filtered result. Thus, certain desired bit locations in the result will contain a zero, all other locations will contain whatever digit was in the original unmasked word at that location. (Further clarified by *mask.*)

final trunk–See *trunk, final.*

fire control–See *control, fire.*

firmware–1: Hardwired computer logic for performing computer functions previously or normally done by programs, for example, hardwired logic to locate available resources such as processors, peripheral devices, input devices, output devices and external storage; hard wired logic for regulation, for facility location, recovery of information, message routing, communications, and multiprogramming. 2: Software and hardware that interact so closely and mutually that the functions of both are inseparable.

155

first-in-first-out—Pertaining to a queuing technique in which the next item to be retrieved from the queue is the item that has been in the queue for the longest time, that is, longer than any other item in the queue. Abbreviated as FIFO. (Related to *storage, pushup* and to *list, pushup.* Contrast with *last-in-first-out.*)

first-level address—Same as *address, direct.*

first-order subroutine—See *subroutine, first-order.*

fitting compaction, curve—See *compaction, curve-fitting.*

five-bit byte—Same as *quintet.*

fixed-cycle operation—See *operation, fixed-cycle.*

fixed field—See *field, fixed.*

fixed length—See *length, fixed.*

fixed-length record—See *record, fixed-length.*

fixed-length record file—See *file, fixed-length record.*

fixed-length word—See *word, fixed-length.*

fixed-logic query—See *query, fixed-logic.*

fixed point—See *point, fixed.*

fixed point, fractional—A fixed-point numeration system used in many binary digital computers wherein all numerical quantities represented by the computer are numerals with a fixed number of digits, with the binary point implicitly located at the left end so that all numerals are less than one. All quantities represented by the computer that lie outside this range must be scaled accordingly.

fixed-point calculation—See *calculation, fixed-point.*

fixed-point computer—See *computer, fixed-point.*

fixed-point operation—Same as *calculation, fixed-point.*

fixed-point part—Same as *coefficient, floating-point.*

fixed-point representation—See *representation, fixed-point.*

fixed-radix notation—See *notation, fixed-radix.*

fixed-radix numeration system—See *system, fixed-radix numeration.*

fixed-radix scale—Same as *notation, fixed-radix.*

fixed routine—See *routine, fixed.*

fixed storage—See *storage, fixed.*

fixed-tolerance-band compaction—See *compaction, fixed-tolerance-band.*

fixed type bar—See *bar, fixed type.*

fixed word length—See *word, fixed-length.*

flag—An indicator, such as a signal, symbol, character, or digit, used for identification; for example, a word mark, a group mark, or a letter that signals the occurrence of some condition or event, such as the end of a word. Flags are usually programmed. (Synonymous with *tag* and *sentinel.*)

FLAIR—An automatic programming system developed by Lockheed Missile Systems Division for the IBM 650 computer or by Convair for the IBM 704 computer.

flange, connector—A projection extending from or around the periphery of a connector. The flange usually has holes to permit mounting the connector to a panel or to another mating connector half.

flash—A thin film of material formed at the sides of a forging or casting where some of the material is forced between the faces of the forging dies or the mold halves.

flash, form—The displaying of graphic data by exposing a stored form, usually at the same time as data related to the form also displayed. Thus, the form is static and is used to explain the nature of the dynamic data that is displayed. (Synonymous with *form overlay.*)

flash card—See *card, flash.*

flat-bed plotter—See *plotter, flat-bed.*

flat cable—Same as *cable, tape.*

flat-card resolving potentiometer—Same as *potentiometer, slab resolving.*

flat fading—See *fading, flat.*

flat file—See *file, flat.*

flicker—In display devices, a blinking or pulsating of the display image that occurs when the refresh rate is so low that regeneration becomes noticeable to the human eye.

FLINT—(Floating Interpretive Language). A programming language developed by the Institute for Advanced Study, for the IAS computer.

FLIP-1: (Floating Indexed Point Arithmetic). A floating-point routine developed by Argonne National Laboratory. 2: (Floating Point Subroutine System). A floating-point routine developed by Consolidated Vultee for the Univac 1103 and 1103A computers. 3: (Floating Point Interpretive Program). A floating-point routine developed by Humble Oil and Refining Company for the Bendix G-15 computer. 4: (Film Library Instantaneous Presentation). A technique developed by Benson-Lehner Corporation.

flip-flop—A circuit or device, usually containing active elements, capable of assuming either one of two stable states. The flip-flop is placed in a particular state by means of an input stimulus, whose nature and place of input determine which state is to be assumed. If the flip-flop is composed of electrical networks, then the coupling network may also be considered part of the flip-flop. If a device is capable of counting modulo-two, it may also be considered a flip-flop. Any sequential logic element having the above properties is in fact, a flip-flop. A multivibrator having two conditions of stable equilibrium may also be a flip-flop. A flip-flop is capable of storing one bit of information and is commonly used in the counters and registers of digital computers to store numbers and to hold gates open or closed. In a digital computer, the flip-flop is usually in the form of a two-tube or two-transistor device in which either one tube or transistor or the other is conducting, but not both. Whether a zero or a one is stored is determined by which tube or transistor is conducting. (Synonymous with *toggle*, with *bistable circuit*, with *bistable multivibrator*, with *bistable trigger circuit*, and with *binary pair*. Further clarified by *trigger, Eccles-Jordan*.)

flip-flop, a-c coupled—A flip-flop constructed of electronic circuits in which the two active elements, such as tubes or transistors, are coupled with capacitors. The circuit is actually a modified multivibrator and depends upon restorer-pulse action for its ability to store information indefinitely. (Contrast with *flip-flop, d-c coupled*.)

flip-flop, capacitance-coupled—Same as *flip-flop, a-c coupled*.

flip-flop, d-c coupled—A flip-flop constructed of electronic circuits in which the two active elements, such as tubes and transistors, are coupled with resistors rather than with capacitors. Thus, direct current flowing in plate or collector load resistors and in coupling resistors establishes the grid or base bias for the tube or transistor operating condition. The d-c coupling refers to the cross-coupling and not to the manner in which the flip-flop input or output signals are coupled to the environment of the flip-flop. (Contrast with *flip-flop, a-c coupled*.)

flip-flop, direct-coupled—Same as *flip-flop, d-c coupled*.

flip-flop, sign—The flip-flop used to store the algebraic sign of a number. (Synonymous with *sign-control flip-flop*.)

flip-flop, sign-control—Same as *flip-flop, sign*.

flip-flop register—See *register, flip-flop*.

flip-flop storage—See *storage, flip-flop*.

float, contact—Same as *alignment, contact*.

floating address—See *address, floating*.

floating bushing—See *bushing, floating*.

floating character—See *character, floating*.

floating point—See *point, floating*.

floating-point base—See *radix, floating-point*.

floating-point calculation—See *calculation, floating-point*.

floating-point coding compaction—See *compaction, floating-point coding*.

floating-point cofficient—See *coefficient, floating-point*.

floating-point computer—See *computer, floating-point*.

floating-point operation—Same as *calculation, floating-point*.

floating-point radix—See *radix, floating-point*.

floating-point register—See *register, floating-point*.

floating-point representation—See *representation, floating-point*.

floating-point routine—See *routine, floating-point*.

FLOP—(Floating Octal Point). A subroutine developed by Lockheed Aircraft Corporation for the IBM 701 computer.

flow—A sequence of events, such as operations or decisions, involved in the solution of a problem or the movement of data. Flow can be mapped, showing the interrelationships among the steps or events.

flow, bidirectional—In flowcharting, flow that can occur in either or both directions and is represented by a single flowline.

flow, control—The time and space sequence of execution of instructions that maintain control of the system, such as executive routine instructions, jump instructions, and decision instructions.

flow, normal-direction—In flowcharting, flow from left to right or from top to bottom. (Further clarified by *flow, reverse-direction*.)

flow, parallel—Same as *work-flow, parallel*.

flow, reverse-direction—In flowcharting, flow in a direction other than left to right or top to bottom. (Further clarified by *flow, normal-direction*.)

flow, serial—Same as *work-flow, serial*.

flow amplification—See *amplification, flow*.

flow analysis—See *analysis, flow*.

flow diagram—Same as *flowchart*.

flow diagram, dynamic—See *diagram, dynamic flow*.

flow diagram, programming—Same as *flowchart, programming*.

flow direction—See *direction, flow*.

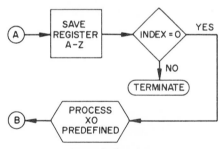

A sample flowchart.

flowchart—A graphical representation for the definition, analysis, or solution of a problem or situation in which symbols are used to represent operations, data, flow, or equipment. Conventional symbols are adopted and used to show the sequence of individual steps or operations. The symbols used on the flowchart may represent documents, machines, actions to be taken, or conditional situations. The flowchart depicts *what* is to be done more than *how* it is to be done and usually contains descriptions of the input-output, arithmetic, and logic operations involved. Types of operations or documents are often indicated by standard symbols, such as those given in the USA Standard Flowchart Symbols in Information Processing (USASFCIP) prepared by the USA Standards Institute. Some operations that may be indicated on a flowchart are jump, read, write, compare, and compute. Some of the symbols shown on a flowchart are operation boxes; alternative, comparison, or decision boxes; fixed connectors, and variable connectors. The flowchart is a master plan of a system having various levels of detail and sophistication. (Synonymous with *process chart* and with *flow diagram.* Further clarified by *diagram, logic.*)

flowchart connector—See *connector, flowchart.*

flowchart, data—A flowchart showing the path of data through the steps of a problem solution or through a system. The phases of data processing, such as operations and disposition of data and various data media, are represented on the data flowchart. (Synonymous with *data flow diagram*)

flowchart, programming—A flowchart that represents or describes the sequence of operations or groups of instructions in a computer program. (Synonymous with *programming flow diagram.*)

flowchart symbol—See *symbol, flowchart.*

flowline—1: In flowcharting, a line, with arrows, representing a connecting path between symbols on a flowchart. **2:** In process control, a line, with arrows, representing the flow of materials in a process. **3:** In data processing and control, a line, with arrows, representing the flow of data and control signals.

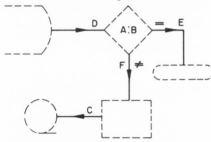

Flowlines *on a flowchart. Flowline C is a reverse-direction flowline. Flowlines D, E, and F are normal-direction flowlines.*

FLOW-MATIC—An automatic programming language developed by Sperry Rand Corporation for the Univac I and Univac II computers.

fluidic—Pertaining to devices that utilize hydraulic principles to accomplish sundry functions such as logic, arithmetic, control, information processing, actuating, and decision functions.

fluidic element—See *element, fluidic.*

fluidics—The branch of science that deals with the study and application of hydraulic phenomena to accomplish logic, data processing, control, and accuation functions such as comparing, adding, negating, amplifying, and differentiating.

flutter—A recurring speed variation of a moving medium. The variation is of relatively low frequency. The speed variation, much like a vibration, is of importance with magnetic tape, audio,

analog, and digital recording, although the condition is less serious with digital recording.

flying spot—See *spot, flying.*

flying-spot scanner—See *scanner, flying-spot.*

FM—See *modulation, frequency.*

FM discriminator—See *discriminator, FM.*

FOCUS—A credit union accounting program developed by International Business Machines Corporation for controlling and reporting credit union operations.

fold—To compact data by interrelating, combining, or operating upon parts of the data; for example, to transform a multiword alphabetic key into a one-word numeric key by adding the numeric equivalents of the letters.

folder, problem—Same as *file, problem.*

follow-up file—See *file, follow-up.*

follower, cathode—See *cathode-follower.*

follower, curve—A device, usually an optical sensing device, that reads data in the form of a graph, such as a line or curve drawn on a piece of paper. (Synonymous with *graph follower.*)

follower, emitter—See *emitter-follower.*

font—A family, set, or particular assortment of consistent size, shape, or style of printer's type or characters, including alphabetic and numeric characters, and other signs and symbols. Pica, elite, block, Old English, and slant are some of the names of different fonts. The size is measured in points. Seventy-two points equals one inch. A typical size and style is twelve-point Gothic. (Further clarified by *style, character.*)

font, type—A type face of a given size; for example, 10-point Gothic or 12-point Old English.

font change character—See *character, font change.*

foot, cross—See *crossfoot.*

FORAST—(Formula Assembler and Translator). A programming language developed for the ORDVAC and BRLESC computers at Ballistic Research Laboratories, Aberdeen Proving Ground, Md.

forbidden character—Same as *character, illegal.*

forbidden code—Same as *code, illegal.*

forbidden combination—Same as *code, illegal.*

forbidden-combination check—See *check, forbidden-combination.*

forbidden digit—Same as *character, illegal.*

forbidden-digit check—Same as *check, forbidden-combination.*

FORC—(Formula Coder). An automatic coding and programming language developed by General Electric Company for the IBM 704 computer.

force—1: In digital-computer programming, to intervene manually in a routine and cause the computer to do a jump instruction. **2:** To substitute one or more digits by specified digits, independently of the values of the digits being replaced.

force, contact engaging—The force required to insert or engage pins into sockets. The force may be determined when the pins or connectors are in or out of their connector inserts. The average maximum or minimum values of the force may be determined for randomly picked samples, special lots, or specific production runs. The performance acceptance levels may vary by specification and/or customer requirements. The force may also be measured after specified numbers of engagements and separations.

force, contact separating—The force required to separate or remove pins from sockets. (Further clarified by *force, contact engaging.*)

forced coding—Same as *programming, minimum-access.*

forced display—See *display, forced.*

foreground—1: Higher priority tasks, jobs, programs, routines, or subroutines that are completed before lower priority programs are allowed to use the system's resources. 2: Pertaining to the execution of higher priority computer programs that are executed before lower priority programs are allowed to use the system's resources. (Contrast with *background.*)

foreground, display—In computer graphics and display systems, those portions of the display image, usually constructed of display elements, that can be changed by a computer program or by the operator of the display device, such as a display terminal operated in an interactive mode. (Contrast with *background, display.*)

foreground scheduler—See *scheduler, foreground.*

foreign exchange service—See *service, foreign exchange.*

form—A document that has blank spaces for the insertion of data, such as a blank bank check.

form, Backus-Naur—Same as *form, Backus normal.*

form, Backus normal—A metalanguage that can be used to specify or describe the syntax of a language in which each symbol, by itself, represents a string of symbols. Abbreviated as BNF (Synonymous with *Backus-Naur form.*)

form, normal—A prescribed arrangement, usually of data; for example, a method of floating-point number representation in which the fixed-point part has a value that lies within a prescribed standard range, in which case the number is said to be normalized; a specific manner of writing a person's name, such as last name first; or a particular way of writing the date and time, such as 1966 Sep 14 A 1605 30; or a descending order, such as millenium, century, decade, year, or time zone, hour, minute, and second. (Synonymous with *standard form.* Further clarified by *normalize.*)

form, normalized—In floating point representation, the form taken when the fixed-point part, that is, the coefficient, lies within a prescribed range. The

normalization must be accomplished so that any given real number can be represented by two numerals, that is, a coefficient and an exponent, the base or radix being expressed or implied.

form, pinfeed—A continuous strip of single or multipart paper that is fed, aligned, and positioned by means of pins or sprockets that fit in marginal holes and used on writing or printing mechanisms, such as high-speed wheel printers. The forms may be preprinted, ruled, or subdivided.

form, printed card—A form, printed on a card, that usually describes the purpose of the card, that designates the precise location of card fields, and that has a layout or format for locating other data related to the use of the card.

form, pseudo-instruction—Same as *form, quasi-instruction.*

form, quasi-instruction—The representation of data in the same form as an instruction. The quasi-instruction form is usually convenient for the representation of small units of data that may occur in a program; for example, preset parameters that are read as instructions, but treated as data. There is no restriction as to the kind of instruction involved, such as computer operation code, input instruction, housekeeping, or any other. (Synonymous with *pseudo-instruction form.*)

form, standard—Same as *form, normal.*

form cards, continuous—See *cards, continuous form.*

form feed character—See *character, form feed.*

form feeding—See *feeding, form.*

form flash—See *flash, form.*

form overlay—Same as *flash, form.*

form stop—See *stop, form.*

formal language—Same as *language, artificial.*

formal logic—See *logic, formal.*

formal system—See *system, formal.*

format—1: A specified or predetermined arrangement of data on a document. Examples include: an arrangement of printed characters on a page; an arrangement of blocks of data, lines, and punctuation on a cathode-ray tube screen; an arrangement of binary digits in magnetic core storage; an arrangement of holes on a card or tape; an arrangement of blocks of data on a magnetic tape or drum; or an arrangement of the contents of a message. (Synonymous with *data layout.* Illustrated by *layout, record.*) 2: The arrangement or layout of data on or in a data medium.

format, address—The arrangement of the address part or parts of an instruction. Typical formats for addresses show the addresses of one or more operands or the address of the next instruction, such as one-plus-one and two-plus-one address formats.

format, horizontal—Pertaining to the left-to-right or right-to-left arrangement of data, as viewed by an observer of a

159

document; for example, the character spacing arrangement for each line of English-language printed text, including word spacing, right and left margins, and indentations. (Contrast with *format, vertical*.)

format, instruction—The arrangement for a digital computer of the component parts of the word used to instruct a computer; for example, the first 10 bits, left to-right, shall be used to express the referenced address; the next six bits to designate the operation; and the last bit to express a parity bit. (Synonymous with *order format* and with *order structure*.)

format, n-address-instruction—The arrangement of the component parts of a digital-computer instruction word that references *n* storage locations; for example, a three-address-instruction format, wherein the first 16 bits specify the storage location of one operand, the second 16 bits specify the storage location of another operand, the third 16 bits specify where to put the results, and the last 12 bits specify the operation to be performed by the operands.

format, order—Same as *format, instruction*.

format, vertical—Pertaining to the top-to-bottom or bottom-to-top or the up-and-down arrangement of data as viewed by an observer of a document; for example, the line spacing arrangement for each line of English-language printed text, including top and bottom margins and spacing between paragraphs. (Contrast with *format, horizontal*.)

format control—See *control, format*.

format effector character—See *character, format effector*.

forms control—See *control, forms*.

forms file—See *file, forms*.

formula manipulation—See *manipulation, formula*.

FORTOCOM—A FORTRAN I compiler developed for the Burroughs 205 computer by Burroughs Corporation (formerly Electrodata Corporation Datatron computer).

FORTRAN—(Formula Translator). A formula translating language designed to instruct computers to solve algebraic problems by permitting mathematical language to be converted automatically to machine language. FORTRAN is a compiling routine for a given machine that accepts a program written in FORTRAN language. Thus, if each FORTRAN language statement is translated into the equivalent machine language statements, one for one or one for many, then a given computer for which such a translator is written, can execute any set of instructions written in FORTRAN. FORTRAN compilers have been written for many digital computers of many manufacturers. FORTRAN permits the expression of algebraic operations, including the use of exponents and up to seven levels of subscripts. Boolean expressions, hierarchies of

subroutines, and other capabilities are possible. For example, a computer routine written in the FORTRAN language might extract data and instructions from a tape, transform the instructions into machine language, and control the execution of the routine. FORTRAN was developed by International Business Machines Corporation and is undergoing standardization by the USA Standards Institute. Many versions or "dialects" of FORTRAN exist.

FORTRAN IV, USASI—See *USASI, FORTRAN IV*.

fortuitous distortion—See *distortion, fortuitous*.

forty-four repeater—See *repeater, forty-four*.

forward channel—See *channel, forward*.

forward supervision—See *supervision, forward*.

FOSDIC—(Film Optical Scanning Device for Input to Computers). A device developed by the United States Bureau of Standards and Bureau of the Census that photoelectrically reads census and business forms and produces properly recorded magnetic tape, which may be used as direct input to computers.

four-address—A machine instruction that explicitly refers to or describes four storage locations or registers. Usually, the four-address instruction specifies the storage location of one operand, say the dividend, in the first address; the storage location of the other operand, say the divisor, in the second address; the storage location of the result in the third address; and the storage location of the next instruction to be executed in the fourth address. Multiple-address machines can be made to operate faster than single-address machines, since a reduced number of instructions are required to produce a given result, and so a reduced number of accesses to storage to fetch instructions. Hardly any four-address machines are being manufactured and nearly all are of the early 1950's vintage. (Synonymous with *quadruple address*.)

four-address code—Same as *instruction, four-address*.

four-address instruction—See *instruction, four-address*.

four-bit byte—Same as *quartet*.

four-plus-one address—See *address, four-plus-one*.

four-tape sort—See *sort, four-tape*.

four-wire channel—See *channel, four-wire*.

four-wire circuit—See *circuit, four-wire*.

fractional fixed point—See *fixed point, fractional*.

fragment—1: To rearrange or restate the contents of a document into a series of parts; for example, to list all the descriptors that would describe the nature of the contents of a document. 2: One of the parts of the contents of a document.

frame—1: A recording or punch position across the width of a tape or film; for example, a row of holes across a punched-paper tape, a row of bits across a magnetic tape, or one complete image on a role of microfilm. 2: In communications, the time period needed to transmit a specified set of bits or bytes, along with parity and other control data. (Further clarified by *interleave, bit.*)

frame, code—One group of a cyclically recurring number of code characters or signals; for example, a single row of holes on a five-level punched paper tape or two rows of bits recorded on a magnetic tape.

frame, connector—The surrounding portion, usually metal, of a multiple-contact connector having a removable body or insert. The frame supports the insert and permits a method for mounting the connector to a panel or to a mating connector half.

frame, film—1: A single photograph on a ribbon of film containing a series of photographs, such as movie film, microfilm, and film strips. 2: The area of film exposed during each exposure, whether or not the area is filled by an image. (Synonymous with *recording area.*)

frame, full—In display systems, pertaining to a display image that is scaled so as to utilize the entire viewing surface or display area of the display device.

frame, main—Same as *unit, central processing.*

frame, time—The limits of time imposed on a particular situation or event; for example, the period or unit of time in which a specific computer program is to be run or the 1965-1970 time frame.

frame ground—See *ground, frame.*

frame grounding circuit—See *circuit, frame grounding.*

free-core pool—Same as *pool, free-storage.*

free field—See *field, free.*

free oscillations—See *oscillations, free.*

free-running multivibrator—See *multivibrator, free-running.*

free-storage list—See *list, free-storage.*

free-storage pool—See *pool, free-storage.*

frequency, carrier—The frequency of a periodic unmodulated carrier wave, usually a sinusoidal electromagnetic wave, such as a radio carrier wave, a video carrier wave, or a radar carrier wave, which is subject to modulation in order to bear intelligence or serve as data for the representation of information in transit. If a periodic pulse-type carrier is used, then the carrier frequency is the pulse repetition rate. In any case, the carrier frequency is the reciprocal of the wave period, for sinusoidal, pulse, square, sawtooth, or any other wave shape or modulation method such as AM or FM.

frequency, clock—The rate, usually in pulses per second, kilohertz, or megahertz, at which pulses of any shape emanate from a generator, or clock to be used for timing or controlling the events in a computing system, usually a synchronous digital computer. Thus, clock pulses may enter every AND gate in order to shape and synchronize the output pulse, if any.

frequency, modulation—The rate in hertz or bits per second at which a sine wave carrier is modulated by an intelligence-bearing signal; for example, a 1000-hertz wave that modulates a 10-megahertz wave for audio purposes in a keyed signal, such as a Morse code transmission.

frequency, pulse repetition—The time rate at which pulses occur, measured in pulses per second, kilohertz, megahertz, or a larger unit. Abbreviated PRF.

frequency, radio—A frequency that lies above the audio range and below the frequency of visible light, thus including microwaves. Abbreviated RF. (Further clarified by *spectrum, frequency.*)

frequency-analysis compaction—See *compaction, frequency-analysis.*

frequency band—Same as *band (3).*

frequency diversity—See *diversity, frequency.*

frequency-division multiplex—See *multiplex, frequency-division.*

frequency-doubling recording—See *recording, frequency-doubling.*

frequency interference, radio—See *interference, radio-frequency.*

frequency modulation—See *modulation, frequency.*

frequency modulation, pulse—See *modulation, pulse-frequency.*

frequency response—See *response, frequency.*

frequency shift—Same as *shift, carrier.*

frequency-shift keying—See *keying, frequency-shift.*

frequency spectrum—See *spectrum, frequency.*

frequency tolerance—See *tolerance, frequency.*

FRINGE—(File and Report Information-Processing Generator). A computer program generator developed by the computer department of General Electric Company.

front, dead—See *dead-front.*

front-end processor—See *processor, front-end.*

front-mounted connector—See *connector, front-mounted.*

frpi—Flux reversals per inch. In the non-return-to-zero-change-on-one (NRZI) method of magnetic recording, a *one* bit is produced, that is, recorded, by a reversal of flux polarity. Thus, packing density of recorded data is measured in frpi, such as 800 frpi.

FS3—A computer programming system using FORTRAN language; developed by General Motors Corporation for use on the IBM 704 computer.

full adder—Same as *adder.*

full-duplex operation—See *operation, full-duplex.*

full-duplex service—See *service, full-duplex.*

full frame—See *frame, full.*

full-read pulse—Same as *pulse, read.*

full-subtracter—Same as *subtracter.*

function–1: The relationship that defines the value of a dependent variable based on the value of the independent variable; for example, $y = 3x^2 + 2x$. 2: A characteristic action or a special purpose action; for example, manually feeding cards into a rack. 3: The relation of one item from a set of items with each item from another set. 4: A computer operation defined by the instruction code; for example, multiplication, transfer, or extract. (Synonymous in this sense with *computer operation*.)

function, Boolean–A switching function that has only two possible values and each of its independent variables has only two possible values.

function, control–Same as *operation, control*.

function, generating–A mathematical function that is represented by simpler functions, such as by an infinite series that has the simpler functions, or constant, as terms in the infinite series or as coefficients of the terms in the series.

function, logic–Same as *function, switching*.

function, mathematical–1: A mathematical entity whose value depends on the values of independent variables. A well behaved mathematical function has only one value of the independent variable corresponding to each permissable combination of values from respective ranges of the independent variables. 2: A set of ordered pairs, one element of each pair being an argument of the function, the other member of the pair being the corresponding value; for example in $y = \sin x$, the ordered pairs would be $0,0$; $\pi/6$, $1/2$; $\pi/3$, $\sqrt{3}/2$; $\pi/2$, 1.

function, recursive–1: A mathematical function defined in terms of itself; that is, a function defined by an operator and an operand, in which the operand includes the function itself and perhaps other variables, such as $e^x = \int_{-\infty}^{x} e^x \, dx$. Thus, in automatic data processing a recursive operation is one that takes advantage of the recursive definition of the function, resulting in either repetition of calculations using the same function repeatedly or using the same function with a slight modification, repeatedly. In actual practice, the algorithm evaluates the function in terms of less accurate approximations of the function. 2: A mathematical function that uses the natural numbers, with natural number values, and which is defined by substitution formula in which the function appears as an operand, for example, the Nth term of a Fibonacci series is defined as $FIB(N) = FIB(N - 1) + FIB(N - 2)$, and the value of factorial N is defined as $FACT(N) = N \cdot FACT(N - 1)$.

function, switching–A function that can assume only a finite number of possible values or states and the independent variable of which have only a finite number of possible values or states. (Synonymous with *logic function*.)

function, threshold–A switching function that can take either of two values depending on whether or not a specified mathematical function of given arguments exceeds a certain specified threshold value. For example, a function that takes a value of one if a specified function of Boolean arguments exceeds a given threshold value, and takes a value of zero if the specified threshold value is not exceeded. Thus, a gate, or binary element, with five inputs, would be designed so that it would yield a one at its output only if three or more of its inputs are a one. The threshold would be three.

function, transfer–A mathematical expression that relates the input signals or variables to the output signals or variables, usually showing the operations performed on the variables by the process or the control element. Transfer functions are useful in the study or control problems, servomechanisms, and systems analysis. By extension, a transfer function can be a detailed description of the operations in a given computer program, since this is indicative of the transformations and operations performed on the input.

function declaration statement–See *statement, function declaration*.

function digits–Same as *part, operation*.

function element–Same as *element, logic*.

function generator–See *generator, function*.

function generator, diode–See *generator, diode function*.

function generator, empiric–See *generator, empiric function*.

function generator, loaded-potentiometer–See *generator, loaded-potentiometer function*.

function generator, tapped-potentiometer–See *generator, tapped-potentiometer function*.

function hole–Same as *punch, designation*.

function key–See *key, function*.

function keyboard–See *keyboard, function*.

function multiplier–See *multiplier, function*.

function part–Same as *part, operation*.

function punch–Same as *punch, designation*.

function switch–See *switch, function*.

function table–See *table, function*.

functional-address instruction–Same as *instruction, source-destination*.

functional character–Same as *character, control*.

functional design–See *design, functional*.

functional diagram–See *diagram, functional*.

functional unit–See *unit, functional*.

functor–Same as *element, logic*.

g

G-dimension—Same as *T-dimension*.

gain—The ratio of the strength or effectiveness of an output signal to the strength or effectiveness of an input signal relative to a device or to a point in space or time; the ratio of the voltage output to the voltage input of an electronic amplifier; the power out divided by the power in; the current out divided by the current in of a transistor amplifier; or the torque out divided by the torque in of a torque amplifier. Power gain is measured in decibels, given as 10 times the logarithm to base 10 of the power ratio or 20 times the log of the voltage ratio. Gain is required at successive stages of computer logic, such as in a sequence of gating operations, to overcome the electrical losses involved. Most logic elements, such as AND, OR, and NOT circuit packages, have an amplifier at the end of the last stage of logic to drive the requisite number of inputs to other packages, thereby accomplishing the total logic required.

gain, insertion—The ratio of the power measured at the receiver before insertion to the power measured at the receiver after insertion, when a transmission system whose insertion gain is being considered is inserted between two impedances, that of a transmitter, Z_e, and a receiver, Z_r. The insertion gain is expressed in decibels and is equal to 10 times the logarithm to base 10 of the power ratio. If the resulting number is negative, an insertion loss is indicated. (Further clarified by *loss, insertion*.)

galley proof—See *proof, galley*.

GAMM—(Gesellschaft für Angewandte Mathematik und Mechanik. Association for Applied Mathematics and Mechanics).

gang punch—See *punch, gang*.

gap—An interval of space or time used to accomplish a separation or apartness for a specific purpose; an absence of a specific mark. A gap does represent information, however, such as in the expressions *factor* and *fact or*, and is therefore considered data.

gap, block—Same as *gap, interblock*.

gap, file—An interval of space or time deliberately placed in a recording, a storage medium, or a transmission to signal the end of a file.

gap, interblock—The distance or physical space between blocks of data on a tape storage medium; an unrecorded or blank length of tape used to separate blocks of data. Gaps are inserted by timed interruptions of recording during acceleration, deceleration, or regular writing, either by automatic means for fixed block lengths or under program control for variable block lengths. Within the gap, the tape can be stopped or brought up to speed again. Reading or writing in the gap is not permitted since the tape speed is changing, which may cause reading or writing errors. Primarily magnetic tape is used. (Synonymous with *block gap*.)

gap, interrecord—The distance or physical space between records of data on a tape storage medium; an unrecorded or blank length of tape used to separate records. Gaps are inserted by timed interruptions of recording during acceleration, deceleration, or regular writing, either by automatic means for fixed record lengths or under program control for variable record lengths. Within the gap, the tape can be stopped or brought up to speed again. Reading or writing in the gap is not permitted since the tape speed is changing, which may cause reading or writing errors. The interrecord gap serves to separate a number of blocks, so that if any instruction requires the reading of a complete record, all the blocks in that record will be read; the tape drive will then stop unless the next record is to be read. Primarily magnetic tape is used.

gap, interword—Same as *space, interword*.

gap, record—An area used to indicate the end of a record on a storage medium or data carrier; for example, a short section of blank tape between records.

gap, word—Same as *space, interword*.

gap character—See *character, gap*.

gap digit—See *digit, gap*.

gap-filler input—See *input, gap-filler*.

gap scatter—See *scatter, gap*.

garbage—Same as *hash*.

garbage collection—See *collection, garbage*.

GASP—General Activity Simulation Program. A generic class of FORTRAN-based, discrete, transaction-oriented simulation languages.

GAT – gate, AND

GAT–(Generalized Algebraic Translator). A program translator developed by the University of Michigan for use on the IBM 650 computer. There is also GAT-2, a second version of the translator.

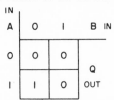

IN			
A	0	I	B IN
0	0	0	
			Q
I	I	0	OUT

A truth table showing the behavior of the A AND NOT B gate.

gate, A AND NOT B–A two-input, binary, logic coincidence circuit capable of performing the logic operations of A AND NOT B. Thus, if A is a statement and B is a statement, the result is true only if A is true and B is false. For the other three combinations of A and B, the result is false. (Synonymous with *exclusion gate*, with *A except B gate*, with *AND NOT gate*, with *NOT if-then gate*, with *sine-junction gate*, and with *subjunction gate*.)

gate, A except B–Same as *gate, A AND NOT B*.

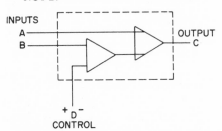

A logic diagram of an OR gate that can be converted to an A ignore B gate by means of a control signal.

gate, A ignore B–A two-input, binary, logic coincidence circuit or device whose normal operation can be interrupted by a control signal, which enables the gate to function so as to pass the A input signal and completely disregard the B input signal. The output is therefore the same as the A input signal and completely independent of the B input signal. (Synonymous with *ignore gate*. Further clarified by *gate, B ignore A*.)

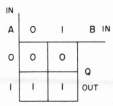

IN			
A	0	I	B IN
0	0	0	
			Q
I	I	I	OUT

A truth table showing the behavior of the A ignore B gate.

gate, A implies B–Same as *gate, B OR NOT A*.

gate, A OR NOT B–A two-input, binary, logic coincidence circuit or device capable of performing the logic operations of A OR NOT B. Thus, if A is a statement and B is a statement, the result is false only if A is false and B is true. For the other three combinations of A and B, the result is true. (Synonymous with *B implies A gate*, with *if-B-then-A-gate*, with *implication gate*, and with *inclusion gate*.)

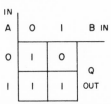

IN			
A	0	I	B IN
0	I	0	
			Q
I	I	I	OUT

A truth table showing the behavior of the A OR NOT B gate.

gate, addition-without-carry–Same as *gate, exclusive-OR*.

gate, alternation–Same as *gate, OR*.

gate, alternative denial–Same as *gate, NAND*.

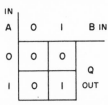

IN			
A	0	I	B IN
0	0	0	
			Q
I	0	I	OUT

A truth table showing the behavior of the AND gate.

gate, AND–A binary, logic coincidence circuit or device capable of performing the logic operation of AND. Thus, if A is a statement, B is a statement, C is a statement,..., the result is true only if all the input statements are true. Otherwise the result is false. (Synonymous with *positive AND gate*, with *intersection gate*, with *conjunction gate*, with *coincidence*

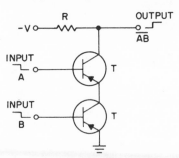

Series electrical schematic diagram of a two-input AND gate with negative inputs and positive output.

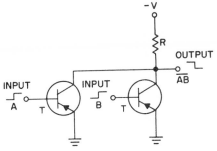

Parallel electrical schematic diagram of a two-input AND gate with positive inputs and negative output.

unit, with *logic product gate,* with *coincidence gate,* with *coincidence circuit,* with *AND circuit,* with *AND unit,* and with *AND element.* Further clarified by *Boolean.*)

gate, AND NOT—1: Same as *gate, A AND NOT B.* 2: Same as *gate, B AND NOT A.*

gate, anticoincidence—Same as *gate, exclusive-OR.*

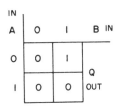

A truth table showing the behavior of the B AND NOT A gate.

gate, B AND NOT A—A two-input, binary, logic coincidence circuit or device capable of performing the logic operations of B AND NOT A. Thus, if A is a statement and B is a statement, the result is true only if B is true and A is false. For the other three combinations of A and B, the result is false. (Synonymous with *B except A gate* and with *negative (B implies A) gate.*)

gate, B EXCEPT A—Same as *gate, B AND NOT A.*

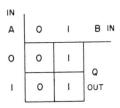

A truth table showing the behavior of the B ignore A gate.

gate, B ignore A—A two-input, binary, logic coincidence circuit or device whose normal operation can be interrupted by a control signal, which enables the gate to function so as to pass the B input signal

and completely disregard the A input signal. The output signal is therefore the same as the B input signal and completely independent of the A input signal. This behavior is usually temporary and controllable. Normal operation might be that of an OR gate.

gate, B implies A—Same as *gate, A OR NOT B.*

gate, B OR NOT A—A two-input, binary, logic coincidence circuit or device capable of performing the logic operations of B OR NOT A, which is the reverse of A OR NOT B. Thus, if A is a statement and B is a statement, the result is false only when A is true and B is false. For the other three combinations of A and B, the result is true. (Synonymous with *A implies B gate,* with *if-A-then-B gate,* with *implication gate,* and with *inclusion gate.*)

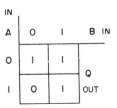

A truth table showing the behavior of the B OR NOT A gate.

gate, biconditional—Same as *gate, exclusive-NOR.*

gate, buffer—Same as *gate, OR.*

gate, coincidence—Same as *gate, AND.*

gate, conditional implication—1: Same as *gate, A OR NOT B.* 2: Same as *gate, B OR NOT A.*

gate, conjunction—Same as *gate, AND.*

gate, difference—Same as *gate, exclusive-OR.*

gate, disjunction—Same as *gate, OR.*

gate, dispersion—Same as *gate, NAND.*

gate, distance—Same as *gate, exclusive-OR.*

gate, diversity—Same as *gate, exclusive-OR.*

gate, don't-care—A logic coincidence gate whose normal operation can be interrupted upon receipt of a control signal and whose operation from then on is such that the output is independent of one or more of the inputs. For example, upon the receipt of a control signal, an AND gate can be converted to an A-ignore-B gate. The output will now equal A, regardless of what B is. A can be the output from another AND gate. The net result is the logic product of two binary variables, with a third variable entered either as a logic multiplier or ignored, depending on some other condition that dispatches the control signal. (Further clarified by *gate, A ignore B.*)

gate, equality—Same as *gate, exclusive-NOR.*

gate, equivalence—Same as *gate, exclusive-NOR.*

gate, except—A coincidence gate that yields an output pulse corresponding to a one or true when one or more input lines are one

165

or true and one or more other input lines are zero or false.

gate, exclusion—1: Same as *gate, A AND NOT B.* **2:** Same as *gate, B AND NOT A.*

gate, exclusive-NOR—A two-input, binary, logic coincidence circuit or device capable of performing the logic operation of exclusive-NOR. In this operation, if A is an input statement and B is an input statement, the result is true when both A and B are true or when both A and B are false. The result is false when A and B differ. (Synonymous with *equivalence gate*, with *biconditional gate*, with *equality gate*, with *identity gate*, and with *match gate*.)

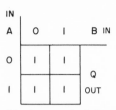

A *truth table showing the behavior of the* exclusive-NOR gate.

gate, exclusive-OR—A two-input, binary, logic coincidence circuit or device capable of performing the logic operation of exclusive-OR. In this operation, if A is an input statement and B is an input statement, the result is true when A is true and B is false or when A is false and B is true. The result is false when A and B are both true or when A and B are both false. (Synonymous with *difference gate*, with *nonequivalence gate*, with *anticoincidence gate*, with *anticoincidence unit*, with *add-without-carry gate*, with *distance gate*, with *diversity gate*, with *exjunction gate*, with *modulo-two sum gate*, with *nonequality gate*, with *partial-sum gate*, and with *symmetric difference gate*. Further clarified by *comparison, logic*.)

A *truth table showing the behavior of the* exclusive-OR gate.

gate, exjunction—Same as *gate, exclusive-OR.*
gate, generator—A circuit or device that produces signals that represent strings of ones in a given system. (Contrast with *gate, null*.)

A *truth table showing the behavior of the* generator gate.

gate, identity—An n-input gate that yields an output signal of a specified kind when all of the n-input signals are alike. If n = 2, the gate is called an exclusive-NOR gate. (Synonymous with *identity unit*.)
gate, if-A-then-B—Same as *gate, B OR NOT A.*
gate, if-A-then-NOT-B—Same as *gate, NAND.*
gate, if-B-then-A—Same as *gate, A OR NOT B.*
gate, if-B-then-NOT-A—Same as *gate, NAND.*
gate, if-then—1: Same as *gate, A OR NOT B.* **2:** Same as *gate, B OR NOT A.*
gate, ignore—1: Same as *gate, A ignore B.* **2:** Same as *gate, B ignore A.*
gate, implication—1: Same as *gate, A OR NOT B.* **2:** Same as *gate, B OR NOT A.*
gate, inclusion—1: Same as *gate, A OR NOT B.* **2:** Same as *gate, B OR NOT A.*
gate, inclusive-NOR—Same as *gate, NOR.*
gate, inclusive-OR—Same as *gate, OR.*
gate, intersection—Same as *gate, AND.*
gate, join—Same as *gate, OR.*
gate, joint denial—Same as *gate, NOR.*
gate, logic product—Same as *gate, AND.*
gate, logic sum—Same as *gate, OR.*
gate, majority decision—A binary input device capable of implementing the *majority* logic operator. In this operation, if A is a statement, B is a statement, C is a statement, . . ., the result is true if more than half of the statements are true and false if half or more of the input statements are false. The majority decision is a special case of the threshold decision. (Further clarified by *element, threshold*.)

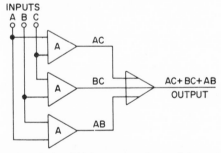

A majority decision gate *made up of three AND gates and one OR gate.*

gate, match—Same as *gate, exclusive-NOR.*
gate, mix—Same as *gate, OR.*
gate, modulo-two sum—Same as *gate, exclusive-OR.*

gate, NAND–A binary, logic coincidence circuit or device capable of performing the NAND, or negative AND, logic operation. In this operation, if A is an input statement, B is an input statement, C is an input statement, . . . , the result is false only when all the input statements are true; otherwise, the result is true. The NAND gate behaves like an AND gate whose output is negated. In terms of binary notation, with zeros and ones as input digits, the NAND gate will yield a one output digit only when all inputs are zero. (Synonymous with *Sheffer stroke gate*, with *if-B-then-NOT-A gate*, with *if-A-then-NOT-B gate*, with *negative AND gate*, with *nonconjunction gate*, with *NOT-AND gate*, with *NOT-both gate*, with *alternative denial gate*, with *dispersion gate*, and with *NAND element*.)

IN

A	0	1	B IN
0	1	1	
1	1	0	Q OUT

A truth table showing the behavior of the NAND gate.

gate, negation–Same as *element, negation*.

gate, negative (A ignore B)–A two-input, binary, logic coincidence circuit or device that is capable of performing the logic operation of negative (A ignore B). In this operation, if A is an input statement and B is an input statement, the result is true when A is false and false when A is true. Thus, the output is independent of B. The gate is the same as an A ignore B gate whose output is negated. The output is the reverse of A. This behavior is usually temporary and controllable. Normal operation might be that of a NOR gate, which, upon signal, is converted to the negative (A ignore B) gate.

IN

A	0	1	B IN
0	1	1	
1	0	0	Q OUT

A truth table showing the behavior of the negative (A ignore B) gate.

gate, negative (A implies B)–Same as *gate, A AND NOT B*.
gate, negative AND–Same as *gate, NAND*.
gate, negative (B ignore A)–A two-input,

binary, logic coincidence circuit or device that can function in a manner identical to the negative (A ignore B) gate, but with the labels on the input leads reversed. Thus, if A is a statement and B is a statement, the result is true if B is false and false if B is true. Thus, the output is the negated, inverted, or reversed value of B and independent of A. This behavior is usually temporary and controllable. Normal operation might be that of a NOR gate, which, upon receipt of a signal at the A input, say a semipermanent false value, will cause the B signal to be inverted and the gate to behave as an inverter for the B input signal.

IN

A	0	1	B IN
0	1	0	
1	1	0	Q OUT

A truth table showing the behavior of the negative (B ignore A) gate.

gate, negative (B implies A)–Same as *gate, B AND NOT A*.
gate, negative ignore–1: Same as *gate, negative (A ignore B)*. **2:** Same as *gate, negative (B ignore A)*.
gate, negative-OR–Same as *gate, NOR*.
gate, neither-nor–Same as *gate, NOR*.
gate, nonconjunction–Same as *gate, NAND*.
gate, nondisjunction–Same as *gate, NOR*.
gate, nonequality–Same as *gate, exclusive-OR*.
gate, nonequivalence–Same as *gate, exclusive-OR*.

IN

A	0	1	B IN
0	1	0	
1	0	0	Q OUT

A truth table showing the behavior of a NOR gate.

gate, NOR–A binary, logic coincidence circuit or device capable of performing the logic operation of NOR, or negative OR. Thus, if A is a statement, B is a statement, C is a statement, . . . , the result is false if at least one of the input statements is false and true only if all the input statements are false. The behavior of the NOR gate is like that of an OR gate whose output is inverted or reversed. (Synonymous with *inclusive-NOR gate*, with *negative-OR*

gate, with *neither-NOR gate,* with *non-disjunction gate,* with *joint denial,* with *rejection gate,* and with *zero-match gate.*)
gate, NOT—Same as *element, negation.*
gate, NOT-AND—Same as *gate, NAND.*
gate, NOT-both—Same as *gate, NAND.*
gate, NOT if-then—**1:** Same as *gate, A AND NOT B.* **2:** Same as *gate, B AND NOT A.*

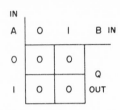

IN			
A	0	1	B IN
0	0	0	
			Q
1	0	0	OUT

A truth table showing the behavior of the null gate.

gate, null—A device that · produces signals representing strings of zeros in a given system, continually as long as power is applied to the device. (Contrast with *gate, generator.*)
gate, one—Same as *gate, OR.*

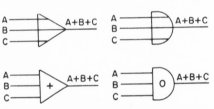

Various logic symbols used to represent a three-input OR gate.

gate, OR—A binary, logic coincidence circuit or device capable of performing the logic operation of OR. Thus, if A is a statement, B is a statement, C is a statement, . . . ,the result is true if at least one of the statements is true and false only if all the statements are false. The OR gate serves as a buffer, since all signals on inputs are· carried through to the output, without having input signals going out on other input lines. (Synonymous with *inclusive-OR gate,* with *alternation gate,* with *buffer gate,* with *disjunction gate,*

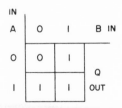

IN			
A	0	1	B IN
0	0	1	
			Q
1	1	1	OUT

A truth table showing the behavior of an OR gate.

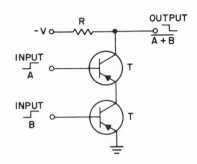

Series electrical schematic diagram of an inclusive-OR gate with positive inputs and negative output.

with *join gate,* with *logic-sum gate,* with *mix gate,* with *positive-OR gate,* with *one gate,* with *union gate,* with *OR unit,* with *OR circuit,* and with *OR element.* Further clarified by *Boolean.*)

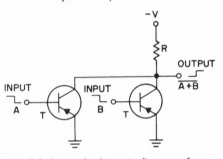

Parallel electrical schematic diagram of an inclusive-OR gate with negative inputs and positive output.

gate, OR NOT—**1:** Same as *gate, A OR NOT B.* **2:** Same as *gate, B OR NOT A.*
gate, partial-sum—Same as *gate, exclusive-OR.*
gate, positive AND—Same as *gate, AND.*
gate, positive OR—Same as *gate, OR.*
gate, rejection—Same as *gate, NOR.*
gate, Sheffer stroke—Same as *gate, NAND.*
gate, sine-junction—**1:** Same as *gate, A AND NOT B.* **2:** Same as *gate, B AND NOT A.*
gate, subjunction—**1:** Same as *gate, A AND NOT B.* **2:** Same as *gate, B AND NOT A.*
gate, symmetric difference—Same as *gate, exclusive-OR.*
gate, union—Same as *gate, OR.*
gate, zero-match—Same as *gate, NOR.*
gate generator—Same as *generator, clock-pulse.*
gate tube—See *tube, gate.*
gear, differential—A mechanical adder with two input variables and one output variable that are represented by the angular position of three shafts, θ, ϕ, and ψ. The shafts are interconnected with epicyclic gearing designed so that $\theta + \phi = 2\psi$. Any two shafts may be taken as inputs. For example, an automobile rear

differential and axle, where the amount of rotation of the right and left wheel shafts, $\theta + \phi$, equal twice the rotation of the motor shaft, ψ. When a mechanism of this type is used as an adder, the inputs are the right and left wheel shafts, and the output corresponds to the motor drive shaft. Thus, if one car wheel rotates through an angle, θ, and the other wheel through an angle, ϕ, then the motor drive shaft rotates through an angle $(\theta + \phi)/2$. If both rear wheels of a car are raised and the motor drive shaft is locked, rotation of one wheel forces the other wheel to rotate through the same angle in the opposite direction. (Further clarified by *autobalance.*)

gear, integrating—An integrator consisting of a pair of gears of variable gear ratio in which the input and output variables are represented by angles of rotation of shafts. The input gear transmits the drive torque from the input shaft (X) to the output shaft (Z). The relationship between these rotations is $dz = y\,dx$ or $z = \int y\,dx$; for example, the wheel and disc integrator, in which a disc is rotated about its polar axis by the X shaft and a wheel whose edge is in contact with the face of the disc is rotated about its own axis by friction with the disc to drive the shaft. The point of contact of the wheel can be moved radially on the disc by a lead screw driven from the Y input shaft. Higher output torque can be obtained in the ball and disc integrator; ball, disc, and cylinder integrator; and the potter's wheel, although the principle is the same in each. The gear is used in mechanical analog computers. (Synonymous with *variable speed gear*, and with *V.S.G.* Further clarified by *amplifier, capstan*, by *amplifier, torque*, and by *autobalance.*)

gear, variable-speed—Same as *gear, integrating.*

GECOM—(General Compiler). A program compiler developed by General Electric Company for use on the GE 225 computer.

GECOS—(General Comprehensive Operating Supervisor). A software package developed by General Electric Company for handling multiprocessing operations.

general escape—See *escape, general.*

general program—See *program, general.*

general-purpose computer—See *computer, general-purpose.*

general-purpose paper card—See *card, general-purpose paper.*

general purpose register—See *register, general purpose.*

general routine—See *routine, general.*

generate—To produce a computer coding or program automatically by means of a computer program generator; for example, to produce a computer program by using a computer to prepare a routine from skeletal coding and specific parameters. Thus, a program that writes another

program is called a program generator. (Related to *generator, program.*)

generated address—Same as *address, synthetic.*

generated error—See *error, generated.*

generating function—See *function, generating.*

generating program, macro—Same as *macrogenerator.*

generating routine—Same as *generator.*

generation—In micrographics, an indication of the remoteness or reproductive distance of a specified copy from the original material. Thus, a contact print from an original negative would be a first generation print; a first microfilm representation is first generation microfilm. Second generation microfilm would be a microfilm made from the first generation microfilm.

generation, load module—The conversion of machine language program instructions into a form that can be transferred directly into main storage and executed.

generation, operating system—The creation of a uniquely specified particular computer operating system. In order to create the operating system, user options and parameters are combined with general-purpose or nonspecialized software, usually supplied by the computer manufacturers, to produce an operating system or set of software, of the desired form and capability.

generation, report—The preparation of reports by machine methods from information and instructions. The input file, format, and content are described, and the machine output is the report. The computer instructions for preparing the report is a report generator.

generation, third—A characterization of general-purpose electronic digital computers introduced during the 1960s. The characteristics used to establish the generation of a computer are the nature of the circuitry of the electronic hardware components and their features; the system logical organization; and the software or programming techniques that are used. (Further clarified by *hardware, third-generation;* by *logical-organization, third-generation;* and by *software, third-generation.*)

generation, vector—In graphic display systems, the drawing of lines on a display surface.

generator—A computer routine that prepares machine instructions from skeletal definitions and from given data or parameters. Thus, a generator is a type of routine that produces other routines by substituting parameters in skeletal sections of coding. Generating routines may be stored in a library of generators until needed. In a very general sense, a generator is any processor that produces a result by following an algorithm. (Synonymous with *routine, generating.*

Further clarified by *assembler*, by *interpreter*, by *translator*, and by *compiler*. Related to *generate*.)

generator, analytical-function—A function generator, usually an analog device or a programmed digital computer, whose operation is based on a physical law or a mathematical identity. Some examples are a thermionic diode, whose current-voltage relationship in the retarding field region can be used to generate a logarithm, or a small auxiliary computer, used to solve a definitive differential equation, that can generate sinusoidal or exponential functions. (Synonymous with *natural-function generator* and with *natural-law generator.*)

generator, arbitrary-function—A function generator that is not committed by its design to a specific function only; thus, the function that it generates may be changed at the discretion of the operator.

generator, character-controlled—A generator that behaves like a compiler in that it takes entries from a library tape, but unlike a simple compiler, it examines control characters associated with each entry and alters the instructions found in the library according to the directions specified by the control characters.

generator, clock-pulse—A device that generates pulses used for timing or gating purposes in a digital computer, such as pulses that are used as inputs to gates to assist in pulse-shaping and timing operations. Usually an oscillator and associated pulse-forming circuits are used as the clock-pulse generator to provide a sequence of pulses at proper intervals. (Synonymous with *restorer-pulse generator*, with *time-pulse generator*, with *timing pulse generator*, and with *gate generator.*)

generator, compiler—A translator or an interpreter that is used to construct compilers.

generator, diode function—A device that is capable of generating an arbitrarily specified, and usually fixed function or fixed family of functions, using an amplifier whose input and/or feedback impedance consists of networks of resistors and diodes with connections to bias supplies. The different diodes start to conduct at different values of input signal voltage (or current), altering the instantaneous effective gain of the unit. The plot of output voltage vs. input voltage can be made to approximate the desired function by a series of segments of approximately straight lines or curves. (Further clarified by *generator, function*.)

generator, display character—The hardware or software that is capable of generating the signals that will generate characters for graphic display, usually from a set of elemental geometric entities that can be focussed on a CRT screen.

generator, empiric function—A device or computer program that generates a mathematical function, curve, or set of values from another set of values, such as test data or laboratory measurement. The function generator may operate by reference to a stored set of values, with or without interpolation between the values in the set. Examples include a cam for mechanical analog representation, a tapped-potentiometer function generator for analog representation by means of a voltage, or a set of numbers stored on a digital computer drum loop constantly being read and thereby circulating.

generator, function—1: An analog device, a programmed digital computer, or a digital computer program that generates a mathematical relationship between an input and an output variable; for example, a diode or amplifier whose characteristics are such that the current that flows is proportional to the logarithm of the input voltage or a digital computer programmed to compute the sine of an argument, usually by summing a series expansion Thus, the device produces the value of a given function as the independent variable changes. The generator may have one or more input variables and one or more output variables, each output variable being equal to some particular function of the input variable or variables. (Further clarified by *generator, diode function*.) 2: In computer simulation, a computer program that is called within a simulation run to calculate a logical or mathematical function, the results of which are needed in subsequent processing, decisions, events, or operations.

generator, gate—Same as *generator, clock-pulse*.

generator, loaded-potentiometer function—An empiric function generator that operates on the principle of variation of resistance in accordance with angular shaft position of a contact or wiper, such as is used in the shaped-card potentiometer. The potentiometer element is uniformly wound with equally spaced taps between which are connected fixed resistors of values designed to give the desired local change of resistance with change of angular shaft position. The loading resistors may be connected between the slider contact terminal and the ends of the element instead of between the taps.

generator, manual number—Same as *unit, manual input*.

generator, manual word—Same as *unit, manual input*.

generator, natural-law—Same as *generator, analytical-function*.

generator, natural function—Same as *generator, analytical-function*.

generator, program—A processor that modifies and combines general purpose object program modules based on source program control statements and prepares a complete object or target program in the appropriate language for computer entry and execution.

generator, pure—A generator that is a routine that writes another routine. When associated with an assembler, a pure generator is usually a section of program found on a library tape called into storage by the assembler. The generator then writes one or more entries in the routine.

generator, random number—1: A device, such as a computer, either with built-in control or under program control, capable of producing a random number or a series of random numbers or digits, according to specified limitations or criteria. Sometimes the computer control routine itself is called a random number generator, though it should properly be called a random number generating routine or subroutine. 2: In computer simulation, a computer program, routine or subroutine designed to produce, in a specified range, numbers that are uniformly distributed throughout the range, are statistically independent, are reproducible, and are nonrepeating.

generator, report—A computer routine designed to prepare a report or a display of data; a computer routine designed to prepare an object routine that will produce a desired report when later run on a computer; or a technique for producing reports using automatic data-processing methods, given only a description of the content and format of the output report and certain information concerning the input file.

generator, restorer-pulse—Same as generator, clock-pulse.

generator, tapped-potentiometer function—An empiric function generator for single variable functions in which the potentiometer resistive element has a number of taps that are held at voltage levels determined by the table of values for the function. The output voltage, taken from the slide contact, is an interpolation of the voltages at adjacent taps. The input (independent) variable determines the angular position of the potentiometer shaft that moves the slide contact. Such a device is used in electromechanical analog computers.

generator, time-pulse—Same as generator, clock-pulse.

generator, timing-pulse—Same as generator, clock-pulse.

generator gate—See gate, generator.

GEPURS—A program compiler developed by General Electric Company as a general-purpose compiler for use on the IBM 701 computer.

germanium diode—See diode, germanium.

gibberish—Same as hash.

gibberish total—Same as total, hash.

GIF—(Gulf IT to FORTRAN). An IT to FORTRAN computer programming language translator developed by Gulf Oil Corporation for use on the IBM 650 computer.

gigahertz circuit—Same as circuit, nanosecond.

GIGO—An acronym that represents the expression "garbage-in-garbage-out." The implication of this expression is that if meaningless, incoherent, inconsistent, wrong or otherwise nonsensical data, or garbage, is inserted into a computing or information processing system, and any operations are performed on this data, that nonsensical data will emerge from the system. The sometimes equivalent expression, to the effect that the output can be no better than the input, may not always be correct, since a computer can effect improvements by insertion of stored data, error correction, translation, or other techniques. (Further clarified by hash.)

global—In computer programming, pertaining to an item that is defined in one part or subdivision of a computer program and used in at least one other subdivision of the program. (Contrast with local.)

global variable—See variable, global.

glossary—An ordered word list with a definition for each word in a given discipline or field or for each word peculiar to a given field, and often contained in a book or report as an ordered list of words specifically used in that document. A glossary applies more to a text, concept, or document than to a discipline or a language.

GLOTRAC—(Global Tracking). A worldwide tracking system developed by General Dynamics Corporation.

G-0—A modification of the Univac I Flowmatic programming language; developed by Sperry-Rand Corporation.

GOE—(Ground Operation Equipment). Communication equipment on the ground, developed by Westinghouse Electric Corporation for use with the Orbiting Astronomical Observatory.

GOTRAN—A programming language developed by International Business Machines Corporation. It is used on the IBM 1620 Model 2 computer as a load-and-go FORTRAN.

GP-1: (Generalized Programming). A common programming procedure developed by Sperry-Rand Corporation for use on the Univac I and II computers. 2: An abbreviation for general processor. 3: An abbreviation for general purpose.

GPC—An abbreviation for general-purpose computer.

GPS—(General Problem Solver). A general programming procedure developed by Rand Corporation for use on the IBM 704 computer.

GPSS—1: Generic Problem Statement Simulator. In computer simulation, a generic class of discrete, transaction-oriented simulation languages that are based on the use of block diagrams to express problem statements. 2: A standard programming language used for simulation. The term GPSS is derived from the expression, "General Purpose Systems Simulator."

GPX—(Generalized Programming Extended). An extension of GP, Sperry-Rand Corporation for use on Univac II.

grandfather cycle—See *cycle, grandfather.*

grandfather tape—See *tape, grandfather.*

graph follower—Same as *follower, curve.*

grapheme—A graphic representation of a semanteme, such as X-roads for crossroads. (Further clarified by *semanteme.*)

graphic—1: Pertaining to representational or pictorial material, usually legible to humans and applied to the printed or written form of data, such as mathematical curves, printed letters of the English alphabet, or a display on a radar scope. 2: A symbol produced by a process that renders the symbol visible on a medium; for example, a symbol produced on paper by handwriting, drawing, or printing. (Synonymous with *graphic symbol.*)

graphic character—See *character, graphic.*

graphic data structure—See *structure, graphic data.*

graphic language—See *language, graphic.*

graphic panel—See *panel, graphic.*

graphic symbol—Same as *graphic.*

graphics, computer—The branch of science and technology that includes the study and application of methods and techniques for processing information on both computers and display devices.

graphics, interactive—In graphic display systems, the use of a display terminal and a computer in a conversational or interactive mode. (Contrast with *graphics, passive.*)

graphics, passive—The use of display terminals and display devices such as plotters, printers, and film viewers, in a non-interactive or non-conversational mode. (Contrast with *graphics, interactive.*)

Gray code—See *code, Gray.*

grid—1: Two sets of parallel lines in the same plane, the members of one set orthogonal to the members of the other set. The grid provides a basis for a Cartesian coordinate system, for such applications as mathematical curve plotting, map coordinate systems, or specifying or measuring character images in optical character recognition equipment. 2: A control electrode in an electronic tube, such as a vacuum tube of the type used in radio or television receivers.

grid, control—The electrode of an electronic tube, usually formed in the shape of a wire mesh, spiral, or coil around the cathode, upon which a signal is impressed in order to control the current to the plate. It is usually called the number one grid. The electric field, caused by electric charge on the grid, accelerates or retards the flow of electrons en route from the cathode to the plate. In a single triode, there is only one control grid. A twin triode has two, one for each triode half. The control grid in a

gas tube, such as a thyratron, loses control once plate current starts to flow.

grid-spaced contacts—See *contacts, grid-spaced.*

grommet—An insulating material used to protect an insulated cable when it passes through a hole in a conductor, such as a metal chassis or a connector body; for example, a rubber seal used on the cable side of a multiple-contact connector to seal the connector against moisture, dirt, or air. Usually the grommet lines the hole.

gross error—1: See *error, gross.* 2: Same as *mistake.*

ground, frame—The electrical reference potential established by the frame or chassis of an electrical communication or power system. Frame ground is usually connected to earth in order to remove static charges and provide safety. (Contrast with *ground, signal.*)

ground, signal—A conductor that establishes electrical ground reference potential for all transmission circuits throughout a communication network. Signal ground is usually separate from frame ground, thus avoiding high-frequency signals in the frame, which may cause radiation, coupling, or induction, and so create unwanted signals in other circuits. (Contrast with *ground, frame.*)

grounding circuit, frame—See *circuit, frame grounding.*

group, display—A group of associated display elements that can be manipulated as a unit. A display group can usually be associated with other groups to form larger groups that also can be manipulated as a unit. (Further clarified by *grouping, automatic.*)

group, link—A set of communications links that connect the same multiplexed terminal equipments.

group, trunk—A set of trunk lines between two switching centers or message distribution points, thus employing the same set of multiplex terminal equipment.

group indicate—See *indicate, group.*

group mark—See *mark, group.*

group record—See *record, group.*

group theory—See *theory, group.*

grouping, automatic—In display systems, a collection of display elements that are associated with common boundaries to form a display group and that may be manipulated automatically as though the group is a single unit. (Further clarified by *group, display.*)

guard band—See *band, guard.*

guard signal—See *signal, guard.*

GUIDE—A group of computer users who share programs for the IBM 702, 705, 7070, and 7080 computers.

guide edge—See *edge, guide.*

guide margin—See *margin, guide.*

gulp—A group of bytes treated as a unit; thus, similar to a character or a word. Gulps and bytes are usually sets of binary digits.

gun, electron—An electron source with associated anodes that accelerate the electrons in a given direction, focusing or diffusing them as required. An electron gun is usually mounted in the base section of cathode-ray tubes, for producing a narrow electron beam used for creating images on a screen. The tubes are used as oscilloscopes, TV picture tubes, and radar scopes and display tubes.

gun, holding—An electron gun that produces the holding beam in an electrostatic storage cathode-ray tube. (Further clarified by *beam, holding.*)

gun, light—Same as *pen, light.*

h

half-adder—1: A device or logic element which has two input channels to which signals may be applied, representing two input digits (addend and augend), and two output channels from which signals may emerge, representing the sum and carry digits. When a half-adder is used for performing operations in signals representing numbers to base two, it is more precisely called a binary half-adder. (Synonymous with *binary half-adder*, with *one-digit adder*, and with *two-input adder.* Contrast with *adder.*) **2:** Refer to the logic diagram illustration for the half-adder. A and B are input signals representing the binary digits of the addend and augend. The S and C are output signals representing the "sum without carry" and the carry digits. The logic diagram shows one method of assembling a half-adder from basic AND, OR, and negation gates. The Boolean functions are also shown. A half-adder may also be said to consist of a nonequivalence element, whose output is a representation of the sum digit $(S = A\bar{B} + \bar{A}B)$, and an AND gate, whose output is a representation of the carry digit $(C = AB)$. The nonequivalence element and the AND gate have common inputs, as shown in the logic diagram. The carry digit is carried forward to the next stage in a parallel adder, but delayed for one digit period in a serial adder. The name half-adder arises because two half-adders, properly connected, may be used to form a full binary adder for performing binary addition. Sometimes the delay element for the carry and an OR gate for combining the delayed carry with the added input signal are an integral part of the half-adder so that all necessary elements are present for making a full serial adder. (Synonymous with *two-input adder.*)

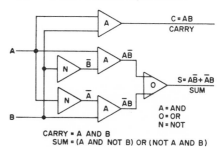

A half-adder *logic diagram, where N is the negation element, A is the AND gate, and O is the OR gate.*

half-adder binary—Same as *half-adder (1).*

half-adjust—To round a number so that the least significant digits or digit determine whether a one is or is not to be added to the next more significant digit than the one(s) used to make the determination. After the adjustment, if necessary, is made, the least significant digit(s) used to make the determination is dropped. If the least significant digit(s) represents less than half of the number base, it is simply dropped and nothing is added to the next more significant digit; if the least significant digit(s) represents one-half or more, then a one is added to the next more significant digit, the least significant digit(s) is dropped, and all carries are propagated; for example, 432.784 is

INPUT		OUTPUT	
A	B	S	C
0	0	0	0
0	I	I	0
I	0	I	0
I	I	0	I

An input-output truth table for a half-adder.

rounded to 432.78, 47.34 is rounded to 47.3 or 47, 48.398 is rounded to 48.4, 439 to 440, 46.5 to 47, 46.51 to 46.5, 473 to 470, 475 to 480 for all decimal numbers; and 10111 is rounded to 1100; 10110 is rounded to 110; 110.101 to 110.11 for binary numbers.

half-duplex channel—See *channel, half-duplex.*

half-duplex operation—See *operation, half-duplex.*

half-duplex service—See *service, half-duplex.*

half-pulse, read—A pulse of magnitude which alone cannot switch a magnetic core, and so cannot interrogate core content, but which combined with a second pulse in the same direction can switch the core to a prescribed state no matter what state the core was in. Thus, it is a partial read pulse, or one that is ineffective by itself in interrogation. One read half-pulse will drive a row of cores in an array. Another will drive a column. Only the core at the intersection can be switched. (Contrast with *pulse, read* and with *half-pulse, write.*)

half-pulse, write—A pulse of magnitude which alone cannot switch a core; and so cannot store a digit, but which combined with a second pulse in the same direction can switch the core to a prescribed state, and so can store or write a one, or a zero, according to convention. One write half-pulse will drive a row of cores in an array. Another will drive a column. Only the core at the intersection can be switched. (Contrast with *half-pulse, read.*)

half-sinusoid—The entire positive or negative portion of a single cycle of a sine wave. Thus, the plot obtained by plotting the projection distance on a diameter vs. the angular displacement of a point on a circle for one half of a circle. (Further clarified by *sine wave.*)

half-subtracter—A logic element having two inputs, a minuend and a subtrahend, and two outputs, the difference digit and the borrow digit, to be used in the digit position of the next higher significance. Two such logic elements may be combined to form a complete subtracter. The half-subtracter and the two-input subtracter are identical, except for the internal handling of the borrow digit in the half-subtracter and the external handling of the borrow digit in the two-input subtracter. (Synonymous with *two-input subtracter* and with *one-digit subtracter.* Further explained by *half-subtracter, serial;* by *half-subtracter, parallel,* and by *subtracter.*)

half-subtracter, parallel—A half-subtracter formed from as many half-subtracters as there are digits in the input numerals, with the borrow output of each half-subtracter connected to the subtrahend input of the half-subtracter corresponding to the next higher significant digit position. Two such parallel half-subtracters thus formed may

be used to form a full parallel subtracter. (Contrast with *half-subtracter, serial.*)

half-subtracter, serial—A half-subtracter with a digit delay element connected between the borrow output and the subtrahend input so that the borrow digit may be used in the digit position having the next higher significance. Two half-subtracters may be used to form a subtracter, with two inputs for externally entered signals and one output for the proper difference digit. One method of constructing a subtracter from two half-subtracters is to apply to the first signals, which represent borrow and minuend, and to the second the difference output of the first and the subtrahend. Another method is to use a half-adder to form the sum of borrow and subtrahend, followed by using a half-subtracter to subtract the sum from the minuend. A third method is to use half-adders and add the twos complement of the subtrahend; or to add the ones complement, followed by adding a one to the resulting sum in the least significant position and propagating all carries. A delay element and an OR gate are required to properly combine the delayed borrow and subtrahend input signals. (Contrast with *half-subtracter, parallel.*)

half-time emitter—See *emitter, half-time.*

half-word—A continuous group, such as a string, of characters that comprise half of a computer word and that can be addressed as a unit when stored.

halt, breakpoint—Same as *instruction, breakpoint.*

halt, drop-dead—A cessation of machine operations, from which there is no recovery back to the point in the program where the last successfully executed program step was performed. The drop-dead halt may occur as a result of a logical error in the program, which is not deliberate, such as division by zero, directing transfer to a nonexistent or improper instruction word, calling for a nonexistent piece of equipment, calling data from an empty storage unit, or a drop-dead halt may be deliberately programmed so as to occur only if a certain condition or situation occurs.

halt, nonprogrammed—A machine stoppage that does not occur automatically as a result of an instruction in a program. The halt may occur as a result of an automatic interruption for effecting a change of program, a manual intervention, a termination of a time period, a machine malfunction, a power failure, or other cause. (Contrast with *halt, programmed.*)

halt, programmed—A stoppage, cessation, or interruption of machine operations deliberately and intentionally caused by a program instruction inserted by the programmer. The halt occurs automatically. The operator is signaled by an audio or visual signal. The purpose is to examine the status of some storage device, insert data, exercise an option, or perform some other operation that can only be done while the machine is halted. (Synonymous with *coded stop* and with *programmed stop*. Contrast with *halt, nonprogrammed*.)

halt instruction–See *instruction, halt*.

halt instruction, optional–See *instruction, optional halt*.

Hamming code–See *code, Hamming*.

Hamming distance–Same as *distance, signal*.

hand-feed punch–See *punch, hand-feed*.

handling, data–Pertaining to that collection of activities which involves the performance of operations on data, such as computer processing, abstracting, transferring, indexing, storing, retrieving, and sorting. Several of these handling activities taken as a group may comprise another; for example, several extracts may result in producing an abstract, or computer processing may involve adding, subtracting, sorting, and storing.

hang-up–An unplanned, nonprogrammed halting of machine operations; for example, a nonprogrammed stop in a computer routine, caused by the use of a nonexistent or illegal operation or by the inability of a computing machine to escape from a loop. A hang-up is usually an unwanted halt, and in the event of intermittent malfunctions, is sometimes unexplained.

hard adder–See *adder, hard*.

hard copy–See *copy, hard*.

hardware–Physical equipment, such as the mechanical, magnetic, electronic, or electrical devices or components from which assemblies are made, or the assemblies themselves; for example, the assembly of material that forms a computer, as distinct from data, routines, or programs. An entire computing system is considered a hardware item. Previously, only metal attachments, such as clamps, nuts, bolts, hinges, and screws, were considered as hardware items; now, any sort of apparatus is considered hardware. (Contrast with *software*.)

hardware, common–Items or components that have multiple application, usually expendable items, such as plugs, sockets, resistors, nuts, bolts, and screws. Stocks of common items are used to construct or repair many machines or many components. (Contrast with *software, common*.)

hardware, third-generation–System hardware that is constructed from integrated circuits. (Further clarified by *generation, third*.)

hardware check–Same as *check, machine*.

hardware language–See *language, hardware*.

harmonic distortion, single–See *distortion, single-harmonic*.

harmonic distortion, total–See *distortion, total harmonic*.

Hartley–A unit of logarithmic measure of information. One Hartley is equal to the decision content of a set of ten mutually exclusive events expressed by the logarithm to the base ten; for example, the decision content of a character set of eight characters equals 0.903 Hartley, since the logarithm of 8 to base 10 is 0.903. (Synonymous with *information-content decimal unit*.)

hash–Obviously meaningless data, usually resulting from an equipment malfunction; for example, a sequence of miscellaneous alphanumeric characters whose meaning is unintelligible. Hash may also result from improper programming, causing wrong associations of characters, giving the appearance of being meaningless, since the reason for, or the cause of, the association is unknown. Hash may result also from human mistakes or equipment malfunction. (Synonymous with *garbage* and *gibberish*. Further clarified by *GIGO*.)

hash address–See *address, hash*.

hash total–See *total, hash*.

HAYSTAQ–An information retrieval method used for document storage and retrieval in connection with patent searching in the field of chemistry. Topological tracing of chemical compound structures is performed. The SEAC system at the National Bureau of Standards is used to implement the retrieval scheme. The solution is coded directly in machine language. The HAYSTAQ system provides facilities for searching for chemical compounds, mixtures of materials, and processes. The file is prepared by chemists from information contained in patents. All the compounds treated in a document are recorded, structure diagrams are drawn, and the data is encoded on paper tape. The data is checked by a routine called SWEEP, corrected, compressed, and assembled in final formats. The program is sponsored by the United States Patent Office and the National Bureau of Standards.

HD–An abbreviation for high density.

head–A device that reads, records, or erases data on a storage medium, usually a moving medium, such as a magnetic or paper tape and magnetic drums or discs, for example, a small electromagnet used to record data on magnetic tape, or the set of perforating, reading, or marking devices used for punching, reading, or printing on paper tape. In many applications, heads are mounted in groups or blocks, so as to read, write, or erase in several tracks simultaneously. A mechanical sensing head for perforated tape or punched cards is shaped very much like a set of fingers. The head actually converts data in the static form, such as holes in tape or magnetically polarized spots on a drum, into electrical signals that represent the same information. (Further clarified by *head, write*.)

head, combined–Same as *head, read-write*.

head, erase–A magnetic head whose sole function is to erase or obliterate information prior to writing new information. Usually, an erase head will restore the magnetic medium to an unpolarized or neutral state, though it might also uniformly polarize the tape, aligning all magnetic dipoles in the same direction in the area being erased. An area uniformly magnetized will not yield a signal while passing under a read head. Erasing is not the same as recording all zeros, since in some number systems, zeros are represented as a particular combination of binary ones and zeros. In most applications, erasing is performed by the write head. In magnetic application, all functions of reading, writing, and erasing are usually performed by one head. For paper tape, the read head, mechanical or photo, is different from the write head, more often called the punch or perforate head, since a mechanical cutting operation is involved when perforating paper tape.

head, magnetic–A head, usually consisting of a small horseshoe-shaped, core electromagnet with a winding and a gap, such that the magnetic flux generated in the core by the winding in accordance with an applied signal, will pass into the recording medium, which is usually a moving magnetic medium, such as a magnetic tape, magnetic drum, magnetic card, or a magnetic disc. The magnetic circuit of the head includes the storage medium, the flux being required to enter the medium because of the reluctance of the head gap. Thus, there is a point of entry and a point of exit for the flux at any instant, giving rise to a polarized or magnetized spot on the medium whenever a signal current flows in the head. (Further clarified by *head, write* and by *head.*)

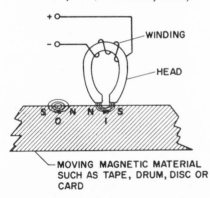

A magnetic recording, reading, writing or erase head.

head, playback–Same as *head, read*.

head, preread–A read head placed relative to a second read head so that the first head may be used to read data on a track of a moving medium, such as a tape, disc, or drum, before the data reaches or passes under the second head.

head, read–A head used for reading data on a medium that is moving relative to the head, such as tape, discs, drums, cards, or optical sensor. (Synonymous with *playback head*. Further clarified by *head* and by *head, write*.)

head, read-write–A magnetic head used for both sensing and recording data. The head may have a single winding connected to a reading or a writing amplifier by means of a switching device, so as to use the same amplifier; two amplifiers may be used; or there may be separate windings, each connected to its own amplifier. (Synonymous with *combined head*.)

head, record–Same as *head, write*.

head, recording–Same as *head, write*.

head, write–A head, usually a magnetic head, used for transferring analog or digital data to a storage device, such as a drum, tape, disc, or magnetic card. The write head may be a separate unit used exclusively for recording; it may operate in a read as well as a write mode, or in an erase mode, a special case of the write mode. (Synonymous with *record head*, with *writing head*, and with *recording head*. Further clarified by *head* and by *head, magnetic*.)

head, write-read–See *head, read-write*.

head, writing–Same as *head, write*.

head azimuth–See *azimuth, head*.

head stack–See *stack, head*.

header card–See *card, header*.

header label–See *label, header*.

header record–See *record, header*.

heading–1: In communications, a string of characters that are machine readable and represent message routing and destination information and that are usually placed at the beginning of a message. 2: In communications, the characters that precede the text of a message, enabling the receiving station to receive and process the text.

heading character–Same as *character, start-of-heading*.

HEEP–(Highway Engineering Exchange Program). An exchange plan for interchanging civil engineering computer programs used in design and construction of highways. The programs are designed to run on the IBM 650 computer.

hermaphroditic connector–See *connector, hermaphroditic*.

hesitation–In computer operation, a temporary halt or brief suspension of operations in a sequence of operations in order to perform all or part of an operation from another sequence; or, during an autonomous peripheral transfer of a block of data, the periodic suspension of the operation of a simultaneous routine in order to transfer each word of the block to or from storage.

heuristic–Pertaining to a method of problem solving in which solutions are discovered by evaluation of the progress made toward the final solution, such as a controlled trial and error method, an exploratory method of tackling a problem, or a sequencing of investigation, experimentation, and trial solution in closed loops, gradually closing in on the solution. A heuristic approach usually implies or encourages further investigation, and makes use of intuitive decisions and inductive logic in the absence of direct proof known to the user. Thus, heuristic methods lead to solutions of problems or inventions through continuous analysis of results obtained thus far, permitting a determination of the next step. A stochastic method assumes a solution on the basis of intuitive conjecture or speculation and testing the solution against known evidence, observations, or measurements. The stochastic approach tends to omit intervening or intermediate steps toward a solution. (Contrast with *stochastic* and with *algorithm.*)

heuristic method—See *method, heuristic.*

heuristic routine—See *routine, heuristic.*

hexadecimal—Same as *sexadecimal.*

hexadecimal notation—Same as *notation, sexadecimal.*

hexadecimal number—Same as *numeral, sexadecimal.*

hexadecimal numeral—Same as *numeral, sexadecimal.*

HF—(High Frequency). Frequencies between 3 and 30 megahertz. (Further clarified by *spectrum, frequency.*)

Hg delay-line—Same as *delay-line, mercury.*

hidden lines—See *lines, hidden.*

hierarchy—1: A specified rank or order of items; for example, a classification scheme based on magnitude, such as bit, byte, gulp, character, word, block, record, file, and bank. 2: A series of items classifed by rank or order.

hierarchy, data—A structuring of data into subsets within sets; for example, bits form a byte, bytes form a character, characters form a word, words form a block, blocks form a record, records form a file, and files form a bank.

high-level language—Same as *language, higher-order.*

high-level modulation—See *modulation, high-level.*

high-low bias check—Same as *check, marginal.*

high-order digit—See *digit, high-order.*

high-performance equipment—See *equipment, high-performance.*

high-speed bus—Same as *register, storage.*

high-speed carry—See *carry, high-speed.*

high-speed loop—Same as *revolver.*

high-speed printer—See *printer, high-speed.*

high-speed storage—See *storage, high-speed.*

high-usage trunk—See *trunk, high-usage.*

higher-order language—See *language, higher-order.*

highpass—Pertaining to the operation of a circuit or device, such as a filter, that permits the passage of high-frequency

signals and highly attenuates the low-frequency signals. (Further clarified by *bandpass.*)

highway—Same as *bus.*

history, track—A radar scope presentation trace of past and present positions of a target being tracked. The trace shows as a line on the radar screen.

hit—1: A match or comparison reached or made when a file is searched for specific data items; for example, in automatic information-retrieval systems, a find made when the label of a stored item matches the search key. 2: In file maintenance, the finding of a detail record for a master record. 3: A transient or temporary disturbance or perturbation in a communication or data processing system.

hit-on-the-fly printer—See *printer, hit-on-the-fly.*

hold—1: To retain data in its location after also moving it to another location. The data is held because it is still needed for some future purpose in the program, even though it is transferred to a register or another storage location in order that it may enter into an operation from that location. (Synonymous with *preserve.*) 2: To make a copy in order to preserve the data for some future use, as in a storage dump or a postmortem dump.

hold facility—See *facility, hold.*

hold instruction—See *instruction, hold.*

holding beam—See *beam, holding.*

holding gun—See *gun, holding.*

hole—In transistor theory, a vacancy in a crystal lattice caused by the absence of an electron in an order structure of covalent bonds. Thermal agitation will break the bond, causing the electron to move away from its atom, leaving the hole behind. The electron may fill another hole left by another electron. The hole may be considered to have a positive charge equal to that of an electron. It is not as mobile as an electron, for an electron can drift readily from atom to atom, or hole to hole, or replace an electron in another atom but the crystal atom itself is locked in an ordered structure, and before a hole can move, it must wait for an electron from an adjacent atom to fill it in, at which time a hole appears in the adjacent atom. From an external point of view, the hole may be considered to move, but with much less mobility than that of an electron. The movement of holes and electrons constitutes current flow, and, upon the application of an electric field, the flow becomes ordered, rather than random as it is under thermal agitation. The external current is a measure of the extent of the ordered flow. Holes also demonstrate the characteristic of possessing mass as well as positive charge. (Further clarified by *semiconductor, intrinsic,* by *acceptor,* by *donor,* by

177

carrier (2), by *semiconductor, p-type,* and by *semiconductor, n-type.*)

hole, control—Same as *punch, designation.*

hole, function—Same as *punch, designation.*

holes, code—The data holes in perforated tape that represent the information, as opposed to the feed holes that are used to control the movement and positioning of the tape.

holes, feed—Same as *holes, sprocket.*

holes, sprocket—Holes punched in a tape to control the movement and positioning of the tape. The movement, or feeding, and the positioning, or indexing, is usually controlled by a longitudinal row of evenly spaced holes at or near the center of tape, which are engaged by a toothed wheel. Some tapes, especially control tapes, such as the type that may be used to program the carriage movement of a tabulator, may have a longitudinal row of holes along both edges of the tape. (Synonymous with *feed holes.*)

hole, binder—See *card, binder-hole.*

Hollerith—Pertaining to a widely used system of encoding alphanumeric information on punched cards. The punched cards, used in electrical accounting machines and computer input card readers, have come to be known as Hollerith cards, after their orginator Herman Hollerith. Developed around 1890, the cards were first used on the census data of that year. (Further clarified by *code, card* and by *code, Hollerith.*)

Hollerith card—See *card, Hollerith.*

Hollerith code—See *code, Hollerith.*

hologram—A photochemical or crystal recording of an image that has been distributed over the surface of a film or in a crystalline structure through the use of interference patterns obtained by causing interference between monochromatic light directly from the same source that is used to illuminate the image. Recovery of the image is obtained by mixing light reflected or transmitted from the recording with light directly from the source. The image can be focused in free space or on a screen. Three dimensional images in free space are possible, giving the viewer the impression of being in the scene he is viewing. The advantages of the use of holograms for data storage are that flaws in the storage medium do not result in the loss of a character or a piece of the image and that extremely high packing densities are achievable; for example, a one inch cubic crystal might hold 12,000 pages of alphanumeric text. (Contrast with *holograph.*)

holograph—A manuscript or other document that is written entirely in the author's own handwriting. (Contrast with *hologram.*)

home record—See *record, home.*

homeostasis—The dynamic condition of a system wherein the input and output of the system are so precisely balanced that there is no appearance of change.

hopper, card—A device, usually an integral part of a machine, that holds cards and makes them available to a card feed mechanism. The punched cards are placed in the hopper prior to their being read by the machine, such as a card-reader input device connected to a digital computer. (Synonymous with *card input magazine.* Contrast with *stacker, card.*)

horizontal feed—See *feed, horizontal.*

horizontal format—See *format, horizontal.*

horizontal position, addressable—See *position, addressable horizontal.*

horizontal tabulation character—See *character, horizontal tabulation.*

housekeeping operation—Same as *operation, red-tape.*

HSM—An abbreviation for high-speed memory.

HSP—An abbreviation for high-speed printer.

HSR—An abbreviation for high-speed reader.

HT—The horizontal tabulation character.

hub—An electrical socket on a control panel or plugboard into which leads or plug wires may be inserted or connected. A hub usually has a single input point and many output points or many input points and a single output point. It may be likened to the hub of a many-spoked wheel, except that electrical signals are carried rather than mechanical stress.

human language—Same as *language, natural.*

hunting—A continuous attempt on the part of an automatically controlled or influenced system to seek an equilibrium condition. The system usually contains a standard or an equilibrium condition, a method of determining the deviation of the state of the system from the standard or equilibrium condition, and a method of

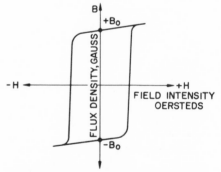

Magnetic flux density vs. a reversing field intensity (magnetomotive force) in a square-loop material. The magnetization flux density will remain at $+B_0$ or $-B_0$ when the mmf field H is removed, depending on whether H is removed from $+H$ or $-H$. This plot is called a hysteresis loop.

influencing the system in such a way that the difference between the standard, or equilibrium condition, and the state of the system tends toward zero. Hunting occurs when the system overshoots its equilibrium, or zero-deviation-from-standard condition, and seeks, or is forced, to return.

hybrid computer—See *computer, hybrid.*

hysteresis—The lagging of an effect behind the cause that is producing it; for example, the lagging of the magnetic flux or polarization of a magnetic material behind the magnetizing force that is producing it. The effect is caused by molecular friction, inertia, crystal and grain structure, and other effects, such as impurities, nonhomogeneity and other characteristics of materials. A hysteresis loop is formed when plotting polarization against magnetizing force. Two curves are formed, spaced a distance apart, one for increasing values of magnetizing force and one for decreasing values. (Further clarified by *loop, hysteresis.*)

hysteresis loop—See *loop, hysteresis.*

i

IAD—(Initiation Area Discriminator). A cathode-ray tube and a photoelectric-cell combination that picks up unmapped, uncorrelated, long-range radar data for processing by the automatic-initiation program of a computer.

IAL—(International Algebraic Language). A programming language for preparing computer programs, now replaced by ALGOL, and designed primarily for solving mathematical problems on digital computers.

IC—1: An abbreviation for integrated circuit. 2: An abbreviation for instruction counter.

icand—An abbreviation of multiplicand.

icand register—See *register, icand.*

ICC—(International Computation Center). A computer service and center made available to member nations; located in Rome and sponsored by UNESCO.

ICIP—International Conference on Information Processing.

identification—1: A name used as a tag or label and usually written or otherwise expressed in some alphabet, such as a numerical or alphabetical code, which uniquely identifies or represents a person, place, or thing, such as an item or a unit of information, like a block, record, or file. The identification might be a unique name, an address, the name of a parameter, or an indirect address. (Further clarified by *identifier.*) 2: The study or determination of the nature of a person, place, or thing by an analysis of its outward characteristics, such as the determination of the hostility or friendliness of an aircraft by flight plan correlation, mode of approach, visual markings, or mode of formation.

identification, file—An identification, such as a label or tag, used to describe, identify, or name a physical medium containing data, such as computer input or output data; for example, the label put on a reel of digital magnetic tape to identify its contents or the tag attached to a box of punched cards, which is the output of a computer run.

identification, terminal—In data transmission networks, a facility that automatically transmits an agreed identification code to a user's terminal before data is transmitted.

identifier—In information retrieval, a symbol whose purpose is to indicate or label a body of data. (Further clarified by *identification.*)

identifier, data element use—Same as *identifier, data use.*

identifier, data use—A name or a title given to the use to be made of the data items for a data element; for example, the data item 1922 October 5, for the data element *date,* must be identified as to its use, such as *date of birth, initial occupancy, arrival, departure,* or *marriage.* (Synonymous with *data element use identifier.*)

identifier, location—An identification, such as a label or tag, assigned to a specific geographic area, city, town, map coordinate, airport, place in computer storage, or any other location.

identify—To attach or assign a unique label or name to a person, place, or thing; for example, to put a label on a reel for magnetic tape so as to permit its retrieval.

identity gate-See *gate, identity.*

identity operation—See *operation, identity.*

idle character, synchronous—See *character, synchronous idle.*

idle time—See *time, idle.*

IDP—An abbreviation for integrated data processing.

IDS—(Integrated Data Store). A technique developed by General Electric Company for organizing business data.

IEC—International Electrotechnical Commission.

IEEE—Institute of Electrical and Electronics Engineers.

ier—An abbreviation of multiplier.

ier register—See *register, ier.*

if-A-then-B gate—Same as *gate, B OR NOT A.*

if-A-then-NOT-B gate—Same as *gate, NAND.*

if-B-then-A gate—Same as *gate, A OR NOT B.*

if-B-then-NOT-A gate—Same as *gate, NAND.*

if-and-only-if operation—Same as *operation, equivalence.*

if-then gate—1: Same as *gate, A OR NOT B.* 2: Same as *gate, B OR NOT A.*

IFCS—International Federation of Computer Sciences.

IFIP—(International Federation for Information Processing). A technical society devoted to furthering the interests of the field of information processing and data communication on an international basis. Formerly IFIPS.

IFIPS—(International Federation of Information Processing Societies). The forerunner of the International Federation for Information Processing (IFIP).

ignore character—See *character, ignore.*

ignore gate—1: Same as *gate, A ignore B.* 2: Same as *gate, B ignore A.*

ignore instruction—See *instruction, ignore.*

illegal character—See *character, illegal.*

illegal code—See *code, illegal.*

illegal command—Same as *character, illegal.*

illegal-command check—Same as *check, forbidden-combination.*

ILLIAD—A version of MAD, a computer programming language developed for the IBM 650 computer at Southern Illinois University.

image—A representation of information in one storage medium of information in another storage medium, wherein there is a one-to-one relationship between the characters; the contents of a two-dimensional array of binary magnetic storage cores represented as a two-dimensional array of holes on a punched card, where magnetization of each core in the clockwise direction represents a one and magnetization in the counter-clockwise direction represents a zero; a hole in the card represents a one and no-hole at a punch position represents a zero. Thus, there is an "image" of the core storage contents on the card.

image, card—An image of the ones and zeros, represented by holes and spaces in a punched card, formed or stored in another medium; for example, a matrix of ones and zeros in core storage, which represent the ones and zeros on a punched card, on a one-to-one basis, where the binary digit is represented by the direction of magnetization, for the magnetic core storage, and by the presence or absence of a hole in the card at each punch position, for the card. Thus, the card image is a one-to-one representation of the contents of a punched card.

image, cine-oriented—An image placed on roll microfilm in such a manner that the top edge of the image is perpendicular to the long edge of the film. The top edge is the upper edge when the image is held for normal human viewing. (Contrast with *image, comic-strip-oriented.*)

Cine-oriented images *on a section of roll microfilm.*

image, comic-strip-oriented—An image on roll microfilm appearing in such a manner that the top edge of the image is parallel to the long edge of the film. The top edge of the image is the upper edge when normally viewed by humans. (Contrast with *image, cine-oriented.*)

image, core—An image of the ones and zeros, represented by polarized magnetic cores, formed or stored in another medium; for example, a matrix of ones and zeros represented by a two-dimensional array of neon lights, on a one-to-one basis, where each binary digit is represented by the light being on or off, for the neon lights, and by the direction of magnetization, for the magnetic core storage unit; or the contents of a core storage plane represented as magnetized spots on the surface of a magnetic storage drum, on a one-to-one basis.

image, display—The display elements and groups that are visually shown on the viewing surface of a display device.

image area—See *area, image.*

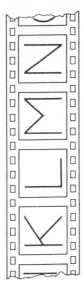

Comic-strip-oriented images *on a section of roll microfilm.*

image dissector—See *dissector, image.*
immediate access—See *access, immediate.*
immediate-access storage—See *storage, immediate-access.*
immediate address—See *address, immediate.*
immediate addressing—See *addressing, immediate.*
immediate instruction—See *instruction, immediate.*
impact modulator amplifier—See *amplifier, impact modulator.*
impedance—The reaction of an electric circuit against the flow of alternating current when an alternating voltage is applied; thus, the ratio of the applied voltage to the resulting current in any given circuit or circuit element. Resistance, inductive reactance, and capacitive reactance are special cases of impedance. In a general case, impedance is a complex quantity, having a real and imaginary part, representing a resistive and reactive part, respectively. The basic unit of impedance is the ohm. The reciprocal of the impedance is called the admittance. The impedance of a circuit or circuit depends on such basic things as the type of material, the shape of the material, temperature, environment, and the frequency of the applied voltage.
impedance, characteristic—The ratio of the voltage to the current at every point along a transmission line on which there are no standing waves. It may be measured by obtaining the square-root of the product of the open- and short-circuit impedance of the line. When a transmission line is terminated in its characteristic impedance, energy is not reflected from the end of the line, but is fully absorbed in the terminating impedance.

impedance, input—Impedance measured at the input terminals of an electrical circuit or device, such as a transmission line, gate, or amplifier, under no-load conditions. The measurement conditions are the same as for terminal impedance measurement. (Contrast with *impedance, output.*)
impedance, output—Impedance measured at the output terminals of an electrical circuit or device, such as a transmission line, gate, or amplifier, under no-load conditions. The measurement conditions are the same as for terminal impedance measurement. (Contrast with *impedance, input.*)
impedance, terminal—The impedance of a device, such as a transmission line, measured at the output or input terminals under no-load conditions. The measurement of terminal impedance between any two terminals of a network is made with all sources of voltage shorted by their internal impedance and all sources of current open-circuited.
imperative statement—Same as *instruction.*
implication—Same as *inclusion.*
implication gate—1: Same as *gate, A OR NOT B.* 2: Same as *gate, B OR NOT A.*
implied addressing—See *addressing, implied.*
imprinter—A device used to make marks, patterns, or impressions on a surface, for example, printing presses, typewriters, pens, cash registers, embossers, raised-seal makers, and pressure devices such as those used with credit cards and address plates.
imprinting—1: The use of an imprinter. 2: The mark, pattern, or impression made by an imprinter.
improper character—Same as *character, illegal.*
improper code—Same as *code, illegal.*
improper command—Same as *character, illegal.*
improper command check—Same as *check, forbidden-combination.*
impulse—Same as *pulse.*
inactive file—See *file, inactive.*
incidentals time—See *time, incidentals.*
incipient failure—See *failure, incipient.*
inclusion—1: A particle of foreign material imbedded in a uniform or homogeneous material; for example, in optical character recognition, a particle of foreign material imbedded in a sheet of paper that changes the optical reflectance of the paper in the vicinity of the particle. 2: A logic operator having the property that if P is a statement and Q is a statement, then P inclusion Q is false if P is true and Q is false, true if P is false and Q is true, and true if both statements are true. P inclusion Q is often represented by P $>$ Q. (Synonymous with *if-then* and with *implication.*)
inclusion gate—1: Same as *gate, A OR NOT B.* 2: Same as *gate, B OR NOT A.*
inclusive-NOR gate—Same as *gate, NOR.*
inclusive-OR gate—Same as *gate, OR.*

inconsistent network—See *network, inconsistent.*

increment—1: To add a quantity to another quantity; for example, to advance the count or number stored in a counter or register. 2: The quantity that is added. (Contrast with *decrement.*)

increment size—See *size, increment.*

incremental binary representation—Same as *representation, binary incremental.*

incremental compaction—See *compaction, incremental.*

incremental computer—See *computer, incremental.*

incremental coordinate—See *coordinate, incremental.*

incremental data—See *data, incremental.*

incremental representation—See *representation, incremental.*

incremental representation, ternary—See *representation, ternary incremental.*

independent operation—See *operation, independent.*

independent-sideband transmission—See *transmission, independent-sideband.*

independent variable—See *variable, independent.*

index—1: A symbol used to identify a particular quantity in an array of similar quantities; for example, the terms of an array represented by x(1), x(2), ..., x(100) have the indexes 1, 2, ..., 100, respectively. 2: An ordered list of references to the contents of a larger body of data, such as a file or record, together with the keys or reference notations for identifying, locating, searching, or retrieving the contents. 3: Pertaining to an index register. 4: To prepare an ordered list of references to the contents of a larger body of data, such as a file or record. 5: To place an item at a particular location or to orient an item in a particular direction. 6: In computer programming, a subscript of integer value, that identifies the position of an item of data with respect to some other item of data. 7: In micrographics, a method or symbol for locating data on a roll of microfilm or microfiche, such as optical codes like targets, flash cards, lines, bars or other marks.

index, citation—An index or list of references to other documents that are mentioned or cited in a particular document or a set of documents. A reference is directly mentioned or quoted in running text. The citation index is a list of these references. The bibliography is a list of supporting documents. (Further clarified by *reference* and by *bibliography.*)

index, code line—A visual index that consists of a set of transparent and opaque bars or lines parallel to the long edge of a roll of microfilm and located between images. The index is used to automatically find a specific frame on the film, since each image may be associated with a unique pattern of code lines.

index, cooperation—In diametral, or facsimile, image transmission, the product of the drum diameter, in inches, and the line scan advance, in scanning lines per inch.

index, cycle—In digital computer programming, the number of times a cycle has been executed. The cycle index number may be the difference or the negative of the difference between the number of times a cycle has been executed and the number of repetitions desired, a kind of countdown. Thus, a cycle index register may be set to the number of cycles desired. Each time a cycle is completed, the count in the register is reduced by one. When the register reaches zero, the series of cycles is completed. (Further clarified by *reset, cycle.*)

index, inverted—An index created by sequencing, according to some criterion, the data elements, items, or codes that are the attributes of a given index; for example, given a conventional telephone listing, an inverted index would enable finding the name of the party given his telephone number.

GIVEN INDEX		INVERTED INDEX	
NAME	ADDRESS	ADDRESS	NAME
BUD, R	6 RECTOR	CANAL 12	RIT, T
DOE, J	18 MAINE	MAINE 18	DOE, J
KEM, J	21 ORIOLE	ORIOLE 7	POT, A
RIT, T	12 CANAL	ORIOLE 21	KEM, J
POT, A	7 ORIOLE	RECTOR 6	BUD, R

An inverted index *derived from a given* index.

index, permutation—An index or listing generated by listing alphabetically all or some of the words of a title of a document such that each word appears once as the first word, followed in the normal sequence by all the other words shifted in circular fashion. Thus, the title Sodium Vapor Corrosive Effects would appear as Sodium Vapor Corrosive Effects; Vapor Corrossive Effects Sodium; Corrosive Effects Sodium Vapor, and Effects Sodium Vapor Corrosive. These would be alphabetized with all other permuted titles, thus permitting look-up and retrieval of particular documents. (Synonymous with *permuted-title index.* Further clarified by *KWIC.*)

index, permuted-title—Same as *index, permutation.*

index entry—See *entry, index.*

index point—See *point, index.*

index register—See *register, index.*

index word—Same as *modifier.*

indexed access—See *access, indexed.*

indexed address—See *address, indexed.*

indexing, coordinate—A technique of indexing individual units of information, such as documents of items in computer storage, by the joint use of two or more terms, such as descriptors or uniterms, usually of equal rank, with retrieval being performed by logical associations among the terms, such as logical product, sum and complement; for example, find all documents treating of cryogenics and microminiaturization, or cryotrons. Thus, the contents of a library can be searched for specific information. The indexing technique uses logical connectives to couple terms and show their interrelationships, such as or, and, not. Sometimes the technique is called concept coordination, uniterm indexing, correlative indexing, multiple aspect indexing, manipulative index, and Zatocoding system. The logical connective words are sometimes called link and role indicators. (Synonymous with *correlative indexing*, with *manipulative indexing*, with *multiple-aspect indexing*, with *Zatocode indexing*, and with *Zatocoding system*.)

indexing, correlative—Same as *indexing, coordinate*.

indexing, cumulative—The assigning of two or more indices to a single address in the instruction word of a digital computer.

indexing, manipulative—Same as *indexing, coordinate*.

indexing, multiple-aspect—Same as *indexing, coordinate*.

indexing, uniterm—A system of coordinate indexing that utilizes single terms to define or describe the contents of a document with some measure of uniqueness. Mortimer Taube called the single terms uniterms. The system is used for document retrieval.

indexing, word—A system of coordinate indexing that utilizes a word or sets of words to define or describe the contents of a document, especially for retrieval purposes. Often, insufficient thought is given to synonymous, ambiguous terms, and more generic concepts related to the term selected.

indexing, Zatocode—Same as *indexing, coordinate*.

indicate, group—To print indicative information from only the first record of a group of records.

indicator—A device, signal, or mark that may be set or placed into a prescribed state or form in accordance with the results of a process, action, or event; for example, a flag. The state of the indicator may be used by a control unit to make a selection of alternative processes. The state of an indicator may or may not be displayed. A register may be used as an indicator to display or hold the results of a comparison. A sequence of operations within a procedure may be varied in accordance with the signals from an indicator. A light used to show that a circuit is in a certain state or condition is an indicator.

indicator, check—A device that indicates whether or not certain conditions or events are occurring in a machine; for example, a light that turns on when a malfunction has occurred at a specific place. Thus, there may be a separate light on a console for each of the built-in checking circuits, such as one light to show that an echo check failed, one to show that a parity check failed, or one to show that a comparison of duplicate hardware output failed. For a computer, a decision in the program can be based on the status of the indicator, or the condition can be ignored. Following the activation of the indicator, fault diagnostic routines and other test routines may be used to locate the failing parts if the check indicator itself does not indicate the location of the failing part.

indicator, end-of-file—**1:** A device that signals or marks the end of a file. The end condition, such as the end of a reel of tape has been reached, must be made known to the routine or the operator in control of the equipment. **2:** A character that signals the end of a file, usually recorded in the same medium as is the file.

indicator, instruction-check—A signal device, such as a light or buzzer, that is turned on to call a machine operator's attention to the fact that a discrepancy, a machine malfunction, or a program error in the instruction currently being executed, has occurred.

indicator, overflow—A device that signals the occurrence of an overflow, such as a number too large for a given register to hold; for example, a bistable trigger, or flip-flop, that changes state when an overflow occurs in the register with which it is associated. The overflow indicator may be interrogated and restored to its original state. Generally speaking, an overflow indicator may be actuated by any unplanned or incorrect operation in the execution of an arithmetic instruction. (Synonymous with *overflow-check indicator*.)

indicator, overflow-check—Same as *indicator, overflow*.

indicator, priority—Information or data used to order a queue; for example, the originating station or address of incoming data may be used as a basis for determining which of several programs is to be run first on a computer.

indicator, read-write check—A device used to signal or determine whether errors have been made in reading or writing; for example, a device that interrogates what has been written, compares the results with what was to be written, and signals the operator or halts the computer if an error was made.

indicator, role—A code assigned to a word, such as a keyword, descriptor, or uniterm, to indicate the nature, part of speech, or any other particular function that the word is to play in the text in which it occurs; for example, a character used to indicate that the associated word is a noun.

indicator, routing—An address, label, or code that identifies or defines the path and the final destination or addressee of a message or call.

indicator, sign-check—An error-checking device that indicates or signals the occurrence of an error in the sign of a number or field. The device might indicate "no sign" or "improper sign." The indicator may be interrogated and appropriate action initiated, such as having the machine halt or enter into a correction routine or a diagnostic routine.

indicator, stack—Same as *pointer, stack.*

indicator, switch—An indicator that displays the setting of a switch, that is, the condition or state the switch is in.

indicator bit—See *bit, indicator.*

indirect address—See *address, indirect.*

indirect addressing—See *addressing, indirect.*

indirect instruction—See *instruction, indirect.*

indirect output—See *output, indirect.*

induced failure—See *failure, induced.*

induction, mathematical—A method of proving the validity, value, or truth of a statement concerning terms based on natural numbers not less than N by showing that the statement is valid for the term based on N, and that if it is valid for an arbitrary value, n, that is greater than N, it is also valid for the term based on (n + 1).

industrial data processing—See *processing, industrial data.*

inequivalence—Same as *exclusive-OR.*

inferential analysis—See *analysis, inferential.*

infinite-pad method—See *method, infinite-pad.*

infinity—1: Unlimited in extent of time, space, or quantity. 2: For computers, any number larger than the largest number a computer can store in a given register or in any of its registers or storage locations. When such a number occurs, the computer may halt and signal by an indicator that an overflow has occurred. A computer may be made to interpret the largest number it is capable of storing in its register or storage locations or is capable of expressing in its fixed word length, as being infinity, which the computer may automatically substitute for any number greater than a stated limit.

infix notation—See *notation, infix.*

infix notation, distributed—See *notation, distributed infix.*

information—The meaning assigned to data by known conventions. Thus, data are the marks, such as characters, signs, or symbols themselves, whereas the knowledge assigned to them is information. In this context, information need not necessarily be new to any person or group of persons. Strictly speaking, computers, data processors, or communication equipment can only handle data: the signs and symbols, in various forms, such as holes, pulses, printed letters, or magnetized spots. The meaning that humans or machines have assigned to the data is another issue.

information, selective dissemination of—See *SDI.*

information, transferred—Same as *content, transinformation.*

information center, technical—See *center, technical information.*

information content—See *content, information.*

information content, conditional—See *content, conditional information.*

information-content decimal unit—Same as *Hartley.*

information-content natural unit—See *unit, information content natural.*

information feedback system—See *system, information feedback.*

information interchange—See *interchange, information.*

information link—Same as *link, communication.*

information measure—See *measure, information.*

information processing—See *processing, information.*

information rate, average—See *rate, average information.*

information retrieval—See *retrieval, information.*

information science—See *science, information.*

information separator—See *separator, information.*

information source—Same as *source, message.*

information source, stationary—Same as *source, stationary message.*

information system—See *system, information.*

information system, management—See *system, management information.*

information theory—See *theory, information.*

information word—See *word, information.*

informative abstract—See *abstract, informative.*

INFRAL—(Information Retrieval Automatic Language). A special programming language, developed at the National Biomedical Research Foundation, and providing the ability to construct bibliographies from indexed information. An adaptation of COBOL, using ALGOL statements, is used to effect the retrieval of information. The language is used to retrieve data stored in machine-readable form.

inherent error—Same as *error, inherited.*

inherited error—See *error, inherited.*

inhibit pulse—See *pulse, inhibit.*

inhibit signal—See *signal, inhibit.*

inhibiting input—See *input, inhibiting.*

initial address—Same as *origin, computer program.*

initial error—See *error, initial.*

initial program loader—See *loader, initial program.*

initialize–Same as *preset*.

initialization, loop–The parts of a loop that determine the starting values of the parameters of the loop. A loop is often executed many times, each iteration causing an adjustment of specified variables. The initial or starting values are used during the first execution of the instructions in the loop.

initialization, system–The overall process of loading an operating system into a computer, defining all the necessary parameters and options, and establishing the proper environment for the execution of programs under the direction of the supervisor. (Synonymous with *system start-up*.)

initiate button–See *button, initiate*.

initiate key–Same as *button, initiate*.

initiation area discriminator–See *IAD*.

ink, extraneous–During the printing of characters, any ink deposited that is not confined to the printed characters themselves and that lies within the clear band. (Further clarified by *band, clear*.)

ink, magnetic–An ink containing particles of a magnetic substance that can be detected by automatic devices and therefore can be read automatically. The art of reading these characters by machine is called magnetic ink character recognition (MICR), in contrast to optical character recognition (OCR). Characters written in magnetic ink may also be read by humans and by optical character recognition devices. Most banks utilize MICR for check indentification. A USA Standard character set exists for MICR characters; it was developed by the American Banking Association with the cooperation of the American National Standards Institute.

ink bleed–See *bleed, ink*.

ink character recognition, magnetic–See *MICR*.

ink reflectance–See *reflectance, ink*.

ink smudge–See *smudge, ink*.

ink squeezeout–See *squeezeout, ink*.

ink uniformity–See *uniformity, ink*.

inline data processing–See *data processing, inline*.

inline procedures–See *procedures, inline*.

inline subroutine–See *subroutine, inline*.

inner face–See *face, inner*.

input–1: Data that is to be processed or operated upon; for example, the state or the sequence of states on a specified channel known as the input channel or device; a device or collective set of devices used for bringing data into another device; a channel for impressing a state on a device or logic element; the process of transferring data from an external storage device to an internal storage device; or pertaining to the computer subroutines that control devices that bring data into a computer. Data transferred from any device, such as auxiliary storage, peripheral devices, or remote stations into a computer, is considered input data to the computer or to any of its operating registers, buffers, or storage locations. Thus, card readers, tape readers, and data links are considered input, though it is preferable to say *input data* or *card input* to avoid confusion between the data and the data handler. 2: The process of transferring data from external storage to internal storage of a computer, or from its peripheral or online equipment, or from a human being. 3: A device or set of devices used to insert data into another device. 4: Pertaining to processes, hardware, or software, related to the insertion of data into a place, such as in input equipment, input media, input terminals, input programs, and input data. Often these are simply referred to as input.

input, card–Pertaining to a method of introducing data to a device through the use of punched cards; the data link or channel over which data read from punched cards is fed into a machine; the card reader itself; or the data read from punched cards and fed into a machine.

input, gap-filler–Data generated by a gap-filler type radar and transmitted by way of ground data links to the input lines of a computer.

input, inhibiting–1: A logic gate input channel, such as an input lead to an AND or an OR gate, which, if in its prescribed state, prevents any output that might otherwise occur. 2: The signal that prevents any output from a gate.

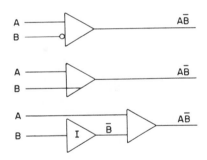

Various logic symbols used to represent an inhibiting input.

input, manual–The entry of data, the data itself, the channel or device used to enter data into a machine through the direct manipulation of a device by a human being; for example, a keyboard used to insert data into a computer; a set of hand toggle switches used to insert a binary number into a computer register or storage location; or a track status associated with surveillance radar information reported from a manual source and inserted into a computer.

input, output–See *input-output*.

input, real-time–Input data, received by a data processing system within time limits determined by the requirements or characteristics of another system or at instants of time that are determined by the other system; for example, data received by airborne radar to determine the aircraft's position for calculating control signals to place the aircraft on course. (Contrast with *output, real-time*.)

input, tape—1: Pertaining to a method of introducing data to a device through the use of tape, such as plastic or metallic magnetic tape, perforated paper tape of the chadding or chadless type, or fabric tape loops. **2:** The data link or channel over which data read from tape is fed into a machine. **3:** The tape reader, station, handler, or transport itself. **4:** The data read from tape and fed into a machine.

input area—See *area, input.*

input block—See *block, input.*

input buffer—See *buffer, input.*

input channel—See *channel, input.*

input data—See *data, input.*

input device— See *device, input.*

input equipment—See *equipment, input.*

input impedance—See *impedance, input.*

input instruction code—See *code, input instruction.*

input magazine—See *magazine, input.*

input magazine, card—Same as *hopper, card.*

input-output—The medium or device used to insert information, data, or instructions into a computing system or the medium or device used to transfer information or data, usually processed data, from a computing system to the "outside" world. Examples of input-output media or devices are paper tape, magnetic tape, punched cards, printers, plotters, illuminated panels, typewriters, cathode-ray display tubes and character-sensing devices. Thus, input-output may be the media or data-carrier handling devices, the data-carrier itself, or the data itself. Input-output permits a computer to communicate with humans or other machines. Abbreviated I-O.

input-output, logical—In a computer operating system, conceptual or virtual input-output operations that are executed by user programs and that do not involve a physical input-output data or device, but perhaps only blocking or deblocking. (Contrast with *input-output, physical*.)

input-output, physical—In a computer operating system, actual input-output operations that involve physical input-output data and devices and that involves the movement of data between main storage and peripheral devices. (Contrast with *input-output, logical*.)

input-output, real-time—The data involved in an operating situation in which a machine accepts the data as it is generated by a sensor, processes or operates on the data, and furnishes the results so as to affect the operations of the data generator or some other device; for example, the data received from an industrial process under the control of a computer or the data received from a missile under the guidance control of a computer.

input-output, simultaneous—Pertaining to the capability of a computer to handle other operations concurrently with input and output operations, usually through the use of a buffer that holds input-output data as it arrives temporarily while other operations are executed, whereupon the contents of the buffer are transferred to and from the computer storage en masse rapidly during a short halt in the other operations. This avoids the necessity of having the computer wait for data arrival or slow down for output rates, say on card punching.

input-output area—See *area, input-output.*

input-output channel—See *channel, input-output.*

input-output controller—See *controller, input-output.*

input-output exchange—See *exchange, input-output.*

input-output medium—See *medium, input-output.*

input-output register—See *register, input-output.*

input-output storage—Same as *area, input-output.*

input process—See *process, input.*

input program—See *program, input.*

input pulse, partial select—Same as *pulse, partial write.*

input reader—Same as *routine, input.*

input register—See *register, input.*

input routine—See *routine, input.*

input station, data—See *station, data input.*

input storage—Same as *area, input.*

input stream—See *stream, input.*

input unit—Same as *input (3).*

inquiry—In the field of information storage and retrieval, a request for information from storage, or from an information network or system; for example, a request for a document from a library, a request for information from a stored collection of data, a machine statement to initiate a search of data in storage, or a request for the number of available airline seats on a specific flight. The request may be in the form of a question or an order. It may be inserted into the data-processing system or network by any means, such as keyboard, pushbutton, punched card reader or telephone.

inquiry application—See *application, inquiry.*

inquiry station—See *station, inquiry.*

insertion, switch—The process by which information is inserted into a data-processing system by an operator who manually operates switches. (Compare with *switch, insertion*.)

insertion gain—See *gain, insertion.*

insertion loss—See *loss, insertion.*

insertion sort—See *sort, insertion.*

insertion switch—See *switch, insertion.*

installation, computer—1: A computing facility or computation center, usually consisting of one or more general-purpose, electronic, digital computing machines, offline data conversion equipment, peripheral online equipment, satellite computers, communication equipment, and operating personnel. **2:** The process of onsite arrival, arrangement, connection, and initiation of the testing procedure of a computer.

installation, terminal—1: A group of operable data terminal equipment and any related equipment. **2:** In a communication system or a teleprocessing system, a data terminal, signal conversion equipment, and any intermediate or associated equipment required for operation, such as a computer or other data processing equipment.

installation date—See *date, installation.*

installation review, post—See *review, post-installation.*

installation time—See *time, installation.*

instantaneous access—Same as *access, immediate.*

instantaneous data-transfer rate—See *rate, instantaneous data-transfer.*

instantaneous storage—Same as *storage, immediate-access.*

instantaneous transmission rate—Same as *rate, instantaneous data-transfer.*

instruction—A statement that specifies an operation and the values or locations of all operands. In computers, instructions are given to, interpreted by, and executed by the computer. The instruction specifies the elementary operations to be performed. The instruction is a basic syntactical unit; for example, add the contents of A to the contents of B; it usually assumes the form of a statement, expression, or declaration, and may be in an interrogative, imperative, or declarative form, depending on the nature of the programming language. The instruction word in a digital computer usually contains an operator, or command part, one or more address parts, and sometimes other items, such as tags. Instructions are usually expressed in plain English or through the use of special codes. For example, in the Control Data 924 computer, of the 64 instructions permissible with the 6-bit code, there are 8 fixed-point arithmetic, 4 logic, 6 indexing, one input-output, 11 conditional and unconditional jumps and stops, 5 storage searching and masking, 7 shifting, 9 loading and storing, 10 accumulator, and 3 other instructions. *Instruction* is preferred to *order* or *command*, in order to avoid ambiguity. (Further explained by *repertory, instruction.* Synonymous with *imperative statement* and with *procedural statement.*)

instruction, absolute—A machine instruction that is in its final form for execution by

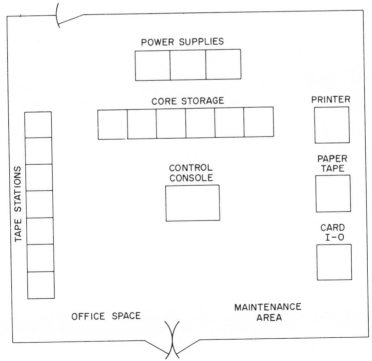

A typical computer installation *site arrangement.*

a computer. Absolute instructions are represented in electrical or other physical form in a machine code for direct decoding, interpretation, and execution by the arithmetic and logic unit of the computer. (Closely related to *instruction, machine.*)

instruction, alphanumeric–An instruction, usually a computer instruction, designed for use with either alphabetic data or numeric data, or both, and which makes use of alphanumeric characters to express the instruction.

instruction, arithmetic–An instruction in which the operator part specifies an arithmetic operation, such as add, subtract, multiply, divide, raise to a specific power, or square-root. These operations are in contrast to logic operations, such as logic sum, logic multiply, or compare.

instruction, blank–Same as *instruction, dummy.*

instruction, branch–An instruction, usually a computer instruction, that requires that the selection of the next instruction be based on the result or outcome of some arithmetic or logic operation, or on the state of some indicator. Thus, the result of the branch instruction is the selection of one of several possible branches in a computer program.

instruction, breakpoint–A computer instruction that will cause a computer to stop, transfer control to a supervisory routine which will serve as a monitor for the interrupted program, or take some other special or remedial action. A breakpoint instruction may be in the regular program or may be entered by a switch or by a computer interrupt device that permits transfer to a higher priority program. (Synonymous with *breakpoint halt.*)

instruction, computer–An instruction, usually consisting of an operator part, one or more address parts, and perhaps special indicators, which serves to define operations and operands for a computer. When the instruction, stated as a structured group of characters, is transferred to the computer, the specified operation is executed. If the computer instruction is written in a machine language and is represented in a machine-readable medium, it is called a machine instruction. (Further clarified by *instruction, machine.*)

instruction, conditional breakpoint–A breakpoint instruction that will be executed only if some specified criterion is satisfied, condition is met, or situation exists. The breakpoint instruction may cause the computer to stop, transfer control to some other routine, or take some other special or remedial action. The routine may be continued as coded or a jump may be forced.

instruction, conditional control transfer–Same as *instruction, conditional jump.*

instruction, conditional jump–An instruction that may or may not cause a jump, or the execution of a jump instruction, depending on the result of an arithmetic operation, a logic operation, or the state of some register or indicator. Usually the jump or transfer occurs only when a certain condition exists or occurs at the time the jump instruction is to be executed. (Synonymous with *conditional control transfer instruction* and *conditional transfer instruction.* Contrast with *instruction, unconditional jump.*)

instruction, conditional transfer–Same as *instruction, conditional jump.*

instruction, control–Same as *instruction, jump.*

instruction, control-transfer–Same as *instruction, jump.*

instruction, decision–A computer instruction that will cause a computer to select one of several alternative courses in accordance with certain criteria or conditions; for example, a jump instruction, a conditional jump instruction, or a branch instruction. (Synonymous with *discrimination instruction.*)

instruction, direct–A computer instruction word that contains the direct address of an operand for the specified operation.

instruction, discrimination–Same as *instruction, decision.*

instruction, do-nothing–Same as *instruction, dummy.*

instruction, dummy–An instruction that specifically instructs a computer to do nothing except proceed to the next instruction in sequence. Hence, an instruction inserted in a sequence of instructions to serve a purpose other than as a meaningful instruction. Thus, it has no functional significance. Some examples of its use are to provide scope for future changes in a computer program or fulfill some prescribed condition, such as the completion of a block of instructions. Since a dummy instruction is not intended to be executed, no result should occur if it is executed. The dummy instruction may be used to express data, so that when the dummy instruction is called for from storage, actual data is called for use in the program. Usually, a dummy instruction implies that no program operation is to be performed. One effect of the instruction is that it might advance an instruction counter by one count. (Synonymous with *no-operation instruction*, with *no-op instruction*, with *do-nothing instruction*, with *waste instruction*, with *skip instruction*, and with *blank instruction.*)

instruction, effective–A computer instruction that can be executed without prior modification.

instruction, executive—In a routine or program, an instruction designed to control the operation or execution of other routines. (Synonymous with *supervisory instruction.*)

instruction, extract—An instruction that requests and directs the formation of a new expression from selected parts of a given expression or expressions. The selection of the parts is usually accomplished through the use of a mask.

instruction, four-address—A computer instruction, or code, that makes a reference to four addresses or four storage locations; for example, add the contents of storage location 149 to the contents of storage location 582, put the sum in storage location 983, and go to storage location 044 for the next instruction. (Synonymous with *code, four-address.*)

instruction, functional-address—Same as *instruction, source-destination.*

instruction, halt—An instruction that stops the further execution of the program being run. The halt instruction will cause a programmed halt, rather than a halt due to other causes, such as errors, loss of power, or malfunctions. (Synonymous with *stop instruction.*)

instruction, hold—A computer instruction that will cause data called from a storage device to be also retained at the storage location after it is called out and transferred to a new location. If data is transferred out of a storage location without the hold instruction, the location will remain cleared after transfer. The hold instruction causes the regeneration and reinsertion of the data after interrogation; that is, after the "read and hold" instruction is given.

instruction, ignore—A machine instruction that requires nonperformance of what normally might be executed. The ignore instruction refers or is directed toward an instruction other than itself. This is in contradistinction to the no-op instruction, which is an instruction to do nothing at this point. The ignore instruction is represented or designated by characters, or codes, as is any other instruction. In paper-tape punched-hole codes, for example, the ignore character is an all-holes-punched character. Thus, any incorrect punching

can be erased or deleted simply by converting into an ignore character.

instruction, immediate—An instruction in which the address part is an operand for the operation specified by the operation part.

instruction, indirect—An instruction that has as its address part the indirect address of an operand for the operation specified in the operation part.

instruction, jump—A computer instruction that causes a jump to occur; that is, a departure from the normal sequence of executing instructions. Jump instructions include both unconditional and conditional jumps. (Synonymous with *control-transfer instruction*, with *transfer instruction*, and with *control instruction.*)

instruction, logic—An instruction that causes the execution of an operation that is defined in symbolic logic statements or operators, such as AND, OR, and NOR. These are distinguished from arithmetic instructions, which cause the execution of operations that are defined in arithmetic operation statements or operators, such as add, multiply, and divide. It is pointed out, however, that the arithmetic operations may be composed by a proper sequence of logic operations, obtained electrically through the proper use of gates.

instruction, machine—An instruction that can be recognized and executed by a machine. Usually, the machine instruction is written in machine language and so can be obeyed directly by the machine, such as a computer, as opposed to an instruction that must first be interpreted or translated by an appropriate routine. (Further clarified by *instruction, computer.*)

instruction, multiaddress—Same as *instruction, multiple-address.*

instruction, multiple-address—An instruction that contains more than one address, in addition to the operation part and perhaps other parts. The multiple-address instruction is usually specified as a two-address, three-address, four-address, etc., instruction. The addresses specify the locations of operands or other instructions. The operands may be data or other instructions that are to be operated upon. Thus, any instruction that makes reference to more than one address or

BITS

I	10	II	20	21	30	31	40	41	44
ADD A		ADD B		ADD R		ADD N		OP	

ADD A	ADDRESS OF OPERAND A	10 BITS	*A four-address instruction*
ADD B	ADDRESS OF OPERAND B	10 BITS	*word for a computer.*
ADD R	ADDRESS OF RESULT OF OPERATION	10 BITS	
ADD N	ADDRESS OF NEXT INSTRUCTION	10 BITS	
OP	OPERATION PERFORMED	4 BITS	

189

location is a multiple-address instruction, (Synonymous with *instruction, multiaddress.* Further clarified by *code, multiple-address;* by *instruction, two-address;* by *instruction, three-address;* by *instruction, four-address;* and by *code, instruction.* Contrast with *instruction, one-address.*)

instruction, n-address—An instruction that has an address part containing n addresses, where n is a natural number.

instruction, N-plus-one-address—A multiple-address instruction in which one of the address parts specifies the location of the next instruction to be executed.

instruction, no-address—An instruction that can be executed by a machine without having to obtain an operand from the storage unit.

instruction, no-op—Same as *instruction, dummy.*

instruction, no-operation—Same as *instruction, dummy.*

instruction, nonprint—An instruction, usually transmitted in the form of an inhibit signal which prevents the printing of a line or character of a printer that is otherwise under machine control.

instruction, one-address—An instruction consisting of an operation part, exactly one address part, and any other parts, such as tags, special characters, or indexes. The address part contains only one address, either of a storage location, of a register, or of a piece of equipment. The instruction code of a one-address computer may include both zero-address and multiple-address instructions as special cases. (Synonymous with *one-address code,* with *single-address code,* and with *single-address instruction.* Further clarified by *one-address.*)

instruction, one-plus-one-address—An instruction consisting of an operation part; exactly two address parts, one of which specifies explicitly the location of the next instruction to be executed; and any other parts, such as tags, special characters, or indexes. This instruction is usually used on computers whose storage has a latency factor; that is, a serial delay time. The instruction simplifies minimal-access programming.

instruction, operational-address—Same as *instruction, source-destination.*

instruction, optional-halt—A halt instruction that includes the option of stopping the computer either before or after the instruction is obeyed, depending on some criterion. The instruction may specify some other operation that is to take place either immediately before or immediately after the execution of the optional-halt instruction. (Synonymous with *optional-stop instruction.* Closely related to *instruction, optional-pause.*)

instruction, optional-pause—An instruction that permits manual interruption of the execution of a computer program.

(Closely related to *instruction, optional-halt.*)

instruction, optional-stop—Same as *instruction, optional-halt.*

instruction, pause—An instruction that specifies the temporary suspension or interruption of the execution of a computer program. A pause instruction is usually not an exit from a computer program.

instruction, presumptive—1: An instruction that has not yet been subjected to modification, but in all likelihood will be modified. 2: An instruction that is not effective until it has been modified in a prescribed manner.

instruction, repetition—An instruction that causes one or more specified instructions to be executed a specified number of times.

instruction rescue—Same as *instruction, restart.*

instruction, restart—An instruction in a computer program at which the program may be restarted. (Synonymous with *rescue instruction.*)

instruction, single-address—Same as *instruction, one-address.*

instruction, skip—Same as *instruction, dummy.*

instruction, source-destination—A computer instruction that has no operation part as such, the operation being implicitly specified by the address parts; for example, the two addresses that are specified may designate storage locations whose contents are always added. (Synonymous with *operational-address instruction.*)

instruction, stop—Same as *instruction, halt.*

instruction, supervisory—Same as *instruction, executive.*

instruction, symbolic—An instruction in which symbols are used to represent or express the operator part and the address parts. The symbols are merely a convenience for the programmer, making the code simpler and more mnemonic. Symbolic instructions are converted into machine language instructions by an assembly routine or a program translator. Thus, ADD is more convenient to express an addition operation than 1000001, 0010001, 0010001, which might be the machine language code. This example is mnemonic as well as more convenient.

instruction, table-look-up—An instruction designed to facilitate reference to systematically arranged, stored data; for example, an instruction that will direct a computer to automatically search for a specified argument in a table in order to locate and retrieve a required result. A table-look-up operation may be performed in lieu of a calculation; for example, given the argument for sin x or e^x, one could calculate the value of the function or one could store a table and look up the value. One method requires more computer time, the other method requires more storage space. The method selected might depend on the characteristics of the available computer.

instruction, three-address–A computer instruction that makes a reference to three addresses. For example, add the contents of storage location 128 to the contents of storage location 149 and store the sum in storage location 492. This might be coded as, add 128, 149, 492. (Synonymous with *three-address code.*)

instruction, three-plus-one address–An instruction consisting of an operation part; exactly four address parts, one of which specifies explicitly the location of the next instruction to be executed; and any other parts, such as tags, special characters, or indexes. This instruction is often used on computers whose storage has a latency factor; that is, a serial delay time. The instruction facilitates minimal-access programming and provides flexibility. Two addresses usually specify the location of two operands; one address specifies the location where the result is to be stored. Three-plus-one address instructions are often called four-address instructions.

instruction, transfer–Same as *instruction, jump.*

instruction, two-address–A computer instruction that makes a reference to two addresses. For example, add the contents of storage location 396 to the contents of storage location 432 and place the sum in register A. This may be coded as add 396, 432. (Synonymous with *two-address code.*)

instruction, two-plus-one address–An instruction consisting of an operation part; exactly three address parts, one of which specifies explicitly the location of the next instruction to be executed; and any other parts, such as tags, special characters, or indexes. This instruction is usually used on computers whose storage has a latency factor; that is, a serial delay time. The instruction facilitates minimal-access programming. Two of the addresses specify the location of two operands.

instruction, unconditional-jump–An instruction that always causes a jump to occur. (Synonymous with *unconditional-transfer instruction.* Contrast with *instruction, conditional-jump.*)

instruction, unconditional-transfer–Same as *instruction, unconditional jump.*

instruction, waste–Same as *instruction, dummy.*

instruction, zero-address–An instruction that specifies an operation in its operation part, but contains no address in its address part; for example shift left 0003 has in its address part the amount of shift desired. The address may be given by the program code so that no address need be stated explicitly.

instruction address–See *address, instruction.*

instruction address register–See *register, instruction address.*

instruction area–See *area, instruction.*

instruction character–Same as *character, control.*

instruction check, unallowable–Same as *check, forbidden-combination.*

instruction-check indicator–See *indicator, instruction-check.*

instruction code–See *code, instruction.*

instruction code, input–See *code, input instruction.*

instruction code, machine–Same as *code, instruction.*

instruction code, mnemonic–See *code, mnemonic instruction.*

instruction constant–See *constant, instruction.*

instruction control–See *control, instruction.*

instruction counter–See *counter, instruction.*

instruction cycle–See *cycle, instruction.*

instruction deck–See *deck, instruction.*

instruction digit, unallowable–Same as *character, illegal.*

instruction format–See *format, instruction.*

instruction format, n-address–See *format, n-address instruction.*

instruction mix–See *mix, instruction.*

instruction modifier–See *modifier, instruction.*

instruction register–See *register, instruction.*

instruction repertoire–Same as *repertory, instruction.*

instruction repertory–See *repertory, instruction.*

instruction set–Same as *repertory, instruction.*

instruction set, computer–Same as *set, machine instruction.*

instruction set, machine–See *set, machine instruction.*

instruction storage–Same as *area, instruction.*

instruction tape–Same as *tape, program.*

instruction tape, master–See *tape, master instruction.*

instruction time–See *time, instruction.*

instruction word–See *word, instruction.*

instrument, end–A device connected to one terminal of a communication loop or channel and capable of converting data from one form to electrical signals, or vice versa; for example, teletypewriter, telegraph key, page printer, tape perforator, or telephone. The device includes all generating, signal converting, or loop terminating devices employed at the transmitting or receiving location.

integer–A whole number, thus, a number without a fractional part. Zero is considered an integer; mixed numbers are not. Digital computers can deal with integers, fractions, and mixed numbers. There is a distinction between digit, integer, number and numeral.

integral–In the calculus, the result of the process of integration performed on a mathematical function. Thus, differentiation of the integral yields the integrand. Both integration and differentiation may be performed by programming digital and analog computers. (Further clarified by *integrand*.)

integrand—In the calculus, the mathematical function that is operated upon in the process of integration. Thus, differentiation of the integral yields the integrand. Both integration and differentiation may be performed by programming digital and analog computers. (Further clarified by *integral*.)

integrated circuit—See *circuit, integrated* and *circuit, large-scale integrated*.

integrated circuit, monolithic—See *circuit, monolithic integrated*.

integrated data processing—See *data processing, integrated*.

integrated monolithic circuit—Same as *circuit, monolithic integrated*.

integrating amplifier—See *amplifier, integrating*.

integrating circuit—Same as *integrator*.

integrating gear—See *gear, integrating*.

integrating motor—See *motor, integrating*.

integrator—A device whose output function is proportional to the integral of the input function with respect to a specified variable; for example, a watthour meter. Integration need not be performed only with respect to time. In digital machines, the device accomplishes a numerical approximation of the process of integration. The integrator may have two input variables and one output variable, with the output variable proportional to the integral of one variable with respect to the other; for example, an integrating gear. The integrating device may have one input variable and one output variable, with the output variable proportional to the integral of the input variable with respect to elapsed time; for example, an integrating amplifier. The integrator is a device whose output signal is proportional to the integral, or cumulative sum, of the input signal values. Thus, if the input signal is a square wave, the output signal is a straight-line rise for as long as the signal is present; when the square-wave pulse returns to zero and the internal impedance of the square-wave generator is infinite, the output signal of the integrating circuit remains constant. If the internal impedance of the square-wave generator is zero, the output voltage decays exponentially. If the input signal is alternate spikes, the output wave may be rectangular. An example of an integrating analog network would be a resistance-capacitance series network of appropriately sized elements, with output signal voltage taken from across the capacitor. The odometer (cumulative miles) is an example of an integrator, whereas the speedometer is an example of a distance differentiator. (Contrast with *differentiator*.)

integrator, decision—Same as *servointegrator*.

integrator, incremental—A digital integrating device whose output signal is a maximum negative, a maximum positive, or a zero value according to whether the sign of the instantaneous input signal is negative, positive, or zero.

integrator, summing—An analog computer amplifier capable of forming, as output, the time integral of the weighted sum of several input voltages or currents. (Further clarified by *amplifier, summing* and by *amplifier, integrating*.)

intellectronics—The application of electronics to the extension of man's intellect, such as the use of an electronic computer to remember facts, store rules, apply logic, and arrive at new conclusions.

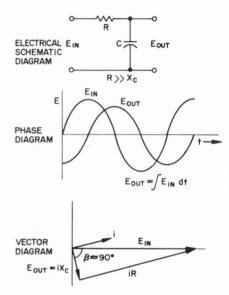

$$E_{OUT} = \int E_{IN} \, dt$$

For the integrator shown, if resistance R is very much greater than capacitive reactance X_C of capacitor C, the current will be nearly in phase with input voltage E_{IN}, but output voltage E_{OUT} across capacitor C will lag E_{IN} by nearly $90°$; see the phase and vector diagrams. Hence, E_{OUT} is the time integral of E_{IN}.

intelligence, artificial—The capability of a device to perform functions that are normally associated with human intelligence, such as reasoning, learning, and self-improvement. It includes the study of computers and computer-related techniques to increase the intellectual capabilities of man. Just as tools and powered machinery extend the physical power of man, computers, data-processing machines, and other programmed equipment extend his mental powers. The field of artificial intelligence includes the study of techniques for making more effective use of digital computers by improved programming; optical character recognition and other forms of perception and identification; artificial learning; and the study of self-organizing, self-adaptive, self-repairing, automatic fault detection, location, and correction techniques. In a general sense, artificial intelligence includes the study of the use of programmed machinery for the solution of problems involving logic or reasoning, with the additional requirement that performance improves with experience or operation, such as the ability to play a game, like chess or checkers, improves with each game played, as long as the machine is informed of the results of each game.

intensity—In optical character recognition, the depth of a black or colored image produced by a carbon or ribbon on paper.

interactive file maintenance—See *maintenance, interactive file.*

interactive graphics—See *graphics, interactive.*

interactive mode—Same as *mode, conversational.*

interactive query—See *query, interactive.*

interblock gap—See *gap, interblock.*

intercalate—To file, place, or insert among or between; for example, to interpolate a value between two others in accordance with some function, or to insert a card in its proper place in a card catalog.

INTERCARD—A programming interpreter-compiler developed by North American Aviation Corporation for the Bendix G-15 computer.

interchange, information—The sending and receiving of data in such a manner that the content or meaning assigned to the data is not altered during the transmission.

interchange code, extended binary-coded decimal—See *code, extended binary-coded decimal interchange.*

interchange point—See *point, interchange.*

interchangeable connector—See *connector, interchangeable.*

interchangeable type bar—See *bar, interchangeable type.*

INTERCOM—An automatic coding system developed by Bendix Corporation for use on the Bendix G-15 computer. Intercom programming languages include INTERCOM 101 and INTERCOM 1000.

intercycle—A step in the sequence of steps of a punched-card machine's main shaft during which time the card feed is stopped, usually because of a change in control. In some machines, the programmer or operator may predetermine the number of intercycles that are to arise for a control change; in others, the determination is made within the machine.

interest profile—See *profile, interest.*

interface—1: A shared boundary; for example, the boundary between two

systems or two devices; the points of separation between two programs, such as a development program and a production program; the points of contact between organizations; the boundaries separating two elements or aspects of a system, such as the boundary between a person using an information system and the input or output station itself. The interface may be mechanical, such as surfaces and spacings in mating parts, modules, components, or subsystems; or any other transition point, such as a human vs. machine boundary, machine vs. outside environment boundary, or machine vs. machine boundary. In accordance with the definition of system, every element or part of a system must interface; that is, react or associate, with one or more other parts of the system. If the system is to be useful, it must interface with something outside itself, such as humans, its environment, materials, or another system. 2: Linkages and other arrangements and conventions established for communication between independent elements or components, such as between one program and another, between a computer operator and the computer, and between a terminal user and a computer.

interface, compiler—Functions that are performed by a computer operating system and that provide supporting services to the system language compilers.

interface, standard—A form of interface previously agreed upon so that two or more systems may be readily joined or associated; for example, a set of output signal levels from a register that will serve as input signals to a logic network in a digital computer.

interference, adjacent channel—Distorting, spurious, unwanted, or other signals interfering with the operation of a communications channel and caused by signals in neighboring channels adjacent in frequency, in spatial position, such as adjacent tracks on tape, discs, or drums, or other forms of adjacency, the adjacency causing coupling and hence crosstalk. (Further clarified by *crosstalk.*)

interference, radio-frequency—See *RFI.*

interfile search—See *search, interfile.*

interfix—A technique that allows the relationship between key words, such as descriptors or uniterms, to be described, by such means as links or role indicators, in order to reduce the number of false retrievals that might be obtained due to crosstalk among the key words. Thus, if searching on tape readers and card punches, obtaining card readers is not a desired retrieval, or if searching on combustion of methane in excess oxygen, combustion of oxygen in excess methane is not a desired retrieval, key words must be interfixed.

INTERFOR — interrupt

INTERFOR—A floating-point interpretive routine developed by Control Data Corporation for use on the Control Data 160A computer.

interior label—See *label, interior.*

interlace—Same as *interleave.*

interleave—To arrange the members of one sequence of things or events so that they alternate with members of one or more other sequences of things, with each original sequence retaining its identity in the new sequence; for example, to assign numerically consecutive storage addresses to physically separated, nonconsecutive, storage locations, such as on a magnetic drum or tape, usually for the express purpose of reducing access time; to insert segments of one program into another program such that the two programs can be executed simultaneously, such as in multiprogramming; or to allocate digits to cells in a track on a magnetic tape such that cells allocated to successive digits of a particular word are separated by a specific number of intermediate cells which may be allocated similarly to digits of other words. (Synonymous with *interlace.*)

interleave, bit—In a communication system, to multiplex a line, circuit, or channel so as to transmit many bits by time-dividing a single time frame. (Further clarified by *frame.*)

interlock—A device or arrangement that controls the operation of machines or devices so that their operation is interdependent and their proper coordination is thus assured; for example, a device that will prevent a computer from initiating further operations until the current operation is successfully completed; an arrangement that would prevent a signal from being transferred if the receiving station is not ready to receive it; or a device that would require a fixed sequence of operations specifically to safeguard against injury, damage, or loss of information.

interlock circuit—See *circuit, interlock.*

interlude—A small program designed to do some preliminary computation or organization of data; for example, to calculate the value of a parameter on the side, or to clear certain parts of a store. The interlude is usually overwritten after it has served its purpose, since it is usually no longer needed after it is once used or accomplished.

intermediate control change—See *change, intermediate control.*

intermediate language—See *language, intermediate.*

intermediate product—Same as *product, partial.*

intermediate total—See *total, intermediate.*

internal arithmetic—See *arithmetic, internal.*

internal bias—See *bias, internal.*

internal sort—See *sort, internal.*

internal storage—See *storage, internal.*

internally stored program—See *program, internally stored.*

interpolator—Same as *collator.*

interpret—To translate and execute each statement in a computer program written in a source language before translating and executing the next statement in the program.

interpreter—1: A computer program that translates and executes each source language instruction before translating and executing the next one; for example, a program that, as the computation progresses, translates the stored-program expressions in pseudocode into machine language, and performs the indicated operations as they are translated. An interpreter is essentially a closed subroutine that operates successively on an indefinitely long sequence of program parameters. Usually it is entered as a closed subroutine and left by a pseudocode exit instruction. An interpreter differs from a translator in that where instructions are repeated, as in a succession of loops, the translation is repeated for each instruction in an interpretive routine, whereas the instructions are translated only once in a translating routine. An interpretive routine translates each instruction and immediately executes it, whereas an assembler or a compiler prepares a new routine or subroutine to be executed at a later time. 2: A machine that accepts cards, reads the information punched on the cards, and prints the same data on the cards. Common data on a master card can be printed on a group of detail cards from the punched data on the master card. (Further clarified by *programming, interpretive.*) 3: A translator of nonmachine language into machine language. 4: A decoding device. (Synonymous with *interpretive program* and *interpretive routine.* Further clarified by *assembler*, by *generator*, by *translator*, and by *compiler.*)

interpreter, transfer—A device that prints on a punched card the characters that are equivalent to hole patterns in another card.

interpretive language—See *language, interpretive.*

interpretive program—Same as *interpreter.*

interpretive programming—See *programming, interpretive.*

interpretive routine—Same as *interpreter.*

interrecord gap—See *gap, interrecord.*

interrogation, system—1: An operator-initiated query submitted to a system to determine its status, operating condition, or availability. 2: A query initiated by a problem, user, or utility program to the system supervisor requesting data concerning system status, operating condition, or availability.

interrupt—The stopping of a process in such a way that it can be resumed, such as a temporary suspension of a sequence of operations; or the signal that causes the suspension; for example, a signal generated by an input-output device, representing an operational error, a request for more data or program segments, or a requirement to execute a higher priority program. The interrupt feature on a computer permits adequate control of system functions. After the disruption has ended, usually normal operation can be resumed from the point of interruption. The interrupt signal usually originates in an external source. (Further clarified by *breakpoint.*)

interrupt stacking—See *stacking, interrupt.*

intersection—Same as *AND.*

intersection gate—Same as *gate, AND.*

intersection operation—Same as *operation, conjunction.*

interstage punch—See *punch, interstage.*

interval, unit—The duration of the signal element in a signaling system using an equal length code. Usually, the duration of the shortest signal element in a coding system that makes use of an isochronous modulation.

intervention button—Same as *button, panic.*

intervention switch—Same as *button, panic.*

interword gap—See *space, interword.*

interword space—See *space, interword.*

INTRAN—An input translator developed by IBM for the IBM 709 and 7090 computer systems.

intrinsic semiconductor—Same as *conductor, intrinsic.*

inversion—**1:** In Boolean operations, same as *NOT.* **2:** In mathematics, the taking of a reciprocal of a value; that is, dividing unity by the given value.

invert—To change a physical, logical, mathematical, or two-state value to its opposite state.

inverted file—See *file, inverted.*

inverted index—See *index, inverted.*

inverter—Same as *element, negation.*

inverting amplifier—Same as *amplifier, sign-reversing.*

I-O—1: An abbreviation for input-output. **2:** An abbreviation for input. **3:** An abbreviation for output.

IOCS—An abbreviation for Input-Output Control System.

IOPKG—(Input-Output Package). Developed by International Business Machines Corporation for the IBM 705 III computer.

IOR—An abbreviation for input-output register.

IPC—An abbreviation for Industrial Process Control.

IPL—An abbreviation for Information Processing Language.

irrational number—See *number, irrational.*

IRE—(Institute of Radio Engineers). An organization now merged with the American Institute of Electrical Engineers (AIEE) to form the Institute of Electrical and Electronics Engineers (IEEE).

IRL—An abbreviation for Information Retrieval Language.

irregularity, stroke edge—In optical character recognition, the deviation of any point on the edge of character from the stroke edge.

IS—The information separator character.

ISO—An abbreviation for International Organization for Standardization.

isochronous multiplexor—See *multiplexor, isochronous.*

IT—(Internal Translator). A programming language translator developed by Carnegie Institute of Technology for use on the IBM 650 computer.

italics—A form of lettering using a font different from ordinary font. Italicized letters approach script, lean at about a 15° list to the right, and are used for special emphasis, as in the word *italics.*

item—In data processing, a collection of related characters treated as a unit; for example, a set of one or more fields of data representing specific and related information; a unit of correlated information relating to a single entity, such as a person or class of objects; the contents of a single message, or any arbitrary amount of data, expressed in units of bits, bytes, gulps, characters, words, blocks, records, files, or banks, which comprise the hierarchy of data units.

item, data—The name of a member of a set of data denoted by a data element; for example, January, the name of the first member of the set of months of a Gregorian calendar year. *Months of a year,* is the name of the data element, *January* is the data item, and 01 might be the data code. (Contrast with *element, data.*)

item, line—In data processing, an item of data in a given set of items that is on the same level in a data-processing application and that might be printed on the same line of an output printer page; for example, stock number, name, quantity, and price.

item advance—See *advance, item.*

item design—See *design, item.*

iterate—To repeatedly execute a series of steps; for example, to repeat a loop in a routine. The iterative process or series of steps is usually repeated until some condition is satisfied. The sequence of steps may be implemented by repeating sets of instructions calling for a repeated series of arithmetic or logic operations on a digital computer.

iterative process—See *process, iterative.*

j

jack panel–See *panel, jack.*

jam, card–A malfunction of a card handling or processing device in which cards become jammed, that is, become stuck or immovable by the mechanism for moving the cards.

jargon–The special vocabulary used by a specific group of people; for example, a set of terms that have special meanings in the computer field, colloquially known as computerese. Words cease to be jargon when they become generally or universally accepted in fields other than the one in which they originated. The use of jargon establishes a requirement for specialized glossaries, vocabularies, and dictionaries in order to assure communication.

JAZ–An interpretive routine developed by Philco Corporation for use on the LGP 30 computer.

JCL–Job Control Language.

JCS-13–An assembly routine developed by Rand Corporation for use on the IBM 701 computer.

JISC–Japanese Industrial Standards Committee.

jitter–A tendency toward lack of synchronization of one phenomenon with another; for example, intermittent, instantaneous changes in the linear speed of a magnetic tape or the intermittent, instantaneous changes in the position of a picture on a cathode-ray (TV) tube. Eccentricity of revolving parts, vibrations, slippage of belts, or interference, can cause jitter. Changes in equipment, such as transmission systems, causing the delay distortion characteristics of a given circuit to change with time, due to pressure, temperature, or other variations, can bring about jitter, such as delay jitter.

job–The data that defines a specific amount of work for a computer to do, usually including programs, files, instructions to the operating system and any other data needed for the specified work to be accomplished.

job contract–See *contract, job.*

job control–See *control, job.*

job control language–See *language, job control.*

job description–See *description, job.*

job entry, remote–See *entry, remote job.*

job management–See *management, job.*

job-oriented terminal–See *terminal, job-oriented.*

job processing–See *processing, job.*

job queue–See *queue, job.*

job scheduler–See *scheduler, job.*

job status–See *status, job.*

job stream–Same as *stream, input.*

join gate–Same as *gate, OR.*

joint denial gate–Same as *gate, NOR.*

JOVIAL–(Jules Own Version of International Algebraic Language). A generalized programming language developed by System Development Corporation.

joy stick–See *stick, joy.*

JUG–(Joint Users Group). A group of computer users sharing interests, programs, and computers.

jump–A departure from the normal sequence of executing instructions in a digital computer; for example, an instruction used to alter the normal or programmed sequence of executing instructions in a computer. A jump instruction causes the next instruction to be withdrawn from a specified storage location, rather than the next location in the normal sequence. Hardware may be arranged such that a jump may be caused by an operator throwing a switch. The computer interrogates the switch, causing the jump determined by the switch setting. Most jumps occur when certain conditions are satisfied. These are conditional jumps. If a jump is to occur at a particular point in a program without regard to any condition, the jump is unconditional. (Synonymous with *branch* (3) and with *transfer.*)

jump, conditional–A jump that occurs only if specified criteria are met; for example, the result of an instruction that causes departure from the normal sequence of instruction execution in a digital computer only if a specified set of conditions is met. The conditional jump includes the testing of the condition. Conditions are usually expressed as relative values of numbers, such as a certain number being greater than another number. (Synonymous with *conditional branch* and with *conditional transfer.* Contrast with *jump, unconditional.*)

jump, unconditional–A jump that occurs when the instruction to execute a jump is given or when the instruction to jump occurs in the normal sequence of instructions; for example, the result of an instruction that causes departure from the normal sequence of instruction execution in a digital computer. The jump instruction specifies the address from which the next instruction to be executed is to be obtained. Thus, jumping is simply skipping over to a specific address rather than executing the instruction located at the next or adjacent address. (Synonymous with *unconditional branch* and with *unconditional transfer*. Contrast with *jump, conditional*.)

jump instruction—See *instruction, jump*.

jump instruction, conditional—See *instruction, conditional jump*.

jump instruction, unconditional—See *instruction, unconditional jump*.

jump operation—See *operation, jump*.

jumper—A relatively short length of electrical conductor used to permanently or temporarily complete another circuit or to bypass an existing circuit.

junction—The contact interface surface or immediate region between n-type and p-type semiconducting material. It is at the junction of these differently doped materials that transistor action takes place. Thus, junction transistors may be of the p-n-p type or the n-p-n type for the emitter, base, and collector electrode materials, respectively. At each junction, a potential gradient or potential energy barrier occurs, due to the migration of charges to the junction and the accumulation of unlike charges, that is, holes and electrons, on either side of the junction.

junction, p-n type—A region between p and n; that is, positively and negatively doped or acceptor and donor type, semiconductor materials. Such transition regions provide the necessary electric charge distributions and potential (voltage) gradients to permit diode and transistor action.

justified margin—See *margin, justified*.

justify—1: To shift a data item in a storage medium so that a particular part of the item assumes a particular position relative to some reference point in the medium; for example, to adjust the positions of

words on a printed page so that the left, the right, or both, margins are flush, or to shift an item in a register so that the most or least significant digit is at some specified position in the register. The justification may take place with regard to any specified pattern or reference, such as a circle, triangle, or any mathematical curve or surface. (Illustrated by *justify, left* and by *justify, right*.) 2: To align data in or on a medium to fit the positioning constraints of a required format.

justify, left—1: To preserve a left margin for the words on a printed page. Western world typewriters maintain a left justified margin. (Illustrative of *justify*.) 2: To arrange, place, or position data in or on a medium so as to align the left edge of the data when viewing the data from the normal or conventional direction; for example, to shift the content of a register so that the character at the left-hand end of the data in the register is at a specified position in the register, to control printing positions of characters on a page so that the left margin of the printing is straight or regular, or to align characters of a string horizontally so that the left-most character of the string is in a specified position. (Contrast with *justify, right*.)

justify, right—1: To preserve a right margin for words on a printed page. Since English text is usually typed or printed from left to right, right justification is more difficult. Certain typewriters permit easy right margin justification. (Illustrative of *justify*.) 2: To arrange or position data in or on a medium so as to align the right edge of the data when viewing the data from the normal or conventional direction; for example, to shift the content of a register so that the character at the right hand end of the data in the register is at a specified position in the register, to control printing positions of characters on a page so that the right margin of the printing is straight or regular, or to align characters of a string horizontally so that the right-most character of the string is in a specified position. (Contrast with *justify, left*.)

k

Karnaugh map—See *map, Karnaugh.*
key—1: A marked button or lever manually operated for copying a character; for example, the lever that is depressed on a typewriter, paper tape perforator, card punch, manual typewriter, digitizer, or manual keyboard; the toggle on a telephone switchboard for inserting signals on lines; the lever or switch on a computer console for the purpose of manually altering computer action; or the hand-operated switching device, ordinarily formed of concealed spring contacts with an exposed handle or push button, capable of switching one or more parts of a circuit. **2:** In data processing, one or more characters used to identify a body of data, such as a group of data elements, data items, data codes, data chains, an abstract, or a document. The key may itself be a code. (Further clarified by *label.*) **3:** Same as *password.*
key, activate—Same as *button, initiate.*
key, actual—In COBOL, a data item that may be used as a machine address and that expresses the location of a record in a storage medium.
key, attention—In teleprocessing systems, a function key on a data terminal that causes program execution by a central processing unit to be interrupted.
key, function—In data display systems, a button, switch, lever, dial or other similar manually operated device that is actuated to initiate and dispatch a signal representing an instruction to a display monitor. (Further clarified by *keyboard, function.*)
key, initiate—Same as *button, initiate.*
key, load—A manual control key, or similar device, used to initiate the input of data or instructions into a machine, such as a computer or control system. The instructions are usually computer routines.
key, sequencing—Same as *key, sort.*
key, sort—A key used to determine the sequence of the items in a set. The keys may be in or a part of the items being sequenced. (Synonymous with *sequencing criterion* and *sequencing key.*)
key, start—Same as *button, initiate.*
key search—Data that is to be compared with specific parts of data items, labels, or identifiers for purposes of identification when conducting a search.
key transformation—See *transformation, key.*
key verify—See *verify, key.*
keyboard—A set or panel consisting of an array of keys; for example, manually activated marked levers. Depressing a key causes the generation of a specific character or symbol in electrical, printed, or other form. Used in conjunction with appropriate gating elements, the keyboard permits the generation of coded symbols for interpretation by or storage in a computer. Thus, the keyboard may be part of a manual input device for a computer, part of a keypunch, part of a paper tape perforator, or part of an electric typewriter monitor.
keyboard, function—In display systems, a group of function keys mounted together to form an input device panel for an interactive display terminal. (Further clarified by *key, function.*)
keyboard entry—See *entry, keyboard.*
keyboard perforator—See *perforator, keyboard (1).*
keyboard punch—Same as *keypunch.*
keyed access—See *access, keyed.*
keyed file structure—See *structure, keyed file.*
key-in—To enter data into a system by means of a keyboard.
keying, frequency-shift—Modulation of the frequency of a carrier signal by a modulating signal that can vary among a fixed number of discrete values. Thus, the modulation signal is a digital signal, such as is used in the touch-tone telephone dialing and signaling system. This type of frequency modulation differs from continuous spectrum modulation, permitting all values of modulating frequency, such as voice modulation, resulting in an analog type of frequency modulation.
keypunch—A device, with a set of manually operated keys, arranged so that depression of a particular key will cause holes to be punched in some medium or data carrier, such as cards or tape, so as to represent information. The device moves the medium, such as to the next column on cards or the next row on tape. In some card keypunches, depressing a single key

enters the character on the card, even if multiple punching is involved. In others, more than one key must be depressed, to accomplish multiple punching, for each character. Most paper tape keypunches will punch a feed or sprocket hole, as well as the code holes, automatically, at each punch position. Usually, a keypunch is a keyboard-actuated device that inserts data on a card in the form of punched holes to represent information. (Synonymous with *keyboard perforator* and with *keyboard punch*.)

keyword—A more informative or more significant word in a title, abstract, body, or any other part of text that might be contained in a document. A set of keywords might describe the contents of the document, be used as a label, and can assist in identifying and retrieving the document. (Closely related to *descriptor*; to *uniterm*; to *entry, index*; and to *docuterm*.)

kilobit—One thousand binary digits.

kilomegabit—One-thousand-million binary digit. Pertaining to one U. S. billion binary digits, such as a one-billion-bit storage device. (Synonymous with *billibit*.)

Kipp relay—Same as *multivibrator, one-shot*.

KISS—An automatic coding system used by Computer Usage, Inc. on the IBM 704 computer and by Chrysler Corporation on the IBM 650 computer.

kludge—An ill-assorted collection of poorly matching parts forming a distressing and disconnected whole. The term might be derived from the German *klug*, meaning smart or witty. In typical variations of language, it eventually came to mean not so smart, actually ridiculous. The term is usually facetiously applied to a computer whose design and behavior characteristics are rather undesirable, somewhat like the concept of a *Rube Goldberg* type of device, except perhaps in a more modern or electronic sense. The term expresses thoroughgoing disdain and is destructively critical.

KOMPILER—A programming compiler developed by University of California Radiation Laboratories for the Atomic Energy Commission for use on the IBM 704 computer.

KWIC—(Key Word in Context). A method of listing text, say titles of documents, in permuted forms and alphabetizing the various permutations. Assuming that titles are descriptive of contents, the various permutations of the words in titles aid in searching and enhance retrieval. The technique has been considerably advanced by International Business Machines Corporation. Thus, the scheme makes use of permuted title indexing. It may also be applied to text other than titles. The resulting KWIC index can be computer generated. Certain words are excluded from indexing to avoid ambiguity, redundancy, and other problems. Many KWIC indexes have been prepared for selected bibliographies by various computers. The limitation of the index usually results from the limited information content of titles. It has been proposed that permutations of more descriptive concept statements, strings of keywords specially selected for permutation, and the use of links and roles might improve the recall ratio and relevance ratio when retrieving documents from a collection. (Further clarified by *index, permutation*.)

l

label—In information processing, a key, consisting of one or more symbols, used to identify a body of data and usually attached to the data. However, the label may not necessarily be attached to the item. The label might indicate the location of an item, such as an address, or cite the name, length, date of origin, structure, nature of contents, related files, and similar information. The label is usually visible or is capable of being sensed by a computer, and is used to identify something so as to distinguish it from its surroundings. Thus, the label is usually a key attached to the body of data it identifies.

label, header—A record at the beginning of a file, record, or volume that contains control and other data about the file, record or volume. (Contrast with *label, trailer*.)

label, interior—A label recorded or stored with the data it identifies; for example, a label recorded on magnetic tape, which may be used to identify the data on the tape to a computer under the control of a program. Interior labels are usually read by the machine.

label, trailer–A record at the end of a file, record, or volume that contains data about the file, record, or volume. (Contrast with *label, header.*)

lace–To punch all the holes in a given area on a punch card; for example, to punch all rows of a card column or all columns of a card row.

laced card–See *card, laced.*

lag–A measure of time delay between two events, such as successive states or conditions, or the distance between two moving objects.

language–A set of representations, conventions, and associated rules used to convey information. A language has a defined set of characters or symbols, combinations of which may be assigned meanings. In order to permit only meaningful and logical statements certain rules govern the combinations that are permitted. Most spoken and written languages consist of a set of characters, called an alphabet; groups of characters to which meaning may be assigned, called words; and various rules for combining the words into logical expressions, called syntax. Languages are devised primarily for communication among men, men and machines, and among machines. Examples of languages include English, French, Russian, Hebrew, ALGOL, FORTRAN, and COBOL. A language may be conveniently constructed from a set of code elements in accordance with the rules for combining them to form characters, words, sentences, statements, or other expressions for communicating information.

language, absolute–Same as *language, machine.*

language, algebraic–A language designed and used to describe situations, operations, relationships, and procedures in an algebraic style; that is, using various symbols to express operators, operands, parameters, variables, equivalences, logical relationships, and matters of such nature. Each form of algebra may have its own language; that is, its own set of symbols for writing its expressions. In turn, each algebra has its own set of rules that are independent of its language, but that can be defined in the terms of the language. Some algebraic languages are extensions of natural languages.

Language, Algebraic Oriented–A misnomer for ALGOL.

language, algorithmic–1: A language that is primarily procedure oriented and is designed for ease of expressing and communicating sets of well-defined rules or processes for the solution of a problem in a finite number of steps, such as a full statement of a procedure for the evaluation of sin x to a given precision. 2: Same as ALGOL.

language, application-oriented–A problem-oriented language containing statements that resemble or use the terminology of the occupation or profession of the user of the language; for example, a report program generator, or APT, a numerical control language for machine tools.

language, artificial–A language based on a set of rules that are established prior to construction or use of the language. Usually, the language is specifically designed for use in a particular field of interest and did not naturally grow in that area. (Synonymous with *fabricated language*, with *synthetic language*, with *formal language*, and with *mechanical language*. Contrast with *language, natural.*)

language, assembly–A computer programming language, similar to a computer language, designed to be used to write or express statements of an assembly program. The instructions written in an assembly language usually have a one-to-one correspondence with computer instructions in machine language or any other pseudolanguage. However, there may be a one-to-many correspondence with computer instructions, the assembly language itself having then the beginning appearances of an assembly program. The instruction code written in an assembly language is often a mnemonic code for assembling machine language computer instructions.

language, command–A source language consisting primarily of procedural instructions, each capable of specifying a function to be executed.

language, common–A computer programming language that is sensible to two or more computers with different machine languages; for example, COBOL, FORTRAN, and ALGOL. Usually each machine that has a common language capability has an automatic built-in translator that accepts common language notation and translates it into its own machine language for execution. This is what is meant by a common language capability. For example, as each FORTRAN statement is read, it is translated into the equivalent set of machine language instructions. The translation may be programmed, but if this is necessary, the machine is said not to have the common language capability per se.

language, computer–Same as *language, machine.*

language, computer-dependent–Same as *language, machine-oriented.*

language, computer-oriented–Same as *language, machine-oriented.*

language, computer-sensitive–A programming language that is somewhat dependent upon the type of computer that is to execute a program written in the language. Abbreviated CSL.

language, extensible–A computer programming language that allows the definition of new elements, such as data types, operators, statements, or structures in terms of the existing language. ALGOL 68 is an example of an extensible language.

language, fabricated–Same as *language, artificial.*

language, formal–Same as *language, artificial.*

language, graphic–In computer graphics, a language used to program a computer that interacts with a display device.

language, hardware–A reference language that uses symbols particularly suitable for direct input to a computer.

language, high-level–Same as *language, higher-order.*

language, higher-order–1: A programming language that tends toward being more independent of the limitations of a specific computer; for example, pseudolanguages; problem-oriented languages; common languages, such as COBOL, FORTRAN, and ALGOL; and assembly languages. 2: A computer programming language that does not reflect or imply the structure of any given computer or class of computers. (Synonymous with *high-level language.*)

language, human–Same as *language, natural.*

language, intermediate–1: A computer programming language that lies between an absolute language and a higher-order language, such as a highly problem-oriented language. The use of an intermediate programming language permits a computer to compile a program in machine language for execution, while the problem is more easily translated from the natural, logic, or algebraic languages to an intermediate programming language, which might also be a common language, like COBOL, or might be a compiler for a specific computer. 2: A language for which there are translators to or from any two or more other languages. Thus, if there are translators between German and Russian, and between English and German, then one could translate between English and Russian, with German as the intermediate language. This is one method of attacking the problem of mechanical translation of languages. It is possible that the intermediate language could be a completely artificial, or a composite language, with translators to and from it and all other languages. This eliminates the requirement that there be a translator constructed to go from each to every other language. Thus, if one translates from any source language to any target language, by way of any other language, then the other language is an intermediate language.

language, interpretive–A language used to write a program that translates and executes each source language expression before translating and executing the next one. Thus, the interpretive language expresses the statements in an interpreter.

language, job control–A problem-oriented language that expresses the statements of a job and that are used to identify the job or describe its requirements, usually to an operating system. Abbreviated JCL.

language, machine–A programming language or instruction code used directly by a machine. The code is in a form directly acceptable to a machine and requires no translation. Transliteration from data in one form, such as a pattern of holes on a card or magnetization on tape, to another, such as electrical pulse patterns in a wire, are all that is necessary. The machine language uses absolute, or machine addresses, and machine notation for the representation of operation codes. The machine language is directly intelligible to the control unit of the machine. Thus, numbers and instructions in machine language are expressed in a form that a computer can process or execute directly without conversion, translation, or programmed interpretation. Machine languages are usually not convenient for human use, although their use can often result in a more efficient program in terms of computer running time and storage space utilization. (Synonymous with *computer language* and with *absolute language.* Closely related to *language, machine-oriented.*)

language, machine-independent–A language, usually a programming language, that is not written for use with a particular computing or data-processing system or class of machines. Most procedure- or problem-oriented languages are machine-independent languages, such as ALGOL, FORTRAN, and COBOL. (Contrast with *language, machine-oriented.*)

language, machine-oriented–1: A computer programming language designed for convenient conversion to a machine-language computer-instruction code, yet much more convenient to the programmer than the machine language itself. The instructions are expressed in a number system that is basic to the machine; symbolic operation codes are used with absolute addresses or relative addresses. Generally, one line, or unit, of coding specifies one instruction to the computer. Thus, a program might be written in a problem-oriented language, translated into a machine-oriented language, and then automatically translated into the machine language for execution on a specific machine. The terms problem-oriented and machine-oriented, or computer-oriented, are relative; for example, a programmer may find a computer-oriented language generally more convenient for problem specification than a machine-language instruction code, but perhaps less convenient than a problem-oriented code. The machine-oriented code may be a type of pseudocode that is designed for a particular machine or class of machines. Usually, natural language words, such as English words, are found in the language. Abbreviated as *MOL*. (Synonymous with *computer-oriented language* and with *computer-dependent language*. Contrast with *language, machine-independent*, and compare also with *language, computer-sensitive*. Closely related to *language, machine*.) 2: A computer programming language having words and syntax that are designed for use on a specific computer or on a specific class of computers. (Synonymous with *native language*.)

language, mechanical–Same as *language, artificial*.

language, multidimension–A language that has expressions assembled with more than one class of symbols and codes, such as flowcharts, logic diagrams, block diagrams, and decision tables. (Contrast with *language, one-dimensional*.)

language, native–Same as *language, machine-oriented*.

language, natural–A language whose syntax reflects and describes current usage rather than prescribed usage. The rules are developed *ex post facto*. The language evolves from usage. An artificial language is determined prior to usage. To a newcomer, they may appear to be the same, since he has to learn both. Computers can handle and develop natural languages, as well as artificial languages. (Synonymous with *human language*. Contrast with *language, artificial*.)

language, object–Same as *language, target*.

language, OCR-common–A system of notation acceptable to the optical character recognition (OCR) equipment of various manufacturers. Universally acceptable language primarily implies universally acceptable character shapes.

language, one-dimensional–A language that has expressions assembled with only one class of symbols and codes, such as flowcharts, logic diagrams, block diagrams, and decision tables. (Contrast with *language, multidimensional*.)

language, original–Same as *language, source*.

language, problem-oriented–A programming language designed for ease of problem definition and problem solution for specific classes of problems; for example, a language specifically convenient for expressing a specific problem in mathematical form, such as the ordinary algebraic languages or the symbolic notation of the Boolean algebra applied to

a special problem; a special language for machine tool control; a programming language for medical diagnosis; a language for programming accounting problems; or a language for electrical circuit design engineers. There is usually little resemblance to machine instructions in these languages. Using these languages, a compiler will prepare the appropriate machine language programs for execution on a machine. The concepts of machine-oriented, machine-independent, problem-oriented, and procedure oriented languages are not all mutually exclusive; however, problem-oriented languages are usually machine-independent; that is, not machine-oriented. (Contrast with *language, procedure-oriented*. Synonymous with *application oriented problem*.)

language, procedure-oriented–A programming language designed for convenience in expressing the technique or sequence of steps required to carry out a process or flow. It is usually a source language and is usually not machine oriented. Since many classes of problems involve similar procedures for their solution, the procedure-oriented language lends itself more readily to describing how a problem is to be solved. Flow diagrams, process control languages, and many of the common programming languages, such as COBOL, FORTRAN, and ALGOL are considered procedure-oriented languages, since they are applicable to universal or broad classes of problems. Procedure-oriented languages are usually computer independent; that is, are not machine-oriented. (Contrast with *language, problem-oriented*.)

language, programming–A language used to prepare computer programs; that is, sets of rules or conventions that govern the manner and sequence in which instructions are written or specified for execution by a computer. Programming languages permit describing the method of solution to a program to a computer. They are ruly languages. They may be machine languages, machine-oriented languages, procedure-oriented, or problem-oriented. They may be source or target, or even intermediate languages. Basically, they permit communication between men and machines. There are translators between programming languages and natural languages. Programming languages are usually artificial languages. ALGOL, FORTRAN, COBOL, JOVIAL, FORAST, and IT are examples of programming languages. The machine language of a specific computer may be considered a programming language.

language, publication–A reference language that uses symbols suitable for printing.

language, reference–A set of characters and the rules used to define or describe a computer programming language. A reference language is not a metalanguage. (Further clarified by *metalanguage*.)

language, simulation—A language used in creating, describing, operating, or using models of systems, concepts, processes, or other models; for example, Simscript, Simula, GASP, or GPSS.

language, source—A language from which another language is to be derived; therefore, one that is an input to a given translation process. Several sequential translations from a source language may occur. Any natural or artificial language may be the source language. In any series of translations from one language to another, and to another, and so on, what has been the target language in the prior translation process becomes the source language for the next translation. In computer programming practice, the source language is usually the procedure-oriented, problem-oriented, or common language in which the program is initially written. Translators, assemblers, or compilers prepare the machine-language program from the source language. (Synonymous with *original language*. Contrast with *language, target*.)

language, stratified—A language that cannot be used as its own metalanguage, that is, a language that cannot be used to describe or specify itself. (Contrast with *language, unstratified*.)

language, symbolic—A computer programming language that is used to express addresses, operation codes, and other parts of computer instructions in symbols convenient to humans rather than in machine language; for example, a language in which the symbols or groups of symbols that express operation codes are mnemonic.

language, syntax—A language used to specify the syntax of another language, thus, a syntax language is a metalanguage, since it is used to describe an attribute namely syntax, of another language.

language, synthetic—Same as *language, artificial*.

language, target—1: A language into which a given language is to be translated; therefore, one that is an output from a given translation process. Several translations may occur before the final target language is reached. Any natural or artificial language may be the target language. In any series of translations of several languages, what has been the target language in the prior translation process becomes the source language for the next translation. In computer programming practice, the target language is usually the machine language, although the computer programmer writes the program in a source language that is different from the machine language. Translators, assemblers, or compilers prepare the target-language program. (Synonymous with

object language. Contrast with *language, source*.) 2: Any language specified by another language, that is, specified by a metalanguage. The language that is specified by the metalanguage is often also called the object language.

language, universal—A language that can serve as the target language of any translator or into which any language can be translated.

language, unstratified—A language that can be used to describe or specify itself, that is, that can be used as its own metalanguage with respect to itself as an object language; for example, English and computer languages are unstratified; FORTRAN is not. (Contrast with *language, stratified*.)

language processor—See *processor, language*.

large-scale integrated circuit—See *circuit, large-scale integrated*.

laser-emulsion storage—See *storage, laser-emulsion*.

last-in-first-out—Pertaining to a queuing technique in which the next item to be retrieved from the queue is the item most recently placed in the queue. Abbreviated as LIFO. (Related to *storage, pushdown* and to *list, pushdown*. Contrast with *first-in-first-out*.)

latency—The time between the completion of the interpretation of an address and the start of the actual transfer from the addressed location; for example, in a serial storage system, the access time less the word time, the time spent waiting for a desired word or storage location to appear under the heads of a magnetic drum or at the end of an acoustic delay line; or the delay while waiting for information called for from storage to be delivered to the arithmetic unit.

Law, Zipfs—See *Zipfs Law*.

layer, barrier—An electrical double layer formed at the contact surface between a metal and a semiconductor, or between two metals, in order that the Fermi levels in each material be the same. The action influences semiconductor and contact conductivity.

layout, data—Same as *format*.

layout, file—1: The format of a file, including structure, sequence, size and nature of parts of the file. 2: The arrangement of data in a file. A file layout description would also include the order, size, location, and shape of the components of the file.

layout, record—The arrangement of data items in a record; for example, the sequence of occurrence of items in a linear record or the two dimensional format of a printed page. Size, as well as distribution, is a significant factor in record layout. (Illustrative of *format*.)

L C—(Library of Congress). A prefix or suffix to indicate a Library of Congress subject or document classification number.

LD trunk—Same as *trunk, long-distance.*
LDRI—An abbreviation for Low Data-Rate Input.
leader—The blank section at the beginning of tape or roll of film.
leader, tape—A strip or length of tape at the beginning of a reel of tape, which may be blank to permit initial threading on a tape handler or may contain some start-of-tape marker, such as a hole, notch, conducting surface, magnetization, or some other easily detected mark, and may also contain a header record, indicating the nature of the data stored on the tape.
leader record—See *record, leader.*
leading decision—See *decision, leading.*
leading edge, card—See *edge, card leading.*
leading end—See *end, leading.*
leading zero—See *zero, leading.*
leapfrog test—See *test, leapfrog.*
leapfrog test, crippled—See *test, crippled-leap-frog.*
learning, machine—The ability of a computer and its program to improve its performance in solving a class of problems based on its own experience. This is achieved by a preplanned strategy wherein the program modifies itself based on results that have been obtained thus far in the handling of similar problems. As a result of experience and evaluation of prior results, the machine induces or guesses a rule and behaves accordingly until experience forces it to modify the rule. Machine learning refers to inductive rather than the deductive ability of a machine with its program.
leased-line network—See *network, leased-line.*
least significant digit—See *digit, least significant.*
LED—Light-emitting diode.
left justify—See *justify, left.*
Legal Retrieval—An information retrieval language for legal studies. The language embraces a variety of statutes, regulations, wordings, citations, and other legal documents, references, and literature. The use of the language, along with a computer and a program, provides assistance to lawyers for the retrieval of information in legal studies. An IBM 7070 computer has been used for conducting studies, using the statutes of Pennsylvania, at the University of Pittsburgh. Use has been made of a special abbreviated English language and KWIC programs.
length, block—The number of data items, such as words or characters, contained in one block. In most computing and data-processing systems, a block usually contains a fixed or variable number of words.
length, field—The number of columns or characters in a given field. Fixed storage areas, such as cards and channels on drums or discs are subdivided into fields, in order to simplify access, addressing, and programming. Thus, it becomes necessary to address the field and cause the contents of specific fields to be stored in specific

areas of storage only when data is transferred to internal storage.
length, fixed—Pertaining to the number of characters that may be contained in a particular storage location or data element, wherein the number of characters that may be handled as a unit may not be changed by the programmer, and there will be a loss of storage space due to inherent variations in the length of data elements. Thus, if variable-length data elements are placed in fixed-length storage locations, say blocks on tape, blank or unused spaces will result and the word-packing density along the tape will not be uniform. (Contrast with *length, variable.*)
length, fixed word—Same as *word, fixed-length.*
length, pulse—Same as *width, pulse.*
length, record—The number of data units, such as digits, characters, words or blocks, that are contained in a given record; for example, 128 blocks, each containing 48 characters.
length, register—The capacity of a register. The capacity is usually expressed as a number of digits or characters. A register may be called long, medium or short, in order to distinguish imprecisely between registers of different capacities in a particular system. (Synonymous with *register capacity.*)
length, variable—Pertaining to the number of characters that may be contained in a particular storage location or data element, wherein the number of characters that may be handled as a unit is subject to the discretion of the programmer, and there is no loss of storage space due to the variation in length of the data item. Thus, a variable-length block implies that each successive block on tape may have a different number of words and there are no blank spaces within each block; that is, the word-packing density remains constant along the tape. (Contrast with *length, fixed.*)
length, variable word—Same as *word, variable-length.*
length, word—The number of digits or characters in a word; for example, 40 binary digits. In many digital computers the word length is fixed; the fixed number of characters are handled as a unit. In variable word-length machines, each character may be considered a word. However, then the number of binary digits required to express a character is fixed. Each word is handled as a unit by a computer. (Synonymous with *word capacity.* Further clarified by *numeral, double-length.*)
length modulation, pulse—See *modulation, pulse-length.*
LESS—(Least-Cost Estimating and Scheduling System). A management procedure developed by International Business Machines Corporation.
letter—1: An alphabetic character used for the representation of sounds in a spoken

language. A phonetic sound may be assigned to each letter; each letter is a member of a set, called an alphabet, and the letters are combined to form words, to which meaning is assigned; or, words may be assigned to a meaning or a concept. 2: A graphic character that may be used alone or combined with others and that represents, in a written language, one or more sound elements of a spoken language. Diacritical marks used alone and punctuation marks are usually not considered letters.

level-1: A given relative rank or position in a hierarchy of a given class of entities; for example, nesting level, recursion level, noise level, signal level, and addressing level. 2: The degree of subordination or seniority of an item in a hierarchic arrangement.

level, addressing—A measure of the number of steps of indirect addressing that have been applied at a particular point or throughout a computer program. Thus, first-level addressing is direct addressing; that is, the address part of the instruction word contains the address, or location in storage, of the operand. In second-level addressing, or indirect addressing, the address part of the instruction word gives the storage location where the address of the operand may be found. (Illustrated by *addressing, two-level* and by *addressing, three-level.*)

level, average effectiveness—For measurement of the effectiveness of equipment, a percentage figure determined by dividing the operational use time by the total performance period.

level, carrier noise—The noise level produced by undesired variations of a carrier, such as its amplitude, frequency, or phase, in the absence of any intended modulation.

level, Fermi—The point of an energy level diagram corresponding to the top of the Fermi distribution, or the energy level in a semiconductor for which the Fermi-Dirac distribution function has a value of one-half.

level, reference—In single sideband equipment for voice frequency input power, the power of one of two equal tones which together cause the transmitter to develop its full rated power output.

level, relative transmission—The ratio of the test tone power at the given point in a transmission system to the test tone power at some point in the system chosen as a reference point. The ratio is expressed in decibels (dB). The transmission level at the transmitting switchboard is frequently taken as the zero-level reference point.

level, signal—In optical character recognition, the amplitude of the electronic response that results from the contrast ratio between the area of a printed character and the area of a document background.

level number—See *number, level.*

lexeme—Same as *semanteme.*

lexicon—A glossary or vocabulary, with definitions or explanations for all terms, not necessarily in alphabetical order.

LF-1: (Low Frequency). Frequencies between 30 and 300 kilohertz. (Further clarified by *spectrum, frequency.*) 2: The line feed character.

Liberator—A concept developed by Honeywell Data Processing Division for permitting programs written for other manufacturers' systems to be converted to Honeywell 200 computer language under program control.

library-1: An organized collection of documents used for reference or study. 2: An organized collection of data associated with a program or group of programs; for example, a set of physical properties for each of a set of elements. A look-up procedure, as in a table, is also involved. Thus, it is an automatic library of sorts.

library, data—A collection of files that are physically or logically related; for example, the files used for stock control or the files of an insurance company.

library, program—Same as *library, routine.*

library, public—In a computer operational environment, the collection of software, such as user programs, utility programs, report generators, general-purpose programs, and compilers, generally available to all users of the computer system. (Synonymous with *system library.*)

library, routine—A collection of proven computer programs, routines, and subroutines, through the use of which problems and parts of problems may be solved. The routines drawn from the library can be combined with other programs or inserted into a specific program by various methods. The programs in the library are often stored on magnetic tape for ease and speed of access. (Synonymous with *subroutine library* and with *program library.* Further clarified by *library, tape* and by *tape, library.*)

library, system—Same as *library, public.*

library, tape—A collection of tapes, usually magnetic tapes, organized so that data, routines, programs, or subroutines may be obtained and placed on a tape unit. The tape library usually is the collection of routines required to operate a computing facility. The majority of working routines, executive routines, assemblers, compilers, and translators are held on magnetic tapes in a tape library. The tapes are appropriately labeled and indexed and withdrawn or loaned as required. (Further clarified by *library, routine* and by *tape, library.*)

library program—See *program, library.*

library routine—See *routine, library.*

library subroutine—See *subroutine, library.*

library support, compiler—See *support, compiler library.*

library tape—See *tape, library.*

library track—See *track, library.*

life, shelf—See *shelf-life.*

LIFO—See *last-in-first-out.*

LIFT—1: (Logically Integrated FORTRAN Translator). A software package that automatically converts programs written in FORTRAN II to FORTRAN IV; developed by the Univac Division of Sperry-Rand Corporation. **2:** (Leven-o-seven Internal FORTRAN Translator). A program translator and compiler used on the Univac 1107 for the translation of programs written in IBM FORTRAN so they may be run on the Univac 1107 automatic data-processing system.

light, Nixie—A device based on a glow tube which converts a combination of electrical pulses, such as a binary number as a pattern of pulses, into a visual number. The light is used to give a visual display of decimal numbers on computer consoles, usually to show the contents of registers or storage locations, particularly those that are subject to changes at rapid rates to which mechanical devices are unable to respond. (Synonymous with *Nixie tube.*)

light-emitting diode—See *diode, light-emitting.*

light-emitting diode display—See *display, light-emitting diode.*

light gun—Same as *pen, light.*

light pen—See *pen, light.*

light stability—See *stability, light.*

limited, computer—See *computer-limited.*

limited, tape—Pertaining to a condition of computer operation wherein the time required for tape reading, writing, or punching exceeds the time required for some other type of operation, such as computing or printing. Such a situation often occurs in computers executing business types of programs. The condition may occur only at certain times during the execution of a routine; for example, when items are being sought on magnetic tape and most of the time is spent moving the tape. Thus, the operational speed of the operating system is reduced because of the slow speed of the tape units. (Synonymous with *tape bound.*)

limiter—1: In electronic computers, a device that has one input variable and one output variable and operates such that the output equals the input whenever a is less than or equal to the input or the input is less than or equal to b; the output equals a when the input is less than or equal to a; and the output equals b when the input is greater than or equal to b. Thus, the device has a saturating characteristic; that is, for input u and output v, $v = u$ when $a \leqslant u \leqslant b$, $v = a$ when $u \leqslant a$, and $v = b$ when $u \geqslant b$. **2:** In communications, a device that reduces the power of an electrical signal when it exceeds a specified value. The amount of reduction or compression increases with increase of input power.

line—1: In data processing, a horizontal row of characters printed across a page or card. Many printers print a line at a time as a unit before the paper moves. (Closely related to *row.*) **2:** In signal communications, a channel or conductor capable of transmitting signals. **3:** In flowchart symbols, a flowline.

line, access—In telecommunication systems, a line that continuously connects a remote station or terminal to a switching center or a data processor.

line, acoustic delay—Same as *delay-line, sonic.*

line, action—In a cathode-ray storage tube, also called Williams tube or electrostatic storage tube, operating in the serial mode, that line of the raster that is used during the action period. (Further clarified by *period, action* and by *spot, action.*)

line, B—Same as *register, index.*

line, balanced—A transmission line consisting of two conductors in the presence of ground, capable of being operated in such a way that the voltages of the two conductors at any transverse plane are equal in magnitude and opposite in polarity with respect to ground and the currents in the two conductors are equal in magnitude and opposite in direction.

line, character-spacing reference—See *reference-line, character-spacing.*

line, coding—Same as *word, instruction.*

line, control—In electronic or electromechanical computers, a transmission line, usually consisting of a simple single conductor, along which logic signals are sent, usually to control gates and flip-flops. The control signals in the control lines are developed as a result of logic decisions, which, in turn, create control signals. Thus, decision-making in a computer controls further decision-making. Initial control is obtained by placing certain control lines in specific states.

line, delay—See *delay-line.*

line, electric delay—See *delay-line, electric.*

line, electromagnetic delay—See *delay-line, electromagnetic.*

line, magnetic delay—See *delay-line, magnetic.*

line, magnetostrictive delay—See *delay-line, magnetostrictive.*

line, mercury delay—See *delay-line, mercury.*

line, nickel delay—See *delay-line, nickel.*

line, quartz delay—See *delay-line, quartz.*

line, sonic delay—Same as *delay-line, acoustic.*

line, tie—Same as *link, communication.*

line, transmission—A path for sending power or signals from point to point; for example, in communications, a length of coaxial cable having a low characteristic impedance, of the order of 100 ohms, and high velocity of propagation, as contrasted with a delay-line; or in power transmission, a high-voltage, cross-country, low-resistance cable, usually mounted on steel frame towers. Thus, a transmission line is used to carry electrical energy from a source to a load.

line, X-datum—An imaginary line, used as a reference line, along the top edge of a punch card, that is, a line along the edge nearest the twelve-punch row of a Hollerith punch card. (Contrast with *line, Y-datum*.)

line, Y-datum—An imaginary line, used as a reference line, along the right edge of a punch card and at right angles to the X-datum line. (Contrast with *line, X-datum*.)

line-at-a-time printer—Same as *printer, line*.

line driver—Same as *driver, bus*.

line driver, analog—Same as *ALD*.

line feed character—See *character, line feed*.

line index, code—See *index, code-line*.

line item—See *item, line*.

line printer—See *printer, line*.

line printing—See *printing, line*.

line side—See *side, line*.

line switching—Same as *switching, circuit*.

linear optimization—See *optimization, linear*.

linear programming—See *programming, linear*.

linear selection switch—Same as *storage, core-rope*.

linear unit—See *unit, linear*.

lines, hidden—In graphic display systems, line segments that are obscured from view in an orthogonal projection of a three-dimensional object. The hidden lines are usually represented in the graphic data structure so that many different orthogonal views may be displayed or so as to allow the image to move or rotate.

linguistics—The science of natural languages, their properties, and their interrelationships. The science of linguistics is normally divided into two parts: descriptive linguistics and comparative linguistics.

linguistics, comparative—The branch of linguistics that deals with the relationships between languages, such as the historical aspects of languages, the geographical distribution of language families, and similarities and differences among languages.

linguistics, descriptive—The branch of linguistics that deals with the characteristics of languages, such as phonology, grammar, morphology, syntax and semantics.

link—A part of a computer program, such as a computer instruction or an address, that passes control or parameters to and among separate portions of the computer program.

link, communication—The physical equipment used to connect one location to another for the purpose of transmitting and receiving information. (Synonymous with *data link*, with *information link*, and with *tie line*.)

link, data—Same as *link, communication*.

link, information—Same as *link, communication*.

link escape character, data—See *character, data link escape*.

link group—See *group, link*.

linkage—In computer programming, coding that connects two separately coded

routines or subroutines. (Further clarified by *subroutine, open*; by *subroutine, first-order*; by *subroutine, second-order*; and by *subroutine, closed*.)

linkage, basic—A linkage that is used repeatedly in one routine, program or operating system and that is used in accordance with the same set of rules each time.

linkage editing—Same as *binding*.

linkage editor—See *editor, linkage*.

linkage editor-loader—See *editor-loader, linkage*.

linked subroutine—Same as *subroutine, closed*.

LISP—A standard programming language intended for list processing. Applications include artificial intelligence and text manipulation. The term LISP is derived from the expression, "List Processing."

list—1: To place data items in a column, or data items placed in a column; for example, a column of names, or a column of numbers, or a column of words. A column of tangible items, such as cars, ships, or troops, is called a column rather than a list. (Contrast with *tabulate*.) 2: An ordered set of items, such as data; for example a passenger list, a stock list, or a grocery list.

list, attribute—Same as *list, description*.

list, backward-linked—A chained list in which each item in the list has an identifier or pointer for locating the preceding item in the list.

list, bi-directional—A chained list in which each item in the list contains an identifier or pointer for locating the preceding and the following item in the list. (Synonymous with *both-way list*, with *doubly-linked list*, with *symmetric list*, and with *two-way list*.)

list, both-way—Same as *list, bi-directional*.

list, chained—A list in which data items may be scattered but in which each item contains an identifier for locating the next item to be considered.

list, circular—A chained list that always allows return to the preceding item after passing through all the following items in the list.

list, description—A list of data elements and their corresponding values of an entity. (Synonymous with *attribute list* and with *property list*.)

list, free storage—A list of available storage space that may be assigned without loss of needed programs or data.

list, one-way—Same as *list, uni-directional*.

list, property—Same as *list, description*.

list, pushdown—A list so constructed and maintained that the next item to be retrieved is the most recently stored item in the list; that is, last in, first out. (Contrast with *list, pushup*. Related to *last-in-first-out*. Synonymous with *stack*.)

list, pushup—A list so constructed and maintained that the next item to be retrieved is the oldest item in the list; that is, first in, first out. (Contrast with *list, pushdown*. Further clarified by *storage, pushup*. Related to *first-in-first-out*.)

list, two way—Same as *list, bi-directional*.

list, uni-directional—A chained list that has identifiers or pointers for locating either the preceding item or the following item in the list, but not both. (Synonymous with *one-way list*.)

list processing—See *processing, list*.

literal—In a source program, an explicit representation of an item that must remain unaltered during any translation of the program; for example the word STOP in the instruction "If a = 1, print STOP." Thus, a representation of an item that is not to be interpreted and therefore must remain unaltered during any translation.

literature search—See *search, literature*.

load—1: In computer programming, to place data into a storage unit, such as by means of an input routine. (Further clarified by *routine, input*.) 2: To transfer a load module into main storage before it is executed.

load-and-go—A computer operating technique in which there are no stops or delays between the loading phase and the execution phase of a program. The technique may include assembling or compiling, or both.

load key—See *key, load*.

load module—See *module, load*.

load module generation—See *generation, load module*.

load point—See *point, load*.

loaded origin—See *origin, loaded*.

loaded-potentiometer function generator—See *generator, loaded-potentiometer function*.

loader—Same as *routine, input*.

loader, absolute—An input routine that causes a computer program to be brought into main storage, usually beginning at the assembled origin.

loader, bootstrap—An automatic built-in subroutine that has the capability of initiating the reading of a subroutine whose first few instructions will bring in the rest of the subroutine.

loader, initial program—The routine that causes the initial part of a computer program to be loaded into storage so that the computer program can proceed under its own control.

loader, relocating—A loader that adjusts addresses of the programs it handles relative to the assembled origin by using the relocation factors.

loading, dynamic program—In a computer operating system, the loading of a program module into main storage upon demand for that program module by an executive program or supervisor.

loading error, potentiometer—See *error, potentiometer loading*.

loading routine—Same as *routine, input*.

local—In computer programming, pertaining to items that are defined and used only in one subdivision of a computer program. (Contrast with *global*.)

local center—Same as *center, local switching*.

local center, telephone—Same as *center, local switching*.

local exchange center—Same as *center, local exchange switching*.

local exchange center, telephone—Same as *center, local exchange switching*.

local exchange switching center—See *center, local exchange switching*.

local side—See *side, local*.

local switching center—See *center, local switching*.

local variable—See *variable, local*.

locate-mode buffering—See *buffering, locate-mode*.

location—In data processing, any place in which data may be stored. Locations are usually designated by the address part of an instruction word.

location, protected—1: A storage location reserved for certain special purposes in which data are stored after having undergone a screening process to establish suitability for storage therein. 2: A storage location whose contents are protected against unauthorized access, inadvertant alteration, or improper alteration.

location, storage—A place in or a part of a storage device that can usually be explicitly and uniquely identified by an address.

location counter—Same as *counter, instruction*.

location delimiter—See *delimiter, location*.

location identifier—See *identifier, location*.

lock code—See *code, lock*.

locking—Pertaining to the use of code extension or escape characters such that the change in characters or the change in the interpretation of characters applies to all coded representations that follow or to all coded representations of a given class, until the next code extension or escape character occurs. (Contrast with *non-locking*.)

locking escape—See *escape, locking*.

lockout—Same as *protection*.

log drum—See *drum, log*.

log-in—To insert certain specified identification data to a computer system remote terminal preliminary to entering a query or engaging in a conversation. The purposes of logging-in may include user identification, determination of system status, and determination of file availability.

logger—1: A device that records events or conditions, usually with respect to time. 2: A device that enables a user of a system, of which the device is a part, to identify himself or itself, its purpose and the time of entry, that is, to log-in; and to log out with similar information so that accounting procedures may be carried out in accordance with the operating system.

logic, double-rail—Pertaining to circuits in which each logic variable may be represented by a pair of electrical lines which can assume three meaningful states, such as zero, one, and don't care or undecided.

logic, formal—The study of the structure and form of valid argument without regard to the meaning of the terms in the argument; for example, the Boolean algebra.

logic, N-level—In digital computer design, an arrangement of gates so connected that not more than N gates are connected in series in a particular component or frame.

logic, programmed—Internal logic design that can be changed in accordance with a prepared program that controls various electronic interconnections among gating elements, thus permitting the instruction repertory to be electrically altered. Rearrangement of the internal structure permits matching the machine capability to the problem requirement, allowing for more rapid or efficient operation. (Synonymous with *variable logic*.)

logic, symbolic—The subject, field, study or discipline that treats of formal logic by means of a formalized artificial language, such as a symbolic calculus, whose purpose is to avoid the inadequacies of natural language, such as ambiguities, inconsistencies, and illogical constructions.

logic, variable—Same as *logic, programmed*.

logic add—See *add, logic*.

logic analysis—See *analysis, logic*.

logic-arithmetic unit—Same as *unit, arithmetic*.

logic comparison—See *comparison, logic*.

logic-controlled sequential computer—See *computer, logic-controlled sequential*.

logic decision—See *decision, logic*.

logic device—See *device, logic*.

logic diagram—See *diagram, logic*.

logic diagram, engineering—See *diagram, engineering logic*.

logic design—See *design, logic*.

logic difference—See *difference, logic*.

logic element—See *element, logic*.

logic function—Same as *function, switching*.

logic instruction—See *instruction, logic*.

logic multiply—See *multiply, logic*.

logic operation—See *operation, logic*.

logic product—See *product, logic*.

logic product gate—Same as *gate, AND*.

logic query, fixed—See *query, fixed-logic*.

logic shift—See *shift, logic*.

logic sum—See *sum, logic*.

logic-sum gate—Same as *gate, OR*.

logic switch—See *switch, logic*.

logic symbol—See *symbol, logic*.

logic unit—Same as *unit, arithmetic*.

logic variable—Same as *variable, switching*.

logical add—Same as *add, logic*.

logical connective—See *connective, logical*.

logical connector—Same as *connective, logical*.

logical decision—Same as *decision, logic*.

logical diagram—Same as *diagram, logic*.

logical design—Same as *design, logic*.

logical difference—Same as *difference, logic*.

logical file maintenance—See *maintenance, logical file*.

logical input-output—See *input-output, logical*.

logical multiply—Same as *multiply, logic*.

logical-organization, third-generation—For computer, data processing, and communications systems, features that permit the ability to handle many programs at the same time; for example storage protection circuits, hardware address modification, modular components, such as modular CPU components, storage modules, and data channels, and telecommunication capabilities. (Further clarified by *generation, third*.)

logical product—Same as *product, logic*.

logical record—See *record, logical*.

logical shift—Same as *shift, logic*.

logical sum—Same as *sum, logic*.

logical trace—See *trace, logical*.

logical tracing—See *tracing, logical*.

login—Same as *log-in*.

logout—1: To record the occurrence of an event, such as the entry of a load program under the control of the supervisor. 2: The document or record of the occurrence of an event, such as the print-out of a statement of satisfactory completion of a diagnostic routine.

logout, diagnostic—A detailed record of the status of hardware, such as the status of registers, switches, indicators, and keys, made at the time of occurrence of a hardware malfunction, a software error, or a human operator mistake.

long-distance trunk—See *trunk, long-distance*.

long word—See *word, long*.

look-up, table—A procedure, such as a program, routine, or subroutine, for obtaining the value of a function corresponding to a specified value of the argument, such as the independent variable, from a table of values of the function. Thus, the sine of 36 degrees could be looked up in a table of trigonometric function values. The function value for sine 36 degrees could also be computed from a trigonometric series by means of an appropriate subroutine. This would not be table look-up.

loop—1: A closed path or any sequence of events that repeats itself, is closed back on itself, or connected back on itself, such as output connected back to input. (Synonymous with *cycle*. Further clarified by *cycle (2), (3) and (4)*.) 2: A set of instructions that may be executed repeatedly while certain conditions prevail. Often, no test is made to discover whether the conditions prevail until the loop has been executed once.

loop, closed—A loop without an exit, the execution of which can be interrupted only by intervention from outside the program that contains the loop.

loop, high-speed—Same as *revolver*.

loop, hysteresis—A rectangular coordinate plot of a cause and effect during a complete cycle of the cause from its increase to a certain value, its decrease to zero, its reversal in the opposite direction or polarity, and its decrease in magnitude to zero and return to its original value, with a plot of the value of the effect for each value of the cause; for example, a complete cycle of the magnetization level obtained in a piece of magnetic material as plotted against the applied magnetic field intensity; a complete cycle of the polarization of a dielectric material produced as the result of an applied electric displacement field, or the mechanical strain developed in a material under the influence of an applied stress. Except for the initial curve, or initial several curves, the plot of applied forces or fields makes the effects appear as a closed loop when they are plotted as the dependent variable against the cause as the independent variable. (Further clarified by *ratio, squareness*; by *loop, square*; and by *hysteresis*.)

loop, rapid-access—Same as *revolver*.

loop, rectangular—Same as *loop, square*.

loop, square—A hysteresis loop that is fairly or nearly rectangular in shape rather than more nearly like an S-shaped curve. In square curves, the residual value of the effect after all cause is removed is nearly equal to the maximum possible or saturated level of effect. Thus, for ferrite magnetic storage cores, the residual magnetization is nearly equal to the saturated value, making the top and bottom of the loop nearly horizontal, and sudden switching at the threshold or coercive value of applied field makes the sides of the loop nearly vertical. (Synonymous with *rectangular loop*. Further clarified by *loop, hysteresis* and by *ratio, squareness*.)

loop body—See *body, loop*.

loop box—See *box, loop*.

loop control—See *control, loop*.

loop control statement—See *statement, loop control*.

loop control variable—See *variable, loop control*.

loop initialization—See *initialization, loop*.

loop storage—Same as *storage, tape-loop*.

loss, insertion—A negative insertion gain; that is, an attenuation. (Further clarified by *gain, insertion*.)

low-level modulation—See *modulation, low-level*.

low-order digit—See *digit, low-order*.

low-performance equipment—See *equipment, low-performance*.

low-speed storage—See *storage, low-speed*.

lower curtate—See *curtate, lower*.

lowpass—Pertaining to the operation of a circuit or device, such as a filter, that permits the passage of low-frequency signals and highly attenuates high-frequency signals. (Further clarified by *bandpass*.)

LSD—Abbreviation for least significant digit.

LSI—Large-scale integrated circuits.

Luhn scanner—See *scanner, Luhn*.

luminescence—The property of emitting light while exposed to excitation. The phosphors, such as Aquadag, used as a coating on the interior surface of a cathode-ray-tube screen, emit light when excited by the electron beam. Persistence, or the tendency to phosphoresce, must be low or else there would be no dark areas, as, for instance, in a television picture. There is a slight amount of phosphorescence, however, as can be seen in the television screen after the set is turned off in a darkened room.

m

m-out-of-n code—See *code, m-out-of-n*.

MAC—1: An autocoding program for the Norwegian Defense Research Establishment on the Ferranti Mercury computer. 2: Multiple Access Computer. 3: Machine Aided Cognition. 4: Memory-Assisted Cognition. 5: A technique for the development of new ways in which computers can aid people in creative work; a program supported by federal and private agencies through the Massachusetts Institute of Technology.

machinable—Same as *readable, machine*.

machine—In data processing, a computer, such as an electronic data-processing machine or an automatic data-processing machine, or any individual component of an overall data-processing system, such as a tape unit, a card reader, or a central processing unit.

machine, accounting–A machine that prepares accounting records, usually actuated by a keyboard, but that may also read data from external storage media, such as cards or tapes, and automatically produces accounting records or tabulations, usually on continuous forms.

machine, asynchronous–A machine whose speed of operation is not related to any fixed frequency in the system to which it is connected; for example, a machine whose next operation is initiated when the completion of the prior operation is signaled. There is no fixed period or clock pulse that signals each event. (Contrast with *machine, synchronous.*)

machine, data-processing–Same as *machine.*

machine, electric accounting–See *EAM.*

machine, electronic data-processing–A system of interconnected electromechanical and electronic units for high-speed processing of data, usually under the control of a stored program. Each electronic, digital, data-processing machine consists of input, output, central processing (arithmetic and logical), storage and control units. Abbreviated as *EDPM.*

machine, punched-card–A machine that operates with punched cards, usually either reading them or punching them; thus, a card punch or a card reader. Punched card machines (PCM) are a class of card handling machines, including readers, punches, tabulators, sorters, collators, and keypunches.

machine, punched-tape–A machine that handles perforated tape, usually paper tape.

machine, self-organizing–A class of machines that may be characterized as containing a variable network in which the various elements or components are organized by the machine itself, without intervention or external control, to meet the criteria for successful operation; for example, a digital computer that automatically rearranges its internal logic connections in order to minimize the running time for the solution to a problem.

machine, synchronous–A machine whose speed of operation is related to a fixed frequency in the system to which it is connected; for example, a machine whose next operation is timed in accordance with a fixed-frequency clock-pulse generator. Each event in the machine is timed by the constant frequency source. (Contrast with *machine, asynchronous.*)

machine, Turing–A mathematical model of a device that changes its internal state and reads from, writes on, and moves a potentially infinite tape, all in accordance with its present state, thereby constituting a model for computerlike behavior. The behavior of a Turing machine is specified by listing an alphabet, a set of

internal states, and a mapping of alphabet and internal states, which determine what the symbol written and tape motion will be, and also what internal state will follow when the machine is in a given internal state and reads a given symbol. These are the minimal requirements of a digital computer.

machine, universal Turing–A Turing machine that can simulate any other Turing machine.

machine address–Same as *address, absolute.*

machine check–See *check, machine.*

machine code–See *code, machine.*

machine cognition–Same as *perception, artificial.*

machine cycle–See *cycle, machine.*

machine error–See *error, machine.*

machine-fault time, no-charge–See *time, no-charge machine-fault.*

machine-independent language–Same as *language, machine-independent.*

machine instruction–See *instruction, machine.*

machine instruction code–Same as *code, instruction.*

machine instruction set–See *set, machine instruction.*

machine language–See *language, machine.*

machine learning–See *learning, machine.*

machine-oriented language–See *language, machine-oriented.*

machine readable–See *readable, machine.*

machine-readable data–See *data, machine-readable.*

machine-readable medium–See *medium, machine-readable.*

machine recognizable–Same as *readable, machine.*

machine run–Same as *run.*

machine script–Same as *data, machine-readable.*

machine sensible–Same as *readable, machine.*

machine-spoiled time–See *time, machine-spoiled.*

machine translation–Same as *translation, mechanical.*

machine word–Same as *word, computer.*

machinery, computing–A system of equipment capable of handling data in accordance with instructions and usually consisting of interconnected input, storage, arithmetic and logical, control, and output units. An individual component is called a machine, such as a punched-card machine.

macro–Same as *macroinstruction.*

MACRO-10–A computer assembly language.

macro declaration–Same as *definition, macro.*

macro definition–See *definition, macro.*

macro generating program–Same as *macrogenerator.*

macrocode–A computer coding and programming language that assembles groups of computer instructions into single instructions. Thus, the computer must interpret or translate these macrocoded instructions into sets of smaller instructions, or clusters of

211

microcoded instructions, so that the computer can follow them, unless the computer is wired so as to directly interpret and execute the macrocoded instruction. Most modern computers operate on a macrocode basis, with such instructions as multiply, merge, sift, sort, and search.

macroelement, data–A usually ordered set of two or more data elements used as one data element, often with a single data use identifier; for example, the identifier *date* may be the data macroelement for the data elements *year, month* and *day.* The data macroelement may be the name of a set of data elements. (Synonymous with *data element chain.* Contrast with *element, data.*)

macrogenerator–A computer program that replaces macroinstructions in the source language with defined sequences of instructions in the source language. (Synonymous with *macro generating program.*)

macroinstruction–An instruction that is equivalent to a specified sequence of instructions and usually written in a source language. In an assembly routine, the macroinstruction calls for the insertion into the object program of a sequence of instructions generated from a skeletal definition of the specified macroinstruction by the insertion of supplied parameters. The macroinstruction can be a kind of pseudoinstruction, designating a predetermined and limited group of computer instructions for performing a particular task. Thus, the macroinstruction has no single equivalent operational instruction, but is usually replaced in a routine by a predetermined set of machine instructions. If the macroinstruction is machine independent, it is not written in machine format, and during assembly, the macroinstruction requires that a special subroutine be called or generated. It may be implemented on any of a large class of machines. If the macroinstruction is machine associated, or machine dependent, the instruction is usually written in machine format, in which case the programmer treats the instruction as a machine instruction. This macroinstruction does not have any corresponding single instruction in the operation code of the machine, but it does direct the machine to the proper subroutine. The macroinstruction might be an instruction that designates or represents a group of instructions for performing a particular task. Thus, a macroinstruction may be composed of two or more smaller or more basic instructions; for example, a multiply instruction in some computers causes the machine to proceed through a series of smaller, or microinstructions, such as fetch, subtract, shift, add, and compare. (Contrast with *microinstruction.* Synonymous with *macro.*)

macroprogramming–The process of preparing computer programs as a series of macroinstructions. Most computer programs are macroinstruction programs, since many computers now have macroinstructions wired in as part of the instruction repertory.

MADCAP–An algebraic translator and compiler programming language developed by Los Alamos Scientific Laboratories, UCLA, for use on the MANIAC II computer.

MADE–(Microalloy Diffused Electrode). A technique of transistor manufacture developed by Philco Corporation.

MADT–An abbreviation for Microalloy Diffused Base Transistor.

magamp–An abbreviation for magnetic amplifier.

magazine, card input–Same as *hopper, card.*

magazine, input–A containerlike device that holds and feeds a data input medium, such as cards, paper tape, magnetic tape, magnetic discs, film chips, or roll film; for example, a device that holds cards and makes them available to a card feed mechanism.

MAGIC–1: (MIDAC Automatic General Integrated Computation). A programming language and compiler developed in 1953 by the University of Michigan for use on the early MIDAC system. **2:** A generalized program control system for the AN/FSQ 7 computer.

Magnacard–A movable, accessible, and addressable magnetic surfaced card system developed by Magnavox Company for the storage of digital data.

MAGNET–A computer programming language and compiler developed by Shell Oil Company for use on the IBM 709 and 7090 computers.

magnetic, all–See *all-magnetic.*

magnetic card–See *card, magnetic.*

magnetic card storage–See *storage, magnetic card.*

magnetic cell–See *cell, magnetic.*

magnetic core–See *core, magnetic.*

magnetic core storage–Same as *storage, core.*

magnetic delay-line–See *delay-line, magnetic.*

magnetic disc–See *disc, magnetic.*

magnetic drum–See *drum, magnetic.*

magnetic drum storage–See *storage, magnetic drum.*

magnetic head–See *head, magnetic.*

magnetic ink–See *ink, magnetic.*

magnetic ink character recognition–See *MICR.*

magnetic path–See *path, magnetic.*

magnetic recording–See *recording, magnetic.*

magnetic rod storage–See *storage, magnetic rod.*

magnetic shift register–See *register, magnetic shift.*

magnetic slug storage–See *storage, magnetic slug.*

magnetic storage–See *storage, magnetic.*

magnetic storage, static–Same as *storage, core.*

magnetic tape–See *tape, magnetic.*

magnetic-tape reader—See *reader, magnetic-tape.*

magnetic-tape station—Same as *unit, magnetic-tape.*

magnetic-tape storage—See *storage, magnetic-tape.*

magnetic-tape unit—See *unit, magnetic-tape.*

magnetic thin-film—See *thin-film, magnetic.*

magnetic thin-film storage—See *storage, magnetic thin-film.*

magnetic wire—See *wire, magnetic.*

magnetic wire storage—Same as *wire, magnetic.*

magnetostriction—The physical phenomenon involving the change in dimensions which occurs when a magnetic material is magnetized. The sudden change in dimension permits the use of magnetic materials as a hammer to launch a shock down a length of elastic material, and since a change in dimension occurs as the sound wave passes, the resulting change in magnetic reluctance permits sensing of the wave. This permits time delay of data and data storage as a sonic delay line. (Further clarified by *electrostrictive* and by *piezoelectric.*)

magnetostrictive—Pertaining to an effect or phenomenon in which magnetic materials develop mechanical strains or stresses when they are magnetized. The mechanical strain is approximately proportional to the square of the applied magnetic field. Magnetostrictive devices are used as transducers, such as in nickel delay-lines, to change electric pulses into a kind of acoustic wave in the material, such as is produced by a hammer blow. (Compare with *electrostrictive.* Further clarified by *piezoelectric.*)

magnetostrictive delay-line—See *delay-line, magnetostrictive.*

magnitude—In mathematics, the absolute value of a number or quantity; for example, the absolute value or magnitude of -8 is 8; of a velocity of 6 feet per second northeast, the magnitude, or speed, is 6 fps.

magnitude, relative—The magnitude of one quantity as compared to the magnitude of another. Relative magnitudes, like relative addressing in computer programming, usually are expressed in terms of or with reference to a base magnitude. The relative magnitude is usually expressed as a difference from or a percentage of the base or reference magnitude.

Magslip—Same as *synchro.*

MAID—(Monrobot Automatic Internal Diagnosis). A computer diagnostic malfunction detection and location program developed by Monroe Calculating Machine Company for the Monrobot computers.

main control unit—See *unit, main control.*

main frame—Same as *unit, central processing.*

main program—See *program, main.*

main routine—Same as *program, main.*

main storage—See *storage, main.*

maintainability—The probability that a device can be retained in or restored to a specified state within a given period of time when the maintenance is performed in accordance with prescribed procedures, resources and conditions.

maintenance—Activity intended to keep equipment (hardware) or programs (software) in satisfactory working condition, including tests, measurements, replacements, adjustments, repairs, program copying, and program improvement. Maintenance is either preventive or corrective.

maintenance, corrective—Maintenance performed to clear a known fault or malfunction, including repairs, replacements, adjustments, measurements, and tests to detect, locate, and remove the fault, and to ensure satisfactory performance of the equipment.. Thus, corrective maintenance is performed on an unscheduled basis. (Synonymous with *remedial maintenance* and *unscheduled maintenance.*)

maintenance, emergency—Same as *maintenance, corrective.*

maintenance, dynamic system—The maintenance of a system by its own automatic action whereby the system reconfigures itself, or rearranges its components to adjust to operator addition or deletion of some of its processing components, or reconfigures itself to continue operation in a degraded state of operation when some of its processing components fail. In particular, for a computer operating system, the process of updating the system is performed automatically in response to changes in the operating environment or to changes in the programs within the operating system. (Further clarified by *maintenance, operating system.*)

maintenance, file—The activity of keeping a file up to date by adding, changing, or deleting data. The updating may be performed as each change occurs; changes may be processed in batches when the batch size makes it practical to do so; the maintenance may be performed periodically, or the maintence may be subject to any other rule. Correcting errors and improving format, style, and changing recording medium, are additional examples of file maintenance activities.

maintenance, interactive file—The updating, correction, and purging of a file in real time from an online terminal usually operating in an interactive, that is, conversational, mode. (Contrast with *maintenance, logical file.*)

maintenance, logical file—The updating, correction and purging of a file through the use of computer programs and, perhaps, transaction or change files. (Contrast with *maintenance, interactive file.*)

maintenance, operating system–The group of functions devoted to the updating and correction of the computer operating system in response to operating environment and program changes that occur over time. User programs must be changed when user needs change. Computer modification and improved software make changes in other software necessary. Both of these changing conditions necessitate updating of the computer operating system. (Further clarified by *maintenance, dynamic system*.)

maintenance, preventive–Tests, measurements, replacements, adjustments, repairs, and similar activities carried out with the intention of preventing faults or malfunctions from occurring during subsequent operation. Preventive maintenance is designed to keep equipment and programs in proper operating condition and is performed on a scheduled basis. It is based on the ability to predict, with a certain degree of probability, which components are likely to fail during normal operation by means of time and behavior studies.

maintenance, program–The group of support functions that modify, update, and correct application programs for the user.

maintenance, remedial–Same as *maintenance, corrective*.

maintenance, routine–Same as *maintenance, scheduled*.

maintenance, scheduled–Maintenance performed in accordance with an established and agreed on timetable. Scheduled maintenance is planned long in advance. The timetable is published for all personnel, such as programmers, coders, operators, maintenance technicians, engineers, and others concerned. It is not intended to include occasional periods of maintenance work done to fill idle time or to correct trends toward poor performance. Thus, supplementary maintenance is not considered scheduled maintenance. Scheduled maintenance is considered regularly scheduled maintenance. (Synonymous with *routine maintenance*.)

maintenance, supplementary–Maintenance performed outside the periods of scheduled maintenance by prior arrangements among the maintenance and operating personnel. Supplementary maintenance is commonly performed during periods of idle time or after regularly scheduled operating periods, to introduce modifications for performance improvement or reliability improvement. Corrective maintenance is not considered as supplementary maintenance, since corrective maintenance is performed when a malfunction occurs.

maintenance, unscheduled–Same as *maintenance, corrective*.

maintenance, volume–In a computer operating system, the group of functions and activities that diagnose, correct, and remove error conditions and their causes from the volumes that comprise the system they are a part of. (Further clarified by *purging, file* and by *analysis, surface*.)

maintenance panel–See *panel, maintenance*.

maintenance period, principal–See *period, principal maintenance*.

maintenance program–See *program, maintenance*.

maintenance standby time–See *time, maintenance standby*.

maintenance time, deferred–See *time, deferred maintenance*.

maintenance time, nonscheduled–See *time, nonscheduled maintenance*.

maintenance time, scheduled–See *time, scheduled maintenance*.

maintenance time, supplementary–See *time, supplementary maintenance*.

major control change–See *change, major control*.

major cycle–See *cycle, major*.

major total–See *total, major*.

MAJORITY–A logic operator having the property that if P is a statement, Q is a statement, R is a statement, . . . , then the majority of P, Q, R, . . . is true if more than half the statements are true, false if half or less than half are true.

majority carrier–See *carrier, majority*.

majority decision element–Same as *gate, majority decision*.

majority decision gate–See *gate, majority decision*.

majority operation–See *operation, majority*.

make connection–See *connection, make*.

makeup time–See *time, makeup*.

malfunction–The effect of a fault or failure in the operation of the hardware of a system; for example, an improper sum obtained from a set of gates containing a shorted diode. Thus, the malfunction causes an operational or a machine error. A mistake in programming cannot be said to cause a machine error, since the machine is executing the instructions properly and requires no corrective maintenance. (Further clarified by *failure, equipment*. Contrast with *accuracy, error* and with *mistake*.)

malfunction, program-sensitive–A malfunction, due to a fault or failure in the operation of the hardware of a system, which occurs only when some particular combination of instructions are executed; for example, oscillations built up by periodic occurrences of certain binary pulse patterns or peculiar behavior of a set of logic elements (gates) due to the nature of a particular set of logic instructions.

management, computer-assisted–Management performed with the aid of automatic data processing hardware, software, or both.

management, data–1: The function of controlling or directing the acquisition, analysis, indexing, storage, retrieval, and distribution of data. 2: In an operating system, the programs used to handle data, such as providing access to data, performing or monitoring the storage of data, or controlling input/output devices. (Contrast with *data, management*.)

management, job–In a computer operating system, the real-time initiating, scheduling, monitoring and controlling of all system operations and functions, including the allocation and scheduling of the use of system resources, for each job. (Closely related to *control, job*.)

management, operating system–The development, generation, and maintenance of an operating system for a computer or data processing system.

management, record–To provide economy, efficiency, and effectiveness in the creation, organization, maintenance, use, and disposition of records, assuring that needless records will not be created or kept and that valuable records will be preserved.

management data–See *data, management*.

management routine, file–See *routine, file management*.

management system, data–See *system, data management*.

manifolding–Pertaining to the use of many sheets of paper and carbon paper in order to produce many copies at a single printing. Thus, five-part paper implies printing five copies at once, using four sheets of carbon paper and including the original.

manipulated variable–Same as *variable, controlled*.

manipulation, algebraic–The processing of mathematical expressions, in accordance with specified rules or algorithms, without regard to the numeric values of the symbols that represent numbers; for example, the determination of the expansion series for a trigonometric function or proving the validity of transformation of a Boolean expression.

manipulation, formula–Algebraic manipulation of mathematical formulae. For example, transposing expressions in an equation from one side of the equals sign to the other, with appropriate change of mathematical sign.

manipulation, symbol–The processing of symbols usually in accordance with prescribed rules that have logical significance or correlation but that do not have explicit numerical values; for example, to transform AB into $A + B$, that is, not (A AND B) into notA OR notB; or in a string processing language, such as SNOBOL, to write SUB-FUZE; SUB 'Z' = "S"; OUTPUT = SUB; and execute would result in the new string FUSE.

manipulative indexing–Same as *indexing, coordinate*.

mantissa–The fractional part of the logarithm of a number; for example, in decimal notation, the base 10 logarithm of 2000 is 3.3010; therefore, the mantissa of the logarithm is .3010. The mantissa is always positive. When the logarithm is given and

the number, or antilog, is to be obtained, the mantissa is used to obtain the significant digits of the antilog. The characteristic of the logarithm, 3 in the example, sets the decimal point. Thus, the antilog of .3010 is 2. The characteristic 3 sets the antilog decimal point at 2000.

manual control–See *control, manual*.

manual exchange–See *exchange, manual*.

manual input–See *input, manual*.

manual input unit–See *unit, manual input*.

manual number generator–Same as *unit, manual input*.

manual read–See *read, manual*.

manual reconfiguration–See *reconfiguration, manual*.

manual-switch storage–See *storage, manual-switch*.

manual telephone switchboard–Same as *exchange, manual*.

manual word generator–Same as *unit, manual input*.

many-to-one–Pertaining to the relationship between members of one set and members of another set wherein the correspondences are such that two or more members of one set correspond to one member of the other set. For example, several expressions in a source language may be equivalent to only one statement in a target language; several microinstructions equivalent to one macroinstruction, or many cables connected to a single trunk or bus. A many-to-one relationship is involved in a computer when many logic elements are wired together to execute a single computer instruction, such as add, shift, sort, and square-root. (Contrast with *one-to-one* and with *one-to-many*.)

map–In data processing, to establish a correspondence or relationship between the members of one set and the members of another set and to perform a transformation from one set to another; for example, to form a set of truth tables from a set of Boolean expressions. Information should not be lost or added when transforming the map from one to another.

map, Karnaugh–A tabular method of representing the relationship between Boolean switching functions. Thus, an orderly extension, into tabular form, of the Venn diagram, especially for functions with more than two variables. The Karnaugh map may be used to show each adjacent state, the right-most column being adjacent to the left-most column and the top row being adjacent to the bottom row. In the illustration, note that each possible term is represented as an intersection of a row and column. A one signifies the presence of the term and a zero signifies its absence. Thus, the four ones indicate the presence of four terms in the function; namely $ABCD$, $A\overline{B}CD$, $\overline{A}BCD$, and $\overline{A}\overline{B}CD$. Note that the intersection is taken as logical multiplication. Logical addition, or union, results in the functional representation F =

$A\overline{B}\overline{C}D + ABCD + \overline{A}BCD + \overline{A}BC\overline{D} = ABD + \overline{A}BC$. Thus, the Karnaugh map shown is a map of this function. Note that adjacent squares permit the immediate elimination of redundant literals, that is, variables. (Further clarified by *diagram, Veitch.*)

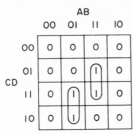

A Karnaugh map *of the function* $F = \Sigma$ (6, 7, 13, 15), that is $F = \overline{A}BC + ABD$.

mapping device—See *device, mapping.*

margin, guide—On paper tape, the distance, measured across the tape, from the guide edge to the center of the nearest track; that is, line of data holes.

margin, justified—An arrangement of data printed on a page in such a manner that the left or right end characters of each horizontal line or row lie in the same left or right column; that is, under one another.

margin-perforated card—Same as *card, edge-punched.*

margin-punched card—Same as *card, edge-punched.*

marginal check—See *check, marginal.*

marginal check, programmed—See *check, programmed marginal.*

marginal test—See *test, marginal.*

mark—A character used to indicate a situation, signal an event, or serve as a reference; for example, an end-of-file mark on a magnetic tape; a character used for signaling the beginning or end of a set of data units, such as field, word, block, record, or file; or a sentinel, tag, or flag bit that indicates whether a floating-point or a fixed-point instruction is to be executed.

mark, admissible—Any one of the set of symbols acceptable to a specific system; for example, the symbols 7, 8, and 9 are admissible marks for a decimal computer but are not admissible for a binary computer; the Roman alphabet is a set of admissible marks for a given optical character reader, but all the Russian Cyrillic characters are not admissible.

mark, bench—See *benchmark.*

mark, document—An optical mark, inside the recording area but outside the image area, on each frame of a roll of microfilm. The mark is used to count images and frames automatically.

mark, end—A mark that signifies the end of a unit of information; for example, an end-of-file mark, such as a special word recorded on the tape in the usual manner

of recording; a metallic strip at the end of a tape, whose conductivity signals that the end of the tape is at hand and to stop the drive in that direction; or a special character used to signify the end of a record on a drum.

mark, group—A symbol, such as a character, that marks or signals the beginning or the end of a group of data recorded, represented, or handled in a serial fashion.

mark, record—A symbol used to signal the beginning or end of a record. Such marks are used to separate serially handled records.

mark, word—A symbol used to signal the beginning or end of a word when data elements are presented serially.

mark scan—See *scan, mark.*

mark-sense—The process of detecting data in the form of marks on a card or sheet, usually made with a special conducting-lead pencil so as to be easily detectable electrically. The marks are detected by their low electrical resistance compared with the unmarked paper. The position of the mark indicates the nature of the data. It might be marked like a standard punch card or a simple choice of one-out-of-several might be indicated by a mark in the selected box. The marks may be converted automatically to hole punches on the same or another card for computer input that can only accept cards or the mark-sense reader may be connected directly to the computer. The device that makes corresponding holes in a punched card is a mark sense punch.

mark-sense column—See *column, mark-sense.*

mark-sense punch—See *punch, mark-sense.*

mark-sense row—See *row, mark-sense.*

mark-space multiplier—See *multiplier, mark-space.*

marker, beginning-of-tape—A mark on, or a special characteristic of, a magnetic tape, used to indicate the beginning of the magnetic recording area; for example, a reflective strip, a perforation, or a transparent section.

marker, end-of-tape—A mark on, or a special characteristic of, a magnetic tape, used to indicate the end of the magnetic recording area; for example, a reflective strip, a perforation, a transparent section, or a special bit pattern.

marking pulse, teletypewriter—See *pulse, teletypewriter marking.*

Markov chain—See *chain, Markov.*

MARLIS—(Multi-Aspect Relevance Linkage Information System). An information storage and retrieval system developed by Imperial Chemical Industries, Ltd., Herefordshire, England.

MARS—(Multiple Apertured Reluctance Switch). The International Business Machines version of the multiapertured magnetic-core switching device used for performing logic functions in digital computers.

MASCOT–(Motorola Automatic Sequential Computer Operated Tester). A device for computer-controlled testing of electronic components.

mask–1: In computer programming, a filter consisting of a pattern of characters that is used to control the retention or elimination of portions of another pattern of characters. (Synonymous with *extractor*. Further clarified by *filter*.) 2: To use a pattern of characters for controlling the retention or elimination of portions of another pattern of characters. 3: In an operating system, to discontinue the recognition of interrupts, that is, to allow interrupts to be ignored. (Contrast with *unmask*.)

MASS–(Multiple Access Sequential Selection). A method of data storage and retrieval, utilizing magnetic tapes, which combines the increased volumetric packing density of magnetic tapes with the faster and more random access achievable on magnetic discs in order to provide increased mass data storage with decreased serial access time.

mass data–See *data, mass*.

mass storage–See *storage, mass*.

master clock–See *clock, master*.

master control–Same as *program, master-control*.

master-control program–See *program, master-control*.

master data–See *data, master*.

master file–See *file, master*.

master instruction tape–See *tape, master instruction*.

master program–Same as *program, main*.

master program tape–Same as *tape, master instruction*.

master routine–Same as *routine, executive*.

master station–See *station, master*.

master synchronizer–Same as *clock, master*.

master tape–See *tape, master*.

master timer–Same as *clock, master*.

match–To determine the extent of identity, similarity, or agreement between members of one set and members of another set in order to select or separate comparable members. Thus, if only matched members are removed, only data items that are in both sets are considered as matched items. It is a data-processing operation similar to merge, except that instead of producing a sequence of items made up of two or more inputs sequenced, a sequence of items is made up that has members that exist in both original sets. Frequently, matching is performed in conjunction with merging.

match gate–Same as *gate, exclusive-NOR*.

mate–In connectors, the other half of a connector with reference to a given half.

MATH-MATIC–Univac MATH-MATIC Programming System. A programming language developed by Sperry-Rand Corporation for use on the Univac I and II computers.

mathematical check–See *check, mathematical*.

mathematical function–See *function, mathematical*.

mathematical induction–See *induction, mathematical*.

mathematical model–See *model, mathematical*.

mathematical programming–Same as *programming, linear*.

matrix–1: In mathematics, a two-dimensional rectangular array of quantities. Matrices may be manipulated in accordance with rules, such as the rules of a matrix algebra. By extension a matrix may be any multidimensional array of any kind in any pattern. 2: In electric circuits, an array of circuit elements interconnected in such a manner as to perform a specific function according to the manner of interconnection. The elements may be transistor, diode, or relay gates, thus performing logic functions, such as transliteration of characters, encoding, decoding, path selection, number system transformation, or word translation. Usually in a rectangular planar array, input is taken along one dimension and output is taken along the other. (Synonymous with *matrix switch*.)

(A)

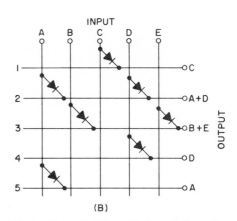

(B)

(A) A matrix *of mathematical symbols, and (B) a* diode *matrix for decoding binary numerals.*

matrix, dot–An array of dots used to generate a graphic symbol.

matrix, program timing–An array of connections in a synchronous digital computer which supplies timing pulses at regular intervals in proper sequence to permanently selected groups of lines, thus setting up an operation for execution. The timing pulses are also called clock pulses and the program timing matrix a clock-pulse generator.

matrix printer—See *printer, matrix.*

matrix switch—Same as *matrix (2).*

maximal—Pertaining to the most, greatest, largest, highest, longest, or similar superlative. (Contrast with *minimal.*)

MDE—An abbreviation for Magnetic Decision Element. (Further clarified by *element, logic.*)

mean entropy, character—See *entropy, character mean.*

mean repair time—Same as *mean-time-to-repair.*

mean-time-between-failures—The limit of the ratio of operating time of equipment to the number of observed failures as the number of failures approaches infinity. Abbreviated MTBF. (Contrast with *mean-time-to-failure.*)

mean-time-to-failure—The average or mean time between initial operation and the first occurrence of a failure or malfunction, as the number of measurements of such time on many pieces of identical equipment approaches infinity. Abbreviated MTTF. (Contrast with *mean-time-between-failures.*)

mean-time-to-repair—The average time required to accomplish corrective maintenance. (Abbreviated MTTR. Synonymous with *mean repair time.*)

mean transinformation content—See *content, mean transinformation.*

measure, information—A function of the frequency of occurrence of a specified event from a set of possible events. The term event is to be understood as used in probability theory. An event might be the occurrence or presence of a given element in a set, or the occurrence of a specified character or word in a given position of a message.

measurement, work—A method of establishing a relationship between the quantity and quality of work performed and the man and machine power utilized.

mechanical dictionary—Same as *dictionary, automatic.*

mechanical differential analyzer—See *analyzer, mechanical differential.*

mechanical language—Same as *language, artificial.*

mechanical replacement—See *replacement, mechanical.*

mechanical translation—See *translation, mechanical.*

mechanized—Same as *readable, machine.*

mechanized data—Same as *data, machine-readable.*

medium—A material or method for storing or otherwise handling data; for example, magnetic cores, paper tape, magnetic tape, punched cards, microfiche, laser emulsion, delay-lines, and microfilm. These data carriers provide for storage, mobility, and transportability of data. (Synonymous with *data medium.* Further clarified by *carrier, data* and by *medium, input-output.*)

medium, data—1: The material may be represented, usually as a physical variable of the medium, that is, the material itself; for example magnetic tape, magnetic cores, punched cards, punched tape, or magnetic discs. 2: The physical quantity that may be varied to represent data; for example the liquid in a thermometer.

medium, empty—A data medium that does not contain data and usually has a frame of reference enabling it to hold addtional data; for example, a blank form, blank tape, or an unrecorded disc.

medium, input-output—A material substance intended for carrying recorded data and designed to be transportable independently of the reading and writing mechanism; for example, a punched card, a magnetic card, a magnetic tape, paper tape, a paper sheet, preprinted stationery, or microfilm. The medium is handled by an input-output device, such as a card reader-punch, a magnetic tape handler, a paper tape perforator, a high-speed printer, or a camera. The medium is used to insert data and instructions into a computer and to remove results. (Further clarified by *medium* and by *carrier, data.*)

medium, machine-readable—A data medium that can be used to convey data to a sensing device; for example punched cards, punched tapes, and magnetic tapes. (Synonymous with *automated data medium* and with *mechanized data medium.*)

medium, storage—The material, or its configuration, on which data is recorded; for example, paper tape, çards, magnetic cores, magnetic tape, drums, discs, or laser-emulsion.

medium, transfer—A material that transfers a solid or liquid ink during printing, usually consisting of a sheet or ribbon of fabric, paper, or plastic film as a supporting base, with liquid or solid ink absorbed into or coated on the supporting base.

medium, virgin—A data medium in or on which data has not been recorded; for example unmarked paper, paper tape that has no holes in it, or magnetic discs on which no recording has been made.

meet—Same as *AND.*

meet operation—Same as *operation, conjunction.*

megabit—One million binary digits.

megahertz—One million cycles per second.

member, print—See *print-member.*

memory—Same as *storage.*

memory, core-rope—Same as *storage, core-rope.*

memory, Olsen—Same as *storage, core-rope.*

memory, plated-wire—A storage device consisting of an array of elements, each made up of a thin cylindrical shell of electro-deposited magnetic material on a bare copper wire substrate. The memory element is formed by making a coil about the coated wire with an insulated wire. A current is passed along the substrate wire during the plating process to achieve circumferential polarization. A binary digit is stored by the interaction of circumferential and transverse fields caused by coincident current selection. Non-destructive sensing is accomplished by application of current in the transverse field alone.

memory, rope—Same as *storage, core-rope.*

memory, virtual—Same as *storage, virtual.*

memory, woven-wire-screen—A storage device consisting of an array of rectangular storage cells formed by weaving bare copper wire intermixed with insulated wire. The resulting screen is plated with a magnetic material. Plating does not adhere to insulation, thus providing rectangular torroids at the intersections. Weaving is accomplished at high speeds. Fabrication is simple and economical. Properties of the memory are in some respects superior to standard ferrite cores.

memory capacity—Same as *capacity, storage.*

memory cycle—Same as *cycle, storage.*

memory dump—Same as *dump.*

memory exchange—Same as *exchange, storage.*

memory protection—Same as *protection, storage.*

menu, display—In display systems and devices, the options listed on a display for selection by the operator. Usually the operator indicates the next action by means of an input device, such as a keyboard or a light pen.

mercury delay-line—See *delay-line, mercury.*

mercury storage—See *storage, mercury.*

mercury tank—See *tank, mercury.*

merge—To combine two or more sets of items into one, usually in a specified sequence. Thus, a single ordered file is formed by combining two or more ordered files. Merging is a special case of collating. The form of the items are not changed during a merging operation. A merging-sort is the putting of items into sequence by repeated merging, splitting, and remerging. This process is also called sequencing by merging. (Synonymous with *mesh.* Contrast with *split.* Related to *collate.*)

merge, balanced—An external sort in which strings, created by an internal sort, are placed on half of the available storage devices and then merged by moving them back and forth between an equal number of devices until the merging process is complete.

merge-sort—To sort; that is, to produce a single sequence of items, ordered according to some rule, from two or more previously unordered sequences, without changing the items in size, structure, or total number, although more than one pass may be required for a complete sort. Items are selected during each pass on the basis of the entire key. A merge-sort

program can be written in which items in a set are divided into subsets, the items in each subset are sorted, and then the sorted subsets are merged. Such a program would be called a sort-merge program. The overall operation would be called a sort-merge operation.

merge-sort, balanced—See *sort, balanced merge.*

merge-sort, unbalanced—See *sort, unbalanced merge.*

mesh—Same as *merge.*

message—1: An amount of information whose beginning and end are defined or implied, such as a communication of information or advice from a source to one or more destinations in suitable language or code; for example, a group of words or lines of data transported as a unit, or a selection from an agreed set of signals intended to communicate information. In telegraphic and data communications, a message is composed of: (1) a heading, containing a suitable indicator of the beginning of the specific message together with information on any or all of the following: source and destination, date and time of filing, and routing or other transmission information; (2) a body, containing the information or advice to be communicated; and (3) an ending, containing a suitable indicator of the conclusion of the specific message, either explicit or implicit. 2: An ordered set of characters to which meaning has been assigned in order to convey information.

message, multiple-address—A message that is to be delivered to two or more destinations. (Contrast with *message, single-address.*)

message, single-address—A message that is to be delivered to one destination. (Contrast with *message, multiple-address.*)

message block—See *block, message.*

message exchange—See *exchange, message.*

message routing—See *routing, message.*

message sink—See *sink, message.*

message source—See *source, message.*

message source, stationary—See *source, stationary message.*

message switching—See *switching, message.*

message switching, automatic—See *switching, automatic message.*

message switching center—Same as *center, data switching.*

message switching center, semiautomatic—See *center, semiautomatic message switching.*

messmotor—Same as *motor, integrating.*

metacompilation—The process of preparing and using compilers to assemble or compile other compilers that are used to assemble or compile computer programs that are actually executed on or by a computer. Thus, compilers may be used to assemble computer programs that are executed as they are compiled or the computer program may be compiled and stored for future use. A metacompiler prepares compilers. Compiling time and the number of compilers are increasing in data processing center applications.

metal, base—Metal on which one or more other metals or coatings may be deposited. Coated base metals are often used in printed circuits for connecting computer logic elements.

metalanguage—A language that is used to specify or describe another language. (Further clarified by *language, reference.* Contrast with *catalanguage.*)

method—1: The details and mechanics of accomplishing the individual steps toward a goal; for example, an arrangement or sequencing of operations or events to secure a result. (Synonymous with *technique*, with *approach*, and with *procedure.* Contrast with *structure.*) 2: In data processing, the action taken in order to solve a problem, such as a procedure involving the steps to evaluate or produce the results obtainable from or indicated by a mathematical equation; for example Horner's method or Amble's method for finding solutions to equations.

Method, Amble's—Same as *connection, regenerative.*

method, heuristic—An exploratory method of solving problems in which an evaluation is made of the progress made toward an acceptable result by using a series of approximations that lead toward that result.

method, infinite-pad—In optical character recognition, a method of measuring the reflectiveness of paper stock wherein doubling the number of backing sheets of the same paper does not measurably change the measured reflectiveness.

method, monte carlo—A procedure that involves probabilistic techniques in order to obtain an approximation to the solution of a problem; for example, a trial-and-error method of repeated calculations to discover the best solution or a random-walk method. The monte carlo method is often used when a great number of variables are present, with interrelationships so extremely complex as to forestall straightforward or classical analytical handling. The technique permits computer simulation of a brute-force empirical approach, involving the construction of a number of possible mathematical models that are appropriately tested. Usually intractable mathematical functions are computed, using tables of random numbers, powerful statistical methods, and very fast numerical calculations on large digital computers.

MF—(Medium Frequency). Frequencies between 300 and 3000 kilohertz. (Further clarified by *spectrum, frequency.*)

MICA—(Macroinstruction Compiler Assembler). A computer program assembler-compiler developed by North American Aviation, Los Angeles.

MICR—(Magnetic Ink Character Recognition).

A standardized procedure developed by American Banking Association and various manufacturers to expedite bank document processing. Standard characters are preprinted with magnetic ink, containing a ferrite, on documents, such as checks, in advance of usage, to permit document identification and sorting. Also, after a check is written, magnetic characters are printed for control and amount. Special scanners read the magnetic characters, which are also visible to the eye, to sort, sum, and control the flow of commercial paper. The use of magnetic ink reduces error that might occur from extraneous marks that are scanned by optical scanners. (Contrast with *OCR*. Further clarified by *recognition, character* and by *recognition, pattern.*)

MICR code—See *code, MICR.*

MICR scan—See *scan, MICR.*

microcode—A code that represents the smaller and simpler concepts, instructions, or operations; for example, a code that represents computer instructions, such as add, compare, fetch, move tape, read, write, or transfer to storage. Often several microinstructions form a single macroinstruction. Each of these microcoded instructions involves only one simple step. Sometimes microcoding makes use of certain suboperations not ordinarily accessible to the programmer such as parts of multiplication or division operations.

microcomputer—1: A complete general or special-purpose electronic digital computer, with central processing unit, storage, and I-O bus, usually constructed of one LSI chip, with up to 16,000 32-bit words of high-speed internal (main) storage. 2: An analog computer built of microcircuits.

microelectronic—Pertaining to microscopically small electronic circuit elements. The etched, deposited, carved, or otherwise formed passive and active circuit elements, usually on a single piece of semiconducting material, which are fabricated and can only be seen under a microscope, are considered microelectronic circuits. Microelectronic is smaller than microminiature, but larger than molecular.

microfarad—One-millionth of a farad.

microfiche—A photographic negative film in the form of a single sheet containing an array of frames, each frame being a photograph of a page, drawing, hardware item, or similar item. One standard microfiche has a reduction ratio of one to twenty and measures four by six inches, with six rows of twelve frames each. This permits 72 pages of data to be stored on a single sheet of microfiche. (Further clarified by *fiche.*)

microfilm—A photo film used to photograph documents in reduced sizes for storage and subsequent viewing, enlargement, or printing.

microfilm, computer output—1: Microfilm

that contains data from a computer. 2: To place data from a computer or microfilm. Abbreviated as COM.

microform—A data medium that contains microimages, that is, images that cannot be read by the unaided eye.

micrographics—The branch of science and technology concerned with methods and techniques for converting any form of information to or from microform.

microimage—A representation of information too small to be read by the unaided human eye under normal conditions of light, proximity, and other environmental factors.

microinstruction—Small, simple, basic instructions that a computer is capable of executing. Sets of microinstructions might make up macroinstructions or microprograms. Microinstructions, even sets of them, might be permanently wired or built in and so are executed automatically. In variable logic computers, different combinations of microinstructions or microoperations, can be programmed. In most modern computers, microinstructions are not used and the macroinstructions are wired in. (Contrast with *macroinstruction*.)

micromation—The field of microforms associated with automatic data processing by computer, including computer output microfilm (COM). The term is derived from microfilm and automation. Micromation refers to the overall systems that makes use of computers and microfilms.

microminiaturization—A reduction in size of parts further than miniaturization. Miniaturized parts are simply smaller parts packed tighter. Microminiaturized circuits are usually composed of circuits of special construction, such as etched, electrodeposited, evaporated or monolithic integrated etched circuits. Microminiature circuits include extremely small conventional circuit elements, somewhat smaller than miniature but larger than microelectronic or molecular electronic.

micron—A unit of length equal to one-thousandth of a millimeter, one-millionth of a meter, or 39-millionths of an inch.

microprocessor—1: The arithmetic, logic, or control unit of a minicomputer, usually constructed of a single LSI chip. 2: A processor that executes the micro-instructions of a microprogram.

microprogram—A computer program written in the most basic or elemental instructions or subcommands a computer is capable of executing; for example, addition can be programmed in terms of a set of Boolean AND and NOT, or OR and NOT, logic operations; division can be programmed as a set of add and subtract operations, and multiplication as a set of shift and add operations. When the microprograms are written for the macroinstructions, then computer programs may be written in terms of the macroinstructions only. Microprogramming is done to utilize the subcommand structure of a computer in an optimum fashion.

microprogramming—A method of operating the control unit of a computer, wherein each instruction initiates or calls for the execution of a sequence of more elementary instructions; that is, a sequence of small, separate operational steps, called microinstructions, each sequence of small steps being called a microprogram. The microprogram is generally stored in a nonvolatile, fixed storage unit, such as one wired with a matrix of ferrite cores permanently fixing the contents of the storage unit. The instruction repertory of a computer can be altered by changing the storage unit of the microprogram without otherwise affecting the construction of the computer. Thus, control signals corresponding to the instruction are appropriately generated. The method permits machine language coding in which the coder builds machine instructions from the primitive, basic subinstructions (microinstructions) that are built into the hardware of the computer. This allows construction of various analytic instructions as needed from the subcommand or microinstruction structure of the computer. Thus, the instruction repertory is defined in the microinstruction sets, set up and controlled by the fixed storage unit.

microsecond—One-millionth of a second. Usually abbreviated as μsec or usec. Also written as 0.000001 sec, 10^{-6} sec, us, and μs.

microwave—An electromagnetic wave in the super-high-frequency radio band of the radio frequencies; that is, from 3,000 to 30,000 Megahertz.

migration—The movement of atoms within a metal or among metals in contact; for example, silver atoms moving through gold plating to the surface when gold is plated over silver. The silver atoms can then oxidize or otherwise corrode, which prevents the gold from performing its purpose as a protective coating. The problem is encountered in using gold-plated electrical contacts on printed-circuit boards.

millimicrosecond—Same as *nanosecond*.

millisecond—One-thousandth of a second, usually abbreviated as msec. Also written as 0.001 sec, 10^{-3} sec, or ms.

miniaturization—The reduction in the size and the increase in packing density of electrical, electromechanical, mechanical, and electronic parts, components, and circuit elements. Miniaturization results in less space and power requirement and reduced delay in propagation of signals. Thus, equipment can operate faster.

minicomputer—A small computer, about the size of a typewriter, built for on-site installation, that does not require a closely controlled environment, often used for specific tasks, such as manufacturing, mostly of a repetitive nature, and available at a price comparable to the monthly rate of a large scale computer. The minicomputer is usually mass produced, can be maintained by the user or the vendors own staff, and can be programmed and operated by people who are not computer experts. It normally has a small word size, a minimum main storage, accepts a wide variety of peripherals, such as magnetic tape units, discs, and line printers, and is able to communicate with a wide variety of devices, such as plant machinery, laboratory equipment and other computers.

minimal—Pertaining to the least, smallest, shortest, or similar superlative. (Contrast with *maximal*.)

minimal-access routine—Same as *routine, minimal-latency.*

minimal-latency coding—See *coding, minimal-latency.*

minimal-latency program—Same as *routine, minimal-latency.*

minimal-latency programming—Same as *programming, minimum-access.*

minimal-latency routine—See *routine, minimal latency.*

minimal-latency subroutine—Same as *routine, minimal-latency.*

minimum-access coding—Same as *coding, minimal-latency.*

minimum-access programming—See *programming, minimum-access.*

minimum-delay coding—Same as *coding, minimal-latency.*

minimum-distance code—See *code, minimum-distance.*

minor control change—See *change, minor control.*

minor cycle—See *cycle, minor.*

minor total—See *total, minor.*

minority carrier—See *carrier, minority.*

minuend—A quantity from which another quantity, called a subtrahend, is subtracted, to obtain a result called the difference.

minus zone—See *zone, minus.*

mirror-image projection—See *projection, mirror-image.*

MIS—Abbreviation for management information system.

misfeed—The failure of cards, tape, or other media to pass into or through a machine or device in the proper manner. This may be the cause or the result of damaged media or incorrectly sensed data.

MISHAP—An automatic coding system developed by Lockheed Missile Systems Division for use on the Univac 1103 and 1103A computers.

mistake—In data processing, a *human* action causing an unintended and usually undesirable result; for example, the failure of a human operator to carry out an operation in the required or proper manner, such as in writing a program or in

operating equipment. Incorrectly used in place of *error, fault,* and *malfunction,* which have other meanings in data processing. (Synonymous with *gross error,* with *blunder,* and with *booboo.* Contrast with *accuracy,* with *error,* and with *malfunction.*)

MISTRAM—A missile trajectory measurement system developed by General Electric Company.

MIT—1: An abbreviation for master instruction tape. 2: An abbreviation for Massachusetts Institute of Technology.

MITILAC—An automatic coding system developed by the Massachusetts Institute of Technology for use on the IBM 650 computer.

mix, instruction—The set of computer instructions chosen to solve a specified problem. The speed with which a problem is solved is dependent upon the instructions selected and their sequence. If the optimum mix is made the set is called an optimum program.

mix gate—Same as *gate, OR.*

mixed-base notation—Same as *notation, mixed-radix.*

mixed-base numeration system—See *system, mixed-base numeration.*

mixed-radix notation—See *notation, mixed-radix.*

mixed-radix numeration system—See *system, mixed-radix numeration.*

MJS—An automatic coding system developed by the University of California Radiation Laboratory at Livermore, California, for use on the Univac I and II computers.

ML programmer—See *programmer, ML.*

mnemonic—Assisting, or intended to assist, human memory. Mnemonics makes use of established conventions, prior training, and memory aids, such as the use of an abbreviated symbol that assists human memory; for example, *mpy* for multiply and *dvd* for divide. Mnemonic symbols are widely used in computer programming to assist programmers in remembering instruction codes by having the mnemonic symbols serve as the codes or pseudolanguage terms for writing programs.

mnemonic code—See *code, mnemonic.*

mnemonic instruction code—See *code, mnemonic instruction.*

mnemonic operation code—Same as *code, mnemonic instruction.*

MOBL—(Macro-oriented Business Language). A specific set of macroinstructions particularly suited or designed to accomplish specific tasks of business data processing; tasks such as sorting, merging, collating, sifting, searching, etc. MOBL is designed for use with MICA (Macroinstruction Compiler Assembler), which is a preprocessor for the SOS system used on the IBM 7090 computer. The sequence is as follows: MICA receives a MOBL program, which is written in macroinstructions, and converts it into a series of symbolic language instructions, then assembles the symbolic language instructions and produces 7090 machine-language instructions. The Integrated Data Processing Division of North American Rockwell, International Airport, Los Angeles, is associated with MOBL techniques.

mod—In computer programming, any modification made in a program after it is written. Each mod is identified to show that it is the latest modification to the identified program. This identification is known as the mod number.

MOD/DEM—Abbreviation for modulating and demodulating units. (Synonymous with *modem.*)

mode—A status; for example, a manner, method, or fashion, such as binary mode, interpretive mode, parallel mode, or the most frequent value in the statistical sense. Computers may operate in various modes, subject to expression of option and nature of application.

mode, access—In COBOL programming language, the name of the technique used to obtain a specific record from, or to place a specific record into, a file held in a mass storage device.

mode, card—A computer operational status in which punched cards are being read or punched.

mode, conversational—A mode of operation of a data processing system such that the user, at an input-output terminal, carries on a conversation or dialogue with the system. As each unit of input data is entered a prompt response is obtained from the system. Thus, a sequence of runs can take place between the user and the system such that the average time of and between runs is of the order of magnitude typical for a conversation among humans. (Synonymous with *interactive mode.*)

mode, interactive—Same as *mode, conversationaal.*

mode, load—Data transmission such that data delimiters are transmitted with the data. (Contrast with *mode, move.*)

mode, move—Data transmission such that data delimiters are not transmitted with the data. (Contrast with *mode, load.*)

mode, noisy—A mode of floating-point arithmetic operation associated with normalization of numerals in which digits other than zero are introduced in the low order, or less significant, positions during the left shift.

mode, system production—A mode of operating a computer operating system in such a manner that an operating environment is created to execute user programs as efficiently as possible, usually without the use of special debugging facilities that are made available to programs that are executed in the system test mode. (Contrast with *mode, system test.*)

mode, system test—A mode of operating a computer operating system in such a

manner that an operating environment is created in order that executing programs are tested, usually with special debugging facilities that are not made available to programs that are executed in the production mode. (Contrast with *mode, system production.*)

model, deterministic—In computer simulation, a representation of a concept, system, model, or operation that has a unique output for each given set of inputs. (Contrast with *model, stochastic.*)

model, dynamic—In computer simulation, a model in which one or more significant variables are functions of time. (Contrast with *model, static.*)

model, expected-value—In computer simulation, a model in which the variables or parameters are assigned expected values, rather than be allowed to assume values determined purely by chance. The expected values are the values that are most probable according to available facts and known relationships.

model, mathematical—1: A mathematical representation, usually of a process, device, or concept, which permits mathematical manipulation of variables as a means of determining how the process, device, or concept would behave in various situations, such as under application of specific stimulation. Mathematical models are often used as a step in the application of simulation techniques, such as the simulation of an industrial process on a digital computer. (Further clarified by *simulate.*) 2: In computer simulation, an explicit mathematical representation of a system, concept, model, or operation with all probabilities elements either removed or replaced with expected or fixed value elements or variables.

model, probabilistic—Same as *model, stochastic.*

model, static—In computer simulation, a model in which none of the variables are functions of time. (Contrast with *model, dynamic.*)

model, stochastic—In computer simulation, a model in which functional relationships among component parts of the model depend upon chance parameters that affect the values of variables and in which the output for given input can be predicted only in a probabilistic sense. (Contrast with *model, deterministic.* Synonymous with *probabilistic model.*)

modem—(Modulator-demodulator). The modulator and demodulator circuits of a carrier terminal are normally mounted together on a single panel and may have common elements. Thus, *modem* is used to refer to this portion of a carrier terminal. (Synonymous with *MOD/DEM.*)

modification, address—1: The process of changing the address part of a computer instruction. Address modification may be accomplished through the use of computer instructions developed from the results obtained thus far in the execution of a program. The process may be performed automatically, as in indirect addressing or programmed address modification. 2: An arithmetic, algebraic, logic, or syntactic operation that is performed on an address. 3: The change that is produced by performing an arithmetic or logic operation on an address. 4: The result obtained by performing an arithmetic or logic operation on an address, that is, the resulting address.

modifier—In computer programming, a word or quantity used to alter an instruction so as to cause the interpretation and execution of an instruction that is different from the original instruction; for example, an index tag, an indirect address tag, cycle index, or base address. Thus, the modifier may· alter the address, the operation, or other parts of an instruction word, such as flags or tags. The modifier is usually stored in an index register for ready reference. (Synonymous with *index word*.)

modifier, instruction—A computer word or a part of a computer word that alters an instruction.

modifier register—Same as *register, index*.

modify—In computer programming, to alter an instruction in a prescribed way, thus producing another instruction, which either may be executed or further modified. The instruction to be modified is sometimes called the presumptive or unmodified instruction, and the modified instruction, which is actually executed, is sometimes called the effective or actual instruction. The operation, called modification, involves one or more words or parts of words, called modifiers, or index words, which are combined with the presumptive instruction in some logical manner in the arithmetic and logic unit of the computer. Instruction modification is usually programmed and accomplished by the computer itself. It is this capability of an internally-stored-program digital computer to modify and even write its o w n instructions that m a k e s the computer so powerful. The most common form of instruction modification is modification of the address part, through the use of index registers containing a base address. In some applications, the modification is only temporary and affects only the current execution of the instruction.

modular—The property of a system that permits it to be constructed or assembled from sets of components or subassemblies; for example, a computer assembly technique in which logic packages containing sets of gates are wired together to form the computer, or the assembly of a large scale computer from a set of major components, such as storage units, input units, output units, logic units, buffers, control units, and communications links. Modularity permits maximum utilization of equipment and variation of system capability to meet a specific application. (Contrast with *polymorphic*.)

modular connector—See *connector, modular*.

modulation—The process of varying some characteristic of a wave in accordance with another wave; for example, the process of varying the radio frequency of one wave (a carrier) in accordance with the audio frequency of another wave (modulator); or the process of varying the amplitude of a radio-frequency carrier with the audio-frequency amplitude, thus having the audio wave serve as the amplitude envelope of the radio wave. Upon demodulation, or detection, the carrier is eliminated and the original audio wave is recovered. In acoustic delay-line storage units for digital computers, the high-frequency carrier wave is modulated by the binary pulses, so that each binary one, for example, is represented by a packet of radio-frequency waves. Thus, the carrier is modulated in accordance with the intelligence-bearing signal. Keying, or turning a carrier wave on and off, as in Morse code transmission, is a form of modulation, specifically amplitude modulation.

modulation, amplitude—Modulation in which the amplitude of the carrier wave is varied in accordance with the instantaneous value of the modulating, or intelligence bearing, signal. Abbreviated AM. (Further clarified by *carrier (1)*.)

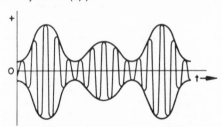

Amplitude modulation *of a carrier wave*.

modulation, angle—Modulation in which the phase angle (leading or lagging a given reference) of the sine wave carrier is varied in accordance with the intelligence-bearing signal. Phase and frequency modulation are specific forms of angle modulation.

modulation, dipole—A method of representing binary digits on a magnetic surface medium, such as drums, discs, tapes, or cards, in which a specified part of each cell is magnetically saturated in one of two opposing senses, depending on the digit value represented, the remainder of the cell being magnetized in a predetermined sense that remains fixed.

modulation, frequency—Modulation in which the instantaneous frequency of a sine wave carrier is caused to depart from its reference frequency by an amount proportional to the instantaneous value of the modulating wave. The shift in frequency of the sine wave carrier varies in accordance with the amplitude of the modulating signal. Frequency modulation is a form of angle modulation.

Abbreviated FM. (Further clarified by *carrier (1)*.)

modulation, high-level—Modulation at a point in a system where the power level approximates that at the output of the system. (Contrast with *modulation, low-level*.)

modulation, low-level—Modulation at a point in a system where the power level is low compared with the power level at the output of the system. (Contrast with *modulation, high-level*.)

modulation, multiple—Modulation in which the modulated wave from one process becomes the modulating wave for the next.

modulation, phase—1: In communications, modulation in which the electrical angle is varied in accordance with the instantaneous value of the amplitude of the modulating signal. The angle is measured relative to the unmodulated carrier angle. (Further clarified by *carrier*.) 2: In magnetic tape recording, a method of representing binary digits on a magnetic surface, such as tape, disc, drum or card, in which each cell is divided into two parts that are magnetically saturated in opposing senses, the sequence of these senses indicating the value of the binary digit represented.

modulation, pulse—The modulation of a pulse train or carrier; that is, a series of pulses bearing no intelligence, such as is obtained from a pulse generating source, so that the amplitude, duration, position, or time or frequency of occurrence of the individual pulses or series of them, is caused to vary in accordance with some impressed signal.

modulation, pulse-amplitude—Modulation in which the amplitude of a series of pulses bearing no intelligence, such as is obtained from a pulse generating source, is varied in accordance with a modulating signal.

modulation, pulse-code—Modulation in which the amplitude of the modulating signal is sampled and each sample is quantized; that is, represented by a set of pulses that expresses a numerical value proportional to the instantaneous value of the modulating signal. Each set of pulses may represent a different number. Different values of the modulating signal amplitude are represented by correspondingly different shapes, sizes, quantities, or spacings of pulses in each set. For example, if pulses, all of the same shape, are appropriately spaced, binary numerals can be represented whose values are directly proportional to the modulating signal amplitude, as is accomplished in some analog-digital converters. Thus, sequences of these numerals can describe the shape of the modulating signal.

modulation, pulse-duration—Same as *modulation, pulse-length*.

modulation, pulse-frequency—Modulation in which the pulse repetition frequency of the pulse carrier is varied in accordance with the modulating signal's frequency, amplitude, or other characteristic. The

carrier is a pulse wave rather than a sine wave. However, a sine wave might be considered as a special case of a pulse wave.

modulation, pulse-length—Modulation in which the time duration of the pulses of a pulse-type carrier is varied in accordance with a characteristic of the modulating wave, such as its amplitude. The modulating wave may vary the time of occurrence of the leading edge, trailing edge, or both edges, of the individual pulses in order to achieve pulse-length modulation. (Synonymous with *pulse-duration modulation* and *pulse-width modulation*.)

modulation, pulse-position—Modulation of a pulse-type carrier in which the pulse time of occurrence, with reference to the unmodulated position time, is varied in accordance with a characteristic of the modulating signal, such as its amplitude. This mode of modulation corresponds to phase modulation of a sine wave carrier. Pulse-position modulation, in actual practice, is equivalent to the introduction of a delay time proportional to the value of the modulating signal.

modulation, pulse-time—Modulation in which the time of occurrence of some characteristic or feature of the carrier wave pulses are varied in accordance with a modulating signal. Pulse-time modulation includes pulse-position modulation, pulse-length, pulse-duration, and pulse-width modulation.

modulation, pulse-width—Same as *modulation, pulse-length*.

modulation, two-tone—In telegraph operation, a modulation method in which two different carrier frequencies are employed for the two signal conditions of the code. The transition from one frequency to the other is abrupt, with resulting phase discontinuities.

modulation frequency—See *frequency, modulation*.

modulation recording, polarized dipole—Same as *recording, polarized return-to-zero*.

modulation recording, phase—See *recording, phase modulation*.

modulator—A device that receives two signals and causes a characteristic of one of the signals to vary in accordance with a characteristic of the other. The output signal is varied, or modulated, according to the modulating signal; for example, a device that receives a high-frequency carrier and a voice wave, and in which the amplitude of the voice wave causes the amplitude of the carrier frequency (envelope) to vary.

modulator amplifier, impact—See *amplifier, impact modulator*.

module—An interchangeable unit that contains components, parts, or subunits; for example, a logic subunit, such as a printed-circuit card, that may be easily detached from the whole system; a machine subassembly that has characteristics common to more than one machine or device; major components of a computing system, such as tape units, drums, processors, and storage planes; or other pluggable units.

module, load—A computer program that is in a form suitable for transfer into main storage for execution.

module, object—1: A program module, routine, subroutine or part of a subroutine, prepared by an assembler or compiler for execution by a computer. 2: A program module that is the output of a single execution of a language processor and that is input to a linkage editor or that serves as a load module.

module, program—A discrete and identifiable part of a program. The module is usually the input to or output from a single execution of a language processor or linkage editor. The module can be a part of a source, object, or load program. The program module is usually handled as a unit with respect to compiling and loading.

module, programming—A set of computer program instructions treated as a unit by an assembler, compiler, translator, loader or other routine or subroutine.

module, refreshable program—A computer program module that can be replaced dynamically, that is, during its execution, without changing the sequence of execution or the results of the processing that is underway. Thus, a refreshable program module can never be modified by itself, or be modified by another program module, during execution.

module, relocatable program—A computer program module, such as an object program module or a load program module, that can be moved within main storage.

module, sort—In a computer operating system, a program module that performs a sort or a sort-merge function.

module generation, load—See *generation, load module.*

modulo—A mathematical operator that yields the remainder of a division operation. Thus, decimal 46 modulo-6 to 4.

modulo-n check—See *check, modulo-n.*

modulo-n counter—See *counter, modulo-n.*

modulo-n residue—See *residue, modulo-n.*

modulo-two sum—Same as *operatio non-equivalence.*

modulo-two sum gate—Same as *gate, exclusive-OR.*

moisture-proof paper card—See *card, moisture-proof paper.*

MOL—An abbreviation for machine-oriented language.

molecular electronic—See *electronic, molecular.*

monadic operation—See *operation, monadic.*

monadic operator—See *operator, monadic.*

monitor—To supervise and verify the correct operation of a program during its execution, usually by a diagnostic routine used from time to time to answer questions about the program. Usually, significant departures from the norm are indicated. A primary purpose of monitoring is to control the operation of several unrelated routines and machine runs so that the computer is used efficiently and effectively. A monitor may also be a device or routine used to warn of faults.

monitor program—Same as *program, control.*

monitor routine—Same as *routine, executive.*

monitor system—Same as *system, operating.*

monitor unit—See *unit, monitor.*

monitoring, program-limit—The monitoring of computer programs, tasks, and jobs to insure that certain system or user limits and bounds are not exceeded, such as limits on central processing unit time, main storage space, numbers of cards, and numbers of output channels.

monitoring event—In a computer operating system, the maintenance of control over the execution of programs, such as processing interrupts, trapping error conditions, notifying on external conditions that require attention, and allocating central processing unit time to contending programs.

monolithic integrated circuit—See *circuit, monolithic integrated.*

monostable—A device that has one stable state; for example, a spring, a one-shot multivibrator, or a right circular cone on its base. The monostable device will return to its stable state when any applied force causing it to depart from its stable state is removed. In most instances, damped oscillations will occur. (Contrast with *bistable.*)

monostable circuit—See *circuit, monostable.*

monostable multivibrator—Same as *multivibrator, one-shot.*

monostable trigger—Same as *multivibrator, one-shot.*

monte carlo—Statistical sampling techniques involved in obtaining probabilistic approximations to the solution of mathematical or physical problems. Digital computers, because of inherent high speed in handling numbers, lend themselves to trial and error techniques, as exemplified by monte carlo methods. The methods of computation are based on probability theory using random numbers and statistical methods to find solutions to various types of problems. The name is derived from the random occurrence of numbers obtained from honest dice, roulette wheels, and pin-wheels, such as are used in the casinos of Monte Carlo.

monte carlo method—See *method, monte carlo.*

Moore's Law—An information system will tend not to be used whenever it is more painful and troublesome for an individual to have information than for him not to have it.

morpheme—An element or property of language that indicates relationships between words or expressed ideas or images in sentences, such as a meaningful linguistic unit that contains no smaller meaningful parts; a connective, such as and, or, with, or not, that performs a meaningful function; or a phrase or sentence. (Further clarified by *semanteme* and by *primitive.*)

morphology—The branch of linguistic study that deals with the history and functions of inflections and derivational forms of language. Morphological studies are required before satisfactory mechanical translation of languages is possible through the use of electronic digital computers and computer programs. (Related to *semantics.*)

mortem, post—See *post mortem.*

MOSAIC 636—(Macro-Operation Symbolic Assembler and Information Compiler). A programming language which specifies the compilation of subroutines on the Daystrom 636 automatic data-processing system.

most significant digit—See *digit, most significant.*

motor, integrating—A direct-current (d-c) motor, usually of the permanent magnet type and designed to give a constant ratio of output shaft rotational speed to input voltage. Thus, the angle of rotation of the shaft is proportional to the integral, with respect to time, of the applied voltage. Integrating motors are often used in electromechanical types of analog computers. The output can also be used to mechanically actuate devices such as radar antennas and industrial process control equipment. (Synonymous with *messmotor.*)

motor, mess—Same as *motor, integrating.*

mounted, back—See *back-mounted.*

mouth—The cable entrance of a connector barrel.

mouth, belled—A flared or widened entrance to the barrel of an electrical connector, permitting easier insertion of the conductor.

move mode—See *mode, move.*

move-mode buffering—See *buffering, move-mode.*

movement data, air—See *data, air-movement.*

MQ—An abbreviation for the multiplier-quotient register in some electronic digital computers.

ms—An abbreviation for millisecond, or one-thousandth part of a second.

MSD—An abbreviation for most significant digit.

MSI—Medium scale integrated circuits.

MT—An abbreviation for mechanical translation or machine translation.

MTBF—An abbreviation of mean-time-between failures.

MTTF—An abbreviation of mean-time-to-failure.

MTTR—Mean-time-to-repair.

multiaddress—Same as *address, multiple.*

multiaddress instruction—Same as *instruction, multiple-address.*

multiaspect—Information storage and retrieval systems that permit more than one aspect; for example, subject, discipline, or topic, information to be used in combination to effect identification, selection, and retrieval of information from the files.

multicomputer—A computing system in which there are many arithmetic and logic units operating in parallel, usually on the same program, but also possible on several programs.

multicomputing unit—Same as *multiprocessor.*

multicycle feeding—Same as *feeding, multiread.*

multidimensional language—See *language, multidimensional.*

multifile search—See *search, multifile.*

multilevel addressing—Same as *addressing, indirect.*

multipass sort—See *sort, multipass.*

multiple access—See *access, multiple.*

multiple-address—See *address, multiple.*

multiple-address code—See *code, multiple-address.*

multiple-address instruction—See *instruction, multiple-address.*

multiple-address message—See *message, multiple-address.*

multiple-aperture core—See *core, multiple-aperture.*

multiple arithmetic—See *arithmetic, multiple.*

multiple-aspect indexing—Same as *indexing, coordinate.*

multiple connector—See *connector, multiple.*

multiple-length numeral—See *numeral, multiple-length.*

multiple-length working—See *working, multiple-length.*

multiple modulation—See *modulation, multiple.*

multiple precision—See *precision, multiple.*

multiple punch—See *punch, multiple.*

multiplex—1: To interleave or simultaneously transmit two or more messages on a single channel. 2: The arranging of the capability of a transmission facility or link into two or more channels so as to permit more than one message to be transmitted at a time. 3: To connect input/output channels to designated peripheral devices. 4: To execute two or more functions at the same time; for example, to coordinate several input, output, or calculation operations at the same time, or to use a communication to transmit two or more messages at the same time. 5: To arrange buffering in such a manner that, when transferring data from several storage devices operating at relatively low transfer rates to one storage device operating at a high transfer rate, the high-speed device is not obliged to wait for the low-speed units.

multiplex, frequency-division—A signaling process or device in which each signal channel modulates a separate subcarrier, the subcarrier frequency being spaced to avoid overlapping of the subcarrier sidebands, and the selection and demodulation of each signal channel is accomplished on the basis of its frequency.

multiplex, time-division—A signaling process or device in which two or more signals or messages are sent on the same channel using different time intervals for the different signals. (Synonymous with *chop.*)

multiplex data terminal—See *terminal, multiplex data.*

multiplexed operation—See *operation, multiplexed.*

multiplexor—A device that is capable of interleaving the events of two or more activities or that is capable of distributing the events of an interleaved sequence to the respective activities, operations, systems, or processes.

multiplexor, isochronous—A multiplexor that can interleave two time-independent data streams into one higher-speed stream independent of the master timing control required by a synchronous multiplexor. (Contrast with *multiplexor, synchronous.*)

multiplexor, synchronous—A multiplexor that can time interleave two data streams into one higher-speed stream on a single line, circuit, or channel. In a system that uses these types of multiplexors, all of the peripheral equipment in the system must be under the control of a master synchronizing device or clock. (Contrast with *multiplexor, isochronous.*)

multiplicand—A quantity, expressed as a numeral, that is, or is to be, multiplied by another quantity, called the multiplier. The result of the arithmetic operation of multiplication is called the product.

multiplication—An arithmetic process or operation that produces the product of two numbers; for example, 6 X 5 = 30 is a multiplication operation. The numbers being multiplied are called the multiplicand and the multiplier. In binary computers, multiplication is accomplished by a process of shifting and adding. (Contrast with *multiply, logic.*)

multiplication, arithmetic—Same as *multiplication.*

multiplier—1: A quantity, expressed as a numeral, that is or is to be used to multiply another quantity, called the multiplicand. The result of the arithmetic operation of multiplication is called the product. **2:** A device that has two or more inputs and whose output is a representation of the product of the quantities represented by the input signals.

multiplier, analog—A device that generates an analog product from two or more analog input signals, by having the output variable proportional to the product of the input variables. Usually, a varying output

product signal is generated that is proportional to the instantaneous value of the varying input signals. If input and output signals are continuous, the device is then called a function multiplier, such as a crossed-fields multiplier or a servomultiplier.

multiplier, crossed-fields—An analog device incorporating a cathode-ray tube, usually especially designed for this purpose, in which one input signal produces a proportional electrostatic field perpendicular to the axis of the tube. The other input signal, representing the other variable, produces an axial magnetic field. The resulting deflection of the beam perpendicular to the two fields is proportional to the product of the input signals. The output signal is obtained from a servo system, incorporating sensing and deflecting electrodes, that annuls the deflection and produces an output signal proportional to the product of the two input signals.

multiplier, digital—A device that generates a digital product from the digital representation of two numbers. A digital product may be formed by additions of the multiplicand, in accordance with the value of the digits in the multiplier. In the case of binary digital multiplication, it is necessary only to shift the multiplicand and add it to the product if the multiplier digit is a one, and just shift the multiplicand without adding, if the multiplier digit is a zero, for each successive digit of the multiplier.

multiplier, function—A device that generates a continuously varying analog representation of a product of two continuously varying analog input signals, as some independent variable, such as time or distance, changes. (Synonymous with *variable multiplier.*)

multiplier, mark-space—An analog multiplier, in which one input variable, represented as a current or voltage, is used to control the mark-to-space ratio of a repetitive rectangular wave, whose amplitude is made proportional to the other variable also represented by a current or voltage. The output voltage, proportional to the area of the pulse voltage-time curve, represents the product of the input variables. The output voltage or current waveform is averaged by a smoothing circuit. Since the average is still proportional to the area under the pulse curves, with a fixed-time base, the average value is proportional to the product of the input variables. (Synonymous with *time-division multiplier.*)

multiplier, potentiometer—Same as *servomultiplier.*

multiplier, quarter-squares—An analog multiplier whose operation is based on the identity $xy = (1/4)(x + y)^2 - (1/4)(x - y)^2$, and contains sign-reversal units, adders, and square-law function generators that are usually electronic, using the principle of a diode function generator. The unit accomplishes multiplication by summing, differencing, squaring, and dividing by four, all of which are relatively simple to accomplish, compared to multiplication.

multiplier, servo—See *servomultiplier.*

multiplier, time-division—Same as *multiplier, mark-space.*

multiplier, variable—Same as *multiplier, function.*

multiplier coefficient unit—Same as *scalar.*

multiplier coefficient unit, constant—Same as *scalar.*

multiplier-quotient register—See *register, multiplier-quotient.*

multiply, logic—An operation performed in the Boolean algebra on two binary digits (operands) at a time such that the result is a one if and only if both digits are a one, and a zero if either digit, or both, is a zero. The operator is referred to as the AND operator. The word AND comes from the English statement, "if, and only if, one digit *and* the other digit are a one, the result (logic product) is a one. the operation is related to arithmetic multiplication; that is, $1 \cdot 0 = 0$, $0 \cdot 1 = 0$, $0 \cdot 0 = 0$, and $1 \cdot 1 = 1$. The · is often used to indicate logical multiplication. Sometimes no sign at all is used; that is, if A and B are operands, then AB is a statement indicating the logic product. (Synonymous with *logical multiply*. Further clarified by *AND*. Contrast with *OR*, with *add, logic,* and with *multiplication*. Further clarified by *product, logic*.)

multiply, logical—Same as *multiply, logic.*

multiply operation—See *operation, multiply.*

multiplying punch—Same as *punch, calculating.*

multipoint circuit—See *circuit, multipoint.*

multipoint network—See *network, multipoint.*

multiprocessing—1: Pertaining to either the simultaneous or the interleaved execution, or both, of two or more programs or sequences of instructions by a computer component, a computer, or a computer network. Thus, multiprocessing may be accomplished by multiprogramming, parallel processing, or both. 2: A manner of operating a computer having two or more arithmetic or logic units such that two or more computer programs are executed simultaneously.

multiprocessor—A computer having multiple arithmetic or logic units that can be used simultaneously. Two or more programs, or parts of the same program, can be run on a multiprocessor at the same time. Thus, parallel processing can be accomplished by multiprogramming. (Synonymous with *multicomputing unit*. Further clarified by *multiprogramming;* by *processing, parallel;* and by *multiprocessing*.)

multiprogramming—Pertaining to the interleaved execution of two or more programs by a computer or data-processing system. Thus, two or more programs share the time of a given piece of

equipment on a one-at-a-time basis; however, the outward appearances might be that the several programs are being executed simultaneously. Improved utilization of computer components can thus be achieved, since other programs can be executed while a unit might otherwise be waiting for completion of some other operation, such as a search, look-up, storage, or input-output operation. The processor, such as an arithmetic unit, might be directed to switch back and forth among programs under control of a master-control program. (Synonymous with *multirunning*. Contrast with *processing, parallel*.)

multiread feeding—See *feeding, multiread.*

multirunning—Same as *multiprogramming.*

multisequencing—The simultaneous execution of several parts of a program by separate central processing units.

multitasking—Pertaining to the concurrent execution of two or more tasks by a computer, usually under program control.

multivibrator, astable—Same as *multivibrator, free-running.*

multivibrator, bistable—Same as *flip-flop.*

multivibrator, free-running—An oscillator that generates desired shapes of signals, usually nonsinusoidal shapes and usually of the relaxation type. Operation is dependent upon two interacting circuits; for example, two tubes or transistors so connected that one governs the operation of the other; one tube causes the charging of a capacitor, causing a rise in voltage, which triggers the other tube to discharge the capacitor, causing an output voltage wave. The name implies a signal rich in harmonic content or multiplicity of frequencies. (Synonymous with *astable multivibrator*.)

multivibrator, monostable—Same as *multivibrator, one-shot.*

multivibrator, one-shot—A type of multivibrator that has one stable or quasistable state and one unstable state and that goes through a complete change cycle; that is, stable state to unstable state and return, with each triggering action. The circuit provides a single signal of proper form and timing from a varying shaped, randomly timed signal. Thus, upon receipt of a trigger signal, it assumes another state for a specified length of time, at the end of which it returns, of its own accord, to its original state. (Synonymous with *Kipp relay*, with *single-shot multivibrator*, with *monostable multivibrator*, with *monostable trigger*, and with *start-stop multivibrator*.)

multivibrator, single-shot—Same as *multivibrator, one-shot.*

multivibrator, start-stop—Same as *multivibrator, one-shot.*

mutual information—Same as *content, transinformation.*

Mylar—A type of polyester plastic film widely used as a base for magnetic tape. Mylar is a registered trademark of E. I. DuPont de Nemours and Company.

Mylar tape—See *tape, Mylar.*

Mystic–An automatic coding system for computer programming developed by the United States Air Force Missile Test Center, Patrick Air Force Base, for use on the Univac 1103 and 1103A and the IBM 650 and IBM 704 computers.

n

n-address instruction–See *instruction, n-address.*

n-address-instruction format–See *format, n-address-instruction.*

n-adic–Pertaining to a selection, choice, or condition that has n possible values or states. (Synonymous with *n-ary.*)

n-adic Boolean operation–See *operation, n-adic Boolean.*

n-adic operation–See *operation, n-adic.*

n-ary–Same as *n-adic.*

n-ary Boolean operation–Same as *operation, n-adic Boolean.*

n-ary operation–Same as *operation, n-adic.*

n-ary operator–See *operator, n-ary.*

n-bit byte–See *byte, n-bit.*

n-core-per-bit storage–See *storage, n-core-per-bit.*

N-cube–In switching theory, two N-1 cubes with corresponding points connected.

N-level logic–See *logic, N-level.*

N-plus-one-address instruction–See *instruction, N-plus-one-address.*

N-tuple–A collection or multiplicity of an arbitrary number of elements, specified by N; for example, $x_1, x_2, x_3, \ldots, x_N$.

n-tuple-length register–See *register, n-tuple-length.*

n-tuple register–Same as *register, n-tuple-length.*

n-type semiconductor–See *semiconductor, n-type.*

N-way switch–Same as *connector, variable.*

NAK–The negative acknowledge character.

name–One or more words used to identify a single member or other subset of a class of persons, places, things, or concepts. Usually names are the whole or part of a label, whereas the label includes the medium on which it is recorded or represented. Thus, for a magnetic tape, the name written on the leader may together form the label. If the label is cut off, the tape still has a name, but its label is gone. A computer with a nameplate is labeled. If the nameplate is removed, the machine is no longer labeled, but it still has a name.

name, data–An identifier, label or tag for an item of data; for example, estimated arrival time.

name, qualified–A data name with its specification as to which class it belongs to in a classification system.

NAND–A logical operator having the property that if P is a statement, Q is a statement, R is a statement, . . . , then the NAND of P, Q, R,. . . is true if at least one statement is false, false if all statements are true. (Synonymous with *NAND operator.*)

A Venn diagram showing the NAND logic function.

NAND element–Same as *gate, NAND.*

NAND gate–See *gate, NAND.*

NAND operation–Same as *operation, non-conjunction.*

NAND operator–Same as *NAND.*

nanosecond–One-billionth of a second, usually abbreviated as mμsec. Also written as 10^{-9} sec. In some European countries, to avoid confusion with the use of billion and billionth, a nanosecond is also described as one-thousandth of a millionth of a second. (Synonymous with *milli-microsecond* and with *billisecond.*)

nanosecond circuit–See *circuit, nanosecond.*

NANWEP–(Navy Numerical Weather Prediction). A development of the Control Data Corporation, utilizing digital computers.

NASA–National Aeronautics and Space Administration.

NAT–An abbreviation for natural units of information.

native language–Same as *language, machine-oriented.*

natural-function generator–Same as *generator, analytical-function.*

natural language—See *language, natural*.
natural-law generator—Same as *generator, analytical-function*.
natural number—See *number, natural*.
natural unit, information-content—See *unit, information-content natural*.
Naur form, Backus—Same as *form, Backus normal*.
NCA—(Northwest Computing Association). An organization devoted to mutual support in computing affairs and advancement of computer art, located at Box 836, Seahurst, Washington.
NDR—Nondestructive read.
NDRO—(Non-destructive Read Out). Pertaining to the interrogation of the nondestructive type of storage systems. (Further clarified by *storage, nondestructive* and by *read, nondestructive*.)
NEAT—(National Cash Register Electronic Autocoding Technique). A computer programming language and compiler developed by National Cash Register Company for use on NCR computer systems.
needle—In edge-punched cards, a long wire probe used on decks of cards. When the needle is inserted in the margin of a deck and the deck is vibrated, all cards having a notch cut at the hole position will drop out; all having just a hole will be retained.
negate—To perform the logic NOT operation. (Further clarified by *NOT* and by *element, negation*.)
negation—Same as *NOT*.
negation gate—Same as *element, negation*.
negative—In combinational logic gating, the same as NOT. Thus negative AND is the same as NOT AND, or NAND; negative OR is the same as NOT OR, or NOR; and negative A is the same as NOT A, rather than minus A, as it might be in the arithmetic sense.
negative acknowledge character—See *character, negative acknowledge*.
negative feedback—See *feedback, negative*.
negative film—See *film, negative*.
negative (A ignore B) gate—See *gate, negative (A ignore B)*.
negative (A implies B) gate—Same as *gate, A AND NOT B*.
negative AND gate—Same as *gate, NAND*.
negative (B ignore A) gate—See *gate, negative (B ignore A)*.
negative (B implies A) gate—Same as *gate, B AND NOT A*.
negative ignore gate—1: Same as *gate, negative (A ignore B)*. 2: Same as *gate, negative (B ignore A)*.
negative-OR gate—Same as *gate, OR*.
negator—Same as *element, negation*.
neither-NOR gate—Same as *gate, NOR*.
neither-NOR operation—Same as *operation, non-disjunction*.
NELIAC—(Naval Electronics Laboratory International Algebraic Compiler). An algebraic compiler in common use on many machines, such as the M-460,

M-490, and CDC 1604 computers at the Naval Electronics Laboratory; the IBM 704 computer at the University of California, Berkeley; the IBM 709 computer at Ramo-Wooldridge; and the IBM 7090 at the Lockheed Missiles and Space Division.
nest—1: To include an item, such as a subroutine or block of data, within a larger similar item; for example, including in a subroutine, a loop of instructions that contains an inner loop. Subroutines may be nested by placing a subroutine in a subroutine of higher order. 2: To evaluate an nth-degree polynomial with a particular algorithm that uses $(n - 1)$ multiply and $(n - 1)$ add operations in succession.
nesting storage—Same as *storage, push-down*.
network—An interconnected set of points or objects, such as electrical circuit elements, power stations, communications equipment, or terminals; for example, a telephone system or a power distribution system.
network, analog—A network, usually electrical, which is used to represent, simulate, or serve as a model for a usually nonelectrical system; for example, a mechanical system. Thus, a network of resistors, capacitors, inductors, and amplifiers can be an analog network for a mechanical system of springs, weights, frictional surfaces, and motors. Equations written for the network pertain to the physical system. Stimuli applied to the network can be used to study the effect of a corresponding stimuli applied to the physical system. Usually differential equations express the relationships between the physical and corresponding electrical quantities involved. (Further clarified by *analog* and by *analog, network*.)

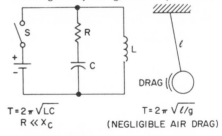

$$T = 2\pi \sqrt{LC}$$
$$R \ll X_C$$

$$T = 2\pi \sqrt{\ell/g}$$
(NEGLIGIBLE AIR DRAG)

Periods of oscillation can be made the same for the pendulum on the right and for the analog network on the left.

network, computer—Two or more interconnected computers. A computer network permits geographical distribution of computer capability to meet local information processing needs and at the same time permits local available capacity to meet requirements from remote locations that are unable to handle local needs. Parallel processing may also be used by having several processors simultaneously occupied with different parts of the same general problem. Data and programs can be transmitted around the network. For information storage and retrieval systems, a network of computers permits multipoint entry, query analysis, locally maintained data banks, availability of local data banks to all stations of the network, use of common languages, central control points or information switching centers, and mutual support activities, such as rapid data transfer, immediate response, reduced interference with local missions, and a reduced necessity for new centralized facilities.

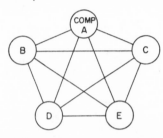

A five-station computer network.

network, consistent—In computer simulation, a network in which one and only one specific event occurs in each and every path. (Contrast with *network, inconsistent.*)

network, data—An assembly of data terminal equipment, data communication equipment, and data links.

network, inconsistent—In computer simulation, a network in which a specific event occurs more than once in at least one of the paths of the network. (Contrast with *network, consistent.*)

network, leased-line—A communications network consisting of leased communication channels and therefore for the exclusive use of one party or his designee. (Synonymous with *private wire network.*)

network, multipoint—A data network configuration in which a connection is made among three or more terminal installations and that usually includes switching facilities.

network, private telephone—A network consisting of leased voice grade telephone lines for the exclusive use of one party or his designee.

network, private wire—Same as *network, leased-line.*

network analog—See *analog, network.*

network analyzer—See *analyzer, network.*

network calculator—Same as *analyzer, network.*

neutral zone—See *zone, neutral.*

new-line character—See *character, new-line.*

nexus—A connection or interconnection, such as a tie, link, or network of modes and branches.

NICAP—An assembler developed by the University of Illinois for use on the ILLIAC II computer.

nickel delay-line—See *delay-line, nickel.*

nim—A game, wherein a number of piles of objects, each containing any number of objects, is set forth. Each of two contestants is allowed, in turn, to take any number of objects from any one pile. The one who takes the last object wins or loses, as is decided in the beginning. It is a trivial game and has been used in its various forms to test computers.

nines check—Same as *check, casting-out-nines.*

nines complement—See *complement, nines.*

ninety-column card—See *card, ninety-column.*

Nixie light—See *light, Nixie.*

Nixie tube—Same as *light, Nixie.*

NL—The new-line character.

NMAA—National Machine Accountants Association.

no-address instruction—See *instruction, no-address.*

no-charge machine-fault time—See *time, no-charge machine-fault.*

no-charge nonmachine-fault time—See *time, no-charge nonmachine-fault.*

no-op—No-operation instruction.

no-op instruction—Same as *instruction, dummy.*

no-operation instruction—Same as *instruction, dummy.*

node—1: A point of convergence on a diagram. Nodes may be used to designate a state, an event, time coincidence, or convergence of paths or flow. 2: A point of divergence on a diagram; for example, in a tree structure, a point at which subordinate items, such as data, originate.

noise—1: Random variations of one or more characteristics of any entity, such as voltage, current, sound or data. Noise is usually unwanted, although some types of noise are used. In the case of data, the noise, appearing as meaningless extra bits, characters, or words, must be removed from the data at the time they are used. 2: In communications, the sum of all unwanted or disturbing power introduced into a communication system from any sources, such as crosstalk, power induction, atmospheric conditions, or electronic circuit components. (Synonymous with *static (2).*)

noise level, carrier—See *level, carrier noise.*

noise ratio—See *ratio, noise.*

noisy mode—See *mode, noisy.*

NOMA—National Office Management Association.

nominal bandwidth—See *bandwidth, nominal.*

nonarithmetic shift—Same as *shift, cyclic.*

nonconjunction gate—Same as *gate, NAND.*

nonconjunction operation—See *operation, nonconjunction.*

nondestructive addition—See *addition, nondestructive.*

nondestructive read—See *read, nondestructive.*

nondestructive read-out—See *NDRO.*

nondestructive storage—See *storage, nondestructive.*

nondisjunction gate—Same as *gate, NOR.*

nondisjunction operation—See *operation, nondisjunction.*

nonequality gate—Same as *gate, exclusive-OR.*

nonequivalence gate—Same as *gate, exclusive-OR.*

nonequivalence operation—See *operation, nonequivalence.*

nonerasable storage—Same as *storage, fixed.*

nonexistent code—Same as *character, illegal.*

nonexistent code check—Same as *check, forbidden-combination.*

nonidentity operation—See *operation, nonidentity.*

noninferential analysis—See *analysis, noninferential.*

nonlinear optimization—See *optimization, nonlinear.*

nonlocking—Pertaining to the use of code extension or escape characters such that the change in characters or the change in the interpretation of characters applies to a specified number of coded representations or characters that follow, usually only to the one character that follows the code extension character, that is, the escape character. (Contrast with *locking.*)

nonlocking escape—See *escape, nonlocking.*

nonnegative number—Same as *number, natural*

nonpolarized return-to-zero recording—See *recording, nonpolarized return-to-zero.*

nonprint instruction—See *instruction, nonprint.*

nonprogrammed halt—See *halt, nonprogrammed.*

non-return-to-reference recording—See *recording, non-return-to-reference.*

non-return-to-zero—Pertaining to a method of binary digital data representation, such as a voltage signal displayed on a cathode-ray oscilloscope or magnetic recording, in which a change in signal level, or in the case of electric signals, a change in voltage or current level, occurs only when a change in the digit of the binary number being represented occurs. Thus, the binary number 001111011 would require four levels and four changes (assuming all

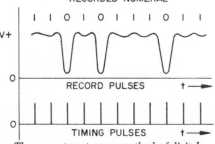

RECORDED NUMERAL

The non-return-to-zero *method of digital data representation.*

representations start and stop at zero). (Contrast with *return-to-zero.*)

non-return-to-zero recording—See *recording, non-return-to-zero.*

non-return-to-zero (change) recording—See *recording, non-return-to-zero (change).*

non-return-to-zero change-on-ones recording—See *recording, non-return-to-zero change-on-ones.*

non-return-to-zero (mark) recording—Same as *recording, non-return-to-zero change-on-ones.*

nonscheduled maintenance time—See *time, nonscheduled maintenance.*

nonvolatile storage—See *storage, nonvolatile.*

NOR—A logic operator having the property that if P is a statement, Q is a statement, R is a statement . . . , then the NOR of P, Q, R, . . . is true if all statements are false and false if at least one statement is true. (Synonymous with *NOR-operator.*)

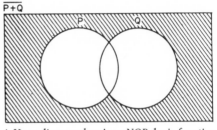

A Venn diagram showing a NOR logic function.

NOR element—Same as *gate, NOR.*

NOR gate—See *gate, NOR.*

NOR gate, neither—Same as *gate, NOR.*

NOR operation—Same as *operation, non-disjunction.*

NOR-operator—Same as *NOR.*

normal binary—Same as *binary, straight.*

normal direction flow—See *flow, normal direction.*

normal form—See *form, normal.*

normal form, Backus—See *form, Backus normal.*

normal random number—See *number, normal random.*

normal-stage punch—See *punch, normal-stage.*

normal termination—See *termination, normal.*

normalization, pulse—Same as *standardization, pulse.*

normalization, signal—Same as *standardization, signal.*

normalize—1: To adjust the representation of a quantity so that the representation lies in a prescribed range; for example, to multiply a variable by a numerical coefficient in order to make the result be within a specified or desired range of values; to adjust the exponent and fractional part of a floating-point number so that the fractional part lies within a prescribed range, such as between plus one and minus one for a fixed-point, binary computer, with the binary point at the left

233

end of the number; or to make the maximum of a set of quantities equal to unity. (Further clarified by *form, normal.*) 2: Same as *standardize.*

normalized form–See *form, normalized.*

normally closed contact–See *contact, normally closed.*

normally open contact–See *contact, normally open.*

NOT–A logic operator that has the property that if P is a statement, then NOT P is false if P is true and NOT P is true if P is false. NOT P may be written as P′, P̄, ~ P, >P, (1 – P), or NP. If the two possible states of the operand are written as 0 and 1, the corresponding results are 1 and 0. The NOT logic operation is the only nontrivial Boolean operation on one operand. The NOT operator produces the alternative value of the operand. (Synonymous with *Boolean complementation,* with *NOT-operator,* with *inversion,* and with *negation.* Further clarified by *negate* and by *element, negation.*)

NOT-AND gate–Same as *gate, NAND.*

NOT-AND operation–Same as *operation, nonconjunction.*

NOT-both gate–Same as *gate, NAND.*

NOT-BOTH operation–Same as *operation, nonconjunction.*

NOT circuit–Same as *element, negation.*

NOT gate–Same as *element, negation.*

NOT if-then–A logic operator having the property that if A is a statement and B is a statement, then NOT (if A then B) is true if A is true and B is false, false if A is false and B is true, and false if both statements are true. (Synonymous with *exclusion.*

NOT if-then gate–1: Same as *gate, A AND NOT B.* 2: Same as *gate, B AND NOT A.*

NOT operator–Same as *NOT.*

NOT-OR operation–Same as *operation, nondisjunction.*

notation–A systematic or conventional method for representing information through the use of signs and symbols, such as numerals, alphabetic characters, and special signs, and most commonly applied to number systems employing forms of *positional notation.* Thus, groups of symbols have special meaning, according to positional relationships; for example, *saw* is different from *was* in a given language, and 368 is different from 863.

notation, base–Same as *notation, radix.*

notation, binary–A numeration system with a radix of two. Usually, a positional notation system in which only two symbols are allowed, such as *zero* and *one,* or 0 and 1. Numbers are characterized by the arrangement of digits in sequence with the understanding that successive digits are interpreted as coefficients of successive powers of the radix, which is two. One such system of binary notation indicates the first dozen numbers, zero to eleven, as 0, 1, 10, 11, 100, 101, 110, 111, 1000,

1001, 1010, and 1011. Thus, 1010 means one times two cubed, or 8, plus zero times two squared, or 0, plus one times two, or 2, plus zero times one, or 0, totaling ten. Thus, 1010 in binary notation is equivalent to 10 in decimal notation. To avoid confusion with decimal notation, 1010 is read as one zero one zero, *not as* ten ten, or one thousand ten. (Synonymous with *binary number system,* with *binary scale,* and with *two-scale.*)

notation, binary-coded–A binary notation system or arrangement in which each character is represented by a binary numeral consisting of a set of binary digits.

notation, binary-coded-decimal–A numeration system in which each digit in a decimal numeration system is represented by a group of binary digits. Thus, a binary notation system is used to represent each digit of a decimal notation system. In a straight binary-coded-decimal system, each decimal digit is represented by its pure or straight binary equivalent, such as 0101 for 5, or 1001 for 9. In an excess-three binary-coded-decimal system, three is added to each straight binary numeral equivalent to the decimal digit, so that 1100 represents 9 and 1000 represents 5. Many other forms of binary-coded-decimal notation systems may be used. (Further clarified by *decimal, binary-coded.*)

notation, biquinary–A numeration system in which each decimal digit N is represented by the digit pair AB, where N = 5 A + B, and where A = 0 or 1 and B = 0, 1, 2, 3, or 4, depending on the decimal digit being represented. Thus, decimal 7 is represented by biquinary 12; that is, 5 times 1, plus 2. Biquinary notation is a type of mixed radix notation, with radices of 2 and 5, with the more significant position having a weight of five, and so biquinary. As in binary-coded decimal, each decimal digit is separately represented. Perhaps the term *biquinary-coded-decimal notation* is more descriptive of the actual case than simply *biquinary notation system.* The contemporary forms of the Chinese abacus use slight variations of biquinary notation. Some modern computers were built using the biquinary notation system. The contemporary form of Japanese abacus uses biquinary notation.

notation, coded-decimal–A numeration system in which the digits used are decimal digits and each decimal digit is represented by a code, usually a binary code; for example, biquinary, excess-three binary-coded decimal.

notation, decimal–1: A numeration system with a radix of 10. Usually a positional notation system allowing 10 symbols representing the digits zero through nine. Numbers are characterized by the arrangement of digits in a sequence with the understanding that successive digits are interpreted as coefficients of successive powers of the radix, which is 10. Thus, 569 implies five times 100, plus six times 10, plus nine times one, or $5 \times 10^2 + 6 \times 10^1 + 9 \times 10^0$. Note the ascending powers of ten, from right to left, starting at zero. Unless otherwise stated, notation is assumed to be decimal. (Synonymous with *decimal number system*.) 2: A notation that uses ten different characters, usually the decimal digits; for example, the decimal digit string 19740101000159 might represent the beginning of the sixtieth second of the second minute of the year 1974, or the representation used in the Universal Decimal Classification (UDC). These examples use decimal notation but they do not satisfy the definition of the decimal numeration system, which assigns increasing powers of ten to succeeding digit positions from right to left. (Contrast with *system, decimal numeration.*)

notation, distributed infix—An infix notation system for forming mathematical expressions according to rules of operator precedence and using parenthesis in which operators are dispersed among the operands, each operator indicating the operation to be performed on the operands or on the intermediate results adjacent to it, and in which there are more than two operands for each operator and operation. (Further clarified by *notation, infix.*)

notation, fixed-radix—A positional numeration system in which the significance of successive digit positions are successive integral powers of an integer, called the radix or sometimes called the base. Since the radix is usually positive, permissible values of each digit range from zero to one less than the radix. Negative integral powers of the radix allow the representation of fractions. Thus, if the radix is 10, or decimal, the numeral 896.38, represents $8 \times 10^2 + 9 \times 10^1 + 6 \times 10^0 + 3 \times 10^{-1} + 8 \times 10^{-2}$. Most radix notation systems are fixed-radix notation systems. *Fixed-radix* should not be confused with *fixed-point*. In fixed-radix systems, the ratio of weights for each consecutive or successive pair of digit positions is a constant. (Synonymous with *fixed-radix scale*. Further clarified by *notation, radix.*)

notation, hexadecimal—Same as *notation, sexadecimal.*

notation, infix—A notation system for linearly expressing arithmetic and logic statements by alternating single operands and operators. Any operator performs its indicated function on its adjacent term. The notation system is subject to the rule of operator precedence and grouping brackets to eliminate ambiguity. For

example, in infix notation, the expression "a plus b multiplied by c" would be represented as (a + b) $\times$ c. (Further clarified by *notation, distributed infix.*)

notation, mixed-base—Same as *notation, mixed-radix.*

notation, mixed-radix—A numeration system that makes use of more than one radix, such as the numeration system used in biquinary notation. The significance (weight) of any two adjacent digit positions have an integral ratio, called the radix of the less significant of the two positions. Permissible values of the digit in any position range from zero to one less than the radix of that position, as in any single radix notation. A time notation system to represent hours, minutes, and seconds, or the British coinage system, might conveniently use a mixed-radix notation. Usually mixed-radix notation employs pairs of digits, each with a different radix, to express or represent a single digit in another system using a single radix, such as a biquinary pair to represent a decimal digit. (Further clarified by *notation, radix.*)

notation, octal—A numeration system with a radix of eight; usually a positional notation system, allowing eight symbols representing the digits zero through seven. Numbers are characterized by the arrangement of digits in a sequence with the understanding that successive digits are interpreted as coefficients of successive powers of the radix, which is eight. Thus 476.2 implies four times 64 (decimal) plus seven times eight (decimal) plus six times one plus two times one-eighth, or $4 \times 8^2 + 7 \times 8^1 + 6 \times 8^0 + 2 \times 8^{-1}$, or 318.25 decimal. Note the ascending powers of eight, from right to left, starting at -1. Octal numerals may be coded; represented by three binary digits, so that octal 476.2 may be represented as 100 111 110 . 010, actually obtained digit-by-digit. Conversion to straight binary is obtained by running the digits together, as 100111110.010. Thus, octal notation is a convenient form for binary digital computers. (Synonymous with *octal number system*. Further clarified by *notation, positional.*)

notation, parenthesis-free—Same as *notation, prefix.*

notation, Polish—A form of prefix notation, used for writing logical, arithmetic, and algebraic expressions, without the use of parentheses. The method was originated by the Polish logician J. Lukasiewicz. Thus $(Z + Y) \times (A - B)$ may be written in Polish notation as $ZY + AB - \times$, which implies: Fetch Z and Y and add; fetch A and B and subtract B from A; then multiply the sum and difference.

notation, positional—A number representation or numeration system that makes use of an ordered set of digits, such that the value contributed by each digit position depends on its position in the numeral, relative to the other digits, as well as on the digit value. One such system, in common use, is characterized by the arrangement of digits in sequence, so that successive digits are interpreted as coefficients of successive powers of an integer called the radix of the numeration system. In the binary numeration system, the successive digits of a numeral are interpreted as the coefficients of successive powers of two. In the decimal system the digits relate to the successive powers of ten, starting with the zero power and ascending in positive powers to the left of the decimal point. Each digit is a character that represents zero or a positive integer smaller than the radix. The ratio of weights for each successive pair of digit positions is a constant in fixed-radix positional notation systems. (Further clarified by *notation, radix.*)

notation, postfix—A method of forming mathematical expressions in such a manner that each operator is preceded by its operands; for example, ab + c × could mean, by convention a and b are to be added and c is to be multiplied by their sum. (Contrast with *notation, prefix.*)

notation, prefix—1: A notation system of linear, that is, one-dimensional strings of symbols (operators and operands), used to indicate or state various logic, arithmetic, and algebraic expressions without the use of parentheses. Each sequence or string of operands may itself contain operators and operands. Polish notation is a form of prefix notation. Thus, × + *AB* − *CD* implies the product of the sum of *A* and *B* and the difference of *C* and *D*. Certain rules must be followed; for example, it is *D* that is subtracted from *C*, since *D* follows *C*. Also, the operands could, by convention, precede the operators. Thus, *AB* + *CD* − × states that *A* and *B* are to be fetched (as in a computer) and added; *C* and *D* are to be fetched, *D* subtracted from *C*, and the sum and difference are to be multiplied. Note that in these examples, *AB* does not imply multiplication, as in ordinary algebra, nor does it imply *A* AND *B* as in Boolean algebra. (Synonymous with *parenthesis-free notation.*) 2: A method of forming mathematical expressions in such a manner that each operator precedes its operands; for example, × + abc could mean, by convention, that a and b are to be added and their sum multiplied by c. (Contrast with *notation, postfix.*)

notation, radix—A numeration system in which the successive digits of a numeral in the system have a value or weight according to its position in the numeral and the radix assigned to the position. In a fixed-radix notation, the radix is the same for each position, the weight for the

position being determined by the radix raised to a power, and also, usually, the ratio of weights for successive positions is a constant. In decimal notation, each digit position has a weight 10 times higher (or lower) than the weight of the adjacent position. In mixed-radix notation, this is not the case. In any case, the total value of a digit in a numeral is determined by the value assigned to the digit itself, and by the weight of the digit position. In most numeration systems, the total value of a numeral is determined by adding the total values obtained from each digit. (Synonymous with *base notation*, with *radix numeration system*, and with *radix scale.* Further clarified by *notation, fixed-radix;* by *notation, mixed-radix;* and by *notation, positional.*)

notation, sexadecimal—A numeration system with a radix of 16. As a positional notation system, 16 symbols are used. In one such system used in digital computers, such as the ORDVAC, the usual decimal characters up to nine are used and K, S, N, J, F, and L are used for the digits beyond nine. Such a system is convenient in a digital computer, since each sexadecimal digit can be represented by a group of four binary digits; that is, a tetrad. Thus 5N might be used to represent 5 × 16 + 12, or 92 decimal. Using binary, the numeral sexadecimal 5N is represented as 0101 1100 in binary tetrad sexadecimal groupings, and as 1011100 in straight binary, which, of course, is the same sequence of binary digits, save for the initial zero. (Synonymous with *hexadecimal notation.*)

notation, suffix—1: A method of forming mathematical expressions in which each operator or set of operators follows its or their operands; for example, to indicate that a and b are to be added, and their sum is to be multiplied by c, one may write abc + x. It is necessary to establish rules for correlating the operands with the operators. 2: Same as *notation, postfix.* Contrast with *notation, infix* and with *notation, prefix.*

notation, symbolic—A system for representing or displaying abstractions and interrelationships between elements of concepts; for example, a method of writing computer programs using relative numerals for the addresses of storage locations; a method of using special signs or symbols to represent instructions to be executed by a computer, or the use of symbols to represent the operators and operands in an algebra. In many applications, a machine can recognize, interpret, and act in accordance with symbolic notation used.

notation, ternary—A numeration system with a radix of three. Usually a positional notation system; only three symbols are allowed, such as zero, one and two, or 0, 1, and 2.

notched card, edge—See *card, edge-notched.*

notice, event−In computer simulation, a temporary entity that is an announcement of the occurrence of an event.

noughts complement−Same as *complement, radix.*

n-p-n transistor−See *transistor, n-p-n.*

NRZ−Non-return-to-zero recording.

NRZ (C)−Non-return-to-zero (change) recording.

NRZI−*Non-return-to-zero change-on-ones recording.*

NRZ (M)−*Non-return-to-zero (mark) recording.*

NTDS−An abbreviation for Naval Tactical Data System.

NUCOM−A version of the APT machine-tool control language developed by Autonetics Division of Ford Motor Company for the RECOMP III computer.

NUL−The null character.

null−Pertaining to a negligible value or a lack of information in contrast to a zero or a blank that conveys information, such as in numerals and spaces between words. Thus, 50 is distinguished from 500 because of the presence or absence of a zero, and *standin* is different from *stand in* because of a space. A null is an indication of complete emptiness or nothingness. However, under certain conditions, a null situation can occur that does have a meaning, such as the null indication in the balancing of a Wheatstone bridge.

null character−See *character, null.*

null gate−See *gate, null.*

null set−Same as *set, empty.*

null string−See *string, null.*

number−1: A mathematical entity or abstraction to indicate quantity or amount of units, such as a number of feet or the number of miles per hour. Number is distinguished from numeral in that the numeral is the figure or device used to represent a quantity, or number, of things. Thus, as an example of usage: Let the *numeral* 25 indicate the *number* of years required for the man to be in business in order to qualify for the contract. In automatic data processing, the term *number* is used in its normal mathematical sense, including examples such as integer, cardinal number, ordinal number, rational number, real number, and mixed number. These concepts of numbers exist independently of any method of representing numbers; that is, any type of numerals used to represent quantities. There is a distinction between digit, integer, number, and numeral, however. 2: Loosely, a numeral.

number, binary−Same as *numeral, binary.*

number, call−A set of digits that identifies or labels a subroutine and contains data to be inserted into the subroutine, data to be used in generating the subroutine, or other data relating to the operands. The call number usually identifies a closed subroutine. (Further clarified by *call* and *word, call.*)

number, complex−A number, more properly called a numeral, consisting of an ordered pair of real numbers, expressible in the form a + bi, where a and b are real numbers and $i \times i = -1$.

number, counting−Same as *number, natural.*

number, decimal−See *numeral, decimal.*

number, designation−Same as *numeral, designation.*

number, double-length−Same as *numeral, double-length.*

number, double-precision−Same as *numeral, double-length.*

number, duodecimal−Same as *numeral, duodecimal.*

number, Fibonacci−An integer in the Fibonacci series.

number, hexadecimal−Same as *numeral, sexadecimal.*

number, irrational−A real number that is not a rational number, thus a number that cannot be expressed or generated as a quotient of an integer divided by an integer other than zero. (Contrast with *number, rational.*)

number, level−A number that indicates the position of an item in a hierarchic arrangement, that is, a number that indicates the rank of an item.

number, natural−One of the whole numbers; for example, one of the integers 0,1,2,3...n. Natural numbers are positive and include zero. They are established by counting whole objects, and are therefore also called counting numbers. A natural number would be one member of the set of positive integers. (Synonymous with *counting number* and with *non-negative number.*)

number, nonnegative−Same as *number, natural.*

number, normal random−A number selected by chance from a set of numbers, in which each number has an equal chance of being selected and the distribution of numbers in the set follows a normal or Gaussian distribution. (Further clarified by *number, random.*)

number, octal−Same as *numeral, octal.*

number, operation−In the sequence of operations that form a computer routine, the number assigned to identify an operation or its equivalent subroutine. Thus, an operation number can serve to relate program steps written in a symbolic or pseudocode to the corresponding steps written in a mnemonic or natural language code.

number, random−A number whose successive digits are determined by a process under which each digit is equally likely to be any one of the set of permissible digits from which the number may be represented. The random number must be selected according to some rule or process for randomness. Thus, a sequence of random numbers is not affected by any unwanted cause or hypothesis that might bias the selection of numbers or their digits.

Sequences of random numbers are often used in calculations in which the laws of chance are applicable and computer direction in accordance with these laws is desirable. A random number sequence generator is required to allow these numbers to be fed into the calculations, such as might be required in simulation by calculation of real situations containing an element of uncertainty and methods of integration which use formulas derived from statistical theory as in the Monte Carlo or random-walk methods. It is possible that a sequence of numbers that satisfy one criterion for randomness may not satisfy another. A number is considered random if it satisfies at least one statistical test for randomness; however, it is necessary to identify the nature of the criteria in each case. (Synonymous with *uniform random number.* Further clarified by *number, normal random.*)

number, rational—A real number that can be expressed or generated as the quotient of an integer divided by an integer other than zero. (Contrast with *number, irrational.*)

number, real—1: A member of the set of all positive and negative numbers, including integers, zero, mixed, whole, rational, and irrational numbers, but excluding any imaginary or complex numbers. 2: A number that may be represented by a numeral in a fixed radix numeration system.

number, serial—A numeral assigned to an item as a label, usually to denote the time sequence or spatial position of the item relative to other items. Usually, no arithmetic significance is given to a serial number, except for control purposes, such as determining the quantity of items produced in a given time period or at a certain place. Often, the numerals representing the serial number are attached to the item as a label.

number, sexadecimal—Same as *numeral, sexadecimal.*

number, uniform random—Same as *number, random.*

number generator, manual—Same as *unit, manual input.*

number generator, random—See *generator, random number.*

number range—See *range, number.*

number representation system—Same as *system, numeration.*

number sequence, random—1: Same as *sequence, psuedorandom number.* 2: See *sequence, random number.*

number system—Same as *system, numeration.*

number system, binary—Same as *notation, binary.*

number system, decimal—Same as *notation, decimal.*

numeral—1: The design or symbol, or set of designs or symbols, used for the representation of a number; thus, the set

of digits that represent a quantity of items. The numerals 365, CCCLXV, and 101101101 all may represent the number of days in a solar year. Numerals may be written or be represented as Morse code; they may consist of pulse trains in wires, or may be represented as holes in punched cards, as polarized spots on magnetic tape, or in any conventional form, even as lanterns in a bell tower. There is a distinction between digit, integer, number, and numeral. (Synonymous with *figure.*) 2: Loosely, a number.

numeral, binary—A numeral written in the binary numeration system; thus, a numeric word, or set of digits, that represents a quantity, displayed or represented in a binary form. The binary numeral is often expressed or represented as a set of binary digits. The usual representation of a number expressed in binary notation is by means of a sum of a series of terms, thus, a positional notation system; that is, the binary numeral 1011 represents $1 \times 2^3 + 0 \times 2^2 + 1 \times 2^1 + 1 \times 2^0 =$ decimal 11. Binary numerals are easily represented and handled in digital computers, since an on or off, open or closed condition can be used to represent the digits 0 or 1, as the state of a switch, the flow of current, presence of a voltage, or direction of magnetic polarization. Correctly stated one should say that 101 is the binary numeral, 5 is the decimal numeral, and V is the Roman numeral for the number of fingers on one hand. (Synonymous with *binary number.*)

numeral, decimal—1: A numeral formed in a positional notation system of radix 10; for example, 579, indicating $5 \times 10^2 + 7 \times 10^1 + 9 \times 10^0$. Unless otherwise indicated, numerals are assumed to be decimal numerals. There are 10 different digits from which decimal numerals may be formed. (Synonymous with *decimal number.*) 2: A numeral in the decimal numeration system.

VARIABLE	DESIGNATION	NUMERAL			
1	A	0	0	1	1
2	B	0	1	0	1
3	AB	0	0	0	1
4	$\overline{AB}$	1	1	1	0
5	$\overline{A}$	1	1	0	0
6	$\overline{B}$	1	0	0	0
7	A+B	1	1	1	0
8	$\overline{\overline{A+B}}$	0	0	0	1

Designation numerals, *proving the Boolean algebra proposition that* $\overline{AB} = \overline{A} + \overline{B}$, i.e., *NOT (A AND B) = NOT A OR NOT B and also that* $AB = \overline{\overline{A} + \overline{B}}$.

numeral, designation—In a truth table, that is, a table that represents all possible combinations of binary states of a set of variables, the set of digits that represents a particular Boolean expression, usually as a line or column in the table. Since all possible states are accounted for, various Boolean identities can be proved by designation numerals. In the table shown, each line of binary digits is a designation number. Note that line 4 is the same as line 7. Since the designation numbers are the same, $\overline{AB} = \overline{A} + \overline{B}$. Thus, the same operation is performed when A and B are fed into an AND gate and the output is negated, as when A and B are first fed into a negation gate, or negated, and the outputs of both are fed into an inclusive-OR gate. (Synonymous with *designation number.*)

numeral, double-length—A numeral that has twice as many digits as in ordinary numerals in a given computer. These double-length numeric words usually require two registers or storage locations to hold them and are capable of expressing quantities more precisely. Thus, in multiplication, the more significant half and the less significant half of a product can be represented and retained by the double-length numeral. (Synonymous with *double-length number,* with *double-precision number,* and with *double-precision numeral.* Further clarified by *length, word.*)

numeral, double-precision—Same as *numeral, double-length.*

numeral, duodecimal—A numeral written in the radix 12 notation system. The notation system is positional and allows 12 different characters, usually including the 10 characters of the decimal notation system. A duodecimal system has advantages over a decimal system in that there are more factors of the radix; namely, 1, 2, 3, 4, 6 and 12, than of ten; namely, 1, 2, 5, and 10. This permits more convenient whole subdivision. The duodecimal system has not been widely used, save in the mixed British system of currency and Troy and apothecary weights and measures. The sexadecimal, and the included octal and binary, notation systems are far more practical than a duodecimal system for digital computer use.

numeral, hexadecimal—Same as *numeral, sexadecimal.*

numeral, multiple-length—A numeral, representing a quantity of items, that has twice or more digits than the numeric words ordinarily encountered in a given computer. These numerals will require two or more registers or storage locations for operations or storage. Multiple-length numerals permit higher precision calculations or allow longer, fixed word lengths for representing alphanumeric data.

numeral, octal—A numeral written in the octal notation system. Thus, a positional notation system is used with a radix of eight. The octal numeral may be written as

a set of digits, as there are eight different characters. Usually, the zero through seven integers of the decimal system of notation are used. Each set of three successive digits, starting from the decimal point and going leftward, might be considered as a single octal digit. Thus, the binary numeral 101110 is represented as the octal numeral 56. Note the direct conversion of the right three binary digits; namely, 110 to octal 6 and the left three digits to 5, which are the ordinary transformations of binary to decimal and octal. Octal has been found convenient to use on many digital computers; however, for greater ease of operation, the binary-coded-decimal notation system has found broader application. (Synonymous with *octal number.*)

numeral, self-checking—A numeral containing check digits; for example, 1011011 may be a six-bit numeral, with the seventh bit serving as an odd-parity bit; that is, the total number of one marks in the numeral must always be odd.

numeral, sexadecimal—A numeral written or represented in a notation system whose radix is 16. Usually a positional notation system is used, with 16 different symbols, such as the zero through nine of the decimal system and K, S, N, J, F, and L, as is used on the ORDVAC computer. A radix of 16 allows for easy binary notation, in which four binary digits, that is, a tetrad, can be used to represent each sexadecimal digit. Sexadecimal numerals are convenient for use in binary digital computers. (Synonymous with *hexadecimal numeral,* with *hexadecimal number,* and with *sexadecimal number.*)

numeral system—Same as *system, numeration.*

numeration system—See *system, numeration.*

numeration system, decimal—See *system, decimal numeration.*

numeration system, fixed-radix—See *system, fixed-radix numeration.*

numeration system, mixed-base—See *system, mixed-base numeration.*

numeration system, mixed-radix—See *system, mixed-radix numeration.*

numeration system, pure binary—See *system, pure binary numeration.*

numeration system, radix—Same as *notation, radix.*

numeric—Pertaining to numerals in contrast to letters or other special signs and symbols. (Synonymous with *numerical.*)

numeric-alphabetic—Same as *alphanumeric.*

numeric character—Same as *digit.*

numeric character set—See *set, numeric character.*

numeric character subset—See *subset, numeric character.*

numeric code—See *code, numeric.*

numeric coded character set—See *set, numeric coded character.*

numeric data—See *data, numeric.*

numeric data code—See *code, numeric data.*

numeric punch—See *punch, numeric.*

numeric representation—See *representation, numeric.*
numeric word—See *word, numeric.*
numerical—Same as *numeric.*
numerical analysis—See *analysis, numerical.*

numerical control—See *control, numerical.*
NYAP—(New York Assembly Program). A computer assembly program written by Service Bureau Corporation for the IBM 704 computer.

O

OAO—(Orbiting Astronomical Observatory). An observatory in an earth satellite, a development of the Westinghouse Corporation.
Oarac—(Office of Air Research Automatic Computer). Same as *computer, Oarac.*
object code—See *code, object.*
object language—Same as *language, target.*
object module—See *module, object.*
object program—Same as *program, target.*
object routine—Same as *program, target.*
objective, design—A projected or planned software or hardware performance characteristic, chosen prior to development and based on reasonable technical estimates of the performance required but which have not necessarily been confirmed by actual measurement. The design objective serves as a projected standard until actual measurement under operating conditions can be made to determine whether or not, or to what extent, the design objective has been met. Thus, a design objective of a new computer may be a storage cycle time of 0.50 microseconds. After construction and testing of the unit, the actual value for satisfactory operation may prove to be 0.46 microseconds, in which case it may be stated that the design objective has been met.
OCR—(Optical Character Recognition). The machine identification of printed characters through the use of light-sensitive materials or devices. (Further clarified by *recognition, character* and by *recognition, pattern.* Contrast with *MICR.*)
OCR common language—See *language, OCR common.*
octal—1: Pertaining to a characteristic or property involving a selection, choice, or condition in which there are eight possibilities, such as a numeration system with a radix of eight. 2: Pertaining to eight, the radix eight, or numerals or number systems with a radix of eight. Thus, the octal numeral 214 represents $2 \times 8^2 + 1 \times 8^1 + 4 \times 8^0$, or $128 + 8 + 4$, or decimal 140. In binary notation, the same quantity is represented by the numeral 010, 001, 100; or simply 10001100 in straight binary. Note the simple conversion, digit by digit, from octal to binary, wherein each octal digit is represented by three binary digits. Many early computers made use of octal notation, such as the EDVAC computer.
octal, binary-coded—A form of numeral representation in which binary numerals are used to represent the octal digits of an octal numeral. The binary numeral may be written in any one of many codes, such as the common 4-2-1 code, where 111 represents octal 7 and 101 octal 5. Levels of redundancy and other check digits, such as parity bits may be added. (Abbreviated as BCO.)
octal digit—See *digit, octal.*
octal notation—See *notation, octal.*
octal number—Same as *numeral, octal.*
octal number system—Same as *notation, octal.*
octal numeral—See *numeral, octal.*
octet—A sequence of eight binary digits operated on or considered as a unit. (Synonymous with *eight-bit byte.*)
odd-even check—Same as *check, parity.*
odd parity—See *parity, odd.*
off, round—See *round-off.*
off-the-shelf—Pertaining to an item that is available from stock and need not be manufactured after receipt of order.
off time—See *time, off.*
office exchange, central—See *exchange, central office.*
offline—With reference to given equipment, pertaining to other equipment not in direct communication with nor under the control of the reference equipment, such as a processing or other control unit. Thus, tabulators; converters, such as card-to-tape and tape-to-printer; and key-punches, which operate independently of the main computing system, preparing input or processing output without the use of main frame or central computer time, are said to be operating offline. A teletypewriter used as a typewriter and not connected to

a communication link over which messages are being received is being used offline. (Contrast with *online*.)

offline operation—See *operation, offline*.
offline output—Same as *output, indirect*.
offline storage—See *storage, offline*.
offline working—See *working, offline*.
offset stacker—See *stacker, offset*.
Olsen memory—Same as *storage, core-rope*.
omission ratio—See *ratio, omission*.
OMNICODE—An automatic coding system developed by General Electric Company for use on the IBM 702 computer.
OMNIFAX—An automatic coding system developed by New York University for use on the Univac I and Univac II computers.
OMNIFLEX—An integrated service routine developed by Sperry-Rand Corporation for use with the Univac II computer.
on-the-fly printer—Same as *printer, hit-on-the-fly*.
one, binary—Of the two possible binary digits, that which has the value of unity assigned to it as a matter of convention. Usually written as 1, it may be represented as the presence or absence of a voltage or current at a given point, the set or reset state of a flip-flop, the clockwise or counterclockwise magnetization of an annular core, or the presence or absence of a pulse at a given point in time or place, in accordance with the adopted convention. The other of the two states is used to represent the binary zero. For numerical purposes, the binary one has the same value as a decimal one or a one in any other numeration system using similar positional notation and other conventions. The notation systems of binary and decimal in the conventional sense differ only in the number of permissible digits and the weights or values assigned to the positions of the digits, not the digits themselves.
one-address—Pertaining to a machine instruction which explicitly refers to or describes one storage location and one operation to be performed on or with the contents of that storage location. A typical one-address instruction is to add the contents of a particular storage location to the contents of an accumulator, holding the sum in the accumulator. Examples of one-address computers are the ORDVAC, Control Data 1604, GE 225, IBM 7090, Philco 2000, and the Univac 1107. One-address instructions permit greater flexibility, but require an increased number of program steps to produce the same result as say a three-address or a four-address instruction program. One-address instructions make more practical use of shorter words. (Synonymous with *single-address*. Further clarified by *instruction, one-address*. Contrast with *address, multiple*.)
one-address code—Same as *instruction, one-address*.
one-address instruction—See *instruction, one-address*.

one-ahead addressing—See *addressing, one-ahead*.
one-core-per-bit storage—See *storage, one-core-per-bit*.
one-digit adder—Same as *half-adder*.
one-digit subtracter—Same as *half-subtracter*.
one-dimensional language—See *language, one-dimensional*.
one gate—Same as *gate, OR*.
one-level address—Same as *address, direct*.
one-plus-one address—See *address, one-plus-one*.
one-plus-one-address instruction—See *instruction, one-plus-one-address*.
one-shot multivibrator—See *multivibrator, one-shot*.
one-shot operation—Same as *operation, single-step*.
one-step operation—Same as *operation, single-step*.
one-to-many—Pertaining to the relationship between members of one set and members of another set wherein the correspondences are such that one member of one set corresponds to several members of the other set. For example, one expression in a source language may be equivalent to many expressions in a target language. When a common-language compiler or assembler of machine code operates, usually one instruction in the common language is equivalent or will be made equivalent to several instructions or statements in the machine language. (Contrast with *one-to-one* and *many-to-one*.)
one-to-one—Pertaining to the relationship between individual members of one set and individual members of another set wherein each member of one set has a distinct relationship to one member of the other set. For example, a one-to-one relationship exists between two languages, such as a source language and a machine language, when each expression in one language is equivalent to one expression in the other language. If a different combination of six bits is used to represent each alphanumeric character, then a one-to-one relationship exists between the bit combinations and the alphanumeric characters. (Contrast with *one-to-many* and *many-to-one*.)
one-to-partial-select ratio—See *ratio, one-to-partial-select*.
one-way list—Same as *list, uni-directional*.
one-way operation—See *operation, one-way*.
one-way-reversible telegraph operation—See *operation, one-way-reversible telegraph*.
ones complement—See *complement, ones*.
online—1: With reference to given equipment, pertaining to other equipment in direct communication with or under the direct control of the reference equipment. Thus, a printer is operating online with a central processing unit when the printer is connected to and is controlled by the processing unit. Sometimes real-time operations may imply online operations. For example, if

data from a wind-tunnel or a target-tracking run is fed directly into a computer from the sensors, then it may be said that the computer is operating *online* with the other equipment; that is, the wind tunnel or the radar equipment. However, online does not imply real time, since online refers to a physical or electrical relationship whereas real time involves the time relationship between equipment and an ongoing process or event. (Contrast with *offline*.) 2: Pertaining to the access to a computer by a person via a terminal.

online data reduction—See *reduction, online data.*

online diagnostics—See *diagnostics, online.*

online operation—See *operation, online.*

online output—Same as *output, direct.*

online storage—See *storage, online.*

online working—See *working, online.*

onomasticon—A vocabulary of proper nouns or special names; for example, an alphabetical list of document titles, chemical compound names, corporation names, or names of persons.

op, pseudo—Same as *pseudoinstruction.*

open amplifier—See *amplifier, open.*

open contact, normally—See *contact, normally open.*

open-ended—Pertaining to any process or system that has no inherent restriction on its magnitude or extent, thus having the quality or capability of being extended, expanded, or augmented; for example, in an information retrieval scheme, pertaining to the quality by which the addition of new terms, subject headings, or classifications does not disturb the preexisting system.

open routine—See *routine, open.*

open shop—See *shop, open.*

open subroutine—See *subroutine, open.*

operand—That which is operated upon. In digital computers, an operand is usually identified by the address part of an instruction; for example, it may be any one of the quantities or items of information entering into or arising from an arithmetic or logic operation. An operand may be an argument, a result, a parameter, a variable, a function, the next instruction, a name, or a quantity. The operator indicates the nature of the operation to be performed on the operand. The operator and operand together form an algorithm. In the expression "add sin x," *add* is the operator and *sin x* is the operand. In the expression "sin x," *sin* is the operator and *x* is the operand.

operating delay—See *delay, operating.*

operating ratio—See *ratio, operating.*

operating system—See *system, operating.*

operating system generation—See *generation, operating system.*

operating system maintenance—See *maintenance, operating system.*

operating system management—See *management, operating system.*

operating system reconfiguration—See *reconfiguration, operating system.*

operating system residence device—See *device, operating system residence.*

operating time—See *time, operating.*

operation—1: A defined action, namely the act of obtaining a result from one or more operands in accordance with a rule that completely specifies the result for any permissible combination of operands. 2: The set of acts specified by a rule or the rule itself. 3: The act specified by a computer instruction. 4: A program step undertaken or executed by a computer; for example, transfer. The operation is usually specified by the operator part of an instruction. 5: The event or specific action performed by a logic element. 6: Loosely, one member of the instruction code set for a computer. 7: The act that is specified by an operator and the operand itself. Thus, the derivation of a result from an operator and operand.

operation, add—The operation indicated by the instruction "to add," in an arithmetic sense. In addition, the operands are the addend and the augend, and the result is the sum. The addend and the augend are distinguishable if the result appears in the storage location previously occupied by one of the operands. In this case, the displaced operand is the augend and the surviving operand is the addend.

operation, AND—Same as *operation, conjunction.*

operation, arithmetic—An operation performed in accordance with the rules of arithmetic, involving numerical quantities or their representation. The ordinary basic arithmetic operations are addition, subtraction, multiplication, and division. In addition, the operands are the addend and augend; the result is the sum. When addition is actually carried out, such as by a digital computer, the addend and augend are distinguishable as follows: in destructive addition, the sum appears in the location previously occupied by the augend, which is lost, and the addend remains in its original location; in nondestructive addition, the first operand placed in the arithmetic register is the augend. The succeeding operand is the addend, and the sum then replaces the augend in the arithmetic register. The sum may then become the augend for a subsequent addition. In subtraction, the subtrahend is subtracted from the minuend to form the difference. In multiplication, the operands are the factors and the result is the product. When the method of performing multiplication makes a distinction between the two factors useful, they are called the multiplier and the multiplicand. In a binary digital computer, the multiplier determines how many times the multiplicand is to be shifted and added. In division, the dividend is divided by the divisor to give the quotient and the remainder. Thus, dividend = (divisor X quotient) + remainder, relates the three quantities. Their exact values are determined by the precision required in the quotient, the rule for terminating it (that is, whether truncated, rounded off, etc.), and the rules governing the sign of the remainder. Thus, quotient and remainder may be regarded as less precise terms than sum, difference, or product. The process of negation and absolute value are also considered arithmetic operations. (Contrast with *operation, logic*.)

operation, asynchronous—The execution of a sequence of operations such that each operation is initiated upon completion of the previous operation. A clock signal is not used. (Synonymous with *asynchronous working*. Contrast with *operation, synchronous*.)

operation, auxiliary—In a computing system, an operation performed by equipment that is not under direct or continuous control of the central processing or control unit.

operation, average calculating—In a digital computer, a typical or representative operation that could serve as an indication of the calculating speed of the machine, usually longer than an addition time but shorter than a multiplication time, such as the mean time for nine additions and one multiplication. The average calculating operation serves as an indication of computer speed.

operation, binary—Same as *operation, dyadic*.

operation, binary arithmetic—An arithmetic operation, such as addition, subtraction, multiplication, and division, performed with operands and results represented in binary notation, such as is performed in most electronic digital computers.

operation, bookkeeping—Same as *operation, red-tape*.

operation, Boolean—A mathematical or logic operation that depends on the application of the rules of the Boolean algebra. The operands and results assume either one of two values or states when evaluated for either of the two states that any variable may assume in any of the expressions. A Boolean operation may involve any number of operands.

operation, Boolean add—Same as *operation, disjunction*.

operation, both-way—Same as *operation, full-duplex*.

operation, collation—Same as *AND*.

operation, complementary—A Boolean operation whose result is the negation of another Boolean operation. It may be represented by writing zero for one and one for zero in the tabulated values of the result for the original operation. For example, disjunction is complementary to nondisjunction, NAND is complementary to AND, and NOR to OR.

operation, complete—A computer operation that includes obtaining the instruction, interpreting the instruction, obtaining all operands, executing the command or operation part, and returning the results to storage.

operation, computer—The electronic, mechanical, or other physical action of the hardware of a computer, usually resulting from the execution of instructions designed to obtain computed results; for example, one of the predetermined set of operations that a computer is built to perform directly, such as a transfer, a jump, or an addition operation.

operation, concurrent—A mode of operating a computing system in such a manner that two or more operations, such as reading, writing, adding, printing, seeking, and storing, proceed simultaneously in different parts of the system, usually under program control. (Contrast with *operation, sequential*.)

operation, conjunction—The dyadic Boolean operation that has the Boolean value of 1 if and only if each operand has the Boolean value of 1. If any one of the operands has the value of 0, the result of the operation is 0. Thus, the operation result is designated false if one or more of the operands are false. (Synonymous with *AND operation*, with *intersection operation*, and with *meet operation*. Contrast with *operation, non-conjunction*.)

operation, control—1: An action performed by a device; for example, the starting or stopping of a device or process, a carriage return, a font change, or a rewind. The simple reading, transmission, or receiving of data, such as operation control symbols, are not considered as control operations. 2: Any action or event that affects the recording, transmission, interpretation, or other processing of data; for example, the starting or stopping of a process; effecting a carriage return; changing a type font; rewinding; or ending a transmission. (Synonymous with *control function*.)

operation, decoded—An operation that has been interpreted, usually by a matrix, and one that a computer is capable of sensing, interpreting, and executing. The command or operation part of an instruction word is furnished to a decoding matrix, the output being a set of signals that, perhaps by means of flip-flops, enables certain sets of gates to function as an adder, shifter, comparator, transfer unit, or whatever the particular input instruction specifies.

operation, disjunction—The dyadic Boolean operation that has the Boolean value of 0 if and only if all operands have the value 0. If one or more of the operands have the value 1, the result of the operation is 1. (Synonymous with *OR operation*, with *Boolean add operation*, and with *union operation*. Contrast with *operation, non-disjunction*.)

operation, dual−A Boolean operation whose result is the negation of the result of another Boolean operation that is applied to the negation of the operands. It may be represented by writing zero for one and one for zero in the tabulated values for the operands and results for the original operation. The new table is the dual of the old function; for example, the OR operation is the dual of the AND operation, or disjunction is the dual of conjunction.

operation, dyadic−An operation performed on or with two operands. (Synonymous with *binary operation*.)

operation, dyadic Boolean−An operation in the Boolean algebra performed on or with two operands, the result of which depends on both of them. If the values that the operands and the result can assume are denoted by 0 and 1, any Boolean operation specified by a connective can be designated by a table showing the value of the result that is obtained from each of the four possible combinations of the values of the two operands. There are sixteen possible truth tables that can be written, of which only ten represent dyadic operations. In the other six, the result is independent of one or both operands. An operation on or with two operands is usually represented by writing a symbol before or between the two operands. The symbol is often called a connective. Some Boolean dyadic operations can be extended in a straightforward fashion to apply to more than two operands.

operation, either-way−Same as *operation, half-duplex*.

operation, equivalence−The dyadic Boolean operation that produces the Boolean value of one if and only if the operands have the same Boolean value, that is they are both zero or both one. (Synonymous with *if-and-only-if operation*. Contrast with *operation, nonequivalence*.

operation, exclusive-OR−Same as *operation, non-equivalence*.

operation, fixed-cycle−A type of machine operation or performance whereby a fixed length of time is allocated for the execution of an operation or sequence of operations, such as synchronous or clock-type operation of a computer in which events occur as a function of, or in time coincidence with, measured periodic time intervals. Thus, the fixed-cycle operation is completed in a specified number of regularly timed execution cycles.

operation, fixed-point−Same as *calculation, fixed-point*.

operation, floating-point−Same as *calculation, floating-point*.

operation, full-duplex−A mode of communication between two points in which communication takes place between the two points in both directions simultaneously. Thus, both ends can simultaneously send and receive. When used on radio transmission, duplex operation requires the use of two frequencies; in wire communication, two insulated wires are required or a special coil is required to permit two channels over one wire, such as in one-wire duplex telegraph transmission. (Contrast with *operation, half duplex*. Synonymous with *both-way operation*.)

operation, half-duplex−A mode of communication between two points in which communication takes place in only one direction at a time, with or without a break or interrupt feature. The break feature enables the receiving station to interrupt the sending station. Thus, *half-duplex* requires use of a modifier such as send only (SO), receive only (RO), or send or receive (SR). (Contrast with *operation, full duplex*. Synonymous with *either-way operation*.)

operation, housekeeping−Same as *operation, red-tape*.

operation, identity−An operation that has a Boolean result of one if and only if all the operands have the same Boolean value. If there are only two operands, the operation is an equivalence operation. (Contrast with *operation, non-identity*.)

operation, if-and-only-if−Same as *operation, equivalence*.

operation, independent−In electronic computers, an operation that does not inhibit the operation of any unit not directly concerned in the operation.

operation, intersection−Same as *operation, conjunction*.

operation, jump−An operation in which a computer departs from the regular sequence of executing instructions in a computer program. (Synonymous with *transfer operation (1)*.)

operation, logic−1: An operation in which the operands and results are single digits; for example, a comparison on the two state variables A and B, each represented by zero or one, which yields zero when A is less than B, and one when A is equal to or greater than B; also, the dyadic Boolean operations; the operations of compare, select, match, sort, and merge; any nonarithmetic computer operation, such as extract, jump, shift, and transfer; and those operations expressible in the Boolean algebra. (Contrast with *operation, arithmetic*.) 2: An operation performed according to the rules of symbolic logic.

operation, majority−An operation on several operands, each of which may assume the value of zero or one, such that the result of the operation is one if and only if the number of operands having the value of one is greater than the number of operands having the value zero.

operation, meet–Same as *operation, conjunction.*

operation, monadic–An operation performed on one operand; for example, negation, formation of absolute value, and circular shift. (Synonymous with *unary operation.*)

operation, monadic Boolean–A Boolean operation on only one operand; for example, NOT.

operation, multiplexed–1: Simultaneous operations that share the use of a common unit in such a way that they can be considered as independent operations. **2:** A mode of operation in which the events of two or more activities are interleaved and wherein, the events are usually distributed to the respective activities after having been interleaved.

operation, multiply–An arithmetic operation in which the operands are factors and the result is the product, the product being the same as is obtained by adding the multiplicand as many times as is specified by the multiplier.

operation, n-adic–An operation that has exactly n operands, where n is a natural integer. (Synonymous with *n-ary operation.*)

operation, n-adic Boolean–A Boolean operation that has exactly n operands, where n is a natural integer. (Synonymous with *n-ary Boolean operation.*)

operation, n-ary–Same as *operation, n-adic.*

operation, n-ary Boolean–Same as *operation, n-adic Boolean.*

operation, NAND–Same as *operation, non-conjunction.*

operation, neither-NOR–Same as *operation, non-disjunction.*

operation, nonconjunction–The dyadic Boolean operation that has the Boolean value of 0 if and only if each operand has the Boolean value of 1. Thus, the operation result is designated false if all the operands are true. (Synonymous with *NAND operation,* with *NOT AND operation,* and with *NOT BOTH operation.* Contrast with *operation, conjunction.*)

operation, nondisjunction–The dyadic Boolean operation that has the Boolean value of 1 if and only if each operand has the Boolean value of 0. (Synonymous with *neither-NOR operation,* with *NOR operation,* and with *NOT-OR operation.* Contrast with *operation, disjunction.*)

operation, nonequivalence–The dyadic Boolean operation that produces the Boolean value of one if and only if the operands have different Boolean values, that is, one operand has a value of one and the other has a value of zero. (Synonymous with *addition-without-carry,* with *exclusive-OR operation.* and with *modulo-two sum.* Contrast with *operation, equivalence.*)

operation, nonidentity–An operation that has a Boolean result of one if and only if all the operands do not have the same Boolean value. If there are only two operands, the operation is a nonequivalence operation. (Contrast with *operation, identify.*)

operation, NOR–Same as *operation, nondisjunction.*

operation, NOT- AND–Same as *operation, nonconjunction.*

operation, NOT- BOTH–Same as *operation, nonconjunction.*

operation, NOT-OR–Same as *operation, nondisjunction.*

operation, offline–An operation that is performed on equipment or devices that are not under the direct control of a central processing or control unit of a system. Usually, offline operations are performed on peripheral equipment. The operations are in support of, or closely related to, operations that have been or will be performed on the main frame of the system being supported by the peripheral devices. (Contrast with *operation, online.*)

operation, one-shot–Same as *operation, single-step.*

operation, one-step–Same as *operation, single-step.*

operation, one-way–A mode of operation of a data link such that data are transmitted in a pre-assigned direction over one channel. (Synonymous with *simplex operation.*)

operation, one-way-reversible telegraph–Telegraph, or any communication operation, on a circuit in one direction at a time without a break feature.

operation, online–An operation performed on equipment or devices that are under the direct control of a central processing or control unit of a system. Online operations are not performed on peripheral equipment unless the peripheral equipment is, at least temporarily, under the control of the central processing or control unit. If data is gathered, processed, and made available so as to control an ongoing process or situation, such as a continuous strip rolling mill in which the output product is continuously monitored for quality and the results, even the trend in results, are measured continuously and fed back to the mill control devices, the operation is considered to be taking place in real time. In these cases, all the devices that are physically or electrically connected, even the product under control, are all considered to be online. In a target-radar-launcher-missile system, all units are performing online and in real time except the target. It is performing in real time, but not online, since it is not subject to the control of the system. (Contrast with *operation, offline.*)

operation, OR–Same as *operation, disjunction.*

operation, parallel–An operation in which two or more parts of the operation are executed simultaneously, or two or more parts of the operands are handled simultaneously; for example, an addition operation in which all the bits of a computer word are obtained from storage simultaneously and added simultaneously. In this example, a parallel storage unit and a parallel adder are being used to perform the parallel operation. Parallel operation is performed to save time over serial operation. Parallel operation may be mixed with serial operation; thus one might add the binary digits representing a decimal numeral as a parallel operation, but add the decimal numerals as a serial operation. (Contrast with *running, parallel* and with *operation, serial*.)

operation, push-to-talk–A voice communication operation in one direction at a time in which operation of a switch is required prior to and during transmission.

operation, push-to-type–A teletype and telegraph operation in one direction at a time in which operation of a switch is required prior to and during transmission.

operation, real-time–Operations performed by a system during the actual time that a related physical process takes place in order that the results of the operations can be made available soon enough so as to influence or control the physical process. In such operations, a computer might be used as an element of a processing system in which the times of data transmission are determined by other portions of the system, such as a rolling mill motor for handling sheet steel, or by physical events outside the system but sensed by the system, and so cannot be modified for convenience in programming. When a computer or data processor is connected to an ongoing physical process, the computer is considered to be online to the process equipment. Thus, real-time is a time relationship whereas online is a spatial relationship, and each must be related to an ongoing process or a reference piece of equipment. A simulation is said to be operating in real-time if the simulation proceeds at the same speed as the events being simulated. (Synonymous with *real-time working* and *true-time operation*.)

operation, red-tape–In computer programming and operations, an operation that does not directly contribute to the result; therefore, an operation that is primarily organizational. For example, arithmetic, logic, and transfer operations used to modify the address parts of other instructions, to count cycles, to rearrange data; operations that must be performed before actual computations begin, such as establishing controlling marks, reading in the first record, initiating registers, setting up verification operations, and identifying files; and the recording of the storage locations used by different parts of a routine or subroutine to ensure that data is not overwritten unless it is no longer needed. Usually, those portions of each set of microinstructions that are identical for all macroinstructions are red-tape instructions, which are required to operate the computer or execute the program; for example, packing or unpacking data, rearranging data and subroutine linkages, translating, and setting up constants and variables to be used in the program. Most red-tape operations are accomplished prior to the running of the main program. At times it is difficult to distinguish between a main program operation and a red-tape operation, much as it is difficult to distinguish between a main operational event and a supporting operation. (Synonymous with *housekeeping operation* and *bookkeeping operation*.)

operation, repetitive–In computers, operation in such a manner that repeated solutions of the same set of equations, with the same set of initial conditions and parameters, are obtained. The repetition rate is sufficiently high so that a steady-state solution becomes apparent when displayed on a cathode-ray oscilloscope screen. Repetitive operation may be used to permit manual adjustment of parameters, to permit optimization, smoothing, or fitting. Transients, temporary changes, and spurious signals may be ignored as noise in the system. Thus, in radar tracking of aircraft, the predicted position indicator output is based on repetitive solution of the same equation with relatively slowly changing parameters. The aircraft cannot accelerate rapidly compared to the repetition rate of the equation solutions.

operation, representative calculating–Same as *operation, average calculating*.

operation, sequential–The execution of operations one after the other; that is, in time sequence; for example, the execution of an addition, a multiplication, and another multiplication, as given by the expression $(a + b)cd$, in sequence. The individual digits expressing the operands may be handled serially or in parallel. Thus, a computer with a serial, or bit-by-bit, adder may execute operations sequentially or concurrently, depending on whether or not other operations such as read, write, print, punch, transfer, or compare, are performed simultaneously. Usually serial operation pertains to smaller logic operations, such as bit-by-bit comparison or addition within a computer word, whereas sequential pertains to larger operations, such as the addition of a computer word as a whole. (Contrast with *operation, concurrent*.)

operation, serial–An operation whose individual parts or processes are performed in time sequence; for example, an addition in which each pair of digits, one from each operand, are added in time sequence, usually starting with the least significant digit first and propagating all carries to the end. In this example, a full serial adder might be used. (Contrast with *operation, parallel.*)

operation, simplex—Same as *operation, one-way.*

operation, simultaneous—A mode of operation in which two or more events occur at the same instant or in time coincidence.

operation, single-shot—Same as *operation, single-step.*

operation, single-step—Manual operation of a computer in such a manner that one instruction or part of an instruction is executed in response to a manual control device, such as a button or switch. Single-step operation permits checking of various outputs, registers, and storage locations for detecting program mistakes and equipment malfunctions, and so may be used by programmers to debug programs and by engineers to detect and locate malfunctions. (Synonymous with *one-shot operation*, with *single-shot operation*, with *step-by-step operation*, and with *one-step operation.*)

operation, step-by-step—Same as *operation, single-step.*

operation, storage—A computer operation involving a storage unit, such as a reading, writing, transferring, storing, or holding operation, or a movement of data within storage from one location to another.

operation, synchronous—The execution of a sequence of operations controlled by regular, time-spaced, clock signals, such as clock pulses. In a synchronous computer, each instruction step is executed in accordance with a clock signal. (Synonymous with *synchronous working.* Contrast with *operation, asynchronous.*)

operation, threshold—An operation performed so as to obtain the value of a threshold function.

operation, transfer—1: Same as *operation, jump.* 2: Same as *operation, transmit.*

operation, transmit—An operation in which a computer moves data from one location to another location. (Synonymous with *transfer operation (2).*)

operation, true-time—Same as *operation, real-time.*

operation, unary—Same as *operation, monadic.*

operation, union—Same as *operation, disjunction.*

operation, variable-cycle—Computer operation in which any operation is initiated immediately after the previous cycle is completed, each cycle time period being not necessarily of the same length. Thus, the execution of operations are not regularly timed. This type of operation is characteristic of asynchronous computers.

operation code—See *code, operation.*

operation code, augmented—See *code, augmented operation.*

operation code, mnemonic—Same as *code, mnemonic instruction.*

operation control—See *control, operation.*

operation-control switch—See *switch, operation-control.*

operation decoder—See *decoder, operation.*

operation number—See *number, operation.*

operation part—See *part, operation.*

operation register—See *register, operation.*

operation table—Same as *table, truth.*

operation table, Boolean—See *table, Boolean operation.*

operation time—See *time, operation.*

operation time, average—See *time, average operation.*

operational-address instruction—Same as *instruction, source-destination.*

operational amplifier—Same as *amplifier, computing.*

operational character—Same as *character, control.*

operational rules—See *rules, operational.*

operational-use time—Same as *time, effective.*

operations, asynchronous—A sequence of operations that are executed not necessarily in time coincidence with any event, that is, the operations are executed without a regular or predictable time relationship.

operations analysis—Same as *research, operations.*

operations research—See *research, operations.*

operator—1: In the description of a process, such as an arithmetic or logic operation, that which performs an action or indicates the action to be performed on an object or item called an operand, such as an addend or augend. The operator may be a symbol, a machine, a person or anything capable of action. 2: The person who actually manipulates the computer controls, places data media into the input devices, removes output, mounts reels of tapes, pushes initiate buttons, and performs a number of other similar duties.

operator, AND—Same as *AND.*

operator, binary—Same as *operator, dyadic.*

operator, Boolean—An operator that has operands and results that take one of two possible values; for example, the AND, OR, NAND and NOR operators.

operator, complementary—An operator whose result is the NOT of a given operator; for example, NOR or NAND.

operator, dyadic—An operator that uses, operates upon, or requires, two and only two operands. (Synonymous with *binary operator.*)

operator, exclusive-OR—Same as *exclusive-OR.*

operator, monadic—An operator that operates on one and only one operand, such as an algebraic sign, a negation operator, or an inverse (reciprocal) operator. (Synonymous with *unary operator.*)

operator, n-ary—An operator that operates upon or requires exactly n operands; for example, a binary operator requires two operands, such as a difference operator, a multiply operator, or an AND operator with two operands.

operator, NAND—Same as *NAND.*

operator, NOR—Same as *NOR.*

operator, NOT—Same as *NOT.*

operator, OR—Same as *OR.*

operator, quaternary—An operator that uses or requires exactly four operands.

operator, relational—1: An operator that indicates the relationship between two values, such as *equal to, greater than, less than,* or *greater than or equal to.* 2: An operator that operates on two or more operands and yields a truth (or false) value, such as 3 *is greater than or equal to* 5 is false.

operator, ternary—An operator that requires or operates upon three operands; for example the operator that produces the vector cross-product.

operator, unary—Same as *operator, monadic.*

operator command—See *command, operator.*

operator console—See *console, operator.*

operator control panel—See *panel, operator control.*

operator part—Same as *part, operation.*

optical character recognition—See *OCR.*

optical scanner—See *scanner, optical.*

optimization—A method of arriving at the most desirable set of conditions based on a set of criteria or constraints; for example, to determine the least cost method of shipping fragile goods to the interior of foreign countries; to determine which depot or which plant should ship which goods to which customers so as to maximize profit or minimize cost; or in computer operations, to minimize the machine time required to solve a problem, as in minimal-latency programming. (Related to *suboptimization.*)

optimization, linear—1: The process or procedure for locating the maximum, minimum, or other optimum value or values of a function of variables that are themselves subject to mathematically linear constraints and inequalities. The values or ranges of the variables that yield the optimized value of the function need also be determined in most instances. (Contrast with *optimization, nonlinear.*) 2: Same as *programming, linear.*

optimization, nonlinear—The process or procedure for locating the maximum, minimum, or other optimum value or values of a function of variables that are themselves subject to mathematically nonlinear constraints and inequalities. The values or ranges of the variables that yield the optimized value of the function need also be determined in most applications. (Contrast with *optimization, linear.*)

optimum coding—See *coding, optimum.*

optimum programming—Same as *programming, linear.*

option, default—In a computer operating system, an option that will be assumed automatically if it is not overridden by the specification of a parameter; for example, an option that is implied when no option is explicitly stated.

optional-halt instruction—See *instruction, optional-halt.*

optional-pause instruction—See *instruction, optional pause.*

optional-stop instruction—Same as *instruction, optional-halt.*

P + Q

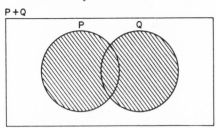

A Venn diagram showing the OR logic function.

OR—1: A logical operator having the property that if P is a statement, Q is a statement, R is a statement, . . ., then the OR of P, Q, R, . . . , is true if at least one statement is true, false if all statements are false. P OR Q OR R is often represented by P + R, P ∨ Q ∨ R, or P∪Q∪R. The positive inclusive-OR is implied. (Synonymous with *OR operator,* with *disjunction,* with *OR else,* with *Boolean add,* and with *union.* Further clarified by *add, logic* and by *gate, OR.* Contrast with *NOR* and *AND.*) 2: Abbreviation for operations research.

OR circuit—Same as *gate, OR.*

OR element—Same as *gate, OR.*

OR else—Same as *OR.*

OR gate—See *gate, OR.*

OR gate, exclusive—See *gate, exclusive-OR.*

OR gate, negative—Same as *gate, NOR.*

OR gate, positive—Same as *OR.*

OR NOT gate—1: Same as *gate, A OR NOT B.* 2: Same as *gate, B OR NOT A.*

OR operation—Same as *operation, disjunction.*

OR operator—Same as *OR.*

OR unit—Same as *gate, OR.*

ORBIT—(ORACLE Binary Internal Translator). An algebraic programming system developed by Union Carbide Corporation for use on the ORACLE computer.

order—1: To put items in a given sequence, usually by sorting and then sequencing. The ordering is accomplished in accordance with specified rules, usually through the use of identifying keys following a prescribed pattern, such as alphabetical order, numerical order, or size place. In the early days of digital computer development and use, order was used to mean instruction or command. Thus, one spoke of the order code or the order part of an instruction word, to distinguish it from the address part of the instruction word. In data processing today, order is used as defined above. (Synonymous with *sequence*.) 2: In mathematics, the relative level or degree of the elements in an equation or digits in a numeral; for example, the level of a derivative, the level of an exponential, the place or weight of a digit in a numeral, such as the high-order or more significant digits. (Further explained by *rank*.)

order, expanded—Same as *pseudoinstruction*.

order-by-merging—To order items, usually data, by repeated splitting and then merging.

order code—Same as *code, operation*.

order format—Same as *format, instruction*.

order structure—Same as *format, instruction*.

order wire—See *wire, order*.

ordering bias—See *bias, ordering*.

ordinary binary—Same as *binary, straight*.

organization, computer service—1: An organization that under a contract provides maintenance to computers owned by other organizations. 2: An organization that provides computer, analyst, programmer, and other related support to a customer who requires the use of a computer and such services.

oriented language, application—See *language, application-oriented*.

origin—In relative addressing of a digital computer program, the absolute address of the beginning of a program or block of coding; thus, the origin is the absolute address of the base address.

origin, assembled—1: The computer program origin that is assigned by another program, such as an assembler, a compiler, or an editor. 2: The address of the first or initial storage location assigned to a computer program by an assembler, a compiler, or an editor such as a linkage editor.

origin, computer program—The address in main storage assigned to the initial storage location of a computer program. The initial storage location will contain the first instruction to be executed in the program. The next and subsequent instructions will either be in consecutive storage locations, or each instruction to be executed will contain the address of the next instruction to be executed. (Synonymous with *initial address*.)

origin, loaded—The address of the first or initial storage location used by a computer program at the time the computer program is located into storage; usually main or internal storage.

original language—Same as *language, source*.

origination, data—To put data in machine-sensible form, usually at the source.

ORSA—Operations Research Society of America.

OSAS—A symbolic assembly language developed by Control Data Corporation for use on the Control Data 160A computer.

oscillating sort—See *sort, oscillating*.

oscillations, free—Oscillating currents and voltages which continue to flow in a circuit after the impressed voltage has been removed or applied. The frequency is the natural resonant frequency of the circuit, which must be a closed loop or be closed by coupling. The oscillations are due to the interchange of electromagnetic and electrostatic energy, and the fact that a time rate of change of charge at a point is an electric current which stores energy in the form of a magnetic field and a time rate of change of a magnetic field produces a voltage which stores energy in the form of an electric field. With the fields changing, the energy swings from one form to the other, as a pendulum swings from kinetic energy to potential energy. In computer circuits, it becomes necessary to dampen these oscillations to avoid gate leakage; that is, having a pulse appear where it should not.

oscilloscope—An instrument containing a focused electron beam gun, a means of beam deflection, and a screen that indicates the point of impact of the beam. The instrument is used to show visually the changes in a varying current or voltage. The cathode-ray-tube 'scope is used for storage and display (output) purposes in analog and digital computers.

oscilloscope tube—See *tube, oscilloscope*.

OTRAC—(Oscillogram Trace Reader). A trace reader developed by Non-Linear Systems, Inc.

outconnector—On a flowchart, a symbol that indicates a place at which a flowline is broken or interrupted for continuation at another place. (Further clarified by *connector, flowchart*. Contrast with *inconnector*.)

outer face—See *face, outer*.

outline, character—The graphic pattern, that is, printed shape, established by the stroke edges of a character. It is implied that the character is drawn or printed rather than in forms such as punched holes, magnetized tape, or magnetized cores.

output—1: Data that has been processed. 2: The process of transferring data from internal storage to external storage of a computer or to its peripheral or online equipment or to a human being. 3: A device or set of devices used to take data out of another device. 4: Pertaining to processes, hardware, or software related to the removal of data from a place, such as output equipment, output media, output terminals, output programs, and output data. Often these are simply referred to as output.

output, direct—Output data obtained from online output equipment or the online output equipment itself. Thus, direct output involves a system in which the final output is produced by equipment connected directly to the computer; for example, data obtained from an online high-speed printer connected to the computer and directly under the computer program control. (Synonymous with *online output*. Contrast with *output, indirect*.)

output, disturbed-one—Same as *signal, disturbed-one output*.

output, disturbed-zero—Same as *signal, disturbed-zero output*.

output, indirect—Output data originating from a given data-processing system, but now obtained from offline equipment, or the offline output equipment itself, Thus, indirect output involves a system in which the final output is produced by equipment not connected directly to the computer; for example, data that was taken from an output card punch and placed in a tabulator for further editing, format arrangement, and display. (Synonymous with *offline output*. Contrast with *output, direct*.)

output, offline—Same as *output, indirect*.

output, online—Same as *output, direct*.

output, real-time—Output data, delivered by a data processing system within time limits determined by the requirements or characteristics of another system or at instants of time that are determined by the other system; for example data delivered by airborne radar to the aircraft computer to determine the aircraft's position. (Contrast with *input, real-time*.)

output area—See *area, output*.

output block—See *block, output*.

output buffer—See *buffer, output*.

output equipment—See *equipment, output*.

output impedance—See *impedance, output*.

output-input—See *input-output*.

output microfilm, computer—See *microfilm, computer output*.

output port—See *port, output*.

output process—See *process, output*.

output program—See *program, output*.

output rating, carrier power—See *rating, carrier power output*.

output routine—See *routine, output*.

output stacker—Same as *stacker, card*.

output storage—Same as *area, output*.

output table—Same as *board, plotting*.

output tape punch—Same as *punch, automatic tape*.

output unit—Same as *output (3)*.

OUTRAN—An output translator developed for the IBM 709 and 7090 series of computers.

overflow—The portion of the result of an operation that cannot be fitted into an intended storage unit because of the limited capacity of the unit, such as a register, punched card, printer line, or internal storage location; for example, the sum of 689 and 782 cannot be held in a three-digit register; the one in the most significant position of the sum is an overflow that either must be given special consideration or must be prevented from occurring. If a product is obtained, the number of digits is approximately equal to the total number of digits in both the operands. Overflow will result if special arrangements are not made, such as retaining the more significant and less significant parts of the product in separate registers. This is called multiprecision arithemetic. In a floating-point operation, if a result is so small as to require a negative exponent so large in magnitude (absolute value) as to be beyond the capacity of the storage unit to retain it, the situation is referred to as an underflow condition, although the situation in the register is the same as in an overflow condition. All sorts of tests, traps, and indicators exist for detection of overflow, since errors can result if overflow is ignored. Scaling techniques are used to avoid overflow. Floating-point representation has allowed greater number range to help avoid overflow, at the sacrifice of precision, unless other special arrangements are made to retain precision. (Contrast with *underflow*.)

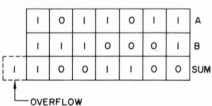

Registers A, B, and Sum are seven-bit registers. Thus, the leftmost digit of the sum is an overflow.

overflow-check indicator—Same as *indicator, overflow*.

overflow indicator—See *indicator, overflow*.

overflow position—See *position, overflow*.

overlay—1: To repeatedly use the same blocks of internal storage during different stages in the solution of a problem; for example, when one routine is no longer needed in storage, another routine can replace all or part of it. The technique can be used when total storage requirements for instructions exceed the available storage capacity. Thus, any data or routines no longer needed in the solution of the same problem or same main program constitute overlaying. 2: In a computer program, a segment or part that is not maintained in internal storage. 3: In the execution of a computer program, to load a segment of the program in a storage area that was occupied by parts of the program that are not currently needed.

overlay, form—Same as *flash, form*.

overlay program—See *program, overlay.*

overprinting—In optical character recognition, any marks placed in the clear band; that is, areas set aside for machine reading, after a document is ready for machine sensing.

overpunch—Same as *punch, zone.*

overpunching—1: In punched cards, the punching of cards so as to permit the representation of alphabetic or special characters by punching a hole in one of the top three rows and a second hole in one of the nine lower rows. The top three rows are the zero, X, and Y punch positions. These are called zone punches. (Further clarified by *punch, zone.* 2: The adding of holes in a card column that already contains holes. Overpunching is used to represent special characters. 3: The adding of holes to perforated tape to change a character, usually to produce a delete character.

own code—See *code, own.*

owner, file—The individual or corporate entity that controls access to a file.

p

P-pulse—Same as *pulse, commutator.*

p-type semiconductor—See *semiconductor, p-type.*

PABX—An abbreviation for private automatic branch exchange.

PACC—(Product Administration and Contract Control.) A concept for business data management developed by Univac Division of Sperry-Rand Corporation.

pack—1: To compress data; that is, to increase the storage density of data, in a storage medium without losing the ability to recover the data. Packing makes more efficient use of available storage medium; for example, to include two or more data items in one machine word by allocating groups of digits to the individual data item; to store only the nonzero items of a table, those not stored being assumed to be zero; to replace consecutive strings of zeros by an indicator of the number of zeros replaced; or to include the fields of an employee's pay number, weekly pay rate, and tax exemptions in one word or in consecutive columns across a card. 2: Same as *deck.*

pack, disc—1: An assembly of magnetic discs built into a single unit capable of being easily connected and disconnected from a computer. The packs can be easily dedicated to a specific application and contain all the data and programs for that application. The disc pack is usually a portable set of flat, circular recording surfaces. 2: An assembly of magnetic discs that can be easily removed from a drive unit. A disc pack is often used for applications that make use of dedicated storage.

package, parallel-plate—A packaging, that is, circuit construction and wiring, technique for logic and other computer circuitry developed by Burroughs Corporation to achieve high packing density, ease of automatic production and assembly, and simple maintenance.

packet—A group of binary digits that is switched in a data transmission network as a single unit. The packet usually includes data bits, call control signals, and error control bits arranged in a prescribed format.

packet, switching—See *switching, packet.*

packing density—See *density, packing.*

PACT I—(Project for the Advancement of Coding Techniques). A coding technique project supported by Douglas Aircraft Corporation, Lockheed Aircraft Corporation, Naval Ordnance Test Station, North American Aviation, and Rand Corporation for use on the IBM 701 computer.

PACT IA—PACT for the IBM 704 computer.

pad—1: To fill out a unit of data, such as a word, block, record, or file, with smaller units of dummy data, such as zeros, letters, or any other meaningless data. 2: To incorporate filler in data. (Synonymous with *fill.*)

padding—1: Meaningless data used to fill out a unit of data such as a word, block, record, or file. 2: The technique of applying padding to a unit of data.

page—1: One side of a single piece of paper containing data. 2: A fixed-length block, or a fixed number of blocks, of instructions or data or both. The segmentation and loading of these blocks is usually automatically controlled by a computer. Pages are created in a size convenient for transmission between main storage and auxiliary storage.

page, common—A page that is allocated to two or more computer programs, usually used for the movement of data among separate programs.

page entry—See *entry, page.*

page exit—See *exit, page.*

page printer—See *printer, page.*

page swapping—See *swapping, page.*

page turning—Same as *paging.*

paging—A technique in which pages are loaded into main or internal storage only when needed. The pages are usually referenced during program execution. (Synonymous with *page turning.*)

pair, binary—Same as *flip-flop.*

paired cable—See *cable, paired.*

palindromic program—See *program, palindromic.*

panel—A surface, such as a sheet of metal or chassis, upon which hardware components, such as buttons, switches, lights, tubes, and meters, are mounted.

panel, control—1: A panel, usually consisting of a surface containing an assortment or an array of switches, wires, plugs, meters, lights, or other devices used by an operator to control the operations of a specific device, such as a computer, calculator, printer, card reader, or tape station; for example, an ordered array of terminals that use removable wires to direct the operation of a computer or punched card machine. (Synonymous with *patch panel.*) 2: Same as *plugboard.*

panel, graphic—A master control panel that displays the relationship of control equipment and the operation of a system or process. It permits a system operator to monitor or check the status of operation or pending operation of a distributed or far-flung system. Various dials, valves, scales, lights, paths, and colors are used to reflect conditions, status, or situations in ongoing activities, such as computation, military force deployment, power plant operation, and chemical, paper, and petroleum processes.

A jack panel showing jumper wires connecting terminals 4D with 4F and 7E with 7F.

panel, jack—A control panel that uses electrical connectors, such as short wires

or plugs, called jacks, to control the operation of a device, such as a computer or punched card machine. A type of jack panel opened like a cooking range oven door, or like a jackknife, to expose the wiring panel, also giving rise to the name jack panel.

panel, maintenance—A part of a system or a unit of equipment that is used for communication between the system or unit of equipment and a maintenance engineer or technician.

panel, operator control—A part of an operator console that contains components used to control all or part of a system and that may contain indicators giving information on the functioning of the system.

panel, patch—1: Same as *plugboard.* 2: Same as *panel, control (1).*

panel, wing—A panel added on the side of an existing and usually larger panel; for example, the panel containing intervention switches and warning lights that may be added to either or both sides of a SAGE computer system display or auxiliary console.

panic button—See *button, panic.*

paper card, general-purpose—See *card, general-purpose paper.*

paper card, moisture proof—See *card, moisture-proof paper.*

paper card, special-purpose—See *card, special-purpose paper.*

paper slew—Same as *throw, paper.*

paper tape—See *tape, paper.*

paper tape, perforated—Same as *tape, punched-paper.*

paper tape, punched—See *tape, punched paper.*

paper-tape code—Same as *code, punched-tape.*

paper-tape coil—See *coil, paper-tape.*

paper-tape coil, blank—See *coil, blank paper-tape.*

paper-tape coil, virgin—See *coil, virgin paper-tape.*

paper-tape reader—See *reader, paper-tape.*

paper-tape punch—See *punch, paper-tape.*

paper throw—See *throw, paper.*

paragraph—A group of sentences logically related; for example, five sentences concerning one person.

parallel—Pertaining to the simultaneous occurrence of two or more processes or events. The events may be different, similar, or identical, and may include the processing of the individual parts of a whole, such as the bits of a character, the characters of a word, or the words of a record, even if separate facilities are used for the various parts. Usually, pertaining to operations that are handled in separate facilities at the same time. (Contrast with *serial.*)

parallel access—See *access, parallel.*

parallel adder—See *adder, parallel.*

parallel addition—See *addition, parallel.*

parallel arithmetic—See *arithmetic, parallel.*

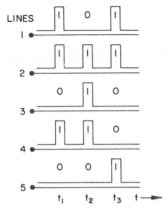

LINES

1

2

3

4

5

t_1 t_2 t_3 $t \longrightarrow$

At time t_1, the binary numeral 11010 is represented as parallel digits on the five lines. At time t_2, 01110 is represented, and at t_3, 11001.

parallel-by-bit—Pertaining to the handling of all binary digits of a byte or character simultaneously in separate equipment, such as separate wires, gates, or switches.

parallel-by-character—In digital computers, pertaining to the handling of all the characters of a computer word simultaneously in separate equipment, such as separate wires, gates, or switches.

parallel computer—See *computer, parallel*.

parallel flow—Same as *work-flow, parallel*.

parallel half-subtracter—See *half-subtracter, parallel*.

parallel operation—See *operation, parallel*.

parallel-plate package—See *package, parallel-plate*.

parallel processing—See *processing, parallel*.

parallel programming—See *programming, parallel*.

parallel running—See *running, parallel*.

parallel-search storage—Same as *storage, associative*.

parallel-serial—See *serial-parallel*.

parallel storage—See *storage, parallel*.

parallel transmission—See *transmission, parallel*.

parallel work-flow—See *work-flow, parallel*.

parameter—1: A variable that is assigned a constant value for a specific purpose or process; for example, in a subroutine, a quantity whose value specifies the process to be performed, such as when a subroutine is used in different main routines, or in different parts of one main routine, the quantity remaining unchanged throughout any one such use; in a subroutine for the multiplication of matrices, the number of rows and the number of columns are parameters; in stock control, the reorder level is a parameter; in the function $y = ax + b$, the a and b are considered parameters, their choice of values determining the angles and distances at which the line crosses the coordinate axis; in programming,

parameters may determine the number of columns in a field, the number of times a cycle is to be repeated, the computer system configuration, the subroutines to be run, or their sequence; in mathematics, a variable that is held constant in a given equation representing a curve, then allowed to assume different fixed values, giving rise to a family of curves, such as the bias voltage in a set of vacuum tube static plate characteristics; or a quantity that is a constant within a system but a variable outside the system. (Related to *constant* and *variable*.) 2: In computer simulation, an attribute of a transaction. The attribute usually remains unchanged for a specific simulation run.

parameter, chance—A parameter that is allowed to assume values determined purely by chance; for example, in computer simulation, the variables of a model that are determined using Monte Carlo methods.

parameter, dynamic—Same as *parameter, program-generated*.

parameter, external program—A parameter or variable in a computer program that must be bound during the calling of the computer program. A parameter is bound when a value is assigned to it, that is, the parameter is fixed at some value.

parameter, preset—1: In computer programming, a parameter incorporated into a subroutine before or during input. 2: A parameter that is bound or defined when the computer program that contains it is constructed, that is, flowcharted, coded, or compiled. (Contrast with *parameter, program-generated*.)

parameter, program—A parameter incorporated into a computer subroutine prior to or during execution, usually by means of an instruction. A program parameter frequently is in the form of a computer word, stored relative to either the subroutine or the entry point and dealt with by the subroutine. It may be altered by the routine or it may vary from one point of entry to another.

parameter, program-generated—A parameter that is bound or defined when the computer program that contains it is executed. (Synonymous with *dynamic parameter*. Contrast with *parameter, preset*.)

parameter word—See *word, parameter*.

parametric analysis—See *analysis, parametric*.

parametron—A device that has two stable states of oscillation, one at twice the frequency of the other, and is therefore capable of storing one binary digit.

parenthesis-free notation—Same as *notation, prefix*.

parity—In computers, pertaining to maintaining a given level or count, such as maintaining the number of binary ones in all words of a given computer as an even number.

parity, drum—The use of parity checking when transferring data to or from the drum storage of a digital computer.

parity, even—In a parity check, a count in the computer word or character of the number of binary ones which is always maintained as an even number. If the ones in the data part of the word or character is even, the parity bit is a zero; if the ones in the data part of the word or character is odd, the parity bit is a one. In either case, the word or character length is the same. (Contrast with *parity, odd*. Further clarified by *check, parity*.)

parity, odd—In a parity check, a count of the number of binary ones in a computer word or character that is always maintained as an odd number. If the ones in the data part of the word or character is even, the parity bit is a one; if the ones in the data part of the word or character is odd, the parity bit is a zero. In either case, the word or character length is the same. (Contrast with *parity, even*. Further clarified by *check, parity*.)

parity, storage—The use of parity checking when transferring data to or from storage, such as the drum, disc, or core storage of a digital computer.

parity, tape—The use of parity checking when transferring data to or from magnetic or paper tape.

parity bit—See *bit, parity*.

parity check—See *check, parity*.

part, address—The part of a computer instruction word that specifies the address of an operand or the next instruction. An instruction may have several address parts which may specify the addresses of various locations that may contain operands, instructions, references, or other addresses. Such instructions are called multiple address or multiaddress instructions. The locations may be storage devices, specific locations within these devices, or special registers, such as arithmetic or index registers.

A computer instruction showing the operation part, OP, and the address parts, A and B. This instruction states that the contents of storage location 0148 be added to the contents of storage location 3219. The two numerals are the addresses of the storage locations at which the operands are stored.

part, fixed-point—Same as *coefficient, floating-point*.

part, function—Same as *part, operation*.

part, operation—The operator part of an instruction; that is, the part of a computer instruction word that specifies an operation. (Synonymous with *operator part*, with *function part*, and with *function digits*.)

part, operator—Same as *part, operation*.

partial arithmetic—See *arithmetic, partial*.

partial carry—See *carry, partial*.

partial drive pulse—Same as *pulse, partial write*.

partial dump—See *dump, partial*.

partial-one output signal—Same as *signal, disturbed-one output*.

partial product—See *product, partial*.

partial read pulse—See *pulse, partial read*.

partial-select input pulse—Same as *pulse, partial write*.

partial-select output pulse—Same as *pulse, partial read*.

partial sum—See *sum, partial*.

partial-sum gate—Same as *gate, exclusive-OR*.

partial write pulse—See *pulse, partial write*.

partial-zero output signal—Same as *signal, disturbed-zero output*.

partition—Same as *segment*.

pass—In automatic data processing, to process, such as scan, search, or examine, the data contained in a given file for a specific purpose; for example, each complete reading and updating of the contents of a reel of magnetic tape.

pass, band—See *bandpass*.

pass, high—See *highpass*.

pass, low—See *lowpass*.

pass, sort—In the execution of a sort, that is, during sorting, a single processing of all the items to be sorted in order to reduce the number of strings of unsorted items and to increase the number of items in the sorted strings, until all the items are in the sorted strings.

passage—In fluidics, a connecting line between two points either within a device or between two devices.

passive element—See *element, passive*.

passive graphics—See *graphics, passive*.

password—A computer word that must be used in a prescribed manner in order that a user may gain access to protected storage areas, files, or devices. (Synonymous with *key*. Related to *control, file access*; to *protection, storage*; and to *protection, volume*.)

PAT—(Programmer Aptitude Tester). Developed by Wolf Research and Development Corporation, Boston.

patch—1: To change a routine by adding a section of coding at a particular place, usually by inserting a transfer instruction at that place and by adding elsewhere the new instructions and the return transfer instruction. Patching is done to correct mistakes or to build into the routine new instructions to take care of a newly arisen situation and still permit the old routine to be salvaged. 2: A temporary electrical connection. 3: To make an improvised change, modification, or repair.

patch panel—1: Same as *plugboard*. 2: Same as *panel, control (1)*.

patch-program plugboard–See *plugboard, patch-program.*

patchboard–Same as *plugboard.*

patchcord–A flexible conductor with connectors at both ends used to interconnect the sockets of a plugboard.

patchplug–A plug, usually a piece of metal with an insulating handle, that performs the function of a patchcord. The patchplug is cordless, whereas the standard plug has a wire for jumping, or connecting, two terminals.

path, magnetic–The route taken by magnetic flux lines. The path is closed and involves all media through which the lines of flux pass; for example, the interior of a ferrite toroidal core or the horseshoe-shaped magnetic core of a magnetic recording head and the section of drum, tape, or disc, along with a small air gap in some cases, through which the magnetic flux must thread. The length of this path may be taken as a mean value for each part of the path.

path, sneak–An undesired or unintentional electrical path within a circuit.

paths, conjunctive–In computer simulation, two or more paths, of a flowchart or block diagram that originate at the same decision box event, all of which must be executed. (Contrast with *paths, disjunctive.*)

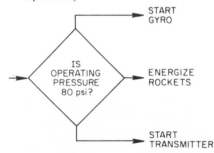

Three conjunctive paths *that originate at a decision element, all of which must be performed.*

paths, disjunctive–In computer simulation, two or more paths, of a flowchart or block diagram that originate at the same decision box event, only one of which must be performed. (Contrast with *paths, conjunctive.*)

pattern, bit–An arrangement of binary digits; for example, 101101. There are eight different linearly arranged bit patterns possible when three bits are used; four bits permit sixteen patterns; or 2^n patterns are possible with n bits, if the bits are arranged in a single straight row.

pattern, hole–A punching array or configuration; for example, the letter A represented as holes in a single column or a punched card or in a single frame of paper tape.

pattern recognition–See *recognition, pattern.*

pattern-sensitive fault–See *fault, pattern-sensitive.*

pause instruction–See *instruction, pause.*

pause instruction, optional–See *instruction, optional pause.*

PAVE–(Position and Velocity Extraction.) A program used in the SAGE Defense System computers.

PAX–An abbreviation for private automatic exchange.

PBX–An abbreviation for private branch exchange.

PCM–1: An abbreviation for punched card machine. 2: An abbreviation for pulse code modulation.

PCMI–(PhotoChromic MicroImage). A National Cash Register Company trademark which describes a microimage process that permits reductions of 1:40,000 in area. The process permits 1.6 billion words, or 7.5 billion characters, on less than 2 sq. in. of the surface of a film.

PDPS–(Parts Data Processing System). A system developed by Bell Telephone Company for storing and retrieving parts data.

PE–Phase encoded recording.

peak data-transfer rate–Same as *rate, instantaneous data-transfer.*

peak transmission rate–Same as *rate, instantaneous data-transfer.*

peek-a-boo–In information retrieval, pertaining to a method of sighting or passing light through a deck of evenly stacked cards in order to determine which hole locations have a hole punched in every card in the deck. For example, cards representing the aspects of information of interest in a search are superimposed. The holes through which light passes serve to locate or identify the documents relating to all aspects of interest represented by the superimposed cards. (Synonymous with *Batten* and with *Cordonnier.*)

peek-a-boo check–Same as *check, sight.*

pen, light–A photosensitive device that is held against the face of a cathode-ray tube and whose position can be determined by a computer. The light pen permits communication between man and computer by indicating a sequence of locations on the face of the cathode-ray tube. Thus, points or lines can be drawn

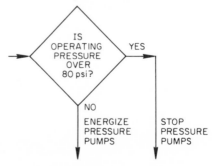

Two disjunctive paths *that originate at a decision element, only one of which must be performed.*

on the tube, and the coordinates of the successive points on the line transferred to computer storage. A computer program can compare the input coordinates with specific sets of geometric figures. Thus, if an approximate circle is drawn by the pen, the computer will convert the circle into a precise circle and display the precise circle, will dynamically display the circle rotating, will increase or decrease the size, or will produce other situations. (Synonymous with *light gun*.)

pence coding, single-column—See *coding, single-column pence.*

pence conversion equipment—See *equipment, pence conversion.*

pentode—A five-electrode vacuum tube, containing a cathode, control grid, screen grid, suppressor grid, and a plate. If two or more of the electrodes can control the flow of current, the tube can be used in a computer as a logic element; that is, a gate. If any one of the electrodes can stop or force the flow of current from the cathode to the plate independently of the condition of the other electrodes, the tube can function as an OR gate. If it is required that all of the electrodes must be in a certain state to halt or force the flow of current, the tube will function as an AND gate. In usual computer applications, the tube functions as a NOR or a NAND gate, since usually the tube also serves as an inverter if the output is taken off the plate. If the output is taken off the cathode, as in a cathode-follower, the output will not be inverted and the normal AND or OR functions are executed.

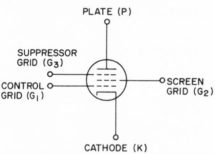

PLATE (P)

SUPPRESSOR GRID (G₃)

CONTROL GRID (G₁)

SCREEN GRID (G₂)

CATHODE (K)

A pentode showing the plate, cathode, and three grids.

perception, artificial—The ability of a machine to optically sense a displayed character and select from a given repertory of characters a character that is nearest in shape to the character displayed. If the difference between the shape of the character displayed and the nearest in shape in the repertory exceeds a certain threshold, the character may be interpreted as a new one and added to the repertory of acceptable characters. The shapes of characters in the repertory can be based on a statistical norm. Thus, the

system approaches the characteristic of artificial learning, since perception and interpretation are based on experience. Optical character recognition or some other form of character recognition must take place before artificial perception can occur. Machine learning is an extension of artificial perception. (Synonymous with *artificial cognition* and *machine cognition.*)

perceptron—A model of the behavior of the human brain; for example, a theoretical nerve net. Usually, a determined part and a self-teaching part are necessary. Thus, a perceptron is a generic name for all types of theoretical nerve nets, rather than a device for pattern recognition.

perforated—Punched with holes. Perforated is often used in connection with tapes or continuous paper, but punched is used even more often in connection with both cards and tapes. Thus, punched and punch are usually preferred to perforated, perforate, and perforator.

perforated card, edge—Same as *card, edge-punched.*

perforated card, margin—Same as *card, edge-punched.*

perforated card, verge—See *card, verge-perforated.*

perforated paper tape—Same as *tape, punched paper.*

perforated tape—Same as *tape, punched.*

perforated-tape code—Same as *code, punched-tape.*

perforated-tape reader—Same as *reader, paper-tape.*

perforation rate—See *rate, perforation.*

perforator, keyboard—1: A device with a bank of keys, such that when a key is depressed or touched, a pattern of holes is punched in a tape to represent a character, each key corresponding to a different character. 2: Same as *keypunch.*

perforator, tape—Same as *punch, tape.*

performance evaluation—See *evaluation, performance.*

performance period—See *period, performance.*

period, action—In an electrostatic storage tube, the time during which the stored data is read or new data is written at a storage location. (Further clarified by *line, action* and by *spot, action.*)

period, digit—The time interval between the occurrence of successive digit signals.

period, performance—A specified time interval that a device is to operate; for example, the scheduled hours of operation, which is not to include certain test or preparatory operations, nor those hours rescheduled as a result of equipment malfunction. (Further clarified by *time, up.*)

period, principal maintenance—Any period of time specifically scheduled each day in order to perform preventive maintenance.

period, regeneration—In an electrostatic storage tube, the time during which the screen is swept by the electron beam solely to regenerate or restore the charge distribution that represents the stored data. (Synonymous with *scan period*.)

period, retention—In file maintenance, the time interval that records must be kept before they may be disposed of, usually stated as a term of months or years, a specific terminal date, or after the occurrence of a specified event.

period, scan—Same as *period, regeneration*.

peripheral equipment—See *equipment, peripheral*.

peripheral transfer—See *transfer, peripheral*.

permanence, water—The extent to which an image is capable of resisting deformation of shape or change of color on immersion in water for a specified period, at a specified temperature, or at other stated conditions.

permanent connection—See *connection, permanent*.

permanent entity—See *entity, permanent*.

permanent storage—Same as *storage, fixed*.

permanent store—Same as *storage, fixed*.

permeability—A measure of the capacity of a substance to permit another substance to pass through it, such as a solvent through a membrane, or in the case of magnetic materials, the capacity to conduct or concentrate lines of magnetic flux, in which case the magnetic permeability is given by the magnetic flux density (gauss) divided by the magnetomotive force (oersteds), or $\mu = B/H$.

permutation—1: A spatial arrangement or distribution of the members of a set; for example, abc and acb are two permutations of the three letters abc. The letter arrangements ab and ba are two different permutations of the same combination. The number of permutations of n things taken r at a time is always equal to or greater than the number of combinations of the same n things also taken r at a time; or, $nPr \geqslant nCr$. (Contrast with *combination*.) 2: An ordered arrangement of a given number of different elements selected from a set.

permutation index—See *index, permutation*.

permuted code, cyclic—Same as *code, unit distance*.

permuted-title index—Same as *index, permutation*.

PERT—(Program Evaluation and Review Technique). A management tool for defining and interrelating on a time scale the jobs and events that must take place in order to accomplish desired objectives. One may start at the required completion date and work backward, thus establishing the completion date for each subtask or work unit, based on the estimate of time required to complete the subsequent work unit. The interdependency of tasks establishes a network. The longest path through the network is the critical path and it determines the duration of the overall project. A reallocation of resources from other subtasks might result in a shortening of the critical path. The application of computers permits rapid determination of allocations, schedules, impact of changing conditions, cost analysis, and related matters.

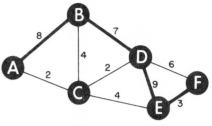

The critical path of the PERT *diagram is shown by the heavy line.*

PGEC—(Professional Group on Electronic Computers). A technical professional group devoted to the advancement of computer-related sciences, such as computer programming, computer engineering, storage devices, and combinational logic, formerly of the Institute of Radio Engineers (IRE) and now of the Institute of Electrical and Electronics Engineers (IEEE).

phase, assembly—The logical subdivision or part of a run that includes the execution of the assembler, that is, the assembly program. Upon completion of the assembly phase, the assembled program may be executed, or it may be stored for future execution.

phase, compile—That part of a computer run that includes the execution of a compiler.

phase, execute—A logical subdivision of a computer run that includes the execution of the object or target program. Other phases of a computer run might be an assembly phase, a compile phase, a sort phase, and a translate phase.

phase, sort—A part of a sort procedure or sort program, for example, an initialization phase, an internal phase, a merge phase, or a sort phase.

phase, translate—A logical subdivision of a computer run that includes the execution of a translator. Other phases of a computer run might be an assembly phase, a compile phase, a sort phase, or a translate phase.

phase distortion—Same as *distortion, delay*.

phase-distortion coefficient—See *coefficient phase-distortion*.

phase encoded recording—Same as *recording, phase modulation*.

phase modulation—See *modulation, phase*.

phase modulation recording—See *recording, phase modulation*.

phase shift—See *shift, phase*.

PHLAG—(Phillips Load and Go). A load-and-go programming system developed by Phillips Petroleum Corporation for the IBM 709 computer.

phone, data—See *Data-phone.*

phoneme—A basic or primitive sound unit of speech in a specified language. Spoken words consist of one or more phonemes. In English, the spoken word or letter "I" consists of at least two phonemes, "ah" and "eeh"; in German, the same letter consists of only one, namely "eeh."

phosphorescence—The property of emitting light for some time after the source of excitation is removed. Electrostatic storage tubes and cathode-ray display tubes make use of this phenomenon to allow a trace on a screen to remain after the transient signal causing the signal is removed. This extends the persistence of vision natural to the human eye and is a form of temporary storage.

photoconductive—Pertaining to an effect or a phenomenon in which the electrical conductivity of certain materials is dependent upon the intensity and frequency of electromagnetic radiation incident upon the material. (Compare with *photoemissive* and with *photovoltaic.*)

photoelectric reader—See *reader, photoelectric.*

photoemissive—Pertaining to an effect or a phenomenon in which electrons are caused to be emitted from the surfaces of certain materials at certain threshold levels of frequency of incident electromagnetic radiation, such as visible light, infrared, or ultraviolet. The effect is used in the operation of phototubes, in which a sensitive surface emits electrons that are captured by a positively biased collector, all contained within an evacuated envelope. (Compare with *photoconductive* and with *photovoltaic.*)

photon—A quantum of electromagnetic energy, given as Planck's constant times the frequency.

photo-optic storage—See *storage, photo-optic.*

photovoltaic—Pertaining to an effect or phenomenon in which certain materials produce an electromotive force, that is, a voltage or electric potential difference, when incident electromagnetic energy, such as visible light, ultraviolet light, or infrared light, falls on the junction of two dissimilar materials, such as on a p-n junction or a metal-semiconductor junction. The photovoltaic effect is utilized in the construction of exposure, or light, meters used to measure brightness for photographic work. (Compare with *photoemissive* and with *photoconductive.*)

photovoltaic cell—See *cell, photovoltaic.*

photovoltaic cell, back-wall—See *cell, back-wall photovoltaic.*

physical input-output—See *input-output, physical.*

physical record—See *record, physical.*

pica—A unit of measure in printing, approximately one-sixth of an inch.

pickup plate—See *plate, pickup.*

picofarad—One-millionth of one-millionth of a farad, a unit of electrical capacity; equal also to one-thousandth of a millimicrofarad or to a micromicrofarad, and also called a puff. Abbreviated $\mu\mu$F or pF.

picosecond—One-millionth of one-millionth of a second, or one-thousandth of a nanosecond, or one micromicrosecond, or 1×10^{-12} seconds. Abbreviated as psec.

picture—In a programming language, a character string, or its description, in which each position has associated with it a symbol representing the properties of the character that may occupy it; for example, in COBOL, "9999" is used as a picture of any four-digit numeric word.

piezoelectric—Pertaining to a phenomenon or an effect in which certain crystalline electrical insulating materials develop mechanical strains and stresses when they are placed in an electric field; that is, electrified. The mechanical strain is directly proportional to the applied electric field strength. In the converse, an output voltage is obtained only while there is a time rate of change of an applied stress. Piezoelectric materials are used as transducers at both ends of a mercury delay-line, both to launch the acoustic wave, like a hammer, at one end, and to generate a signal voltage, proportional to the time derivative of the incident acoustic wave, at the other end. The piezoelectric effect is demonstrated only by those types of crystals that do not possess a center of symmetry; that is, zero-point symmetry. The direction in which tension, torsion, or compression stresses develop electric polarization parallel to the strain is called the piezoelectric axis of the crystal. Certain quartz crystals demonstrate the effect. (Compare with *electrostrictive.* Further clarified by *magnetostrictive* and *magnetostriction.*)

pilot—In a transmission system, a signal, usually of single frequency, transmitted over the system to test, indicate, or control its characteristics.

pin contact—See *contact, pin.*

pinboard—A board containing an array of holes into which pins may be inserted to represent different sequences of operations that the computer it controls is to execute. In some computers, the pinboard is removable with the pins intact in order to preserve the program. The rows of pins are scanned successively much like data on a magnetic tape. Pinboards differ from plugboards in that pins are cordless, whereas plugs have wires that permit jumping from one terminal hole to another on the face of the board. Generally both are used for much the same purpose. The pinboard is used generally for short programs and on small computers, converters, punch card machines, and other peripheral equipment.

pinfeed form—See *form, pinfeed.*

pinfeed platen—See *platen, pinfeed.*

ping-pong—In computer programming, a technique of alternately switching back and forth between two units, such as two magnetic tape units, until the complete file on the two units is processed.

pitch, array—Same as *pitch, row.*

pitch, character—The distance from the vertical reference axis of a character to the vertical reference axis of the adjacent character in a line of text or in a printed word.

pitch, feed—The distance between the centers of adjacent feed holes in perforated tape. Usually the feed pitch is the same as the row pitch, since there is one row of holes at each feed hole.

pitch, row—The distance, measured along perforated tape, between the centers of adjacent rows of holes. The pitch is measured along the tape longitudinally, whereas the holes in a row are transverse to the tape axis. The row pitch is usually the same as the feed pitch. (Synonymous with *array pitch.*)

pitch, track—The distance between centers of adjacent tracks. The tracks may be on magnetic tape, discs, drums, or cards, or on paper tape, in which case the distance between centers of holes is measured across, or transverse to, the longitudinal axis; that is, transverse to the direction of motion of the tape. In any case, the track pitch is always measured transverse to the direction of motion of the recording medium. The track pitch is the inverse of the track density. Thus, if the pitch is 0.1 inch, the density is 10 tracks per inch. (Contrast with *density, track.*)

PL-1—A common programming language that looks and behaves like an extension of FORTRAN and that has been characterized as being simpler than FORTRAN, more powerful, less restrictive, and has fewer rules. The language philosophy is to use a standard set of instructions to accomplish a specific purpose. Thus, programming is rapid but the program may not be optimum. If the program is to be used many times, a more optimum program may be written using the full power of the language. Instructions are explicitly written. PL-1 is as well suited as COBOL, ALGOL, and FORTRAN for mass data handling, such as in business data applications and mass data storage and retrieval. It is also well suited for scientific applications.

place—1: In a positional notation system, a location or position in which a digit may occur in a numeral. Thus, a nine-place numeral has nine digits. 2: Any of the permissible locations or position at which a character may appear in a word. In many computers, the places are numbered from left to right for purposes of identification and reference. Thus, the ninth and tenth place may be used to express the

command part of an instruction word, the first eight places being used to express two addresses of the operands involved. (Synonymous with *position.*)

place, digit—1: In a positional notation system, the site of a digit in a numeral. 2: In a positional representation system, a site that can be occupied by a character and that may be identified by an ordinal number or by an equivalent identifier. (Synonymous with *digit, position.*)

plane, digit—In a digital computer storage unit and in an array of binary storage cells in three dimensions, the plane that contains the corresponding binary digit of every word. Thus, if there are 1024, or 32 X 32, bits in the digit plane, there are 1024 words in the array. There are as many digit planes in the storage array, or stack, as there are bits in a word. As many stacks are used as are required to make up a desired size storage unit or the size of the digit plane can be increased to increase the storage capacity.

plane driver, digit—See *DPD.*

plant—In computer programming, to put or place an instruction that has been formed during the execution of a routine in a storage location such that it will be obeyed at some later stage in the execution of the routine. By means of plants and with the ability to prepare instructions based on results thus far obtained, the computer has the ability to control and execute its own program.

plate, pickup—In a cathode-ray storage tube, a conducting plate, such as copper foil or a fine copper-wire mesh, situated close to or cemented on the face or screen of the tube. The plate is capacitively coupled to each element of the screen inside the tube; any alteration of the charge stored on the element causes an output signal to be developed by the pickup plate, thus forming the basis for electrostatic storage storing and interrogating. (Synonymous with *signal plate.*)

plate, signal—Same as *plate, pickup.*

plated-wire memory—See *memory, plated-wire.*

platen—A smooth, tough surface, often cylindrical, against which printing mechanisms, usually type, strike to produce an impression.

platen, pinfeed—A cylindrical platen that drives material by means of lugs or pins, which are an integral part of the platen, by engaging holes in the material. Most printers and tabulators for computers require pinfeed platens to ensure positive drive and proper registration of lines of print.

plates, deflection—In a cathode-ray tube, a pair of electrodes shaped like a pair of bent, square postage stamps, set a short distance apart and parallel, between which a focused electron beam is sent. If the plates are horizontal, the beam is deflected vertically by an amount

259

playback head — pocket

proportional to the voltage across the plates. The type of deflection is called electrostatic deflection. If the plates are vertical, the deflection is horizontal. Thus, the electron beam can be controlled in two dimensions, and made to strike anywhere on the screen, forming the basis for an oscilloscope, television display tube, or electrostatic storage tube for a computer.

playback head—Same as *head, read.*

plot—To draw a map, graph, diagram, or other line drawing type of display. The resulting figure is a plot representing the variation of variables as a function of others, such as a plot of the variation of voltage with time, of temperature with time or with distance, or of pressure with altitude. Plotters are used as output devices with computers to display the results of computations.

plotter—A device capable of presenting data in graphic form, such as two-dimensional curves or line drawings; thus, an analog curve or point tracer. The dependent variable is graphed as a function of the independent variable by a controlled pen that moves along a moving bar, permitting access to any place in a plane. The pen can be up or down as the bar moves. If the pen can move in only one dimension and the paper is moved or fed in the other perpendicular direction, the instrument is considered a recorder rather than a plotter. Plotters are often used as a computer output device to display the results of computation. (Further clarified by *board, plotting.*)

plotter, drum—A device that draws an image on a data medium such as paper or film mounted on a drum that rotates for one coordinate axis and with a stylus that moves parallel to the drum access of rotation for the other coordinate axis in order to draw a two dimensional figure.

plotter, flat-bed—A device that draws an image on a data medium, such as paper or film, that is mounted on a flat surface, such as a table.

plotter step size—Same as *size, increment.*

plotting board—See *board, plotting.*

plotting table—Same as *board, plotting.*

plug—Same as *connector, electrical.*

plug, patch—See *patchplug.*

plugboard—A perforated board that accepts manually inserted plugs to control the operation of equipment, such as a removable panel containing an ordered array of terminals which may be interconnected by short electrical leads (plugged in by hand) according to a prescribed pattern and thereby designating a specific program or sequence of specified program steps. The panel is rewired for different programs. Many computers and peripheral equipment are programmed by means of a plugboard. In some applications, a set of plugboards is maintained, one wired plugboard for each program. Thus the plugboards need not be

rewired each time they are used. The entire prewired plugboard is inserted as a unit. It may be a wiring board or sometimes referred to as a control panel or terminal board. One type of plugboard has an array of terminal sockets or holes that are connected by an output plug to logic elements, such as gates, registers, and relays, permitting the logic or the program of a computer to be varied by means of pins, plugs, or interconnecting wires. To change a program, one wired-up plugboard can be removed and another inserted in its place. The data represented by the interconnections stored on the face of the plugboard can be read like data stored on tape, or the connections may actually wire the logic elements of the computer. In some instances, the interpretation of interconnections on the plugboard is made in association with holes on punched cards. The primary difference between plugboards and pinboards is that plugboards use jump wires, plugs, and patchcords, while pinboards use patchplugs, pins, or cordless plugs. The plugboard may also be used simply to route data or interconnect communication links, such as a telephone switchboard. It consists of a row of holes, or sockets, connected to incoming and outgoing lines, and a row of plugs, or jacks, to connect any incoming call on any line to any other line. Most plugboards in computer applications are removable with the connections intact so as to preserve the wired-up program for future use, and so, quickly change jobs. The Univac 1004 computer uses a plugboard for program control. (Synonymous with *control panel,* with *patch panel,* with *problem board,* with *wiring board,* and with *patchboard.*)

plugboard, detachable—A plugboard that can be removed or detached from the computer or other system without disturbing the positions of the cords and plugs. Thus, programs can be preserved and programs can be wired-up on boards prior to connection to the system, allowing for quick change from one job to another. (Synonymous with *removable plugboard.*)

plugboard, patch-program—A small plugboard containing a program change or variation in the form of pin or patchcord arrangements and mounted on a larger plugboard containing the main program.

plugboard, removable—Same as *plugboard, detachable.*

plugboard chart—See *chart, plugboard.*

plugging chart—Same as *chart, plugboard.*

plus zone—See *zone, plus.*

PM—See *modulation, phase.*

p-n type junction—See *junction, p-n type.*

p-n-p transistor—See *transistor, p-n-p.*

pocket—In a sorter, the card stacker assigned to each key position; a card storage location corresponding to each key. Pocketing for a given key eliminates the

260

need for sorting on that key before tabulating, totals for each key value being accumulated in its corresponding pocket.

point, addressable—In display systems, a position on a display surface that may be specified in absolute data, that is, absolute coordinates of the device. Usually there are a finite number of addressable points for a specified display device, forming a grid or raster over the display surface.

point, arithmetic—In positional notation, the character, expressed or implied, that separates the integral part of a numerical expression from the fractional part; for example, a decimal point, a binary point. Thus, the point falls between the zero and the minus one power of the base in the series that defines the number, as in 765.98, which represents $7 \times 10^2 + 6 \times 10^1 + 5 \times 10^0 + 9 \times 10^{-1} + 8 \times 10^{-2}$. The last dot is a period, not an arithmetic point. If there is no point, it is implied to be located at the right end of the integer. In computer representation of numerals, the arithmetic point is fixed or arranged for in the logic design of the computer, and so, from an external view, is understood or implied to be at a certain location. (Synonymous with *base point* and with *radix point*. Illustrated by *point, decimal*.)

point, base—Same as *point, arithmetic*.

point, binary—In a numeral written with a radix of two in positional notation, the arithmetic point that separates the integral part of a numeral from the fractional part. Thus, the binary point is the arithmetic point in a binary numeral. Thus, in binary notation, 110.101 is equivalent in decimal notation to $4 + 2 + \frac{1}{2} + \frac{1}{8}$, or $6\frac{5}{8}$, or 6.625.

point, branch—See *branchpoint*.

point, break—See *breakpoint*.

point, check—See *checkpoint*.

point, decimal—1: In positional notation, the arithmetic point, expressed or implied, in a numeral written with a radix of 10. (Illustrative of *arithmetic point*.) 2: The radix point in the decimal numeration system. Among the conventions used to represent the decimal point are the comma, the period, and the point or dot at the mid-height of the digits.

point, entry—1: In a routine, any point to which control can be passed, such as the address or identifier of the first executed instruction in a computer routine. A routine may have a number of different entry points each of which corresponds to a different purpose of the routine. The point at which a routine is reentered from a sub-routine is called a reentry point. 2: The address, label, or tag associated with the first instruction executed when entering a computer program, routine or subroutine. A computer program, routine, or subroutine may have many different entry points, each entry point

corresponding to a different function or purpose. (Synonymous with *return address*.) 3: The address of the location of the instruction in a computer program to which a subroutine is to return control. Such control is normally returned after the subroutine is completed and the original program is to be resumed. 4: In computer simulation, the place in a flowchart or block diagram where a system, process, or operation is initiated.

point, fixed—Pertaining to a system of numeration in which the position of the arithmetic point is placed at a given position with respect to a given end of the numerals in that system, according to some convention. In many computers, the binary point is considered fixed at the left end of the numerals, thus scaling all numerals between plus one and minus one. Unless otherwise stated, most numeration systems hold all numerals to the left of the point to be whole, all numerals to the right to be fractional. Thus, in a fixed-point computer, the arithmetic point is not located by the programmer, but always remains located in a predetermined or wired-in position. (Contrast with *point, floating* and with *point, variable*.)

point, floating—Pertaining to a system of numeration in which the position of the arithmetic point is not placed and held at a given position with respect to a given end of all numerals in that system. The position of the arithmetic point is expressed by a given convention, such as by an exponent of the radix of the numeration system. In floating-point notation, a number is usually expressed as a fixed-point numeral that serves as a multiplying coefficient and an exponential part that consists of the radix of the numeration system raised to a power, which, in effect, locates the arithmetic point; hence, the term floating point. In the numeral 0.397×10^4, or 0.397×04, the 0.397 is the coefficient, sometimes called the fractional part, if it is less than unity, and the 04, or 4, is the power to which the radix is to be raised. The product is the magnitude of the number. In this case, 0.397×04 is equivalent to 3970. Floating-point notation permits wide ranges of numbers to be expressed and helps to reduce scaling problems in computers, when it is difficult to predict the magnitude of computed quantities. A numeral resulting from an operation, such as 94,000,000 that might exceed the capacity of a register, might be represented as 9.4,7, or 94,6, where the third digit in the examples is an exponent of the radix. The radix, raised to the indicated power, is then multiplied by the remaining two digits, usually a fixed-point number. By proper selection of the value of the exponent, representing the power to which the radix is to be raised, the fractional part of the number may be held within a given range, still permitting the expression of numbers of greater magnitude. (Contrast with *point, fixed* and with *point, variable*.)

point, index—In punch-card machines containing rotating machinery driven by a main shaft, one of the equally spaced rotational reference positions of the main shaft. The equally spaced reference positions are usually chosen to be those at which successive card rows or columns are at the sensing or punching station of the card reader or punch. Extra index points may be required to allow for a gap between cards while they are traversing the card track. The index point may be labeled according to the row or column, if any, to which it corresponds.

point, interchange—A location, usually in a data network, where interface signals are transmitted between equipment by means of planned electrical interconnection.

point, load—A marked position on magnetic tape that is positioned under the recording head when the reel is mounted in a tape station. Reading and writing begin and end at this point. A metallic strip may be used to mark the load point, indicating to both the operator and the machine where to start or stop reading or writing.

point, radix—Same as *point, arithmetic*.

point, reentry—In a computer program, the instruction at which the program is reentered from another program, routine, or subroutine. The reentry point is usually designated by the address or the label of the instruction that is designated as the reentry point.

point, rerun—A location or a point in a computer program at which all information required to repeat the program from the last rerun point is available either to the program itself or to a restart routine. This permits repeating the routine from the last rerun or checkpoint in the event of an error or a malfunction. The rerun points may be only three to five minutes apart, so that instead of returning to the beginning of a program in the event of an error, it is only necessary to return to the last rerun point. All information pertinent to a rerun is available in stored or recorded form during the whole time from one rerun point to the next. One purpose of a checkpoint is to permit the rerunning of the program from the checkpoint; thus, a checkpoint may serve as a rerun point. In any case, a computer run may be reconstituted and run again from a rerun point or a checkpoint. (Synonymous with *restart point*, and with *rescue point*.)

point, rescue—Same as *point, rerun*.
point, restart—Same as *point, rerun*.
point, variable—A radix numeration system in which each number is represented by a numeral; that is, a set of digits, with the arithmetic point explicitly indicated by a character placed among the digits by the

writer according to the magnitude of the number desired to be expressed; for example, 85.96, 8.596, or 859P6. Usually the point is a dot or period, and its position separates the coefficients of the negative powers of the radix from the coefficients of the positive powers of the radix, being just to the right of the coefficient of the zero power of the radix; that is, just to the right of the units position. (Contrast with *point, floating* and with *point, fixed*.)

point, zero-level transmission reference—An arbitrarily chosen physical point in a circuit to which all transmission levels, such as current, voltage, and power levels, are referred or referenced, and so are measured from. The transmission level at the transmitting switchboard is frequently taken as the zero-level transmission reference level, and thus the transmitting switchboard becomes the zero-level transmission reference point.

point-through—The transfer of a recorded signal from one layer of magnetic tape to adjacent layers when the tape is wound on a hub or reel.

point-to-point connection—See *connection, point-to-point*.

pointer—An identifier or indicator of the location of data; for example, an address, an algorithm for generating an address, a keyword, a code for generating an address, or a destination or source designator.

pointer, stack—The address of the first one of a sequence of storage locations that are used for a pushdown storage. The address is usually held in a preassigned register. (Synonymous with *stack indicator*.)

polarization diversity—See *diversity, polarization*.

polarized dipole modulation recording—Same as *recording, polarized return-to-zero*.

polarized return-to-zero recording—See *recording, polarized return-to-zero*.

Polish notation—See *notation, Polish*.

poll—1: In switching networks, to request a station to send data. 2: In a computer operating system, to periodically interrogate a device to determine if an interaction is required between the device doing the polling and the device that is being polled. 3: To interrogate a set of devices sequentially; for example, to interrogate each of a set of terminals sharing a communication channel periodically to determine if it requires use of the channel.

polymorphic—Pertaining to a mode of computing system organization, configuration, or arrangement of major component parts in a manner such that all components at a given installation are held in a common pool, and, as each program to be executed is selected, a specific set of components is chosen from the pool, electrically connected, used to execute the program, and, upon completion, returned to the pool. Each configuration of equipment is matched to the program, and as many programs can be run simultaneously as systems can be constructed from the pool. For example, to run Program A, a control unit, two arithmetic and logic units, a core storage unit, two disc units, four tapes, a card reader and a printer are automatically connected. Program B may require only one arithmetic unit and no disc units. When Program A is completed, the units are returned to ready status for reassignment to Program C, and so forth. A modular system, however, is relatively a fixed configuration, somewhat changeable in the sense that a given program will only use what it needs, with perhaps the remaining equipment going unused. Polymorphic implies variable modularity. (Contrast with *modular*.)

polyphase sort—See *sort, polyphase*.

pool, buffer—A group of buffers that may be allocated as needed to various jobs.

pool, free-core—Same as *pool, free-storage*.

pool, free-storage—An area, or areas, of computer main storage that may be dynamically allocated to sundry uses, such as input-output buffering, program expansion, and scratch-padding. (Synonymous with *free-core pool*.)

POPS—(Pantograph Optical Projection System). A radar data-plotting system technique wherein targets are projected on a plotting board as a point of light and a plotter in the rear marks the target with a grease pencil. Similar to DOPS and TOPS, except as to input devices.

port—In a fluidic device, an opening or exit to another environment from a different environment; for example an opening from an internal passage to the atmosphere or to a constant-pressure chamber; or an opening from a controlled-pressure chamber to an internal passage of a fluidic device.

port, bias—In a fluidic device, a port at which a biasing signal, such as a controlled-pressure stream, is applied.

port, control—In a fluidic device, a port at which a control signal, such as a variable pressure, is applied.

port, output—In a fluidic device, a port at which an output signal occurs.

port, supply—In a fluidic device, the port at which power is provided to an active device, such as an amplifier.

port, vent—In a fluidic device, the port at which a reference pressure is applied.

port-a-punch card—See *card, port-a-punch*.

portable data medium—Same as *carrier, data*.

position—Same as *place*.

position, addressable horizontal—In micrographics, a position along a horizontal, x-axis, or abscissa, within a specified film frame, at which a vertical line can be placed. (Contrast with *position, addressable vertical*.)

position, addressable vertical—In micrographics, a position along a vertical, y-axis, or ordinate, within a specified film frame, at which a horizontal line can be placed. (Contrast with *position, addressable horizontal*.)

position, bit—A character position in a computer word expressed in binary notation.

position, code—The sites in a data-recording medium or data carrier where data may be entered, such as a hole punched, a character printed, or a magnetic mark made. In a punched card, the rows and column code positions are located with reference to the card edges. The intersection of a row and column marks a code position. A paper tape is divided into a number of tracks parallel to the edges and transversely into rows. The intersection of each track and row marks a code position where a single hole may or may not be punched. A character may be represented by an array of holes at a group of code positions, on tape or cards, such as a column of code positions, with one or more code positions having holes to represent an alphanumeric character; a part of a row of code positions on a card to represent a character; or a row of code positions on paper tape to represent a character. Conventions must be adopted in order to describe the locations of code positions in any medium used as a data carrier. In an 80-column card with 12 rows, there are 960 punch positions. The code position on a punched card or a punched tape or sheet is called a punch position.

position, digit—Same as *place, digit*.

position, overflow—An extra place in a register in which an overflow digit, such as the carry digit resulting from adding the two most significant digits of two numerals, may be developed or stored. The position condition may be sensed in a computer and used to indicate an excess magnitude, to trigger an overflow alarm, or to indicate that a possible error in scaling has been made.

position, punch—The location on a data carrier, usually registered or indexed with reference to edges of the medium, such as cards, tapes, or sheets, where a hole may be made. (Further explained by *track*, card. Contrast with *station, punching*. Synonymous with *punching position*.)

position, punching—Same as *position, punch*.

position, sign—The position at which the sign of a number is located. The sign position in a computer word is usually located at the left end or most significant position when written or when viewing a computer register. Since the sign may be either positive or negative, a binary digit is sufficient to designate the sign of a number, such as a zero for a minus sign and a one for a plus sign. As a result, and for other arithmetic purposes, such as complementing, it sometimes becomes necessary to associate a sign with zero as expressed in the computer. The binary digit in the sign position is detected and used to determine how to process the number in an arithmetic operation; for example, since the addition of a positive number to a negative number is equivalent to subtraction, the negative sign digit causes the computer to add the positive number to the complement of the negative number, which is always available anyway as the opposite side of each flip-flop of the register that is used to express or store the operands. (Further clarified by *digit, sign.*)

position modulation, pulse—See *modulation, pulse-position.*

position pulse—Same as *pulse, commutator.*

positional notation—See *notation, positional.*

positional representation—Same as *notation, positional.*

positional representation system—See *system, positional representation.*

positioning time—See *time, positioning.*

positive-AND gate—Same as *gate, AND.*

positive feedback—See *feedback, positive.*

positive film—See *film, positive.*

positive-OR gate—Same as *gate, OR.*

post—To record a unit of data; for example, to enter the type, quantity, and source of a load of material that just arrived at a warehouse in a ledger or log, or to print out the results of a set of computations after each iteration.

post-edit—To edit the results of data that has been processed; for example, to edit output data from a computer computation run, or to edit the output of a mechanical translation of a natural language; that is, to edit the target language output for consistency, ambiguity, grammar, and logic. (Contrast with *pre-edit.*)

postfix notation—See *notation, postfix.*

post-installation review—See *review, post-installation.*

post mortem—Pertaining to the analysis of an operation after its completion; for example, in digital computer programming, a diagnostic routine that automatically or on demand prints out information concerning the contents of registers and storage locations at the time the routine stopped in order to assist in the location and correction of a mistake in coding or a malfunction of the computer.

post mortem dump—See *dump, post mortem.*

post mortem routine—See *routine, post mortem.*

post-write disturb pulse—See *pulse, post-write disturb.*

posting, event—Saving programs and data related to a task or job and establishing the programs and data of another task or job to which control is to be passed, based on the occurrence of an event, such as completion of loading of data into storage or completion of execution of a task or job.

posting, facsimile—The process of transferring, by means of a duplicating process, a printed line on a record to another ledger, usually on a selective basis. This form of posting may be used to post customer ledgers, employee earning records, and stock ledger cards.

posting, terminal-digit—Posting in accordance with the final or least significant digits of identifying numerals, such as arranging and recording of serial numbers of documents on the basis of the final digits of the numerals.

postprocessor—A computer program that performs some final computation or data processing after the completion of certain other processing, such as after completion of a program or a run. (Contrast with preprocessor.)

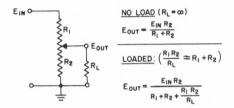

Loaded and unloaded potentiometer, *i.e., a voltage divider, used in analog and digital computers.*

potentiometer—A voltage divider, consisting of a fixed resistor with two fixed end terminals and a third terminal, usually a slider or wiper, capable of being positioned between the end terminals, which permits a fraction of the voltage applied across the end terminals to be tapped off, with reference to one of the ends. Such a device may be used in analog computers to perform multiplication, division, and other functions, especially in electromechanical systems.

potentiometer, flat-card resolving—Same as *potentiometer, slab resolving.*

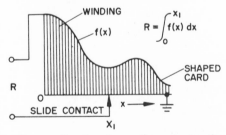

For any function given as the perimeter of the shaped-card potentiometer, *the resistance to point* x_1 *is proportional to the integral of function to* x_1 *from origin 0.*

potentiometer, shaped-card—A function generator in analog form for generating functions of one variable, in which the input variable sets the angular position of a potentiometer shaft. The resistor card, on which the resistance wire forming the potentiometer is wound, is shaped so that the length of each turn of wire is proportional to the derivative of the desired function. A reference supply voltage is connected to the card resistance and the output voltage, representing the desired function, is taken from the potentiometer slider that moves along the card. Thus, since the voltage at the slider is proportional to the resistance, and the resistance is proportional to the total resistance to the slider, that is, to the integral of all resistance elements or turns up to the slider, the output is proportional to the desired function. The device can be used to generate only the particular function for which it has been constructed.

potentiometer, slab resolving—A potentiometer whose resistance element is wound on a square slab. The input variable is made to set the angle of rotation of the slab about an axis through the center perpendicular (normal) to its plane and the plane of rotation. Four fixed sliders or wipers are positioned symmetrically about the center of rotation, forming a square whose diagonal is less than the side of the slab. The input variable is used to apply voltages representing plus and minus R to the ends of the resistance element, and the four output voltages from the wipers then are proportional to $\pm R \cos \theta$ and $\pm R \sin \theta$, where θ is the angle of rotation of the slab. The wipers could rotate and the slab remain fixed. A unit of this type is used in electromechanical analog computers. (Synonymous with *flat-card resolving potentiometer*.)

potentiometer function-generator, loaded—See *generator, loaded-potentiometer function*.

potentiometer function-generator, tapped—See *generator, tapped-potentiometer function*.

potentiometer loading error—See *error, potentiometer loading*.

potentiometer multiplier—Same as *multiplier, servo*.

power—In mathematics, pertaining to the number of times a numeral or quantity is to be multiplied by itself; for example, 8 raised to the second power is 64; $x + x^2 + x^3 + \ldots + x^n$ is a power series; and 1000 is an integral power of 10, namely 3.

power, standard test tone—One-milliwatt (0 dBm) at 1000 hertz.

power dump—See *dump, power*.

power output rating, carrier—See *rating, carrier power output*.

power-supply, reference—Same as *supply, reference*.

powered telephone, electrically—See *telephone, electrically powered*.

powered telephone, sound—See *telephone, sound-powered*.

pragmatics—1: The study, discipline, or subject field concerning the relationships between symbols and their users or interpreters. 2: The relationship between

groups of characters, their interpretation, and their use.

preanalysis—In computer programming, a review of the task to be accomplished by the computer prior to programming in order to increase the efficiency of task performance by the programmer and the computer.

preburning—Same as *burn-in*.

precision—The degree of discrimination with which a quantity is described or stated. Thus, a three-digit numeral discriminates among eight possibilities in a binary numeration system and among 1000 in a decimal system. Precision is the degree of exactness with which a quantity is stated, not the correctness with which it is stated. Thus, if 3.14189 is used to represent the value of pi, there is an attempt to be precise to six places; however, the figure is accurate to only four places, the fifth place being inaccurate, that is, incorrect or wrong. Precision is to be distinguished from accuracy, with which it is often confused. Again, the value of e, radix of the natural logarithms, has been computed with a precision of over 1000 places by means of a digital computer, confirming that a hand computation was inaccurate in the 808th place. Precision is measured in terms of the number of significant digits required to express its value, such as the measurement 2.7500 ± 0.0001 inches being more precisely determined than 2.75 ± 0.01 inches. (Contrast with *accuracy*.)

precision, double—In computer operation and programming, pertaining to the use of two computer words to represent a number. Thus, twice as many digits as are normally carried in a fixed-length computer word are used to express numbers, by keeping track of the more significant and less significant halves of the numbers. Often, matrix manipulation imposes a requirement to resort to multiprecision numbers, even in floating-point computers. For example, in multiplication, the product may have twice as many digits as the factors, and if the product is used as a factor, precision is lost even if the less significant half of a product is discarded. (Contrast with *precision, single*. Compare with *precision, multiple*.)

precision, multiple—In computer operation and programming, pertaining to the use of two or more computer words to represent a single numeric quantity or numeral. Thus, twice as many, or more, digits as are normally carried in a fixed-length computer word are used to express numbers by keeping track of the several parts of each numeral as they are handled and placed in storage. Matrix manipulation often requires the use of multiple precision arithmetic, even in floating-point computers. (Contrast with *precision, single*. Compare with *precision, double*.)

precision, single—In computer operation and programming, pertaining to the use of numeric quantities containing not more than the number of digits as in one word length of the computer. Single precision is implied in computer programming, unless multiple precision is specifically resorted to or specified. (Contrast with *precision, double* and with *precision, multiple*.)

precision, triple—In computer operation and programming, pertaining to the use of three computer words to express the value of numeric quantities; that is, numerals. As triple and double precision arithmetic is performed, the computer programmer must arrange to keep track of each part of each numeral by his program. (Contrast with *precision, single* and compare with *precision, multiple*.)

predefined process—See *process, predefined*.

predicate—In deductive logic or mathematics, that which is affirmed or denied; for example, statement P is true, but statement Q is false.

pre-edit—To edit data prior to processing; for example, to edit input data to be used in a computer run or to edit a source natural language before it undergoes machine translation into a target language in order to remove inconsistency, ambiguity, grammatical errors, and idiomatic expressions that might not be translatable, so that the machine can produce a higher quality product in the target language. (Contrast with *post-edit*.)

prefix notation—See *notation, prefix*.

preliminary review—See *review, preliminary*.

preparation, volume—For a computer operating system, the group of functions and activities that are performed when a new volume is to be added to the system; for example the writing of standard volume labels, formatting tracks, and creating a volume directory.

preprocessor—A computer program that performs some initial computation or data processing before initiation of certain other processing, such as before initiation of a program or a run. (Contrast with *postprocessor*.)

preread disturb pulse—See *pulse, preread disturb*.

preread head—See *head, preread*.

preselection—Pertaining to a computer programming technique in which a block of data on tape is transferred, from the next tape to be read, into a buffer so that it may be rapidly transferred from the buffer to internal storage, thus preventing the main frame from waiting for data to be transferred from tape to internal storage and speeding up operations. It is the next tape to be read that is preselected by the program prior to the time that the data is actually needed.

presence bit—See *bit, presence*.

preserve—Same as *hold*.

preset—To establish an initial condition or starting state; for example, to set the

contents of a storage location to a given initial value, to set all registers in a computer to specific values prior to the running of a program, to establish the initial control value for a loop, or to set an initial value for the address of an operand or a cycle index. (Synonymous with *initialize*.)

preset parameter—See *parameter, preset*.

pressure amplification—See *amplification, pressure*.

prestore—To store data that will be required by a subroutine before the subroutine execution starts. The data is usually stored in a location that is most convenient to the subroutine, usually in the internal storage, having been taken from external storage.

pre-stored query—See *query, pre-stored*.

presumptive address—Same as *address, base*.

presumptive instruction—See *instruction, presumptive*.

preventive maintenance—See *maintenance, preventive*.

PRF—(Pulse Repetition Frequency). Same as *frequency, pulse repetition*.

primary center—Same as *center, primary switching*.

primary center, telephone—Same as *center, primary switching*.

primary storage—Same as *storage, main*.

primary switching center—See *center, primary switching*.

primitive—The smallest, most basic, most fundamental unit of data, such as a single letter, a syllable, a digit, a machine code, a pseudocode element, or a symbol. In a sense, primitives may form semantemes which may be grouped to form morphemes.

principal maintenance period—See *period, principal maintenance*.

print contrast ratio—See *ratio, print contrast*.

print control character—See *character, print control*.

print-member—The component of a printing device that is responsible for the form of the printed character; for example, a print bar, type bar, or print wheel. An interchangeable print member allows the operator to change the available alphabet.

print-out, dynamic—The printing of data resulting from a computer run during the run as one or more of the sequential operations in the routine. (Contrast with *print-out, static*.)

print-out, static—The printing of data resulting from a computer run after the run occurs; thus, the print operations are not among the sequential operations in the routine. (Contrast with *print-out, dynamic*.)

print-punch editor—See *editor, print-punch*.

print wheel—See *wheel, print*.

print-wheel assembly—See *assembly, print-wheel*.

printed card form—See *form, printed card*.

printed circuit—See *circuit, printed*.

printed-circuit card—See *card, printed-circuit*.

printer−A device that forms a visible permanent image on a surface by the application of ink. The printer is often used as an online or offline output mechanism for digital computers to permit communication between the machine and the man, both immediately and subsequently to the operation or computation. Printers for computers are available in a variety of types and with a variety of characteristics. The printed record obtained from a printer can be visually read by a person or optically or magnetically sensed by optical character recognition and magnetic-ink character recognition equipment. (Contrast with *tabular*.)

printer, bar−A printer that has its type at each print position held in a long narrow box or magazine from which the type projects. A particular character is selected for printing by moving the box vertically until the desired character is opposite the printing position. Each bar contains the entire alphabet or font available to a particular print position. The erratic motion required of the bar made the bar printer slower than the newer wheel printers. Only paper feed control was necessary, not carriage lateral motion. (Further clarified by *bar, type*.)

printer, chain−A high-speed printer in which the type is carried on a moving closed loop chain or belt that is hit on-the-fly by an appropriate hammer as the type moves across the paper, with each character printing in its proper location, thus forming a line of print. The chain travels in a horizontal plane, each character being printed as it is positioned opposite a magnet-driven hammer that presses the paper against the type on the chain.

printer, character−A printer in which a single character at a time is selected, or composed, and determined within the device prior to its being printed. Thus, similar to a typewriter action, a laterally moving carriage is involved to move the paper or the type font to the next print position on a line.

printer, drum−A line printer that has the type mounted on a rotating drum that contains a full character set for each of the printing positions. An entire line may be printed during one rotation of the drum; usually the same character, for example, all the letter A's, are printed at once at all the positions at which an A occurs.

printer, high-speed−A printer capable of printing at relatively rapid printing rates, usually expressed in terms of characters per second, lines per minute, or pages per minute. The relatively high rate is relative to the state of the art. About 600 lines per minute is considered high speed, though 2400 lines per minute is practical. If a printer can efficiently operate online with a computer, it is considered high speed

relative to that system. Most wheel, chain, matrix, and cathode-ray-tube-based printers are considered high-speed printers.

printer, hit-on-the-fly−A printer in which the type does not stop moving during the impression time. High-speed hammers strike the paper or the type while the type is moving relative to the paper at the precise instant that the proper type is at the appropriate print position. Wheel and chain printers hit on-the-fly. Thus, the type or print head is in continuous motion, avoiding the necessity of overcoming inertia in starting and stopping type, and so saving time and wear. (Synonymous with *on-the-fly printer*.)

printer, line−A printer in which an entire line of print is composed and determined within the printer prior to printing, and the entire line thus composed is printed during a single cycle of operation, such as during a single revolution of the type cylinder or wheel or a single revolution of the chain, each character printed in its position on a line as it comes opposite the print line and the hammer. It may appear from outside the printer as though the entire line is printed simultaneously, as the paper feeds a line at a time. There is no lateral movement of a carriage as in a character printer. (Synonymous with *line-at-a-time printer*.)

printer, line-at-a-time−Same as *printer, line*.

printer, matrix−A printer that forms characters by forcing a set of selected styli or wires against the ribbon or paper, such as the specific wires of a 5 × 7 array chosen so as to form a character. On close examination, the printed character appears as a pattern of dots. The print heads are located in a single line at each character position. When the paper is positioned for a new line, all heads simultaneously print the appropriate character for their respective positions along the line of print. (Synonymous with *stylus printer* and with *wire printer*.)

printer, on-the-fly−Same as *printer, hit-on-the-fly*.

printer, page−A printer in which an entire page of characters is composed and determined within the printer prior to printing and the entire page is printed during a single cycle of operation, such as in a xerographic printer or in a cathode-ray tube, camera, and film printer.

printer, stylus−Same as *printer, matrix*.

printer, wheel−A printer that has the type face mounted or engraved on the outside of the rim of a disc or wheel. There is a wheel for each print or character position in a line of print. The wheels are keyed to a shaft, forming a cylinder which is rotated at high speed. As each character type, on each wheel, that is to be printed comes opposite the print position on the line to be printed on the paper, a signal is given to a magnetically driven hammer to press the paper against the ribbon to print the character. An entire line may be printed during each revolution of the type wheel, unless time is required to move the paper or to permit recovery of the hammer driving mechanism, in which case it may be necessary to skip one or more revolutions of the wheel. (Further explained by *wheel, print* and by *assembly, print-wheel.*)

printer, wire—Same as *printer, matrix.*

printer, xerographic—A printer that forms an optical image such that dark areas are electrostatically charged and light areas are electrostatically uncharged. The paper is dusted with particles of finely powdered dry ink. The particles adhere only to the electrostatically charged areas. The paper is heated, causing the ink to melt, permanently fixing an image of characters to the paper.

printing, line—The printing of an entire line, or row, of characters at a time and as a unit.

printing equipment—See *equipment, printing.*

priority, program—The relative position assigned to a computer program in the sequencing of programs on the computer. The priority of all programs to be run are taken into consideration by the master control program or executive routine in order to arrive at a schedule. Interrupt features permit a program to be interrupted in favor of a program of higher priority. Time-sharing is accomplished by a carefully worked out time distribution among interleaved programs, each program being assured a length of time according to its priority or other criteria, the lower priority programs receiving shorter running time, only occasional time, or only when-available time. Sometimes higher priority is given to short programs, lower priority to long programs. Priority decisions must be made when operating a computing system in order to get the most important work accomplished and to avoid difficulties among the using organizations. (Further clarified by *processing, priority.*)

priority indicator—See *indicator, priority.*

priority processing—See *processing, priority.*

private automatic branch exchange—See *exchange, private automatic branch.*

private automatic exchange—See *exchange, private automatic.*

private branch exchange—See *exchange, private branch.*

private telephone network—See *network, private telephone.*

private wire network—Same as *network, leased-line.*

probabilistic model—Same as *model, stochastic.*

probability-analysis compaction—See *compaction, probability-analysis.*

probability theory—See *theory, probability.*

problem, benchmark—In computer operation, a problem used to evaluate and measure the performance of computers relative to

each other; for example, obtaining the solution of a set of differential equations, inverting a group of matrices, or handling a specific payroll computation. Benchmark problems are selected in a given area of application or class of problems to be solved. Computer selection is based on the performance time and cost to execute the benchmark problems.

problem, check—In computer operation, a problem whose solution is known, chosen and run specifically to determine whether a computer is operating properly. (Synonymous with *test problem.*)

problem, fault-location—In computer operation, a problem whose solution provides information that identifies the location of faulty equipment. It is usually run after a rapid check problem shows that a fault exists. The fault-location and check problem may be one and the same problem in the form of a diagnostic routine. (Synonymous with *trouble-location problem.*)

problem, test—Same as *problem, check.*

problem, trouble-location—Same as *problem, fault-location.*

problem board—Same as *plugboard.*

problem definition—Same as *description, problem.*

problem description—See *description, problem.*

problem file—See *file, problem.*

problem folder—Same as *file, problem.*

problem-oriented language—See *language, problem-oriented.*

problem program—See *program, problem.*

problem time—See *time, problem.*

procedural statement—Same as *instruction.*

procedure—Same as *method.*

procedure, recovery—In a communications network, a process by which a network control or master station attempts to resolve erroneous or conflicting conditions arising from network operations.

procedure-oriented language—See *language, procedure-oriented.*

procedures, inline—In COBOL, procedural instructions that are part of the main sequential and controlling instructions of the program.

process—1: In data processing, to handle, manipulate, or perform some operation or sequence of operations on data in accordance with a specified or implied algorithm, usually as a series of discrete steps, including operations such as compute, assemble, compile, interpret, generate, translate, store, retrieve, transfer, select, extract, shift, search, sort, merge, transliterate, read, write, print, erase, and punch. The processing usually results in a solution to a problem. 2: A course or sequence of events that takes place according to an intended purpose or to create an intended effect.

process, input—A process consisting of the reception of data into a data processing system, subsystem or device. (Contrast with *process, output*.)

process, iterative—A process for calculating a desired result by means of repeating a cycle or sequence of operations, each cycle bringing the result closer and closer to the solution or true value.

process, output—The process of delivering data from a device such as a data processing system or a computer. (Contrast with *process, input*.)

process, predefined—An identified process that is defined elsewhere in greater detail.

process, sequential—A process that has component events that have no simultaneity or overlap in time or space, respectively.

process chart—Same as *flowchart*.

process control—See *control, process*.

processable scored card—See *card, processable scored*.

processing, automatic data—The handling, manipulating, or performing of some operation or sequence of operations by machine on data in accordance with a specified or implied algorithm, such as a computer program, usually as a series of discrete steps, including operations such as compute, assemble, compile, interpret, generate, translate, store, retrieve, transfer, select, extract, shift, search, sort, merge, transliterate, read, write, print, erase, and punch. Automatic data processing (ADP) involves the use of computer, control, and other data-processing machinery, such as printers, sorters, storage devices, and tape stations. Most automatic data-processing equipment involves an electronic digital or analog computer surrounded by a collection of online and offline peripheral equipment. The basic steps in automatic data processing might include obtaining input data, operating on the data by machine in accordance with a stored program with a minimum of manual intervention, and producing the desired output.

processing, batch—1: The processing of data that has been accumulated over a period of time. 2: The processing of a group of items prepared or required for one or more related operations. 3: The processing of data that has been accumulated in advance such that each accumulation of data or batch thus formed is processed during one computer run.

processing, concurrent batch—A mode of operating a computer such that batched programs are run concurrently using multiprogramming or parallel processing techniques. (Contrast with *processing, sequential batch*.)

processing, data—See *data processing*.

processing, demand—1: A mode of operation of a data processing system in such a manner that data is accepted by the system immediately, if possible, upon receipt of a signal from an external device that usually also is the transmitter

of the data. 2: In teleprocessing systems, the processing of data by a network computer immediately on demand from a network station, subject only to priorities, queues, and system saturation, in contrast to batch processing, where the batching may occur at the sending or receiving station.

processing, electronic data—The processing of data automatically through the use of electronic machinery, such as electronic digital computers. Abbreviated EDP. (Further clarified by *processing, automatic data*.)

processing, industrial data—Data processing of industrial data for control of industrial processes, such as control of machine tools, control of manufacture and production, and control of materials flow and handling.

processing, information—1: Same as *data processing*. 2: The entire field of computers, data processing, process control, and numerical control. Information processing adheres more closely to the meaning assigned to the data involved, interprets the meaning, and encompasses the totality of scientific and business operations performed on computers, as well as data reduction, data sensing, and communications.

processing, job—In a computer operating system, the reading of control statements in an input stream, the initiating, controlling and execution of job steps defined in the program statements, and the writing of output messages reflecting the status and results of the jobs.

processing, list—The processing of data in the format of lists; for example the processing of data in pushup lists, pushdown lists, or chained lists. If chained lists are used, the order of the items can be changed without altering their physical locations.

processing, parallel—1: Pertaining to the simultaneous execution of two or more sequences of instructions by a device having multiple processing units, such as by a computer having multiple arithmetic or logic units. (Contrast with *multiprogramming*. Synonymous with *simultaneous working*.) 2: The concurrent or simultaneous execution of two or more processes in a single system or device.

processing, priority—A system of time-sharing of computing facilities where the programs to be run are selected in accordance with a system of priorities, such as in accordance with the length or nature of the program, or the source of the problem (sponsor). Priorities are assigned to programs beforehand. Interrupt features permit running programs to be interrupted to allow programs of higher priority to run. (Further clarified by *priority program*.)

processing, program termination—The functions that are performed when a computer subroutine, routine, program, job, task, or run comes to either a normal or abnormal halt.

processing, real-time—1: A mode of operation of a data processing system such that the system processes incoming requests or instructions at either random or programmed points in time, the execution of operations being subjected to certain conditions, such as those concerning the availability of results within specified time limits. **2:** Pertaining to data processing in such a manner that the disadvantage or difficulty of not getting results rises sharply when a specified time limit is passed; for example, pertaining to a data processing system operated in a conversational mode.

processing, remote batch—Batch processing in which input devices or output devices used in handling the data and programs being processed and executed, have access to the computer through communication links rather than through direct electrical connection on site at the central processing unit of the computer. Thus, data and programs, although the programs could be resident at the site of the CPU and on call from peripheral or external storage, are sent to the CPU via communication links. Results could be returned via communication links or sent by other means.

processing, sequential batch—A mode of operating a computer such that a run or program is completed before another program or run is started. (Contrast with *processing, concurrent batch*.)

processing, stacked-job—A technique of operating a computer system in such a manner that job-to-job transition is performed automatically and thus with little or no operator intervention.

processing center, data—See *center, data-processing.*

processing machine, data—Same as *machine.*

processing machine, electronic data—See *machine, electronic data-processing.*

processing system, data—See *system, data processing.*

processor—1: In computer hardware, a data processing system; for example, a computer. **2:** In computer software, a program that might include such functions as compiling, assembling, translating, and related functions, usually for a specific programming language, such as COBOL.

processor, data—Equipment capable of performing operations on data with its program, which sequences its operations, or the program itself. Data processors include accounting machines; tabulators; punch card machines, such as card readers; punches, sorters, and collators; automatic computers, and automatic data processors, with their peripheral equipment, such as tape stations, high-speed printers, visual display, and storage devices. Processors may exist as hardware, or as software.

processor, front-end—A computer or data processor connected between input channels and another computer, usually to preprocess data before entry into a larger computer so as to save time on the larger computer. A front end processor might be used to reformat, handle input priority, and perform minor computation prior to further processing on a higher performance computer. Preprocessing is intended to save time and conserve utilization of the larger computer so as to reduce overall cost.

processor, language—A computer program that performs specific functions, such as compiling, assembling, and translating, for a specified programming language; for example, a COBOL processor or a FORTRAN processor.

PROCOMP—(Program Compiler). A program compiler for the TRW 340 computer.

product—The result obtained from the AND logic operation or from the arithmetic multiplication of two numbers. Unless explicitly stated otherwise, the arithmetic product is implied by the word product alone. Thus, in the decimal numeration system, the product of 9 and 8 is 72. (Contrast with *sum*, with *quotient*, and with *difference*.)

product, arithmetic—The result obtained when two numbers are multiplied arithmetically. The arithmetic product is implied when the word product is used alone, unless explicitly stated otherwise. Thus, the product of 9 and 8 is 72 in the decimal system of numeration. (Contrast with *product, logic*.)

product gate, logic—See *gate, logic product.*

product, intermediate—Same as *product, partial.*

product, logic—The result obtained from the AND operation. (Contrast with *product, arithmetic*. Further clarified by *multiply, logic*.)

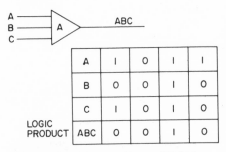

A	I	O	I	I
B	O	O	I	O
C	I	O	I	O
LOGIC PRODUCT ABC	O	O	I	O

The logic product is binary 0010, i.e., decimal 2. The arithmetic product is decimal 220.

product, partial—The result obtained by multiplying the multiplicand by one of the digits of the multiplier. There are as many partial products in a multiplication operation as there are significant digits in a multiplier. The partial sums are appropriately shifted and added to obtain the final product, called simply the product. (Synonymous with *intermediate product*.)

I I 0 I 0 I	MULTIPLICAND
I 0 I I	MULTIPLIER
I I 0 I 0 I	FIRST PARTIAL PRODUCT
I I 0 I 0 I	
I 0 0 I I I I I	SECOND PARTIAL PRODUCT
I I 0 I 0 I 0	
I 0 0 I 0 0 0 I I I	PRODUCT

Multiplication showing partial products.

production mode system—See *mode, system production.*

production routine—See *routine, production.*

production time—See *time, production.*

profile, interest—The subjects of interest or concern to a person or an organization. The descriptions of these subjects form the profile. The profiles are used for the selective dissemination of information to the person or organization.

PROGENY—An automatic report generator developed by Sperry-Rand Corporation, Univac Division, for use on the Univac Solid State II 80/90 computer.

program—The plan or specification of steps for solving a problem, including an analysis of the problem, to arrive at the steps, the steps themselves, and any associated actions, such as flow diagraming, development of computer routines or subroutines, allocation of storage, specification of input and output formats, and any other action required to set up for a computer run, and including coding; or to devise a plan for solving a problem. It may involve problem analysis, writing of routines, and coding, or just selection of a few existing routines from a library. The primary steps in computer programming are problem analysis, flow-charting, writing of routines, and coding, as performed by the analyst, programmer, and coder, respectively, with some overlap of duties and responsibilities. (Further clarified by *subroutine,* by *routine,* and by *program, computer.*)

program, assembly—Same as *assembler.*

program, baseball computer—1: An automatic question answerer; that is a computer program that answers questions, phrased in ordinary English, concerning stored data on a particular subject. The replies generated by the computer need not necessarily be phrased in grammatically correct English sentences. For example, in response to the question, "Who discovered America in 1492?", the reply might simply be, "Columbus." 2: A computer program specifically designed to analyze questions concerning baseball and phrased in ordinary English text. At the present time, replies are not in grammatically correct, ordinary English text. "Did Whitey Ford ever pitch for the Cleveland Indians?"

might be a typical question. The questions are inserted on punch cards. The program causes the computer to look up the words and idioms in a stored glossary. The program extracts the information from the data matching the specifications. The extracted data are processed and the results are printed. The program is coded in IPL V (Information Processing Language, Version 5), using an IBM 7090 computer.

program, benchmark—A standard program used to evaluate the performance of different computers relative to each other and relative to preselected evaluation criteria.

program, blue-ribbon—Same as *program, star.*

program, check—A routine used to run a check problem on a computer to determine if a malfunction or fault exists. If the check problem runs correctly, there is no need for running a diagnostic routine.

program, checking—A computer program that examines data, such as other computer programs, for mistakes or errors of all types, such as syntax errors, spelling errors, coding errors, logical errors, and punctuation errors.

program, coded—A list of computer instructions which have been written in a language or code acceptable to the computer.

program, common—A program that is used by two or more jobs, tasks, or runs, only one copy of which is stored in main storage.

program, compiling—Same as *compiler.*

program, computer—1: A plan or a procedure for solving a problem with a computer, as contrasted with terms such as fiscal program, military program, research and development program, safety program, quality-control program, and technical information program. 2: A sequence of instructions or statements in a form acceptable to, and intended for execution on, a computer.

program, control—1: A computer program that observes, regulates, controls or verifies the operations of a data processing system, such as the execution of other programs. 2: A computer program that schedules and supervises the execution of the programs, routines, and subroutines of a computing system. 3: A computer program that is part of the operating system supervisor. (Synonymous with *monitor program.*)

program, dependent—A user or nonsupervisory computer program, such as a utility program, that is called by the operating system when needed.

program, driver—A computer program that controls the use or operation of a device connected online to the computer, such as a disc, tape, or input-output unit.

program, dynamic—1: A computer program structured with more than one module

271

and in which each module can be loaded into main storage, relocated in main storage, and executed independently, subject to program structure control by the operating system. (Contrast with *program, overlay* and with *program, simple*.) 2: A computer program structured in such a manner that values can be assigned to certain parameters by the computer before or during its execution depending on the specific application or on results obtained thus far during a particular run.

program, editor—A computer program that performs editing functions, such as the rearrangement, modification, deletion, or addition of data in accordance with prescribed rules. An editor program may be used for format control, code conversion, zero-suppression, and other standard processes that have become routine for a given application area. (Contrast with *editor, linkage*.)

program, executive—Same as *routine, executive*.

program, externally stored—A computer program that is stored in an input medium, such as punched cards, removed disc packs, removed tapes, and removed film. The program must be read from the medium, by connection and subsequent interpretation. Plugboard and pinboard programs may be considered internally stored when wired and inserted and externally stored programs when not plugged in or connected to a computer, but stacked in a storage rack. (Contrast with *program, internally stored*.)

program, general—A computer program designed to solve a class of problems, becoming applicable to a specific problem only when appropriate parametric values are supplied. (Contrast with *program, specific*.

program, input—A program, usually a utility program, that controls or organizes the input process of a computer. (Contrast with *program, output*.)

program, internally stored—A computer program that is stored in the internal storage of a computer, perhaps in the same storage area as the data to be operated on, usually stored in high-speed storage, so that instructions may be accessed or obtained rapidly for execution. Programs are considered to be internally stored if they are immediately and directly accessible to the control and arithmetic or logic unit. This is in contrast with externally stored programs on cards, tapes, or pinboards, although pinboards and plugboards are often considered as internal storage, since they are electrically so rapidly accessible to the computer. Most high-speed electronic digital computers are internally stored program computers. (Contrast with *program, externally stored*.)

program, interpretive—Same as *interpreter*.

program, library—A computer program that is in or taken from a group of programs that is considered to be a library of programs.

program, macro generating—Same as *macrogenerator*.

program, main—A computer program that controls all operations except those specified by other programs, routines, subroutines, or loops entered from it. After completion of specific sequences of instructions, control reverts back to the main program. The main program minimizes the requirement for human intervention. It might perform one or more of the following functions: schedule programs and routines; initiate segments of programs; control input-output operations; allocate storage dynamically; issue instructions to a human operator and verify that his actions are correct; perform corrective actions on mistakes in a program; or take corrective action when a piece of equipment fails to function properly. (Synonymous with *master program* and *main routine*.)

program, maintenance—A computer program usually consisting of diagnostic routines, test routines, checking routines, and similar routines designed to assist in removing or reducing malfunctions in a computer or to maintain programs and routines in proper working order, ready for use and up to date.

program, master—Same as *program, main*.

program, master-control—An application-oriented program, which performs the highest level of control in a hierarchy of subroutines, routines, and programs. (Synonymous with *master control*. Closely related to *system, operating*.)

program, minimal-latency—Same as *routine, minimal-latency*.

program, monitor—Same as *program, control*.

program, object—Same as *program, target*.

program, output—A program, usually a utility program, that organizes or controls the output process of a computer. (Contrast with *program, input*.)

program, overlay—A segmented computer program structured and executed in such a manner that the segment being executed uses the same main storage area as was occupied by the previously executed segment. (Contrast with *program, dynamic* and with *program, simple*.)

program, palindromic—1: A computer program that accomplishes the same result whether executed forward or backward. Such forward and reverse execution provides a good check of correctness of execution and results. A palindrome is a word, phrase, or sentence that reads the same forward as backward; for example, level, madam, mom, able was I ere I saw Elba, radar, or rotor. 2: A computer program that can be executed in reverse sequence, that is, from the last instruction to the first, thereby reversing the effect that is accomplished when executed in its normal forward sequence. Thus, if a series of instructions transforms a computer from state A to state B, reverse execution would transform state B back to state A.

program, problem–A computer program that, when executed, performs processing of data of the type for which a computing system is intended; for example programs that solve problems of a scientific nature, monitor and control industrial processes, sort and merge records, perform computations, process transactions against stored data, or update records, rather than serve as supervisors or compilers. (Closely related to *software, application*. Synonymous with *user program*.)

program, reenterable–Same as *program, reentrant*.

program, reentrant–A computer program that may be entered repeatedly before execution of the program is completed, subject to the requirement that neither its external program parameters nor any instructions are modified during its execution. A reentrant program may be used simultaneously by several computer programs. (Synonymous with *reenterable program*, with *reentrant code* and with *reentrant subroutine*.)

program, resident–A computer program that is executed from and that remains somewhat permanently in main storage during a succession of runs, jobs, or tasks.

program, reusable–A computer program that can be loaded once and executed repeatedly, subject to the conditions that instructions modified during its execution are returned to their initial values and that its external parameters are unchanged.

program, self-adapting–A program that can change its performance characteristics in response to changes in its environment; for example, a program that can alter itself depending on the nature of the problems it is required to resolve.

program, self-organizing–A program that can automatically rearrange its internal structure while it is being executed or simply by being placed on the computer for the sole purpose of having it change itself by operating upon itself in accordance with specified criteria.

program, service–Same as *program, utility*.

program, simple–A computer program structured in such a manner that it consists of but one module that occupies one fixed area of main storage. (Contrast with *program, dynamic* and with *program, overlay*.)

program, snapshot–A trace program that produces output for selected instructions, under selected conditions, or in accordance with specified criteria; for example a trace program that executes a selective dump, prints out addresses of specified storage locations, or displays the content of certain registers.

program, sort–A computer program that accomplishes a sort on a computer, given the items to be sorted in storage. Sort programs can be written so as to accomplish the sort in many different ways, depending on the characteristics of the computer and the nature of the items being sorted.

program, source–A program written in a source language; that is, a language designed for ease and convenience of expression, in a class of problems, by humans. A generator, assembler, compiler, or translator is used to perform the mechanics of transforming a source language program to a target language program. The target program is usually acceptable to the computer that will eventually run the program. (Synonymous with *subject program* and with *source routine*. Contrast with *program, target*.)

program, specific–A computer program that can only be used to solve a particular problem. (Contrast with *program, general*.)

program, standard–A program that meets certain specified criteria; for example, a program written in a standard or common programming language, such as ALGOL, FORTRAN, or COBOL; a program that yields an approved solution to a problem, such as calculating a payroll in accordance with standard rules, such as standard tax deductions; or a program that is commonly used to yield accepted solutions, such as might be in a library of programs that direct machine tools to fabricate certain parts.

program, star–A handwritten, that is, programmer prepared, computer program in which no mistakes were made and so containing no bugs. Assuming no computer malfunctions, a star program runs correctly the first time it is run and no programming errors are discovered. (Synonymous with *blue-ribbon program*. Further clarified by *debug*.)

program, stored–A computer program that has been placed in storage and is accessible to the computer automatically.

program, subject–Same as *program, source*.

program, supervisory–Same as *routine, executive*.

program, support–A subroutine, routine, or program, usually within or part of a supervisor, that accomplishes one or more of a variety of miscellaneous services for an application program. Support programs may also be part of an operating system for a computer.

program, target–A computer program written in target language; that is, in a language acceptable to the computer, or in an intermediate language. The target program usually results from a generator, assembler, compiler, or translator output and is usually in machine language that has evolved from a source language after a series of transformations. (Synonymous with *object program*, with *target routine*, and with *object routine*. Contrast with *program, source*.)

program, test—Same as *routine, test*.

program, trace—A computer program that checks another computer program by exhibiting the instructions of the program being traced in the sequence in which they are executed. The results of execution of the program being traced are also usually shown by the trace program.

program, transient—In a computer operating system, a program that is normally permanently stored in a resident device, loaded into a transient area in main storage when needed for execution, and usually used to accomplish selected supervisory functions but not often enough to be made part of the resident supervisor.

program, user—Same as *program, problem*.

program, utility—A general-purpose program, supplied by a manufacturer with his equipment, for executing standard or typical operations, such as sorting, indexing, translating, assembling, compiling, or merging. (Synonymous with *service program*.)

program analyzer—Same as *analyzer (1)*.

program block—See *block, program*.

program card—See *card, program*.

program checkout—See *checkout, program*.

program compiler—Same as *compiler*.

program control—See *control, program*.

program-controlled sequential computer—See *computer, program-controlled sequential*.

program counter—Same as *counter, instruction*.

program development time—See *time, program development*.

program drum—See *drum, program*.

program error—See *error, program*.

program execution time—See *time, program execution*.

program-generated parameter—See *parameter, program-generated*.

program generator—See *generator, program*.

program library—Same as *library, routine*.

program-limit monitoring—See *monitoring, program-limit*.

program loader, initial—See *loader, initial program*.

program loading, dynamic—See *loading, dynamic program*.

program maintenance—See *maintenance, program*.

program module—See *module, program*.

program module, refreshable—See *module, refreshable program*.

program module, relocatable—See *module, relocatable program*.

program origin, computer—See *origin, computer program*.

program parameter—See *parameter, program*.

program parameter, external—See *parameter, external program*.

program priority—See *priority, program*.

program register—Same as *register, instruction*.

program relocation, dynamic—See *relocation, dynamic program*.

program-sensitive error—See *error, program-sensitive*.

program-sensitive fault—See *fault, program-sensitive*.

program-sensitive malfunction—See *malfunction, program-sensitive*.

program step—See *step, program*.

program storage—See *storage, program*.

program structure—See *structure, program*.

program structure control—See *control, program structure*.

program suspension—See *suspension, program*.

program swapping—See *swapping, program*.

program tape—See *tape, program*.

program tape, master—Same as *tape, master instruction*.

program termination processing—See *processing, program termination*.

program test—See *test, program*.

program timing matrix—See *matrix, program timing*.

program translation—See *translation, program*.

programatics—The study, use, and application of computer programming methods, languages, and codes.

programmed, card—See *card-programmed*.

programmed check—See *check, programmed*.

programmed halt—See *halt, programmed*.

programmed logic—See *logic, programmed*.

programmed marginal check—See *check, programmed marginal*.

programmed stop—Same as *halt, programmed*.

programmed switch—1: See *switch, programmed*. 2: Same as *connector, variable*.

programmer—A person who prepares and plans the sequences of events that a computer must undertake in order that a problem may be solved. He usually works and writes instructions in the source language, leaving it up to the coder or automatic translator to write object programs in machine language. The programmer may prepare a flowchart, translating this into a set of instructions, or the actions portrayed on the flowchart, which is an algorithm for the solution of the problem, may be implemented by judicious selection of existing subroutines from a library of subroutines. The programmer must understand the language of the sponsor who has stated the problem, or of the analyst who has analyzed the problem and restated it or has written an algorithm to permit machine solution, such as reducing the problem to a set of equations. The programmer uses his knowledge of the computer's capability and of the existing programs, which can be amended to suit a particular problem, to prepare his program. He works between the analyst and the coder. If they are not available, he must perform their functions as well, or seek the help of a theoretician for the analytical aspects and either code, write a translator to machine language and have the computer code, or find the help of a coder. It is usually the programmer who is held responsible for satisfactory and efficient solution of the problem. (Further clarified by *programming.*)

programmer, ML—A computer programmer who writes computer programs in machine language.

programming—1: The field of interest devoted to the art and science of planning the solution of problems by reducing the plan to a set of machine-sensible instructions that can direct the actions of a computing or data-processing system capable of performing logic operations that will yield solutions to the problems. (Further clarified by *programmer.*) 2: The planning, designing, writing and debugging of programs.

programming, automatic—The process of using a computer to assist in the task of preparing a computer program. Activities include the use of machine translators, compilers, generators, assemblers, and coders. Other tasks that might be included as machine-assisted activities are assignment of absolute addresses, integration of subroutines into the main program, and interpretation of instructions. To be fully automatic would be to prepare the computer program directly from the problem definition in either English common language, a general algorithm, or a set of general instructions, entirely by machine.

programming, convex—In operations research, a special case of nonlinear programming in which the function to be optimized and the constraints are convex or concave functions of the independent variables.

programming, interpretive—The writing of computer programs in a pseudo, or a "pretend," language, usually mnemonic, which is translated by the machine into machine language either in toto before being run or one by one as the instructions are executed. (Further clarified by *interpreter.*)

programming, linear—Pertaining to the technique of finding the maximum or minimum value of a linear function of variables that are subject to linear constraints, usually in the form of inequalities. The linear expressions involved are of the form $a_1 x_1 + a_2 x_2 + \ldots + a_n x_n$. The techniques of mathematics, operations research, and systems science for solving problems involving many variables, where a best value or a set of best values is to be found, are involved. When the quantity to be optimized, sometimes called the objective function, can be stated as a mathematical expression with terms representing the various activities and conditions within the system, and when the activities and conditions are in simple proportion to the measure of the activities and conditions; and when all other imposed restrictions are linear, then the problem is one of linear programming. For example, a problem to determine the ratio of quantities to blend for an optimum mixture, say to prepare a cattle feed blend to achieve a certain balanced ratio of vitamins, minerals, protein, carbohydrate, etc., at least cost from available basic feed grains. *Programming* is used here in its general sense, not in the sense of computer programming, although when linear programming problems are best solved with computers, computer programs will be written to solve the linear programming problem. The process or procedure for determining or locating the maximum, minimum, or other preferred or optimum value or values of a function of variables that are themselves subject to mathematically linear constraints and inequalities is called linear optimization. In most applications it becomes necessary to find the values or ranges of the variables that yield the optimum value of the function. (Synonymous with *optimum programming,* with *mathematical programming,* and with *linear optimization.*)

programming, mathematical—Same as *programming, linear.*

programming, minimal-latency—See *programming, minimum-access.*

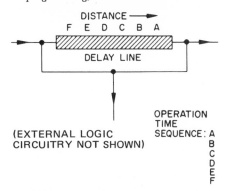

DISTANCE ⟶

F   E   D   C   B   A

DELAY LINE

OPERATION
TIME

(EXTERNAL LOGIC   SEQUENCE: A
CIRCUITRY NOT SHOWN)   B
                                                       C
                                                       D
                                                       E
                                                       F

Operations are executed in the sequence with which they emerge from serial (drum, disc, tape, delay-line) storage in order to achieve minimum-access programming benefit.

programming, minimum-access—Preparing a computer program so as to reduce to a minimum the waiting time for obtaining data or instructions from storage, particularly serial access storage. Thus, if there are multiword high-speed loops in drum storage or multiword lengths of delay-lines, a set of instructions can be so arranged that the next instruction to be executed is just emerging from the end of the loop or line, or the next operand to be obtained is just emerging from the loop or line. If no attention is paid to minimizing the waiting time, the average access time will be about half of the delay length of the loop, line, disc, or drum. When used, minimum-access programming is inapplicable. (Synonymous with *forced programming* and with *minimal-latency programming*. Contrast with *programming, random-access*. Closely related to *coding, minimal-latency*.)

programming, nonlinear—In operations research, a procedure for locating maxima or minima of a function whose variables are subject to constraints, when the function or the constraints are nonlinear.

programming, optimum—Same as *programming, linear*.

programming, parallel—Programming a computer in such a manner that two or more arithmetic or logic operations are executed simultaneously, even though there may be only one arithmetic and logic unit, by using different parts of a word for holding the operands; parallel programming can involve timesharing of computer parts, giving rise to two or more separate sequences of instructions, which on paper have the appearance of being written in parallel.

programming, random-access—Programming a computer without regard for the time required to wait for access to a storage position when placing or calling data and instructions in and out of storage. When using random-access storage, all programming is random-access programming. When using serial storage involving a delay time for a string of words, such as a drum, disc, delay-line, or tape loop, the average delay time will be half the time-length of the loop, if random-access programming is applied. (Contrast with *programming, minimum-access*.)

programming, sequential—Programming a computer in such a manner that only one logic or arithmetic operation is performed at a time, without timesharing among two or more programs and without using more than one arithmetic or logic unit. *Programming* implies sequential programming unless another modifier is used. (Contrast with *multiprogramming*, with *processing, parallel*, and with *multiprocessing*.)

programming, symbolic—Same as *coding, symbolic*.

programming flow diagram—Same as *flowchart, programming*.

programming flowchart—See *flowchart, programming*.

programming language—See *language, programming*.

programming system—See *system, programming*.

progress report—See *report, progress*.

progression code, continuous—Same as *code, unit-distance*.

progressive code, continuous—Same as *code, unit-distance*.

projection, mirror-image—In computer graphic display systems, the reflection, movement, or transfer of display elements or groups with respect to a specified straight line or plane by a perpendicular distance on the opposite side of the line or plane equal to the distance the display elements or groups are located on the given side of the line or plane.

prompting—In computer graphic display systems, the informing of the user of the alternative courses of action and the options open, usually when the system is operated in an interactive or conversational mode.

prompting query—See *query, prompting*.

PRONTO—(Program for Numerical Tool Operation). A program that translates parts drawings to numerically coded machine tool language for positioning a cutting tool. English sentences may be used to describe the machining operations to be performed. PRONTO was developed by General Electric Company.

proof, galley—An impression made from type that has been set before it is made up into pages. The name comes from *galley*, a tray for holding type when it is set. (Synonymous with *slip proof*.)

proof, slip—Same as *proof, galley*.

proof total—See *total, proof*.

propagated error—See *error, propagated*.

proper subset—See *subset, proper*.

property list—Same as *list, description*.

property sort—See *sort, property*.

proportional band—Same as *range, proportional*.

proportional control—See *control, proportional*.

proportional range—See *range, proportional*.

protected location—See *location, protected*.

protection—A method or arrangement for restricting or preventing access, use, or modification of the whole or part of a system. (Synonymous with *lock-out*.)

protection, memory—Same as *protection, storage*.

protection, storage—In a computer operating system, the measures taken to protect a storage unit or storage area against unauthorized access for purposes of reading, writing, or both. (Related to *password*.)

protection, volume—In a computer operating system, the measures taken to protect a volume against unauthorized access for purpose of reading, writing, or both. (Related to *password*.)

protection character—See *character, protection.*

Proto Synthetic Indexing—Same as *PSI*.

proving—Demonstrating that a machine is free from faults, is not malfunctioning, and is capable of performing particular tasks, particularly after preventive or corrective maintenance has been performed. In machines capable of timesharing, the functioning of the machine may be checked automatically by including a program for that purpose among the other operating programs.

proving time—See *time, proving.*

psec—Abbreviation for *picosecond.*

pseudocode—A code or language in which a computer program may be written, but which is not itself a computer instruction code and so must be translated into machine code, or interpreted, before the instructions may be executed. A pseudocode is usually a mnemonic code; that is, the instructions and addresses are easier for a human to remember and handle. The pseudocode may be independent of the hardware of the computer. There is hardly a distinction between a symbolic code and a pseudocode, except that the pseudocodes tend to direct attention to meaning, while symbolic codes tend to direct attention to representation. The instructions represented by the pseudocode may not specify operations physically and individually built into the computer. For example, in addition to being translated into machine language and interpreted, absolute addresses must be assigned before the finished and assembled program can be run. The pseudocode may not be natural to the computer on which the program is to be run. (Closely related to *code, symbolic.*)

pseudoinstruction—A computer instruction written in a pseudocode, thus an instruction that must be translated or interpreted before it can be executed by a computer; for example, a group of characters representing information for a compiler or interpreter; a mnemonic operation code; operations addressed to an interpreter; certain macroinstructions that are not built into the hardware, such as a floating-add instruction in a machine that does not have built-in automatic floating point; calls for subroutines or macroinstructions; or instructions that effect the way in which following instructions are to be interpreted, located, or defined, such as in expanded instruction repertories. (Synonymous with *quasi-instruction*, with *expanded order*, and with *pseudo-op.*)

pseudoinstruction form—Same as *form, quasi-instruction.*

pseudolanguage—An artificial language specially constructed to accomplish a specific purpose. A set of rules is devised and meanings are assigned to somewhat arbitrarily selected expressions. It may have mnemonic qualities to assist human usage. Usually somewhat independent of the hardware, computer programs are more easily written in a pseudolanguage than in machine language. Most problem-oriented and procedure-oriented programming languages are pseudolanguages, although expressions may resemble English statements for mnemonic, semantic, syntactical, and logical purposes.

pseudo-offline working—See *working, pseudo-offline.*

pseudo-op—See *pseudoinstruction.*

pseudorandom—Pertaining to the characteristic of satisfying one or more criteria for randomness, such as equal probability of occurrence of given digits in sequence, an equal number of each digit occurring in a large number of digits, uniform distribution, or Gaussian distribution. Usually the randomness is determined by some defined arithmetic process, and, if numbers are involved, the randomness of the numbers is produced by a definite calculation process, such as is obtained in calculating the digits of π, e, or certain irrational numbers. (Further clarified by *sequence, pseudorandom number.*)

pseudorandom number sequence—See *sequence, pseudorandom number.*

PSI—(Proto Syntex Indexing). A SMASHT program written to index the occurrence of each word in running English text by a tape address scheme. The system also includes a semiautomatic word-combining program to combine indexes for words on the basis of morphological or semantic similarity. Inputs include the input and output from FEAT. The system has been applied to the IBM 7090 computer. Application has been made by System Development Corporation.

public library—See *library, public.*

publication language—See *language, publication.*

pulse—A change in the intensity or level of a physical or electrical condition for a relatively short period of time and the return to the original condition, where the time required to change is much shorter than the time in the original or normal state. An ideal pulse for some purposes may be one of infinite magnitude and zero duration, or for other purposes, a perfectly rectangular pulse of finite amplitude and duration may be ideal. In computer applications, pulses are primarily electrical, sonic, or magnetic. Usually a pulse is used to represent a bit, the presence of a pulse signifying a one and the absence of a pulse signifying a zero. If, in a computer, at a particular time interval, the voltage at a point rises from a −10-volt level to a +20-volt level for a period of 0.4 microseconds, then it may be said that a 0.4-microsecond 30-volt pulse passed, which might signify that a binary one "passed by." Digital computers manipulate pulses in the execution of logic and arithmetic operations, where pulses represent bits, groups of bits represent characters, and groups of characters represent words or numerals. Logic operations are performed by coincidence gating to perform Boolean operations. Pulse parameters include repetition rate, width, amplitude, and squareness. (Synonymous with *impulse.*)

pulse, clock—Same as *pulse, timing.*

pulse, commutator—A pulse issued at a particular instant of time relative to a reference pulse, such as a major or minor cycle pulse, and used to define, mark, clock, or control a particular binary digit position in a computer word. The pulses are commutated on to a set of lines such that adjacent lines have their pulses phased one pulse period apart. In each line, the pulses are spaced according to the period of a cycle, such as a major or minor cycle. (Synonymous with *position pulse* and *P-pulse.*)

pulse, drive—A pulse capable of accomplishing a result beyond that of simple coincidence gating; for example, a pulse capable of driving a set of logic gates distributed around a computer; a pulse capable of switching a magnetic core, with or without the aid of another drive pulse; or a pulse capable of driving the hammers of a printer.

pulse, emitter—In a punched-card machine, one of the group of pulses that is used to define a particular row within the columns of a card.

pulse, full-read—Same as *pulse, read.*

pulse, half-read—Same as *half-pulse, read.*

pulse, half-write—Same as *half-pulse, write.*

pulse, inhibit—A pulse that prevents or does not permit an action that would otherwise happen if the inhibit pulse were not present; for example, a pulse that prevents a gate from functioning, or closes it; a pulse that prevents a core from being read out of or written into; a pulse that stops a counter from counting, or stops pulses from arriving at a counter.

pulse, P—Same as *pulse, commutator.*

pulse, partial drive—Same as *pulse, partial write.*

pulse, partial read—In coincident-current magnetic-core storage devices, one of two or more pulses that are required to effect the selection or the switching of a core when interrogating or transferring data, that is, a binary digit, out of the storage device. (Synonymous with *partial-select output pulse.*)

pulse, partial-select input—Same as *pulse, partial write.*

pulse, partial-select output—Same as *pulse, partial read;*

pulse, partial write—In coincident-current, magnetic-core storage devices, one of two

or more pulses that are required to effect the selection or the switching, of a core when entering or storing data; that is, a binary digit, into the storage device. (Synonymous with *partial-select input pulse* and with *partial drive pulse.*)

pulse, position—Same as *pulse, commutator.*

pulse, post-write disturb—In a coincident-current, magnetic-core storage device, a pulse applied after a write pulse to put all cores in the disturbed state. (Contrast with *pulse, preread disturb.*)

pulse, preread disturb—In a coincident-current, magnetic-core storage device, a pulse applied before a read pulse to ensure that the core about to be read is in the disturbed state. (Contrast with *pulse, post-write disturb.*)

pulse, read—In coincident-current core storage devices, a pulse, or the sum of several simultaneous pulses, capable of switching a core, or producing a change in its residual flux density so as to produce an output signal on the read winding provided for this purpose. The amplitude of the output pulse is determined by whether or not the core had switched, which signifies whether or not a one was stored. (Synonymous with *full-read pulse.* Contrast with *half-pulse, read.*)

pulse, reset—A pulse used to place a binary storage cell, such as a flip-flop or a magnetic core, back to its original, reset, or specified condition or state.

pulse, set—A pulse used to place a binary storage cell, such as a flip-flop or a magnetic core, into a specified state or condition initially. After changing from this state, it may be reset to this state by a reset pulse.

pulse, sprocket—Same as *pulse, timing.*

pulse, teletypewriter marking—A signal pulse that corresponds to a circuit-closed or current-on condition, in d-c or neutral teletype operation.

pulse, timing—A pulse placed adjacent to recorded characters on media such as tapes, drums, and discs in order to regulate the timing of read circuits, to count characters, and to perform related functions of the type that a clock pulse would perform inside the computer. (Synonymous with *sprocket pulse,* with *clock pulse,* and with *clock signal.*)

pulse amplitude—See *amplitude, pulse.*

pulse-amplitude modulation—See *modulation, pulse-amplitude.*

pulse code—See *code, pulse.*

pulse-code modulation—See *modulation, pulse-code.*

pulse decay time—See *time, pulse decay.*

pulse duration—Same as *width, pulse.*

pulse-duration modulation—Same as *modulation, pulse-length.*

pulse-frequency modulation—See *modulation, pulse-frequency.*

pulse generator, clock—See *generator, clock-pulse.*

pulse generator, restorer–Same as *generator, clock-pulse.*

pulse generator, time–Same as *generator, clock-pulse.*

pulse generator, timing–Same as *generator, clock-pulse.*

pulse length–Same as *width, pulse.*

pulse-length modulation–See *modulation, pulse-length.*

pulse modulation–See *modulation, pulse.*

pulse normalization–Same as *standardization, pulse.*

pulse-position modulation–See *modulation, pulse-position.*

pulse regeneration–Same as *standardization, pulse.*

pulse repetition frequency–See *frequency, pulse repetition.*

pulse repetition rate–See *rate, pulse repetition.*

pulse reshaping–Same as *standardization, pulse.*

pulse rise time–See *time, pulse rise.*

pulse shaping–Same as *standardization, pulse.*

pulse spacing, teletypewriter–See *spacing, teletypewriter pulse.*

pulse standardization–See *standardization, pulse.*

pulse string–See *string, pulse.*

pulse-time modulation–See *modulation, pulse-time.*

pulse train–Same as *string, pulse.*

pulse transformer–See *transformer, pulse.*

pulse width–See *width, pulse.*

pulse-width modulation–Same as *modulation, pulse-length.*

pulse-width recording–See *recording, pulse-width.*

pulses, synchronization–Pulses introduced into a system to keep all components operating in step; for example, pulses introduced into transmitters and receivers to keep them in step, or timing pulses introduced by a master clock to keep all logic gates operating in step in a synchronous digital computer.

punch–1: A device that will make holes to represent information in any medium in accordance with signals sent to it from another source, such as a computer, a communication link, or a human being through a keyboard. 2: A hole in a data carrier or medium, such as tape, cards, or sheets of paper, usually made in arrays with other holes to represent information. (Further clarified by *punch, designation.*)

punch, automatic feed–A punch that has a card hopper, a card track, and a card stacker, and is constructed in such a manner that the card moves automatically along the track to the hopper during keyboard operations. A buffer storage with a capacity adequate for one card may be provided. The keyboard may have 12 keys, one for each row, or be a conventional typewriter keyboard.

punch, automatic tape–A device that punches patterns of holes representing or forming characters on tape, the tape moving automatically as each character is formed. Usually the holes for each character are placed across the tape, one row for each character. The characters arrive at the punch in the form of coded electrical signals, the punch automatically transcribing the coded electrical signals into rows of holes and moving the tape as necessary for each character. The device has been called a reperforator, from its use in telegraphy, as a contraction of receiving perforator. (Synonymous with *output tape punch.* Further clarified by *reperforator.*)

punch, calculating–A punch-card machine that reads the data on a card, performs some arithmetic or logic operations on the data, and punches the results on another card or the same card. (Synonymous with *multiplying punch.*)

punch, card–A device that will make holes in cards in certain patterns so as to represent data. The holes are punched at specific locations in accordance with signals received by the punch. Usually, provisions are made to automatically remove a card from a feeder hopper, move the card along a track as a pattern of holes are punched to represent characters, in accordance with coded signals received, and then place the card in a stacking hopper. Card punches range from a small portable card holder and a hand-held tool that makes holes to a high-speed electronic punch used as an online output device on an electronic high-speed digital computer, punching cards at rates over 600 cards per minute.

punch, control–Same as *punch, designation.*

punch, designation–A hole placed in a punch card to indicate to a machine the nature of the data on the card or which functions the machine is to perform, since computer instructions may be placed on the card in the same manner as other data. (Synonymous with *control hole,* with *control punch,* with *function hole,* and with *designation hole.* Further clarified by *punch (2).*)

punch, double–To place two holes in a single column of a punch card. Without double, or multiple punching, only 12 different digits can be represented on some types of punch cards. Multiple punching, or zone punching, permits many more characters to be represented in a single column; many more than the number of rows or hole positions in a column. The theoretical maximum number of different characters that can be represented in a single column on a punch card is 2^n, where n is the number of rows, or hole positions, in the card column. Double punch is reserved for two holes in a column, rather than three or more, which may be called *multiple punching.* (Further explained by *punch, zone.* Contrast with *punch, single.*)

punch, function–Same as *punch, designation.*

punch, gang—To punch identical data into a group or deck of punch cards. A type of gang punch has a single track, with a punching station followed by a sensing, or reading, station. Each card with data to be gang punched is followed by as many cards as are to be gang punched with the data on the lead card. This combination is followed by another lead card with different data to be gang punched, followed by again as many cards as are to be gang punched, and so on. When a card reaches the read station, the data on the card being read is punched on the card at the punching station. Arrangements must be made for transition between combinations. Another type holds the control card, sensing and resensing it, directing the punch station to punch successive cards identically.

punch, hand-feed—A card punch, with a manual keyboard, into which punch cards are fed by hand one at a time. Each card is moved as it is punched by the actuating manual keys. Upon completion of punching, the card is removed by hand.

punch, interstage—To punch holes in a punch card only in the odd numbered rows in each card. (Contrast with *punch, normal-stage.*)

punch, key—See *keypunch.*

punch, keyboard—Same as *keypunch.*

punch, mark-sense—To punch holes in a card automatically, based on electrically conductive marks made on another card or the card being punched with a special pencil. Thus, data may be entered on the cards at the source and sent to a central place for punching and processing.

punch, multiple—To place two or more holes in a single column of a punch card. Multiple punching permits the representation of an increased number of different characters in each column on the card, one character in each column. The theoretical maximum number of different characters that can be represented in a column, one character at a time, is 2^n, where n is the number of punch positions in a column.

punch, multiplying—Same as *punch, calculating.*

punch, normal-stage—To punch holes in a punch card only in the even numbered rows in each card. (Contrast with *punch, interstage.*)

punch, numeric—The punching of holes in a card column such that only a single hole, in rows one through nine, is punched in the given column being considered. (Synonymous with *digit punch.*)

punch, output tape—Same as *punch, automatic tape.*

punch, paper-tape—A device that makes feed holes and code holes in paper tape to represent information.

punch, reproducing—Same as *reproducer.*

punch, single—Pertaining to a system of punch card coding wherein any one of the numeric values zero to 11 can be represented by one hole punched in a specific position (row) in a column. (Contrast with *punch, double.*)

punch, spot—A card punch for punching a single hole at a time in any desired punch position.

punch, summary—A card punch that may be connected to another machine, such as a tabulator or other accounting machine, that will punch cards, entering data that was produced, calculated, or summarized by the other machine. It is called a summary punch because originally such a machine punched a summary or part of a tabulation for purposes of carry forward, thus behaving somewhat as a temporary storage device for holding intermediate results.

punch, tape—A machine that makes holes in tape in accordance with codes so as to represent information. The tape punch may or may not make feed or sprocket holes. (Synonymous with *tape, perforator.*)

punch, X—See *X-punch.*

punch, Y—See *Y-punch.*

punch, zone—1: A punched hole in the zero, X, or Y row on a Hollerith punch card. The use of zone punching permits the number of characters that may be represented in a single column to be increased. (Further explained by *punch, double* and by *overpunching.*) 2: A hole punched in one of the punch rows designated as twelve, eleven, or zero, and sometimes nine or eight. A zero punch, and sometimes a nine punch, by itself, may be considered a numeric punch. 3: A zero punch in combination with a numeric punch. (Synonymous with *overpunch.*)

punch column—See *column, punch.*

punch position—See *position, punch.*

punch-print editor—See *editor, print-punch.*

punch rate—See *rate, punch.*

punch row—See *row, punch.*

punched card—See *card, punched.*

punched-card, border—Same as *card, edge-punched.*

punched card, ducol—See *card, ducol-punched.*

punched card, edge—See *card, edge-punched.*

punched card, margin—Same as *card, edge-punched.*

punched card, verge—Same as *card, edge-punched.*

punched-card machine—See *machine, punched-card.*

punched paper tape—See *tape, punched paper.*

punched tape—See *tape, punched.*

punched-tape code—See *code, punched-tape.*

punched-tape machine—See *machine, punched-tape.*

punched-tape reader—Same as *reader, paper-tape.*

punching, card—The set of actions related to entering data on punch cards to represent information. The operator of a card punch reads the source document, and by depressing keys in proper sequence, enters the data on the cards. The machine feeds, positions, and ejects the cards. Similar to typing, the operator's primary concern is to depress the proper keys in correct sequence. Some card punches are equipped with printing mechanisms that print, sometimes called interpret, the punched information at each column top.

punching position—Same as *position, punch.*

punching station—See *station, punching.*

punctuation symbol—Same as *delimiter.*

pure binary—Same as *binary, straight.*

pure binary numeration system—See *system. pure binary numeration.*

pure generator—See *generator, pure.*

purging, file—The destruction of the contents of a file, either with or without the removal of the name of the file from the list of files or system catalog. (Further clarified by *maintenance, volume.*)

push-to-talk operation—See *operation, push-to-talk.*

push-to-type operation—See *operation, push-to-type.*

pushdown list—See *list, pushdown.*

pushdown storage—See *storage, pushdown.*

pushup list—See *list, pushup.*

pushup storage—See *storage, pushup.*

put, through—See *throughput.*

q

Q-1: A figure of merit, a measure of sharpness of tuning or resonance, equal to $\omega L/R$ for an inductor, where ωL is the inductive reactance, ω is 2π times the frequency, in hertz, L is the inductance, in henries, and R is the series resistance, in ohms. A high ratio indicates low-loss, highly selective tuning, a high reactive factor, and high performance. For a capacitor, Q is $1/\omega CR$, where C is the capacity in farads. For a given medium, that is, material, circuit element, or substance, Q is the ratio of displacement current density to conduction current density. The basic equation may be expanded to include series and parallel resonant circuits. **2:** A measure or quantity of nuclear disintegration energy.

quad—Four separately insulated conductors twisted together, or two twisted pairs of conductors. Quads are structural elements employed in cables.

quadded cable—See *cable, quadded.*

quadrature—**1:** A relationship between two sinusoidally varying quantities such that the phase difference between them is one-fourth of the period, or 90 degrees. **2:** Pertaining to vector quantities or phasors, that are 90 degrees apart; that is, at right angles in the same plane; for example, two fields, such as magnetic and electric fields, are said to be in quadrature if they are at right angles to one another; two forces are in quadrature if they pull at right angles to one another.

quadrature component—See *component, quadrature.*

quadripuntal—Pertaining to having four punches; for example, having four randomly punched holes on a punched card as a tool in determinative documentation.

quadruple-address—Same as *four-address.*

quadruple-length register—See *register, quadruple-length.*

quadruple register—Same as *register, quadruple-length.*

qualified name—See *name, qualified.*

quantity—An entity or an amount of something that is measurable, the measure or size usually being expressable in terms of numbers. Thus, in a mathematical sense, a quantity is expressed as a positive or negative number or as a symbol that represents a number, such as the quantity x in the equation $y = mx + b$.

quantity, double-precision—A quantity whose value is expressed with twice as many digits as are normally used to express quantities; for example, in a fixed word-length computer, a product may contain twice as many digits as were in the multiplier or multiplicand, two computer words being used to express the product, and the two halves must be properly handled in all subsequent operations.

quantity, scalar—A quantity that possesses magnitude and not direction, or the magnitude of a vector quantity; for example, volume, size, temperature, or the scalar product of two vector quantities. (Contrast with *quantity, vector.*)

quantity, vector—A quantity that possesses both magnitude and direction; for example, electric field intensity, magnetic field intensity, wind velocity, momentum, angular velocity, or their cross product. (Contrast with *quantity, scalar.*)

quantization—The subdivision of the range of values that a variable may assume into a finite number of nonoverlapping intervals or subranges; for example, the expressing of temperature in the centigrade scale as a number from 0 to 100 in the range from freezing to boiling points of water; or the subdivision of the earth's surface into 24 time zones, each designated by a name or number; or expressing latitude as units of degrees from 0 to 90. Computers, working with numerals, require that data be in quantized form.

quantize—1: To subdivide the range of values of a variable into a finite number of nonoverlapping subranges or intervals, each of which is represented by an assigned value within the subrange; for example, to represent a person's age as a number of whole years or the temperature as a number of whole degrees. 2: To divide the difference between the maximum and minimum values a variable may have into a finite number of nonoverlapping intervals that are not necessarily equal and to designate each interval by an assigned value within that interval.

quantizer—A device that accepts an analog quantity and selects the particular subdivision or range that the quantity should be placed in so that the quantity may be digitized, such as by an analog-to-digital converter.

quantum—An amount, usually resulting from a subdivision; for example, one of the subranges resulting from quantization, such as a year, when expressing a man's age.

quarter-squares multiplier—See *multiplier, quarter-squares.*

quartet—A byte composed of four binary elements; for example, a group of four binary electrical pulses that might be used to represent a decimal digit. (Synonymous with *four-bit byte.* Closely related to *tetrad.*)

quartz delay-line—See *delay-line, quartz.*

quasi-instruction—Same as *pseudoinstruction.*

quasi-instruction form—See *form, quasi-instruction.*

quaternary operator—See *operator, quaternary.*

QUEASY—An automatic coding system developed by the Naval Ordnance Test Station at China Lake (Inyokern), California, for use on the IBM 701 computer.

query—A question or statement that specifies the criteria that are needed to locate and retrieve data in a file. Queries may assume various forms and modes, such as batch, cue-response, fixed-logic, pre-stored, prompting, and skeletal.

query, batch—A query that is processed on a computer operated in the batch processing mode.

query, cue-response—A query that is processed on a computer in a manner such that the user participates in a question-answer dialogue with the system and in which the response contains a cue leading to the next query.

query, fixed-logic—A query that is processed on a computer in a manner such that the operands and operators in the query or related instructions cannot be altered by the user at the time of execution. (Contrast with *query, skeletal* and with *query, interactive.*

query, interactive—A query that is processed on a computer in a manner such that the query is formulated and posed or entered on-line to the data processing system. (Contrast with *query, fixed-logic.*)

query, pre-stored—A query that is processed on a computer in a manner such that the query is stored in a system library and at execution time is loaded into the computer directly from the library.

query, prompting—A query that is processed on a computer in a manner such that aid is provided by the data processing system so as to assist the user in formulating meaningful questions or retrieval statements by prompting or leading the inquirer through the interrogation process.

query, skeletal—A query that is processed on a computer in a manner such that the query is pre-sorted in an outline or skeletal form and the user defines specific operands, operators or other options, at execution time. (Contrast with *query, fixed-logic.*)

query stacking—See *stacking, query.*

queue—In computer simulation, the set of transactions that are waiting to enter a specific piece of equipment.

queue, channel—1: A queue of requests for the use of a data channel. 2: A queue of data waiting to be processed by a channel.

queue, device—A queue of requests for the use or services of a device; not a queue of devices waiting for the use of another device; for example, a queue of data or requests for the use of a communication channel, not a group of input-output devices seeking the use of a data link.

queue, dispatcher—In a computer operating system, a queue of tasks, jobs, or programs ready for dispatch and execution.

queue, double-ended—A queue, or list, whose length or content may be changed by adding or removing items at either end, top or bottom.

queue, job—The backlog of jobs waiting to be executed by a computer operating system.

queue, scheduling–In a computer, data processing, or communication system, a queue of jobs that are ready to be scheduled for execution or transmission.

queue control–See *control, queue.*

queuing–Pertaining to the movement in time and space of discrete units through channels; for example, the movement of vehicular traffic through toll booths or tunnels; problems, programs, or data arriving at a computer; movement of aircraft arriving at a terminal and waiting for runway availability while the aircraft are stacked in the air; movement of heavy traffic on a highway; or lining up of employees in a cafeteria line. (Further clarified by *theory, queuing.*)

queuing theory–See *theory, queuing.*

quibinary code–See *code, quibinary.*

quick-access storage–Same as *storage, high-speed.*

quick-disconnect–Pertaining to a type of connector shell which permits rapid locking and unlocking of two connector halves.

quiescing–The bringing of a multiprogrammed computer to a halt by denying it new jobs.

quinary–Pertaining to a characteristic or property involving a selection, choice, or condition in which there are five possibilities; or, pertaining to five. (Further clarified by *biquinary.*)

quintet–A byte composed of five binary elements, for example, a packet of five binary pulses in a delay line, the presence or absence of a pulse at each position in the packet indicating the presence or absence of a binary one, the absence of the pulse usually indicating a zero. (Synonymous with *five-bit byte.*)

quotient–The result obtained from dividing two numbers. The dividend is divided by the divisor into a number of parts equal to the quotient, such as fifteen (dividend) is divided by five (divisor) into three (quotient) parts. The quotient may be a whole or mixed number, and it may be rounded. (Contrast with *product*, with *sum,* and with *difference.*)

quotient-multiplier register–Same as *register, multiplier-quotient.*

r

rack–1: A metal frame on which several panels of electrical equipment or a chassis may be mounted. In computer applications, the rack may hold power supplies, amplifiers, tape drives, control equipment and other apparatus. 2: A metal frame and all the electrical equipment mounted on it. A typical standard rack holds a panel 17 inches wide.

radial transfer–See *transfer, radial.*

radio frequency–See *frequency, radio.*

radio-frequency interference–See *RFI.*

radix–1: In a positional numeration system, a quantity whose successive integral powers are the implicit multipliers of the sequence of integers that represent a number; for example, if the radix is five, then 1342 is $1 \times 5^3 + 3 \times 5^2 + 4 \times 5^1 + 2 \times 5^0$, which is equivalent to 222 in radix 10, or decimal, representation. In radix two, or binary, representation, the binary number 101101 is $1 \times 2^5 + 0 \times 2^4 + 1 \times 2^3 + 1 \times 2^2 + 0 \times 2^1 + 1 \times 2^0$, which is equivalent to 45 in decimal. Thus, loosely, the radix is the quantity used to define a system of number representation by means of positional notation. It is the radix that is raised to the successive powers, the result then being multiplied by the given digits of the specified number. The radix number also is equal to the number of symbols, that is, character designs or different digits, required for the particular system of number representation. For example, in a radix 10 number system, there are 10 characters; namely, 0, 1, 2, 3, 4, 5, 6, 7, 8, and 9. (Synonymous with *base (2).*) 2: In a positional notation system, the positive integer by which the weight assigned to the digit place is multiplied to obtain the weight of the digit place with the next higher weight; for example in the decimal numeration system the radix is ten, in binary, it is two. Thus, the radix is the ratio of the weights of higher to lower adjacent digit positions.

radix, floating-point–In the floating-point numeration system, the fixed positive integer that is the radix of the power. (Synonymous with *floating-point base.*)

radix complement–See *complement, radix.*

radix complement, diminished–See *complement, diminished-radix.*

radix-minus-one complement–See *complement, radix-minus-one.*

radix notation–See *notation, radix.*

radix numeration system—Same as *notation, radix.*

radix numeration system, fixed—See *system, fixed-radix numeration.*

radix numeration system, mixed—See *system, mixed-radix numeration system.*

radix point—Same as *point, arithmetic.*

radix scale—Same as *notation, radix.*

rail logic, double—See *logic, double-rail.*

Rajchman selection switch—Same as *storage, core-rope.*

RAM—An abbreviation for random access memory.

RAMAC—(Random Access Method of Accounting and Control). A development of IBM Corporation.

random access—See *access, random.*

random-access programming—See *programming, random-access.*

random-access storage—See *storage, random-access.*

random number—See *number, random.*

random number, normal—See *number, normal random.*

random number, uniform—See *number, uniform random.*

random number generator—See *generator, random number.*

random number sequence—1: Same as *sequence, pseudorandom number.* 2: See *sequence, random number.*

random-walk—Pertaining to the movement of a body to its next position, such that it is likely to move in any direction with equal probability by a specified fixed distance from its present position. Numbers may be involved that correspond to the distances. Monte carlo methods are used to produce random walks. (Further clarified by *method, monte carlo.*)

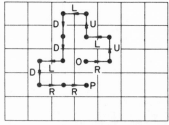

Starting at 0, the point moved either right, up, left, or down at random, i.e., with equal probability of moving in any of the four directions, arriving at point P. The point executed a random-walk.

randomize—To make random or scatter randomly, such as to assign random or pseudorandom codes or characters to particular locations in storage.

range—1: The set or span of values that a quantity or function may have or assume. 2: The difference between the highest and lowest values that a quantity or function may assume. (Synonymous with *span.*)

range, error—1: The set or span of all possible values that the error in a quantity or function may have; for example, in specifying a tolerance of 1.875 ± 0.005, the latter figure specifies the error range in the resulting manufactured part or mathematical parameter. 2: The difference between the highest and lowest values that an error may assume; for example, in the value 1.875 ± 0.005, the error range is 0.010.

range, number—The range or span of values that a number may assume, usually expressed as ranging from a lower limit to an upper limit. A statement must also be made as to whether or not either or both of the limits are included in the range of values; for example, a set of integers of values greater than 199 and less than 300, in which case all three-digit numerals with 2 as the most significant digit are included in the specified range. (Synonymous with *computer capacity.*)

range, proportional—The range or band of values of a condition or phenomenon being regulated which will cause the controller to operate over its full linear range. The proportional range is usually expressed by engineers in terms of percentage of full scale of the associated instrument. (Synonymous with *proportional band.*)

rank—Relative position in an ordered sequence, with the higher order position considered to be of higher rank. Thus, the letter A might be ranked above B in an alphabetical ordering of letters. Rank must be defined in each system or hierarchy specifically, such as ranking by size, distance from a reference, position or authority, intensity, or any other quantity or characteristic. (Further clarified by *order.*)

rapid-access loop—Same as *revolver.*

rapid-access storage—Same as *storage, high-speed.*

raster—In graphic display systems and devices, the coordinate grid that divides the display area into discrete positions or rectangular coordinate locations.

raster count—See *count, raster.*

raster scan—See *scan, raster.*

raster unit—See *unit, raster.*

rate, average data-transfer—Same as *rate, effective data-transfer.*

rate, average information—The mean entropy per character per unit of time. The average information rate may be expressed in such units as the shannon per second.

rate, average transinformation—The mean transinformation content per character per unit time. The average transinformation rate may be expressed in such units as shannon per second per unit time.

rate, average transmission—Same as *rate, effective-data-transfer.*

rate, bit—The time rate, in bits per second, that binary digits are handled, such as transmitted over a communication channel, passed through a magnetic recording head, or handled at a paper-tape perforating head. Usually, bit rate refers to a single channel, so that the bit rate is not considered to increase if the channels are placed in parallel. If a set of parallel channels simultaneously handle the bits of a character, the character rate is the same as the bit rate.

rate, clock—The basic pulse repetition frequency in an electronic machine. Usually, this is the rate at which bits of a word in a serial operation machine, or corresponding bits in succeeding words of a parallel operation machine, are handled, such as transmitted, gated, shifted, or counted. If computer instructions, such as multiplication, require several successive combinations of basic instructions, or micro-instructions, several clock cycles will be required to complete the major instruction.

rate, data signalling—In communications, the data transmission capacity of a channel, expressed in bits per second.

rate, effective data-transfer—The rate at which data is transmitted through a channel over an extended period of time, so as to allow for gaps between words, blocks, records, files, or fields. Starting, stopping, rewinding, searching, or any other operations subject to program control in the case of magnetic tape, discs, or drums, are not included. Regeneration time for electro-static or core storage is included, since this time delays continuous transfer from storage and is not subject to program control. (Synonymous with *average transmission rate*, with *effective transmission rate*, and with *average data-transfer rate*.)

rate, effective transmission—Same as *rate, effective data-transfer*.

rate, instantaneous data-transfer—The rate at which data is transmitted through a channel, measured during the time data is actually being transmitted. For tape, the rate is measured in terms of characters per second and is dependent only on the packing density, the linear tape speed, and the number of tracks, and not on the gaps between words, blocks, records or files. (Synonymous with *instantaneous transmission rate*, with *peak transmission rate*, and with *peak data-transfer rate*.)

rate, instantaneous transmission—Same as *rate, instantaneous data-transfer*.

rate, peak data-transfer—Same as *rate, instantaneous data-transfer*.

rate, peak transmission—Same as *rate, instantaneous data-transfer*.

rate, perforation—The rate at which characters or words are punched in a tape, usually measured in characters per second. The instantaneous rate, rather than the effective rate, is usually implied.

rate, pulse repetition—The number of pulses experienced at a given point, or passing a given point, in a unit of time, usually measured in pulses per second. The different functions performed within a computer may require different pulse repetition

rates. The bit rate at which the binary digits of a serial computer word pass a point, usually at the basic gating or clock rate of the computer, might be one pulse repetition rate. The recording rate of a magnetic head may be a fraction of this bit rate, since heads will not respond to a pulse repetition rate of several megahertz. In core storage operation, several pulse repetition rates are involved for interrogating, storing, regenerating, and disturbing. In magnetic drum, disc, or tape recording, a word or block count pulse may be involved. Thus, various pulse rates are required in computers for gating, timing, counting, controlling, and performing other functions.

rate, punch—The number of units of data punched as holes in a medium, such as cards or tape, in a unit of time. The punch rate may be expressed as words, blocks, fields, cards, holes, inches, or similar units per second, minute, or hour.

rate, read—The number of units of data that are sensed by a device in a unit of time. The read rate may be expressed as bits, characters, words, blocks, cards, holes, inches (of tape), pages, or similar units per second, minute, or hour.

rate, reset—The rate at which output signals are sampled to determine deviation from norm or control level, and the input is corrected so as to restore the output to norm. The reset rate is usually expressed as a number of repeats per minute.

rate, sampling—The time rate at which physical quantities are measured, or sampled. The purpose of sampling is to obtain data to feed to a computing system so that the results of the computations can be made available to accomplish a purpose, usually in real time and online, such as predicting the future position of a missile, controlling a mixing process, or preparing a regional coordinate weather map. Sampling permits working with discrete values, timesharing of equipment, and the use of many sensors.

rate, telegraph—The reciprocal of the unit interval expressed in seconds. The telegraph rate is measured in baud. Thus, if the unit interval for the on-off condition of a signalling device is one twenty-fifth of a second, the telegraph rate or speed is 25 baud. (Synonymous with *data speed*.)

rating, carrier power output—The unmodulated power nominally available at the output terminals of the transmitter when connected to its normal antenna or to an equivalent circuit. The carrier power output rating is the normal rating of a transmitter.

ratio, activity—Same as *ratio, file activity*.

ratio, data transmission utilization—In a data transmission system, the ratio of useful or satisfactory data output to the total data input.

ratio, elimination–In an information retrieval system, the ratio of the number of documents or records not retrieved by a search to the total number of documents or records in the file. Thus, the elimination ratio is one minus the retrieval ratio.

ratio, file activity–The ratio of the number of file elements, such as records, for which a transaction or a change is made during a given updating run or during a given period to the number of file elements in the file. Thus, in a file of employees' pay rates, if over a period of one month 20 out of 1000 employees receive a pay increase and the files are updated during the month, the activity ratio for the month is 2 percent for this file. (Synonymous with *activity ratio.*)

ratio, noise–In an information retrieval system, the ratio of the number of documents or records that are relevant to a particular search criterion to the number of documents or records that were retrieved by the search. Thus, the noise ratio is one minus the relevance ratio.

ratio, omission–In an information retrieval system, the ratio of the number of relevant documents or records not retrieved by a search to the number of relevant documents or records in the file. Thus, the omission ratio is one minus the recall ratio.

ratio, one-to-partial-select–In a coincident-current, magnetic-core storage output line, the ratio of the magnitude of the signal representing a full, or one, output signal to a signal representing a partial switching, or noncoincidence, of a core or cores.

ratio, operating–In machine operation, the ratio of the number of correct or satisfactory hours of machine operation to the total number of hours of scheduled operation, including scheduled preventive maintenance, as unsatisfactory time; for example, if 100 hours of operation are scheduled, and 20 hours of preventive maintenance are scheduled, resulting in 120 scheduled hours, and 10 hours of unscheduled down-time or corrective maintenance is required, then the operating ratio is $(120-20-10)/120 = 75$ percent. (Further clarified by *time, available* and by *availability*)

ratio, print contrast–In optical character recognition, the ratio of the difference between the maximum reflectance, or coefficient of reflection, within a specified distance from the given area at which the ratio is being determined and the reflectance of the given area, to the maximum reflectance at the specified distance. Usually, the print contrast ratio is simply the reflectance of the paper minus the reflectance of the inked area and the result divided by the reflectance of the paper. Thus if the reflectance of the ink is zero, say for jet black ink, the contrast ratio comes out as unity. If the ink is grayish and consequently reflects 25 percent of the incident light and the paper reflectance coefficient is 75 percent of the incident light, then the print contrast ratio would be $(75 - 25)/75$ or 0.67. If the paper and the ink have the same coefficient of reflectance, then there is no contrast and the print contrast ratio comes out as zero, no matter what the reflectance coefficient or the intensity of the incident or reflected light is. The coefficient of reflectance is the ratio of the intensity of reflected light from a surface to the intensity of the incident light. (Further clarified by *coefficient, reflection* and by *contrast.*)

ratio, read-around–In electrostatic storage, the ratio of the number of times a specific location may be interrogated as a matter of programming policy to the number of times a spot may be consulted, that is, read and regenerated, before spillover will cause a loss of data stored in surrounding spots. The read-around number is the denominator of the ratio, or the minimum number of interrogations that will cause spillover in a given storage tube. Operational practice holds the number reduced so as to preclude any possibility of spillover occurring.

ratio, recall–In a document retrieval system, the ratio of the number of pertinent documents retrieved by a particular query to the total number of pertinent documents in the collection, as determined by the query criteria. (Contrast with *ratio, relevance.*)

ratio, reflectance–The reciprocal of the ratio of the intensity of light reflected from an image area of a picture or graphic representation dark area, to the intensity of light reflected from the background or light area; for example, in optical character recognition, the ratio of the light reflected from the inked area to the intensity of light reflected from the background area. (Further clarified by *contrast.*)

ratio, relevance–In a document retrieval system, the ratio of the number of pertinent documents retrieved by a particular query to the total number of documents retrieved by the query criteria. (Contrast with *ratio, recall.*)

ratio, resolution–In an information retrieval system, the ratio of the number of documents or records retrieved by a search to the total number of documents or records in the file.

ratio, retrieval efficiency–In an information retrieval system, one of the ratios that are used to express the efficiency of retrieval when the system is searched or queried; for example, the resolution, elimination, relevancy, noise, recall, and omission ratio.

ratio, selection–The ratio of the amplitude of

the smallest pulse that switches a magnetic cell, that is, reverses its magnetization, to the amplitude of the largest pulse that does not switch the cell.

ratio, sensitivity—Same as *sensitivity*.

ratio, signal-to-noise—The ratio of the power of the signal to the power of the noise. The ratio is expressed in peak values in case of impulse noise and in root-mean-square (rms) values in case of random noise.

ratio, squareness—For a magnetic material in a symmetrically cyclically magnetized condition, the ratio of the residual magnetic flux density, or the flux density at zero magnetizing force, to the maximum flux, or density. The ratio is a function of the magnetizing force and is a measure of the squareness of the hysteresis loop. It varies between 0.75 and 0.95 for most square materials, such as square-loop ferrites used in storage cores for digital computers, each core storing one binary digit. (Further clarified by *loop, hysteresis* and by *loop, square*.)

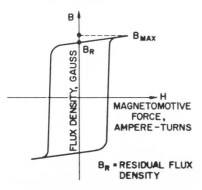

Squareness ratio *is* B_R/B_{MAX}.

rational number—See *number, rational*.

raw data—See *data, raw*.

read—To sense or obtain data from a record, medium, data carrier, document, storage, or other form. Usually, a transcription is made, also leaving the data in its pre-read form. It is preferable to use the phrases "to read from" and "to write to" or "to write on," rather than "to read to" and "to write from." Actually, it is only a question of viewpoint and direction of transmission. *Reading* implies nondestructive reading, unless otherwise stated. *Read* also implies interpretation of the data read. (Contrast with *scan* and with *write*.)

RB—Same as *recording, return-to-bias*.

read, destructive—To sense data with a process that inherently destroys the record of the data that has been read. In electrostatic and some core storage, reading is destructive, requiring that the data be regenerated after each

interrogation. In tape, disc, drum, punched-card, or punched-tape storage, reading is accomplished without destroying the data in the medium. (Synonymous with *DRO*, or *destructive read-out*. Contrast with *read, nondestructive*. Further clarified by *storage, destructive*.)

read, manual—A computer operation in which the computer senses the contents or settings of manually set switches or registers. (Further clarified by *unit, manual input*.)

read, nondestructive—To sense data in a storage medium without destroying or erasing the data stored in the medium, and therefore without requiring that the data be regenerated after being read. Fixed core storage, magnetic tape, and punched cards and tape may be read nondestructively. Ordinary core storage and cathode-ray-tube (electrostatic) storage are destructively read and the data must be regenerated after reading if the data is to be retained. (Synonymous with *NDRO*, or *nondestructive read-out*. Contrast with *read, destructive*. Further clarified by *storage, nondestructive*.)

read, regenerative—Same as *regenerate*.

read-around ratio—See *ratio, read-around*.

read-back check—Same as *check, echo*.

read cycle time—See *time, read cycle*.

read half-pulse—See *half-pulse, read*.

read head—See *head, read*.

read-in—To sense, read, or transcribe data into a device from an external medium; for example, to transcribe data from external storage or medium to internal storage. (Contrast with *read-out*.)

read-only storage—Same as *storage, fixed*.

read-out—To sense, read, or transcribe data, transferring the data to an external device; for example, to transcribe data from internal storage or medium to external storage. (Contrast with *read-in*.)

read-out device—Same as *device, character display*.

read pulse—See *pulse, read*.

read pulse, partial—See *pulse, partial read*.

read-punch unit—Same as *reader-punch, card*.

read rate—See *rate, read*.

read-write—Pertaining to the capability of both reading and writing, and generally used to denote input-output functions of a system.

read-write check—See *check, read-write*.

read-write check indicator—See *indicator, read-write check*.

read-write head—See *head, read-write*.

readable, machine—Pertaining to the characteristic of being able to be sensed or read by a device, usually by a device that has been designed and built specifically to perform the reading or sensing function. Thus, data on tapes, cards, drums, discs, and similar media are machine readable. A register of flip-flops can contain data that is rapidly readable; indeed, the register may do the reading by serving as an input to a matrix that is designed to sense the contents of another medium of storage.

Optical character readers and magnetic ink character readers are available and serve as examples of equipment capable of reading machine-readable data, in addition to card readers, paper tape readers and magnetic tape units. (Synonymous with *machine sensible,* with *machine recognizable,* with *machinable,* and with *mechanized.* Further clarified by *data, machine-readable.*)

readable medium, machine—See *medium, machine-readable.*

reader—Any device capable of sensing, detecting, or converting data. Usually transformation to another form or medium is involved. However, data that is read is neither translated, transliterated, nor operated upon in any analytical way. Thus, a magnetic read head merely transforms data from magnetic spots on tape to a series of electrical pulses, as the tape moves past the head. For example, in micrographics, a reader is a device for viewing enlarged microimages.

reader, card—A device that reads, or senses, holes in cards, transforming the data from patterns of holes to patterns of electrical pulses. Usually, a card reader has facilities for holding a deck of cards, feeding the cards past sensing stations, generating pulse patterns corresponding to the data on the cards, and stacking the cards that have been read. The holes may be sensed by means of wire brushes, metal pin-type feelers, or photoelectric devices. Card readers are often used as input devices for digital computers, printers, tabulators, and plotters.

reader, character—A device capable of reading printed characters; that is, converting printed characters into electrical pulses corresponding to the characters. The reader may operate electronically, magnetically, or photoelectrically, and may sense data printed with ordinary or magnetic ink. The reader may convert the printed characters to pulse patterns corresponding to the standard pulse code patterns for each character, for direct input to a computer. Character readers usually have provisions for handling the documents that are read.

reader, film—1: A device that projects or displays photofilm to permit human reading of the data on the film. Usually, microfilm readers have provision for holding and moving the film at the discretion of the operator. **2:** A device that converts patterns of opaque and transparent spots on a photofilm to electrical pulses corresponding to the patterns.

reader, input—Same as *routine, input.*

reader, magnetic-tape—A device capable of converting the patterns of magnetic spots (dipoles) on magnetic tape to sequences of electrical pulses. The pulse patterns correspond with the magnetization of the tape. The data is read and transmitted to another device, such as a computer, printer, plotter, or another tape unit for writing, that is, recording. Most magnetic tape readers also have the capability of writing data on tape as well as reading data from tape. The reader is equipped with controls, a mechanism for moving the tape, and necessary input and output buffers or registers for handling the data. The same magnetic head is usually used for reading and writing.

reader, paper-tape—A device capable of converting the pattern of holes, or cuts, in a paper tape to sequences of electrical pulses, usually for transmitting the data to another storage medium, such as the internal storage of a computer or a printed page. The reader includes a mechanism for holding, feeding, and disposing of the tape, a sensing station for detecting the holes, and equipment for generating electrical pulses. The holes may be sensed mechanically or photoelectrically. (Synonymous with *perforated tape reader* and with *punched tape reader.*)

reader, perforated-tape—Same as *reader, paper-tape.*

reader, photoelectric—A device capable of converting data in the form of patterns of holes in storage media such as cards, tape, or sheets, into electric pulse patterns by means of photosensitive components, such as photocells or photosensitive diodes and transistors. The reader also includes mechanisms for holding, feeding, and taking up the media. The photoelectric reader is often used as a computer input device or is used to drive a printer, plotter, or card punch.

reader, punched-tape—Same as *reader, paper-tape.*

reader, tape—A device capable of sensing data on tapes, such as paper tape or plastic and metallic magnetic tape. The reader includes mechanisms for holding, feeding, controlling, and reeling up the tape, as well as a device for sensing the data on the tape. Tape readers are usually used as computer input devices; to drive printers, plotters, card punches; or to transmit data over a communications line. (Synonymous with *automatic tape transmitter* and with *tape transmitter-distributor.*)

reader-printer—In micrographics, a device that reads and prints so as to produce hard copy enlargements of selected microimages.

reader-punch, card—A device that both reads and punches data on cards. One such device consists of an input hopper, a card feed, a read station, a punch station, another read station, and two output card stackers.

readiness review—See *review, readiness.*

reading—The acquiring or the interpreting of data from a data source, such as from a storage device, from a data medium, or from a transducer or sensor.

reading station—Same as *station, sensing.*
real address—See *address, real.*
real number—See *number, real.*
real time—See *time, real.*
real-time address—Same as *address, immediate.*
real-time addressing—Same as *addressing, immediate.*
real-time control—See *control, real-time.*
real-time data reduction—See *reduction, real-time data.*
real-time input—See *input, real-time.*
real-time input-output—See *input-output, real-time.*
real-time operation—See *operation, real-time.*
real-time output—See *output, real-time.*
real-time processing—See *processing, real-time.*
real-time simulation—See *simulation, real-time.*
real-time working—Same as *operation, real-time.*
rearrange—To change the sequence or location of items in a collection or array.
recall ratio—See *ratio, recall.*
receive-only service—See *service, receive-only.*
received data circuit—See *circuit, received data.*
receiver, card—Same as *stacker, card.*
reception, exalted carrier—A method of handling received signals, either amplitude or phase modulated, in which the carrier is separated from the sidebands, filtered and amplified, and then combined with the sidebands again at a higher level prior to demodulation.
reckoning, dead—A method of computing the present position of a moving body, based on an earlier known position; elapsed time; speed; direction; and other applied forces, such as wind, tide, currents, and gravity.
recognition, character—The identification of phonic, graphic or other types of characters, usually by automatic means; for example, optical recognition or magnetic recognition. The technology of character recognition includes handling the characters to be read, sensing the characters, and converting them to patterns of electrical signals.
recognition, magnetic ink character—See *MICR.*
recognition, optical character—See *OCR.*
recognition, pattern—The identification of graphic patterns through the use of devices capable of scanning, sensing, and converting graphic patterns into electrical signals, such as digital pulse patterns, which may be compared with pulse patterns in storage. The patterns in storage have been assigned meaning. Thus, the device is capable of recognition. If read patterns are not identical to stored patterns, the nearest or closest pattern is used to identify the perceived pattern. If a pattern is sensed that is nearly the same as one in the repertory, it may be recognized as such. When the deviation exceeds a

threshold value, it may be identified as a new or strange pattern and added to the repertory, with appropriate meaning assignment. Cognition, abstraction, and perception are involved. The device can be made capable of recognizing or rejecting graphic patterns shown to it and taking appropriate action in accordance with what it sees.
recognizable, machine—Same as *readable, machine.*
reconfiguration, manual—The changing of the configuration of a system, that is, the changing of the kinds and types of components and their interconnection, by means of keyboard input or punched card input.
reconfiguration, operating system—The modification of a computer operating system, usually in order to compensate for changes in the quantity or capability of system resources.
record—A collection of related data elements, items, or codes, treated as a unit. In the hierarchy of data units, one might consider, in ascending order, bit, byte, alphanumeric character, word, field, block, record, file, and bank. For the verb form of record, *write* is preferred in data processing; that is, to write on tape, discs, or cathode-ray tube.
record, addition—A new record added to a file without moving or deleting any existing record in the file. (Contrast with *record, deletion.*)
record, deletion—A new record added to a file, removing and replacing an existing record in the file. (Contrast with *record, addition.*)
record, fixed-length—A record in which the number of data units, such as blocks, words, characters, or digits, is limited to a given number. Usually, the restriction is caused by the equipment design. The amount of data in a given record may be less than the allowable limit. In some semifixed length record systems, a choice between a few predetermined record lengths is available to the programmer. (Contrast with *record, semifixed length,* and with *record, variable length.*)
record, group—Two or more records placed together; that is, associated and identified with a single key in one of the records. One purpose of grouping is to conserve space and save running, acceleration, and deceleration time on magnetic tape.
record, header—A record that contains data pertaining to and heading a group of records. The data might be common to all records, might identify records, or might summarize the contents of records in the group it leads. For example, a header record might be the first record on a reel of tape and it might contain the date, program identification, report number, tape identification and special notes. (Contrast with *record, trailer.* Further clarified by *end, leading.*)

289

record, home—The first record in a chain of records. The home record is used with the chaining method of file organization.

record, leader—Same as *record, header.*

record, logical—A collection or an association of records on the basis of their content rather than their physical location; for example, all data relating to a given person forms a logical record regardless of where or how the data may be located, dispersed or distributed. (Contrast with *record, physical.*)

record, physical—A record that is defined or structured in terms of the way in which it is recorded such as the unit record on a punched card or volume on a reel of magnetic tape, without regard to conceptual relationships of the content of the record or without regard to the use of the record. (Contrast with *record, logical.*)

record, reference—An output of a compiler, listing the operations with their position in the final specific routine, and containing information describing the segmentation and storage allocation of the routine.

record, semifixed length—A fixed-length record whose length may be changed at the discretion of the programmer. Usually, a choice is offered between a few predetermined lengths and remains fixed for a given application, problem, or run. (Contrast with *record, fixed-length* and with *record, variable length.*)

record, trailer—A record that contains data pertaining to and following a group of records. The data might be common to all records, might identify records, or might summarize the contents of records in the group it follows. (Contrast with *record, header.* Further clarified by *end, trailing.*)

record, unit—A member of a set of records, each identical in format and data elements. Only the data items and data codes in the records differ from each other. For example, an employee's statement of earnings and deductions might be treated as a unit record. Sometimes a unit record can conveniently be placed on a punched card.

record, variable-length—A record in which the number of constituent parts, such as blocks, words, or characters, is not fixed. The record is only as long as is necessary to contain or write the data, rather than of a fixed-length or a fixed allowed space in storage. (Contrast with *record, fixed-length* and *record, semifixed length.*)

record control schedule—See *schedule, record control.*

record gap—See *gap, record.*

record head—Same as *head, write.*

record layout—See *layout, record.*

record length—See *length, record.*

record management—See *management, record.*

record mark—See *mark, record.*

recorder, film—A device that makes a record; that is, places data on film, usually in the form of light and dark or opaque and transparent spots on photographic roll film. The data may be digital output data from a computer or it may be data from a sensor and intended for computer input to be processed. To record the data, a light beam modulated according to the binary digital data is used to expose the film. A light beam passing through the film to a photocell is used to read the data. The film recorder has necessary mechanisms for holding and feeding the unexposed film, recording the data, and reeling up the exposed film.

recording, double-pulse—Magnetic recording in such a manner that each storage cell is composed of two regions each magnetized in opposite polarity. Thus, a zero may be represented by a cell composed of a negative region followed by a positive region and a one by a positive region followed by a negative region, or vice versa.

recording, electron beam—A method of obtaining microfilm output from a computer by directing a beam of electrons onto an energy sensitive film. Abbreviated as EBR.

recording, frequency-doubling—The magnetic recording of bits such that each storage cell is comprised of a single pulse or sine wave of magnetization for a one and two pulses of sine waves for a zero, or vice versa.

recording, magnetic—A method of storing data by selectively magnetizing portions of a magnetic material.

recording, nonpolarized return-to-zero—A return-to-reference recording in which zeros are represented by the absence of magnetization and ones are represented by a specified condition of magnetization, and the reference condition is zero magnetization. Also, the absence of magnetization can be used to represent ones, and the magnetized condition can be used to represent zeros. Abbreviated RZ(NP).

recording, non-return-to-reference—A magnetic recording in which the patterns of magnetization used to represent zeros and ones occupy the entire storage cell, and no part of the cell area is magnetized to a reference condition, except perhaps in a transition region.

recording, non-return-to-zero—A method of recording such that the change of magnetization representing either a zero or a one provides the reference condition. It is a non-return-to-reference recording method in which the reference condition is zero magnetization. Abbreviated as NRZ.

recording, non-return-to-zero (change)—Non-return-to-reference recording of bits such that zeros are represented by magnetization to one condition and ones are represented by magnetization to a different or alternative condition. The two conditions may be saturation and zero magnetization, but more often the conditions are saturation in opposite senses, that is, opposite directions. In this method of recording the recorded magnetic condition is changed only when the recorded bit changes from zero to one or from one to zero.

recording, non-return-to-zero change-on-ones—A non-return-to-reference recording in which ones are represented by a change of the magnetization condition, whereas zeros are represented by the absence of a change. Thus, the recording method is called NRZ (mark) because only the one, or mark, signals are explicitly recorded. Abbreviated N R Z I . (Synonymous with *non-return-to-zero (mark) recording, NRZ*(M).

recording, non-return-to-zero (mark)—Same as *recording, non-return-to-zero change-on-ones.*

recording, phase encoded—Same as *recording, phase modulation.*

recording, phase modulation—The recording of bits such that each binary storage cell or area is divided into two parts, each of which is magnetized in different senses, usually in opposite directions, the sequence of these senses indicating whether the bit represented is a zero or a one. Abbreviated PM or PE. (Synonymous with *phase encoded recording.*)

recording, polarized dipole modulation—Same as *recording, polarized return-to-zero.*

recording, polarized return-to-zero—A method of return-to-reference recording in which zeros are represented by polarization in one sense, that is, in one direction, and ones are represented by polarization in the opposite sense, that is, in the opposite direction, and the reference condition is the absence of magnetization, that is, zero magnetization. Abbreviated as RZ(P). (Synonymous with *polarized dipole modulation recording.*)

recording, pulse-width—The magnetic recording of bits such that the condition of magnetization changes at each boundary between cells, and in which ones are represented by an additional change of magnetization within the cell, whereas for zeros there is no such additional change, or vice versa. Pulse-width recording may be either non-return-to-reference or return-to-reference, the reference condition being either zero or a bias condition.

recording, return-to-bias—A type of return-to-reference recording where in ones (or zeros) are represented by magnetization to a specified bias, that is, polarization condition, zeros (or ones) are represented by a different specified

condition, and the bias condition is also the reference condition. Usually the bias condition is magnetic saturation in one sense, that is, direction of polarization, and the alternative condition is saturation in the opposite sense, that is, opposite direction. The use of different intensities of magnetization in the same direction for the bias and signalling conditions reduces the strength of the recording without a compensating advantage. Thus, nonpolarized return-to-bias recording is not used and return-to-bias recording implies polarized operation. Abbreviated as RB.

recording, return-to-reference—A magnetic recording in which the magnetization patterns used to represent zeros and ones occupy only a part of the storage cell, with the remainder of the cell magnetized to a reference condition. The reference condition may be either the absence of magnetization or polarized or non-polarized magnetization to a specified bias condition. Either polarized or non-polarized or recording may be used.

recording area—Same as *frame, film.*

recording head—Same as *head, write.*

recovery procedure—See *procedure, recovery.*

rectangular loop—Same as *loop, square.*

rectifier, crystal—Same as *diode, crystal.*

recursive function—See *function, recursive.*

recursive routine—See *routine, recursive.*

recursive subroutine—See *subroutine, recursive.*

recursively-defined sequence—See *sequence, recursively-defined.*

red-tape operation—See *operation, red-tape.*

redact—To revise or edit a publication.

redaction—A revised edition or a new edition of a publication.

reduction—1: Pertaining to the process of transforming raw data obtained from instruments, such as transducers, into useful data and intelligence. 2: A measure of the number of times the linear dimension of an object are reduced when photographed or otherwise displayed in graphic form, the measure being expressed as 16X, 24X, or other value.

reduction, data—The process of transforming masses of raw or test data into useful, organized, condensed, and simplified information; that is, into intelligence. The data is usually obtained during an experiment or a test, gathered by instruments and sensors, and by means of smoothing, adjusting, scaling, ordering, and formulation is transformed into summaries, results, tabulations, or mathematical formulas. In many instances, data reduction is performed prior to computer input, such as transforming filmed data to punch cards by means of a film-to-punched-card converter. In other instances, raw data is fed directly to a computer for reduction, such as a radar-to-computer, airspeed-to-computer, fuel-level-to computer, etc., arrangement in an aircraft for flight control. Very often data reduction involves conversion from one form to another, such as analog to digital, or from one medium to another, such as pen-records to magnetic tapes or films to cards.

reduction, online data—The immediate reduction of data as rapidly as the data is received by the data-reduction equipment or the reduction of data as rapidly as it is sensed or generated by the source; for example, reducing satellite position data vs. time as it is received from tracking instruments, for further processing and orbital path calculations and determination of future position. (Contrast with *reduction, real-time data*.)

reduction, real-time data—The reduction of data as rapidly as it is received at the data reduction processor, such as the computer, or as rapidly as it is generated by the source. Thus, if the computer simply stores the raw data for an extended period, before the reduction process begins, the data reduction may be performed online, but not in real time. (Contrast with *reduction, online data*.)

redundancy—The amount by which the decision content of a message exceeds the entropy. Usually, messages can be represented with fewer characters than are actually used by using suitable codes. The redundancy may be considered as a measure of the decrease of the length of the message thus achieved.

redundancy check—See *check, redundancy*.

redundancy check bit—See *bit, redundancy check*.

redundant—Equipment, facilities, or data over and above the minimum required for a specific purpose or effect. Redundant equipment and redundant characters often serve to facilitate a check. A parity bit is redundant as far as the intelligence in the data is concerned. One of two arithmetic units performing identical operations at the same time is redundant. Redundancy is observable in natural language in that information in text is not lost when some characters in some words are omitted. However, when too many characters are omitted and redundancy is reduced to a low level, then ambiguity begins to increase.

reel—In data processing, a tape-holding spindle, usually flanged, for holding a roll of tape, during storage, operation, or shipment. A reel of tape includes both the reel and the tape. A roll of tape is the tape alone. (Synonymous with *spool*.)

reel, feed—A reel from which tape is being unwound.

reel, take-up—A reel on which tape is being wound or may be wound.

reenterable program—Same as *program, reentrant*.

reentrant code—Same as *program, reentrant*.

reentrant program—See *program, reentrant*.

reentrant subroutine—Same as *program, reentrant*.

reentry point—See *point, reentry*.

reference—In documentation, data that serves to indicate the location or title of specific information, such as identification of a document, an author, or a computer instruction. A reference is usually directly referred to, specifically mentioned, or directly quoted in the running text of a document, whereas a bibliography is a list of related, supporting, or otherwise pertinent documents, usually listed by author, title, publisher, date, and other annotation, at the end of a given document. (Further clarified by *bibliography* and by *index, citation*.)

reference address—Same as *address, base*.

reference axis—See *axis, reference*.

reference edge—See *edge, reference*.

reference edge, document—See *edge, document reference*.

reference language—See *language, reference*.

reference level—See *level, reference*.

reference-line, character-spacing—In character recognition, a vertical line used to evaluate the horizontal spacing of characters. It may equally divide the distance between the sides of a character boundary or it may coincide with the centerline of a vertical stroke.

reference point, zero-level transmission—See *point, zero-level transmission reference*.

reference power-supply—Same as *supply, reference*.

reference record—See *record, reference*.

reference supply—See *supply, reference*.

reference time—See *time, reference*.

reflectance, background—In optical character recognition, the reflectance of the background, that is, the document surface within the clear band (the area to be printed on), compared to a reference standard. (Further clarified by *contrast*.)

reflectance, ink—In optical character recognition, the reflectance of the ink deposited on the surface of a document compared to a reference standard. (Further clarified by *contrast*.)

reflectance, spectral—The reflectance for a specific wavelength of incident light from a specified surface. (Further clarified by *contrast*.)

reflectance ratio—See *ratio, reflectance*.

reflected binary unit-distance code—Same as *code, Gray*.

reflection coefficient—See *coefficient, reflection*.

refreshable program module—See *module, refreshable program*.

regenerate—In data storage, to restore data that is about to be lost or that has been destructively read; for example, to restore data stored on a cathode-ray-tube screen or in a magnetic core that has been sensed, since interrogation destroys the data in these devices; or in some instances, to rewrite data that must be restored, periodically, to prevent decay, such as might occur in a cathode-ray tube or in some nondestructive core-storage units after repeated interrogation of the same cell. (Synonymous with *regenerative read*.)

regeneration, pulse—Same as *standardization, pulse*.

regeneration, signal—Same as *standardization, signal*.

regeneration period—See *period, regeneration*.

regenerative connection—See *connection, regenerative*.

regenerative feedback—Same as *feedback, positive*.

regenerative read—Same as *regenerate*.

regenerative storage—See *storage, regenerative*.

regenerative track—Same as *revolver*.

region—In computer programming, a group of storage locations, each of whose relative address refers to the same base address.

region, communication—In an operating system, the part of a supervisor or executive routine that monitors or controls interprogram or intraprogram movement of data.

regional address—See *address, regional*.

register—A device capable of storing a specific amount of data, such as a character, a word, or a 10-digit numeral, in a digital computer. The data is usually held in the register only long enough to accomplish a specific purpose. Often, registers are constructed of a row of high-speed flip-flops that control logic gates. Registers may store data words or instruction words, may operate on the data in them, and are often used for control purposes.

BINARY NUMERAL

FLIP-FLOPS

S = SET CONDITION   R = RESET CONDITION

Flip-flops 2, 4, and 5 are in the positive reset condition, representing a one digit, while flip-flops 1 and 3 are in the positive set condition, representing a zero digit for the register *shown above.*

register, A—Same as *register arithmetic*.

register, address—In a computer, a register that holds the address part of an instruction word while the instruction is interpreted for execution, the addresses are decoded, and the operands are being obtained from storage.

register, arithmetic—A register in the arithmetic or logic unit of a computer that holds the operands that are to be operated upon; that is, the words that enter into arithmetic or logic operations. Thus, it may hold the addend for addition, the

multiplier for multiplication, or one of the words to be shifted or compared. (Synonymous with *A-register*.)

register, B—Same as *register, index*.

register, base—Same as *register, index*.

register, base-address—A register used to hold the base address. (Further clarified by *register index*.)

register, check—A register used to temporarily store transferred data in order to compare the data transferred with a second transfer of the same data in order to verify the accuracy of the transfer. Thus, a register used for checking purposes only.

register, circulating—A shift register in which data moved out of one end of the register is reentered into the other end as in a closed loop, such as a register consisting of a means for storing, delaying, removing, regenerating, and reinserting data; for example, a pair of heads and a tape, drum, or disc track, such that data written serially is read later and fed back to the write head, thus forming a loop or a string of flip-flops used as a cyclic shift register, wherein data removed at one end is reinserted, serially, at the other end and the data within is shifted character by character or bit by bit.

register, control—Any one of the registers in a computer used to direct or control events in the computer, such as an instruction register, an instruction counter, an index register, or an input-output register. (Illustrated by *counter, control*.)

register, delay-line—A circulating register, constructed of a delay-line, a means for returning data from the end of the line to the beginning, and a means for changing the data that is continually circulating. Storage is accomplished serially. Outside of the delay element itself, the pulses representing information must be received at the end, amplified, shaped, clocked, gated, and returned to the beginning and transmitted. Taps along the line permit simultaneous examination of characters stored along the line. Data stored is changed at the external gates.

register, exchange—Same as *register, storage*.

register, flip-flop—A series of flip-flops connected in a chainlike fashion and used to store binary digits. The data may be stored in parallel, that is, all flip-flops set to the desired state simultaneously, or data may be fed serially from one end and shifted in bit by bit. (Illustrative of *storage, flip-flop*.)

register, floating-point—A register designed to effectively handle numerals expressed in floating-point representation.

register, general purpose—A register that can be used for different purposes. It is often explicitly addressable within a set of registers in a given computer program. Examples of general purpose registers are accumulators, index registers and other registers that can be used for several purposes other than their name implies.

register, icand–In multiplication by a computer, the register used to hold the multiplicand during the multiplication process. (Contrast with *register, ier*.)

register, ier–In multiplication by a computer, the register used to hold the multiplier during the multiplication operation. (Contrast with *register, icand*.)

register, index–A register whose contents are used to modify an instruction prior to its execution; for example, a register whose content is added to or subtracted from the operand address of an instruction prior to its execution. The index register is used to control events, under the direction of the computer program. In relative addressing, the index register holds the base address, or the number to be added to the relative address, to obtain the absolute address. (Synonymous with *B-box*, with *B-line*, with *base register*, with *B-register*, with *B-store*, and with *modifier register*. (Further clarified by *register, base-address*.)

register, input–A computer register that receives data from input devices and holds the data long enough only to effect transfer to internal storage or to the arithmetic unit register, as directed by the program.

register, input-output–A computer register that receives data from input devices, from which the data is transferred to internal devices, such as the storage, arithmetic, or control unit, and also receives data from the internal devices, transferring the data to external devices, such as printers, punches, perforators, plotters, or other computers by way of a data link. A single register often holds one word. If a number of registers is used, particularly to avoid queuing, the device is usually called a buffer, or an input-output buffer. However, sometimes the buffer is part of the external device, rather than an input-output register to the computer proper.

register, instruction–A register that stores the current instruction being, or to be, executed. The register usually holds the instruction during a complete instruction cycle, including the interpretation of the address and operation parts. When interpretation of the instruction word in the register is completed by the control unit, a new instruction may be transferred from storage to the register. The contents of the instruction register actually control computer events during the execution of the instruction, usually by enabling and disabling various gates that perform logic functions. (Synonymous with *program register*.)

register, instruction address–A register whose contents are used to derive the address of the next instruction to be executed. The register may be a portion of a storage device specifically designated for the derivation of the address of the next instruction. A translator, compiler, interpreter, language processor, executive routine, operating system or other software may handle the designation of the portion of storage that is to serve as the instruction address register.

register, magnetic shift–A register capable of storing and moving data a number of positions to the right or left and entirely constructed of wire and magnetic cores, for performing storage, logic, and amplification functions.

register, modifier–Same as *register, index*.

register, multiplier-quotient–A register in the arithmetic and logic unit of a computer, in which the multiplier for multiplication is placed and in which the quotient for division is formed. (Synonymous with *quotient-multiplier register*.)

register, n-tuple–Same as *register, n-tuple-length*.

register, n-tuple-length–A group of n registers logically or physically connected or otherwise associated so as to function or be considered as a single register. Usually each register may be individually addressed. (Synonymous with *n-tuple-register*.)

register, operation–In a computer, a portion of circuitry in the form of a register where the operation part of an instruction word is held for decoding, interpretation, analysis, setting of logic conditions, and enabling and inhibiting of various gates required for the execution cycle of the instruction.

register, program–Same as *register, instruction*.

register, quadruple–Same as *register, quadruple-length*.

register, quadruple-length–A group of four registers logically or physically connected or otherwise associated so as to function or be considered as a single register. Usually each register may be individually accessed or addressed. (Synonymous with *quadruple register*.)

register, quotient-multiplier–Same as *register, multiplier-quotient*.

register, return code–A register used to store data that controls the execution of subsequent programs. (Further clarified by *code, return*.)

register, sequence control–Same as *counter, instruction*.

register, shift–A register capable of moving data within itself relative to the register frame in accordance with signals received. Usually, data is shifted to the right or left if a line of data is involved. If a column of data is involved, the data is shifted vertically. The register may assume any form, such as a row of flip-flops of tubes or transistors, or a row or column of magnetic cores and appropriate driving pulses and gates. Operation may be accomplished by storing data in parallel; that is, filling all positions simultaneously, and shifting out the data position by position, serially. Also, the data could be read in by shifting serially, and read out in parallel. Special design and arrangements need to be made to accomplish some of these special operations. (Synonymous with *stepping register*.)

register, standby—A register in which verified or validated data is stored so as to be available for a rerun or other use in the event data is spoiled by a mistake in the program or a malfunction in the computer.

register, stepping—Same as *register, shift*.

register, storage—A register in the storage unit of a computer that is involved in all transfers of data to and from the storage unit and all other units of the computer, such as the arithmetic unit, the control unit, and input-output units. (Synonymous with *high-speed bus*, with *distributor*, and with *exchange register*.)

register, triple—Same as *register, triple-length*.

register, triple-length—Three registers that are logically or physically, usually electrically, connected so as to function as a single register capable of storing three computer words. Usually, each register may be separately addressed and accessed. (Synonymous with *triple register*.)

register capacity—Same as *length, register*.

register length—See *length, register*.

registration—Pertaining to accurate positioning relative to a reference; for example, in optical character recognition, the positioning of characters relative to a specified location. Registration is measured in terms of displacement distance from the specified location.

regular binary—Same as *binary, straight*.

regulation—A statement having the force of law, prescribing the manner, place, and time for the discharge of assigned duties or responsibilities; or the invocation of rights established by law or by rule based on law. Regulations are established in order to permit groups of persons engaged in related pursuits to reach a stated goal through a concerted effort. The concert is achieved by regulations.

regulation, voltage—A measure of the degree to which an electrical power source maintains its output voltage stability under varying load conditions. Specifically, the voltage regulation is defined as the no-load voltage minus the full-load voltage, all divided by the full-load voltage, and then all multiplied by 100, giving the regulation in percent.

rejection gate—Same as *gate, NOR*.

relational operator—See *operator, relational*.

relative address—See *address, relative*.

relative coding—See *coding, relative*.

relative error—See *error, relative*.

relative magnitude—See *magnitude, relative*.

relative transmission level—See *level, relative transmission*.

relative vector—See *vector, relative*.

relay, Kipp—Same as *multivibrator, one-shot*.

relay center—Same as *center, data-switching*.

RELCODE—A relative coding procedure developed by Sperry-Rand Corporation for use on the Univac I and Univac II computers.

release connection—See *connection, release*.

relevance ratio—See *ratio, relevance*.

reliability—The probability that a device will function without failure over a specified period of time or amount of usage. Thus, the extent to which something is free of error or malfunction, for example, the probability that when required a device will perform to a specified standard without remedial action. Reliability is sometimes appraised in terms of mean-time-between-failures or mean-repair-time. It is measured as the probability of no fault occurring in a specified period, with the usual difficulties of statistical measurement, or that there is no error in the item whose reliability is being determined. (Contrast with *validity*.)

reliability, data—The extent to which data meets a specified standard; for example, accuracy of data, the degree to which data is free of error, the probability that the data is correct, or a measure of the extent to which a given set of data is unchanged after only transmission, recording, or similar types of operations have been performed. (Contrast with *validity, data*.)

relocatable address—See *address, relocatable*.

relocatable program module—See *module, relocatable program*.

relocatable routine—See *routine, relocatable*.

relocate—To move a routine from one storage area to another, making appropriate adjustments in addresses so that the routine can be executed from the new location. Relative addresses may be automatically adjusted in most systems when a routine is relocated.

relocating loader—See *loader, relocating*.

relocation, dynamic—A method of assigning new absolute addresses to a computer program during execution so that it may be stored in and executed from a difference area of main storage.

relocation, dynamic program—The transferring or moving of a computer program to another part of storage before it has completed execution, without modification, and with continued execution from the new location.

relocation dictionary—See *dictionary, relocation*.

relocation factor—See *factor, relocation*.

remainder—1: In a division operation, the quantity that is left over after the divisor is successively subtracted from the dividend an integral number of times until the difference that results from the subtraction operations is smaller than the divisor, the final difference being the remainder. 2: The fractional part of a quotient. 3: The undivided part, less than the divisor, left after a division operation is completed.

remedial maintenance—Same as *maintenance, corrective.*

remote batch processing—See *processing, remote batch.*

remote control equipment—See *equipment, remote control.*

remote job entry—See *entry, remote job.*

removable plugboard—Same as *plugboard, detachable.*

reorder—Same as *order (1).*

reorganization, file—The facility in a computer operating system that supports or accomplishes the restructuring of a file.

repair delay time—See *time, repair delay.*

repair time—See *time, repair.*

repair time, mean—Same as *mean-time-to-repair.*

repairing, self—See *self-repairing.*

repeatability—In graphic display systems, the ability of hardware, given the same data, to retrace a display element or image.

repeated selection sort—See *sort, repeated selection.*

repeater, forty-four—A telephone repeater that employs two amplifiers, operates on a four-wire system, and does not make use of hybrid arrangements.

repeater station—See *station, repeater.*

reperforator—Originally in communications, a receiving paper-tape perforator and now any paper-tape punch that automatically converts coded electrical signals into patterns of holes, with provisions for automatically advancing the tape, usually for each character. The tape punch operates without direct human control. (Synonymous with *receiving perforator.* Further clarified by *punch, automatic tape.*)

repertoire, code—Same as *code, instruction.*

repertoire, instruction—Same as *repertory, instruction.*

repertory, code—Same as *code, instruction.*

repertory, instruction—The set of computer operations that can be represented in a given operation code and that a given computer or automatic coding system is capable of executing. Some programming languages and automatic coding systems are of such a nature that the concept of instruction repertory does not apply. A given computer language may have an instruction repertory independent of any computer. Then, however, there may be instructions in the language that a given computer cannot execute. (Synonymous with *instruction set* and with *instruction repertoire.*)

repetition frequency, pulse—See *frequency, pulse repetition.*

repetition instruction—See *instruction, repetition.*

repetition rate, pulse—See *rate, pulse repetition.*

repetitive addressing—See *addressing, repetitive.*

repetitive operation—See *operation, repetitive.*

replacement, mechanical—The substitution of a machine or component of a system for another that is installed at a given site. The substitution is usually occasioned by the operating condition of the equipment being replaced.

replacement, track—The substitution of an alternate track for a track found to be defective during a surface analysis. Track replacement is normally accomplished on magnetic cards, discs and drums, rather than on magnetic tapes. (Further clarified by *analysis, surface.*)

report, progress—A report on the current status of an activity; for example, an output from a computer summarizing the results of a run at a particular point in the program.

report generation—See *generation, report.*

report generator—See *generator, report.*

representation—In data processing, the use of a symbol for identification of or in lieu of an item, entity, or unit of data.

representation, analog—The representation of a variable or an item by means of a physical quantity, such as a continuously varying voltage, an angular position, or a column of liquid. The physical quantity that represents the variable behaves as some function of the variable, such as direct proportion, inverse proportion, or square-law relationship. Interaction of the physical quantities is made equivalent to indicated operations among the variables.

representation, binary incremental—1: Incremental representation in which the value of an increment is limited to one of the two values of plus one or minus one, for each quantum step. The maximum positive rate of change is represented as a continuous string of plus ones, the maximum negative rate of change is a continuous string of minus ones. The closest approximation to zero is a string of alternating plus ones and minus ones. In-between values are represented as an average over a sufficiently large number of steps, such as +1, +1, −1, +1, +1, −1 representing $+1/3$. 2: Representation of changes in variables through the use of binary numbers. Thus, each millisecond, the change in range to a target is expressed as a binary number, like 1011101. In this case, the rate of change of range is 1011101 divided by one millisecond. (Further clarified by *representation, incremental.*)

representation, coded—The representation of data established by a code or the representation of a character defined by a coded character set; for example, DIA as the representation for Dulles International Airport in the code for three-letter identification for airports; or the seven binary elements representing the carriage return character in the

ANSCII 7 bit coded character set. (Synonymous with *code value*.)

representation, digital—The representation of variables, in the form of data, by means of digits, or discrete quantities, usually by their presence or absence, or by their presence in a form and its inverse; for example, a voltage level represented by a pattern of binary digits, in which case the binary digits themselves exist as patterns of voltage pulses. In a digital computer, variables are represented as patterns of pulses, either as a pulse train on a single wire (serial) or as a set of time-coincident pulses on a set of wires (parallel).

representation, excess-fifty—A binary number representation system in which any number *n* is represented by the binary equivalent of *n* + 50. Thus, the decimal number 12 is represented as 0111110, which is the binary equivalent of decimal 62. In this system, −50 is represented as 0000000. All numbers above −50 are therefore expressed as positive binary numbers. (Synonymous with *excess-fifty code*.)

representation, fixed-point—A positional numeration system in which each number is represented by a numeral with a single set of digits and with the radix, or arithmetic, point fixed with respect to one end of the set of digits, according to some rule or convention.

representation, floating-point—A numeration system in which each numeral representing a number consists of a pair of numerals, one of which is a coefficient for a fixed positive integer radix raised to a power by an exponent, which is the second numeral of the pair; for example, 0.0148 may be represented as 148 −4; that is 148 X 10⁻⁴.

representation, incremental—The representation of variables in which changes in the variables are represented, rather than the absolute values of the variables. If equations are being solved, the changes in the independent variables correspond to changes in the dependent variables, in the manner defined by the equations. Thus, if velocity is being determined, only the changes in distance and time are required; for acceleration, only the changes in velocity and time are necessary anyway. (Further clarified by *representation, binary incremental*.)

representation, numeric—A discrete representation of data using numerals; for example a representation of letters of the alphabet using binary numerals, such as the ASCII, or the representation of post offices with five-digit ZIP codes.

representation, ternary incremental—Incremental representation in which the value of an increment is rounded to plus one, zero, or minus one. The maximum positive rate of change is represented as a continuous string of plus ones. Lesser positive values are obtained by inserting more and more zeros with

plus ones. Zero is represented as a continuous string of zeros. Negative values are represented by inserting minus ones with the zeros. The maximum negative value is a continuous string of minus ones. The averaging is usually accomplished over a specific time interval or sample.

representation system, positional—See *system, positional representation*.

representation system, variable-point—See *system, variable-point representation*.

representative calculating operation—Same as *operation, average calculating*.

reproduce—In data processing, to prepare a duplicate of stored data; for example, to make another printed page or another punched card, with the same words or holes, in the same arrangement, language, and alphabet.

reproducer—A punch-card machine that prepares a punched card from a punched card, changing all, some, or none of the data on the card that is read. New data may be inserted on the card being punched. Usually, the reproducer has a reading station and a punching station, each fed by a hopper. As cards are read, data from them are punched on blank or prepunched cards at the punching station. The cards read and punched enter separate stackers. (Synonymous with *reproducing punch*.)

reproducing punch—Same as *reproducer*.

request-send circuit—Same as *circuit, send-request*.

request stacking—See *stacking, request*.

rerun—To repeat all or part of a routine on a computer. Reruns become necessary because of interruptions, false starts, the need for corrections of variables, or similar reasons. (Synonymous with *rollback*.)

rerun point—See *point, rerun*.

rerun routine—See *routine, rerun*.

rescue instruction—Same as *instruction, restart*.

rescue point—Same as *point, rerun*.

research operations—1: The use of the analytic methods of the sciences for solving operational problems. The objective is to provide management with a more quantitative basis for making sound predictions and decisions. Some of the more common scientific techniques used in operations research are linear programming, probability theory, information theory, game theory, monte carlo methods, queuing theory, critical-path analysis, PERT, statistical theory, and systems engineering. The use of these tools permit more optimum solutions to problems, proper control of systems, and effective management. 2: The application of scientific or analytic methods to the solution of complex problems that usually involve the optimal allocation of resources. Abbreviated as OR. (Synonymous with *operations analysis*.)

reserve—Same as *allocate*.

reserved word—See *word, reserved.*

reset—To return the state of a device to an initial or arbitrarily selected state or condition; for example, to place a binary cell in the state representing zero, to place a binary storage cell into the alternative state, such as the state alternative to the set state, or to insert a zero into a flip-flop by pulsing the control grid of the proper tube. (Synonymous with *clear*, with *restore*, and with *unset*. Contrast with *set* (2).)

reset, cycle—The returning or resetting of a cycle counter, or a parameter, such as a count, numeral, variable, or reiteration, to its initial or other specified value. The parameter is usually one used within the cycle of events, and the reset may take place each time a cycle is completed. (Further clarified by *index, cycle.*)

reset pulse—See *pulse, reset.*

reset rate—See *rate, reset.*

reset-to-n—To set a device, such as a counter or a register, so as to store or display a given value, herein arbitrarily called n; for example, to return a counting device to an initial state representing n.

reshaping, pulse—Same as *standardization, pulse.*

reshaping, signal—Same as *standardization, signal.*

residence device, operating system—See *device, operating system residence.*

resident program—See *program, resident.*

resident segment—Same as *segment, root.*

resident supervisor—See *supervisor, resident.*

residual error—See *error, residual.*

residue, modulo-n—The remainder after dividing a number by the number n; for example, the residue for 60 modulo-7 is 4, since 60 divided by 7 is 8 with a remainder of 4. (Further clarified by *check, modulo-n.*)

residue check—Same as *check, modulo-n.*

resistance, breakage—In paper handling, the combination of tear resistance and tensile strength.

resistance, color-bleeding—In multiple-colored ribbons, the resistance to the intermixing or "running" of inks.

resistance, smudge—The resistance to inadvertent transfer of ink from a printed image in normal use.

resistance, wear—In printing ribbons and carbons, the ability of a ribbon or carbon to resist reduction of its ability to produce an image after repeated use.

resistance-coupled amplifier—Same as *amplifier, direct-coupled.*

resistor—1: An electrical element across which a voltage drop occurs when an electric current flows in it; power dissipation occurs when current flows in it, and the current in it is always in phase with the voltage drop across it. The resistor resists the flow of electric current. 2: In a fluidic device, a component or element that produces a

linear or nonlinear drop in pressure as a function of fluid flow through it.

resolution—In a display device, the smallest distance between two display elements that can be detected to be two distinct elements under normal operating conditions.

resolution, digital—The value assigned to the least significant digit of a numeral.

resolution ratio—See *ratio, resolution.*

resolver—A device whose inputs are vector quantities and whose outputs are components of the inputs; for example, a device capable of separating a quantity into constituent parts or elements; a device that forms two mutually perpendicualr components of a vector; a function generator that generates the values of the cartesian coordinates, as output, from the input polar coordinates; that is, a device that generates R cos θ and R sin θ from R and θ, or a ball resolver.

resolver, ball—A resolver consisting of a ball that can rotate about an axis through its center, zero. The ball is in contact tangentially with three mutually prependicular wheels, at the points X, Y, and Z, such that OX, OY, and OZ are mutually perpendicular. The ball is driven at a speed R by the wheel at point Z, whose axis is parallel to the OXY plane and makes an angle θ with the direction OY. The ball drives the two wheels, whose speeds are R cos θ and R sin θ. (Synonymous with *spherical resolver.*)

resolver, spherical—Same as *resolver, ball.*

resolving potentiometer, flat-card—Same as *potentiometer, slab resolving.*

resolving potentiometer, slab—See *potentiometer, slab resolving.*

resource, system—A facility, component, piece of equipment, or item of software, that is part of or available to a computing system or its operating system for accomplishment of a task or job, such as main storage, input-output devices, the central processing unit, files, and programs.

resource allocation—See *allocation, resource.*

resource deallocation—See *deallocation, resource.*

response, frequency—The ability of a device to take into account, follow, or act upon a rapidly varying condition; for example, a measure of the output of a device when an input sine-wave signal is applied whose magnitude is constant, but whose frequency is varied from zero to infinity; the frequency band over which the gain of an amplifier is greater than 0.707 of the midband gain; the maximum periodic change that can be followed by a system; or the inverse Fourier transform of the time response of a system to a unit impulse.

response, spectral—1: The variation in sensitivity of a device to light of various wavelengths. 2: The response of a device

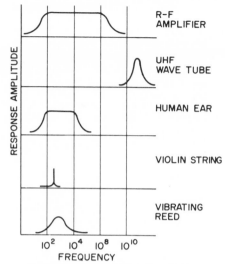

R-F AMPLIFIER

UHF WAVE TUBE

HUMAN EAR

VIOLIN STRING

VIBRATING REED

RESPONSE AMPLITUDE

10^2 10^4 10^8 10^{10}
FREQUENCY

Frequency response *of various items.*

to light; that is, radiant energy, of a particular wavelength or band of frequencies.

response time—See *time, response.*

restart—To reestablish the execution of a computer routine, using the data recorded at a checkpoint. Restarting usually involves returning to a specific previously planned point in a routine in order to overcome a malfunction in the computer system. The length of time between restart points in a given routine should be a function of the mean-free-error time of the machine itself. (Further clarified by *return.*)

restart, automatic—A restart that is initiated by a computer system supervisor or other executive software independently of either user or operator direction or intervention.

restart, deferred—A restart that is initiated by a computer operator or user and that usually requires a rerun or that the job be resubmitted to the data processing center.

restart condition—See *condition, restart.*

restart instruction—See *instruction, restart.*

restart point—Same as *point, rerun.*

restart routine—Same as *routine, rerun.*

restore—Same as *reset.*

restorer-pulse generator—Same as *generator, clock-pulse.*

result—1: The outcome of the performance or application of an operation by an operator on an operand. 2: An entity produced by the execution of an operation; for example, a sum, product, difference, quotient, square root, or reciprocal.

RETA—(Retrieval of Enriched Textual Abstracts). A set of computer programs

which performs the basic functions of storage of text contained in punched cards and the retrieval of information which satisfies the logic expressed in requests. SAP is used to implement the scheme on an IBM 7090 computer. The operational programs are designed for great generality, allowing for storage and retrieval of material ranging from variable field running text to encoded language, such as is employed in typical classification systems. Associated with General Electric Company, Washington, D.C.

retention period—See *period, retention.*

retrieval, data—The searching, selecting, and retrieving of actual data contained in a file; for example, the retrieval from a personnel file, or a data bank, of all names and addresses of persons over 40 years old, married, with four or more children, and over four years with the company.

retrieval, document—The indexing, searching, and identification of specific documents that contain desired data concerning a matter of interest. (Contrast with *retrieval, data.*)

retrieval, false—A document, or a reference to a document, such as the title, author, publisher, and date, which is not related, or is only vaguely related, to the subject of search in a retrieval system. False retrievals are often caused by language ambiguities, deficiencies in the retrieval system, such as poor search strategies or poorly stated queries, communication problems, improper coding, wrong combinations of keys, improper terminology, improper keypunching, and similar errors. The false retrieval occurs when a data item is identified as pertinent by a system but proves to be irrelevant to the search requirement. (Synonymous with *false drop.*)

retrieval, information—The recovery and interpretation of stored data, including the procedures, techniques, and related activities involved, such as the selection and utilization of storage devices, the preparation of store and search routines, data mechanization, the indexing of stored data, and the coding of data. It is necessary to distinguish between document retrieval and actual data retrieval. (Compare with *retrieval, data.*)

Retrieval, Legal—See *Legal Retrieval.*

retrieval code—See *code, retrieval.*

retrieval efficiency ratio—See *ratio, retrieval efficiency.*

Retrieval System, WRU—See *WRU Retrieval System.*

retrieve—In information processing, to find, select, and withdraw data from a collection; that is, a file or a bank. (Synonymous with *fetch.*)

retrofit—To adjust an existing system or program in order to accommodate a new or changed part and to make all other appropriate changes in related systems and programs.

return–1: In programming, to go back to a checkpoint in a program and conduct a rerun. (Further clarified by *restart*.) **2:** In a subroutine, routine or program, to bind a variable in the computer program that called the subroutine, routine, or program. **3:** In a subroutine, routine, or program, to effect a link to the computer program that called the subroutine, routine, or program.

return, carriage–The motion of the carriage of a printer, typewriter, teletypewriter, or similar device, back to the starting point or to some intermediate point. The carriage return is usually effected by a signal, a character, or a specific key, thus automatically or manually causing the next character to be printed at the left margin.

return address–Same as *point, entry*.

return character, carriage–See *character, carriage return*.

return code–See *code, return*.

return-to-bias recording–See *recording, return-to-bias*.

return-to-reference recording–See *recording, return-to-reference*.

RECORDED NUMERAL

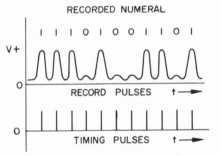

The return-to-zero *method of digital data representation*.

return-to-zero–Pertaining to a method of binary digital data representation, such as a voltage signal displayed on a cathode-ray oscilloscope, or magnetic recording in which a change in signal level, or voltage or current level in the case of electric signals, occurs whenever a binary one digit occurs, returning the signal level to zero between the binary ones and remaining there, or at some equivalent lower level, between the ones as well as during the zeros. The convention could be reversed in terms of binary ones or zeros, Thus, in return-to-zero representation, a string of ones looks like a string of separate pulses, whereas in nonreturn-to-zero representation, a string of ones looks like a single pulse, the signal level not returning to zero, or changing, until a zero occurs. In this discussion, zero and one can be interchanged. (Contrast with *nonreturn-to-zero*.)

return-to-zero recording, nonpolarized–See *recording, nonpolarized return-to-zero*.

return-to-zero recording, polarized–See *recording, polarized return-to-zero*.

reusable program–See *program, reusable*.

reverse-direction flow–See *flow, reverse-direction*.

reversible counter–See *counter, reversible*.

reversible telegraph operation, one-way–See *operation, one-way reversible telegraph*.

reversing amplifier–Same as *amplifier, sign-reversing*.

review, post-installation–In data-processing installation, an on-site examination of the operations and procedures, system utilization, adequacy of results, and related matters pertaining to the automatic data-processing system, to correct deficiencies, determine the extent to which goals have been met, recommend improvements, and provide necessary guidance and assistance where appropriate, all accomplished some time, such as one year, after the system was installed and passed an acceptance test.

review, preliminary–In data-processing installation, a review of matters concerning data processing at an organization or agency to provide guidance in the preparation of plans or proposals for installing automatic data-processing equipment.

review, readiness–In data-processing installation, an on-site examination of the adequacy of preparations for effective utilization upon installation of computing or data-processing equipment and to identify any actions necessary to achieve the required degree of readiness, in both the hardware and the software area, for such installation.

revolver–In magnetic drum or disc storage, a section that has a faster access than that provided by a complete revolution of the drum or disc. The more rapid access is provided by a read head and a write head spaced some distance apart in the same set of tracks, such that data written by one head is read by another head a short time later, and is then sent to the write head. This causes a fixed-length loop of data to revolve. Data may be changed by simple gating. The behavior is similar to that of a delay-line. Revolvers are used primarily for storage of instructions or constants, or for scratch-pad use in computers without high-speed storage, such as core storage. Some revolvers are single-word registers. (Synonymous with *high-speed loop*, with *rapid-access loop*, with *revolver track*, and with *regenerative track*.)

revolver track–Same as *revolver*.

rewind–To return to the beginning of a tape or roll, such as magnetic tape, roll film, or paper tape. Often, rewind speeds are faster than forward reading and recording speeds, since data may not be read or recorded while the tape is rewinding.

rewrite—Same as *regenerate*.

RF—Same as *frequency, radio*.

R-F bandwidth—Same as *bandwidth, R-F emission*.

R-F emission bandwidth—See *bandwidth, R-F emission*.

RFI—(Radio-Frequency Interference). Undesired interference of electromagnetic radiation of radio-frequency signals into operating circuits; for example, high-intensity RFI, say from a radar beam, can completely prevent the successful operation of a digital computer by inducing false and spurious signals; such as, enabling or disabling coincidence gates, causing encoding and decoding errors, and causing erroneous sensing and recording.

right-angle edge connector—See *connector, right-angle edge*.

right justify—See *justify, right*.

ring counter—See *counter, ring*.

ring-file structure—See *structure, ring-file*.

ring shift—Same as *shift, cyclic*.

ringdown signaling—See *signaling, ringdown*.

ringing, AC-DC—A method of telephone ringing that used alternating current to operate a ringer and direct current to actuate a relay that stops the ringing when the called party answers.

ripple-through carry—Same as *carry, high-speed*.

rise time—See *time, rise*.

rise time, pulse—See *time, pulse rise*.

ROAR—(Royal Optimizing Assembly Routing). An assembly program for the Royal McBee RPC 4000 computer.

robot—**1:** A device with sensing instruments capable of detecting input signals or environmental conditions with acting or reacting mechanisms and with guidance mechanisms. The guidance mechanisms receive signals from the sensing instruments, perform calculations on these signals according to stored rules, conventions or logic, and deliver appropriate signals to the acting mechanisms to produce the desired reaction; for example, a thermostatically controlled furnace in a home. **2:** A machine that runs by itself; for example, a thermostatically controlled furnace in a home, an autopilot in an aircraft, or a clock. A clock is not an example of definition (1) above.

rod storage, magnetic—See *storage, magnetic rod*.

role indicator—See *indicator, role*.

rollback—Same as *rerun*.

rollback routine—Same as *routine, rerun*.

roll-in—To return to main or internal storage data that had been previously transferred from main or internal storage to auxiliary or external storage. (Contrast with *roll-out*.)

roll-out—In reading a register or counter, to add ones to each of the digits in the stored number simultaneously, obtaining a signal as each column returns to zero, until all columns have returned to zero. The worst case will require n additions, where n is the number base. The process may be part of a specialized diagnostic routine to determine malfunctions systematically. If the counter counts modulo-n, its contents are read by causing it to count a sequence of n pulses in each place, determining at which stage in the sequence the content passes through zero, the process preserving the original content of the register.

roll-out-roll-in—A computer operating technique for increasing available main storage by temporarily moving data or programs, such as an executive program, from main storage to secondary or auxiliary storage, using the area in main storage that is thus temporarily unoccupied, and then returning the data or programs from secondary or auxiliary storage to main storage, thus restoring their original status.

ROM—Read-only memory.

root segment—See *segment, root*.

rope memory—Same as *storage, core-rope*.

rope storage—Same as *storage, core-rope*.

round—Same as *round-off*.

round-down—To round without making an adjustment to the part of the numeral (being rounded) that is retained. If a numeral is rounded down, its absolute value is not increased. Round-down is a form of truncation. (Contrast with *round-up*.)

round-off—To delete the least significant digit of a numeral, and adjust the remaining part in accordance with some rule; for example, for a fractional numeral, to delete the least significant digit of the decimal numeral, adding one to the next higher significant digit if the least significant digit is 5 or more, and simply deleting the least significant digit without adding one to the next higher significant digit if the least significant digit is 4 or less; or, for whole numerals, to change the least significant digit to zero if it is 4 or less, and adding one to the next higher significant digit if it is 5 or more. Thus, according to these rules, the numeral 32.1828 would be rounded off as 32.183, 32.18, 32.2, 32, and 30. However, 32.1849 would be rounded off as 32.185, 32.18 rather than 32.19. The round-off rule applies to the portion that is left after truncation of the less significant digits of a numeral. Round-off reduces the bias introduced by the truncation of the least significant digits of the numeral. Another round-off statement might be to add one-half of the radix to the next least significant digit before truncation, propagating all resultant carries, and so averaging the effects of truncation. Thus, in decimal notation, a five would be added to one digit position, executing all carries, and then assigning a value of zero to this and all less significant positions, or simply dropping this and all less significant digits. The round-off operation actually increases the size of the quantum used in the representation of a number. (Synonymous with *round*. Contrast with *truncate*.)

round-off error—Same as *error, rounding*.

round-robin scheduling—See *scheduling, round-robin*.

round-up—To round, adjusting the part of the numeral (being rounded) that is retained by adding 1 to the least significant of its digits, and executing any necessary carries if one or more non-zero digits have been deleted. If a numeral is rounded up, its absolute value is not decreased. (Contrast with *round-down*.)

rounding error—See *error, rounding*.

route—In switching networks, the connection, or path, from master to slave, or calling to called, station.

routine—A set of instructions arranged in proper sequence that will cause a computer to perform a desired task, such as solve a problem, retrieve specified data, or control a system. The routine may be a special-purpose routine and a part of a program. The routine may be composed of several subroutines, such as an input-output control subroutine, and a series of subroutines that define mathematical functions, like sine, cosine, and exponential functions. As part of a program, many routines and subroutines are used often, and are held in libraries, on call, usually on magnetic tapes, discs, or drums. The instructions that comprise the routine are coded in a machine or in a common language, such as FORTRAN, COBOL, or ALGOL. (Synonymous with *subprogram*. Further clarified by *program* and by *subroutine*.)

routine, algorithmic—A routine that directs a computer directly toward the solution of a problem in a finite, and usually specified, number of discrete steps, without a trial-and-error process. (Contrast with *routine, heuristic*.)

routine, assembly—Same as *assembler*.

routine, automatic—A computer routine that checks for certain conditions and, if the conditions are met, executes steps that would otherwise require manual intervention, such as selecting another tape station to record data when the tape selected by the program is filled.

routine, check—Same as *routine, test*.

routine, closed—Same as *subroutine, closed*.

routine, compiling—Same as *compiler*.

routine, control—Same as *routine, executive*.

routine, diagnostic—A routine used to detect and locate errors in coding in a program, routine, or subroutine; a mistake by human operators; or malfunctions in a computer. The diagnostic routine may also check and verify data, as well as serve as an aid to debugging and troubleshooting. (Synonymous with *error-detecting routine*. Contrast with *routine, test*.)

routine, direct-insert—Same as *subroutine, open*.

routine, dynamic—Same as *subroutine, dynamic*.

routine, edit—Same as *editor*.

routine, error-correcting—A computer routine designed to correct an error in another program, routine, or subroutine.

routine, error-detecting—Same as *routine, diagnostic*.

routine, executive—A routine that controls the loading and execution of other routines and subroutines. The executive routine organizes and regulates the flow of work in an automatic data-processing system, forming a part of the overall operating system or program. Controls over the flow of work, translations among languages, diagnoses of human mistakes, program and coding errors, equipment malfunctions, priority assignment, checking on releasability of data, and other housekeeping details are exercised by the executive routine. Executive routines might control changeover from one run to the next automatically. Some portions of executive routines may be unknown even to the programmer or the problem sponsor. Thus, the executive routine may often be considered as part of the machine itself. The entire collection of routines normally used in the operation of a computing system, including the executive routines, is considered as comprising the operating system. (Synonymous with *control routine*, with *master routine*, with *monitor routine*, with *supervisory program*, with *supervisory routine*, with *supervisor*, and with *executive*. Further clarified by *system, operating*.)

routine, file management—A routine, usually part of an operating system, that can be used to accomplish one or more of the various file services provided by the system, such as file access control, cataloging, and file protection.

routine, fixed—A routine that cannot be modified by a computer during its execution; for example, a routine on punched cards or in a read-only storage.

routine, floating-point—A set of instructions which permits a computer to execute floating-point operations; that is, perform as though it were performing floating-point operations rather than performing fixed-point operations. Thus, the floating-point operations are programmed. A computer executing a floating-point routine does not have built-in floating-point circuitry; thus, floating-point operations are simulated. With the floating-point routine, floating-point arithmetic instructions may be written as though automatic floating-point circuitry were built-in.

routine, general—A routine designed to solve or process a class or range of problems, specializing in a specific problem when specific parameters are supplied; for example, a routine designed to solve a class of simultaneous differential equations when the coefficients and the exponents defining the order and degree are given; or a routine that will evaluate a matrix or product of matrices, where only the parameters need be supplied.

routine, generating—Same as *generator*.

routine, heuristic—A routine that directs a computer to try various new methods of approach to a solution, like cut-and-try or trial-and-error methods, often involving the act of learning, rather than a routine that directly directs a computer toward a solution in a step-by-step, or algorithmic, procedure. (Contrast with *routine, algorithmic*.)

routine, input—A routine that directs or controls the reading of programs and data for input to a computer for either storage or immediate use. The input routine may be stored permanently in the computer storage, or it may be wired-in computer circuitry, as logic or fixed storage of instructions. Once the input routine is in the computer, it controls the loading of data and other routines. The input routine may control the placement of constants, routines, or other data at appropriate locations in computer storage, or call in such data, as required, from external or peripheral online sources, such as cards, tape, discs, or drums. The input routine may also perform some housekeeping, bookkeeping, red-tape, executive, or operating type instructions, as required, on a limited basis. (Synonymous with *loader, loading routine*, and with *input reader*. Contrast with *routine, output*. Further clarified by *load*.)

routine, interpretive—Same as *interpreter*.

routine, library—A routine held and made available among a collection of routines for possible future use; for example, a checked out routine that may be incorporated into a larger routine and maintained in the library as an aid to programmers. (Further clarified by *subroutine, library*.)

routine, loading—Same as *routine, input*.

routine, main—Same as *program, main*.

routine, master—Same as *routine, executive*.

routine, minimal-access—Same as *routine, minimal-latency*.

routine, minimal-latency—A routine that is judiciously prepared so that the actual latency in serial-access storage is less than the expected random latency that would be experienced if storage locations for storage of data and instructions were chosen without regard to latency. Each routine would have to be prepared with reference to a specific serial storage system. Minimal-latency programming is not necessary or applicable in using random-access storage systems.

(Synonymous with *minimal-latency program* and with *minimal-latency subroutine*.)

routine, monitor—Same as *routine, executive*.

routine, object—Same as *program, target*.

routine, output—A set of computer instructions which organizes and directs all operations related to handling the output data, such as it starts the output equipment, presents data to the output equipment as required, specifies and controls the output equipment as required, specifies and controls the output data format, and monitors output operations. (Further clarified by and contrast with *routine, input*.)

routine, post mortem—A routine used to assist in the performance of an analysis of an operation, or series of operations, after completion. The post mortem routine, may be a diagnostic routine to determine the cause of a failure; a routine designed to permit detailed review of operations; a routine that causes a storage dump for analysis purposes; or a routine that automatically, or on demand, prints the contents of selected storage locations after the main program stops unexpectedly or is stopped deliberately. (Further clarified by *dump, post mortem*.)

routine, production—A routine that accomplishes the purposes for which a computer run is made. Thus, the routine that satisfies the customer's needs, in contrast to those routines that provide support to the production routine, such as translators, compilers, assemblers, and executive routines. (Synonymous with *working routine*.)

routine, recursive—A routine that uses itself as a subroutine, calling itself directly, or calling itself through another routine that it itself has called. The use of a recursive routine usually requires the keeping of records of the status of its unfinished uses, such as in operation of a pushdown list.

routine, relocatable—A routine designed and stored such that it may be easily moved to other storage locations.

routine, rerun—A routine that is designed to be used in the wake of a computer malfunction, program error, or operator mistake, for reconstituting the routine being executed from the last previous rerun point. (Synonymous with *rollback routine* and with *restart routine*.)

routine, restart—Same as *routine, rerun*.

routine, rollback—Same as *routine, rerun*.

routine, selective tracing—A tracing routine that permits only specific instructions to be selected and analyzed, such as only transfer instructions or input-output instructions. (Further clarified by *routine, tracing*.)

routine, sequence-checking—A routine used to check each executed instruction, printing certain results of the checking operation, such as printing the instructions with their addresses, printing selected data, like each transmission instruction and the quantities transmitted, or printing the contents of certain key registers in sequence.

routine, service—A routine that is a member of a broad class of routines standardized at a particular installation for assisting in maintenance and operation of a computer installation and in preparation of programs. Routines designed for actual solution of production problems are not considered as service routines, even though they are held in the same library. Included in the broad class of service routines are executive routines, assemblers, compilers, translators, diagnostic routines, rerun routines, trace routines, post mortem routines, input-output routines, and similar general-purpose routines. The distinguishing quality of service routines is that they are generally standardized so as to serve the needs at a particular installation independent of the specific production type routines. (Synonymous with *utility routine*.)

routine, source—Same as *program, source*.

routine, specific—A routine designed to solve a particular problem, such as the solution of a given equation, a logic situation, or a certain data handling problem, usually in machine language and in which each address refers to explicitly stated registers and locations in storage.

routine, static—Same as *subroutine, static*.

routine, stored—Any routine that has been placed in a storage device, such as a routine placed in fixed storage to control computer operations.

routine, supervisory—Same as *routine, executive*.

routine, target—Same as *program, target*.

routine, test—A routine designed to show whether or not a computer is functioning properly. The test routine usually does not indicate the location of the fault, since it may not be a complete diagnostic routine. The set of instructions in a test routine is specifically designed to reveal computer malfunctions. Some test routines are also diagnostic routines in that they also locate the fault, for instance, by automatically checking all logic circuits and storage elements, and printing out the identification data required to locate each faulty unit. (Synonymous with *check routine* and with *test program*. Contrast with *routine, diagnostic*.)

routine, tracing—A routine that provides a historical record of specified events in the execution of a program, such as the addresses of accessed storage locations. (Further clarified by *routine, selective tracing*.)

routine, utility—Same as *routine, service*.

routine, working—Same as *routine, production*.

routine analyzer—Same as *analyzer (1)*.

routine check—Same as *check, programmed*.

routine library—See *library, routine*.

routine maintenance—Same as *maintenance, scheduled*.

routine maintenance time—Same as *time, scheduled maintenance*.

routine storage—Same as *area, instruction*.

routine support, executive—See *support, executive routine*.

routine test—See *test, routine*.

routing—In communications, selection and assignment of the communication path.

routing, alternate—1: In communications, the assignment of another communications path to a particular destination if the usual or primary path is unavailable. 2: The access of an input-output device to another channel when the device is connected to the central processing unit by more than one channel. 3: The use of a secondary device when the primary device is inoperable; for example, in communications, the use of another trunk line or circuit when the one currently in use malfunctions, is overloaded, is more costly, or is otherwise unavailable.

routing, message—1: In communications, selection and assignment of the communication path over which a specific message, such as a telephone call or a telegram, will be or is sent. Message routing at a particular point might be confined to selection of the next part of the path that the message will follow on its way to the next point in reaching its ultimate destination. Specially designed message-processing equipment may be used to assist in the selection of routes and in message handling. 2: In a computer operating system, the interpreting of a code internal to a teleprocessing message, the directions of the message to the proper program on input, and directing the message to the correct output device on output.

routing indicator—See *indicator, routing*.

A	P	D	4	□	0
I	3	5	C	B	2
8	△	Q	R	F	5
9	7	G	H	J	K
9	4	L	M	R	X
O	4	Y	Z	T	U
V	W	7	6	I	8

The row *is horizontal. Thus, the symbols 135CB2 are said to be in a* row. *The* column *is perpendicular to the* row.

row—A line of horizontal elements in a rectangular matrix or array of elements; for example, one of the 12 lines of 80 punch positions in a standard 80-column punch card, a horizontal line of numerals in a table, a line of printed characters, or the print positions in the line. A line-at-a-time printer is, in fact, a row-at-a-time printer. Rows are usually read from the top down, and are usually so numbered, with the lowest numeral at the top. A single register is usually considered to hold a row of digits. (Closely related to *line*. Contrast with *column*.)

row, binary—See *binary, row*.

row, card—A row of punch positions on a card; that is, a horizontal line of places where holes may be punched to represent data, the data being in binary form, such that a binary one might be a hole and a zero no hole. Typical cards of 12 rows might use a given row to represent a particular digit, such as a row assigned to represent eight. Combinations of holes in specific rows can represent alphanumeric characters. A 12-row card can represent all numerals from zero to 4095, inclusive, in each column. Or, a row in an 80-column card might represent two 40-bit numerals in each row. (Contrast with *column, card*. Further clarified by *binary, row*.)

row, mark-sense—A row or line of mark sense positions. The row is usually considered to be parallel to the X-datum line of a data medium, such as a card or sheet of paper. The X-datum line is an imaginary line along the top edge of the medium when held in its normal viewing position. (Contrast with *column, mark-sense*.)

row, punch—A line of punch positions that is parallel to the X-datum line of a punch card, the X-datum line being parallel to a card column, which is parallel to the longer edge of a card or is horizontal when the card is held for normal human reading of any data printed on the card. (Contrast with *column, punch*.)

row-binary card—See *card, row-binary*.

row pitch—See *pitch, row*.

RPG—Report Program Generator.

rub-out character—Same as *character, delete*.

rubber-banding—In graphic display systems, a technique that allows a straight line to be displayed that has one end fixed and the other end movable and that follows an input device such as a light pen.

RUG—(RECOMP Users Group). A group of users of the RECOMP II computer.

rules, operational—In computer simulation, the part of the data structure of a formal system that comprises the statements of all possible actions to be performed during simulation of the formal system.

rules, syntax—Same as *syntax*.

ruly English—See *English, ruly*.

run—1: In computers and data processing, a single continuous execution of a computer routine, usually complete with regard to some aspect, such as solution of a single problem, conducting a complete search of a file, updating all records, or using up all available storage or reaching a time limit and a rerun point. During a single run, manual intervention does not occur and the computer does not halt. Several linked routines and subroutines may be involved. Input and output operations are usually included in a given run. (Synonymous with *computer run* and with *machine run*.) 2: A single execution of a job on a computer.

run, computer—Same as *run*.

run, machine—Same as *run*.

run book—Same as *file, problem*.

run duration—Same as *time, running*.

running, parallel—Operating a newly developed system concurrently with the system that it is to replace, until there is sufficient confidence in the new system's performance to justify discontinuing the old system. (Contrast with *operation, parallel*.)

running accumulator—Same as *storage, pushdown*.

running time—See *time, running*.

RZ(NP)—Recording, nonpolarized return-to-zero.

RZ(P)—Polarized return-to-zero recording.

S

SABE—(Society for Automation in Business Education).

SABRE—American Airlines SABRE Electronic Reservations System. An American Airlines and IBM seat reservation system based on the IBM 7090 computer.

SACCS—Strategic Air Command Control System.

SAGE—(Semi-Automatic Ground Environment). An air defense data system that correlates radar and other air surveillance data with known flight plans and other information to detect the presence of unknown aircraft and provide automatic guidance of interceptor aircraft.

SAIL–An automatic coding system developed by Sperry-Rand Corporation for the LARC system.

SALE–(Simple Algebraic Language for Engineers). A programming language developed by A. O. Smith Corporation for use on the IBM 705 computer.

sample–To obtain the value of a quantity or the variable itself at periodic intervals or at random intervals. If the sample duration is sufficiently short so that the quantity does not change appreciably during the sample duration, the process is equivalent to quantization. Sampling is often used in process control, to obtain data on the status of various events and conditions in the process. Equipment used to process the data and to direct operations or control the process is time-shared. In statistics, sampling techniques must be carefully planned and applied so that meaningful data is obtained and valid conclusions can be drawn.

sample-change compaction–See *compaction, sample-change.*

sampling rate–See *rate, sampling.*

SAMS–(Satellite Auto-Monitor System). A programming language, procedure, and control system developed by Control Data Corporation for the CDC 1604 system.

SAP–SHARE Assembly Program.

SATIN–(SAGE Air Traffic Integration). An air traffic control system coordinated with air defense, developed by MITRE Corporation.

saturation–A condition that exists when further increases in stimulus or cause produce no corresponding or proportional effect; for example, when a 10 percent increase in magnetomotive force does not produce a 10 percent increase in magnetic flux density in a magnetic material, or when an increase in anode voltage does not produce a correspondingly proportional increase in cathode current, a condition of saturation exists.

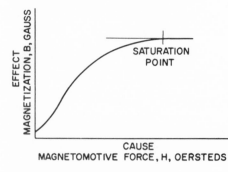

Typical saturation *curve.*

sawtooth wave–See *wave, sawtooth.*

save area–See *area, save.*

scalar–A device that develops an output equal to the input multiplied by a constant; for example, a linear amplifier, a linear attenuator, a voltage divider, a pair of reduction or speed gears, or a set of pulleys. (Synonymous with *coefficient unit,* with *constant multiplier coefficient unit,* and with *multiplier coefficient unit.* Further clarified by *scale* and by *factor, scale.*)

scalar quantity–See *quantity, scalar.*

scale–**1:** In data processing, to change the, representation of a quantity by a factor; that is, multiply it by a number, so as to bring its value or range of values to within prescribed limits. Thus, the range of values might be dictated by the nature of the computer word, such as its length or by the location of the arithmetic point. If a quantity having units is involved, then scaling is equivalent to changing the units; however, when formulas are involved with a consistent set of units, changes in units must be accounted for in the formula, in the computations, and, in any case, in the interpretation of results. The use of floating-point representation in computers has greatly eliminated scaling problems because of the large range of numbers that may be expressed. Scaling includes the determination of scale factors. **2:** In instrumentation, to convert an instrument measurement range into a corresponding range of the quantity measured; for example, for a thermocouple used to measure temperature, to convert, from a calibration instrument, a range of 4 to 20 milliamperes developed by the thermocouple and its milliammeter to a corresponding 300° to 1000°F, and making an instrument scale for the milliammeter marked in °F rather than milliamperes. Enough values in the range must be determined in order to interpolate, that is, scale, all the intermediate values. (Further clarified by *factor, scale* and by *scalar.*)

scale, binary–Same as *notation, binary.*

scale, extended time–A time scale used in data processing when a time scale factor greater than one is used in the processing. (Synonymous with *slow time scale.* Contrast with *scale, fast time* and with *scale, variable time.*)

scale, fast time–A time scale used in data processing when a time scale factor less than one is used in the processing. (Contrast with *scale, extended time* and with *scale, variable time.*)

scale, fixed-radix–Same as *notation, fixed-radix.*

scale, radix–Same as *notation, radix.*

scale, slow time–Same as *scale, extended time.*

scale, time–The relationship between the time required for a process or set of events to take place and the solution time required to predict future events in the process, control the process, or analyze the process. When the machine solution time is greater than the actual physical process time, the time scale is said to be greater than one and the computation is said to be on an extended-time scale or a slow-time scale. If computations proceed faster than the actual physical process, the time scale is less than one and the computation is said to be on a fast-time scale, or a faster-than-real-time scale. If computations proceed in step with the actual process, the time scale is unity and the computations constitute real-time or true-time operations.

scale, two—Same as *notation, binary.*

scale, variable time—A time scale used in data processing when a time scale used in the processing is not held constant. (Contrast with *scale, fast time,* and with *scale, extended time.*)

scale coefficient—Same as *factor, scale.*

scale factor—See *factor, scale.*

scale factor, time—See *factor, time scale.*

scan—To examine sequentially part by part, for example, physical conditions, states of various processes, or items of stored data, usually for a specific purpose and usually as part of the effort required in an information retrieval scheme. Thus, one might scan a file to ensure that all data elements are present, then search the file, seeking a specific item. Thus, a scanner would sweep the entire file, reading all the contents, developing all the signals that result from reading, and accomplish nothing else, save perhaps convert the graphic data to digital signal codes. (Contrast with *read.*)

scan, mark—To scan a document for a specific mark in a specific location. The mark may be made with any pen or pencil, the operation being based on optical scanning and light reflectance. Mark scanning is distinguished from mark sensing in that mark sensing requires an electrographic pencil with a conductive lead, the operation being based on conductivity between two electrodes applied to the paper at precise locations.

scan, MICR—To sense characters printed in magnetic ink. The technique, developed by the American Bankers Association, is used on bank checks, and the character size, shape, and ink used have been standardized by the USA Standards Institute.

scan, raster—To sweep the display area of a display device on a line-by-line basis so as to generate or read an image; for example to generate a picture on a television screen, write alphanumeric text, generate shapes, or read the position of a light pen.

scan period—Same as *period, regeneration.*

scanner—In data processing, a device that automatically samples or interrogates sequentially, the state of various processes, conditions, instruments, sensors, transducers, or other measuring devices, and transfers the data obtained to another device, such as a recorder or a controller. For instance, a scanner might be an instrument that moves a spot of light rapidly across and down a page of printed matter, developing signals that can be interpreted so as to obtain the information on the page in a machine usable form for entry into a digital computer, or a device that checks each of 100 incoming lines continually to determine if signals are arriving, and if so, to accept them and furnish them to a processor.

scanner, flying-spot—In optical character recognition, a device that employs a moving spot of light to scan a sample space or area, the intensity of transmitted or reflected light being sensed by a photoelectric transducer. The intensity of the sensed light varies in accordance with the data being read.

scanner, Luhn—An experimental machine, invented by H. P. Luhn, of the IBM Corporation, which photoelectrically scanned punched cards fed through the machine. Appropriate wiring of the plugboard on the machine permitted searches to be made, based on logic or arithmetic products, sums and differences.

scanner, optical—A device that examines or senses a multidimensional pattern and generates an analog or digital representation of the pattern, usually by optical means, such as a moving spot of light whose reflection is turned on and off in accordance with the light and dark, that is, inked areas on the paper being read; for example, a device that automatically reads printed or written characters and converts them to a digital code. (Synonymous with *visual scanner.*)

scanner, visual—Same as *scanner, optical.*

SCAT—(SHARE Compiler, Assembler, and Translator). A programming package developed by IBM Corporation and SHARE Organization for the IBM 709 computer.

scatter, gap—The deviation from alignment of the magnetic recording head gaps of a group of heads for the several parallel tracks of a magnetic tape unit.

schedule—1: In computer simulation, a time ordered list of events, along with the time they have occurred in the past, are occurring, or will occur in the future within a simulation period, interval, or run. 2: To maintain the calendar of events.

schedule, channel—In an operating system, the part of a supervisor that monitors and controls the movement of data between main storage and input-output devices or other online equipment.

schedule, record control—A comprehensive schedule that designates all actions to be taken in relation to the disposition of the records of a business. Schedules might include instructions for periodic transfer of records from an operating unit to a records center, for disposition, for retention, or other action.

scheduled engineering time—See *time, scheduled engineering.*

scheduled maintenance—See *maintenance, scheduled.*

scheduled maintenance time—See *time, scheduled maintenance.*

scheduler—1: A computer program designed to interpret statements that define jobs and then schedule, initiate and terminate the jobs. 2: A computer program that performs functions in accordance with timing signals, usually sequentially, such as scheduling initiation and termination of jobs. 3: The component of a system that allocates all system resources for a job and performs all necessary initializations prior to execution of the job.

scheduler, foreground—A computer subroutine, routine, or program that processes requests and schedules the execution of appropriate foreground programs in accordance with specified algorithms.

scheduler, job—That part of a control program, or the control program function, that controls input job streams, obtains and allocates input-output resources for jobs or job steps, and regulates the use of the computer system or computer operating system components for each job.

scheduling, round-robin—A technique for scheduling the use of a system or its components, such as the time of a central processing unit of a computer, to a number of controlling users or programs by establishing a circular list of users or programs and allowing a fixed amount of time of the system or component to each user or program in turn, without regard to any priority other than its position in the circular, usually push-up or first-in-first-out, list.

scheduling algorithm—See *algorithm, scheduling.*

scheduling queue—See *queue, scheduling.*

schematic diagram, electrical—See *diagram, electrical schematic.*

science, information—The branch of science devoted to the properties and behavior of information, the forces governing the information transfer process, and the technology necessary to process information for optimum accessibility and use. Interests include the use of codes, transmission, storage, recall, and information processing devices and techniques, such as computers and their operating systems. As an interdisciplinary field, information science is derived from and is related to mathematics, logic, linguistics, psychology, communications and management. It has both a pure and applied science component.

scientific data processing—See *data processing, scientific.*

scissor—In graphic display systems, to remove parts of display elements or images that lie outside a given bound.

scope—1: In computer programming, the portion of a computer program in which the definition of a variable is unchanged. 2: The portion of an expression to which an operator is to be applied.

SCOPT—(Subcommittee on Programming Terminology). A subcommittee of the Standards Committee of the Association for Computing Machinery (ACM).

scored card—See *card, scored.*

scored card, processable—See *card, processable scored.*

SCP—(Symbolic Conversion Program). A one-to-one compiler for symbolic address and operation codes for ITT systems.

scramble time—See *time, scramble.*

scratch-pad storage—Same as *storage, temporary.*

screen—1: To make a preliminary selection of a set of items from a larger set according to given criteria, usually in order to reduce the number of items to be more thoroughly searched at a later time. 2: The inside or outside face of a cathode-ray tube, on the inside face of which data may be displayed or stored. 3: One of the electrodes of a tetrode or pentode vacuum tube. For a pentode, the electrodes are usually called the cathode, plate (or anode), control grid, screen grid, and suppressor grid.

script, machine—Same as *data, machine-readable.*

scrolling—In graphic display systems, the moving of a display image horizontally or vertically in such a manner that as new data appear on the display surface at one edge, other data disappear at the opposite edge. The data that disappear can be automatically scissored as new data are fed in and the image is moved.

SDA—Source Data Automation.

SDI—(Selective Dissemination of Information). A literature searching, notification, and hard copy supply system for selectively serving individuals with internal or external reports, journal articles, and other information. When an item of probable interest to a system subscriber is found, an abstract card suitable for filing is mailed to the subscriber. The subscribers are asked to render an evaluation of each response. The systems that have been used to implement this operational information retrieval scheme are the IBM 650 (tape), IBM 704, IBM 709, IBM 7090, IBM 1401 (tape), and standard card equipment. The programming languages that have been used are machine language for the IBM 650; FORTRAN II for the 704, 709, and 7090; and a symbolic language for the 1401 (tape). SDI now means any system for selectively distributing information in accordance with given profiles.

search—To examine a set of items for a subset that has a specific property; for example, to examine a set of names for all names that begin with J. (Synonymous with *seek (1)*.)

search, area—In information retrieval, to examine a collection of data, such as a group of documents, only within a subset that meets certain criteria, such as within a category, class, scientific discipline, geographical area, or location.

search, binary—A search in which the set of items to be searched is divided into two equal or nearly equal parts, the part not containing the sought items being rejected and the part containing the sought items being processed until those items with the desired property are found. Thus, the binary search is a dichotomizing search in which the two parts are equal or nearly equal. The binary search is often used when it is equally likely that the sought item is anywhere in the collection. If it is more likely to be in certain portions, faster searches are obtained by other forms of dichotomizing searches than binary searches, such as division of the set in accordance with a Fibonacci series.

search, chain—1: A search for an item of data in a file whose items are unordered but interconnected. Thus, to search an unordered but interconnected, or chained, set for an item whose key matches the search key; the search key is transformed to yield an initial address. If the contents of the initial address contain a key that matches the search key, the contents also include the item sought; if not, a further address is found in the contents, and the process is repeated until either the item is found or the chain terminates. **2:** A search in a file constructed so that each item in the file contains a means for locating the next item to be considered in the search.

search, conjunctive—A search to identify items that contain all of a given set of keys; for example, to identify all reports that were published in the last three years *and* treat of biophysics *and* are written in German. The logic product is involved; therefore, all the characteristics must be inherent before the item is selected. (Contrast with *search, disjunctive*.)

search, dichotomizing—1: A search in which the set of items to be searched is divided into two parts, the part not containing the sought items being rejected and the part containing the items being processed until those items with the desired property are found. If the items in the set are divided into two equal, or nearly equal, parts when the dichotomizing search is performed, the search is called a binary search; when the division is in accordance with a Fibonacci series, the search is called a Fibonacci search, and so on. **2:** A search on which an ordered set of items is divided into two parts, one of which is rejected, the other retained because it contains the sought item, the process being repeated on the retained part until the search is completed, that is, the sought item is found.

search, disjunctive—A search to identify items that contain at least one of a given set of keys; for example, to identify all reports that treat of biophysics *or* bionics *or* microbiology, or any combination of these. The logic sum is involved; therefore, only one of the characteristics must be inherent before the item is selected. (Contrast with *search, conjunctive*.)

search, Fibonacci—A dichotomizing search performed such that in each step the original set or remaining subset is subdivided in accordance with successive smaller numbers in the Fibonacci series. If the number of items in the set is not equal to a Fibonacci number, the number of items in the set is assumed to equal the next higher Fibonacci number.

search, interfile—A search, involving two or more files, conducted in such a manner that data retrieved from one file is used to retrieve data from another file. (Contrast with *search, multifile*.)

search, literature—A search of published material for information on a specific subject. A literature search is usually made in order to become familiar with or develop an awareness of the state of the art concerning a certain subject, before undertaking work related to the subject.

search, multifile—A search, involving two or more files, conducted in such a manner

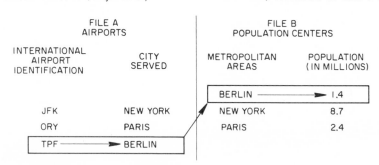

An interfile search for discovering that the Templehof Airport serves a population center of 1.4 million persons.

that data is retrieved from each file, independent of data in the other files. The data thus retrieved is usually assembled in a composite report. (Contrast with *search, interfile*.)

search cycle—See *cycle, search*.

search key—See *key, search*.

search time—See *time, search*.

searching storage—Same as *storage, associative*.

second-level address—See *address, second-level*.

second-level addressing—Same as *addressing, two-level*.

second-order subroutine—See *subroutine, second-order*.

secondary center—Same as *center, secondary switching*.

secondary center, telephone—Same as *center, secondary switching*.

secondary storage—Same as *storage, auxiliary*.

secondary switching center—See *center, secondary switching*.

section, arithmetic—Same as *unit, arithmetic*.

sector—A specified section or area of a track or band on a magnetic recording medium such as a magnetic disc, drum, or card.

SEDIT—A text editor.

see-saw amplifier—Same as *amplifier, sign-reversing*.

see-saw circuit—Same as *amplifier, sign-reversing*.

seek—1: Same as *search*. 2: A single look at a single item of data in a file. Thus, in a search, a number of seeks are made, that is, a number of items are inspected, before the desired item is found. 3: To position, in accordance with given criteria, the access mechanism of a direct access or direct address device; for example, to selectively position the read/write head of a disc storage device or to selectively position a mechanical selector switch of a telephone switching system. (Further clarified by *time, positioning*.)

segment—1: In computer programming, to divide a routine into several parts, or subroutines, each capable of being stored and run, with the instructions necessary to permit jumping to other segments. Segmenting may be automatically accomplished with a compiler, and each segment may be drawn into the computer and executed automatically. (Synonymous with *partition*.) 2: In computer operation, to subdivide a data-processing job into smaller, more easily manageable parts for convenient solution; for example, to subdivide a matrix, such as a determinant, into a function of smaller matrices. (Synonymous with *partition*. Further clarified by *allocate*.) 3: A self-contained portion of a computer program that may be executed without the entire program necessarily being stored in internal storage at any one time.

segment, resident—Same as *segment, root*.

segment, root—The segment of an overlay program that always remains in main storage during execution of successive parts of the overlay program. (Synonymous with *segment, resident*.)

segment buffer, chained—See *buffer, chained-segment*.

select—1: To take alternative A if one condition is met or to take alternative B if the other condition is met. Thus, in a file search, if a condition is met by a file item, remove the item and examine the next item; if the condition is not met, do not remove the item and examine the next item. Selection involves choosing an item from a set of items in accordance with rules and criteria. In selecting cards from a deck, a sorter or collator may select cards with specific digits, all cards with numerals higher than a specific numeral; all cards with numerals lower than a specific numeral; cards with numerals between specific numerals; a specific, such as first, fifth, or last, card in a group; unmatched cards, or cards out of sequence. 2: In switching networks, to request a station to receive data.

selecting—In data transmission networks, a process wherein another station is invited or requested to receive data.

selection, coincident-current—In an array of magnetic cores, the selective switching of one core (cell) in an array by the simultaneous application of two or more drive pulses to the array, which have an additive effect in one core only. Each core in the array must have a threshold value of magnetizing force below which switching will not occur. By proper arrangement of pulse lines threading or winding around the cores, the magnetizing force will exceed the threshold value only in the selected core. The other cores in the array that experience a change in the magnetizing force, for instance, in the same row and column as the selected core, are called partially selected cores. In them, the magnetizing force remains below the threshold value required for selection. The cores involved may be storage cores for holding data, or they may be switch cores for directing currents to appropriate storage cores.

selection check—See *check, selection*.

selection control—See *control, selection*.

selection ratio—See *ratio, selection*.

selection sort—See *sort, selection*.

selection sort, repeated—See *sort, repeated selection*.

selection switch, linear—Same as *storage, core-rope*.

selection switch, Rajchman—Same as *storage, core-rope*.

selective calling—See *calling, selective*.

selective digit emitter—See *emitter, selective digit*.

selective dissemination of information—See *SDI*.

selective dump—See *dump, selective*.

selective fading—See *fading, selective*.

selective trace—See *trace, selective*.

selective tracing—See *tracing, selective.*

selective tracing routine—See *routine, selective tracing.*

selectivity, adjacent channel—The ability of receiving equipment to reject signals on channels whose frequency is close to or near that of the desired signal.

selector—A device that interrogates a condition and initiates one of several possible actions according to the condition interrogated; for example, in punch-card machines, a device that causes a card or an operation to be selected according to some condition or criterion.

selector, digit—A device on a punch-card machine that generates individual pulses corresponding to row positions for each card column.

selectron—An early, now obsolete electronic tube of the cathode-ray type, which stored 256 bits, with rapid access and selection.

self-adapting—Pertaining to the ability of a device, program, or system to change its performance characteristics in response to its environment or to resist changing its performance characteristics as environmental conditions change. For example, a refrigerator continues to develop a 40°F internal temperature although the outside ambient rises from 60°F to 90°F; the unit adapts itself by pumping heat out intermittently for longer periods.

self-adapting computer—See *computer, self-adapting.*

self-adapting program—See *program, self-adapting.*

self-checking code—Same as *code, error-detecting.*

self-checking numeral—See *numeral, self-checking.*

self-demarcating code—See *code, self-demarcating.*

self-learning—Pertaining to the capability of a device to improve its ability to make decisions in accordance with information received, instructions received, calculated results, environmental changes, error history, or other experience.

self-organizing—Pertaining to the capability of a device to adjust its structure, composition, or internal organization in accordance with requirements, such as instructions, rules, or other environmental conditions imposed on it.

self-organizing computer—See *computer, self-organizing.*

self-organizing machine—See *machine, self-organizing.*

self-organizing program—See *program, self-organizing.*

self-relative address—See *address, self-relative.*

self-relative addressing—See *addressing, self-relative.*

self-repairing—Pertaining to the capability of a device to detect, locate, and remove malfunctions during operation without human intervention other than making

parts available to the device for automatic insertion.

Selsyn—Same as *synchro.*

semanteme—An element of language that expresses a definite image or idea, such as a word or a part of a word, and therefore, a data element, item, or code to which meaning has been assigned. Linguistic difficulties occur in communication due to ambiguity among semantemes. (Synonymous with *lexeme.* Illustrated by *grapheme.* Further clarified by *morpheme* and *primitive.*)

semantics—**1:** The study of the meaning of words or expressions and their relationships in a language. (Related to *morphology.*) **2:** The study of the relationships between groups of characters and their meanings independent of their manner of interpretation and use.

Semi-Automatic Ground Environment—Same as *SAGE.*

semiautomatic message switching center—See *center, semiautomatic message switching.*

semiconductor—A material that displays a different electrical resistance in opposite directions. Usual semiconductors, such as germanium and silicon crystals, have a high resistance in one direction, measured in megohms, and a low resistance in the opposite direction, measured in ohms. These make ideal rectifiers, detectors, and gates, which in turn make possible such items as computer logic circuits, voltage multipliers, diode matrices for bit-pattern conversion, and many other devices. A transistor is a diode, or semiconductor, whose resistance, or conductance, is controllable by a third electrode. The resistance of semiconducting material lies in the vast range between a conductor, such as a pure metal, and an insulator, such as glass or rubber.

semiconductor, intrinsic—A substance, usually a crystal such as germanium and silicon, which conducts an electric current upon application of an electric field due to the presence of mobile holes and electrons, but does not conduct to any great extent, such as do copper, silver, gold and aluminum, since the number of charge carriers is only a small proportion of the number of atoms. In a metallic conductor, the carrier density is greater; the electrons are only loosely held to the atoms. Since the property is that of a pure crystal, it is called intrinsic. (Further clarified by *acceptor,* by *donor,* by *hole,* and by *carrier (2).*)

semiconductor, n-type—A semiconducting crystal material which has been doped with minute amounts of an impurity that will produce donor-type centers, or electrons, in the crystal lattice structure. The valence of the impurity might be 5, which leaves an extra electron free to wander about, when all atomic bonds are complete, as with an intrinsic material of valence 4. Conduction takes place by means of electron migration; the electron will freely drift about, moving quite readily from atom to atom, especially under the influence of an externally applied electric field. Since the pentavalent atoms are donating an electron, which is in excess of the 8 electrons required to complete the atomic bonding, they are called donor atoms. Since electrons are negative particles, the material is called n-type. Conduction is primarily by electrons as the majority carrier of electric current. (Further clarified by *carrier, majority*; by *donor*; and by *hole*. Contrast with *semiconductor, p-type*.)

semiconductor, p-type—A semiconducting crystal material which has been doped with minute amounts of an impurity that will produce acceptor-type centers, or holes, in the crystal lattice structure. The valence of the impurity might be 3, which leaves incomplete atomic bonds in the intrinsic material with a valence of 4. Conduction takes place by means of hole migration. The impurity element requires an extra electron to complete its bonding structure, creating a hole in an adjacent intrinsic atom. For example, impurities which create holes in germanium are trivalent and are called acceptors, which are positive and which accept electrons, and so the name p-type material, p for positive. Conduction is by holes as the majority carrier of electric current. (Further clarified by *hole;* by *carrier, majority;* and by *acceptor*. Contrast with *semiconductor, n-type.)*

semifixed length record—See *record, semifixed length.*

semiotics—1: The science that deals with symbols and their syntax. 2: The theory of signs and symbols; their relationships; and their functions in both artificial and natural languages. Semiotics comprises the three branches of syntactics, semantics, and pragmatics.

send-only service—See *service, send-only.*

send-request circuit—See *circuit, send-request.*

sense—To determine the state or condition of an item; for example, to read a magnetic tape, to read or detect holes in a punched card or tape, to determine the status of a switch, to measure the amount of light reflected from a spot on a paper, or to read printed characters or images. Sensing is usually performed relative to some criterion.

sense, mark—See *mark-sense.*

sense switch—Same as *switch, alteration.*

sense wire—See *wire, sense.*

sensible, machine—Same as *readable, machine.*

sensing element—See *element, sensing.*

sensing station—See *station, sensing.*

sensitivity—The ratio of a unit of response on the part of a device, program or system to a unit of input signal or stimulus; for example, in a cathode-ray tube, the ratio of displacement of the electron beam at

impact on the screen per volt of deflecting potential, expressed as centimeters per volt or similar unit; or the angular displacement of a galvanometer as radians per milliampere; or the inches per pound per square inch displacement sensitivity of a stylus-type pressure gauge recorder. (Synonymous with *sensitivity ratio*.)

sensitivity ratio—Same as *sensitivity.*

sentinel—Same as *flag.*

separating character—Same as *separator, information.*

separating force, contact—See *force, contact separating.*

separator—Same as *delimiter.*

separator, information—A control character that delimits like units of data in a hierarchic arrangement of data. The name of the separator may not be indicative of the units of data that it delimits, that is, separates. (Abbreviated as IS. (Synonymous with *separating character*.)

septet—A byte composed of seven binary digits. (Synonymous with *seven-bit byte*.)

septinary—Pertaining to a system of numeration with a radix of seven.

sequence—1: Same as *order (1)*. 2: An arrangement of items in accordance with some criterion that defines their spacewise or timewise succession; for example, a series of numbers or terms in ascending order of magnitude; an orderly progression of items or operations in accordance with some rule, such as alphabetical or numerical order; or a set of instructions executed one after the other on a computer, and so the name sequential machine. 3: To place items into some arrangement in accordance with specified criteria, such as in accordance with the order of the natural numbers. Other natural linear orders may be mapped on to the natural numbers. Thus, by extension, the sequencing may be alphabetical, chronological, or by any other feature such as size or color.

sequence, calling—A group of instructions and data usually arranged in a specified manner necessary to set up and call a given subroutine.

sequence, collating—An ordering assigned to the members of a set so as to establish ranking in procedures such as sorting, collating, or ranking; for example, the alphabetical order assigned to the letters of the English alphabet, the numerical order assigned to a set of numerals, or the chronological order assigned to a set of dates by virtue of the passage of time.

sequence, pseudorandom number—A sequence of numbers, determined by some defined arithmetic process, that is satisfactorily random for a given purpose, such as by satisfying one or more of the standard statistical tests for randomness; for instance, sufficiently random to be used in monte carlo methods involved in statistical sampling techniques. Such a sequence may approximate any one of several statistical distributions, such as uniform distribution or normal Gaussian distribution. (Further clarified by *pseudorandom*. (Synonymous with *random number sequence*.)

sequence, random number—An ordered set of numbers, usually occurring serially in space or time, each of which may not be predicted from any knowledge of its predecessors. (Synonymous with *sequence, psuedorandom number*.)

sequence, recursively defined—1: A sequence that follows an initial set of terms, in which each term is defined by an operation in which some or all operands are terms or are in the terms or expressions that precede the term being defined; for example, a Fibonacci series, a factorial sequence, an arithmetic or geometric series. **2**: A mathematical, algebraic, or semantic series of terms, expressions, or words in which each term, expression, or word is determined by operating upon preceding terms.

sequence-by-merging—To sequence by splitting and merging repeatedly.

sequence check—See *check, sequence*.

sequence-checking routine—See *routine, sequence-checking*.

sequence computer, consecutive—See *computer, consecutive sequence*.

sequence control register—Same as *counter, instruction*.

sequence-control tape—Same as *tape, program*.

sequence counter—Same as *counter, instruction*.

sequencing criterion—Same as *key, sort*.

sequencing key—Same as *key, sort*.

sequential—Pertaining to the occurrence of two or more events in time sequence with only accidental or no time coincidence or overlap of the events. (Contrast with *concurrent*, with *consecutive*, and with *simultaneous*.)

sequential access—See *access, sequential*.

sequential batch processing—See *processing, sequential batch*.

sequential circuit—See *circuit, sequential*.

sequential computer—See *computer, sequential*.

sequential computer, logic-controlled—See *computer, logic-controlled sequential*.

sequential computer, program-controlled—See *computer, program-controlled sequential*.

sequential control—See *control, sequential*.

sequential logic element—See *element, sequential logic*.

sequential operation—See *operation, sequential*.

sequential programming—See *programming, sequential*.

sequential process—See *process, sequential*.

serendipity—In information retrieval, the gift of finding valuable, agreeable, or useful data related to other activities when searching for data for a specific activity.

serial—1: The time-sequencing of two or more processes or events; for example, drilling then tapping, or adding then multiplying. **2**: The time-sequencing of two or more similar or identical processes, using the same facilities for the successive processes; for example, using the same adder first to add, then to multiply (by means of successive addition), or using the same power tool, first to drill, then to countersink. **3**: The time-sequential processing of the individual parts of a whole, such as the bits of a word, using the same facilities for successive parts; for example, handling the individual bits of a word one at a time in the same wire and gate; or handling the data items in a message one after the other in the same device. (Contrast with *parallel*.)

serial access—See *access, serial*.

serial access storage—See *storage, serial access*.

serial adder—See *adder, serial*.

serial addition—See *addition, serial*.

serial arithmetic—See *arithmetic, serial*.

serial computer—See *computer, serial*.

serial flow—Same as *work-flow, serial*.

serial half-subtracter—See *half-subtracter, serial*.

serial number—See *number, serial*.

serial operation—See *operation, serial*.

serial-parallel—A device or procedure that handles data items in both serial and parallel fashion, such as parallel by bit and serial by character, or a device that converts parallel data to serial data for handling over one line, such as a transmission line or a serial adder. For example, an adder may handle the decimal

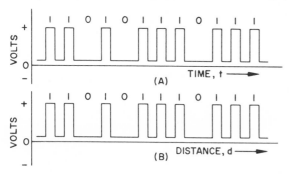

Both plots are serial digits of a numeral. Plot (A) is the voltage of a point on a wire versus time, showing the bits as they pass this point, with the leftmost bit occurring first. Plot (B) is a serial string of pulses on a delay-line at a given instant of time, with the rightmost bit leading the string.

digits of numerals serially, but the bits that represent the decimal digits may be handled in parallel fashion; that is, simultaneously. A serial-parallel converter converts serial data coming in on one wire to parallel data going out on several wires. (Synonymous with *parallel-serial* and with *serioparallel*.)

serial sort—See *sort, serial.*

serial storage—See *storage, serial.*

serial transmission—See *transmission, serial.*

serial work-flow—See *work-flow, serial.*

serializer—Same as *dynamicizer.*

series, Fibonacci—A series of integers in which each integer is equal to the sum of the two preceding integers; mathematically $x_i = x_{i-1} + x_{i-2}$, where $x_0 = 0$ and $x_1 = 1$, that is, $0, 1, 2, 3, 5, 8, 13, 21, 34, 55, 89, \ldots$

series, time—A mathematical series in which each of the terms are functions of time; for example, $t^1 + t^2 + \ldots + t^n$.

serioparallel—Same as *serial-parallel.*

service, exchange—A telephone service permitting interconnection of any pair or any two customer telephones through the use of switching equipment.

service, extended area—A telephone exchange service at increased charge rates, but without toll charges, for a large area or community; for example, a fixed charge for unlimited calls in the five boroughs of New York City, or for Washington, D.C. and the surrounding Maryland and Virginia counties.

service, foreign exchange—Telephone service that connects a customer's telephone to a central office exchange that does not serve the customer's area.

service, full-duplex—The service provided by a single communication channel capable of simultaneous and independent transmission and reception in both directions.

service, half-duplex—The service provided by a duplex communication channel, but limited to simplex operation, that is, one way at a time, and therefore not capable of simultaneous and independent transmission and reception, as in full-duplex service.

service, receive-only—The service provided by a communication channel that is capable of receiving but not of sending signals.

service, send-only—The service provided by a communication channel that is capable of transmitting but not of receiving signals.

Service, Teletypewriter Exchange—A network that provides interconnection for American Telephone and Telegraph Teletypewriter subscribers. (Synonymous with *TWX.*)

service, timing—In a computer operating system, the provision of time measurements and signals to programs that utilize them; for example, providing real clock or actual local time in hours, minutes, and seconds of the day; providing notification of an elapsed interval from a prescribed signal or event; and providing a signal for suspending program execution for a specified interval.

service organization, computer—Same as *organization, computer service.*

service program—Same as *program, utility.*

service routine—See *routine, service.*

serviceable time—Same as *time, up.*

servo—Same as *servomechanism.*

Servo—Abbreviation for *Uniservo.*

servo, velocity—Same as *servointegrator.*

servointegrator—**1:** A servomechanism used to make the rotational speed of its shaft proportional to its input voltage. A tachogenerator on the shaft supplies a feedback voltage proportional to the speed, which allows higher mechanical loading of the output shaft than for the integrating motor. Both devices are used for the same purpose. (Synonymous with *decision integrator,* with *velocity servo,* and with *velodyne.*) **2:** In incremental computers, a digital integrator modified so as to have an output increment that is maximum negative, zero, or maximum positive, according to whether the input is negative, zero, or positive. Thus, the output is of the saturation type. The servointegrator can be used where negative feedback is required, such as in certain types of adders. The output is in a ternary form of incremental representation.

servo swap—Same as *swap, tape-servo.*

servomechanism—**1:** A controlled system in which the output influences the input; that is, in which there is feedback. Abbreviated as servo. **2:** A control system in which the output influences the input, that is, in which there is feedback, and in which at least one of the system's internal signals, inputs, or outputs is or represents mechanical motion. In most servomechanisms, there 'is a built-in capability to reach a condition or state by measuring the deviation from the desired state and stimulating the system so as to reduce the deviation to zero.

servomultiplier—In an analog computer, an analog multiplying unit that has a position control and that is capable of multiplying each of serveral different variables by a single variable, represented by analog voltages. The single variable (multiplier) is used as an input signal to a mechanism that turns the shafts, with a slider or wiper attached to each shaft, through a proportionate angle. One of the potentiometers is energized from the supply reference voltage of the computer and supplies a feedback signal for the mechanism. Each of the multiplicands is used to energize one of the remaining potentiometers. Thus, the product of a multiplicand and the multiplier is available as an output analog signal at the slider of a potentiometer. (Synonymous with *potentiometer multiplier.*)

SESOME—A computer multipurpose routine, to include service, sort, and merge, developed by Sperry-Rand Corporation.

session—In a data processing system operated in a conversational mode, a period of time during which a specific user carries on a dialog with the system.

set—1: A collection of items. Usually the members of a set have something in common, such as a set of numerals, a set of games, a set of china, or a set of computer programs. In a set of miscellaneous items, the items may have nothing in common other than that they are members of the same set. (Contrast with *subset (1).*) 2: To place a storage device into a specified state, usually, other than zero or blank; for example, to place a binary cell in the state representing one. (Contrast with *reset.*) 3: Same as *bind.*

set, alphabetic character—A character set that contains letters; may contain space, control, and other special characters such as punctuation marks; but does not contain digits. (Closely related to *subset, alphabetic character.*)

set, alphabetic coded character—A coded character set with a set of characters that is an alphabetic character set, that is the character set contains letters; may contain control characters, space characters, and other special characters such as punctuation marks; but does not contain digits.

set, alphanumeric character—A character set consisting of letters and digits and usually other special characters such as punctuation marks.

set, alphanumeric coded character—A coded character set with a set of characters that is an alphanumeric character set, that is the character set contains letters and digits, and it may contain control characters, space characters, and other special characters such as punctuation marks.

set, card—Cards and other forms bound so as to provide multiple copies of specific data, like source data for a data system.

set, character—A set of characters that are mutually distinct and designed for a specific purpose, such as a set that is to be recognized by a reader, a set that may be used to form words and write messages, or a set that can be printed by a printer or displayed by a cathode-ray tube. The primary difference between character set and alphabet is that alphabet includes the concept of ordering whereas character set does not. (Contrast with *alphabet.*)

 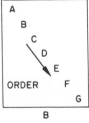

A is a character set *whereas B is an* alphabet.

set, code—A finite, complete, or closed set of representations defined as or by a code; for example, all of the two-letter identifiers for U.S. states, all the three-letter representations for identification of international airports, or all of the five-digit ZIP codes for United States post offices. (Contrast with *code, data.*)

set, coded character—A character set that results from the application of a set of unambiguous rules, there being a one-to-one relationship between the characters of the character set and the coded representations that define the characters.

set, computer instruction—Same as *set, machine instruction.*

set, empty—A set without items or elements. The concept of an empty set is a mathematical or abstractional convenience enabling the number of items in a set to assume all possible values including that of zero. (Synonymous with *null-set.*)

set, instruction—Same as *repertory, instruction.*

set, machine instruction—A set of operators of the instruction repertory of a computer together with a description of the meanings or types of meanings that can be attributed to their operands. (Synonymous with *computer instruction set.*)

set, null—Same as *set, empty.*

set, numeric character—A character set that contains digits, that may contain control characters, special characters, and the space character, and that does not contain letters. (Related to *subset, numeric character.*)

set, numeric coded character—A set of characters each of which are numerically coded.

set, universal—A set that includes all of the elements or items of concern.

set pulse—Same as *pulse, set.*

set theory—Same as *theory, group.*

set-up—In computer operations, a system that has been prepared for operation, including such tasks as putting paper in the printer, mounting reels of tape, loading cards in hoppers, and setting equipment selection switches. Set-up operations are related to an impending run, it being assumed that all parts involved in the set-up are in running order. Maintenance and related operations such as running diagnostic routines and correcting faults are not considered set-up operations. (Contrast with *take-down.*)

set-up diagram—See *diagram, set-up.*

set-up time—See *time, set-up.*

seven-bit byte—Same as *septet.*

sexadecimal—Pertaining to a characteristic or property involving a selection, choice, or condition in which there are 16 possibilities; that is, pertaining to 16. For example, the numeration system with a radix of 16. Many digital computers use a

315

numeration system with a radix of 16, since a tetrad, or four bits, can be used to represent all the digits. The first electronic computers to use a sexadecimal system were the IAS computer and the Army ORDVAC computer. (Synonymous with *hexadecimal*.)

sexadecimal digit—See *digit, sexadecimal.*

sexadecimal notation—See *notation, sexadecimal.*

sexadecimal number—Same as *numeral, sexadecimal.*

sexadecimal numeral—See *numeral, sexadecimal.*

sextet—A byte composed of six binary digits. Synonymous with *six-bit byte.*

shannon—1: A unit of measurement of quantity of information equal to that which can be represented by one or the other of two exclusive and exhaustive states, such as a binary digit. (Synonymous with *binary unit*.) 2: A unit of logarithmic measure of information equal to the decision content of a set of two mutually exclusive events, expressed as a logarithm with the base two; for example, the decision content of a character set of eight characters equals $\log_2 8$, or 3 shannons. (Synonymous with *bit*.)

shape, wave—See *waveshape.*

shaped-card potentiometer—See *potentiometer, shaped-card.*

shaping, pulse—Same as *standardization, pulse.*

shaping, signal—Same as *standardization, signal.*

SHARE—An organization of IBM computer users engaged in mutually exchanging operational experience, computer programs, techniques, and procedures involving the use of IBM computers in the solution of their common problems. Although the IBM Corporation has supplied administrative and logistic support to SHARE, it is an independent organization engaged in mutual support of its members.

share, time—See *timeshare.*

sharing, time—The timewise interleaving of two or more independent processes or events on one operational or functional unit.

sharpness—The clarity of an image; for example, similarity of the geometry of a printed character to the geometry of the original type face.

sheet—In data processing, a single piece of paper containing data on at least one side. One sheet is considered as two pages.

Sheffer stroke gate—Same as *gate, NAND.*

shelf, off the—Same as *off-the-shelf.*

shelf-life—The maximum length of time that an item can remain in stock or in inventory under normal storage conditions and still meet operational requirements when placed in service under design or rated conditions. For many electronic parts, shelf-life is nearly infinite or in-

definite. For some parts, operational life is nearly equal to shelf-life, as is the case for some transistors. Since operation of a component in a circuit might tend to drive off moisture, or for other reasons, it is possible that operational life could exceed shelf-life.

SHF—(Superhigh Frequency). Frequencies between 3000 and 30,000 megahertz. (Further clarified by *spectrum, frequency*.)

shift—To move or displace data, usually to the right or left; or the movement itself. For example, a shift of three digit positions to the left might imply multiplication by 8 for binary digits or by 1000 for decimal digits. The displacement is usually performed in accordance with a set of rules, such as all characters to the left, all characters to the right; characters lost to the right are fed on at the left end (right circular shift), or in a right shift, zeros are fed in at the left end, in order to keep the number of characters constant; that is equal to the number of characters that a register, storage location, or accumulator may hold.

I	I	O	O	I	I	I	O

RIGHT 2	O	O	I	I	O	O	I	I
LEFT 4	O	O	I	I	O	O	O	O
RIGHT I	O	O	O	I	I	O	O	O
RIGHT 4	O	O	O	O	O	O	O	I
LEFT I	O	O	O	O	O	O	I	O

Note the loss of digits during left and right shifts above. Cyclic shift avoids such loss.

shift, arithmetic—A shift of the digits of a number, equivalent to multiplying or dividing the number by a positive number obtained by raising the radix to an integral positive or negative power, without changing the sign of the number. In floating-point numbers, usually only the coefficient is shifted. An arrangement may be made for round-off. Thus, a shift in the number -0.13481 to -0.00134 is considered to be a shift of two places to the right, which is equivalent to dividing by 100, or dividing by 10 raised to the second power. Shifting is applicable to positional notation systems.

shift, carrier—A change in the carrier frequency in a frequency modulation communication system; that is, the difference between the steady-state mark and space frequencies that occur when data is transmitted; for example, in a telegraph teletypewriter operation, the mark signal is one frequency and the space signal a different frequency, the mark usually being the lower frequency.

shift, circular—Same as *shift, cyclic.*

shift, cyclic—A shift in which the data that is moved out of one end of the storage location is moved in at the other, in a circular fashion or as in a closed loop. The net result is a change in position of the data in the location. The circulation may be to the right or to the left. In a right circular shift, the data coming off at the right end is reinserted at the left end and the data in the location is moved to the right. Thus the number 123456 right circular shifted two places becomes 561234. For this number, completely filling the storage location, this is equivalent to a left circular shift of four places. In an arithmetic shift, zeros are fed in at the end opposite to the direction of shift. The sign is treated as any other character. (Synonymous with *end-around shift*, with *end-around-carry shift*, with *circular shift*, with *nonarithmetic shift*, and with *ring shift*. Contrast with *shift, arithmetic*.)

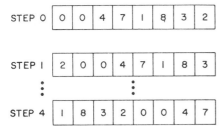

A cyclic shift of the contents of decimal registers.

shift, end-around—Same as *shift, cyclic*.
shift, end-around-carry—Same as *shift, cyclic*.
shift, frequency—Same as *shift, carrier*.
shift, logic—A shift that affects all positions, such as a cyclic shift.
shift, logical—Same as *shift, logic*.
shift, nonarithmetic—Same as *shift, cyclic*.
shift, phase—The difference between the time of occurrence of an input signal and the time of occurrence of the same signal at the output of a circuit, system, or control unit. The phase shift may be measured in units of time, or, for a periodic wave, in electrical or angular degrees, where $360°$ is equivalent to the time of a complete cycle of the periodic wave. A phase shift is a time delay; however, in some periodic waves, such as sinusoidal waves, the phase shift, between voltage and current, can be such that the current leads the applied voltage.
shift, ring—Same as *shift, cyclic*.
shift-in character—See *character, shift-in*.
shift-out character—See *character, shift-out*.
shift register—See *register, shift*.
shift register, magnetic—See *register, magnetic shift*.
shop, closed—In data processing, pertaining to a method of computer installation, programming, and operation wherein programming service, sometimes including problem analysis and formulation, and computer operation and maintenance is the responsibility of a group of specialists who are assigned to the computer facility and who are subject to the supervision of the chief of the facility. Only problems in a general form or general statement are forwarded to the facility for analysis formulation, programming, coding, and running, and only solutions or outputs in proper form, or as requested, are returned to the sponsor. Usually, each problem sponsor is assigned to a computer facility staff member for getting the work through the facility. Thus, no person from outside the computing facility need go beyond the office of his assigned analyst or programmer. (Contrast with *shop, open*.)
shop, open—In data processing, pertaining to a method of computer installation programming and operation wherein programming service, coding, problem analysis, formulation, and all related tasks except perhaps computer operation and maintenance is performed by any qualified staff member of the entire organization to which the computer facility belongs. Usually, in a completely open shop, only computer time is made available; priorities for time are honored or monitored, and maintenance is performed by computer facility personnel. (Contrast with *shop, closed*.)
short card—See *card, short*.
short word—See *word, short*.
SI—The shift-in character.
SIAM—Society for Industrial and Applied Mathematics.
SICOM—A floating-point interpretive routine developed by Control Data Corporation for use on the Control Data 160A computer.
side, line—In communications, data circuit terminal connections to a communications channel between two terminals. (Contrast with *side, local*.)
side, local—In communications, data circuit terminal connections to terminal devices, such as input-output devices like teletypewriters, microphones, or television sets. (Contrast with *side, line*.)
sideband—A band of frequencies that occur on either side of the carrier frequency when a set of frequencies modulates the carrier frequency. The sum of the carrier frequency and the modulation frequencies forms the upper sideband, and the carrier frequency less the modulation frequencies forms the lower sideband. If the carrier frequency is one megahertz, and the modulation signal is an audio signal that varies from 200 to 2000 hertz, then the upper sideband is 1,000,200 to 1,002,000 hertz, and the lower sideband is 998,000 to 999,800 hertz.
sideband transmission, double—See *transmission, double-sideband*.

sideband transmission, independent—See *transmission, independent-sideband.*

sideband transmission, single—See *transmission, single-sideband.*

sideband transmission, vestigial—See *transmission, vestigial sideband.*

sideways sum—See *sum, sideways.*

sifting sort—Same as *sort, bubble.*

sight check—See *check, sight.*

sign—An indicator that designates whether a number is negative or positive. The symbol used for the sign is arbitrary. The symbols + and − are common, though in computers, 0 and 1 and 0 and 9 have been used for the plus and minus signs. The sign is usually held in a predetermined location in a computer word, where its meaning can be interpreted by a person or the machine.

sign, special—Same as *character, special.*

sign bit—See *bit, sign.*

sign-changing amplifier—Same as *amplifier, sign-reversing.*

sign character—See *character, sign.*

sign-check indicator—See *indicator, sign-check.*

sign-control flip-flop—Same as *flip-flop, sign.*

sign digit—See *digit, sign.*

sign flip-flop—See *flip-flop, sign.*

sign position—See *position, sign.*

sign-reversing amplifier—See *amplifier, sign-reversing.*

signal—1: That which is transmitted in order to convey data. Thus, the signal is the physical entity, event, phenomenon or quantity that can be initiated and controlled at a source, transmitted, or recognized at a destination. Signals usually represent data, which, in turn, represent information for a person or a device. 2: A time-dependent value assigned to, and which is itself, a physical phenomenon and which is, represents, or conveys data.

signal, carry-complete—A signal generated by an adder, indicating that all the carries have been added to form the final sum. The signal indicates that no further carries are expected and that the sum now formed is final and complete, whether the addition process involves the use of partial sums, partial carries, or carry propagation throughout the addition, or each addition of a multiplication process.

signal, clock—Same as *pulse, timing.*

signal, delta—In coincident-current magnetic-core storage, the difference in signal magnitude obtained between the partial-select output signal of a cell in the one condition and the partial-select output signal when the same cell is in the zero condition. A partial-select output signal is obtained when only one of the two selection wires is pulsed.

signal, disturbed-one output—The output signal obtained from a binary storage cell that has received a drive pulse tending to partially switch the state of polarization of the ferromagnetic or ferroelectric cell from the one state to the zero state. Such a signal would come from a coincident-current storage cell when only one of the two pulses required to switch the cell occurs at the cell. Disturbed-one and zero outputs occur because of electric and magnetic coupling and because the hysteresis loops of the core or cell material are not rectangular. (Synonymous with *partial-one output signal.*)

signal, disturbed-zero output—The output signal obtained from a binary storage cell that has received a drive pulse tending to partially switch the state of polarization of the ferromagnetic or ferroelectric cell from the zero state to the one state. Such a signal would come from a coincident-current storage cell when only one of the two pulses required to switch the cell occurs at the cell. Disturbed-one and zero outputs occur because of electric and magnetic coupling and because the hysteresis loops of the core or cell material are not rectangular. (Synonymous with *partial-zero output signal.*)

signal, enabling—A signal that permits an event, operation, or phenomenon to take place; for example, a signal to an AND gate to remain open, so that the remaining inputs function according to AND logic. (Contrast with *signal, inhibit.*)

signal, guard—In a digitizer, a digital-analog or analog-digital converter, or another converter, a signal that permits values to be read or converted only when the values are not changing, particularly to avoid ambiguity or error. A set of reading stations may be strobed with the guard signal. An extra output signal, generated when all values are complete and static, may be used as the guard signal.

signal, inhibit—A signal that prevents an event, operation, or phenomenon from taking place; for example, a signal to an AND gate to remain closed, so that no matter what the other inputs are, no output signal occurs. Thus, the inhibit signal prevents the gate from yielding an output even when all other normal input signals are present. (Contrast with *signal, enabling.*)

signal, partial-one output—Same as *signal, disturbed-one output.*

signal, partial-zero output—Same as *signal, disturbed-zero output.*

signal conditioning—See *conditioning, signal.*

signal distance—See *distance, signal.*

signal distortion, teletypewriter—See *distortion, teletypewriter signal.*

signal ground—See *ground, signal.*

signal level—See *level, signal.*

signal normalization—Same as *standardization, signal.*

signal plate—Same as *plate, pickup.*

signal regeneration—Same as *standardization, signal.*

signal reshaping—Same as *standardization, signal.*

signal shaping—Same as *standardization, signal.*

signal standardization—See *standardization, signal.*

signal, start—Same as *bit, start.*

signal, stop—Same as *bit, stop.*

signal-to-noise ratio—See *ratio, signal-to-noise.*

signal transformation—See *transformation, signal.*

signaling, common-battery—A method of bringing a line signal or a supervisory signal to a distant switchboard or end by applying a direct current to the line.

signaling rate, data—See *rate, data signaling.*

signaling, ringdown—A method of bringing a line signal or a supervisory signal to a distant switchboard or end by applying a low-frequency alternating current to the line.

signed field—See *field, signed.*

significance—1: The value or weight given to a position, or to a digit in the position, in a positional numeration system. In most positional numeration systems, positions are grouped in sequence of significance, usually more significant toward the left. A significant digit is one that contributes to the precision of a numeral. The numeral 2300.0 has five significant digits, 2300 probably has two, and 2301 has four. 2: The factor by which the value represented by a character in the digit place of a positional representation system, or numeration system, is multiplied to obtain its additive contribution in the representation of a real number. (Synonymous with *weight.*)

significant digit—See *digit, significant.*

significant digit, least—See *digit, least significant.*

significant digit, most—See *digit, most significant.*

significant-digit arithmetic—See *arithmetic, significant-digit.*

significant figure—Same as *digit, significant.*

silicon diode—See *diode, silicon.*

SIM-8—A PDP-8 computer instruction set simulator with I-O devices, DDT-8 and PAL III assembler.

simple buffering—See *buffering, simple.*

simple program—See *program, simple.*

simplex channel—See *channel, simplex.*

simplex operation—Same as *operation, one-way.*

Simscript—In computer simulation, a generic class of event-oriented and discrete simulation languages.

Simula—In computer simulation, an ALGOL-based, discrete, process-oriented simulation language.

simulate—1: To represent the behavior of one system by another system; for example, represent the behavior of one computer by a computer program written for and executed by another computer. When simulating one computer on another computer, the computer doing the simulating receives data, processes the data, and develops output in such a manner that from outward signs it appears

to be the computer being simulated. It then becomes possible to evaluate the performance of the simulated computer. 2: To represent the behavior of a physical system, such as an industrial process, a servomechanism, or an autopilot, by means of a computer and a program. The computer and program may serve to demonstrate behavior under the influence of stimuli and permit system performance analysis. 3: To represent a system, such as an electrical overland power distribution network by means of a small laboratory analog model. Other examples are to represent a biological system by means of a mathematical model or to represent any physical process or system, such as a war game, a supply system, or a nerve system on a computer by a program. (Further clarified by *model, mathematical.*) 4: To imitate one system with another system using only software and the system doing the simulating. (Compare with *emulate.*)

simulation—The representation or modelling of features or characteristics of a physical or abstract system using another system, thus making the system doing the simulating appear as though it were the simulated system; for example, the representation of physical phenomena by means of operations performed by a computer, or the representation of operations of one computer by another computer, usually using programming techniques rather than hardware, which is called emulation.

simulation, computer—The representation of a concept, system, model, or operation using a programmed analog, digital, or hybrid computer. In order to accomplish simulation by means of a computer, usually a logical or mathematical model must be constructed, which is then programmed for solution using a computer.

simulation, real-time—The operation of a simulator in such a manner that the time scale factor is equal to one for the physical time of the system being simulated and by the corresponding time of the simulator, such as the computer time of the simulator. Thus, the simulator time and the time of the system being simulated, are the same, rather than having the simulator run at faster or slower time than the system being simulated.

simulation language—See *language, simulation.*

simulator—A device or a program that represents the behavior of another device or program. The simulator permits the behavior of the system being simulated to be more easily analyzed, studied, or understood. The simulator usually is less costly than the system being simulated. Also, the simulator may be more practical to construct, whereas the system being simulated may be less practical, such as is the case in simulating military maneuvers and war games.

simulator, computer—A computer program that translates computer programs prepared for one model of computer to be executed on a different model computer. Thus, the simulator is software that performs the same function as an emulator, which is hardware, namely, it makes one computer execute a program as though it were another computer.

simulator, table—A computer program that computes the values in a table, rather than looks them up in a stored table.

simultaneous—Pertaining to the occurrence of two or more events at the same instant, that is, in time coincidence. (Contrast with *concurrent*, with *consecutive*, and with *sequential*.)

simultaneous access—Same as *access, parallel*.

simultaneous computer—See *computer, simultaneous*.

simultaneous input-output—See *input-output, simultaneous*.

simultaneous operation—See *operation, simultaneous*.

simultaneous-operation computer—Same as *computer, simultaneous*.

simultaneous working—Same as *processing, parallel*.

sine-junction gate—1: Same as *gate, A AND NOT B*. 2: Same as *gate, B AND NOT A*.

sine wave—See *wave, sine*.

single-address—Same as *one-address*.

single-address code—Same as *instruction, one-address*.

single-address instruction—Same as *instruction, one-address*.

single-address message—See *message, single-address*.

single-column pence coding—See *coding, single-column pence*.

single-harmonic distortion—See *distortion, single-harmonic*.

single-level address—Same as *address, direct*.

single precision—See *precision, single*.

single punch—See *punch, single*.

single-sheet feeding—See *feeding, single-sheet*.

single-shot multivibrator—Same as *multivibrator, one-shot*.

single-shot operation—Same as *operation, single-step*.

single-sideband transmission—See *transmission, single-sideband*.

single step—See *step, single*.

single-step operation—See *operation, single-step*.

sink, data—In a data transmission system, equipment that accepts data.

sink, message—The part of a communication system into which messages are considered to be received. (Contrast with *source, message*.)

sinusoid—Same as *wave, sine*.

sinusoid, half—See *half-sinusoid*.

SIPROS- (Simultaneous Processing Operating System). An operating system developed by Control Data Corporation for management of all parts and programs of a

system, including equipment selection and storage allocation.

situation display—See *display, situation*.

six-bit byte—Same as *sextet*.

size, increment—In graphic display systems, the horizontal or vertical distance between two adjacent addressable points on a display surface. (Related to *unit, raster*. Synonymous with *plotter step size*.

size, plotter step—Same as *size, increment*.

skeletal code—See *code, skeletal*.

skeletal coding—See *coding, skeletal*.

skeletal query—See *query, skeletal*.

skew—In data processing, a malalignment of the reference edge of data with respect to a given reference; for example, the angle between a given reference axis of a printed character and a given reference edge of the document; the misalignment of bits on magnetic tape with respect to a line perpendicular to the edge of the tape; misalignment of the heads; variances in the magnetic characteristics of the tape or the heads; or errors in timing of the bits as they are written on the tape; or the conditions that combine to cause nonsynchronism or deviation of the received frame from rectangularity due to asynchronism between the scanner and the recorder in facsimile transmission.

skip—1: To ignore a set of instructions in a sequence of instructions. (Further clarified by *instruction, dummy*.) 2: To pass over one or more positions on a data medium; for example, to perform one or more line feed operations on a printer, to leave one or more lines unused on a typewriter, or to leave several spaces on a typed page.

skip, tape—To move a magnetic tape forward and erase a portion of .tape when a defect on the surface causes a write error to persist.

skip instruction—Same as *instruction, dummy*.

slab—1: A part of a computer word. 2: A flat, usually rectangular, material, such as might be used to wind on a potentiometer resistive element.

slab resolving potentiometer—See *potentiometer, slab resolving*.

slave—A component of a system that is under the control of another component, usually of the same system and usually identical or similar to the controlling component; for example, a cathode ray tube display station that displays the same data that is given to another station to display, thus, the slave station tracks the other station.

slave application—See *application, slave*.

slave computer—See *computer, slave*.

slave station—See *station, slave*.

slave system—See *system, slave*.

slave tube—See *tube, slave*.

slew, paper—Same as *throw, paper*.

slicing, time—The dividing of the time of a device among two or more users, applications, or systems; for example, dividing the time of a central processing unit into many intervals and assigning the intervals to several programs, or as might occur in a round-robin scheduling of the use of main storage areas.

slip proof−Same as *proof, galley.*

slope-keypoint compaction−See *compaction, slope-keypoint.*

slow storage−Same as *storage, low-speed.*

slow time scale−Same as *scale, extended time.*

slug-matrix storage−Same as *storage, magnetic slug.*

slug storage, magnetic−See *storage, magnetic slug.*

smooth−To decrease or eliminate rapid or large fluctuations in data; for example, to remove the random variations in an independent function, such as the variations in radar range to a flying object. Since the mass of the object prevents such rapid variations, the range function must be smooth.

smooth contact−See *contact, smooth.*

SMS−(Standard Modular System). A system of computer component and subassembly packaging developed by the IBM Corporation.

smudge, ink−The displacement of ink beyond the original edges of a printed character by means of shearing, smearing, or wiping action. (Contrast with *bleed, ink.*)

smudge resistance−See *resistance, smudge.*

snapshot−Same as *dump, snapshot.*

snapshot dump−See *dump, snapshot.*

snapshot program−See *program, snapshot.*

sneak path−See *path, sneak.*

SNOBOL−A string manipulator based on pattern matching for computer applications.

SNOOP−An information retrieval technique for the IBM 1401, designed to search card files for cards which meet any of a number of criteria. The criteria are specified in a simple code on setup cards. The program permits the 1401 to perform the selection functions of the IBM 101 Statistical Sorter. The IBM 1401 with 4000 storage positions, the 1401 reader, the 1401 printer, the high-low-equal compare, the column-binary device, and an advance programming package are used. An IBM 1401 program is available. The program and the 1401 permit the searching of card files for desired information with less problem preparation and control-panel wiring than would be required when using an IBM 101. Associated with the IBM Corporation.

SO−The shift-out character.

SOAP I, II−(Symbolic Optimum Assembly Programming). A programming language developed by IBM Corporation for the IBM 650 computer.

SOAP III−An improved Symbolic Optimum Assembly Programming language developed for Case Institute of Technology for the IBM 650 computer.

SOAP III, Case−See *SOAP III.*

socket connector−See *connector, socket.*

socket contact−See *contact, socket.*

soft adder−See *adder, soft.*

soft copy−See *copy, soft.*

software−Data and information that are associated with the hardware of a machine or system; for example, a collection of computer programs, routines, compilers, assemblers, translators, manuals, circuit diagrams, and operational procedures. Software must be written, recorded, or represented somehow, even if in the form of a program stored in a plugboard, in which case it is also considered hardware. The hardware and software joined together, such as a program stored in a computer, are considered the operating system. (Contrast with *hardware.*)

software, application−Computer software that is used for, or is oriented toward, specific problems or application areas, such as inventory control, payroll, sales forecasting, scientific calculations or data reduction. (Closely related to *program, problem.*)

software, common−Software items that have multiple application among many systems, such as a subroutine for report generation or a conversion routine that can be used for several programs written in a common language that is acceptable to several computers. (Contrast with *hardware, common.*)

software, third-generation−For computer, data processing, and communications systems, software that supports an operating system that is essential to the functioning of the systems. System efficiency is maximized by an optimized division of functions between hardware logic and software capability. (Further clarified by *generation, third.*)

SOH−The start-of-heading character.

solid state−See *state, solid.*

solid-state component−See *component, solid-state.*

solid-state computer−See *computer, solid-state.*

solid-state device−See *device, solid-state.*

solid-state storage−See *storage, solid-state.*

solver, equation−A device, usually analog, that is designed to solve systems of simultaneous equations, such as linear, nonlinear, or differential equations. The device may also find the roots of polynomials.

sonic delay-line−Same as *delay-line, acoustic.*

SOP−An abbreviation for standard operating procedure.

soroban−Same as *abacus.*

sort−In data processing, to arrange data items in groups according to the specific rules, fields, or keys used to identify and group them; for example, the items may be segregated into pigeonholes, pockets, storage locations, or printed lists in order to collect like items in one place. Sorting does not necessarily involve sequencing, but sorting is usually a prerequisite to sequencing and ordering. In actual practice, many sorts are made according to numerical or alphabetic sequences, resulting in a sort by letters or numbers, and so a resultant ordering occurs in accordance with the collating sequence.

sort, balanced merge–A merge sort, that is an external sort, executed in such a manner that the sorted subsets created by the internal sorts are equally distributed among half of the available storage devices. The subsets are then merged onto the other half of the available storage devices and the process repeated until all the items are in one sorted set. (Contrast with *sort, unbalanced merge.*)

sort, block–A sort performed on one or more of the most significant characters of a key, thus partitioning the items into workable size groups. Items in the segmented groups are then sorted separately, after which all the segments are joined together to form a single sorted sequence. This sorting technique is readily adaptable to punched cards. It is not frequently used in sorting with random-access storage units.

sort, bubble–An exchange sort in which the sequence of the examination of pairs of items being sorted is reversed each time an exchange is made during the execution of the sort. (Synonymous with *sifting sort.*)

sort, digital–To sort first according to the least significant digit, then to re-sort on each next higher order digit until the items are sorted on the most significant digit. This sorting method is readily adaptable to punched cards.

sort, exchange–A sort in which succeeding pairs of items are examined and if the items in the pair are out of sequence according to the specified sort criteria, the relative positions of the items are exchanged. The process is repeated until all items are sorted according to the specified sort criteria.

sort, external–1: A sort that uses auxiliary storage because the items to be sorted cannot be held in internal storage all at once. 2: A sort routine or program, or a phase of a multipass sort, that merges strings of items, using auxiliary storage, until one string is formed.

sort, four-tape–To merge-sort by supplying the data to be sorted on two tapes, which are sorted alternately into two incomplete sequences on two output tapes. The output tapes are used as input on the succeeding pass, resulting in longer and longer sequences after each pass, until the data is all in one sequence on one output tape.

sort, insertion–A sort in which the individual items in a set to be sorted are inserted into proper positions in the sorted set according to specified criteria.

sort, internal–1: A sort that is performed within the internal or main storage of a computer. 2: A sort program or sort phase that sorts two or more items within internal or main storage.

sort, merge–See *merge-sort.*

sort, multipass–1: To sort more items than can be held in main or internal storage at one time. 2: A sort program designed to sort more items than can be held in main or internal storage at one time; for example, the items in main storage are sorted and moved to external storage in batches, and then the batches are merged.

sort, oscillating–A merge sort performed such that sort and merge operations are alternated until all the items in a set are sorted.

sort, polyphase–A merge sort such that the sorted subsets created by the internal sorts are unequally distributed among some of the available auxiliary storage devices. The distribution of sorted subsets is based on a Fibonacci series. The subsets are merged onto the remaining auxiliary storage devices and the process repeated until all items are in one sorted set.

sort, property–To sort by selecting from a group items that have a characteristic meeting certain criteria; for example, to sort employee records first by age, then by length of service within each age group, then by number of dependents within length of service group, so that the oldest employee with the longest service and the most dependents is on top and the youngest employee with the least service and fewest dependents is at the bottom of the sequence. Naturally, each key refers to a span or a range.

sort, repeated selection–A selection sort conducted in such a manner that the set of items to be sorted is divided into subsets and one item meeting certain specified criteria is selected from each subset to form a second level subset. A selection sort is then applied to this second level subset, whereupon the selected item in this second level subset is appended to the sorted set and is replaced by the next item that meets the criteria in the original subset. The process is repeated until all items are in the sorted set. This tree-structure type of sort can be extended to many levels. (Synonymous with *tournament sort* and with *tree-structure sort.*)

sort, selection–A sort in which the items or a set are examined to find items that fit certain criteria; as each item is found it is placed in the sorted set and removed from further consideration, the process being repeated until all items are in the sorted set.

sort, serial–A sort in which sequential access to the items in a set is used. Thus, a serial sort may be performed using only serial access storage devices.

sort, sifting–Same as *sort, bubble.*

322

sort, tournament–Same as *sort, repeated selection.*

sort, tree-structure–Same as *sort, repeated selection.*

sort, unbalanced merge–A merge sort, that is an external sort, executed in such a manner that the sorted subsets created by the internal sorts are unequally distributed among some of the available storage devices. The subsets are merged onto the remaining storage devices and the process is repeated until all items are in one sorted set. (Contrast with *sort, balanced merge.*)

sort key–See *key, sort.*

sort module–See *module, sort.*

sort pass–See *pass, sort.*

sort phase–See *phase, sort.*

sort program–See *program, sort.*

sorter–A person, device, or routine that arranges items in groups according to specific rules, fields, or keys used to identify and group them. A person may sort a deck of playing cards according to suit; a device, such as a punched-card sorter, may sort according to keys in the form of patterns of holes in the cards, dropping certain cards in certain pockets; and a routine might direct sorting in a computer by examining keys and placing data in certain storage areas according to the key.

SOS–(SHARE Operating System). A computer operating system devised and used by the SHARE Organization originally for use on the IBM 709 computer.

sound-powered telephone–See *telephone, sound-powered.*

source, data–In a data-transmission system, equipment that supplies data.

source, information–Same as *source, message.*

source, message–The part of a communication system from which messages are considered to originate. (Synonymous with *information source.* Contrast with *sink, message.*)

source, stationary information–Same as *source, stationary message.*

source, stationary message–A message source, that is, a message dispatch station, operated in such a manner that the probability of occurrence of each message is independent of the time that the message is sent. (Synonymous with *stationary information source.*)

source data–See *data, source.*

source data automation–See *automation, source data.*

source data card–See *card, source data.*

source-destination instruction–See *instruction, source-destination.*

source document–See *document, source.*

source language–See *language, source.*

source program–See *program, source.*

source routine–Same as *program, source.*

SP–The space character.

space–1: A place intended for storage of data; for example, a place on a printed page intended for a character or a location in a storage medium. Thus, a basic unit of area in a record; that is, an area that may contain no more than one printed character, such as the space occupied by a letter in printed text or the blank space between words. One or more blanks constitute a space also. 2: To move or step from one place to another according to a prescribed procedure or format; for example, to move horizontally to the right along a line of print, or to move vertically down a page a prescribed amount. Sometimes a blank or void area is used to designate a blank space. However, since omission might mean error, a symbol might be used to designate a blank space, such as *b*. For example, *in end* might mean *intend*, with the *t* inadvertently omitted, whereas in *in b end* there is no question about the space. The blank space is often used to show the beginning and end of words, as a period is used to delimit sentences and an indentation to delimit paragraphs. 3: One or more blanks.

space, back–See *backspace.*

space, interword–In serial digital computers, the time period and corresponding geometric space allowed between words, such as during transfer, or on tape, disc, or drum. The space allows for control of individual words, such as switching or logic operations to occur. (Synonymous with *word gap* and with *interword gap.* Further clarified by *space, word.*)

space, switching–In an electronic computer, a space left between data items, such as words, blocks, or records, to permit logic or control operations to take place, such as setting flip-flops, enabling gates, inhibiting gates, or allowing switching transients to decay.

space, word–The space occupied by a word and its interword space in serial digital computing devices, such as delay-lines, drums, discs, tapes, and serial lines. (Further clarified by *space, interword.*)

space, working–Same as *storage, temporary.*

space character–See *character, space.*

space diversity–See *diversity, space.*

space suppression–See *suppression, space.*

spacing, teletypewriter pulse–Spacing accomplished on a teletypewriter by an electrical pulse, which in d-c neutral operation corresponds to a circuit-open or no-current condition.

spacing reference-line, character–See *reference-line, character-spacing.*

span–Same as *range (2).*

span, error–The difference between the highest and lowest members of a set of error values.

special add–See *add, special.*

special character–See *character, special.*

special-purpose computer–See *computer, special-purpose.*

special-purpose paper card—See *card, special-purpose paper.*

special sign—Same as *character, special.*

special symbol—Same as *character, special.*

specific address—Same as *address, absolute.*

specific code—Same as *code, absolute.*

specific program—See *program, specific.*

specific routine—See *routine, specific.*

specification, control—The definition of the functions that a set of computer programs, routines, or subroutines are to perform.

spectral reflectance—See *reflectance, spectral.*

spectral response—See *response, spectral.*

spectrum, frequency—The range of frequencies of electromagnetic radiation waves. The range is divided into subranges as follows: VLF (Very-low frequency) below 30 kHz; LF (low frequency) 30-300 kHz; MF (Medium frequency) 300-3000 kHz; HF (high frequency) 3000-30,000 kHz; VHF (very-high frequency) 30-300 MHz; UHF (ultrahigh frequency) 300-3000 MHz; SHF (superhigh frequency) 3000-30,000 MHz; and EHF (extremely high frequency) 30,000-300,000 MHz. VLF is often called audio frequency. The same designation of frequency ranges may be specified in terms of bands of wavelength, where the wavelength is given as the speed of light divided by the frequency. (Further clarified by *frequency, radio.*)

SPEED—(Self-Programmed Electronic Equation Delineator). An LGP-30 computer program used for the solution of equations.

speed, data—Same as *rate, telegraph.*

SPEEDCO—An automatic coding system for the IBM 701 computer.

SPEEDCODE—An automatic programming system used at Redstone Arsenal on the IBM 650 computer and at Convair on the IBM 704 computer.

SPEEDEX—A fixed-point symbolic coding system for longhand, used by North American Aviation Company on the IBM 701 computer.

spherical resolver—Same as *resolver, ball.*

spike file—See *file, spike.*

split—To form two ordered files from one ordered file. (Contrast with *merge.*)

split, column—A facility or device provided on some punched-card machines for sensing a column in two parts; for example, partitioning a card column during the reading or punching by placing the punch positions corresponding to two portions of the column on separate wires. The column split permits certain punch positions within a single column to be ignored or treated separately from other punch positions of the same column.

split catalog—See *catalog, split.*

split detection—See *detection, split.*

spool—Same as *reel.*

SPOOL—A computer programming system for the IBM 7070 computer.

spool, tape—1: A cylinder on which tape may be wound. Usually the spool does not have flanges and is used for perforated tape, rather than magnetic tape, in which case it is called a reel and has flanges. 2: A length of tape, usually perforated, wound in a coil.

spot, action—In an electrostatic storage tube, the actual spot of the raster on the face of the tube, which is used to store a binary digit; that is, hold a charge. (Further clarified by *line, action* and by *period, action.*)

spot, flying—A small, rapidly moving spot of light, generated optically or by means of a cathode-ray tube, used to successively illuminate areas of a printed surface. The light reflected is detected by a photosensitive device. The succession of produced electronic signals can be interpreted to yield the data on the printed page.

spot carbon—See *carbon, spot.*

spot punch—See *punch, spot.*

spring-finger action—See *action, spring-finger.*

sprocket holes—See *holes, sprocket.*

sprocket pulse—Same as *pulse, timing.*

SPS—(Symbolic Programming System). A symbolic programming procedure for use on the IBM 1620 computer.

SPS 1 and 2—Symbolic programming systems for use on the IBM 1401 computer.

SPUR—(Single Precision Unpacked Rounded Floating-point Package). A programming system developed at Consolidated Vultee for use on the Univac 1103 computer.

square loop—See *loop, square.*

squareness ratio—See *ratio, squareness.*

squeezeout, ink—The displacement of ink from the center toward the edges of a character stroke during printing. Squeeze-out causes a heavy character outline and a depleted center of each character stroke.

squoze deck—Same as *deck, condensed.*

stability, carbon—The resistance of carbon paper, ribbon, or other forms of carbons to deterioration and loss of image-producing capacity during storage.

stability, computational—The degree to which a computational process remains valid or reliable when subjected to environmental conditions that produce, or tend to produce, errors, mistakes, or malfunctions.

stability, light—In character recognition, the resistance of an image to changes in its characteristics, such as color, reflectivity, and texture, upon exposure to electromagnetic radiation.

stable state—See *state, stable.*

stack—Same as *list, pushdown.*

stack, head—A group of recording heads mounted together, usually used together, and sometimes all recording in a set of tracks simultaneously, thus forming a recording band or channel.

stack, storage—1: A group of storage elements, such as digit or other arrays or planes, usually piled up and fastened together. 2: A group of data in a storage unit. Such a stack of data might be operated on a last-in-first-out basis; that is, the data item stored last will be the next item to come out of the stack.

stack indicator–Same as *pointer, stack.*

stack pointer–See *pointer, stack.*

stacked-job processing–See *processing, stacked-job.*

stacker, card–A device that accumulates punch cards in a deck, usually after the cards have passed through a machine, such as a reader, a punch, a printer, a sorter, or a collator. The stacker might be a pocket, a bin, or a well. The cards are deposited in the stacker, where they are stacked in a deck and held. (Synonymous with *card receiver* and *output stacker.* Contrast with *hopper, card.*)

stacker, offset–A card stacker that can arrange certain cards selected under machine control so that they protrude from the remainder of the deck for easy physical identification.

stacker, output–Same as *stacker, card.*

stacking, interrupt–Recording a queue of interrupt requests without allowing processing to be interrupted. At some time later, the interrupts may be honored in accordance with some priority algorithm, such as in the order they were received, emergency priority, customer preference, length of job, or economic value.

stacking, query–The placing of a query for the services of a computer or data processing system in a queue for servicing at a later time in accordance with defined criteria. (Related to *stacking, request.*)

stacking, request–The placing of a request for computer or data processing services, such as system service, input-output unit use, message processing, in a queue for servicing at a later time in accordance with defined criteria. (Related to *stacking, query.*)

stand-alone utilities–See *utilities, stand-alone.*

standard–An accepted criterion, established agreement, rule, or test by which an action or item is judged with regard to its characteristics, such as performance, practice, design, terminology, size, shape, or weight.

standard, system–1: In communications, a required electrical performance characteristic of communication circuits which is based on measured performance of circuits under the various operating conditions for which the circuits were designed. 2: The specified characteristic necessary to permit system operation; for example, test tones, center frequencies for telegraph channels, and character patterns for instruction signals.

standard form–Same as *form, normal.*

standard interface–See *interface, standard.*

standard program–See *program, standard.*

standard test tone power–See *power, standard test tone.*

standard subroutine–See *subroutine, standard.*

standardization, pulse–The generation or restoration of pulses that meet specified requirements for amplitude, shape, and timing. The standardized pulse is usually generated from another pulse. The standard specifications usually apply to particular data-processing machines. (Synonymous with *pulse normalization,* with *pulse shaping,* with *pulse reshaping,* and with *pulse regeneration.* Illustrative of *standarization, signal.*)

standardization, signal–The generation or restoration of signals that meet specified requirements for amplitude, shape, and timing. The standardized signal is usually generated from another signal. The requirements usually only apply to specific data-processing machines. There is scarcely any standardization of signals among systems. (Synonymous with *signal normalization,* with *signal reshaping,* with *signal shaping,* and with *signal regeneration.* Illustrated by *standardization, pulse.*)

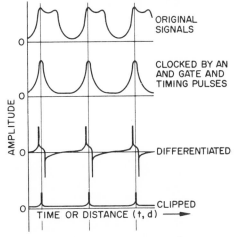

Signal standardization *in time and space.*

standardize–To reduce or eliminate an unnecessary variety of things, particularly in such attributes as dimensions, performance, methods of measurement, terminology, symbols, classification, and methods of expressing performance. (Synonymous with *normalize.*)

standby application–See *application, standby.*

standby block–See *block, standby.*

standby register–See *register, standby.*

standby time–Same as *time, idle* and *time, maintenance standby.*

standing-on-nines carry–See *carry, standing-on-nines.*

star program–See *program, star.*

start–In flowcharting, a beginning point on a flowchart, usually marked with a special symbol.

start bit—See *bit, start.*
start button—Same as *button, initiate.*
start element—Same as *bit, start.*
start key—Same as *button, initiate.*
start-of-heading character—See *character, start-of-heading.*
start-of-text character—See *character, start-of-text.*
start signal—Same as *bit, start.*
start-stop multivibrator—Same as *multivibrator, one-shot.*
start-up, system—Same as *initialization, system.*
start-stop transmission—See *transmission, start-stop.*
state—In a computing system, the condition of all the elements of the system, such as the data in storage, the digits in all registers, and the numbers in control units, as well as the settings of all switches, flip-flops, and power circuits.
state, input—The state or condition of a specified set of input channels; for example, an AND gate input channel may be said to be in the *one* state in contrast to the *zero* state, or it may be said to be in the positive state (of voltage) rather than the negative state. (Contrast with *state, output.*)
state, output—The state or condition of a specified set of output channels; for example, an OR gate output channel may be either in the negative, or *one,* state or in the positive, or *zero,* state. (Contrast with *state, input.*)
state, solid—Electronic components that convey or control electrons within solid materials, such as wires, conducting films or inks, diodes, transistors, thermistors, magnetic films, magnetic cores, inductors, and capacitors. Vacuum, gas, and cathode-ray tubes are not solid-state components.
state, stable—In a trigger circuit, a state in which the circuit remains until a suitable pulse is applied whereupon the circuit changes to another state wherein it may remain temporarily or permanently. (Contrast with *state, unstable.*)
state, unstable—A state in which a trigger circuit may remain for a finite period of time at the end of which it may return to a stable state of its own accord, that is, without the application of a pulse. (Contrast with *state, stable.*)
state vector—See *vector, state.*
state vector, differential—See *vector, differential state.*
statement—1: In computer programming, a generalized instruction in automatic coding; for example, in FORTRAN, statements usually refer to items that will be translated into many instructions. The statement usually describes a step in the solution of a problem or a basic step in a procedure, such as a problem statement or a procedure statement. 2: A set of expressions. Thus, if A is an expression and B is an expression, then A equals B might be a statement of fact concerning A

and B. (Further clarified by *expression.*) 3: In a programming language, a meaningful expression that describes or specifies operations and that is complete in the context of the programming language. 4: An arrangement of symbols; for example, a string of symbols.
statement, assignment—1: A procedural statement that expresses a sequence of computer operations or that assigns operands to specified variables or symbols. 2: In COBOL, a procedural statement that associates a file with the symbolic name of a device.
statement, compound—Two or more statements in a computer program that may be executed as a single statement when the program is run.
statement, conditional—In computer programming, a statement that expresses an assignment, a branch, or a decision, based on specified criteria, for example, an IF-THEN statement, which might be implemented in a computer by an IF-THEN gate. (Further clarified by *connective, logical.*)
statement, control—A computer programming statement that is used to alter the sequential execution of statements; for example, a conditional statement, such as IF, or an imperative statement, such as STOP.
statement, data description—Same as *declaration, data.*
statement, function declaration—A declaration that is used to assign a name to a function.
statement, imperative—Same as *instruction.*
statement, loop control—An executable statement that is used to describe the control to be exercised by a loop, the statements to be executed under the control of the loop, the parameters used in loop execution, and the storage location to which program control is to be passed when the loop is terminated; for example, the FORTRAN DO statement.
statement, procedural—Same as *instruction.*
statement, switch control—A control transfer statement that transfers control, or causes transfer of control, to one of a number of other statements, depending on certain conditions; for example, the switch in ALGOL 60 or the GOTO in FORTRAN.
static—1: Pertaining to a quantity that does not vary with time. Thus, a stable or permanent condition. (Contrast with *dynamic.*) 2: Same as *noise.*
static dump—See *dump, static.*
static magnetic storage—Same as *storage, core.*
static model—See *model, static.*
static print-out—See *print-out, static.*
static routine—Same as *subroutine, static.*
static storage—See *storage, static.*
static subroutine—See *subroutine, static.*
staticize—To convert time-dependent, time-variant, and usually time-sequential data into nontime-variant, that is, into

spatially distributed, data; for example, to enter digits endwise into a register serially, then hold them, then move them out in parallel. An electrostatic storage tube or a magnetic-core storage actually staticizes moving data, such as data entering from moving tapes, entering through transmission lines or delay-lines. The staticizer actually converts a time sequence of states or digits into a space distribution of simultaneous states. In summary, to convert serial or time-dependent parallel data into a static, or nonvariant, form.

staticizer—A device that converts a time sequence of states that represent; data into a corresponding space distribution of simultaneous states that represent the same data. The time-distributed data and the space-distributed data should bear the same meaning.

station, brush—A position where the holes of a punched card are read. A row of wire contacts reaches through the holes, making contact, usually with ground. A contact that reaches through, signals the presence of a hole at its position. The signal enables a particular gate to pass a pulse pattern that corresponds to a given character, thus obtaining the particular character, in electrical form, that is represented by the hole.

station, called—In a switching network, the station that receives a request for a connection from a calling station.

station, calling—In a switching network, the station that initiates a connection. When the connection is made, the calling station becomes the master station.

station, control—In a switching network, the station that directs the network operations or procedures, such as polling, selecting, and recovering.

station, data collection—Same as *station, data input.*

station, data input—A terminal used for the insertion of data into a data processing system. (Synonymous with *data collection station.*)

station, inquiry—A device for inserting queries or questions into a data system. As an input-output device, the inquiry station may be used for inserting data for use by the system as well as for questions for reply from the system. In addition, the inquiry station may serve to furnish replies from the system to the human operator. The inquiry station is usually remote, handles a relatively low volume of data, and is usually manually operated.

station, magnetic-tape—Same as *unit, magnetic-tape.*

station, master—In a switching network, a station that sends data to a slave station and controls the data transfer.

station, punching—The place or position on a card track where the holes that represent information are punched. (Contrast with *station, sensing* and with *position, punch.* Further explained by *track, card.*)

station, reading—Same as *station, sensing.*

station, repeater—A position or location at which an amplifier is located for amplifying or building up the strength of a telephone or telegraph signal in a long line, to compensate for losses, dissipation, or dispersion. In a microwave system, the repeater station receives signals from an adjacent station, amplifies the signals, and retransmits the signals to another adjacent station. The repeater station usually performs its functions in both directions simultaneously.

station, sensing—The place or the position on a card track where the data on the card is read; for example, a brush station. (Synonymous with *reading station.* Contrast with *station, punching.* Further explained by *track, card.*)

station, slave—A station that receives data from a master station, follows or monitors a system, or precisely follows or repeats events, but whose output is not part of the originating or operational system; for example, a radio transmitter receiving and broadcasting data from another system or network, or a cathode-ray-tube display unit receiving and displaying the same data as the master or operational unit.

station, tape—Same as *unit, tape.*

station, tributary—In a switching network, a station subject to direction by the control station.

station, way—In telegraphy, a station along a telegraph line. Signals pass into and through the way station.

stationary information source—Same as *source, stationary message.*

stationary message source—See *source, stationary message.*

status—In computer simulation, the state of a simulated system or a simulation system. The status is defined in terms of the existing entities that comprise the system, the value of each entity, and the sets to which they belong.

status, job—The status of a computer job at a given point in time or space; for example, its position in a job queue, its state or condition of activity, or its extent of completion.

status display—See *display, status.*

stencil bit—See *bit, stencil.*

step—**1:** In computer programming, one operation in a routine. **2:** To cause a computer to execute one operation.

STEP—(Simple Transition to Electronic Processing). **1:** A programming technique developed by Sperry-Rand Corporation, Univac Division. **2:** (Supervisory Tape Executive Program). An executive routine for controlling data on magnetic tape on the National Cash Register NCR 304 computer. Errors during writing are detected and the data is written on another section of tape. **3:** (Standard Tape Executive Program). Same as *STEP (2).*

step, program—The execution of a single instruction, operation, or group of operations.

step, single—Pertaining to a method of operating a computer in which each operation is performed or executed in response to a single manual command.

step-by-step operation—Same as *operation, single-step.*

step change—See *change, step.*

step counter—See *counter, step.*

step size, plotter—Same as *size, increment.*

stepping register—Same as *register, shift.*

stick, joy—In graphic display systems, a lever that can be moved in at least two dimensions, thereby permitting the control of the movement of one or more display elements or cursors. (Further clarified by *cursor.*)

sticking—The tendency of a bistable device, such as a flip-flop or a switch, to remain in or switch back to a particular one of its two stable states.

stochastic—Pertaining to direct solution by trial-and-error, usually without a step-by-step approach, and involving analysis and evaluation of progress made, as in a heuristic approach to trial-and-error methods. In a stochastic approach to a problem solution, intuitive conjecture or speculation is used to select a possible solution, which is then tested against known evidence, observations or measurements. Intervening or intermediate steps toward a solution are omitted. (Contrast with *algorithm* and *heuristic.*)

stochastic model—See *model, stochastic.*

stop, coded—Same as *halt, programmed.*

stop, form—A device on a machine that stops the machine when the supply of paper has run out.

stop, programmed—Same as *halt, programmed.*

stop bit—See *bit, stop.*

stop element—Same as *bit, stop.*

stop instruction—Same as *instruction, halt.*

stop instruction, optional—Same as *instruction, optional-halt.*

stop signal—Same as *bit, stop.*

storage—1: A device or pertaining to a device which receives data, holds and, at a later time, returns data; for example, a plugboard, an array of magnetic cores, a magnetic disc, an electrostatic storage tube, a delay-line, or a bank of flip-flops. Various phenomena, such as electrostatic, ferroelectric, magnetic, acoustic, optical, chemical, electronic, electrical, mechanical and nuclear, are used to effect storage. (Synonymous with *store,* with *memory,* and with *computer store.*) 2: In computer simulation, a specific piece of equipment in which transactions may be stored.

storage, allocate—To assign specific storage areas for specific purposes, such as holding specific routines, holding input/output data or constants, serving as working storage or scratch-pad storage, holding loading programs or executive routines, and storing priority data. (Further clarified by *allocation, storage.*)

storage, annex—Same as *storage, associative.*

storage, associative—A storage device in which the storage locations are identified by their contents rather than by their names,

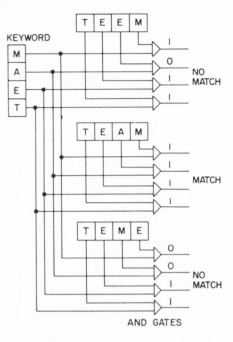

KEYWORD

AND GATES

All storage locations in the above associative storage unit are queried simultaneously to determine if the given keyword is stored. If a match occurs, the appropriate storage location is identified simultaneously and immediately. Many logic elements are required.

addresses, or relative positions. The associative storage is capable of being interrogated in parallel fashion throughout its entire contents to determine whether or not a given word is stored by directly comparing it with all words stored without regard for addressing. For example, if a file consists of many sets of data elements, each element being the label for a set of allowable data items, such as the case of a personnel file, where each set of data elements pertains to a person, then each set of data elements could be put at an addressed storage location. To search for a data item as a key, such as all captains, all storage locations would have to be read and all data items compared to the key. In associative storage, a parallel-read storage operation would immediately identify and retrieve all the data items in the file that were related to the data item matching the key. In a certain sense, the search key is the address of the sought data. Thus, the associative storage quickly answers the question, "Is this word contained in storage?" If the answer is yes, all data associated with the key word may be transferred out. The concept reduces address bookkeeping, since the keys serve as addresses. Information is retrieved by an associative and parallel process without regard for the physical location of the information to be retrieved or its address. A large amount of logic circuitry is involved. A large decoding matrix makes a simultaneous match of all storage location keys. The contents of matching-key locations are immediately dispatched. The programmer does not need to specifiy an address. The machine can store the key and its related data in any available storage location. (Synonymous with *content-addressed storage*, with *parallel-search storage*, with *searching storage*, with *annex storage*, and with *CAM (Content Addressed Memory).*)

storage, auxiliary —A storage that supplements another storage. Usual characteristics of auxiliary storage in a computing system is that it supplements the primary, main, internal, working, or central processor high-speed storage; it is of higher capacity and lower speed, or longer access time, than these storage units; data is usually transferred in blocks to and from auxiliary storage; and the cost is less per unit of storage. Auxiliary storage is usually not an integral part of a given computer, but is directly connected to and controlled by the computer, such as tapes, drums, or discs supporting magnetic core, thin-film, or delay-lines. In a computing system with relatively high-, medium-, and low-speed storage or in a system with two types of storage, the lower-speed storage devices, if any, would be considered auxiliary storage. (Synonymous with *backing storage* and with *secondary storage.* Contrast with *storage, main.*)

storage, backing —Same as *storage, auxiliary.*

storage, buffer —A storage device used to compensate for differences in rate of flow of data or time of occurrence of events when transmitting data from one device to another. The buffer storage, or simply buffer when the meaning is clear from the context, serves as a synchronizing element between two different storage devices or computing elements, usually between internal and external storage or other levices of differing speeds. As an input ɔuffer, data is allowed to queue; data is assembled from input sensors, external, or secondary storage and stored, ready for transmittal to internal storage. As an output buffer, data is transferred from internal storage to the buffer, and held for transmittal to an output device. The buffer serves to permit devices to run at optimum speeds, then be released for other work. Storage buffers are often used in medium conversion, such as cards-to-tape or tape-to-printer, so as to provide smooth operation. Storage is temporary and data is usually only in transit. (Further clarified by *buffer, storage.*)

storage, bulk —Same as *storage, mass.*

storage, capacitor —A storage device that uses the capacitance properties of materials; for example, an electrostatic storage device in which an individual capacitor is used to store each bit. The charged or discharged condition of the capacitor is used to represent a binary digit, such as 0 or 1, respectively. Diodes are used in conjunction with the capacitors to control the flow of data. (Synonymous with *dicap storage* and with *condenser storage.*)

storage, cathode-ray tube —Same as *storage, electrostatic.*

storage, changeable —A storage device whose parts containing data can be removed and replaced by other parts containing different or no data. The data are not destroyed in the process of changing the media, such as discs, tape reels or loops, paper tape magazines, or magnetic card magazines.

storage, circulating —A storage device in which data may be stored dynamically by continuously moving the data in a loop or by moving the medium. For example, transmitting data in a delay-line, sensing the data at the end of the line, amplifying, reshaping, and timing it, and then retransmitting it at the beginning of the line; or writing data on a drum and reading it a short distance away, transmitting the read data to the writing head, and thus continuously circulating it, making it quickly available, rather than waiting for a complete revolution of the drum or disc to gain access to the data. (Synonymous with *dynamic storage* and with *cyclic storage.* Contrast with *storage, static.*)

storage, condenser —Same as *storage, capacitor.*

storage, constant —Same as *area, constant.*

storage, content-addressed —Same as *storage, associative.*

storage, core —A storage consisting of an array of magnetic cores, each core capable of storing one binary digit. The magnetic cores may be arranged in matrices, arrays, and stacks. They are usually arranged in digit planes or word strings. The core storages are high-speed and random access. Usually they are coincident current. They are nonvolatile and usually erasable, though they can be made permanent. The cores may be shaped as annular rings of ferrite, foils of metal tapes on bobbins, or inverted cups or toroids. (Synonymous with *magnetic-core storage* and with *static magnetic storage.*)

storage, core-rope —A fixed or permanent storage device which stores coded information in the form of an array of cores and wires, with the information stored in the wiring rather than in the core itself. The wires are wound in one direction or the other through the core or bypass the core. The resultant pattern, called a rope, permits the selection of a single core for a given pattern or pulses. The selection of this particular core will cause a set of pulses on a set of readout lines, which, in effect, represents the number or code stored. Thus, the size of the word stored per core is arbitrary, depending only on the number of sense lines. The device is highly economical in the use of cores, but does use more lines than a conventional core-storage unit of the destructive variable type. The core may be considered to be more in the nature of a switch than a storage device. The core-rope storage device was invented by Olsen of the Lincoln Laboratory of Massachusetts Institute of Technology. (Synonymous with *Diamond switch*, with *Rajchman selection switch*, with *linear selection switch*, with *core-rope memory*, with *rope memory*, with *rope storage*, and with *Olsen memory*.)

storage, CRT—Same as *storage, electrostatic*.

storage, cryogenic—A storage device that makes use of the superconductive and magnetic properties of certain materials; for example, a device that makes use of the physical phenomenon that the property of superconductivity is destroyed upon application of a magnetic field. (Synonymous with *superconductive storage*.)

storage, cyclic—Same as *storage, circulating*.

storage, dedicated—An area of storage, such as a specified set of storage locations or tracks, that have been committed, obligated, allocated, or otherwise set aside, earmarked, or assigned for a specified use, problem, or user; for example, an area of storage on a disc file assigned to a division of a corporation for its sole use.

storage, delay-line—A circulating storage using a delay-line whose output is amplified, shaped, timed, and gated back into the input of the line. Thus, the pulses circulate indefinitely. The delay-line may be acoustic, such as mercury, nickel, or quartz; it may be magnetostrictive; electric, with distributed or lumped capacitive or inductive elements; or it may be a loop consisting of two read-write heads a short distance apart on a tape, disc, or drum.

storage, destructive—A storage device whose contents at a location need to be regenerated after being read, if it is desired that the contents be retained at the location after reading. Cathode-ray tubes and most core storage are of the destructive type, requiring regeneration immediately after reading if the data is to be retained. Usually this is done automatically within the cycle time. (Further clarified by *read, destructive*. Contrast with *storage, nondestructive*.)

storage, dicap—Same as *storage, capacitor*.

storage, direct-access—Same as *storage, random access*.

storage, disc—Same as *disc, magnetic*.

storage, drum—Same as *drum, magnetic*.

storage, dual—A storage device that permits storage of logic, permitting a programmer to store an operation code of his own design, as well as permitting storage of specific instructions and data. Thus the programmer creates an instruction code

and then utilizes it to write a program of instructions.

storage, dynamic—Same as *storage, circulating*.

storage, electrostatic—A storage device that stores data in the form of electrically charged areas or spots on a nonconducting, surface, such as the screen of a cathode-ray tube. The charges persist for a while after the charging current is removed. The presence or absence of a charge is used to represent a binary digit, say 0 or 1, respectively. The data needs to be regenerated continually, and restored after it is read, since interrogation is destructive. In cathode-ray-tube storage, a stream of electrons is directed at the spot. If a charge is there, no outward effect occurs. If a charge is not there, the storage of a negative charge causes an external pulse. This sequence of events is one type of electrostatic storage operation. (Synonymous with *CRT storage* and with *cathode-ray tube storage*. Further clarified by *tube, Williams* and *tube, cathode-ray*.)

storage, erasable—Storage in which new data can be written in place of the old, such as magnetic tape, drum, disc, or card storage. Punched card or punched tape is not considered erasable storage. Magnetic core can be adapted for both erasable and fixed, permanent, or nonerasable storage. In erasable storage, the storage medium can be used over and over again, even during the course of a single routine; therefore, erasable storage is temporary storage, such as during a given run. (Contrast with *storage, fixed*.)

storage, external—Storage whose contents are in a form acceptable to a computer but not directly accessible to the computer's arithmetic and logic unit, and so, not permanently linked to the computer. External storage assumes a precise meaning with reference to internal storage in connection with a given computer installation. Thus, a rack of magnetic tapes in a cabinet may be external storage, whereas the tapes mounted on a tape handler online may be part of internal storage. On the other hand, tapes in handlers momentarily not connected to a computer may be external storage, whereas a bank of magnetic drums may be internal storage. Usually, magnetic cores are used and considered as internal storage, as are most random-access or high-speed storage devices. (Contrast with *storage, internal*.)

storage, fast—Same as *storage, high-speed*.

storage, fast-access—Same as *storage, high-speed*.

storage, fixed—Storage containing data that cannot be changed by computer instruction, but requires alteration of construction circuits; therefore, data that is nonerasable and reusable, or fixed. Data in fixed storage is usually nonvolatile; that is, it is not lost if the power is turned off. Fixed-storage contents may be changed by changing a disc pack, a tape, a slug matrix, a paper-tape loop, or a prerecorded drum. Fixed-storage units usually contain programs and constants. An erasable storage may be made fixed by a lockout feature that prevents program access for alteration, but that still permits read-out. (Synonymous with *nonerasable storage*, with *permanent storage*, with *permanent store*, and with *read-only storage*. Contrast with *storage, erasable*, with *storage, volatile*, and with *storage, nonvolatile*.)

storage, flip-flop—A storage device, consisting of one or more flip-flops, and so capable of storing a pattern of ones and zeros. Flip-flop storage is often used as a high-speed register due to its ability to control gates, change rapidly, and indicate its state and the nature of its changes. (Illustrated by *register, flip-flop*.)

storage, high-speed—A storage device with a comparatively short access time, usually short compared to the speed of the arithmetic, logic, or central processing unit of the computer; compared to other storage devices in the same computer; or compared to the speed of other storage devices in other computers. Thus in a tape-disc storage system of a computer, core storage may be high-speed and disc storage low-speed. In a disc-tape system, disc storage may be high-speed. (Synonymous with *fast storage*, with *rapid-access storage*, with *fast-access storage*, and with *quick-access storage*. Contrast with *storage, low-speed*.)

storage, immediate-access—A storage whose access time is negligible compared to other operation times. (Synonymous with *zero-access storage* and with *instantaneous storage*.)

storage, input—Same as *area, input*.

storage, input-output—Same as *area, input-output*.

storage, instantaneous—Same as *storage, immediate-access*.

storage, instruction—Same as *area, instruction*.

storage, internal—Storage whose contents are directly accessible to the arithmetic or logic unit of the computer, and so are individually addressable by instructions and capable of controlling and being controlled by the control unit of the computer. Internal storage assumes a precise meaning with reference to external storage in connection with a given computer installation. Internal storage is usually an integral part of the computer. Magnetic-core storage; electrostatic storage; delay-line storage; usually disc, drum and tape loops, and sometimes tapes are forms of internal storage. (Contrast with *storage, external*.)

storage, laser-emulsion—A storage medium for digital data, which utilizes a controlled laser beam to expose minute areas on a photosensitive surface. The process is used in an Itek MCP-1000 disc storage unit. The Kerr effect is used to interrupt the laser beam to produce the desired information pattern.

storage, loop—Same as *storage, tape-loop*.

storage, low-speed—A storage device whose access time is long compared to the speed of the arithmetic, logic, or central-processing unit of the computer, or long compared to other storage devices in the same computer, or long compared to the speed of other storage devices in other computers. (Synonymous with *slow storage*. Contrast with *storage, high-speed*.)

storage, magnetic—A storage device that makes use of the magnetic properties of materials to store information. The information is usually represented as magnetized material in such forms as thin-film spots, annular cores, or continuous media, such as tapes, discs, drums, or cards, in the form of platings, emulsion coatings, or magnetic inks. Magnetic storages may be of stationary media and stationary data, such as magnetic cores and thin-films; stationary media and moving data, such as magnetic delay-lines or a series of magnetic pulse transformer delay-lines; or moving magnetic media and data, such as magnetic drums, discs, tapes, cards, and twistors. The magnetostrictive delay-line is a combination magnetic- and acoustic-action delay-line. All of the magnetic storage devices depend on remaining magnetism, except the magnetic and magnetostrictive delay-lines, to store data.

storage, magnetic-card—A storage device that stores data on the magnetic surfaces of cards. The cards consist of magnetic material coated on any substrate, such as plastic, fiber board laminate, or cardboard. The cards are selected and read or recorded upon as they are moved by mechanical devices. (Further clarified by *card, magnetic*.)

storage, magnetic-core—Same as *storage, core*.

storage, magentic-drum—A storage device that uses a magnetic drum as the storage medium.

storage, magnetic-rod—A static magnetic storage unit that uses small rod-shaped cores about one-tenth of an inch long as cores in the storage planes instead of the annular rings of ferrite that have to be strung on intersecting wires. The rod behaves like the ring-shaped cores.

storage, magnetic-slug—A fixed storage device consisting of two parallel-wire grids set orthogonal to each other, in close proximity, with a piece or slug of magnetic material at each crossing of wires where a one is desired to be stored and therefore coupling between the intersecting wires will occur. Each time one wire of a grid is pulsed, a series of pulses will be generated on the wires that have a slug at the intersections such that a one will occur where there is coupling and a zero where there is no coupling. (Synonymous with *slug-matrix storage*.)

storage, magnetic-tape—Storage that makes use of a ribbon of magnetic material, usually consisting of a substrata of base metal, plastic, such as Mylar, or acetate, coated with a magnetic material. Tape thicknesses are of the order of several mils, widths usually in the range of 0.25 to 2 inches, with 0.5 and 0.75 inches as most popular, five to 10 tracks as quite common, packing up to several thousand binary digits per inch along each track, with 800 to 900 bits per inch being popular usage for digital tapes, and run at a linear speed equivalent to up to 100,000 bits per second in each track. In many tape storage devices, a five- to eight-bit character is placed across the tape, groups of characters forming words serially along the tape. The words in serial sets form blocks, records, and files. The tapes are wound on reels or held in closed loops. Both analog and digital data may be recorded on tapes for capturing, storing, and handling data. (Further clarified by *unit, magnetic-tape*.)

storage, magnetic thin-film—Magnetic storage in which the data medium is a magnetic film usually less than one micrometer thick on a substrate, such as glass, plastic, fiber, or laminate.

storage, magnetic-wire—Same as *wire, magnetic*.

storage, main—The storage that is considered integral, internal, or primary to the computing system. (Synonymous with *primary storage*. Contrast with *storage, auxiliary*.)

storage, manual-switch—Storage, usually in the form of arrays of manually set switches, such as toggle switches, in which data may be entered by manually placing the switch in a position that represents data, controls data flow, or represents instructions. (Synonymous with *switch storage*.)

storage, mass—Relatively large volume storage, online, and directly accessible to the central-processing, arithmetic, logic, or control unit of a computer. Mass storage usually might be large quantities of online discs, drums, tapes, or magnetic cards, rather than limited volume core storage or unlimited volume of offline punched cards. (Synonymous with *bulk storage*.)

storage, matrix—A storage device or medium structured such that two or more coordinates are required to access the data contained in it; for example, cathode-ray tube storage or core storage.

storage, mercury—A storage device that uses the acoustic properties of mercury to store data. Columns or tanks of liquid mercury have pairs of transducers which operate on the piezoelectric effect, transforming elec-

trical pulses into sound waves that pass to the other transducer for transformation back to electrical pulses. The propagation time is sufficiently long to permit storage, in transit, of a number of pulses determined by the distance between the transducers, the pulse duration, and the speed of propagation in mercury, which is somewhat dependent on the temperature. The pulses received at one end are timed, shaped, amplified, and returned to the other end, in a circulating fashion. (Further explained by *delay-line* and by *delay-line, acoustic*.)

storage, n-core-per-bit—A storage device in which each storage cell uses n magnetic cores to store one binary character.

storage, nesting—Same as *storage, push-down*.

storage, nondestructive—A storage device whose contents at a location need not be regenerated after being read if it is desired that the contents be retained at the location after reading. Magnetic tapes, double cores, drums, discs, punched cards, and permanent storage units are examples of nondestructive storage units. Regeneration after reading is not required. (Further clarified by *read, nondestructive*. Contrast with *storage, destructive*.)

storage, nonerasable—Same as *storage, fixed*.

storage, nonvolatile—A storage device that retains stored data after power is removed from the device and that can furnish the data stored upon request after the restoration of power; for example, magnetic tapes, discs, cores, drums, punched cards, and paper tape. Examples of volatile storage devices are acoustic, electric, and magnetostrictive delay-lines and cathode-ray tube storage. (Contrast with *storage, fixed* and with *storage, volatile*.)

storage, offline—Storage not under control of the central processing, arithmetic, logic, or control unit; for example, punched cards in filing cabinets, reels of magnetic tapes in cabinets, packs of discs removed from the control units, and stacks of printed forms in cabinets. (Contrast with *storage, online*.)

storage, one-core-per-bit—A storage device in which each storage cell uses one magnetic core to store one binary character.

storage, online—Storage directly under control of, and so directly accessible to, the central processing, arithmetic, logic, or control unit; for example, core storage, reels of magnetic tapes mounted in tape stations, a deck of cards in an input hopper of a card reader, a magnetic drum, or a magnetic disc unit, each connected as an integral part of a computing system. (Contrast with *storage, offline*.)

storage, output—Same as *area, output*.

storage, parallel—A storage device in which data is put in, held, and taken out in such a manner that each of the parts of the data is handled simultaneously; for example, if a 40 binary-digit number is stored in parallel storage, all 40 bits are stored and retrieved simultaneously over 40 separate lines or wires. Thus, a computer word made up of *n* characters each composed of *m* bits may be stored in parallel storage as an entire word on *m* times *n* parallel lines, or it may be stored serially by character, but the *m* bits of each character may be handled in parallel; that is, simultaneously, on *m* lines. In a parallel storage device, there are as many input and output lines as there are binary digits handled in parallel. In parallel storage, time is not one of the coordinates used to locate a part of that which is being handled in parallel, such as one of the bits of a word whose bits are all handled in parallel; that is, simultaneously. Parallel access should not be confused with random access. (Contrast with *storage, serial* and with *storage, random-access.*)

storage, parallel-search—Same as *storage, associative.*

storage, permanent—Same as *storage, fixed.*

storage, photo-optic—A storage device that uses an optical medium for storage of data; for example, a laser might be used to record data on photographic film.

storage, primary—Same as *storage, main.*

storage, program—Storage used for storing programs, routines, subroutines, or miscellaneous instructions, in a computing system. Usually program storage is some designated portion of internal storage, usually a relatively high-speed storage, particulary for iterative processes, though not necessarily a small, very high-speed portion of storage that might be more effectively used as scratch-pad storage. In some applications, interlocks or other protective devices or measures are taken to prevent inadvertent alteration of the contents of the program storage. In some instances, programs are placed in read-only storage devices; that is, fixed-storage devices. (Closely related to *area, instruction.*)

storage, pushdown— A storage that operates so as to maintain a pushdown list; that is, one that is constructed and maintained so that the next item of data to be retrieved from it is the one that was most recently or last placed in it. Thus, the pushdown storage behaves as though it were constructed of a number of registers arranged in a column, with only the top register connected to the system, and each lower register connected to the one above it. As each word is entered, the words are pushed down to make room at the top. As each word is moved out at the top, the words move from register to register back up the column to fill the space vacated. The effect may be achieved by program or by circuitry. (Synonymous with *nesting storage*, with *running accumulator*, and with *cellar*. Contrast with *storage, pushup*. Further clarified by *list, pushdown*. Related to *last-in-first-out*.)

storage, pushup—A storage that operates so as to maintain a pushup list; that is, one that is constructed and maintained so that the next item of data to be retrieved is the oldest item still in the list. Thus, the push-up storage behaves as though it were constructed of a number of registers arranged in a column, with the bottom register serving as storage input and the top register as storage output. As words are entered at the bottom, they queue, or are pushed from register to register up to the top. The word at the top has been in longest, hence will go out first. The effect may be achieved by program or by circuitry. (Contrast with *storage, pushdown*. Further clarified by *list, pushup*. Related to first-in-first-out.)

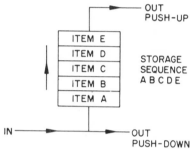

Since item E was stored first, i.e., it's the oldest item in the storage, pushup storage requires that it goes out next. Since item A was stored last, if it goes out first, the unit is operating as a pushdown storage.

storage, quick-access—Same as *storage, high-speed.*

storage, random-access—Storage in which the time required for placing data into it or obtaining data from it is independent of the location of the data most recently obtained from it or placed in it. If each word is addressable, then true random access exists only when the above condition is satisfied for each word. On a disc or drum, each track might be random access, but each word in the track might be serial access. These might be considered as semirandom-access devices. (Contrast with *storage, serial* and with *storage, parallel*. Synonymous with *direct-access storage*.)

storage, rapid-access—Same as *storage, high-speed.*

storage, read-only—Same as *storage, fixed.*

storage, regenerative—A storage device that requires that data stored in it must be read and restored in order to prevent its loss or decay; for example, a delay-line in which attenuation requires that the data be read, reamplified, timed, shaped, and recirculated to prevent its eventual decay, or an electrostatic storage in which the charged spots on the screen of the cathode-ray tube must be read and re-stored in order to prevent decay of the data by a gradual leakage of the charges.

storage, rope—Same as *storage, core-rope.*

storage, routine—Same as *area, instruction.*

storage, scratch-pad—Same as *storage, temporary.*

storage, searching—Same as *storage, associative.*

storage, secondary—Same as *storage, auxiliary.*

storage, serial—A storage device in which data is put in, held, and taken out in such a manner that each of the parts of the data is handled in time sequence, one part at a time, usually on the same circuit or wire in column fashion, rather than by rows or abreast; for example, if a 40 binary-digit number is stored in serial storage, one bit after the other is placed in storage over a single wire, as in single file entering a single delay-line. If the characters of a word are handled in sequence over the same wires, the storage is serial by character, even though the individual bits of the character are handled simultaneously over parallel wires; that is, parallel by bit. In a serial storage device, there are as many input and output lines as there are binary digits handled in parallel. If the device handles one bit at a time, there is only one input and one output line. In serial storage, time is one of the coordinates used to locate data, such as a bit, character, or word. If all of the bits of a word are handled in parallel, but each word is stored in such a manner that latency or waiting time is involved in obtaining specific words, the storage is serial by words, rather than randomly accessible with equal access time no matter where the location in storage. Drums, discs, delay-lines and tapes are constructed as serial storage, while electrostatic and core storage are constructed as parallel storage. (Contrast with *storage, parallel* and with *storage, random-access.*)

storage, serial access—A storage device or medium in which the access time is dependent upon the location of the data; for example, a magnetic tape station, a deck of punched cards, or a paper tape loop.

storage, slow—Same as *storage, low-speed.*

storage, slug-matrix—Same as *storage, magnetic slug.*

storage, solid-state—A storage device in which the memory elements consist of semiconductor circuits, usually integrated circuits. Over 50 million word capacities and 300 nanosecond access times are practical using the MSI type of construction.

storage, static—A storage device in which data may be stored, fixed in space and time, without the data or the medium on which the data is stored move relative to the frame of the storage device. Thus, the static storage may be any storage that is not a circulating storage. Static storage units, such as flip-flop, cathode-ray tube, and magnetic-core storage, have no moving parts, except electric currents. Circulating storage units are dynamic; either the data moves relative to the storage medium, such as in delay-lines, or the medium on which data is recorded moves with the data, such as tapes, discs, and drums. In static storage, the data is stationary. (Contrast with *storage, circulating.*)

storage, static magnetic—Same as *storage, core.*

storage, subroutine—Same as *area, instruction.*

storage, superconductive—storage, cryogenic.

storage, switch—Same as *storage, manual-switch.*

storage, tape—A storage device that makes use of a storage medium consisting of long, relatively narrow strips or ribbons on which data is recorded, such as magnetic or paper tape.

storage, tape-loop—A storage device that uses continuous closed loops of magnetic tape with read-write heads as a storage medium. Usually the loops are read forward or backward for increased speed and reduced access time. A large number of loops held ready to read-write in a chest is called a tape bin. (Synonymous with *loop storage.*)

storage, temporary—Storage used for partial or intermediate results; for example, storage used to hold partial sums, subsums, or evaluated terms involved in the solution of equations; or scratch-pad storage used for performing all sorts of minor computations, small loops or side calculations during execution of a routine. Temporary storage may be part of main storage or auxiliary storage and part of external or internal storage. It is the temporary nature of the data, that is, data representing temporary results that will be used again, that gives temporary storage its name. In programming, temporary storage is storage reserved for intermediate results, like a worksheet in pencil and paper calculations. (Synonymous with *scratch-pad storage,* with *working storage,* with *working area,* and *working space.* Compare with *storage, volatile.*)

storage, two-core-per-bit—A storage device in which each storage cell uses two magnetic cores to store one binary character.

storage, virtual—Notional space on storage devices, appearing to a computer user as main storage. The size of virtual storage is limited only by the addressing scheme of the computing system, rather than by the actual number of main storage locations. (Synonymous with *virtual memory.*)

storage, volatile—A storage device that loses stored data when power is removed from the device and that cannot furnish the stored data when power is reapplied; for example, electric and acoustic delay-lines and electrostatic storage. Delay-lines consisting of drums, tapes, or discs are considered nonvolatile. Special precautions must be taken to prevent loss of data on nonvolatile storage media when a power failure occurs in order to avoid the deleterious effects of the transients that occur when power fails. (Contrast with *storage, fixed* and with *storage, nonvolatile.* Compare with *storage, temporary.*)

storage, wire—Same as *wire, magnetic.*

storage, word-organized—A storage in which only complete computer words may be accessed at a time, that is, only full words may be transferred in or out of the storage unit.

storage, working—Same as *storage, temporary.*

storage, zero-access—Same as *storage, immediate-access.*

storage allocation—See *allocation, storage.*

storage allocation, dynamic—See *allocation, dynamic storage.*

storage area—See *area, storage.*

storage block—See *block, storage.*

storage buffer—See *buffer, storage.*

storage capacity—See *capacity, storage.*

storage cell—See *cell, storage.*

storage compaction—See *compaction, storage.*

storage core—See *core, storage.*

storage cycle—See *cycle, storage.*

storage device—See *device, storage.*

storage dump—Same as *dump.*

storage exchange—See *exchange, storage.*

storage fill—See *fill, storage.*

storage location—See *location, storage.*

storage medium—See *medium, storage.*

storage operation—See *operation, storage.*

storage parity—See *parity, storage.*

storage pool, free—See *pool, free-storage.*

storage protection—See *protection, storage.*

storage register—See *register, storage.*

storage stack—See *stack, storage.*

storage switch—See *switch, storage.*

storage tape—Same as *tape, magnetic.*

storage tube—Same as *tube, Williams.*

storage unit—Same as *device, storage.*

store—1: To enter data into a device from which it can be retrieved at a later time; that is, to enter data into a storage device. 2: To retain data in a device; that is, to hold data in a storage device, from which it can be obtained at a later time. In most storage devices the data can be obtained from the device and still be retained in the device. 3: Same as *storage.*

store, B—Same as *register, index.*

store, computer—Same as *storage.*

store, permanent—Same as *storage, fixed*

store-and-forward switching—Same as *switching, message.*

stored program—See *program, stored.*

stored-program computer—See *computer, stored-program.*

stored routine—See *routine, stored.*

straight binary—See *binary, straight.*

straight-line coding—See *coding, straight-line.*

stratified language—See *language, stratified.*

stream, input—The sequence of control statements and data entered into a computer by an input unit. Entry is usually accomplished under the control of the operating system by a unit usually designated for the purpose of input. The input may occur automatically at system generation time or at any other time designated by the operator. (Synonymous with *job stream.*)

stream, job—Same as *stream, input.*

stream deflection amplifier—See *amplifier, stream deflection.*

string—1: A group of sequenced items, such as words consisting of letters and digits that are sequenced first alphabetically and then numerically within letter groups. Each numerical sequence between alphabetic changes could constitute a string. The sequencing can occur in either time or space or both. Thus, a sequence of pulses at an electrical terminal might constitute a string of pulses; the same pulses moving down a delay-line in a spatial sequence might also constitute a string. The string of items might be strings of words, cars, events, bits, houses, missiles, failures, or thoughts. 2: A linear series of items, entities, or elements such as characters or pulses.

string, alphabetic—A string or sequence of letters from the same alphabet. (Illustrative of *string, character.*)

string, binary element—A string that consists solely of binary elements, namely the constituent elements of the string can assume one of two possible values or states. The binary element is usually a bit, that is, a binary digit, otherwise known as a shannon when the logarithm to the base two of the number of states that can be represented by a binary element string is taken. 2: A series of binary logic elements connected so that the output of one element serves as the input to the next element in the series; for example, a string of flip-flops, a string of AND gates, or a string of OR gates.

string, bit—1: A string or sequence of binary digits in which each bit position is considered to be independent or unweighted. 2: A string that consists solely of binary digits.

string, character—A string or sequence of characters; for example, the character string FG109(4H∗). (Illustrated by *string, alphabetic.*)

string, null—An empty string, that is, a string that contains no entity.

string, pulse—A group of pulses that occur in time sequence at a point in a circuit. An amplitude vs. time plot of the pulses appears as though the pulse group occurs in space sequence, as along a line or string, and so the term pulse string. (Synonymous with *pulse train.*)

string, symbol—A string that consists solely of symbols.

string, unit—1: A string that consists of only one item or one designated entity. 2: A string of designated or defined length used as a unit of measurement of lengths of strings.

string file—See *file, string.*

strobe—To select a desired point or position in a recurring phenomenon, such as a wave, or the device used to make the selection or identify the selected point; for example, to have a narrow pulse beat against a periodic wave with the same frequency, yielding a measure of the amplitude of the periodic wave at each strobe point, or to shine an intermittent light upon a revolving shaft, where the frequency of the light is a multiple or submultiple of the revolutions per unit time of the shaft. If there is a slight difference in light flashes per unit time and revolutions per unit time, the shaft will appear to revolve very slowly. Camera frame speed and revolving stage coach wheels in Western movies show the same stroboscopic effect. In data processing, strobing is often used in signal sampling techniques.

stroke—In character recognition, a straight line, arc, point, or other mark used as a part or segment of a graphic character; for example, the circle of a letter 0, the straight-edge of a letter D, the dot over the i or j, or the cross of a t.

stroke, Sheffer—Same as *NAND.*

stroke centerline—See *centerline, stroke.*

stroke edge—See *edge, stroke.*

stroke edge irregularity—See *irregularity, stroke edge.*

stroke gate, Sheffer—Same as *gate, NAND.*

stroke width—See *width, stroke.*

structure—In a system, the arrangement or relative position of the component parts or elements of the system, such as organization arrangement of an industrial concern or military command, arrangement of the parts of a machine, the parts of a bridge, or arrangement of the parts of a computer. Usually hardware arrangement is implied by *structure.* (Contrast with *method.*)

structure, block—A heirarchical arrangement of program blocks.

structure, data—1: In computer simulation, the state vector and the operational rules that pertain to a formal system. 2: The syntactic structures of expression and their characteristics when assigned to storage.

structure, graphic data—In a computer-driven data display system, a logical scheme for arrangement of the digital data that represents or describes the graphic data. The digital data is stored or otherwise manipulated by the computer for graphic display.

structure, keyed file—A file structured in such a manner that there is a data item in each record that is used to uniquely identify the record.

structure, order—See *format, instruction.*

structure, program—The arrangement of the component parts of a computer program, such as declarations, statements, and identifiers.

structure, ring-file—A list that is circular in that the last data element points back to the first; for example, a threaded list in which the last item in the list contains a pointer that points back to the first item.

structure, tree—A hierarchy of data consisting of nodes, or branches, and items of data.

structure control, program—See *control, program structure.*

structure sort, tree—Same as *sort, repeated selection.*

stub card—See *card, stub.*

study, application—In data-processing applications, an analysis of all available data-processing systems in order to obtain the most economical and effective match between system characteristics and system performance requirements established by the data or operational requirements, including evaluation of all systems against

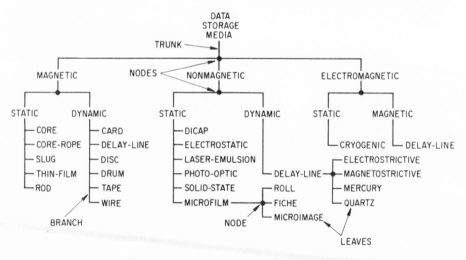

A tree structure *showing the relationships among data storage media.*

the established performance requirements or criteria; that is, to find the most suitable machine for the job. An applications study usually follows a feasibility study, and ends with the selection of a machine or set of machines, in order of preference. Selection criteria are usually weighted. (Contrast with *study, feasibility*. Further clarified by *application, computer*.)

study, feasibility—In data-processing applications, a preliminary study to examine the probable soundness of applying an automatic data-processing system to a given application or set of applications. If it is proved practical, feasible, effective, and economical to use automated means of data processing, the feasibility study is followed by an applications study. (Contrast with *study, applications*. Further clarified by *application, computer*.)

stunt box—See *box, stunt.*

STX—The start-of-text character.

style, character—A distinctive construction, characteristic, or quality of a set of graphic characters, such as the letters of an alphabet, without regard to size, but with regard to shape other than size; for example, old English, gothic, italics, capital block, or roman. Usually styles are variations of the same alphabet, rather than variations between alphabets of different languages. When the size and style are specified, a font has been determined. (Further clarified by *font*.)

styles—In a graphic display device, an instrument that provides coordinate data input or output. (Further clarified by *track* and by *symbol, tracking*.)

stylus printer—Same as *printer, matrix.*

SUB—The substitute character.

subalphabet—A subset of an alphabet, that is, part of an alphabet; for example, all of the first 10 letters of the English alphabet, a through j, inclusive.

subcarrier—A carrier used to modulate another carrier or subcarrier; for example, a kilohertz signal used to modulate a megahertz signal, the kilohertz signal being the subcarrier, which is then keyed by a radio operator sending Morse Code. The purpose of the subcarrier is to render the signal audible.

subject program—Same as *program, source.*

subjunction gate——**1:** Same as *gate, A AND NOT B.* **2:** Same as *gate, B AND NOT A.*

suboptimization—The process of optimizing a system with regard to an intermediate objective or some chosen objective that is an integral part of a broader objective, usually on the supposition that a system is optimized if all its component parts are optimized. The broad objective and the intermediate, or lower level objective, are usually different. (Related to *optimization*.)

subprogram—Same as *routine.*

subroutine—A routine that is part of another routine; examples include a set of

instructions that define a specific mathematical function such as sin x, cube root, log x, or x cubed; a short set of instructions, such as a loop in a main program; or a set of instructions set aside in a particular set of storage locations to be called each time it is to be executed. Programs and routines are usually made up of sets of previously prepared and stored subroutines. Subroutines are often written in relative or symbolic coding. (Further clarified by *program* and by *routine*.)

subroutine, closed—A subroutine that can be stored at one place and can be connected to a routine by linkages, or calling sequences, at one or more locations. Usually, it is stored separately from the main routine, a jump instruction transfers program control to the beginning of the subroutine, and, at the end, another jump instruction transfers control back to the proper point in the main routine. The instructions for entering the subroutine and for returning from the subroutine to the main routine is called a linkage. (Synonymous with *linked subroutine* and with *closed routine*. Further clarified by *linkage*. Contrast with *subroutine, open*.)

subroutine, dating—A subroutine that computes and stores dates and times associated with files and programs and related work associated with computer runs.

subroutine, direct-insert—Same as *subroutine, open.*

subroutine, dynamic—A subroutine containing parameters, such as number of iterations, decimal point position, and byte size, which are selected for a given application. It is often arranged so that the computer generates the subroutine according to the parametric values chosen before the subroutine is executed. (Synonymous with *dynamic routine*. Contrast with *subroutine, static*.)

subroutine, editing—A subroutine, usually with parameters whose values are selected prior to execution, used for performing various operations on input and output data before and after main program operations on these data.

subroutine, first-order—A subroutine entered directly from the main routine or program and returned to it. (Contrast with *subroutine, second-order*. Further clarified by *linkage*.)

subroutine, inline—A subroutine directly inserted into the sequence of operations of a program. Usually the subroutine is stored with the program or it is recopied at each point that it is needed in the routine or program.

subroutine, library—A subroutine held and made available among a collection of subroutines for possible future use. The subroutines in the library are often standardized and kept on file for future use. (Further clarified by *routine, library*.)

subroutine, linked—Same as *subroutine, closed.*

subroutine, minimal-latency—Same as *routine, minimal-latency.*

subroutine, open—A subroutine that must be relocated and inserted into a routine each place it is used, usually without linkage or calling sequence. The open subroutine has fixed reentry points into the routine using it. It is not entered by a jump instruction, and must be recopied at each point it is needed in a routine or program. Sequences of instructions that implement macroinstructions are examples of open subroutines. Generators are often used to copy, prepare and modify open subroutines. (Synonymous with *direct-insert subroutine.* Contrast with *subroutine, closed.* Further clarified by *linkage.*)

subroutine, recursive—A computer program that may call itself as a routine or subroutine during execution, or, in some cases, that may call itself as a subroutine of another subroutine. The concept of a recursive subroutine is the same as the concept of a recursive function wherein the subroutine assumes the role of the function.

subroutine, reentrant—Same as *program, reentrant.*

subroutine, second-order—A subroutine entered from a first-order subroutine and returned to it or to the main routine or program. (Contrast with *subroutine, first-order.* Further clarified by *linkage.*)

subroutine, standard—A subroutine used in solving a class of problems, such as solutions of transcendental functions, payroll computations, and inventory control.

subroutine, static—A subroutine that has no parameters; that is, quantities subject to variation or selection, except addresses of the operands. The addresses may be relative or absolute and may by subject to modification. (Synonymous with *static routine.* Contrast with *subroutine, dynamic.*)

subroutine analyzer—Same as *analyzer (1).*

subroutine call—See *call, subroutine.*

subroutine library—Same as *library, routine.*

subroutine storage—Same as *area, instruction.*

subroutine test—Same as *test, routine.*

A_I	B_n	$(C)_2$	$\|D\|_r$	SUBSCRIPTS
5^3	A^2	a^n	p^v	SUPERSCRIPTS

Subscripts *for indexing and superscripts for exponents are usual applications.*

subscript—In indexing notation, a symbol in typography written below, and usually following, a set name to identify a particular element or elements of the set; for example, A_5 is the fifth element of array A. In ALGOL programming language, A_5 would be written $A[5]$, that is the subscripts are placed in brackets. As

a further example, $B_{5,3}$ might imply the element in the fifth row, third column, of the B array. In ALGOL, this would be written as $B[5,3]$. (Contrast with *superscript.*)

subsequence counter—See *counter, subsequence.*

subset—1: A set contained within a set; for example, the set of digits 1, 3, 5, 6, is a subset of the set of the digits 1, 2, 3, 4, 5, 6, 7. (Contrast with *set (1).*) 2: In communications, a remote station, an input-output device, or terminal equipment that is part of a system, such as a subscriber instrument on a telecommunications network.

subset, alphabetic character—A character subset that contains letters; may contain space, control, and other special characters such as punctuation marks; but does not contain digits. (Closely related to *set, alphabetic character.*)

subset, alphanumeric character—A character subset that contains letters and digits, and that may contain control characters, space characters, and other special characters. (Related to *set, alphabetic character.*)

subset, character—Certain characters from a set of characters, usually comprising all characters with a specified common feature; for example, in an alphanumeric character set, the digits 0 through 9 may constitute a character subset.

subset, numeric character—A character subset that contains digits, that may contain control characters, special characters, the space characters, and that does not contain letters. (Related to *set, numeric character.*)

subset, proper—A subset that does not include all the elements of the set.

substitute—In data processing and information retrieval, to replace one set of data by another set of data.

substitute character—See *character, substitute.*

subtracter—A device capable of forming the algebraic or arithmetic difference between two quantities presented as inputs. Usually, the subtracter cannot retain the difference, which is present only as long as the inputs are time coincidentally present. In other cases, the difference is presented to a register or an accumulator where it may be temporarily stored before being transferred to another location. The subtracter can be considered a logic element with three input channels to which signals representing the minuend, subtrahend, and borrow digit may be applied; and two output channels from which the difference and borrow digits emerge. This device, which is more precisely called a full-subtracter, includes a digit-delay element for the borrow digit, and so has only two external input signal channels for the minuend and subtrahend and one output channel for the difference. Subtracters may be serial or parallel, digital or analog. In actual practice in binary logic elements, a subtracter different from an adder is not necessary, for in most instances, the ones complement of a binary numeral is usually available as the set of bits represented by the opposite side of each flip-flop that represents the bits of the subtrahend. The difference is obtained by adding the minuend to the ones complement of the subtrahend and adding a one to the least significant digit of the result and propagating all carries. The three-input subtracter differs from the full-subtracter only in the handling of the borrow digit; namely, externally vs. internally, respectively. (Synonymous with *three-input subtracter* and with *full-subtracter*. Contrast with *adder*. Further clarified by *adder-subtracter* and by *half-subtracter*.)

subtracter, adder—See *adder-subtracter*.

subtracter, full—Same as *subtracter*.

subtracter, half—See *half-subtracter*.

subtracter, one-digit—Same as *half-subtracter*.

subtracter, three-input—Same as *subtracter*.

subtracter, two-input—Same as *half-subtracter*.

subtraction—An arithmetic process or operation that produces the difference between two numbers; for example, $6-5=1$ is a subtraction operation. The number to be subtracted is the subtrahend; the other is the minuend. The result of a subtraction operation is the difference. Subtraction may be considered a special case of addition in which the subtrahend is a negative quantity. In particular, a binary computer may form the difference by adding a complement of the subtrahend to the minuend. If the ones complement is used, a one will have to be added to the least significant digit of the sum obtained by adding the ones complement to the minuend and propagating the resultant carries.

subtrahend—The quantity subtracted from another quantity, called the minuend, to obtain a result called the difference.

suffix notation—See *notation, suffix*.

sum—The result obtained from the inclusive-OR logic operation, the exclusive-OR operation, or the arithmetic addition of two or more numbers. Unless explicitly stated otherwise, the arithmetic sum is implied by the word sum alone. Thus, in the decimal numeration system, the sum of 9 and 8 is 17. (Contrast with *product*, with *quotient*, and with *difference*.)

sum, arithmetic—The result obtained when two or more numbers are added arithmetically. The arithmetic sum is implied when the word sum is used alone, unless explicitly stated otherwise. Thus, the sum of 9 and 8 is 17 in the decimal system of numeration. (Contrast with *sum, logic*.)

sum, check—The sum, represented by a numeral, used in a summation check; for example, the sum of all the numbers in a given file item, the sum of all the digits in a number, a hash total, or, to arrive at a check digit for the numeral 4516853245, add the last six (arbitrary) digits, to obtain 27, a check sum; or use 7 as the check digit. Such check sums or control totals are compared with previously obtained totals for the same set of records. Any discrepancy signals an error. Often each check sum has some significance, such as the total payroll deductions for a group of employees. Often it may have no significance, such as the sum of all the identification numbers of a group of records. (Synonymous with *control total* and *check total*. Further clarified by *check, summation*.)

sum, logic—The result obtained from either the exclusive-OR operation or the inclusive-OR operation. (Contrast with *sum, arithmetic*. Further clarified by *add, logic*.)

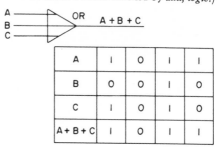

A	I	O	I	I
B	O	O	I	O
C	I	O	I	O
A + B + C	I	O	I	I

The logic sum *is binary 1011, i.e., decimal 11. The arithmetic sum is decimal 23.*

sum, module-two—Same as *operation, non-equivalence*.

sum, partial—The result obtained from the addition of two or more numbers without regard to carries. In the binary numeration system, the partial sum is the same result as is obtained from the exclusive-OR operation.

AUGEND	2 8 9 5 9 4
ADDEND	3 2 0 6 0 7
FIRST (PARTIAL) SUM	5 0 9 1 9 1
PARTIAL CARRY	I 0 I 0 I 0
SECOND (PARTIAL) SUM	6 0 0 I 0 I
PROPAGATED CARRY	0 I 0 I 0 0
THIRD (TRUE) SUM	6 I 0 2 0 I
PROPAGATED CARRY	0 0 0 0 0 0

Addition, showing partial sum *and partial* carry numerals.

sum, sideways—A sum obtained by adding the digits of a numeral without regard to position or significance. Modified sideways sums are obtained by attaching certain weights to the different digit positions. For example, a modulo-nine sideways sum for the decimal numeral 2586 is three; a sideways sum modulo-seven for the octal numeral 64325 is six and for 45723 is zero. The sideways sum forms a good check digit. The odd or even parity check bit is obtained by determining the sideways sum of the digits of a binary numeral modulo-two. If the sum is one, the number of bits in the numeral is odd. Then, if odd parity is used, a zero is the parity bit. If even parity is used, a one is the parity bit, making the sideways sum modulo-two zero, and so even. For the binary numeral 1011011, the sideways sum modulo-two is one; for 1010110, it is zero.

sum check—Same as *check, summation.*

sum check digit—See *digit, sum check.*

summary punch—See *punch, summary.*

summation check—See *check, summation.*

summing amplifier—See *amplifier, summing.*

summing integrator—See *integrator, summing.*

superconductive storage—Same as *storage, cryogenic.*

superconductivity—The physical phenomenon displayed by certain materials wherein below a certain temperature the resistance to the flow of electric current is zero. In some superconductive materials, the conductivity remains zero below a certain threshold temperature, above which the resistance is appreciable. The fact that a magnetic field can change the threshold value of temperature at which superconductivity occurs is made use of in the cryotron, a digital switching and gating device. In essence, at a fixed temperature, the magnetic field tends to destroy superconductivity, which in essence is equivalent to what any manual switch does, or any logic gate or control switch or any flow valve does. In cryotrons, power level requirements are extremely low, flux can be trapped for data storage, and elements can be microminaturized. The field of study related to the phenomenon of superconductivity is called cryogenics, a part of low-temperature physics. The phenomenon has potential application in computer circuitry. (Further explained by *cryogenics,* by *cryostat,* and by *cryotron.*)

superscript—A symbol written above and to the right of another (base) symbol to perform a specified function, such as denote a power that the base symbol is to be raised; denote a derivative; or, if the base symbol is a set name, denote or identify a particular element of the set, in which case it acts like a subscript. (Contrast with *subscript.*)

supervision, backward—In data transmission systems, the use of supervisory control signals sent from a slave station to a master station. (Contrast with *supervision, forward.*)

supervision, forward—In data transmission systems, the use of supervisory control signals sent from a master station to a slave station. (Contrast with *supervision, backward.*)

supervision, through-trunk—Supervision by a telephone operator of a call in a trunk switching system in which the operator maintains control of the call requiring trunk connections through all long-distance switching centers.

supervisor—Same as *routine, executive.*

supervisor, overlay—A routine that controls the location and execution sequence of parts of computer programs during conditions of limited storage space availability.

supervisor, resident—In a computer operating system, the part of the supervisor that remains in main storage at all times in order for the system to function at all.

supervisor call—See *call, supervisor.*

supervisory control—See *control, supervisory.*

supervisory instruction—Same as *instruction, executive.*

supervisory program—Same as *routine, executive.*

supervisory routine—Same as *routine, executive.*

supplementary maintenance—See *maintenance, supplementary.*

supplementary maintenance time—See *time, supplementary maintenance.*

supply, reference—In an electric analog computer, a stable power supply of constant voltage used to assist in improving the accuracy of the computer with voltage analog representation. Initial or boundary conditions are usually derived directly from the reference supply, and voltages representing other values of variables are measured as a fraction of the reference supply, usually by potentiometers. A reference voltage is used to calibrate or regulate the reference supply. (Synonymous with *reference power supply* and with *supply voltage.*)

supply port—See *port, supply.*

supply voltage—Same as *supply, reference.*

support, compiler library—1: The part of an operating system that provides support to maintain compiler libraries; for example, support to maintain compiler source programs, macrostatements, compiler subroutines and other similar libraries. 2: Any support activity to maintain compiler-oriented libraries.

support, executive routine—In a computer operating system, special compiler interface facilities that are provided by the system executive to the compiler, that are usually not available to the problem-oriented programs; for example, the use of certain communication tables in the resident executive.

support program—See *program, support.*

suppressed-carrier transmission—See *transmission, suppressed-carrier.*

suppression—In data representation, the inhibition, elimination, omission, or removal of characters; for example, the elimination of characters that have no meaning in a particular context, such as item separators, initial zeros, or space markers, all in plain text output.

suppression, space—In printing, prevention of the platen or paper movement for a new line of printing, usually where such movement would ordinarily be automatic in the absence of the inhibition of movement.

suppression, zero—The elimination, removal, omission, or inhibition of zeros that have no significance or use, such as zeros to the left of the integral part of a numeral or the zeros to the right of a fractional part of a numeral. Zero suppression may be accomplished just prior to printing as an editing operation. (Synonymous with *zero elimination*.)

surface analysis—See *analysis, surface*.

SURGE—(Sorting, Updating, Report Generating, Etc.) A data-processing compiler developed for the IBM 704 computer and used by Aerojet General CEIR, Douglas Aircraft, Martin, IBM, and North American Rockwell.

surrogate—In a document storage and retrieval system, an item that refers to or can be used in place of a given document, such as an abstract, an index card, a subject classification heading, a coordinate index entry, or a descriptive catalog entry.

suspense file—Same as *file, follow-up*.

suspension, program—The temporary halting of the execution of a computer program until the occurrence of a specified event.

swap, servo—Same as *swap, tape-servo*.

swap, tape-servo—To operate a multitape file of magnetic tapes by mounting the first two tapes of the file on two tape handlers, running the first tape; running the second tape while the first is rewound, removed, and replaced by the third tape; running the third while the second is rewound, removed, and replaced by the fourth, and so on, until all of the tapes have been run. The use of two handlers may be worth the main frame time saved. (Synonymous with *servo swap*.)

swapping, page—The exchanging of pages between two storage devices, such as between main storage and auxiliary storage or between internal storage and external storage.

swapping, program—A method of handling computer programs in such a manner that each program is held in secondary or auxiliary storage until it is loaded into main storage for a limited time interval, usually for a time sufficient to permit execution, after which it is either cleared from main storage, returned to auxiliary storage, or both.

switch—1: A device or programming technique for effecting a selection; for example, toggle; a pivoted blade and jaw for opening or closing a circuit; a conditional jump; a multichoice conditional branchpoint in a program; a device for making, breaking, or changing the path of data flow; an instruction,

numeral, or symbol planted in a routine to select one of a number of alternative paths, enabling the result of a decision to be used at a later point in a routine; or a method of altering normal procedure for a routine or operating system. Programming switches include programmed switches, end-of-file switches, alteration switches, and check indicator switches. 2: To reverse the polarization in a magnetic or a ferroelectric cell by applying a suitable magnetic or electric field. The polarization in a magnetic or ferroelectric material is caused to change from a remaining state in one direction to the remaining state in the other direction. On removal of the applied field, the material will relax from the saturated value to the remaining value.

switch, alteration—A manual switch on a computer console or a switch simulated by a computer program, which can be set so as to control instructions or issue instructions to the computer at such points in the program as a programmed halt, a breakpoint, a rerun point, or at an instruction that calls for the computer to sense or read manually set switches on the console or to read the contents of a specified register or storage location. (Synonymous with *sense switch*.)

switch, breakpoint—A manual switch that permits control of computer operations at a breakpoint in a routine. The switches are used primarily for debugging, checking, or error correction.

switch, Diamond—Same as *storage, core-rope*.

switch, electronic—A switch that operates at electronic speeds and by electronic means; that is, a circuit that opens and closes other circuits at electronic speeds electronically, permitting such switching actions as sampling various waveshapes on different lines so rapidly that all the waveshapes can be displayed on a single-channel oscilloscope in a chopped form by displaying the samples sequentially. Thus, in this application, the electronic switch connects and disconnects the oscilloscope to each circuit for a short time several times during each period of the waves being examined. Such a switch permits rapid sampling of many circuits entering a computer for determination of status, permitting control decisions to be made in accordance with the results of sampling. The switch can cause start and stop actions in a computer at electronic speeds.

switch, emergency—Same as *button, panic*.

switch, function—An electrical network or set of circuits having a fixed number of inputs and outputs designed such that the output data is a function of the input data, each expressed in certain code patterns; thus, a form of code translator. The input may be in the form of switch settings, such as the 10-position settings of arrays of switches; or the switch settings may control the code translation; that is, make it variable, producing different sets of output codes corresponding to given sets of input codes.

switch, insertion—A switch used to insert data or instructions into a data-processing unit or system. (Compare with *insertion, switch*.)

switch, intervention—Same as *button, panic*.

switch, linear selection—Same as *storage, core-rope*.

switch, logic—In computer simulation, a specific piece of equipment that is used for control purposes.

switch, matrix—Same as *matrix (2)*.

switch, N-way—Same as *connector, variable*.

switch, operation-control—A matrix switch that selects the input lines of the matrix whose output controls the logic elements that execute the specific operations to be performed by the computer as directed by the program.

switch, programmed—1: In programming, an instruction, which may be in the form of a numeral, placed in a routine so as to allow the computer to select one of a number of alternative paths in its program. Once a selection is made by or at the switch, the computer persists in this path until altered, perhaps by another switch. This is in contrast to the selection made at a branchpoint, where the selection is made at each iteration or passage according to some criterion. 2: Same as *connector, variable*.

switch, Rajchman selection—Same as *storage, core-rope*.

switch, sense—Same as *switch, alteration*.

switch, storage—A manual switch or bank of switches on the console of a computer, which permits the operator to read, by visual display or print-out, the contents of any register or storage location in the computer. An arrangement can be made to have a specified numeral or word stored at the location selected by the storage switch.

switch, toggle—Same as *toggle*.

switch, whiffletree—A multiposition electronic switch whose gates and flip-flops are so arranged that its circuit diagram resembles a whiffletree; that is, one circuit leads to two circuits, the two lead to four, and so on. The switch and gates permit selection of one or more of many paths at any given instant, under the control of the flip-flops.

switch control statement—See *statement, switch control*.

switch core—See *core, switch*.

switch indicator—See *indicator, switch*.

switch insertion—See *insertion, switch*.

switch storage—Same as *storage, manual-switch*.

switch storage, manual—See *storage, manual-switch*.

switchboard, manual telephone—Same as *exchange, manual*.

switching, automatic message—In communications, a technique of message handling, that is, reading, storing, routing, and transmitting, whereby messages are automatically handled according to information contained in the message, usually according to information in the heading and ending, rather than in the body, which is usually reserved for the writer. (Further clarified by *center, automatic data-switching*.)

switching, circuit—1: In communications, a technique of message handling in which connection is made to the destination prior to the start of the message transmission. Thus, message routing is completed before dispatch, such as is required for full-duplex operation, that is, two-way simultaneous transmission, as required for a telephone conversation. 2: A transmission process that on demand connects two or more data terminals and permits the exclusive use of a data circuit that is maintained until the connection is released. (Synonymous with *line switching*.)

switching, line—Same as *switching, circuit*.

switching, message—In communications, a technique of message handling in which a message is transmitted to the next station, received there, stored until the proper outgoing circuit is available, and then transmitted to the next station. Each station, in turn, must read the address and priority and handle accordingly. (Synonymous with *store-and-forward switching*.)

switching, packet—A data transmission process that transmits addressed packets such that a channel is occupied only for the duration of transmission of a packet.

switching, store-and-forward—Same as *switching, message*.

switching center, automatic data—See *center, automatic data-switching*.

switching center, electronic data—Same as *center, automatic data-switching*.

switching center, local—See *center, local switching*.

switching center, local exchange—See *center, local exchange switching*.

switching center, message—Same as *center, data-switching*.

switching center, primary—See *center, primary switching*.

switching center, secondary—See *center, secondary switching*.

switching center, semiautomatic message—See *center, semiautomatic message-switching*.

switching center, torn-tape—See *center, torn-tape switching*.

switching center, zone—See *center, zone switching*.

switching coefficient—See *coefficient, switching*.

switching function—See *function, switching*.

switching space—See *space, switching*.

switching theory—See *theory, switching*.

switching time—See *time, switching*.

switching tube, beam—See *tube, beam-switching*.

switching variable—See *variable, switching*.

syllable–A character string, such as a binary digit string, a pulse string, or a string of letters, in a word. A syllable is part of a word.

symbol–A representation of something, usually by reason of relationship, association, convention, or form. Symbols are used to assist in handling abstractions, performing computations, permitting logic analysis, and similar actions. Most symbols in data processing assume the form of characters to represent data and information. The use of symbols permits the substitution of representations for the real entities they represent. To· think in the abstract with the use of symbols has been one of man's greatest achievements. Thus, characters, such as letters and numerals, special signs, and similar representations, and their combination into words and phrases, are all considered symbols. Many forms and signs, such as the United States flag, the Christian cross, the shamrock, the fleur-de-lis, the swastika, the hammer and sickle, and the crescent-star have served as symbols. A symbol may even be used to represent nothing, a blank, a space, or a zero.

symbol, abstract–A symbol whose shape or form is not necessarily indicative of its meaning or use. Abstract symbols usually require definition for each specific set of applications.

symbol, breakpoint–A symbol included in an instruction, such as an indicator, tag, flag, sentinel, or designator, to show that at this instruction there is a breakpoint in the program or routine.

symbol, editing–1: A symbol used to indicate an editorial or substantive change in text; for example, a symbol used to indicate insertion of new text, deletion of text or transposition of text, namely ∧, ℯ, and ⌐⌐⌐. 2: In micrographics, a symbol on microfilm that is readable without magnification and is used for conveying preparation instructions such as cutting and loading.

symbol, flowchart–A symbol used to represent operations, data, flow, or equipment, The symbols are usually shown graphically on a flowchart. The symbols are connected by flowlines, which are also symbols for showing decision paths or sequences, or data paths.

symbol, graphic–Same as *graphic*.

symbol, logic–A symbol used to represent a logic element and the nature or type of logic operation that the element is capable of performing; for example, a symbol used to represent an AND gate, and so, too, the AND operation. Such logic symbols will be found on logic diagrams.

symbol, mnemonic–A symbol used to represent information and chosen so as to assist the human memory in recalling its meaning; for example, $>$ to represent *greater than* and SUB to represent the *subtraction instruction*.

symbol, punctuation–Same as *delimiter*.

symbol, special–Same as *character, special*.

symbol, terminating–A symbol placed on tape to indicate the end of a unit of data, such as the end of a block, record, or file.

symbol, tracking–In graphic display systems, a symbol, such as a circle, angle, cross, dot or square, used to indicate the position of a stylus. (Further clarified by *stylus*.)

symbol manipulation–See *manipulation, symbol*.

Standard flowchart symbols.

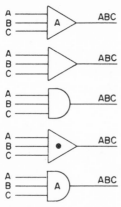

Various logic symbols *used to represent a* three-input AND gate.

symbol string—See *string, symbol.*
symbol table—See *table, symbol.*
symbolic address—See *address, symbolic.*
symbolic code—See *code, symbolic.*
symbolic coding—See *coding, symbolic.*
Symbolic Conversion Program—See SCP.
symbolic deck—See *deck, symbolic.*
symbolic instruction—See *instruction, symbolic.*
symbolic language—Same as *language, symbolic.*
symbolic logic—See *logic, symbolic.*
symbolic notation—See *notation, symbolic.*
symbolic programming—Same as *coding, symbolic.*
symmetric channel, binary—See *channel, binary symmetric.*
symmetric difference gate—Same as *gate, exclusive-OR.*
symmetric list—Same as *list, bi-directional.*
SYN—The synchronous idle character.
synchro—An induction device, consisting of stator and rotor elements, both carrying one or more windings, the mutual inductance depending on the angular position of the rotor with respect to the stator. Uses include remote position indicators, remote position controllers, and components for analog computers for performing trigonometrical operations, such as in a synchro resolver, wherein two stator windings give a-c outputs proportional to R cos a and R sin a, if a-c input R is applied to the rotor winding and a is the mechanically fixed rotor angle. Operation may be dynamic or static. (Synonymous with *Magslip* and with *Selsyn.*)
synchronizer—1: Same as *buffer.* 2: Same as *clock.*
synchronizer, master—Same as *clock, master.*
synchronizer, tape—A device that controls the exchange of data between the central processor and the tape unit. A buffer is usually included and the events are program controlled.
synchronous—A mode of operation such that the execution of each instruction or each event is step-wise controlled by a clock

signal, usually evenly spaced pulses that enable the logic gates for the execution of each logic step. Clocked gates aid pulse shaping, simplify control, and reduce noise. It can cause time delays by causing waiting for clock signals when all other signals at a particular logic gate were available sooner than the next available clock signal. (Contrast with *asynchronous.*)
synchronous computer—See *computer, synchronous.*
synchronous data transmission—See *transmission, synchronous data.*
synchronous idle character—See *character, synchronous idle.*
synchronous machine—See *machine, synchronous.*
synchronous multiplexor—See *multiplexor, synchronous.*
synchronous operation—See *operation, synchronous.*
synchronous working—Same as *operation, synchronous.*
syndetic—Same as *synergic.*
synergic—Pertaining to the capability of working together or cooperating, as in a system, usually such that the capability of the system exceeds the sum of the capabilities of the individual or separate parts. Most computing and data-processing systems are synergic systems, as are most types of systems.
synergistic—Same as *synergic.*
syntax—The structure of expressions in a language or the rules governing the structure. Syntax permits determination of allowable or nonallowable expressions in a language, in contrast to specific meanings assigned to words or expressions. Thus, grammar, sentence structure, order of symbol arrangement, and related rules are all matters of syntax. Syntax deals primarily with relationships between expressions, rather than meaning or even spelling of words. Complexities of syntax makes mechanical translation of languages by means of computers very difficult. A syntactical rule of English is that the letter q may not begin a word unless it is followed by u; a rule of mathematics is that + or − must be followed by a number, a symbol representing a number, or an expression that can be evaluated as a number, and not, for instance, by another +. A language can be completely described by listing the symbols, their uses, and the syntax, which establishes their permissible arrangements. If the rules are never violated, and nothing is permitted, unless explicitly allowed by the rules, the languages are said to be *ruly.* Living, natural languages are usually not ruly, since syntax is often violated. (Synonymous with *syntax rules.*)
syntax rules—Same as *syntax.*
syntax language—See *language, syntax.*
synthesis—The combining of parts to form a whole; for example, to arrive at a circuit, program, or chemical compound, given the

performance requirements or component parts. This is in contrast with analysis, which arrives at the performance or component parts, given the circuit, program, or compound. (Contrast with *analysis.*)

synthetic address—See *address, synthetic.*

synthetic language—See *language, artificial.*

Synthex—A fact-retrieval scheme, from English text in response to English questions. Using the IBM 7090 computer, the scheme is programmed in JOVIAL, an ALGOL-type information-processing language. A prototype Synthex, called Proto-Synthex, is programmed. It can accept simple English questions and frequently find answers for them from a volume of the *Golden Book Encyclopedia.* Proto-Synthex includes a text reader and indexer, a question analyzer, and locator, a grammar analyzer, and a text evaluator. Proto-Synthex is primarily a research tool currently limited to the child's encyclopedia level of English. It interprets text literally. Its performance is greatly dependent on the correspondence of content words in the English question to identical content words in the text. Hundreds of thousands of words of text can be handled.

system—An organized collection of parts or elements, such as men, machines, methods, and information, united by regulated interaction and designed or required to accomplish a specific purpose or reach a specific purpose or reach a specific objective. When the system is computer based, the entire system is called an operating system.

system, addressing—The procedure used to label storage locations in a computer; for example, all the storage locations on a magnetic drum might be numbered from 0000 to 9999, where each block of 1000 locations is on one band; thus, the most significant digit designating the 10 bands, from zero through nine, and the remaining three digits, the word location within the band, around the drum, in consecutive order. Thus, address 4321 is the 322nd word in the fifth band; or in a core storage unit, consisting of four stacks of 4096 words each, the first 4096 locations are in the first stack, addressed as 0000 to 4095, and the next set of addresses, 4096 to 8191, are in the second stack, and so on.

System, Army Fieldata—A family of automatic data-processing systems designed for use in the field; that is, a deployed army, for such applications as logistical control, tactical control, intelligence evaluation, weapons selection, firing or launch schedules, and other administrative, command, and control applications. The equipment is being designed for operational use during the 1965 to 1970 time period. All the latest advances in the state of the computer art are being used. Some examples of the current members of the Fieldata family include the Logipac, Basicpac, Compac, Fadac, and Mobidic A, B, C and 7A. All systems in the Armydata family are compatible with and use the Fieldata Code. (Synonymous with *Armydata.*)

system, binary number—Same as *notation, binary.*

system, bridge duplex—In duplex telegraphy circuits, a connection of sending and receiving apparatus made so as to apply the principle of the Wheatstone bridge to the balancing and neutralization of currents and voltages in the circuits.

system, Brussels classification—Same as *classification, universal decimal.*

system, carrier—In communications, a procedure for obtaining a number of channels over a single path by allowing each channel signal to modulate the one carrier at a different frequency; the demodulator at the receiving end separates out the signals in each channel by selective tuning and then demodulates the output to obtain the intelligence, such as the audio transmission in its original form, in each channel.

system, data management—A group of computer programs, routines, and subroutines, or a computer operating system, designed to create, maintain, and operate a large, organized, and structured collection of data; to interrogate the collection; and to produce various types of output reports.

system, data-processing—A collection of methods, procedures, or techniques united by regulated interaction to form an organized whole for the purpose of handling or performing specified operations on data.

system, decimal number—Same as *notation, decimal.*

system, decimal numeration—The fixed radix numeration system that uses the ten decimal digits, and that has a radix of ten; for example, the decimal numeral 489.3 represents the number $4 \times 10^2 + 8 \times 10^1 + 9 \times 10^0 + 3 \times 10^{-1}$. (Contrast with *notation, decimal* (2)).

system, Dewey decimal—Same as *classification, Dewey decimal.*

system, executive—Same as *system, operating.*

system, Filmorex—A system for electronic selection of microfilm cards devised by Jacques Samain. Each card has a microreproduction of a document, such as a technical report, and a field of 20 five-digit code numbers to identify and index the bibliographic reference and the subjects covered in the document to permit retrieval of the card.

system, fixed-radix numeration—A radix numeration system in which all the digit places have the same radix. The weights of successive digit places are successive integral powers of the radix, each multiplied by the same factor, and negative powers are used to represent fractions. A fixed-radix numeration system is a special case of a mixed-radix numeration system in which, when terms are ordered in descending magnitude of bases, the integral ratio between the bases of adjacent terms is the same; for example, if b is the smallest base and if x represents an integer, the numeral 782 represents the number given by $7x^2 b + 8xb + 2b$. (Contrast with *system, mixed-base numeration,* with *system, mixed radix numeration.*)

system, formal—In computer simulation, a system in which all component parts, entities, events, operations, properties and relationships are either deterministically describable or are describable by sets of rules that define their combinations and interrelationships, with appropriate allowances made for the validity of assertions and assumptions.

system, information—The entire collection of procedures, operations, and functions devoted toward the generation, collection, evaluation, storage, retrieval, and dissemination of data and information within an organization or area in order to promote the flow of information from source to user.

system, information feedback—In data communications, a data transmission system that uses an echo check to verify the accuracy of transmission.

system, management information—An information system designed and operated to assist in decision-making at any specified management level or set of levels. Many modern management information systems are fully automated from source data automation to online, real time storage, retrieval and display of data with operation in a conversational mode.

system, mixed-base numeration—A numeration system that represents a number as the sum of a series of terms, each term consisting of a mantissa, or coefficient, and a base, the base being constant for a given application but there are not necessarily integral ratios between the bases of all the terms; for example if the bases of a number are b_3, , b_2, and b_1, and the mantissae are 7, 5, and 3, the number represented is given by $7b_3 + 5b_2 + 3b_1$. (Contrast with *system, mixed-radix numeration,* and with *system, fixed-radix numeration.*)

system, mixed-radix numeration—A radix numeration system in which digit places do not all have the same radix; for example, the numeration system in which four successive digits, that is adjacent digits, are used to represent tens of hours, hours, tens of minutes, and minutes. Taking one minute as the unit, the weights of the four digit places are 600, 60, 10, and 1 respectively. A numeration system expressing years, months, days, and hours to represent hours would not satisfy the definition of a radix numeration system because the ratio of weights of say the day and tens of hours digit places would not

be an integer. A mixed-radix numeration system is a special case of a mixed-base numeration system in which, when terms are ordered in descending magnitude of bases, there is an integral ratio between the bases of adjacent terms; for example, if b is the smallest base and if x and y represent integers, the numeral 782 represents the number given by $7xyb + 8xb + 2b$. (Contrast with *system, fixed-radix numeration,* and with *system, mixed-base numeration.*)

system, monitor—Same as *system, operating.*

system, number—Same as *system, numeration.*

system, number representation—Same as *system, numeration.*

system, numeral—Same as *system, numeration.*

$$a_1 r^n + a_2 r^{n-1} + a_3 r^{n-2}$$
$$+ \ldots a_{n+1} r^0 \; . + a_{n+2} r^{-1}$$
$$+ a_{n+3} r^{-2} + a_{n+4} r^{-3}$$
$$+ \ldots a_{n+m+1} r^{-m}$$

The general form of a numeral in a fixed-radix positional numeration system. The value represented by the numeral is the sum of the terms. The radix point is immediately to the right of the r^0 term. Thus, decimal 648.53 is $6 \times 10^2 + 4 \times 10^1 + 8 \times 10^0 . + 5 \times 10^{-1} + 3 \times 10^{-2}$.

system, numeration—A method or notation used to represent numbers to indicate quantities. Most numeration systems use sytematic methods for representing numerical quantities in which any quantity is represented by the sequence of digits obtained by having coefficients multiply successive powers of a radix. Usually, each succeeding coefficient from right to left multiplies one higher power of the radix. The first coefficient left of the arithmetic point is associated with the zero power of the radix. In decimal notation, the radix is 10, and 267.43 actually represents $2 \times 10^2 + 6 \times 10^1 + 7 \times 10^0 + 4 \times 10^{-1} + 3 \times 10^{-2}$. The following are the names of number systems sequentially from one to 20; unary, binary, ternary, quaternary, quinary, senary, septenary, octal (octonary), novenary, decimal, unodecimal, duodecimal, terdenary, quaterdenary, quindenary, sexadecimal (hexadecimal), septendecimal, octodenary, novendenary, and vicenary. Duosexadecimal (duotricinary) is 32 and sexagenary (sexagesimal) is 60. Binary, octal, binary-coded-decimal, and sexadecimal are often used in electronic digital computers. Most often the numerals are used to express the radix, such as radix two or radix 16. In most number systems, a positional notation is used such that the weights of adjacent positions bear a constant ratio to one another. This ratio is the radix. Thus, in decimal notation, the thousands position and the hundreds position are adjacent and have a ratio of 10, the radix. In mixed-radix systems, this is not the case; the radices of adjacent positions may differ. (Synonymous with *number representation system*, with *number system*, and with *numeral system*.)

system, octal number—Same as *notation, octal*.

system, operating—In computer programming, the totality of all software, such as executive routines, call routines, loading routines, working routines, together with priorities, associated data, and related software to permit total system operation, including necessary arrangements for assignment of available hardware, storage, and central-processing unit allocation, control of queuing, input-output operations, receipt and transmission, and general control of data flow. Complete operating systems are necessary when organizing multiprocessing by both parallel processing (simultaneous use of several pieces of equipment, particulary main frames or central processing units) and multiprogramming (timesharing of equipment running several interleaved programs). (Synonymous with *monitor system* and with *executive system*. Further clarified by *system, programming* and by *routine, executive*. Closely related to *program, master-control*.)

system, positional representation—A numeration system in which a real number is represented by an ordered set of characters in such a way that the amount contributed by a character to the number depends upon its position in the numeral and on its own value; for example the 8 in the decimal numeral 6853 contributes 800 to the number because it is the third digit from the right and it has a value of eight.

system, programming—The collection of programs and programming languages and techniques for using these for a specific computing system. The programming system forms a part of the operating system. (Further clarified by *system, operating*.)

system, pure-binary numeration—A fixed-radix positional numeration system that uses numerals with binary digits, a radix of 2 and descending powers of 2, from left to right, to indicate the value

each digit contributes to the value expressed by the numeral, the one digit usually indicating the power is to be added, the zero indicating the power is not to be added, thus using straight binary numerals; for example, a numeration system in which 110.01 is equivalent to $2^2 + 2^1 + 2^{-2}$, or decimal 6.25.

system, radix numeration—Same as *notation, radix*.

system, slave—A system connected to another system in such a manner as to follow it, precisely imitating every event or operation within the master system.

system, uniterm—A scheme for the storage and retrieval of information through the use of an index consisting of uniterms. (Further clarified by *descriptor* and by *uniterm*.)

system, variable-length record—Same as *file, variable-length record*.

system, variable-point representation—A radix numeration system in which the position of the radix point, such as the decimal point or the binary point, is explicitly indicated by a special character at that position.

system, Zatocoding—Same as *indexing, coordinate*.

system analysis—See *analysis, system*.

system availability—See *availability, system*.

system check—See *check, system*.

system degradation—See *degradation, system*.

system engineering—See *engineering, system*.

system generation, operating—See *generation, operating system*.

system initialization—See *initialization, system*.

system interrogation—See *interrogation, system*.

system library—Same as *library, public*.

system maintenance, dynamic—See *maintenance, dynamic system*.

system maintenance, operating—See *maintenance, operating system*.

system management, operating—See *management, operating system*.

system production mode—See *mode, system production*.

system reconfiguration, operating—See *reconfiguration, operating system*.

system residence device, operating—See *device, operating system residence*.

system resource—See *resource, system*.

system standard—See *standard, system*.

system start-up—Same as *initialization, system*.

system test—See *test, system*.

system test mode—See *mode, system test*.

t

T-dimension—The dimension of the crimped portion of an electrical connector measured between two opposite points on the crimped surface. (Synonymous with *G-dimension*. Further clarified by *depth, crimp*.)

tab—1: A marker or label, positioned so as to permit quick identification. **2:** Abbreviation for tabulating machine or tabulating equipment.

table—A collection of data, usually arranged in an array where each item in the array is uniquely identifiable by some label or by its relative position. Items in a table are easier to locate or identify, and so provide a ready reference. A table may be stored in a computer, sometimes such that row and column numbers in the table correspond to storage location addresses. Thus, a table is an organized collection of data. Usually, each individual table is a two-dimensional array.

ANGLE θ	SIN θ
0	0
$\pi/6$	0.500
$\pi/4$	0.707
$\pi/3$	0.866
$\pi/2$	1.000

A table of values of the sine of various angles in radian measure.

table, Boolean operation—An operation table that shows how each of a set of operands and results take one of two values.

table, decision—A table of possible courses of action, alternatives, or contingencies to be considered in the description of a problem, with the actions to be taken. Decision tables are often used in place of flowcharts for problem description, analysis, and accompanying documentation.

table, function—Two or more sets of data arranged so that it is possible to have an entry in one set select one or more entries in the remaining sets; for example, a dictionary, a device constructed of hardware, or a routine, which can decode multiple inputs into a single output, or encode a single input into multiple outputs; a tabulation of the values of a function for a set of values of the

independent variable; a bank or an array of interconnected switches for accomplishing specific purposes. The ENIAC computer used function tables in the form of banks of switches that are set to determine program steps and enter constants. DAFT is an example of another type of function table.

table, operation—Same as *table, truth*.

table, output—Same as *board, plotting*.

table, plotting—See *board, plotting*.

table, symbol—A mapping of a set of symbols to words, numerals, or other symbols, usually in the form of an array with corresponding pairs of entries adjacent to one another.

table, truth—A representation of a logic or switching function, in which all possible configurations of the argument, values such as 0 and 1, T and F, or similar representation, for truth and falsity are given, along with the truth or falsity of each configuration. The number of configurations is 2N, where N is the number of arguments, unless the function is incompletely specified; that is, there are *don't care* conditions. Also, if N = 2, there are four configurations of the independent variables, giving rise to 16 possible different sets of values for the function; for example, for the function P AND Q, expressed also as $P \wedge Q$, $P \cdot Q$, or PQ, the truth table is given in the illustration. (Synonymous with *operation, table*.)

P	Q	PQ
0	0	0
0	1	0
1	0	0
1	1	1

A truth table showing the positive AND logic function.

table block—See *block, table*.

table look-up—See *look-up, table*.

table-look-up instruction—See *instruction, table-look-up*.

table simulator—See *simulator, table*.

TABSOL—(Tabular Systems Oriented Language). A programming system developed by General Electric Company for the GE 225 computer.

tabulate—To form data into an array; for example, in punch-card equipment, to print totals, differences, or similar data on the basis of one line of print per group of data, such as a record or set of cards. Each total may be controlled by a separate or different key. Whenever the key changes, such as when a total break occurs, the completed total is usually printed and also added to the next higher level of totals. The completed-total pocket is then reset to zero for accumulation on the next key value. (Contrast with *list*.)

tabulating equipment—See *equipment, tabulating*.

tabulation character, horizontal—See *character, horizontal tabulation*.

tabulation character, vertical—See *character, vertical tabulation*.

tabulator—A machine that reads data from one medium, such as punched cards, paper tape, magnetic tape, or computer storage, and produces lists, tables, and totals on separate sheets, forms, or continuous paper. (Contrast with *printer*.)

TAC—(Transac Assembler Compiler). A compiler system developed by Philco Ford Corporation for the Transac 2000 computer.

tag—1: Same as *flag*. 2: One or more characters attached or associated with a set of data that contains or expresses information about the set, including identification. 3: Same as *flag*.

take-down—Pertaining to actions performed at the end of an equipment operating cycle, preliminary to preparing the equipment for the next setup; for example, to remove tapes of a prior run from the tape handlers or stations, or to remove accumulated cards in sorter hoppers subsequent to a run. (Contrast with *setup*.)

take-down time—See *time, take-down*.

take-up reel—See *reel, take-up*.

talk, cross—See *crosstalk*.

tank—1: Same as *circuit, tank*. 2: Same as *tank, mercury*.

tank, mercury—A container of mercury used as part of an acoustic mercury delay-line. Pairs of transducers, such as quartz crystals, are placed at each end, if the tank is a tube, or diagonally across from one another, if the tank is a tub, and are used to launch the acoustic waves representing the data. (Further explained by *delay-line, acoustic* and by *storage, mercury*.)

tank circuit—See *circuit, tank*.

tape—In computers and data processing, a linear storage medium. The tape may be reeled, spooled, or spindled; used as input, output, internal, or external storage; and is usually paper or magnetic. Some computer tapes are continuous loops.

tape, carriage control—A tape that contains data for controlling the movement of the carriage of a printing device such as controlling vertical or horizontal positioning of a carriage or a paper feed mechanism.

tape, chadded—Tape with the data holes fully punched and so chad results. Most computer paper tapes are chadded types. (Contrast with *tape, chadless*.)

tape, chadless—Punched tape in which chad does not result; that is, the would-be holes are only partially cut, leaving the material that would be removed as chad hanging to the tape like a hinged-lid, permitting mechanical reading of the tape, permitting printing to be placed on the tape, avoiding the presence of chad, and preventing the tapes from being read photoelectrically. Chadless tape is commonly used in teletype operations. (Contrast with *tape, chadded*.)

tape, change—A tape that contains data that will be used to update the data on another tape, usually called a master tape, or the data in another medium, such as disc, drum, or magnetic cards. (Synonymous with *transaction tape*.)

tape, core—A ferromagnetic ribbon or foil used to make a tape-wound core. The ribbon is usually wound on a bobbin for mechanical support.

tape, grandfather—A magnetic tape containing the same data that was also on a second tape which was updated in accordance with transactions or latest changes contained on a third tape. The second tape is thus brought up to date. A copy is made, which becomes the new grandfather tape. The series of grandfather tapes provides a historical record, serves as a data base for statistical analysis, permits an audit trail, permits data to be reconstituted if current files are lost or destroyed, or serves other similar purposes. (Further clarified by *cycle, grandfather*.)

tape, instruction—Same as *tape, program*.

tape, library—A tape, usually a magnetic tape, that has been withdrawn from a stored, indexed collection of tapes held for ready use. The library tape is distinguished from other tapes only in the sense that the library tape is normally kept in the library when it is not in use and also is made generally available, in contrast to other tapes lying around, held by a specific division, available from other sources, or coming from data files. Library tapes usually contain general routines and subroutines required for operation of a computing center. (Further clarified by *library, routine* and by *library, tape*.)

tape, magnetic—A tape with a surface of magnetic material, such as iron oxide, on which data can be stored by selective polarization of portions of the surface or that can be used as the constituent in tape-wound magnetic cores. Most tapes are an oxide-coated polyester film, such as an oriented polyethylene terephthalate film or its equivalent. (Synonymous with *storage tape*. Further clarified by *unit, tape*.)

tape, master—A tape, usually magnetic, that contains the main program or the master file of data. The master tape is updated by the data contained on the change tape. A master tape might contain all the payroll data, 5000 social security accounts, or 1000 inventory items; that is, it is simply a file of data, or it may be a main program tape. In the latter case, the change tape will contain program changes.

tape, master instruction—A tape, usually a magnetic tape, that contains many or all of the routines or programs for a run, or a group of runs, or that forms part of an operating system. Abbreviated MIT. (Synonymous with *master program tape*.)

tape, master program—Same as *tape, master instruction*.

tape, Mylar—In data processing, a tape made of Mylar, a trademarked E. I. Dupont de Nemours and Company polyester film, usually with a magnetic oxide coating for storing data as magnetized spots on its surface.

tape, paper—In data processing, a linear or ribbonlike strip of paper on which data may be stored, such as by punching holes or printing, and which may be reeled, spindled, or looped; for example, punched paper tape, adding machine tape, cash register tape, or chadless teletype tape. Most paper tape is punched tape. (Further explained by *tape, punched paper*.)

tape, perforated—Same as *tape, punched*.

tape, perforated paper—Same as *tape, punched paper*.

tape, program—A tape that contains the sequence of instructions that are to be executed by a computer in solving a problem. The instructions may remain on the tape and be executed as they are read, or the instructions may be stored in internal or high-speed storage and be called from there in sequence and executed, disconnecting the tape reader during program execution. (Synonymous with *instruction tape* and with *sequence-control tape*.)

—| |—ROW PITCH

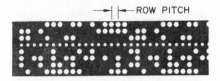

A seven-hole punched tape.

tape, punched—A tape that contains data in the form of a pattern of holes or cuts. Punched tape is usually paper unless it is to be used repeatedly, such as a loop of punched fabric tape used to control

format on a printer. The holes and cuts are in rows and columns. On cards, a character is the hole pattern of a column. On paper tape, the pattern of each row of holes is a character, along with a paper-tape feed-row of holes for moving the tape. If there are holes, it's chadded tape. If there are only cuts, the tape is chadless. (Synonymous with *perforated tape*. Further explained by *tape, punched paper*.)

tape, punched paper—Paper tape on which a pattern of holes or cuts is used to represent data. (Synonymous with *perforated paper tape*. Further explained by *tape, paper* and by *tape, punched*.)

tape, sequence-control—Same as *tape, program*.

tape, transaction—Same as *tape, change*.

tape base—See *base tape*.

tape bin—See *bin, tape*.

tape bound—Same as *limited, tape*.

tape cable—See *cable, tape*.

tape cartridge—See *cartridge tape*.

tape coil, blank paper—See *coil, blank paper tape*.

tape coil, virgin paper—See *coil, virgin paper-tape*.

tape comparator—See *comparator, tape*.

tape-controlled carriage—See *carriage, tape-controlled*.

tape core—Same as *core, tape-wound*.

tape deck—Same as *drive tape*.

tape drive—See *drive, tape*.

tape feed—See *feed, tape*.

tape file—See *file, tape*.

tape input—See *input, tape*.

tape leader—See *leader, tape*.

tape library—See *library, tape*.

tape limited—See *limited, tape*.

tape-loop storage—See *storage, tape-loop*.

tape parity—See *parity, tape*.

tape perforator—Same as *punch, tape*.

tape punch—See *punch, tape*.

tape punch, automatic—See *punch, automatic tape*.

tape punch, output—Same as *punch, automatic tape*.

tape reader—See *reader, tape*.

tape reader, magnetic—See *reader, magnetic-tape*.

tape-servo swap—See *swap, tape-servo*.

tape skip—See *skip tape*.

tape sort, four—See *sort, four-tape*.

tape spool—See *spool, tape*.

tape station—Same as *unit, tape*.

tape storage—Same as *tape, magnetic*.

tape storage, magnetic—See *storage, magnetic-tape*.

tape switching center, torn—See *center, torn-tape switching*.

tape synchronizer—See *synchronizer, tape*.

tape-to-card—Pertaining to equipment or methods that transmit data from tape, such as magnetic or punched tape, to cards, such as magnetic or punched cards. Such conversion or transmission is usually performed offline on peripheral or auxiliary equipment.

tape trailer—See *trailer, tape.*

tape transmitter-distributor—Same as *reader, tape.*

tape transport—Same as *drive, tape.*

tape unit—See *unit, tape.*

tape verifier—See *verifier, tape.*

tape-wound core—See *core, tape-wound.*

tapped-potentiometer function-generator—See *generator, tapped-potentiometer function.*

target computer—See *computer, target.*

target language—See *language, target.*

target program—See *program, target.*

target routine—Same as *program, target.*

tariff—In communications, the cost rate charged for a particular data handling, such as transmission, service of a common carrier.

TASCON—(Television Automatic Sequence Control). A television control technique developed by Bunker-Ramo Corporation.

task—1: A basic unit of work directed by a control program, executive routine, or operating system. 2: A computer program, or a part of a computer program capable of being specified to the control program as a unit of work in a multi-programming, multi-processing or parallel processing environment. Tasks compete for essential and limited system resources. System resources are assigned to tasks and released when the task is completed.

taxonomy—The science of classification. Problems in taxonomy are often handled with the assistance of digital computers.

technical information center—See *center, technical information.*

technique—Same as *method.*

telecommunications—The science of communication by electric, electronic, or electromagnetic means, particularly the transmission of signals over long distances, such as telegraph, radio, television, telephone, or microwave.

telegraph abstract—See *abstract, telegraphic.*

telegraph rate—See *rate, telegraph.*

telemeter—The transmission of measurements over long distances, usually by electric, electronic, or electromagnetic means; for example, to transmit analog or digital signals measuring temperature and pressure from a missile or rocket to a ground station. Usually a transducer is used to convert the quantity being measured to electrical signals, which are transmitted to the distant location, then converted to an analog or digital indicator of the quantity measured, like a pen recorder, a digital numeral for storage on tape, or a visual display.

telephone, electrically powered—A telephone whose operating power is obtained either from batteries located at the telephone (local battery) or from a telephone central office (common battery). (Contrast with *telephone, sound-powered.*)

telephone, sound-powered—A telephone whose operating power is obtained from the speech input only, such as from a diaphragm vibrating in a magnetic field or from the piezoelectric effect. (Contrast with *telephone, electrically powered.*)

telephone circuit, data—See *circuit, data telephone.*

telephone local center—Same as *center, local switching.*

telephone local exchange center—Same as *center, local exchange switching.*

telephone network, private—See *network, private telephone.*

telephone primary center—Same as *center, primary switching.*

telephone secondary center—Same as *center, secondary switching.*

telephone switchboard, manual—Same as *exchange, manual.*

telephone trunk—See *trunk, telephone.*

telephone zone center—Same as *center, zone switching.*

teleprinter—A Western Union telegraphic terminal printer.

teleprocessing—Data processing through the use of a combination of data processors, or computers, and telecommunications facilities.

telesynd—Remote control equipment, such as telemeter equipment, that is synchronous in both speed and position.

teletype—Trademark of Teletype Corporation for its communication system equipment, involving keyboard, paper tape, and printed page, and sending and receiving equipment.

Teletype code—Same as *code, Baudot.*

Teletypewriter—An American Telephone and Telegraph terminal equipment that permits sending by a manual keyboard and receiving on a printed page, much like an electric typewriter, except that it encodes the characters for long distance transmission, and decodes incoming signals into printed characters.

Teletypewriter Exchange Service—See *Service, Teletypewriter Exchange.*

teletypewriter marking pulse—See *pulse, teletypewriter marking.*

teletypewriter pulse spacing—See *spacing, teletypewriter pulse.*

teletypewriter signal distortion—See *distortion, teletypewriter signal.*

Telex—Automatic long-distance printing exchange service provided in the United States by Western Union.

Telpak—A service offered by American Telephone and Telegraph Company in which wide-band communication channels are leased for a specified tariff.

temporary connection—See *connection, temporary.*

temporary entity—See *entity, temporary.*

temporary storage—See *storage, temporary.*

tens complement—See *complement, tens.*

terminal—In communications, a point at which data can enter or leave a communication network.

terminal, data—A device that modulates, encodes, demodulates, or decodes data

terminal, display — test, program

between an input-output device and a data transmission link, line, or network.

terminal, display—In display systems, a terminal consisting of one or more display devices and one or more input-output devices, such as tablets, joy sticks, control balls, light pens, alphanumeric keyboards, function keys, and tape readers.

terminal, job-oriented—In communications, a point at which data for a specific application can enter or leave a communication network; that is, a point at which specific operations are performed on or with the data.

terminal, multiplex data—A device that modulates, encodes, demodulates, or decodes data between two or more input-output devices and a data transmission link.

terminal, user—An input-output unit that a human being may use to communicate with an automatic data processing system usually in a conversational mode, rather than for diagnostics, repair, or maintenance. Such terminals are used in data storage and retrieval systems on a conversational basis rather than in a batch processing mode.

terminal device—Same as *unit, terminal.*

terminal-digit posting—See *posting, terminal-digit.*

terminal equipment—See *equipment, terminal.*

terminal equipment, data—See *unit, terminal.*

terminal identification—See *identification, terminal.*

terminal impedance—See *impedance, terminal.*

terminal installation—See *installation, terminal.*

terminal trunk—See *trunk, terminal.*

terminal unit—See *unit, terminal.*

terminating symbol—See *symbol, terminating.*

termination, abnormal—In a computer run or during computer program execution, the termination of a program, routine, subroutine, job, task, or run prior to its normal completion due to an error condition or malfunction. (Contrast with *termination, normal.*)

termination, normal—The termination of a computer run, job, task, or program after its completion. (Contrast with *termination, abnormal.*)

termination processing, program—See *processing, program termination.*

terminology—The set of words or terms used in a particular discipline or field, such as engineering terminology or medical terminology. When ordered and defined, the terminology becomes a dictionary, a glossary, or a lexicon.

ternary—Pertaining to a characteristic or property involving a selection, choice, or condition in which there are three possibilities, that is, pertaining to three; for example, pertaining to the numeration system with a radix of three. A ternary choice is a choice from among three possibilities.

ternary incremental representation—See *representation, ternary incremental.*

ternary notation—See *notation, ternary.*

ternary operator—See *operator, ternary.*

test, bias—Same as *test, marginal.*

test, compatibility—A test run on a given set of equipment (hardware) and programs (software) to determine how well the components function as a system.

test, crippled-leapfrog—A variation of the leapfrog test; that is, a leapfrog test modified so that the arithmetic and logic operations are repeated from a single set or all of the storage locations rather than from a changing set of locations; hence, the test routine does not leap and is termed crippled. (Further explained by *test, leapfrog.*)

test, destructive—An equipment test which results in a permanent drastic degradation in the performance of the equipment; for example, applying high voltages and currents to computer circuits until elements burn, burst, smoke, shatter, or are otherwise destroyed or lost.

test, diagnostic—A test designed to detect and locate malfunctions or incipient malfunctions in a system, usually through the use of a diagnostic routine.

test, leapfrog—A test of computer storage controlled by a routine designed to discover computer malfunction, characterized by the property that it performs a series of arithmetic and logic operations from one set of storage locations, checks the accuracy of transfer to another set of storage locations, then repeats the set of arithmetic and logic operations over again, repeating the process until all storage locations have been used, checking every possible position in storage, and then beginning again. The actual execution of operations is also checked; however, the primary purpose is to test the storage. The term leapfrog comes from the indicated jump in the position of the test routine as seen on a monitoring cathode-ray tube when the routine moves to a new storage area. (Further clarified by *test, crippled-leapfrog.*)

test, marginal—A test of equipment in which environmental or operating conditions under which the equipment is to perform are altered so as to induce failures or allow the detection of faults so as to measure the permissible operating margins as well as detect incipient failures. For example, the clock-pulse amplitude could be reduced or the frequency increased until a failure occurs and the failed items could be replaced. Marginal checks are made during marginal tests. (Synonymous with *bias test*. Further clarified by *check, marginal.*)

test, program—A test of a computer and its program by running the program in order to discover errors in the program or malfunctions in the computer, usually by built-in checks, programmed checks, or comparison of results with known results. (Closely related to *test, routine*.)

test, routine—A test designed to ensure that a routine has been properly written and that there are no mistakes in it; for example, to run a routine with sample data and known answers so as to check the routine. (Synonymous with *subroutine test*. Closely related to *test, program*.)

test, subroutine—Same as *test, routine*.

test, system—Actual running of all types of applications on the complete system, using actual data and comparing results with known data, for purposes of testing the accuracy, capability, and adequacy of the entire system; for example, a system integration test to determine whether subsystems, operators, and programmed computer functions operate together consistently and reliably under actual operating conditions.

test, volume—A test of a computer based on the use of a large volume of actual data and having a program process the data in order to determine that all conditions have been adequately provided for.

test case—See *case, test*.

test data—See *data, test*.

test mode, system—See *mode, system test*.

test problem—Same as *problem, check*.

test program—Same as *routine, test*.

test routine—See *routine, test*.

test tone power, standard—See *power, standard test tone*.

testing time—Same as *time, proving*.

tetrad—A group of four items; for example, a group of four bits, such as pulses, used to express a decimal digit or a sexadecimal digit in binary form. (Further clarified by *numeral, sexadecimal*. Closely related to *quartet*.)

tetrode—A four-electrode active electronic device; for example, a four-electrode vacuum tube, containing a cathode, a plate or anode, a control grid, and a screen grid; or a four-electrode transistor.

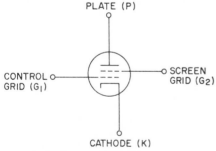

A tetrode showing plate, cathode, and two grids.

TEX—An automatic Teleprinter exchange service provided by Western Union.

text—In communications, the part of the message that contains the information to be conveyed, from the source to the ultimate destination. Usually the text is transmitted as a single entity.

theory, automata—Theory related to the study of the principles of operation, the application, and the behavioral characteristics of automatic devices.

theory, communication—The mathematical discipline dealing with the probabilistic features of data transmission in the presence of noise. Communication theory is usually considered to be included within information theory. (Further clarified by *theory, information*.)

theory, group—Theory related to behavior of combinations of sets and elements, particularly in the mathematical sense, and the application of the rules involved, including the use and application of groups, or sets. (Synonymous with *set theory*.)

theory, information—1: Theory concerned with the likelihood of the transmission of messages, accurate to within specified limits, when the bits of information comprising the message are subject to certain probabilities of transmission failure, distortion, and accidental additions called noise. Related to probability theory and certain analytical processes transferred from the communications field and operations research, information theory evaluates the effectiveness of information within a system. Applied initially to electrical communications networks, it has had an indirect influence in stimulating the examinations of business organizational structures with a view toward improving information flow. 2: The branch of science concerned with measures of information and their properties. Information theory includes communication theory. (Further clarified by *theory, communication*.)

theory, probability—Theory pertaining to the likelihood of occurrence of a chance event. Probability theory is used to analyze, synthesize, and predict the behavior of a group, rather than the behavior of a single item in the group.

theory, queuing—A form of probability theory pertaining to the movement in time and space of discrete units through channels. The capability or characteristics of the channel must in some way restrict or influence the flow in the channel. (Further clarified by *queuing*.)

theory, set—Same as *theory, group*.

theory, switching—Theory pertaining to the operation and behavior of combinational logic; that is, switching networks, sequential logic elements, and types of automata, such as Turing machines, digital computers, and coincidence gating circuits.

thermistor—A resistor whose temperature coefficient of resistance is very high, nonlinear, and negative. It is a solid-state semiconducting material, usually made by sintering mixtures of the oxide powders of various metals. It is made in many shapes of beads, discs, flakes, washers, and rods, to which contact wires are attached. Thus, as the temperature changes, the electrical resistance of the thermistor varies. It can be used as a temperature-sensing or measuring device.

thermocouple—A device consisting of two bimetal joints, such as two wires of different metal whose ends are connected to each other, forming a single loop, and having the property that if the two junctions are maintained at different temperatures, a difference of electric potential is brought into existence, which is equally divided between the two junctions. The thermocouple can be used to measure temperature when the thermocouple is calibrated with a meter inserted into the loop to measure the current.

thesaurus—**1:** A collection of alphabetized terms with other closely related synonyms and near meanings associated with each alphabetized term. The thesaurus is used to seek more precise, more colorful, or more specific terms. **2:** A collection of words or terms used to classify, index, store, and retrieve information in a data bank. The terms serve as labels. They usually are keywords, descriptors, or data elements found in the text or data being indexed. The thesaurus may be an alphabetized word list or it may be hierarchically structured into specialized fields, subareas, or detailed subject matter. The entries may be single words or multiple words. When the references are cited along with the thesaurus, it becomes an index. The terms may be coded for mechanization convenience.

thin-film, magnetic—A layer of magnetic material usually less than one micron, or one-millionth of a meter (10,000 Angstroms) thick, deposited on a substrate material, such as glass or a resin, and used to store binary digits. The films may be continuous, small spots, and multilayer. Deposited or etched conductors are placed under or on top of the films. The films are magnetically polarized by the current in the conductors, at certain spots.

thin-film storage, magnetic—See *storage, magnetic thin-film.*

third generation—See *generation, third.*

third-generation hardware—See *hardware, third-generation.*

third-generation logical-organization—See *logical-organization, third-generation.*

third-generation software—See *software, third-generation.*

third-level address—See *address, third-level.*

thirty-nine feature code—See *code, thirty-nine feature.*

THOR—(Tape Handling Optional Routines). A set of tape routines for controlling magnetic tape operations, such as positioning, copying, writing, correcting, or editing tapes. Any discrepancies are printed. THOR was developed by Honeywell Data Processing Division.

threaded file—Same as *file, chained.*

three-address—Pertaining to a machine instruction which explicitly refers to or describes three storage locations. A typical three-address instruction includes the address of one operand, say the multiplicand; the address of another operand, say the multiplier; the operation to be performed, in this case multiplication; and the address of the storage location for the result, or product. The machine then automatically proceeds to the next instruction to be executed. Examples of three-address machines are the U.S. Army BRLESC, the Datamatic 1000, Honeywell 400, and National 304. Three-address instructions require fairly long words if large storage capacity is to be addressed. (Synonymous with *triple-address.*)

three-address code—Same as *instruction, three-address.*

three-address instruction—See *instruction, three-address.*

three-bit byte—Same as *triplet.*

three-input adder—Same as *adder.*

three-input subtracter—Same as *subtracter.*

three-level addressing—See *addressing, three-level.*

three-plus-one address instruction—See *instruction, three-plus-one address.*

THRESHOLD—A logic operator having the property that if P is a statement, Q is a statement, R is a statement, . . . , then the THRESHOLD of P, Q, R, . . . is true if *n* or more statements are true and false if less than *n* statements are true, where *n* is a specified nonnegative integer called the threshold condition.

threshold element—See *element, threshold.*

threshold function—See *function, threshold.*

threshold operation—See *operation, threshold.*

through, print—See *print-through.*

through-trunk supervision—See *supervision, through-trunk.*

throughput—**1:** The total productive work of a system, all the way from preparing input data and programs through to utilization of output data. Compiling, debugging, production time, and effort are all included, as well as work accomplished by all programmers, system operators, and the system. **2:** A measure of the amount of work performed by a computing system over a given period of time. A unit of measure of throughput might be jobs per day or tasks per hour.

throw, paper—The movement of paper in a printer through a distance greater than the normal line spacing without printing. The speed for throw is usually greater than for the single-line feed. (Synonymous with *paper slew.*)

thyratron—A hot-cathode gas tube in which one or more electrodes control the start of a unidirectional flow of current. Once flow is started, the control electrode loses control. If the flow is stopped, say from a negative anode, the control electrode regains control. The thyratron is a good control device for discharging through the coils of a hammer for a printer, since the precise instant of firing is accurately controllable and a large current can be initiated at this precise time.

ticket converter—See *converter, ticket.*

tickler file—See *file, tickler.*

tie line—Same as *link, communication.*

time, acceleration—In magnetic tape station operation, the time between the interpretation of a tape read or write instruction and the availability of data for transmission from or to the tape, or the initiation of such transmission. This time is nearly the time the tape requires to come up to read or write speed from standstill. (Contrast with *time, deceleration.*)

time, access—The time interval between the instant at which data is called for from a storage device and the instant at which delivery is completed; for example, the time interval between the instant at which data is requested to be stored and the instant at which storage is completed. In some cases the access time can be the read time; the write time; the latency plus the word time (for serial storage); the time required to condition a storage device to receive or transmit data after the instruction to do so is given; the time required to transmit words to or from storage; the time interval between the instant at which the control unit calls for a transmission of data to or from a storage device and the instant at which the operation is completed, that is, the sum of the transmission time and the waiting time; the time required for a computer to locate data in a storage device and to transmit it to an arithmetic unit; the time required to fetch data; or the time required to return it.

time, action—In computer simulation, the number of simulated clock units required for a transaction in a simulation system.

time, actual—Same as *time, real.*

time, add—The time required to perform one addition of two quantities, not including the time required to obtain the quantities from storage and store the result. In most digital computers, the add time is the time required to add two words of specified length, usually the fixed word-length for fixed word-length machines. For variable word-length machines, the word-length must be specified for the add time quoted.

time, assembling—The time required to execute an assembler, that is, an assembly program; thus, the time required to assemble a program.

time, available—The time that a device may be used or is used. During such time, the power is on, and the device is not under maintenance and is known to be in proper operating conditon. Available time can range up to 24 hours in a day. (Contrast with *time, up.* Further clarified by *availability* and by *ratio, operating.*)

time, average operation—The time required for a computer to perform a specified set of operations divided by the number of operations; for example, the average time required to perform one add, one multiply, and one divide operation; that is, the sum of the three operation times divided by three.

time, awaiting-repair—The time interval between the reporting of a suspected fault and the commencement of repair operations, including the time required to trace and diagnose the fault and obtain materials, equipment, assistance, or advice. If the computer is found to be free of faults, the time lost is *operating delay time.* The time between the occurrence of a fault and the commencement of repair operations is unattended time.

time, carry—The time required for transferring all carry digits to their next higher columns; that is, to their respective digit positions, where they are to be added.

time, code checking—Machine time devoted to ensuring that the machine is set up correctly and that the program to be executed is coded correctly.

time, compiling—The elapsed time required to compile a computer program.

time, cycle—**1:** The time interval required to complete a cycle or traverse a loop. **2:** In regenerative or destructive-read storage devices, the time required to obtain data from storage, restore the data that has been read, and ready the device for the next request for data. The cycle time includes the access time and the regeneration time, plus any additional time until a new request can be accepted. (Further clarified by *cycle, storage.*)

time, dead—Any time delay between two successive actions of the same system.

time, debatable—Machine time lost due to unknown or questionable causes; for example, time lost when there is insufficient evidence to show conclusively whether the delay is caused by a computer malfunction, a program, error, or a human operator's mistake.

time, decay—The time required for a transient phenomenon to reach a specified fraction of its original value; for example, the time required for a voltage to reach 10 percent of its full or original value. (Further clarified by *time, pulse decay.*)

time, deceleration—The time required for a moving medium to stop moving, from the instant at which the stopping action is initiated until the instant at which the medium stops; for example, the time required for a moving magnetic tape to come to a halt or the time required for a drum or disc to stop from the time the driving torque is removed. (Contrast with *time, acceleration.*)

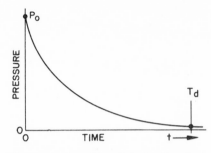

The decay time, T_d, *might be the time required for the pressure to reach 1 percent of its initial value, P_0.*

time, deferred maintenance—Time used to perform corrective maintenance. Corrective maintenance is usually considered to be performed on an unscheduled basis. Preventive maintenance is usually scheduled. Thus, the terms *scheduled maintenance time* and *unscheduled maintenance* time are applicable and are somewhat self-explanatory.

time, development—Computer time used for debugging new routines or new equipment.

time, digit—Same as *period, digit.*

time, down—The time during which a device is not functioning correctly due to a fault or failure. Down time consists of awaiting repair time, repair delay time, repair time, and machine-spoiled work time. Scheduled engineering time may or may not be considered as down time, inasmuch as the machine is not malfunctioning, yet neither is it available for useful work. (Contrast with *delay, operating.*)

time, effective—Time in which equipment is in use, including production time, program development time, and incidental time. (Synonymous with *operational use time.*)

time, elapsed—1: In computer simulation, the time required to complete an activity from start to finish. 2: The time required by an activity from its start to the present or to any specified point in time prior to its completion.

time, engineering improvement—Computer time for installing, commissioning or acceptance testing, and approving equipment being added to increase the capabilities of the facility. Time spent for modification of existing equipment to improve reliability without adding to the facilities is supplementary maintenance time. Engineering improvement time is a part of scheduled engineering time, along with scheduled maintenance time and supplementary maintenance time. Included are all tests to ensure all improvements are operating satisfactorily.

time, execution—In the execution of a computer instruction, the portion of the execution cycle during which actual work is performed; for example, the time required to perform the addition operation. (Further clarified by *time, instruction.*)

time, fault—Same as *time, down.*

time, idle—Time in which equipment is available for use but is not being used, and no fault is believed present. A test program may be run to warn the operator should a fault occur. Idle time may occur between the completion of one run and the start of the next. (Synonymous with *standby time.*)

time, incidentals—Effective or useful computer time for miscellaneous purposes, such as training, demonstrations, and other than production and program development time.

time, installation—The time required to place a system in operation from the time of its delivery or arrival at the site. Installation time may apply to the main system, satellite, or peripheral equipment. System time used to prove, test, and accept equipment being added, such as a new storage bank, is considered engineering improvement time.

time, instruction—The time required to select, prepare, and interpret an instruction and to step to the next instruction, including access time to storage for both instruction and data. Thus, the instruction time is the time required for the entire instruction execution cycle, except for the execution or operation time. (Further clarified by *time, execution.*)

time, machine-spoiled—Computer time wasted on production runs that are spoiled by computer malfunction. The fault may not halt the run but may hamper it so as to cause the computer to overrun its schedule. Such extension of running time is also machine-spoiled time. Machine-spoiled time is part of down time.

time, maintenance standby—Maintenance staff time during which the maintenance staff is on duty but not engaged in scheduled maintenance, supplementary maintenance, installation, or repair. During maintenance standby time the maintenance staff may be employed in other duties such as maintaining a ready-line of spare parts or constructing new equipment. (Synonymous with *time, standby.*)

time, makeup—The part of available time, usually of a computer, that is used for reruns due to failures or mistakes that occurred during a previous operating time.

time, mean repair—Same as *mean-time-to-repair.*

time, no-charge machine-fault—In a computer installation in which charges are being made for machine time, machine time lost due to a computer malfunction, and therefore time not chargeable to a customer.

time, no-charge nonmachine fault—In a computer installation in which charges are being made for machine time, time lost due to causes other than machine malfunction and not justifiably chargeable to a customer; for example, time spent on duplication (program debugging) in a closed-shop type installation, errors in preparation of input data, misinterpretation of instructions by human operators, and time spent in checking a computer on an unscheduled basis when a machine malfunction is suspected but proved not to exist.

time, nonscheduled maintenance—The time that elapses between the determination of a machine malfunction and its placement back into operation. It includes awaiting repair time, repair delay time, and repair time.

time, off—Time during which a machine is not used, maintained, repaired, or modified. No work is being done by it or on it. The power may or may not be turned off.

time, operating—That part of the available time of a computer during which the hardware is operating and apparently correct results are being obtained. Operating time may be considered to include time for program development, testing, and debugging; time for production or execution of programs; time for making up of lost time due to system malfunctions; and time for such miscellaneous purposes as training, demonstrating, and checking online equipment.

time, operation—The time required to interpret and execute an operation, usually an arithmetic or logic operation; for example, add, subtract, multiply, or compare time. In stating operation time, it is always necessary to indicate whether or not access time to storage for instructions or data is included, and if it has, in what way. The overall time to complete a computer run may be related only indirectly to the sum of individual operation times, due to time overlapping of other parts of the instruction cycle, such as accessing storage and decoding or interpreting the operation part of the instruction word. The interval between initiating successive operations may be less than a complete instruction cycle time.

time, operational use—See *time, effective*.

time, positioning—The time required to mechanically position a transducer relative to the location of the required data on a storage medium; for example, the time required to position a read/write head on a magnetic disc plus the time required for the data to arrive at the read/write head. Thus, the positioning time is the total time required for the data to reach the transducer from the time movement of the transducer is initiated, not just the time required for the transducer to reach a reading position. This latter time is the seek time. (Further clarified by *seek*.)

time, problem—The duration of all or part of a process, usually between two specified events; for example the time between start and stop instructions of a computer program.

time, production—Time devoted to the accomplishment of useful work. The part of computer time, without faults, malfunction, and errors, which is effective but does not include program development time, incidentals time, operative delays, and idle time.

time, program development—Time used to test or debug programs including trials conducted for the development and testing of new procedures and techniques. Program development time is a part of up time and a part of effective time, but does not include production time or incidentals time.

time, program execution—The actual time or the length of time, during which the instructions of an object program, that is, a machine language program, are executed.

time, proving—Time used for testing a machine to ensure that no faults exist. Diagnostic routines are run designed to test every circuit, state, event, and condition. Time spent for testing after a specific type of operational time is included therein. Thus, time spent in testing after a fault repair is included in repair time; after scheduled maintenance, it is included in scheduled maintenance time, and so on.

time, pulse decay—The time required for the trailing edge of a pulse to decline. Usually the time is measured as the time required to drop from 90 percent of full amplitude to 10 percent of full amplitude. (Contrast with *time, pulse rise*. Further clarified by *time, decay*.)

time, pulse rise—The time required for the leading edge of a pulse to rise; that is, for the amplitude to reach a specified value. Usually, the time is measured as the time required to rise from 10 percent of full amplitude to 90 percent of full amplitude. (Contrast with *time, pulse decay*. Further clarified by *time, rise*.)

time, read cycle—The interval of time required to execute a read cycle of a magnetic core storage unit that has separate reading and writing cycles. The read cycle time is measured from corresponding instants of successive read cycles, such as the time between successive starts.

time, real—1: The actual time during which a physical process, event, or phenomenon transpires. 2: Pertaining to the performance of computation during the actual time that the related physical process, event, or phenomenon transpires; for example, pertaining to the computations performed by a controlled-approach aircraft landing system to direct the landing of an aircraft on a runway during a period of zero visibility, or to the operation of a data-processing system that proceeds at the same speed as events being simulated or at sufficient speed to permit analysis or control of external events happening concurrently. Thus, for computations to be considered as taking place in real time, they must proceed fast enough so as to permit the results to influence the related process that is underway.

time, reference—A specifically designated instant of time from which all succeeding instants and their intervals may be measured; for example, an instant near the beginning of a magnetic-core switching cycle chosen as an origin for time measurements, such as the first instant at which the instantaneous value of the drive pulse, response voltage, or the integrated voltage reaches 10 percent of its peak amplitude.

time, repair—Time devoted to actual diagnosing and clearing of faults, including fault detection, location, correction, and related testing. Repair time is part of down time; it includes proving time after repair to determine the effectiveness of the repair, but does not include awaiting repair time, repair delay time, machine spoiled work time, and scheduled engineering time.

time, repair delay—Time during which the maintenance staff is on duty, but the repair is held up due to lack of materials, equipment, advice, or assistance. Repair delay time is that part of down time which does not include repair time and machine spoiled work time, but may include some of awaiting repair time.

time, response—The elapsed time between the dispatch of a specified signal to a receiver and the receipt of a specified response signal by the sender from the receiver. Response time is a significant factor in telecommunication operations, in echo checking operations, and other signalling operations.

time, rise—In pulse circuits, the time required for the leading edge of a pulse to reach a specified amplitude from a specified initial reference level. (Further clarified by *time, pulse rise.*)

time, routine maintenance—Same as *time, scheduled maintenance.*

time, running—The elapsed time required for the execution of a run; for example, the time required for the execution of a target program. (Synonymous with *run duration.*)

time, scheduled engineering—Time during which a system is scheduled to be out of service for effecting engineering improvements, maintenance, and installation. The time may be regularly scheduled or scheduled as required in relation to the work load. Scheduled engineering time is out-of-service time, but is not considered down time, since the system is not malfunctioning.

time, scheduled maintenance—Machine time devoted to repair at a predetermined regular pattern of intervals. Preventive maintenance is performed on a regular basis during scheduled maintenance time.

time, scramble—Computer time during which any programmer may have a program run on the computer if his program is on hand and ready to run. Programs run during scramble time usually must be short, usually urgent, and may only be tried once. A set of scramble time rules are usually prepared. The scramble time period is usually short, such as 15 minutes in the early morning, at noon, and at late afternoon. Scramble time permits quick checks or tests of program parts without waiting longer periods for scheduled computer time.

time, search—The time required to find a particular item of data in a file, without prior knowledge of the address or location of the item. Searching requires comparison of each item in the file with a search key, such as a name, number, or group of characters, until a match or identity is found. Search time is different from access time, which is the time required to obtain data from a specified storage location. The associative storage tends to overcome the difficulties encountered in searching. In effect, associative storage devices look at or search the entire contents in parallel; that is, at once.

time, serviceable—Same as *time, up.*

time, set-up—Time before, after, or between machine runs devoted to manual tasks, such as changing reels of tape, moving cards, tapes, and supplies to and from equipment, in preparation for a new run. (Contrast with *time, takedown.*)

time, standby—1: Same as *time, idle.* 2: Same as *time, maintenance standby.*

time, supplementary maintenance—Time devoted to modifying equipment to improve reliability without adding to

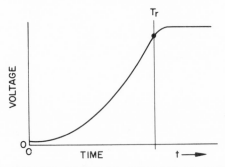

The rise time, T_r, might be the time required for a voltage signal to reach 95 percent of its full value.

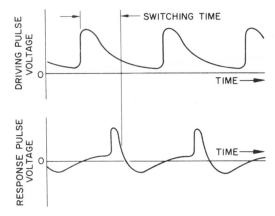

DRIVING PULSE VOLTAGE

SWITCHING TIME

TIME →

RESPONSE PULSE VOLTAGE

TIME →

The switching time *for a magnetic storage cell.*

facility capability. Supplementary maintenance time is a part of scheduled engineering time, along with engineering improvement time, scheduled maintenance time, and installation time.

time, switching—The time interval between a switching or driving pulse intended to switch, or reverse the magnetization, of a magnetic material, such as a magnetic core of a computer storage unit, and the response voltage. The switching time is usually measured between the leading edge of the driving pulse and the instant at which the instantaneous voltage response of a magnetic cell reaches a stated fraction of its peak value, or the trailing edge of the response voltage, which is the voltage induced when the material reverses polarization. It is not considered advisable to measure switching time between reference time and the leading edge of the response voltage.

time, takedown—Time before, after, or between machine runs devoted to manual tasks, such as removing reels of tape, subsequent to a machine run. (Contrast with *time, set-up.*)

time, testing—Same as *time, proving.*

time, total—The full time, such as the 168 hours of a week or 24 hours of a day.

time, training—Time used to train personnel in the operational use of the equipment, such as mounting tapes, console operation, converter operation, input operations, and the conducting of demonstrations. Training time is a part of incidentals time, which is a part of up time.

time, transfer—1: In data transmission, the time between the beginning of transfer of data from a sending station to the complete delivery of the data at a receiving station. The data transferred may be a bit, block, message, or any other unit. If a packet is transferred, then the packet transfer time is the time interval between the dispatch of the first bit of the packet by the sender and the reception of the last bit of the packet by the receiver. 2: In data processing, the

time interval between the instant at which the transfer of a set of data starts and the instant at which the transfer of that set is completed.

time, transit—In computer simulation, the simulated time during which a transaction remains in a simulation system.

time, translating—The time required for a translator to execute a translation; for example, the time required to translate a computer program written in a common language to a machine language for execution by a computer.

time, true—Same as *time, real.*

time, turn-around—1: The time required to reverse the direction of data transmission in a communication channel. 2: In an information retrieval system, the time interval between a request for information by a user and the receipt of the information requested.

time, unscheduled maintenance—Same as *time, nonscheduled maintenance.*

time, unused—Time during which equipment is turned off, not used, and usually not attended by either operators or maintenance personnel. Total time, such as 168 hours a week, is the sum of attended time and unused time.

time, up—Time during which a machine is available for use or is used, and is not known to be malfunctioning; that is, the sum of production time, program development time, incidentals time, operative delay time, and idle time. (Synonymous with *serviceable time.* Further clarified by *time, down.*)

time, word—Same as *word-time.*

time, write cycle—The interval of time required to execute a write cycle of a magnetic core storage unit that has separate reading and writing cycles. The write cycle time is measured from corresponding instants of successive write cycles, such as the time between successive starts.

time constant—See *constant, time.*

time-division multiplex—See *multiplex, time-division.*

time-division multiplier—Same as *multiplier, mark-space.*

time frame—See *frame, time.*

time modulation, pulse—See *modulation, pulse-time.*

time-pulse distributor—See *distributor, time-pulse.*

time-pulse generator—Same as *generator, clock-pulse.*

time scale—See *scale, time.*

time scale, extended—See *scale, extended time.*

time scale, fast—See *scale, fast time.*

time scale, slow—Same as *scale, extended time.*

time scale, variable—See *scale, variable time.*

time scale factor—See *factor, time scale.*

time series—See *series, time.*

time sharing—See *sharing, time.*

time slicing—See *slicing, time.*

timer—Same as *clock.*

timer, master—Same as *clock, master.*

timeshare—To use a device for two or more interleaved purposes; for example, to intersperse the actions of the device among two or more purposes; to make the time of a device available for two different applications, one at a time; to devote the time of a device to the execution of two or more programs on an interleaved basis. Thus, multiprogramming involves timesharing, whereas multicomputing does not.

timing matrix, program—See *matrix, program timing.*

timing pulse—See *pulse, timing.*

timing-pulse generator—Same as *generator, clock-pulse.*

timing service—See *service, timing.*

timing track—See *track, timing.*

toggle—1: Pertaining to any device that has two stable states and the capacity to store or represent one binary digit, and so may be used in arrays to represent binary data, performing such functions as conveying information from the outside into a computer. The device may be manually set, or automatically set by the computer, such as by the routine being executed. (Synonymous with *toggle switch.*) 2: A flip-flop. 3: Loosely, an indicator.

toggle switch—Same as *toggle.*

tolerance, frequency—The maximum permissible deviation of the transmitted carrier frequency with respect to the assigned frequency, expressed as a percentage of the assigned frequency or in hertz.

toll—In telephone communications, a charge for making a connection beyond an exchange boundary.

tone power, standard test—See *power, standard test tone.*

TOPS—(Teletype Optical Projection System.) A radar data-plotting system technique wherein targets are projected on a plotting board as a point of light and a plotter in the rear marks the target with a grease pencil. Similar to DOPS and POPS, except as to input devices.

torn-tape switching center—See *center, torn-tape switching.*

torque amplifier—See *amplifier, torque.*

total, batch—Totals of a certain number or group of specified quantities or unit records used to verify the probable completeness or accuracy of operations on the group; for example, the total number of employees in a department, the total man hours worked in the department over a given period, the total pay for the department, or the number of engines crated during a period.

total, gibberish—Same as *total, hash.*

total, hash—1: A total obtained by adding all the digits in a numeral or group of numerals, without regard to meaning or significance, including numeric values of alphabetic characters, for the purpose of checking transmission, storage, or other operations, and so ensuring that all numerals have been properly handled with a high degree of certainty. (Synonymous with *gibberish total.*) 2: A summation for checking purposes obtained by treating the numerical equivalents of data items.

total, intermediate—A total that is neither a major nor a minor total; that is, the result obtained when a summation is terminated by a change of group being summed that is neither the most nor the least significant in the hierarchy of sums.

total, major—A total obtained when the summation is terminated by the most significant change of group in the hierarchy of sums.

total, minor—1: A sum of numbers, several of which will be totaled to produce an intermediate or major total. When totals are tabulated, certain control changes are necessary to yield the totals desired. Such subtotals are also used for checking purposes. 2: A total obtained when the summation is terminated by the least significant change of group in the hierarchy of sums.

total, proof—A total combined with others to check consistency; for example, in payroll computations, the total gross pay, the total deductions, and the total net pay are proof totals when total net pay and total deductions are added together to produce total gross pay.

total harmonic distortion—See *distortion, total harmonic.*

total time—See *time, total.*

tournament sort—Same as *sort, repeated selection.*

trace—A record of the execution of a computer program, usually showing the instructions that were executed and the sequence in which they were executed.

trace, logical—A selective trace performed only on branch and transfer instructions.

trace, selective—A trace in which only specific parts of computer programs, routines or subroutines are subject to tracing; for example, only those instructions that satisfy certain criteria, such as type of instruction, location of instruction, and location of data, are subject to tracing.

trace program—See *program, trace.*

tracing—A diagnostic technique in which an output device makes a record of events that will permit an analysis of the execution of a program. The instructions and their addresses, the operands and their addresses, and the results produced, along with equipment used, might be some of the data items in the record. The tracing routine permits the identification of trouble in programs and equipment.

tracing, logical—Tracing performed only on jump or transfer instructions.

tracing, selective—Tracing in which only data related to certain specified instructions are subject to tracing, such as only arithmetic or only transfer instructions; only instructions stored in specified locations or storage areas, or only data in certain specified locations.

tracing routine—See *routine, tracing.*

tracing routine, selective—See *routine, selective tracing.*

track—1: The portion of a moving storage medium that is accessible to a specified or a single reading or writing head position; for example, a single path on magnetic tape capable of holding a serial string of pulses; an annulus on a magnetic drum capable of storing serial strings of pulses; a circular loop on a disc available to one head, capable of storing a serial string of binary pulses; or a column of holes on paper tape parallel to the edges. (Further clarified by *band (1).*) 2: In graphic display systems, to cause a display device to follow or determine the position of a moving input device such as the writing tip of a stylus or of a light pen. (Further clarified by *stylus.*)

Recording tracks on a magnetic drum.

track, address—1: On magnetic tape, a track that contains binary codes that locate data stored in other tracks by actual code patterns designating an address, by permitting a count, by their relative position, or by other methods. 2: A track, usually on a rotating or moving medium, that contains addresses to facilitate access. The tracks may contain permanently recorded addresses or may

contain recorded addresses that can be erased or changed.

track, card—The part of a card machine, such as a card reader, punch, tabulator, sorter, keypunch, or transceiver, that moves and guides the cards through the machine, from input hopper to output stacker.

track, clock—Same as *track, timing.*

track, feed—The track that contains the feed holes in paper type.

track, library—A track, on drums, tapes, discs, or cards, used to store reference data, such as titles, document accession numbers, or other labels.

track, regenerative—Same as *revolver.*

track replacement—See *replacement, track.*

track, revolver—Same as *revolver.*

track, timing—A track on magnetic tape, discs, drums, and cards on which a continuous string of pulses is recorded to provide a clock signal as a means for recognizing rows of data by counting or by the position of the pulses or marks in the track. (Synonymous with *clock track.*)

track density—See *density, track.*

track history—See *history, track.*

track pitch—See *pitch, track.*

tracking symbol—See *symbol, tracking.*

trailer, tape—A strip or length of tape at the end of a reel of tape, which may be blank to permit retention on the reel or which may contain some end-of-tape marker, such as a notch, a hole, a conducting surface, special magnetization or other easily detectable mark; or a trailer record.

trailer card—See *card, trailer.*

trailer label—See *label, trailer.*

trailer record—See *record, trailer.*

trailing decision—See *decision, trailing.*

trailing edge, card—See *edge, card trailing.*

trailing end—See *end, trailing.*

trailing zero—See *zero, trailing.*

train, pulse—Same as *string, pulse.*

training time—See *time, training.*

transaction—1: In a data processing system, a change in a data item; for example, a change in the numeral representing the number of hours worked by an employee, the number of items in inventory, or the number of miles driven. 2: In computer simulation, a temporary entity that is handled as an item, or unit of traffic, in the simulation system. The unit need not be individually identified.

transaction data—See *data, transaction.*

transaction file—Same as *file, detail.*

transaction tape—Same as *tape, change.*

transceiver, card—A device that can read data on a punched card and transmit as well as receive data and punch a card. Thus, a transmitting and receiving card reader and punch, and hence a card-to-card converter used for rapid card data transmission and reception. The machines at either end are usually identical and can be used interchangeably for transmitting or receiving.

transcribe–To copy data from one storage medium to another; for example, to copy from an external storage medium to internal storage, to copy from a tape to a printed or typed page, or to copy data from a cathode-ray-tube screen to a printed page. Transcription may include translation, transliteration, conversion, or other process that does not alter the meaning.

transducer–A device that converts energy from one form to another; a transducer enables the conversion of one physical, chemical, biological, mechanical, electrical, hydraulic, pneumatic, optical, or other phenomenon or signal into any other, for transmission, recording, measurement, analysis, actuation, output, input, control, or any other purpose, such as transducers that convert pressure, temperature, acceleration, force, mass time, distance, radiation and many other measurable phenomena into electrical signals proportional to their magnitude, rate of change, or other function. The signals may then be fed to data-processing systems or process controllers. Instrumentation problems often resolve themselves into a proper choice of transducers and data links. Transducers often serve as sensors at hazardous or remote locations.

transfer–1: Same as *jump*. 2: Same as *transmit*.

transfer, block–The process of transmitting blocks of data. The process is usually used when the data is organized in groups of characters such as in blocks. Block transfers are usually initiated by a single action or event.

transfer, conditional–Same as *jump, conditional*.

transfer, peripheral–The transfer of data between two peripheral units of a data processing system; for example, the transfer of data between magnetic tape storage and magnetic disc storage.

transfer, radial–The transfer of data between two units of equipment such that one of the units is more central with respect to the central processing unit (CPU) than the other; for example, transfer between drum storage and magnetic tape, wherein data from the CPU is transferred to the drums and thence to the tapes.

transfer, unconditional–Same as *jump, unconditional*.

transfer bus, digit–See *bus, digit transfer*.

transfer card–Same as *card, transition*.

transfer check–See *check, transfer*.

transfer function–See *function, transfer*.

transfer instruction–Same as *instruction, jump*.

transfer instruction, conditional–Same as *instruction, conditional jump*.

transfer instruction, control–See *instruction, transfer-control*.

transfer instruction, conditional control–Same as *instruction, conditional jump*.

transfer instruction, unconditional–Same as *instruction, unconditional jump*.

transfer interpreter–See *interpreter, transfer*.

transfer medium–See *medium, transfer*.

transfer operation–1: Same as *operation, jump*. 2: Same as *operation, transmit*.

transfer time–See *time, transfer*.

transfer trunk, digit–Same as *bus, digit transfer*.

transferred information–Same as *content, transinformation*.

transform–In data processing, to change the form of data in accordance with specific rules. The change of form may be a change in any characteristic, arrangement, shape, code, language, alphabet, representation, layout, or any other aspect except the meaning. The meaning must remain unchanged by the transformation. This definition is extended to mathematics to include transformations of mathematical expressions brought about by changes in coordinates, functional transformations such as Laplace transforms, and similar changes.

transformation, key–The mapping of a set of keys into a set of integers that can be processed arithmetically to determine the location of the corresponding data.

transformation, signal–The generation of a signal that meets other, usually more stringent, requirements, such as with respect to amplitude, waveform or shape, and relative timing. The requirements usually refer only to a specific data-processing machine. If the signal is transformed or shaped and timed to conform to its original specification, the signal is said to have been regenerated, standardized, or normalized.

transformer, pulse–An electrical transformer that allows impedance matching between circuits or reverses polarity by using square hysteresis loop material for the core and by proper turns ratios among windings, permitting output currents or voltages at proper levels.

transient–A phenomenon or pertaining to a phenomenon that experiences finite changes over relatively short periods of time; thus, an event of a temporary nature. For example, a single rise and decay of a voltage on a line for a period of time that is short compared to the life of the system of which the line is a part. Usually there is a time rate of change of energy storage involved also.

transient area–See *area, transient*.

transient program–See *program, transient*.

transinformation content–See *content, transinformation*.

transinformation content, average–Same as *content, mean transinformation*.

transinformation content, mean–See *content, mean transinformation*.

transinformation rate, average–See *rate, average transinformation*.

transistor—An active device, fabricated of semiconducting material appropriately doped as *n*- or *p*-type, as required, and assembled with at least three electrodes, the minimum three being base, collector, and emitter. The device is capable of amplifying electric signal voltage, current, or power; of mixing signals; of modulation and demodulation; of gating; of buffering; and of many other functions. The transistor was discovered and developed by Bell Telephone Laboratories, a fundamental paper having been written by William Shockley in 1949. It is an electronic device that utilizes the semiconducting properties of materials and the properties of junctions of different semiconducting materials to control the flow of currents from sources in one circuit by currents from different sources in another circuit. A solid-state device, the transistor is applied as a voltage, current or power amplifier; is used for impedance matching; can operate at high frequencies; performs most of the functions of vacuum tubes; has low power dissipation losses; is highly reliable; and serves well as a logic device, as a gate, for performing the Boolean functions of

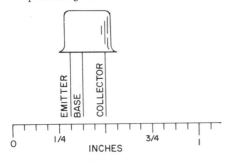

A transistor showing unequal spacing of leads for identification of emitter, base, and collector.

AND, OR, NOR, NAND, and others. As a switching device for logic and high-speed register storage devices, the transistor is the basic building block for computer circuits and, as an amplifier, for communications circuits. (Further clarified by *collector*, by *base*, and by *emitter*.)

transistor, n-p-n—A transistor whose emitter and collector are made of negatively doped or n-type semiconductor material, wherein conduction is predominantly by means of electrons; and the base is made of positively doped or p-type semiconductor material, wherein conduction is predominantly by means of holes. (Contrast with *transistor, p-n-p*. Further clarified by *donor* and by *acceptor*.)

transistor, p-n-p—A transistor whose emitter and collector are made of positively doped

or p-type semiconductor material, wherein conduction is predominantly by means of holes; and the base is negatively doped or n-type semiconductor material, wherein conduction is predominantly by means of electrons. (Contrast with *transistor, n-p-n*. Further clarified by *donor* and by *acceptor*.)

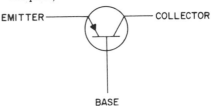

A p-n-p-type transistor *symbol. (The emitter arrow indicates the direction of conventional positive current flow. Thus, this emitter is biased positive and attracts electrons like the plate of a vacuum tube. Conventional positive current flow is opposite in direction to the flow of electrons.)*

transit time—See *time, transit*.

transition card—See *card, transition*.

translate—To convert data from one language to another language without affecting the meaning. Translations may be effected between natural languages, artificial languages, different codes, or different alphabets. Translation takes place from source to target language. Usually, if only alphabetic transformation is involved, the process is called transliteration. If a change of medium is involved, such as punched card to magnetic tape or analog to digital, the process is called conversion. Thus, in the broadest sense, any information represented by a set of data can be considered to have undergone a translation if it is transformed in any way, as long as the meaning is preserved. In telegraphy, the code is considered to be translated to the natural language by the operator.

translate phase—See *phase, translate*.

translating time—See *time, translating*.

translation, machine—Same as *translation, mechanical*.

translation, mechanical—Translation of languages performed through the use of machines, such as electronic computers. Abbreviated MT. (Synonymous with *machine translation*.)

translation, program—The translation of a program written in a source programming language to a target programming language; for example, a translation of a computer program written in ALGOL to a program in IBM 7094 machine language, the instructions being equivalent in both languages and the translation being accomplished by the machine under the control of a translator.

translation algorithm—See *algorithm, translation*.

translator—A routine, program or device capable of directing the translation or transformation of statements or their equivalent codes in one language to equivalent statements or their equivalent codes in another language. The only requirement is that the meaning be the same: The source and target language sequences of statements must be equivalent, whether the individual statements are translated on a one-to-one, a many-to-one, or a one-to-many basis, it being recognized, for example, that often an instruction in one language may require several instructions in another language. Often a translator may be built in as wired logic circuits that accomplish the translation as the instructions are read, transforming the codes of one language to the codes of another language, such as might be accomplished by a diode matrix. (Further clarified by *assembler*, by *generator*, by *interpreter*, and by *compiler*.)

translator, address—1: A computer hardware or software feature that dynamically translates the address part of an instruction word from virtual addresses to real addresses, usually in main storage. (Further clarified by *address, virtual* and by *address, real*.) 2: A software, hardware, or firmware feature of an operating system that translates virtual addresses to main storage addresses.

transliterate—To substitute or convert the characters of one alphabet to the corresponding characters of another alphabet, usually in an attempt to preserve proper pronunciation and also permit the use of available type font; for example, to substitute letters or groups of letters in the Roman or English alphabet for letters of the Cyrillic alphabet in an effort to preserve pronunciation or some semblance of appropriate spelling; or to encode the characters of the English alphabet with the binary codes of the USA Standard Code for Information Interchange. Translation involves meanings whereas transliteration involves alphabets. They both involve words.

transmission—The movement of data from one location to another or the data that is moved; for example, the sending of data from one component of a system to another, the movement of data in coded form by means of electrical signals, or the conveying of electrical energy along a path, channel, or line.

transmission, asynchronous data—A mode of transmission such that the occurrence of each and every character is not related to a fixed time frame of reference, but in which the bits of each character are transmitted synchronously. (Contrast with *transmission, synchronous data*.)

transmission, double-sideband—Transmission in which frequencies produced by modulation of a carrier wave are symmetrically spaced both above and below the carrier frequency and all are transmitted; that is, the upper and lower sidebands as well as the carrier. (Contrast with *transmission, independent-sideband* and with *transmission, single-sideband*.)

transmission, independent-sideband—Transmission in which the sets of frequencies produced by the modulation of a carrier wave above and below the carrier frequency are not related to each other, but are related separately to two separate modulating signals. The carrier frequency may be either transmitted or suppressed. (Contrast with *transmission, double-sideband* and with *transmission, single-sideband*.)

transmission, parallel—Digital data transmission in which the individual bits or another subunit of a character, word, or other data unit, are transmitted simultaneously over separate channels, such as separate wires. (Contrast with *transmission, serial*.)

transmission, serial—Digital data transmission in which the individual bits or another subunit of a character, word, or other data unit, are transmitted in time sequence over the same channel, such as the same wire. Thus, transmission might be parallel by bit and serial by character. (Contrast with *transmission, parallel*.)

transmission, single-sideband—Transmission in which the frequencies produced by modulation of a carrier wave on one side of the carrier frequency are transmitted and those on the other side are suppressed; for example, transmission in which the frequencies above the carrier frequency are transmitted and the frequencies below the carrier are suppressed. The carrier frequency may be either transmitted or suppressed. (Contrast with *transmission, double-sideband* and with *transmission, independent-sideband*.)

transmission, start-stop—Asynchronous transmission in which a group of code signals corresponding to a character is preceded by a start signal that serves to prepare the receiving mechanism for the reception and registration of a character and is followed by a stop signal that serves to bring the receiving mechanism to rest in preparation for the reception of the next character.

transmission, suppressed-carrier—Transmission of a modulated carrier wave in which the carrier frequency is suppressed partially or to the extent possible, and in which one or both of the sidebands are transmitted.

transmission, synchronous data—A mode of data transmission such that the occurrence of each and every character is related to a fixed time frame of reference. (Contrast with *transmission, asynchronous data*.)

transmission, vestigial sideband—Transmission of a modulated carrier wave in which the frequencies of one sideband, the carrier, and only a portion of the other sideband are transmitted.

transmission-block character, end-of—See *character, end-of-transmission-block.*

transmission control character—See *character, transmission control.*

transmission level, relative—See *level, relative transmission.*

transmission line—See *line, transmission.*

transmission rate, average—Same as *rate, effective data-transfer.*

transmission rate, effective—Same as *rate, effective data-transfer.*

transmission rate, instantaneous—Same as *rate, instantaneous data-transfer.*

transmission rate, peak—Same as *rate, instantaneous data-transfer.*

transmission reference point, zero-level—See *point, zero-level transmission reference.*

transmission trap, data—See *trap, data-transmission.*

transmission utilization ratio, data—See *ratio, data transmission utilization.*

transmit—To move data from one location to another location, such as by reading or sensing the data at the source, moving it over a communication channel, and storing it at the destination. The data may be erased at the source and it may be overwritten at the destination, thus removing what was previously there. (Synonymous with *transfer.*)

transmit operation—See *operation, transmit.*

transmitted data circuit—See *circuit, transmitted data.*

transmitter, automatic tape—Same as *reader, tape.*

transmitter-distributor, tape—Same as *reader, tape.*

transparent, code—Pertaining to the capability of transmitting characters regardless of their binary codes.

transport, tape—Same as *drive, tape.*

trap—A nonprogrammed conditional jump to a specified location, automatically activated by hardware, and with the location from which the jump occurred automatically recorded. The trap is a special form of a conditional breakpoint or jump that may be imposed by the operating system, but is usually activated by the hardware itself, sometimes both. Often, a number of internal traps exist in a computer, many of which may be set by unexpected or unpredicted events. Examples of traps that may be enabled or inhibited under program control are overflow traps, traps that provide automatic checking, or traps for communication or signaling between input-output routines and the programs using them.

trap, data transmission—A nonprogrammed conditional jump to a specified location, automatically activated and providing communication or signaling between input-output routines and the programs using them.

trapping—The enabling of a trap, the action performed by a trap, or the executing of a program with an enabled trap. (Further explained by *trap.*)

tree structure—See *structure, tree.*

tree-structure sort—Same as *sort, repeated selection.*

triad—A group of three items; for example, a group of three bits, such as pulses, used to express an octal digit in binary form. (Contrast with *diad* and with *tetrad.* Closely related to *triplet.*)

tributary station—See *station, tributary.*

tributary trunk—See *trunk, tributary.*

trigger—1: To initiate or start an event or operation; for example, to initiate execution of a routine by means of a manually controlled jump to the point of entry or beginning. For a routine, if execution commences automatically after loading, the routine is said to be self-triggering. 2: A device that initiates or starts an action, such as a spring-loaded mechanism that requires a small amount of energy to trip or release the stored larger amount, like the trigger of a gun that releases the hammer, or the small charge that initiates an atomic bomb, or a circuit that initiates a flip-flop action to change its state. Because of this latter action, the flip-flop itself has been called a trigger, since it can initiate and control logic and arithmetic operations in a computer.

trigger, Eccles-Jordan—An early type of direct, cross-coupled multivibrator of the one-shot variety, which led to the development of the flip-flop. (Synonymous with *Eccles-Jordan circuit.* Further clarified by *flip-flop.*)

trigger, monostable—Same as *multivibrator, one-shot.*

trigger circuit—See *circuit, trigger.*

trigger circuit, bistable—Same as *flip-flop.*

trigger tube—See *tube, trigger.*

triode—A three-electrode active electronic device; for example, a three-electrode vacuum tube or a transistor. The triode is used primarily as an amplifier of electronic signals.

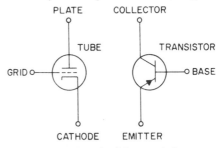

Vacuum and solid-state triodes.

triple-address—Same as *three-address.*

triple-length register—See *register, triple-length.*

triple precision—See *precision, triple.*

triple register—Same as *register, triple-length*.

triplet—A byte that is composed of three binary elements. (Synonymous with *three-bit byte*. Closely related to *triad*.)

trouble-location problem—Same as *problem, fault-location*.

troubleshoot—Same as *debug*.

TRTL—An abbreviation for transistor-resistor-transistor logic.

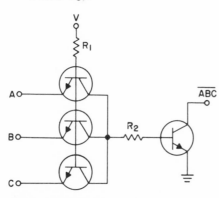

Basic transistor-resistor-transistor logic (TRTL) *NAND gate.*

true complement—Same as *complement, radix*.

true time—Same as *time, real*.

true-time operation—Same as *operation, real-time*.

truncate—To omit, cut off or terminate at a specified place; for example, to terminate a computational process in accordance with some rule, such as ending the evaluation of a power series at a specified term; to omit certain terms of an expression, such as the digits of a numeral in positions of lowest significance or the terms at the end of a series; or to select a finite number of cycles or iterations in an infinitely recursive process. If the value of pi is truncated between the fifth and sixth digit, 3.1415 would result; if rounded to five significant digits, according to one rounding rule, 3.1416 would result. (Contrast with *round-off*.)

truncation—1: The deletion or omission of a leading or of a trailing portion of a string of characters. Usually the truncation must be performed in accordance with specified rules. 2: The termination of a process; for example, the termination of the execution of a computer program before its final conclusion or natural termination. The termination must be accomplished in accordance with specified rules.

trunk—1: A single message circuit between two points, both of which are switching centers or individual message distribution points, such as telephone exchanges, telephone switchboards, telegraph switching centers. or message routing centers. 2: A bus.

trunk, check—Same as *bus, check*.

trunk, digit transfer—Same as *bus, digit transfer*.

trunk, final—In telephone communication the last long-distance trunk that connect switching centers which are adjacent each other in the line of communication such as a local center to its seconda center, a secondary center to its prima center, a primary center to its zone cent or one zone center to another.

trunk, high-usage—In telephon communications, long-distance trunks th interconnect local, secondary, primar and zone centers that are not adjacent the line of communication.

trunk, LD—See *trunk, long-distance*.

trunk, long-distance—In telephon communications, a trunk that permi trunk-to-trunk connection and th interconnects local, secondary, primar and zone centers. (Synonymous with *L trunk*.)

trunk, telephone—A single call circu between two points which are telephon switching exchanges, centers, or individu call distribution points.

trunk, terminal—In telephon communications, a trunk that connec switching centers used in conjunction wit local centers only.

trunk, tributary—In telephon communications, a trunk that connects local exchange with a local center o another local exchange and through whic access to the long-distance network i achieved.

trunk group—See *group, trunk*.

truth table—See *table, truth*.

tube, acorn—A small vacuum tube, usuall with short electron transit time and lo interelectrode capacity; hence, designe for the higher frequency signals.

tube, beam-switching—A vacuum or gas-fille tube constructed so that the cathod electron beam can be directed to any on of two or more anodes; 10 position tube are most common.

tube, cathode-ray—A vacuum tube, with screen and a controlled beam of electrons that may be used as a display or storage device, or both. Data display or data storage is obtained by deflectio of a beam of electrons, in two dimensions on their way to the screen, usually alon the axis of an orthogonal coordinate system. The beam intensity may also be under program control, though usually only on and off control is possible. Digita storage or graphic displays are achievable hence, the tube may be an output device or a storage device for computers. An electron gun, deflection plates, and screen are the essential parts of cathode-ray tube, such as a visual display device for digital computers. Persistence o charge at a spot on the screen permits storage and interrogation of binary data at each spot on the screen. If a screen is divided up into 32 rows and columns,

1024 bits may be stored on the screen. The screen is the inner surface of the face of the tube. Cathode-ray tubes, with minor modifications, serve as data-storage tubes, oscilloscope tubes, television tubes, radar display tubes, and computer output or remote station display tubes. Abbreviated CRT. (Further clarified by *tube, Williams* and by *storage, electrostatic*.)

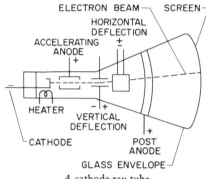

ELECTRON BEAM SCREEN
HORIZONTAL DEFLECTION
ACCELERATING ANODE ±
+
HEATER VERTICAL DEFLECTION
CATHODE POST ANODE
GLASS ENVELOPE

A cathode-ray tube.

tube, display—An electronic tube, usually a cathode-ray tube, used to present data in a graphic, pictorial, or other visual form. Display tubes are used as output devices for computers, particularly to provide the machine-man interface.

tube, electrostatic storage—Same as *tube, Williams*.

tube, gate—A multigrid tube, such as a pentode, that will allow plate current to flow provided grid voltage conditions on two or more grids are met; for example, a tube that conducts only if all grids have a grid voltage of plus one volt or higher, or a tube that will not conduct only if all grids are more negative than minus six volts. Thus, AND and OR gates can be constructed, permitting Boolean operations to be performed electronically. Many radio receiving tubes permitted plate current complete cutoff only if all control grids were driven sufficiently negative. Thus, one could develop the AND function by arranging the circuit such that only a negative pulse on all lines, or grids, would turn off the tube. Or, the same AND function could be accomplished if the tube were normally biased so as to be cut off; that is, no plate current flowing, and either grid could keep the tube cut off, no matter how far positive one grid was driven. In this case, the tube would conduct only if both grid negative biases were removed. With these radio receiving tubes, the early computers like ENIAC, EDVAC, UNIVAC, and ORDVAC were built. It was also realized that diodes permitted the same type logic, and the later tubes were used only for amplification of the outputs of diodes,

both vacuum and crystal, logic and for inversion. From this point of view, the electronic computer technology was spawned by the technology of the radio industry.

tube, Nixie—Same as *light, Nixie*.

tube, oscilloscope—A cathode-ray tube used to display waveshapes and forms, usually as part of a laboratory instrument or measuring device.

tube, slave—A tube, such as a cathode-ray display tube, electrically connected to a master tube, in such a manner that the behavior of both tubes is identical. The master tube is usually the operating tube. The slave tube merely follows it. A slave cathode-ray tube might be used to follow the storage contents of an electrostatic storage tube.

tube, storage—Same as *tube, Williams*.

tube, trigger—An amplifier tube that accepts a logic pulse from the output of another device and delivers a pulse to trigger a flip-flop or other type of multivibrator; for example, a cathode-follower used to apply a drive pulse to one cathode of a flip-flop in order to reset it.

tube, Williams—A cathode-ray tube used in an electrostatic storage unit. Data is stored as discrete charged spots on a secondary-electron emitting surface on the inner face of the tube. Secondary emission is caused by an electron beam. The beam is positioned (addressed) by an electric field applied by a voltage on deflecting electrodes, as in a TV or oscilloscope tube. The read-out or output is obtained from what would otherwise be the final accelerating anode or a conducting film, screen, or mesh placed on the outside adjacent to the storage surface. Detection or interrogation of stored information is accomplished by measuring the change in state of charge of a spot when the electron beam is aimed and it strikes the spot. The cathode-ray tube as an electrostatic storage device was originally proposed by F. C. Williams and T. Kilburn of the University of Manchester, England, during the 1940's and was used in many of the early high-speed electronic digital computers. After several years of widespread use, it was replaced by the magnetic core. Access was random; and so, it was superior to the delay-line. However, volatility, high-potential voltage sources, storage surface irregularities, read-around ratio, destructive sensing, and limited capacity reduced its use as a storage tube. The cathode-ray tube is still widely used as a display device. (Synonymous with *storage tube* and with *electrostatic storage tube*. Further clarified by *storage, electrostatic* and by *tube, cathode-ray*.)

tunnel diode—See *diode, tunnel*.

turbulence amplifier—See *amplifier, turbulence*.

Turing machine—See *machine, Turing*.

Turing machine, universal—See *machine, universal Turing*.

turn-around time—See *time, turn-around.*

turning, page—Same as *paging.*

twelve punch—Same as *Y-punch.*

twenty-nine feature code—See *code, twenty-nine feature.*

twin check—See *check, twin.*

twistor—A storage device that stores data as helical magnetic flux patterns along a wire. The application of tension to the ends of the wire introduces an initial helical strain. Sensing wires wound around the magnetic wire as used to pick up the data as the flux pattern external to the wire changes when the twist is applied. The nature of the change at each location is dependent on the flux pattern stored at that location. No linear motion of the wire is necessary, as in magnetic-wire storage devices. Read-out is as fast as the strain wave can travel down the wire.

two-address—Pertaining to a machine instruction which explicitly refers to or describes two storage locations, and one operation to be performed on or with the contents of these locations. Usually, the two-address instruction specifies the storage location containing the operand, the operation to be performed on it, and the storage location in which the result of the operation is to be stored. The machine then automatically proceeds to the next instruction to be executed. Some two-address machines are the IBM 1401, IBM 1620, MANIAC III, National 315, RCA 501, RW 400, Univac Solid State 80, and Univac 1105. Two-address instruction programs require fewer program steps, make more efficient use of longer words, and require fewer storage accesses than do one-address instruction programs. (Synonymous with *double address.*)

two-address code—Same as *instruction, two-address.*

two-address instruction—See *instruction, two-address.*

two-bit byte—Same as *doublet.*

two-core-per-bit storage—See *storage, two-core-per-bit.*

two-input adder—Same as *half-adder.*

two-input subtracter—Same as *half-subtracter.*

two-level address—Same as *address, second-level.*

two-out-of-five code—See *code, two-out-of-five.*

two-plus-one address instruction—See *instruction, two-plus-one address.*

two-scale—Same as *notation, binary.*

two-state variable—Same as *variable, two-valued.*

two-tone modulation—See *modulation, two-tone.*

two-valued variable—See *variable, two-valued.*

two-way list—Same as *list, bi-directional.*

two-wire channel—See *channel, two-wire.*

two-wire circuit—See *circuit, two-wire.*

twos complement—See *complement, twos.*

TWX—Same as *Service, Teletypewriter Exchange.*

type, data—The structural characteristics, features, properties, and other aspects of data that may be specified by a programming language.

type bar—See *bar, type.*

type bar, fixed—See *bar, fixed type.*

type bar, interchangeable—See *bar, interchangeable type.*

type font—See *font, type.*

typewriter, electric—A typewriter that has a manually operated keyboard, but whose operations, after the keys are touched by human fingers, are all electrically driven or powered.

u

UDC—An abbreviation of Universal Decimal Classification.

UHF—(Ultrahigh Frequency). Frequencies between 300 and 3000 megahertz. (Further clarified by *spectrum, frequency.*)

ultrafiche—Microfiche on which images were reduced ninety or more times the original image in a single dimension; for example, microfiche one page in size, say 8.5 by 11 inches, containing images of more than 8100 pages of the same size.

ultrasonics—The field of science devoted to frequencies of sound above the human audio range, or above 20 kilohertz, such as the high frequencies (one megahertz and above) used in acoustic delay-lines for data storage.

umbilical connector—See *connector, umbilical.*

unallowable instruction check—Same as *check, forbidden-combination.*

unallowable instruction digit—Same as *character, illegal.*

unary operation—Same as *operation, monadic.*

unary operator—Same as *operator, monadic.*

unbalanced error—See *error, unbalanced.*

unbalanced merge sort—See *sort, unbalanced merge.*

unbundle—To separate hardware charges from software charges in the buying and selling of computers and their associated software. Thus when a system is unbundled, there can no longer be a single price for a machine and its programs; the two must be sold separately; for example, a customer can buy a computer from one vendor and hire another to program it or program it himself. Thus, under unbundling arrangements, a computer can be time shared, procured through a service bureau, bought, or rented. A user can write his own programs, hire to have them written, or buy proprietary programs, under unbundling arrangements.

unconditional branch—Same as *jump, unconditional.*

unconditional jump—See *jump, unconditional.*

unconditional-jump instruction—See *instruction, unconditional-jump.*

unconditional transfer—Same as *jump, unconditional.*

unconditional-transfer instruction—Same as *instruction, unconditional-jump.*

underflow—Pertaining to the condition that arises when a computation yields a nonzero result that is smaller than the smallest nonzero quantity that can be represented or stored. Thus, in floating-point numbers, a negative exponent that is too large to be stored is considered as an underflow condition, although from the point of view of the register or storage location, it appears or behaves as overflow. (Contrast with *overflow.*)

underpunch—A second hole, in a punched-card column, that is immediately under the original standard code hole punched in the column.

UNICODE—An automatic coding system developed by Univac Division, Sperry-Rand Corporation, for the Univac 1103-A computer.

UNICOMP—Universal Compiler, FORTRAN Compatible.

unidirectional list—See *list, unidirectional.*

uniform random number—Same as *number, random.*

uniformity, ink—The variation in intensity of light reflectance over the area of a printed character; that is, within the character edges or outline.

union—Same as *OR.*

union gate—Same as *gate, OR.*

union operation—Same as *operation, disjunction.*

unipolar—Pertaining to a signal system wherein a logic true or one input is represented by an electrical voltage or current of a given polarity and a logic false or zero input is represented by an electrical voltage or current of the same or zero polarity; for example, a positive voltage represents true or one and a positive voltage of different magnitude, such as zero voltage, represents false or zero. The unipolar electrical waves or pulses for different representation, such as zero or one may be in terms of magnitude, timing, shape, phase, or other parameter. (Contrast with *bipolar.*)

UNISAP—The SAP assembly system developed at the Case Institute for Univac computers.

Uniservo—A magnetic tape handler developed by Univac Division of Sperry-Rand Corporation. Uniservos may be controlled by program instructions stored within the central processor and coordinated by the tape synchronizer, or may be used offline for data conversions to and from magnetic tape, as can tape handling devices developed by other manufacturers. Abbreviated as Servo. Models include the Uniservo I and II.

unit—A basic element, part, or device having a special function; for example, an arithmetic unit, a tape unit, a control unit, a central processing unit, or a unit of measure, such as a quart or an inch.

unit, AND—Same as *gate, AND.*

unit, anticoincidence—Same as *gate, exclusive-OR.*

unit, arithmetic—The portion of a computer or computing system that contains the circuits that perform the arithmetic, logic, shift, and similar operations. Sometimes called the arithmetic and logic unit, the arithmetic unit usually consists of accumulators, adders, comparator circuits, registers for holding operands and results, and shifting and sequencing circuits for performing multiplication, division, and other desired operations, such as square-rooting. (Synonymous with *arithmetic-logic unit,* with *logic-arithmetic unit,* with *arithmetic section,* and with *logic unit.*)

unit, binary—Same as *Shannon.*

unit, central processing—The part of a computing system that contains the circuits which control the interpretation and execution of instructions, including the necessary arithmetic, logic, and control circuits to execute the instructions. The central processing unit includes two basic components of a computing system, namely, the control unit and the arithmetic unit, the other three basic parts being the storage, input, and output units. (Synonymous with *CPU* and with *main frame.*)

unit, coefficient—Same as *scalar.*

unit, clock—In simulation, an elemented unit of time in a simulation interval, period, or run; for example, a second, minute, day, pulse period, or basic timing interval.

unit, coincidence—Same as *gate, AND.*

unit, comparing—Same as *comparator.*

unit, consistent—A unit in which input variables and output variables have the same form, such as both are in the form of voltage pulses, both as shaft positions, both as current pulses, or both as punched cards or paper tape.

unit, constant multiplier coefficient—Same as *scalar.*

unit, control—In a digital computer, the circuits that effect selection and retrieval of instructions from storage or from outside the computer, in proper sequence, the interpretation of each of the coded instructions, and the development and application of proper signals to the arithmetic unit in accordance with the interpretation, in order to achieve execution of instructions by the arithmetic unit, storage unit, and input-output units. Several control units may be subordinated to a central or main control unit. The control unit, along with the arithmetic unit, forms part of the central processing unit.

unit, delay—A device that produces after a time interval, an output signal essentially similar to a previously introduced input signal.

unit, display—A device or equipment whose output is a graphic, pictorial, or other visual image; for example, a display tube, such as a cathode-ray tube; a point, line, or curve plotter; a matrix of lights; or a film projector.

unit, functional—An entity of hardware, software, or both, that is capable of accomplishing a specified purpose.

unit, identity—Same as *gate, identity.*

unit, information-content decimal—Same as *Hartley.*

unit, information-content natural—A unit of logarithmic measure of information equal to the decision content of a set of two mutually exclusive events expressed by the naperian logarithm; for example, the information content in natural units of a set of eight characters is the decision content of the character set of eight characters, which is equal to $\log_e 8 = \ln 8 = 3 \times \ln 2 = 2.079$ natural units of information. (Abbreviated NAT.)

unit, input—Same as *input (3).*

unit, linear—A device in which the change in output due to any change in an input is proportional to the magnitude of that change and does not depend on the values of the other inputs; for example, an adder, a scalar, or an integrating amplifier. Devices are built that are deliberately nonlinear, such as multipliers and function generators.

unit, logic—Same as *unit, arithmetic.*

unit, magnetic-tape—A device that contains a magnetic-tape drive, together with reading and writing heads and associated controls. Most modern computers have two or more magnetic-tape units for additional high-capacity storage, such as 30,000,000 alphanumeric characters per reel; hence, a tape unit online. (Synonymous with

magnetic-tape station. Further clarified *storage, magnetic-tape.*)

unit, main control—In a computer with m than one instruction control unit, instruction control unit to which other instruction control units subordinated. An instruction control u may be designated as a main control u by hardware or software. A main con unit at one time may be a subordin unit at another time.

unit, manual input—A device into which d may be manually inserted and held, a whose contents can be sensed by computer, data processor, proc controller, or other device. Usually manual input unit is used to manua insert a word into computer storage or hold a manually inserted word until i read during the execution of a progra (Synonymous with *manual word genera* and *manual number generator.* Furtl clarified by *read, manual.*)

unit, monitor—A device that supervises a verifies the operation of another devi such as a computing system, an industr process, a message routing system, or information storage and retrieval syste Usually significant departures from norm are indicated as the state of system is observed or measured. T monitoring unit may also be used to is signals to correct departures from norm and to insert instructions, in wh case it is behaving also as a controller.

unit, multicomputing—Same *multiprocessor.*

unit, multiplier coefficient—Same as *scalar.*

unit, OR—Same as *gate, OR.*

unit, output—Same as *output (3).*

unit, raster—In graphic display systems, horizontal or vertical distance betw two adjacent addressable points on display surface of a cathode ray tu (Related to *size, increment.*)

unit, read-punch—Same as *reader-punch, ca*

unit, storage—Same as *device, storage.*

unit, tape—A device containing a tape dri together with reading and writing he and associated controls. Usually magne tape is implied. (Synonymous with *ta station.*)

unit, terminal—Equipment connected either end of a communication chann line, or link. (Synonymous with *termi device* and with *data terminal equipmen*

unit, volume—The unit of measurement electrical speech power in communicatio as measured by a volume unit (vu) me in the prescribed manner. The vu mete a volume indicator built in accordar with USA Standard C 16.5-1942. decibel scale, dynamic, and otl characteristics are specified in order obtain correlated readings of spee power, since voice currents fluctu rapidly. Zero vu equals zero dBm measurement of sine-wave test-tone pow unit-distance code—See *code, unit-distance.*

unit interval—See *interval, unit.*

unit record—See *record, unit.*

unit string—See *string, unit.*

uniterm—A single-term expression, sets of which are used to define or describe the contents of data holdings, documents, banks, files, records, or other units of data. The term was coined by Mortimer Taube in his original treatises on information and document retrieval. (Closely related to *entry, index,* to *descriptor,* to *keyword,* and to *docuterm.*)

uniterm indexing—See *indexing, uniterm.*

uniterm system—See *system, uniterm.*

UNITRAN—The FORTRANSIT programming language used on the Univac Solid State 80 computer.

Univac—A trade name, formed from the words universal automatic computer, designating a series of computers now manufactured by Sperry-Rand Corporation, usually by Remington Rand Univac Division. The Univac I is the outgrowth of the war-time developments, ENIAC and EDVAC.

universal decimal classification—See *classification, universal decimal.*

universal language—See *language, universal.*

universal set—See *set, universal.*

universal Turing machine—See *machine, universal Turing.*

unload—1: Same as *dump.* 2: For magnetic-tape units, to rewind and disable, sometimes by unthreading.

unmask—In an operating system, to return to the condition in which interrupts are permitted in accordance with the rules established when the system was masked. (Contrast with *mask.*)

unpack—1: To separate data items that have been packed; for example, to separate various sections of a tape record or computer word and store them in separate locations. The sections or pieces of data that are unpacked usually correspond to format fields within a record, block, or word; hence, the unpack operation is similar to an extract operation. 2: To obtain or recover the original form of the data from the packed data.

unscheduled maintenance—Same as *maintenance, corrective.*

unscheduled maintenance time—Same as *time, nonscheduled maintenance.*

unset—Same as *reset.*

unstable state—See *state, unstable.*

unstratified language—See *language, unstratified.*

unused code—Same as *character, illegal.*

unused command—Same as *character, illegal.*

unused command check—Same as *check, forbidden-combination.*

unused time—See *time, unused.*

unwind—1: In programming, to convert a routine loop to an equivalent straight-line sequence of instructions without loops, as a means for trading space for time and usually without using counts, modifiers, and similar aids, in a resulting routine. Unwinding eliminates all sorts of red-tape or housekeeping instructions and may be performed automatically by the computer during assembling, generating, or compiling operations. The process saves operating time but can consume large areas of storage. 2: To fully and explicitly describe, without the use of modifiers, all the instructions that are used in the execution of a loop.

up time—See *time, up.*

update—To process a file in accordance with a specified procedure for inserting, deleting, or altering the data items in the file; for example, to modify a master file in accordance with the latest transaction information.

upper curtate—See *curtate, upper.*

us—A typewriter representation for the Greek letter mu, for micro, and s for second; hence, an abbreviation for microsecond.

U.S. Army Fieldata code—See *code, Fieldata.*

USASI FORTRAN IV—A specified standard programming language.

use identifier, data—See *identifier, data use.*

use identifier, data element—Same as *identifier, data use.*

use time, operational—Same as *time, effective.*

usec—An abbreviation for *microsecond.*

user program—Same as *program, problem.*

user terminal—See *terminal, user.*

utilities, stand-alone—Computer programs, routines, and subroutines that are not under operating system control during their execution.

utility control console—See *console, utility control.*

utility program—See *program, utility.*

utility routine—Same as *routine, service.*

utilization ratio, data transmission—See *ratio, data transmission utilization.*

ν

validation, data—The checking of data for corrections or compliance with applicable standards, rules, or conventions.

validity—The degree to which an event, especially operations, are allowable, permissive, logical, complete, and comprehensible, particularly iterated approximations on data gathered from indigenous or unreliable sources or on data that might have been garbled or ruined in transmission or processing. Validity is a measure of the extent to which a standard has been met or a rule followed. Reliability is a measure of correctness. For example, validity checks indicate whether a particular value lies among a set of possible values, not specifically whether it is the one correct value or not. Of course, invalid data is incorrect, hence unreliable, according to the rules of logic. (Contrast with *reliability.*)

validity, data—A measure of the permissiveness or the extent to which data has been subject to specific tests to ensure that operations performed on the data were performed properly and that the test results have verified the reliability of the data; for example, a measure of the extent to which validity checks have been performed. Thus, data validity refers to whether or not certain criteria have been met, such as a forbidden code has not been used or that all numerals are less than 60. However, even though the data has been thus validated, this is no indication that the data is reliable; that is, that the allowable code used was correct or that the numeral 48 should have been 28 when applying the latter criterion. In other words, when applying the latter criterion, a numeral like 75 would fail the validity check, be invalid, and so also unreliable, incorrect, and inaccurate. The 48 is valid under the given criterion, and can only be proven unreliable by some other check. (Contrast with *reliability, data.*)

validity check—See *check, validity.*

value, code—Same as *representation, coded.*

value, end—A value selected to serve as a minimum or maximum control value and compared with the value of an index, count, or control variable to determine if the selected maximum or minimum has been attained or passed.

variable—The representation of a quantity, or the quantity itself, which can assume any of a given set of values. In most equations, or other mathematical expressions, the quantities involved are represented with symbols, and either the quantities themselves or the symbols are considered as variables. Thus, in the family of straight lines, expressed as $y = mx + b$, y and x are considered variables, whereas m and b are parameters that are constant for a given line, but change in value from line to line. Sometimes variables can only assume the values of a set of values, such as 0 and 1 in binary notation used in computers. (Related to *constant* and *parameter.*)

variable, binary—Same as *variable, two-valued.*

variable, binary-state—Same as *variable, two-valued.*

variable, Boolean—The operand in an expression in the Boolean algebra; that is, a variable that may assume either one of only two values, expressed commonly as true or false, on or off, closed or open, or zero or one. Binary digital computers, nearly all electronic digital computers, make use of two-state Boolean variables.

variable, controlled—A quantity or condition that is subject to regulation by automatic devices. (Synonymous with *manipulated variable.*)

variable, dependent—A variable whose value is determined by some function of another quantity whose value is either constant or varying. In the expression $y = f(x)$, y is considered the dependent variable, since its value is determined by the value of x and the nature of the function. Also, in the cause and effect relationship, the effect is considered as represented by the dependent variable. Thus, if thermal expansion of materials is plotted as a function of temperature, the expansion is considered as dependent, is represented as the dependent variable, such as $s = f(t)$, and the dependent variable is usually plotted as the ordinate; that is, the vertical or y-axis, on a cartesian coordinate graph. (Contrast with *variable, independent.*)

variable, global—A variable that is defined in one portion of a computer program and used in at least one other portion of the same program. Thus, the scope of a global variable is the computer program, and its meaning must remain fixed throughout the program. (Contrast with *variable, local.*)

variable, independent—A variable whose value does not depend on or is not a direct function of some other variable. In the expression $y = f(x)$, x is the independent variable, since its value is not directly determined by y or the nature of the function. Also, in the cause and effect relationship, the cause is considered as represented by the independent variable. Thus, if thermal expansion of materials is plotted as a function of temperature, the temperature is considered as independent, is represented as the independent variable, such as the t in $s = f(t)$, and the independent variable is usually plotted as the abscissa; that is, the horizontal or x-axis, on a cartesian coordinate graph. (Contrast with *variable, dependent.*)

variable, local—A variable that is defined in one portion of a computer program and is not used in any other portion of that program or any other program. (Contrast with *variable, global.*)

variable, logic—Same as *variable, switching.*

variable, loop control—A variable that controls or effects the execution of instructions in a loop body. The loop control variables are operated upon or are modified by the loop control. (Further clarified by *control, loop.*)

variable, manipulated—Same as *variable, controlled.*

variable, switching—A variable that can assume only a finite number of possible values or states. (Synonymous with *logic variable.*)

variable, two-state—Same as *variable, two-valued.*

variable, two-valued—A variable that can assume either one of two values; that is, that can assume the values in a set of two elements, often symbolized as true or false, T or F, 0 or 1, yes or no. The two-valued variable should not be confused with a double-valued variable, such as $\pm x$ or a parabolic, elliptical, or hyperbolic function, which has two values of the independent variable that satisfy or yield the same value of the dependent variable. (Synonymous with *binary-state variable*, with *binary variable*, and with *two-state variable.*)

variable address—Same as *address, floating.*

variable connector—See *connector, variable.*

variable-cycle operation—See *operation, variable-cycle.*

variable length—See *length, variable.*

variable-length record—See *record, variable-length.*

variable-length record file—See *file, variable-length record.*

variable-length record system—Same as *file, variable-length record.*

variable-length word—See *word, variable-length.*

variable logic—Same as *logic, programmed.*

variable multiplier—Same as *multiplier, function.*

variable point—See *point, variable.*

variable-point representation system—See *system, variable-point representation.*

variable-precision coding compaction—See *compaction, variable-precision coding.*

variable-speed gear—Same as *gear, integrating.*

variable time scale—See *scale, variable time.*

variable-tolerance-band compaction—See *compaction, variable-tolerance-band.*

variable word-length—See *word, variable-length.*

variations, calculus of—A calculus devoted to the theory of maxima and minima of definite integrals whose integrands are a function of dependent variables, independent variables, and their derivatives.

varistor—A passive resistor whose resistance is a function of the current through it or the voltage across it. Thus, it may carry constant current independent of the voltage drop across it, or it may drop a constant voltage independent of the current through it. The normal linear form of Ohm's Law for electric current flow in a constant resistance is not obeyed by the varistor. In a certain sense, the varistor is a self-varying resistor and is used as a stabilizer, current limiter, regulator, or other control device, such as preventing current surges or providing ballast.

vector, absolute—In graphic display systems, a line segment whose end points are given in absolute coordinates, that is, whose end points are given in absolute coordinates, that is, whose end points are located or measured from a given origin. (Contrast with *vector, relative.*)

vector, differential state—In computer simulation, an incremental change in the state vector that represents a part of the data structure of a formal system.

vector, relative—In graphic display systems, a line segment whose starting point or end is the end of the preceding display element, and whose finishing point or end is indicated as a distance from the starting point. (Contrast with *vector, absolute.*)

vector, state—In computer simulation, the part of the data structure of a formal system that specifies the current status of a real, model, or simulated, finite system.

vector generation—See *generation, vector.*

vector quantity—See *quantity, vector.*

Veitch chart—Same as *diagram, Veitch.*

Veitch diagram—See *diagram, Veitch.*

velocity servo—Same as *servointegrator.*

velodyne—Same as *servointegrator.*

Venn diagram—See *diagram, Venn.*

vent port—See *port, vent.*

verge-perforated card—Same as *card, edge-punched.*

verge-punched card—Same as *card, edge-punched.*

verification—In graphic display systems, a message that is fed back to a display terminal indicating that an input was detected; for example the brightening of a display element selected by a light pen.

verifier–A machine used for checking the accuracy of transcription of data, usually by comparison with a retranscription; that is, the machine compares a retranscription character by character, as it is rekeyed, somewhat as in proofreading by one person to another who is also reading the text. The verifier compares two manual or two machine transcriptions, or one of each, even as the new transcription is being made.

verifier, tape–A device for checking the accuracy of punched tape by comparing a previously punched tape with a second manual punching of the same data character by character or row by row as the second punching proceeds. The machine signals discrepancies. This process verifies the data on the tapes and permits on-the-spot correction. A comparator will only detect the existence of a discrepancy. (Compare with *comparator, tape.*)

verify–**1:** To determine whether a transcription of data, a copy operation, or other operation has been accomplished accurately; for example, to check the transmission, transcription, or conversion of data, usually immediately following or during the process; to check a transcribing operation by repeating it; to check a transcription by mechanically reading it and comparing the read data with a retranscription; to proofread by two persons; to punch at station one, read at station two, and compare the read data to the original at station three; or to manually key data, then key again and compare the results. **2:** To check the results of keypunching. **3:** Same as *check.*

verify, key–To ensure that the data contained in a punched card or a perforated tape has been properly punched by using a machine, known as a verifier, which has a keyboard. The machine signals when the punched hole and the depressed key disagree. The action is similar to proofreading in which the machine substitutes for one of the readers.

vertical feed–See *feed, vertical.*

vertical format–See *format, vertical.*

vertical position, addressable–See *position, addressable vertical.*

vertical tabulation character–See *character, vertical tabulation.*

vestigial-sideband transmission–See *transmission, vestigial-sideband.*

VHF–(Very-High Frequency). Frequencies between 30 and 300 megahertz. (Further clarified by *spectrum, frequency.*)

video circuit–See *circuit, video.*

VIP–(Variable Information Processing). A generalized information storage and retrieval system. It is organized by file, records within a file, and fields within a record. There are no limitations on either the number of characters in a field or on

the number of fields in a record. The complete character set except asterisk is available for use. Thus, mnemonic codes or abbreviations and plain text language are permissible. The system is most suitable for small, nonformalized files. An IBM 7070, card input/output, two tape channels, and seven tape units are used. Neither coding nor decoding of data is necessary. Basic routines are generalized. Thus, retrieval techniques are available without programming effort. Generalization in files and programs leads to increased running time. Associated with the Naval Ordnance Laboratory, Corona, California.

virgin medium–See *medium, virgin.*

virgin paper-tape coil–See *coil, virgin paper-tape.*

virtual address–**1:** Same as *address, immediate.* **2:** See *address, virtual.*

virtual addressing–Same as *addressing, immediate.*

virtual memory–Same as *storage, virtual.*

virtual storage–See *storage, virtual.*

visible file–See *file, visible.*

visual scanner–Same as *scanner, optical.*

VLF–(Very-Low Frequency). Frequencies below 30,000 hertz. (Further clarified by *spectrum, frequency.*)

vocabulary–An ordered word list with a definition of each word entry in the list. The entry is the word being defined and its definition. The definition usually consists of a defining phrase, explanatory remarks, examples, references, and a usage label. A vocabulary is usually intended for a specific purpose or for a specific class of population, such as Shakespeare's vocabulary, a vocabulary of physics, or a fifth-grade vocabulary. Occasionally a vocabulary may be just a word list without definitions. Vocabulary is generic and should include dictionaries, glossaries, and lexicons. Examples of usage include the USA Standard Vocabulary for Information Processing and the International Standard Organization Technical Committee 97, Subcommittee 1 on Information Processing *Vocabulary.* Vocabulary is not a precise term; its meaning must be inferred by context. Vocabularies are usually limited to nouns and infinitive verbs. Computer programming-language vocabularies may contain highly sophisticated words, such as extract, square-root, divide, linearize, smooth, and select-the-highest.

voice-grade channel–See *channel, voice-grade.*

void–In character recognition, the inadvertent absence of ink within the outline of a character. The void may occur in magnetic ink characters or optical characters and is usually due to defects in the inks, the paper, or the printing process.

volatile–In data processing, pertaining to the characteristic of becoming lost or disappearing when power is removed, especially the loss of data when power is removed and not returned or recovered when power is restored. The state of a system, such as the status of a piece of equipment, as indicated by the condition of a flip-flop may be volatile as well as data in a storage device that cannot be recovered when power is restored. Thus, if a magnetic tape unit was in the process of reading data when power was removed and if it cannot return to this process when power is returned, then the condition of the tape unit was volatile.

volatile storage—See *storage, volatile.*

voltage, supply—Same as *supply, reference.*

voltage regulation—See *regulation, voltage.*

volume—A physical unit of storage or data media that is accessible to a read-write mechanism; for example a reel of magnetic tape, a removable disc pack, a deck of punched cards, or a drum.

volume maintenance—See *maintenance, volume.*

volume preparation—See *preparation, volume.*

volume protection—See *protection, volume.*

volume test—See *test, volume.*

volume unit—See *unit, volume.*

vortex amplifier—See *amplifier, vortex.*

VSG—Same as *gear, integrating.*

VT—The vertical tabulation character.

w

walk, random—See *random-walk.*

wall-attachment amplifier—See *amplifier, wall-attachment.*

waste instruction—Same as *instruction, dummy.*

water permanence—See *permanence, water.*

wave, carrier—A periodic phenomenon that can be modulated so as to bear data or intelligence. Most wireless communications facilities utilize a fixed frequency signal which is pulse, amplitude, or frequency modulated so as to carry information. A direct-current signal that is merely interrupted, as with a telegraph key, is not considered a carrier wave, though such a signal is a carrier. (Further clarified by *carrier.*)

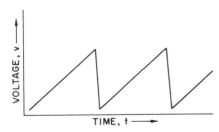

A sawtooth wave such as might be produced by a relaxation oscillator.

wave, sawtooth—A graphic two-dimensional, usually cartesian, plot of a dependent variable vs. an independent variable, characterized by a periodic slow, or low positive-slope ordinate rise, followed by a rapid, high negative-slope ordinate fall, or in reverse order, giving the appearance of a waveshape similar to the teeth of a saw. Thus, a voltage that rises slowly and steadily, then falls suddenly, when plotted against time, resembles a sawtooth. A sawtooth wave is used in the sweep circuits of cathode-ray tubes for horizontal and vertical deflection, in oscilloscopes, and in television picture tubes.

wave, sine—A periodic, mathematical, plotted function or quantity that varies according to $y = R \sin wt$, which is an amplitude-angular-displacement plot of the projection, on a diameter, of a point moving on the circumference of a circle of radius R. In the plot, the angular position of the point is the abscissa, wt; and the distance along a diameter of the orthogonal projection of the point is the ordinate. If the point moves around the circle with uniform speed, hence uniform angular speed, a sine wave of constant frequency, is generated. (Synonymous with *sinusoid.* Further clarified by *half-sinusoid.*)

waveform—The shape, usually of one cycle of a repeated or periodic phenomenon or event, of the graph representing the successive values of a varying quantity, such as voltage, current, pressure, or magnetization, plotted against another variable, such as time or distance, and usually in rectangular, or cartesian, coordinates. The graph represents the characteristics of the varying quantity. It is the variation of the characteristic that is the waveform. The graph is its representation. (Synonymous with *waveshape.*)

waveshape—Same as *waveform.*

way station—See *station, way.*

wear resistance—See *resistance, wear.*

weed—To remove, and usually discard, undesirable or needless information from a file; for example, to remove obsolete documents from a collection of documents.

weight—Same as *significance.*

Western Reserve University Retrieval System—Same as *WRU Retrieval System.*

wheel, print—The single element, in the shape of a disc, that provides a set of type at a single print position of a wheel printer. The type is located at the periphery of the wheel. As many wheels are required as there are print positions across the page on a line, say 120, 160, or 180 characters per line. The required number of print wheels are keyed and tightened on a print wheel assembly, which, during operation, is rotated at high speed. (Further explained by *assembly, print-wheel,* and by *printer, wheel.*)

wheel printer—See *printer, wheel.*

whiffletree switch—See *switch, whiffletree.*

who-are-you character—See *character, who-are-you.*

width, band—See *bandwidth.*

width, pulse—The time interval between points on the leading and trailing edges of a pulse, at which the instantaneous value is a specified fraction of the pulse amplitude. Nominal duration of a standard pulse is the time interval between the half amplitude points of the rise and decay curve of the pulse. The points on the curve must be stated where the width is measured. For rectangular pulses, the time interval between the 10 percent amplitude points of the pulse have also been used to define pulse width. (Synonymous with *pulse duration* and with *pulse length.*)

width, stroke—In character recognition, the distance between the two stroke edges, measured perpendicular to the stroke centerline.

width modulation, pulse—See *modulation, pulse-width.*

Williams tube—See *tube, Williams.*

window—In graphic display systems, an area in a display image in which data that should have been displayed has been scissored, that is, removed. Thus, a window looks like a hole in a set of displayed data.

wing panel—See *panel, wing.*

wiping action—See *action, wiping.*

wire, magnetic—A storage device that makes use of a moving wire containing or coated with magnetic material for storing data in the form of magnetized spots, as dipoles, spaced linearly along the moving wire by means of a stationary head. Storage locations are addressable by means of a counter. Magnetic wire is a serial-by-bit means of data storage; and so, is severely limited in data-processing capability because of limited capacity and long latency time. The direction of magnetization indicates the binary digit stored. (Synonymous with *wire storage* and *magnetic-wire storage.*)

wire, order—An auxiliary wire circuit used by maintenance personnel for communication incident to installation, maintenance, and lineup of communication facilities.

wire, sense—In a core storage device, the wire used to interrogate the storage locations by sending an appropriate pulse down the sense winding. In coincident current storage, each of two sense wires provides only sufficient drive to partially switch the core selected, both together providing sufficient magnetomotive force at the selected core to switch it only.

wire file—Same as *file, string.*

wire network, private—Same as *network, leased-line.*

wire printer—Same as *printer, matrix.*

wire storage—Same as *wire, magnetic.*

wire storage, magnetic—Same as *wire, magnetic.*

wired-program computer—See *computer, wired-program.*

wiring board—Same as *plugboard.*

WIZ—An algebraic and tabular language developed by General Electric Company for the GE 225 computer.

WIZOR—Same as *WIZ.*

WJCC—(Western Joint Computer Conference). These series of conferences, along with the Eastern Joint Computer Conferences, have been replaced by the spring and fall Joint Computer Conferences.

word—1: In computers and information processing, a group of characters treated as a unit and to which meaning can be assigned. (Further clarified by *word, computer.*) 2: A character string or a binary element string that is used, or is convenient, for some purpose, and is considered as an entity.

word, alphabetic—A word consisting entirely of letters of an alphabet, usually as distinct from numerals. Occasionally, special signs and symbols, like comma, hyphen, or apostrophe, are also considered alphabetic characters. Numeric characters may not be included. (Contrast with *word, numeric.*)

word, call—A set of characters used to identify, effect, label, or place a subroutine or data, or both, into the subroutine itself or into a larger routine of which the subroutine is a part. The call word usually identifies a closed subroutine. (Further clarified by *call* and by *number, call.*)

word, computer—A sequence or group of characters, such as bits, treated as a unit and capable of being stored in one computer storage location. Thus, each word is usually addressable, at least in high-speed random-access storage. Random access applies to access to the word. The word may be an instruction word, with address and operation parts, or a data word, of alphanumeric characters or a fixed- or floating-point number. Word lengths may be fixed or variable. Words may be divided into parts for many purposes. Many words have no meaning when taken out of context. The arithmetic, logic, and control units usually operate with or on words as a single entity. Each word has a specific meaning or meanings assigned to it. The characters or bits of a word may be handled serially or in parallel. If a word is sent to the control unit, it is treated as an instruction; if sent to the arithmetic unit, it is, represents, or is treated as if it represents, a quantity, in contrast to an instruction. Thus, a word may be any symbol or symbols to which meaning may be assigned; for example, in telegraphy, six operations or characters are considered as constituting a word for determining speed or traffic capacity; or a single-entry term in a dictionary, glossary, vocabulary, or thesaurus. Parts of computer words have been called syllables, catenas, bytes, slabs, and gulps. (Synonymous with *machine word*. Further clarified by *word*.)

word, control–A computer word that specifies a particular action to be taken; for example, in a subroutine, an instruction word containing one or more parameters that specify the action to be taken; a word that contains the addresses of words that specify control actions; the first or last word of a record or a block that carries indicative information concerning the words in the block or record; a word that specifies input-output operations; or a word that determines whether or when an interruption should take place.

word, data–Same as *word, information*.

word, double–A contiguous set or sequence of characters that comprises two computer words. Usually, the double word can be processed or addressed as a single unit.

word, fixed-length–A computer word in which there is always a constant number of characters, such as 12 alphanumeric characters or 40 binary digits, never more or less. Storage locations, registers, parallel logic wiring, and gating are arranged so as to handle a fixed number of digits at a time. (Synonymous with *fixed word-length*. Contrast with *word, variable-length*.)

word, index–Same as *modifier*.

word, information–A computer word that is regarded as part of the data being manipulated within or by a computer or its program, in contrast to an instruction word. The information word may be used to modify an instruction or it may be operated upon by the arithmetic or logic unit, or combined with other information words, such as added. Instruction words are usually sent to the control unit; information words to the arithmetic and logic unit. (Synonymous with *data word*. Contrast with *word, instruction*.)

word, instruction–A computer word that contains an instruction to a computer and usually consists of one or more operation parts, address parts, and flags, sentinels, check digits, or other special symbols. The instruction word is usually obtained from storage, decoded or interpreted, and the indicated operation executed. (Synonymous with *coding line*. Contrast with *word, information*.)

I	6	7 BITS 17	18	28	29	32
OP CODE	A ADDRESS		B ADDRESS		TAG	

A 32-bit instruction word with one 6-bit operation part, two 11-bit address parts, and a 4-bit tag.

word, long–A computer word of greater or greatest length in a computer capable of handling two or more different lengths of words. Often, the long word is a full word, made up of two half-length words, or the long word may be a double-length word, made up of two full words.

word, machine–Same as *word, computer*.

word, numeric–A word consisting entirely of digits of a numeration system, such as entirely of decimal digits, as distinct from letters of an alphabet that are not normally assigned numeric values. (Contrast with *word, alphabetic*.)

word, parameter–A computer word that directly or indirectly, provides, expresses, represents, or designates one or more parameters.

word, reserved–A word, in a source language, whose meaning is fixed by the particular values of that language and whose meaning is not to be altered in order to suit one computer program written in the source language. By extension, the reserved word shall not have different meanings within the same program, even if it appears in different contexts in the program.

word, short–A computer word of lesser or least length in a computer capable of handling two or more different lengths of words. Often the short word is half the length of the full-length or long word.

word, variable-length–A computer word in which the number of characters in a given word is variable and subject to the discretion of the programmer. Storage locations, registers, parallel logic wiring, and gating are arranged so as to handle a character or digit at a time. In storage, each character is addressable and so may be considered a word. A machine in which limited control of word length is possible, such as half-words or double-words and a machine whose word-length is optional at time of installation and henceforward fixed are not considered variable word-length machines. (Synonymous with *variable word-length*. Contrast with *word, fixed-length*.)

word capacity—Same as *length, word*.

word gap—Same as *space, interword*.

word generator, manual—Same as *unit, manual input*.

word indexing—See *indexing, word*.

word length—See *length, word*.

word-length, fixed—See *word, fixed-length*.

word-length, variable—See *word, variable-length*.

word mark—See *mark, word*.

word-organized storage—See *storage, word-organized*.

word space—See *space, word*.

word-time—The time required for a computer word to pass a given point; for example, in a serial storage device such as a delay-line, the time for all of the bits of a word to pass through the input control gate. For a serial device, the word-time is the sum of all the bit times. In a parallel system, the word-time might be the bit time. (Synonymous with *beat*.)

work cycle—See *cycle, work*.

work-flow, parallel—The conduct of operations or the performance of work such that several operations can be performed simultaneously, such as haircutting, manicuring, and shoe-shining all at the same time. (Synonymous with *parallel flow*. Contrast with *work-flow, serial*.)

work-flow, serial—The conduct of operations or the performance of work such that one operation is performed at a time and the work piece usually moves along a single channel where one type of operation is performed at each of a succession of stations. (Synonymous with *serial flow*. Contrast with *work-flow, parallel*.)

work measurement—See *measurement, work*.

working—In data processing, the mode or method of performing sequences or groups of operations on data.

working, asynchronous—Same as *operation, asynchronous*.

working, autonomous—A mode of performing operations on data such that a set of operations are initiated and executed independently on a portion of the equipment of a system while the remainder of the system is available for other operations.

working, multiple-length—A mode of performing operations on data such that two or more words are used to represent data items, elements, and codes; for example, the use of two or more words to represent a number to enhance precision in arithmetic operations.

working, offline—A mode of performing operations on data such that part of the operations are performed by equipment not under the direct control of the central processing unit or control unit; for example, converting data on punched cards to magnetic tape on a separate converter. The magnetic tape may then be placed on an online tape station, which is under the direct control of the central processing unit. Offline working saves valuable time of the larger system and permits more efficient use of the system. In many offline working operations, the output of the main system is stored intermediately for subsequent processing, under manual control, by the offline unit. (Contrast with *working, online*.)

working, online—A mode of performing operations on data such that the circuits or equipment performing the operations are under the direct control of the central processing or control unit. During online working, data from one unit of the system is accepted by another unit as soon as it is available without manual intervention. The primary criterion that determines whether or not an operation is performed online or offline is based on whether or not the main frame, central processing unit, or arithmetic unit is occupied with the operation. (Contrast with *working, offline*.)

working, pseudo-offline—A mode of performing operations on data such that the operations are performed on equipment connected to the main system but under the control of a separate routine, running concurrently, hence in parallel, with another stage of the operation. Thus, the output of one unit might be stored intermediately for subsequent processing under control of a program by a second unit, such as transferring data from punched cards to magnetic tape for subsequent use by another routine.

working, real-time—Same as *operation, real-time*.

working, simultaneous—Same as *processing, parallel*.

working, synchronous—Same as *operation, synchronous*.

working area—Same as *storage, temporary*.

working routine—Same as *routine, production*.

working space—Same as *storage, temporary*.

working storage—Same as *storage, temporary*.

woven-wire-screen memory—See *memory, woven-wire-screen*.

wrap—In tape-wound magnetic cores, one turn of the metallic magnetic tape. The tape is usually wrapped around a bobbin, with the coils of wire passing through the bobbin. The cores are often used as switching cores in digital computers.

write—In data processing, to deliver data to a storage medium; that is, to record data; for example, to place data on a magnetic tape in the form of a pattern of magnetic dipoles: to punch data on cards in the form of a pattern of holes; to place data in core storage, or drums or discs; to place marks on a mark-sensed card; or to draw patterns on the screen of a cathode-ray tube with a controlled beam of electrons, either for storage or for visual display. (Contrast with *read*.)

write cycle time—See *time, write cycle*.
write half-pulse—See *half-pulse, write*.
write head—See *head, write*.
write pulse, partial—See *pulse, partial write*.
write-read head—Same as *head, read-write*.
writing head—Same as *head, write*.

WRU—The who-are-you character.
WRU Retrieval System—(Western Reserve University Retrieval System.) A method for searching literature. Two programs were developed by General Electric Company for use on the GE 225. One program converts encoded abstracts and writes them on magnetic tape; the other compiles questions posed to the system and performs the search. The GAP Assembly routine performs the search. Associated with Western Reserve University, Cleveland. The operational file subject areas include metallurgy, diabetes, communicable diseases, and educational research.

x

X-datum line—See *line, X-datum*.
X-punch—A punched hole in the second row, one row above the zero row, on a Hollerith punch card. The X-punch is often used to represent a minus sign. (Synonymous with *eleven punch*.)
X-1—An assembly language and system developed by Sperry-Rand Corporation for the Univac I computer.
X-2—An assembly language and system developed by Sperry-Rand Corporation for the Univac UCT system.
X-6—An assembly language and system developed by Sperry-Rand Corporation for the Solid State 80 and 90 computers. The X-6 receives as input a series of operations or subroutines, assigns storage, and prepares program decks as output.

Relative and symbolic addresses are converted to absolute or machine addresses automatically.
XS-3—An abbreviation for excess three.
xerographic printer—See *printer, xerographic*.
xerography—A dry copying process whereby an electrostatic image is produced on the copy paper; a dry resinous powder consisting of ink mixed with a low melting-point binder is dusted over the image; the ink particles adhere to the areas that remain charged; i.e., the dark areas forming the characters being printed; the paper is heated, melting the binder and fusing the ink to the paper. The result can be a copy or used as an offset master.
XTRAN—Experimental computer languages developed by IBM Corporation.

y

Y-datum line—See *line, Y-datum*.
Y-punch—A punched hole in the top row, two rows above the zero row, on a Hollerith punch card. The Y-punch is often used to denote a plus sign. (Synonymous with *twelve punch*.)

yoke—In magnetic recording, a group of heads rigidly fastened and moved together for reading and writing on channels consisting of two or more tracks on magnetic tapes, drums discs, and similar media.

Z

Zatocode indexing–Same as *indexing, coordinate.*

Zatocoding–A system developed by C. N. Mooers of superimposed coding by edge-notching cards.

Zatocoding system–Same as *indexing, coordinate.*

zero–1: A numeral that represents a lack of magnitude and that is often used to convey information, such as designate the value of 56 in the numeral 56,000 or serve as the alternate symbol in a binary system of coding. There may be many representations for zero in a given computer and among different computers. Thus, there may be positive or negative zero. The straight binary representation for zero, such as –.111111111, may be different from the excess-three code, such as 0011. In floating-point notation, the coefficient may be zero or any representation of zero whereas the exponent may vary and assume any value. 2: A number that when added or subtracted from another number does not alter the value of the other number, or, when used as a factor in a multiplication operation, produces a product that has zero or no value.

zero, binary–Of the two possible binary digits, that which has the value of zero assigned to it as a matter of convention. Usually written as 0, it may be represented as the presence or absence of a voltage or current at a given point, the set or reset state of a flip-flop, the clockwise or counterclockwise magnetization of an annular core, or by the presence or absence of a pulse of any physical or electrical phenomenon at a given point in time or place, in accordance with the adopted convention. The other of the two states is used to represent the binary one. For numerical purposes, the binary zero has the same value as a decimal zero or a zero in any other numeration system using similar positional notation and other conventions.

zero, leading–In a positional numeration system, a zero that occupies a more significant digit position than the digit position of the most significant nonzero digit of a numeral; for example, the underlined zeros in the decimal numeral 0028.54. (Contrast with *zero, trailing.*)

zero, trailing–In a positional numeration system, a zero that occupies a less significant digit position than that of the least significant nonzero digit of a numeral usually to the right of the arithmetic point; for example, the underlined zero in the numeral 28.450. (Contrast with *zero, leading.*)

zero access–Same as *access, immediate.*

zero-access addition–See *addition, zero-access.*

zero-access storage–Same as *storage, immediate-access.*

zero-address instruction–See *instruction, zero-address.*

zero complement–Same as *complement, radix.*

zero elimination–Same as *suppression, zero.*

zero-level address–Same as *address, immediate.*

zero-level addressing–Same as *addressing, immediate.*

zero-level transmission reference point–See *point, zero-level transmission reference.*

zero-match gate–Same as *gate, NOR.*

zero suppression–See *suppression, zero.*

zerofill–Same as *zeroize.*

zerography–Same as *xerography.*

zeroize–To fill storage space or to replace with a representation of zero. A storage location may be cleared to zero, but zeroizing may not necessarily be the same as clearing. Thus, in binary storage, clearing might imply that all cells be placed in the state that represents binary zero; however, the decimal numeral for zero may have ones in it if the excess-three system of binary coding is used. (Synonymous with *zerofill.*)

Zipfs Law–An empirical law that relates the frequency of occurrence of words, syllables, or letters, with respect to their rank or position in a list of descending frequency of occurrence. The frequency of occurrence times the rank or position number is a constant and about equal to 0.1 for most languages.

ZMMD–(Zurich, Mainz, Munich, Darmstadt). A joint university effort of ALGOL processors.

zone–1: In a punched card, the top three rows of the upper curtate of the card; namely, the twelve, eleven, and zero rows. Alphabetic characters can be represented by a zone punch and a punch in one of the positions of one through nine in the lower curtate of the card. **2:** Same as *area, storage.*

zone, dead–Same as *band, dead.*

zone, minus–The set of characters in a given code that are associated with the adjacent bit that represents a minus sign; for example, if a binary one represents a minus sign in the left-most place in the numerals from 1000 to 1111, then the 1000 to 1111 are in the minus zone and the numerals from 0000 to 0111 are in the plus zone, or 186 is in the minus zone and 086 is in the plus zone, where the arithmetic sign convention of the previous example applies. (Further clarified by *bit, zone.*)

zone, neutral–In automatic control, a range of values in a control system's parameters in which no control action occurs.

zone, plus–The set of characters in a given code that is associated with the adjacent bit that represents a plus sign; for example, if a binary one represents a plus sign in the left-most place in the numerals from 1000 to 1111, then the numerals 1000 to 1111 are in the plus zone and the numerals from 0000 to 0111 are in the minus zone; or 186 is in the plus zone and 086 is in the minus zone, where the arithmetic sign convention of the previous example applies. (Further clarified by *bit, zone.*)

zone bit–See *bit, zone.*

zone center–Same as *center, zone-switching.*

zone center, telephone–Same as *center, zone-switching.*

zone punch–See *punch, zone.*

zone-switching center–See *center, zone-switching.*

zoom–In graphic display systems, to change the scale of all display elements of a display image so as to more clearly perceive and manipulate small parts and details of an image. Zooming makes images appear larger.

Bibliography

In the Preface, the seven major vocabulary efforts and the additional eighty vocabularies that were used as a data base and reference source for the preparation of the dictionary were discussed. The number eighty was reached by counting each vocabulary or glossary, however small, that contained some trace of original intellectual effort. Direct copies or reprints were not counted, since they are not independent works. The list of vocabularies, glossaries, and dictionaries given below cites each relevant work even if it is a reprint or a copy of another. The reader may wish to avail himself of the contents of the 158 works in the list. However, such an undertaking is not recommended, as this dictionary tends to supersede these works, and besides, redundancy is involved. However, revised editions or new works not indicated below may prove to be of some supplemental value in the years ahead.

Acoustical Society of America. *American Standard Acoustical Terminology*. New York: USASI, 1960.

American Standards Association (ASA). *See* United States of America Standards Institute.

Armed Forces Management. "1968 Glossary of Military Electronic Systems," *Armed Forces Management Magazine* (July 1968).

Association for Computing Machinery (ACM). "The First Glossary of Programming Terminology" by G. M. Hopper, *et al,* from *Report to the Association for Computing Machinery*. New York: ACM, June 1954.

_____.*Glossary of Terms in the Computer and Information Processing Field* by W. B. Fritz (Ed.), Chairman, and the ACM Subcommittee on Programming Terminology. New York: ACM, Oct. 1962.

Auerbach Corporation. *Auerbach Standard EDP Reports, An Analytical Reference Service for Electronic Data Processing Field*, Vol. 1, Chap. 7, pp. 7:101.001-7:263.010.

Bemer, R. W. and Grems, M. *Association for Computing Machinery (ACM) Standard Committee–Terminology Subcommittee Report*. New York: ACM, Nov. 1, 1963.

Berkeley Enterprises, Inc. *Glossary of Terms in The Field of Computers and Automation*. Newtonville, Mass.: Berkeley Enterprises, Inc., 1954.

Berkeley, E. C. and Lovett, L. L. *Glossary of Terms in Computers and Data Processing*. Newtonville, Mass.: Berkeley Enterprises, Inc., June 1960.

Bibero, R. J. *Dictionary of Automatic Control*. New York: Reinhold Publishing Corporation, 1960.

Bolsky, *M. Glossary of Programming Terms*. Santa Monica, Calif.: System Development Corporation, 1961.

Borko, H. *Computer Applications in the Behavioral Sciences, Glossary*. Englewood Cliffs, N.J.: Prentice-Hall, Inc., 1962.

Bormann, W. O. *Glossary—Terms Used in Computer Programming and Engineering.* Poughkeepsie, N.Y.: IBM Corporation, 1960.

British Standards Institution (BSI). *Glossary of Terms Relating to Automatic Data Processing.* D 62/4492, Reference USM/4. London: BSI, July 16, 1962.

Bull-General Electric. *Vocabulaire du Traitement de l'information Anglais-Francais.* Feb. 1967.

Burroughs Corporation. *Electrodata Glossary of Computer Engineering and Programming Terminology.* (Reprint of BRL glossary by M. H. Weik.) Detroit: Electrodata Division, Burroughs Corporation, 1958.

———. *A Short Glossary of Computer Terms,* by J. C. Mihm (Ed.). Washington, D. C.: Electrodata Division, Burroughs Corporation, 1959.

———. *The American Standard Vocabulary for Information Processing.* Reprint of USA Standard Vocabulary for Information Processing, X3.12-1966. New York: USASI, June 14, 1966.

CCITT (International Telegraph and Telephone Consultative Committee.) *Definitions for Data Transmission.* International Organization for Standardization/Technical Committee (97/1 N 19), Nov. 15, 1963.

———. *Data Transmission, Third Plenary Assembly, Blue Book, Volume VIII.* Geneva: International Telecommunication Union, 1964.

Clason, W. F. *Elseviers Dictionary of Automation, Computers, Control and Measuring.* Amsterdam: Elsevier Publishing Co., 1961.

CODASYL COBOL Committee and European Computer Manufacturers Association (ECMA). *COBOL, Edition 1965.* Washington, D.C.: Superintendent of Documents, U.S. Government Printing Office, 1965.

Colilla, R. A. "Time-sharing and Multiprocessing Terminology," *Datamation* (March 1966), pp. 49-51.

Commerce Clearing House, Inc. "Dictionary—Definitions. Terminology, Abbreviations," *Automation Reporter,* Vol. 1 (1964), pp. 1201-1416.

Compagnie IBM France. *Terminologie Du traitement de l'information, Edition 1967.* Paris: Compagnie IBM France, 1967.

Composition Information Services (CIS). *CIS Glossary of Automated Typesetting and Related Computer Terms.* Los Angeles: CIS, 1964.

Control Data Corporation. *The Control Data 8050 Information Control System Glossary.* Publication No. 36822600, March 1965.

Datamation. "Automatic Data Processing Glossary" (reprint of Bureau of the Budget ADP Glossary), *Datamation,* 1965.

Department of Defense (DOD). *Glossary of Terms and Data Configurations for Logistics Data Processing.* Washington, D.C.: DOD, July 1960.

———. *Technical Data and Standardization Glossary.* Philadelphia: Office of the Asst. Secretary, Installations and Logistics, U.S. Naval Supply Depot, December 1965.

———. *COBOL, Edition 1965.* Changes and Corrections. Washington, D.C.: DOD, 1967.

Eastwood, D. E. *SHARE Glossary of Terms,* Murrary Hill, N.J.: Bell Telephone Laboratories, 1960.

Ellsworth, L. *Basic IBM Applied Programming Teaching Glossary*. New York: IBM Data Systems Division, 1960.

Engles, R.W. *Concepts and Terminology for Programmers,* Technical Report TR 00.1663. Poughkeepsie, N.Y.: IBM Systems Development Division, 1967.

Executive Office of the President, Bureau of the Budget. *ADP Glossary*. Washington, D.C.: Superintendent of Documents, U.S. Government Printing Office, Dec. 1962.

————. *Report to the President on the Management of Automatic Data Processing in the Federal Government*. Submitted by J. L. McClellan, Chairman, Committee on Government Operations, U.S. Senate. Washington, D.C.: U.S. Government Printing Office, March 4, 1965.

Fachnormenausschuss Informationsverarbeitung (FNI) in Deutschen Normenausschuss. *Informationsverarbeitung, Begriffe*. [German standard vocabulary on theory concepts.] DIN 44 300. Berlin: Deutscher Normenausschuss, 1968.

————. *Informationstheorie Begriffe*. [German standard vocabulary of information theory concepts] DIN 44 301. Berlin: Deutscher Normenausschuss, 1967.

————. *Magnetbandtechnik fur Informationsverarbeitung, Begriffe*. [German standard vocabulary for magnetic tape technology for information processing.] DIN 66010. Berlin: Deutscher Normenausschuss, 1965.

————. *Datenubertragung,Begriffe.* [German standard vocabulary of data transmission concepts.] DIN 44 302 Berlin: Deutscher Normenausschuss,1967.

Federal Council for Science and Technology (Committee on Scientific Information). *Glossary of Fifty Definitions–Scientific and Technical Information*. Supplement No. 3. Washington, D.C.: Federal Council for Science and Technology, Jan. 1964.

Feldman, J. and Gries, D. "Translator Writing Systems," *Communications of the ACM,* Vol. 11, No. 2 (Feb. 1968), pp. 77-108.

Fox, Phyllis. *Glossary of Terms Frequently Used in Physics and Computers*. New York: American Institute of Physics, May 22, 1962.

Foxboro Company. *Glossary of Analog and Digital Process Control Terms*. Foxboro, Mass.: Foxboro Company, 1967.

Fritz, W. B. "Selected Definitions," *Communications of ACM,* No. 4 (April 1963), pp. 152-158.

General Electric Company. *Glossary of Computer Engineering and Programming Terminology*. (Reprint of BRL glossary by M. H. Weik.) Phoenix, Arizona: General Electric Company, 1958.

————. *Glossary of Computer Terminology*. CPB-93A. Phoenix, Arizona: Computer Department, General Electric Company, 1962.

————. *Glossary of Computer Terminology*. CPB-93B. Phoenix, Arizona: Computer Department, General Electric Company. 1963.

————. *Glossary of Process Computer Terms*. GET-3397-B. Phoenix, Arizona: Process Computer Business Section, General Electric Company.

Gorn, S. "Some Basic Terminology Connected with Mechanical Languages and Their Processors," *Communications of ACM*, Vol. 4, No. 8 (Aug. 1961), pp. 336-339.

Gregory, R. H. and Van Horn, R. L. *Automatic Data Processing Systems, Principles and Procedures.* Second Edition. Belmont, Calif.: Wadsworth Publishing Company, Inc., 1963.

Grems, M.; Bemer, R., and Williams, F. *IBM Glossary for Information Processing.* Preliminary Edition. White Plains, N.Y.: IBM Corporation, May 1, 1961 and August 1, 1961.

————. *IBM Glossary for Information Processing.* Revised Preliminary Edition. White Plains, N.Y.: IBM Corporation, October 1961.

Grems, M. (IBM Research Center). "A Survey of Languages and Systems for Information Retrieval," *Communications of ACM*, Vol. 5, No. 1 (January 1962).

————. "Terms Frequently Combined in Problem Description," *Communications of ACM*, Vol. 6, No. 1 (Jan. 1963), p. 31.

————."Glossary Construction," *Communications of ACM,* Vol. 6, No. 2 (Feb. 1963), pp. 64-65.

von Handel, P. *Electronic Computers: Fundamentals.* Glossary. Englewood Cliffs, N.J.: Prentice-Hall, Inc., 1962.

Hannum, D. E. *Glossary for Data Transmission Study Group.* Downey, Calif.: North American Rockwell.

Head, R. V. *Real-Time Business Systems.* Glossary, pp. 333-359. New York: Holt, Rinehart and Winston, Inc.

Herron, R. M. *Glossary of Terms,* White Plains, N.Y.: IBM Corporation, 1960.

Holmes, James F. *Communications Dictionary.* New York: John F. Rider Publisher, Inc., 1962.

————. *Data Transmission and Data Processing Dictionary.* New York: John F. Rider Publisher, Inc., 1965.

Holmstrom, J. E. *Multilingual Terminology of Information Processing.* Rome: Provisional International Computation Centre, 1959.

Honeywell Electronic Data Processing. *Glossary of Data Processing and Communications Terms.* First and Second Editions, 1964. Wellesley Hills, Mass.: Honeywell Electronic Data Processing.

Horn, J. *Computer and Data Processing Dictionary and Guide.* Englewood Cliffs, N.J.: Prentice-Hall, Inc., 1966.

House of Representatives. "Study No. IV, Documentation and Dissemination of Research and Development Results," 88th Congress, pp. 95-100. Glossary from *Report of the Select Committee on Government Research.* Washington, D.C.: Superintendent of Documents, Government Printing Office, 1964.

Informatics Inc. *Glossary of Data Communications/Message Switching Terms.* Sherman Oaks, Calif.: Informatics Inc., 1967.

Institute of Electrical and Electronics Engineers (IEEE). *Standards on Electronic Computers – Definitions of Terms.* New York: IEEE, 1956.

————. "IRE Standards on Static Magnetic Storage: Definition of Terms," 59 IRE 8. S1, *Proceedings of IRE*, Vol. 47, No. 3 (March 1959).

_____. *Definitions of Terms for Electronic Digital Computers*, Standard No. 162. New York: IEEE, Dec. 1963.

International Business Machines Corporation. *Glossary for Data Processing Machines*. Washington, D.C.: IBM Washington Education Center, 1959.

_____. *Glossary for Information Processing*. White Plains, N.Y.: IBM Corporation, 1962.

_____. *IBM Reference Manual Glossary for Information Processing*. White Plains, N.Y.: IBM Corporation, May, 1963

_____. *IBM Division Programming Standard Glossary*. Cat. DPS. Subject 7-6015, Suffix T. New York: IBM Corporation, August 1964.

_____. *Standard Definitions for Information Processing Terms*. Technical Report TR 00.1357 by P. H. Trautwein. Poughkeepsie, N.Y.: IBM Systems Development Division, November 1, 1965.

_____. *A Data Processing Glossary*. C201619-0. White Plains, N.Y.: IBM Technical Publications Department, 1968.

International Computation Centre (ICC). *Multilingual Terminology of Information Processing*. Incomplete Provisional Draft. Rome:. International Computation Centre, June 1959.

International Federation for Information Processing/International Computation Center (IFIP/ICC). *Vocabulary of Terms Used in Information Processing*. Preprint Edition. IFIP/ICC, June 1964.

_____. *Vocabulary for Information Processing*. First English Language Edition. Amsterdam: North-Holland Publishing Co., 1966.

International Organization for Standardization (ISO). *Proposed ISO Style Manual*. Table of Contents. (Annex to the General Secretariat Circular letter re ISO Style Manual dated Nov. 9, 1962), A:7892-1/E.

_____. *Character Recognition Draft Glossary*. ISO/TC97/SC3 (Secretariat-9) 18. New York: USASI, October 22, 1964.

_____. *Vocabulary of Terminology*. Draft ISO Recommendation No. 761. Geneva: ISO, 1964.

_____. *Guide for the Preparation of Classified Vocabularies*. Draft ISO Recommendation No. 792. Geneva: ISO, 1964.

_____. *International Unification of Concepts and Terms*. Draft ISO Recommendation No. 1189. Geneva: ISO, 1966.

_____. *Naming Principles*. Technical Committee 37 (Terminology). Draft ISO Recommendation No. 676. Geneva: ISO, 1966.

_____. *Programming Language ALGOL*. Technical Committee 97 (Computers and Information Processing). Draft ISO Recommendation No. 1538. Geneva: ISO, 1967.

_____. *Programming Language FORTRAN*. Draft ISO Recommendation No. 1539. Geneva: ISO, 1967.

International Resistance Company (IRC). *Condensed Glossary of Electronics Terminology*. Philadelphia: IRC, June 1, 1964.

James, G. and James, R. C. (Ed.). *Mathematics Dictionary: Multilingual Edition*. Princeton, N.J.: D. Van Nostrand Company, Inc. 1959.

Japanese Industrial Standards Committee (JISC). *Terms Relating to Digital*

Computers (General). JIS Z8111. Tokyo: Japanese Industrial Standards Committee, 1961.

Jeenel, J. *Programming for Business Computers*. Glossary. New York: McGraw-Hill Book Co., Inc., 1959.

Kelly, D. X. *Glossary of Electronic Data Processing Terminology*. Bedford, Mass.: Adams Associates, 1962.

Lambert, C. G. *TABS-3, Terms and Abbreviations*. Field Note FN-580-3. Santa Monica, Calif.: System Development Corporation, 1961.

_____. *TABS-7, A Glossary of Terms and Abbreviations*. TM-90580/000/07. Santa Monica, Calif.: System Development Corporation, 1966.

Mandl, Matthew. *Fundamentals of Digital Computers*. Glossary. Englewood Cliffs, N.J.: Prentice-Hall, Inc., 1958.

Mason, R. M. *A Programming Glossary for Narec Users*. NRL Report 5779, OTS, AD No. 283800. Washington, D.C.: Naval Research Laboratories, 1962.

Massachusetts Institute of Technology (MIT). *Glossary of Computer Terms*. Report R-138, Project Whirlwind, Report to Office of Naval Research. Cambridge: MIT, May 1948.

McKracken, D. D. *Guide to IBM 1401 Programming*. Glossary. New York: John Wiley & Sons, Inc., 1962.

McKracken, D. D., Weiss, H., and Lee, T. *Programming Business Computers*. Glossary. New York: John Wiley & Sons, Inc., 1961.

Meacham, A. D. "Glossary of Punched Card Accounting Terms." *Data Processing Equipment Encyclopedia, Vol. 1: Electromechanical Devices. pp. 370-373. Detroit: Gille Associates, Inc., 1961.*

_____. *"List of Data Processing Abbreviations." Data Processing Equipment Encyclopedia, Vol. 2: Electronic Devices.* Appendix A, pp. 329-338. Detroit: Gille Associates, Inc., 1961.

_____. "Glossary of Computing Terms." *Data Processing Equipment Encyclopedia, Vol. 2: Electronic Devices.* Appendix B, pp. 339-362. Detroit: Gille Associates, Inc., 1961.

Meek, C. *SHARE Glossary*. SHARE, Inc. Buffalo: Computing Center, State University of New York, 1967.

G. & C. Merriam Company. *Webster's Third New International Dictionary*. Springfield, Mass.: G & C. Merriam Company, 1961.

Minneapolis-Honeywell. *Automation Dictionary*. St. Paul, Minn.: Minneapolis-Honeywell, 1954.

Mordy, D. L. *Glossary of Programming and Computer Technology*. New York: IBM Data Systems Division, 1960.

Nathan, R. and Hanes, E. *Computer Programming Handbook*. Glossary. Englewood Cliffs, N. J.: Prentice-Hall, Inc., 1962.

National Cash Register Company. *Bank Terminology*. Dayton, Ohio: NCR, 1954.

National Office Management Association (NOMA). *NOMA Glossary of*

Automation Terms: Willow Grove, Penn.: NOMA, April 1958, revised Jan. 1961.

National Radio Institute. *Radio-Television-Electronics Dictionary.* New York: John F. Rider Publisher, Inc., 1962.

Neuman, A. J. *Glossary of ASTIA Operational Terms.* ASTIA Thesaurus Revision Glossary Committee. Cameron Station, Virginia: Defense Documentation Center (formerly Armed Services Technical Information Agency), July 1, 1962.

Orne, J. "Report on the Fourth Plenary Conference of International Organization for Standardization/Technical Committee 37, Terminology, Principles and Coordination," Berlin: ISO, May 1960.

Parkhill, D. F. *The Challenge of the Computer Utility.* Reading, Mass.: Addison-Wesley Publishing Company, 1966.

Perry, O. W. *Glossary of Computer and Programming Terms.* Poughkeepsie, N. Y.: IBM Corporation, 1959.

Piraux, H. *Dictionnaire Francaise-Anglais des termes relatifs á l'électrotechnique l'électronique et aux applications connexes.* Paris: Editions Eyrolles, 1963.

Prudential Insurance Company. *Introduction to Electronic Computers–Glossary.* New York: Prudential Insurance Co., 1954.

Radio Corporation of America (RCA). *The Language and Symbology of Digital Computer Systems.* Camden, N. J.: RCA Service Co., 1959.

Rhine, D. and Brandon, D. *Operating System Description Standard Definitions.* Santa Monica, Calif.: System Development Corp., 1961.

Roth, G. D. *A Brief Glossary of Data Processing Terms.* White Plains, N. Y.: IBM Data Processing Division, 1959.

Howard W. Sams Technical Staff. *Pocket Dictionary of Computer Terms.* Indianapolis: Howard W. Sams and Co., Inc., 1962.

Savage, T. R. "The Hyphen Controversy," *Communications of ACM,* Vol. 7, No. 4 (April 1964), pp. 203, 263.

Siegel, P. *Understanding Digital Computers.* Glossary. New York: John Wiley & Sons, Inc., 1961.

Sippl, C. J. *The Computerman's Dictionary.* North Hollywood: Western Periodicals Company, 1965.

————. *Computer Dictionary.* Indianapolis: Howard W. Sams and Co., Inc., 1966.

Strong, J. A. "Data Communications Glossary," *Datamation* (March 1962), pp. 66-73.

Taylor, R. S. *Glossary of Terms Frequently Used in Scientific Documentation.* New York: American Institute of Physics, August 1962.

Thiess, H. E. (Ed.). *Side-by-Side Listing of prUSAVIP and IFIP/ICC Vocabulary.* USASI X3.5 Working Paper. Washington, D. C.: Naval Command Systems Support Activity, 1967.

Traub, J. F. "American Standard and IFIP/ICC Vocabularies Compared," *Communications of the ACM,* Vol. 8, No. 6 (June 1965), pp. 361-363.

Trautwein, P. H. *Standard Definition for Information Processing Terms.* Technical Report TR 00.1357. Poughkeepsie: IBM Systems Development Division, November 1, 1965.

TRW (Thompson Ramo Wooldridge) Cleveland, Ohio. *Glossary of Computer and Process Control.* Cleveland: TRW, 1963.

United States Air Force. *Glossary of STINFO Terminology.* AFOSR 5266. Compiled by D. L. Thompson. Washington, D. C.: USAF Office of Aerospace Research, Oct. 1963.

United States Army. *Radar Electronic Fundamentals.* Glossary. TM 11-466. Washington, D. C.: United States Army, The Adjutant General, 1948.

United States of America Standards Institute (USASI) (formerly the American Standards Association—ASA). *Style Manual.* PM117a. New York: USASI, Jan. 1960.

——. *Communications Glossary.* Working Paper. Task Group X3.3.2. New York: USASI, March 1962.

——. *Definitions of Terms for X3.6.* Working Paper. New York: USASI. Sept. 12, 1962.

——. *Guidelines for the Preparation of Definitions.* Informal Paper. Subcommittee X3.5. New York: USASI, Oct. 26, 1962.

——. *Proposed American Standard Print Specification for Magnetic Character Recognition.* Definitions in Sect. 10, Signal Level. Working Paper. Subcommittee X3.7. New York: USASI, May 22, 1963.

——. *An Informal Glossary of Terms Used in Optical Character Recognition Field.* Working Paper. Subcommittee X3.1. New York: USASI, June 10, 1963.

——. *Criteria for a Technical Vocabulary.* Working Paper X3.5/2. Subcommittee X3.5. New York: USASI, April 17, 1964.

——. *American Standard Vocabulary for Information Processing.* X3.12-1966. New York: USASI, June 14, 1966.

——. *Proposed USA Standard COBOL.* Working Group X3.4.4 COBOL Standards. SICPLAN Notices, Vol. 2, No. 4 (April 1967). New York: ACM, 1967.

Univac Solid State Systems. *Systems Design and Programming Terminology Glossary.* Philadelphia: Univac, Division of Sperry Rand Corporation, 1960.

Univac Systems Programming. *Vocabulary for Information Processing.* Philadelphia: Univac, Division of Sperry Rand Corporation, 1968.

Victorian Computer Society. *Thesaurus of Terms and Definitions Used in Automatic Data Processing.* Printer's Draft. Australia: Victorian Computer Society, 1963.

VITRO Corporation of America. "Glossary of Computer and Related Terms," Section 12 of *Electronic Digital Computer Survey.* New York: VITRO Corporation of America, January 30, 1953.

Wagner, F. S., Jr. "A Dictionary of Documentation Terms." *American Documentation,* Vol. XI (April 1960), pp. 102-119.

Weik, M. H. "A Glossary of Computer Engineering and Programming

Terminology," Chapter V from *A Survey of Domestic Electronic Digital Computing Systems.* Report No. 971. Aberdeen Proving Ground, Md.: Ballistic Research Laboratories (BRL), December 1955.

_____. "A Glossary of Computer Engineering and Programming Terminology," Chapter V from *A Survey of Domestic Electronic Digital Computing Systems.* PB11196 (reprint of BRL Report No. 971). Washington, D. C.: U. S. Department of Commerce, Office of Technical Services.

_____. "A Glossary of Computer Engineering and Programming Terminology," Chapter V from *A Second Survey of Electronic Digital Computing Systems.* Report No. 1010. Aberdeen Proving Ground, Md.: Ballistic Research Laboratories (BRL), June 1957.

_____. "A Glossary of Computer Engineering and Programming Terminology," Chapter V from *A Second Survey of Domestic Electronic Digital Computing Systems.* PB 111996R (reprint of BRL Report No. 1010). Washington, D. C.: U. S. Department of Commerce, Office of Technical Services, June 1957.

_____. "BRL Glossary of Computer Programming and Engineering Terminology," *Communications of the ACM*, Vol. 1, No. 6 (June 1958), No. 8 (August 1958), No. 9 (Sept. 1958), No. 10 (Oct. 1958), and No. 11 (Nov. 1958).

_____. "Glossary of Computer Engineering and Programming Terminology," Chapter V from *A Third Survey of Domestic Electronic Digital Computing Systems.* Report No. 1115. Aberdeen Proving Ground, Md.: Ballistic Research Laboratories (BRL), March 1961.

_____. "Glossary of Computer Engineering and Programming Terminology," Chapter V from *A Third Survey of Domestic Electronic Digital Computing Systems.* PB 171265 (reprint of BRL Report No. 1115). Washington, D.C.: U.S. Department of Commerce, Office of Technical Services, March 1961.

_____. *A Revised Glossary of Computer Engineering and Programming.* Aberdeen Proving Ground, Md.: Ballistic Research Laboratories, July 1961.

_____. *A Fourth Survey of Domestic Electronic Digital Computing Systems.* Report No. 1227. Aberdeen Proving Ground, Md.: Ballistic Research Laboratories (BRL), January 1964.

Weik, M. H. and Confer, V. J. *Thesaurus of the Names of Electronic Digital Computers and Processors.* Technical Note No. 1472. Aberdeen Proving Ground, Md.: Ballistic Research Laboratories (BRL), Sept. 1962.

Williams, W. F. *Principles of Automated Information Retrieval.* Elmhurst, Ill.: Business Press, 1965.

Wilmot, E. *Glossary of Terms Used in Automatic Data Processing.* London: Business Publications Ltd., 1960.

Wrubel, M. H. *Programming for Digital Computers.* Glossary. New York: McGraw-Hill Book Co., Inc., 1959.